TAKING SIDES

Clashing Views on

Legal Issues

THIRTEENTH EDITION

Selected, Edited, and with Introductions by

M. Ethan Katsh
University of Massachusetts–Amherst

**McGraw-Hill
Higher Education**

Boston   Burr Ridge, IL   Dubuque, IA   New York   San Francisco   St. Louis
Bangkok   Bogotá   Caracas   Kuala Lumpur   Lisbon   London   Madrid   Mexico City
Milan   Montreal   New Delhi   Santiago   Seoul   Singapore   Sydney   Taipei   Toronto

McGraw-Hill
Higher Education

TAKING SIDES: CLASHING VIEWS ON LEGAL ISSUES,
THIRTEENTH EDITION

Published by McGraw-Hill, a business unit of The McGraw-Hill Companies, Inc., 1221 Avenue of the Americas, New York, NY 10020. Copyright © 2008 by The McGraw-Hill Companies, Inc. All rights reserved. Previous edition(s) 1983–2006. No part of this publication may be reproduced or distributed in any form or by any means, or stored in a database or retrieval system, without the prior written consent of The McGraw-Hill Companies, Inc., including, but not limited to, in any network or other electronic storage or transmission, or broadcast for distance learning.

Some ancillaries, including electronic and print components, may not be available to customers outside the United States.

Taking Sides® is a registered trademark of the McGraw-Hill Companies, Inc.
Taking Sides is published by the **Contemporary Learning Series** group within the McGraw-Hill Higher Education division.

 This book is printed on recycled, acid-free paper containing 10% postcomsumer waste.

1 2 3 4 5 6 7 8 9 DOCDOC 9 8 7

MHID: 0-07-351509-4
ISBN: 978-0-07-351509-0
ISSN: 1098-5395

Managing Editor: *Larry Loeppke*
Production Manager: *Faye Schilling*
Senior Developmental Editor: *Susan Brusch*
Editorial Assistant: *Nancy Meissner*
Production Service Assistant: *Rita Hingtgen*
Permissions Coordinator: *Lori Church*
Senior Marketing Manager: *Julie Keck*
Marketing Communications Specialist: *Mary Klein*
Marketing Coordinator: *Alice Link*
Project Manager: *Jane Mohr*
Design Specialist: *Tara McDermott*
Senior Administrative Assistant: *DeAnna Dausener*
Senior Operations Manager: *Pat Koch Krieger*
Cover Graphics: *Maggie Lytle*

Compositor: ICC Macmillan Inc.
Cover Image: Comstock/JupiterImages

Library of Congress Cataloging-in-Publication Data

Main entry under title:
  Taking sides: clashing views on controversial legal issues/selected, edited, and with introductions by M. Ethan Katsh.—13th ed.
  Includes bibliographical references.
  1. Law—Social aspects—United States. 2. United States—Constitutional law. 3. Justice, Administration of—United States. Katsh, M. Ethan, *comp.*
                        340'.115

www.mhhe.com

Clashing Views on

Legal Issues
THIRTEENTH EDITION

Preface

The study of law should be introduced as part of a liberal education, to train and enrich the mind. . . . I am convinced that, like history, economics, and metaphysics—and perhaps even to a greater degree than these—the law could be advantageously studied with a view to the general development of the mind.

—Justice Louis D. Brandeis

The general study of law in colleges, universities, and even high schools has grown rapidly during the last 30 years. Accompanying this development has been the publication of new curriculum materials that go beyond the analysis of legal cases and doctrines that make up much of professional law study in law schools. This book is part of the effort to view and study law as an institution that continuously interacts with other social institutions. Law should be examined from an interdisciplinary perspective and be accessible to all students.

This book focuses on a series of controversial issues involving law and the legal system. It is, we believe, an appropriate starting point for law study because controversy and conflict are inherent in law. Law is based on an adversary approach to conflict resolution, in which two advocates representing opposing sides are pitted against each other. Judicial decisions often contain both majority and dissenting opinions, which reveal some of the arguments that went on in the judges' chambers. Perhaps most relevant to a discussion of the place of controversy in the legal system is the First Amendment guaranty of freedom of speech and of the press, which presumes that we all benefit by a vigorous debate of important issues.

Since many of the issues in *Taking Sides* are often in the news, you probably already have opinions on them. What you should remember, however, is that there is usually more to learn about any given issue, and the topics discussed here are best approached with an open mind. You should not be surprised if your views change as you read the selections.

Organization of the book   This book contains 38 selections presented in a pro and con format that debate 19 legal issues. Each issue has an issue *introduction,* which sets the stage for the debate as it is argued in the YES and NO selections. Each issue concludes with a *postscript* that makes some final observations, points the way to other questions related to the issue, and provides some *suggestions for further reading* on the issue. Also, the *Internet References* page that accompanies each part opener contains a list of Internet site addresses (URLs) that should prove useful as starting points for further research. At the back of the book is a listing of all the *contributors to this volume,* which provides information on the legal scholars, commentators, and judges whose views are debated here.

Changes to this edition This edition adds a new section on Law and Terrorism in recognition of the significant impact on law of the events on September 11, 2001. In this new section we retain one issue from the last edition, "Should Persons Who Are Declared to Be 'Enemy Combatants' Be Able to Contest Their Detention Before a Judge?" and add three new issues, "Does the President Possess Constitutional Authority to Order Wiretaps on U.S. Citizens?" (Issue 2), "Is the Geneva Convention Irrelevant to Members of al Qaeda Who Are Held Prisoner at Guantanamo Bay?" (Issue 3), and "Should Someone Held by the CIA and Interrogated in a Foreign Country Be Allowed to Sue the U.S. Government?" (Issue 4). We have also added "Is It Constitutional to Ban Partial-Birth Abortions Without Providing for an Exception to Protect the Health of the Mother?" (Issue 5) and "Should the United States Require a Secure Identification System for Citizens?" (Issue 15).

A word to the instructor *An Instructor's Resource Guide With Test Questions* (multiple-choice and essay) is available through the publisher for the instructor using *Taking Sides* in the classroom. A general guidebook, *Using Taking Sides in the Classroom,* which discusses methods and techniques for integrating the pro-con approach into any classroom setting, is also available. An online version of *Using Taking Sides in the Classroom* and a correspondence service for *Taking Sides* adopters can be found at http://www.mhcls.com/usingts/.

Taking Sides: Clashing Views on Legal Issues is only one title in the Taking Sides series. If you are interested in seeing the table of contents for any of the other titles, please visit the Taking Sides Web site at http://www.mhcls.com/takingsides/.

Acknowledgments The new section on Law and Terrorism was suggested by Gabriel Katsh and benefited greatly from his research and writing.

M. Ethan Katsh
University of Massachusetts–Amherst

To Rebecca and Jordy

Contents In Brief

Contents

Supreme Court Justice Sandra Day O'Connor finds that the Authorization for Use of Military Force passed by Congress does not authorize the indefinite detainment of a person found to be an "enemy combatant." Justice Clarence Thomas believes that the detention of an "enemy combatant" is permitted under the federal government's war powers.

The Department of Justice argues that the Constitution gives the president the right to engage in electronic surveillance, with or without congressional approval or judicial oversight. It further claims that the NSA wiretapping program ordered by President Bush does not violate federal law, specifically the Foreign Intelligent Surveillance Act (FISA), because such surveillance falls under the auspices of the military response to the 9/11 attacks that was authorized by Congress. Several lawyers with expertise in constitutional law or experience in the federal government argue that the NSA wiretapping program violates the Foreign Intelligence Surveillance Act (FISA) and the Fourth Amendment of the U.S. Constitution. They further argue that the president does not have any inherent ability either to engage in warrantless wiretapping or to violate federal law that limits such surveillance.

Supreme Court Chief Justice William H. Rehnquist rules that although patients have the right to refuse life-sustaining treatment, physician-assisted suicide is not constitutionally protected. Judge Stephen Reinhardt argues that forbidding physician-assisted suicide in the cases of competent, terminally ill patients violates the due process clause of the Constitution.

Justice Ginsburg believes that the copyright laws are violated by a company when its software is used primarily for illegal file sharing, and lawful uses in the future are unlikely. Justice Breyer does not want the copyright laws to hinder technological innovation and is more willing to take into account the potential use of the software for lawful file sharing.

Supreme Court Justice Anthony Kennedy holds that requiring an individual to identify himself does not violate the right to remain silent and does not infringe rights guaranteed by the Fourth and Fifth Amendments. In a brief filed by the Office of the Nevada State Public Defender, the argument is put forward that when persons are detained on less than probable cause, it is unconstitutional for police to demand that such persons identify themselves and provide the police with their names.

Supreme Court Justice Clarence Thomas affirms the right of religious groups to use school facilities after the school day ends, maintaining that restricting such use is a violation of free speech rights. Supreme Court

Justice David Souter, dissenting from the Court's opinion, contends that the use of school facilities by religious groups blurs the line between public classroom instruction and private religious indoctrination and therefore violates the establishment clause of the Constitution.

Supreme Court Justice Antonin Scalia maintains that thermal imaging devices reveal information "that would previously have been unknowable without physical intrusion" and that using such devices for surveillance without a warrant constitutes a violation of the Fourth Amendment. Supreme Court Justice John Paul Stevens asserts that the Court's application of search and seizure rules to new technology is too broad and that collecting thermal imaging data from outside the home is not a violation of privacy rights.

Supreme Court Chief Justice William H. Rehnquist rules that a federal law withholding funds from public libraries that fail to install filters on computers that are connected to the Internet does not violate the First Amendment. Supreme Court Justice John Paul Stevens argues that filters on computers that are connected to the Internet are flawed and that the Children's Internet Protection Act violates the First Amendment.

Supreme Court Justice Anthony Kennedy holds that the Constitution prohibits the execution of a person who was under the age of eighteen at the time of the offense. Supreme Court Justice Antonin Scalia believes that the Constitution does not preclude the execution of a juvenile.

identifying citizens is a necessary part of the War on Terror and will also reduce identity theft. Timothy D. Sparapani, legislative counsel for the American Civil Liberties Union, argues that the proposed system will require all citizens to carry a national identity card and that such a system will not deter terrorists but will invade privacy.

Supreme Court Justice Sandra Day O'Connor argues that a Virginia statute proscribing all forms of cross burning is unconstitutional because symbolic speech can only be prohibited when done with the intent to intimidate, and such an intent cannot be inferred solely from the type of symbolic speech used. Supreme Court Justice Clarence Thomas argues that the history and nature of cross burning in the United States inextricably links the act to threatening and menacing violence and that the intent to intimidate can therefore be inferred solely from the act of cross burning itself.

Massachusetts Supreme Court Justice Margaret Marshall rules that banning marriage to same-sex couples causes hardship to a segment of the population for no rational reason. Massachusetts Supreme Court Justice Robert Cordy, in dissent, holds that a statute banning same-sex marriage is a valid exercise of the state's police power.

Supreme Court Justice John Paul Stevens interprets the Individuals with Disabilities Education Act as requiring public school districts to provide students who have severe physical disabilities with individualized and continuous nursing services during school hours. Supreme Court Justice

Clarence Thomas argues that such an interpretation will impose serious and unanticipated financial obligations on the states.

Supreme Court Justice Clarence Thomas argues that the University of Michigan Law School's admissions policy discriminates on the basis of race and is therefore in violation of the Fourteenth Amendment's equal protection clause. Supreme Court Justice Sandra Day O'Connor holds that the admissions policy of the University of Michigan Law School, which makes race one factor among many in the process of creating a diverse student body, does not violate the Constitution's guarantee of equal protection under the law.

Introduction

The Role of Law

M. Ethan Katsh

Two hundred years ago, Edmund Burke, the influential British statesman and orator, commented that "in no other country, perhaps, in the world, is the law so general a study as it is in the United States." Today, in America, general knowledge about law is at a disappointing level. In one recent study, 69 percent of those surveyed mistakenly believed that when it was first written, the U.S. Constitution outlawed slavery. Furthermore, a 2002 poll of 800 Americans found that nearly two-thirds (64 percent) could not name a single member of the current U.S. Supreme Court, and just 32 percent knew that there are nine justices. Only five people (two men, three women) in the entire survey could name all nine. In contrast, a whopping majority—75 percent—knew that there are three Rice Krispies characters, and 66 percent proudly cited their names (Snap, Crackle, and Pop). The Supreme Court justice with the highest name recognition (24 percent) was Sandra Day O'Connor.

One purpose of this volume is to provide information about some specific and important legal issues. In your local newspaper today, there is probably at least one story concerning an issue in this book. The quality of your life will be directly affected by how many of these issues are resolved. But affirmative action (Issue 19), abortion (Issue 5), copyrighted material on the Internet (Issue 7), and other issues in this book are often the subject of superficial, misleading, or inaccurate statements. *Taking Sides* is designed to encourage you to become involved in the public debate on these issues and to raise the level of the discussion on them.

The issues that are debated in this book represent some of the most important challenges our society faces. Issue 1, for example, raises questions about the rights of persons suspected of planning terrorist acts. How they are dealt with will influence what kind of society we will have in the future. While it is important to look at and study them separately, it is equally necessary to think about their relationship to each other and about the fact that there is a tool called "law," which is being called upon to solve a series of difficult conflicts. The study of discrete legal issues should enable you to gain insight into some broad theoretical questions about law. This introduction, therefore, will focus on several basic characteristics of law and the legal process that you should keep in mind as you read this book.

The Nature of Law

The eminent legal anthropologist E. Adamson Hoebel once noted that the search for a definition of law is as difficult as the search for the Holy Grail. Law is certainly complicated, and trying to define it precisely can be frustrating. What follows, therefore, is not a definition of law but a framework or perspective for looking at and understanding law.

Law as a Body of Rules

One of the common incorrect assumptions about law is that it is merely a body of rules invoked by those who need them and then applied by a judge. Under this view, the judge is essentially a machine whose task is simply to find and apply the right rule to the dispute in question. This perspective makes the mistake of equating law with the rules of law. It is sometimes even assumed that there exists somewhere in the libraries of lawyers and judges one book with all the rules or laws in it, which can be consulted to answer legal questions. As may already be apparent, such a book could not exist. Rules alone do not supply the solutions to many legal problems. The late Supreme Court justice William O. Douglas once wrote, "The law is not a series of calculating machines where definitions and answers come tumbling out when the right levers are pushed." As you read the debates about the issues in this book, you will see that much more goes into a legal argument than the recitation of rules.

Law as a Process

A more meaningful way of thinking about law is to look at it as a process or system, keeping in mind that legal rules are one of the elements in the process. This approach requires a considerably broader vision of law: to think not only of the written rules but also of the judges, the lawyers, the police, and all the other people in the system. It requires an even further consideration of all the things that influence these people, such as their values and economic status.

"Law," one legal commentator has stated, "is very like an iceberg; only one-tenth of its substance appears above the social surface in the explicit form of documents, institutions, and professions, while the nine-tenths of its substance that supports its visible fragment leads a sub-aquatic existence, living in the habits, attitudes, emotions and aspirations of men."[1]

In reading the discussions of controversial issues in this book, try to identify what forces are influencing the content of the rules and the position of the writers. Three of the most important influences on the nature of law are economics, moral values, and public opinion.

Law and Economics

Laws that talk about equality, such as the Fourteenth Amendment, which guarantees that no state shall "deny to any person . . . equal protection of the laws," suggest that economic status is irrelevant in the making and application of the law. As Anatole France, the nineteenth-century French satirist, once wrote, however, "The law, in its majestic equality, forbids the rich as well as the poor to sleep under bridges, to beg in streets, and to steal bread." Sometimes the purpose and effect of the law cannot be determined merely from the words of the law.

Critics of law in capitalistic societies assert that poverty results from the manipulation of the law by the wealthy and powerful. It is possible to look at several issues in this book and make some tentative judgments about the influence of economic power on law. For example, what role does economics play in the debate over the sharing of music files through the Internet (Issue 7)? Is the controversy over providing incentives for creators and musicians or maximizing profits for record companies?

Law and Values

The relationship between law and values has been a frequent theme of legal writers and a frequent source of debate. Clearly, there is in most societies some relationship between law and morality. One writer has summarized the relationship as follows:

1. *There is a moral order in society.* Out of the many different and often conflicting values of the individuals and institutions that make up society may emerge a dominant moral position, a ìcoreî of the moral order. The position of this core is dynamic, and as it changes, the moral order of society moves in the direction of that change.
2. *There is a moral content to the law.* The moral content of law also changes over time, and as it changes, the law moves in the direction of that change.
3. *The moral content of the law and moral order in society are seldom identical.*
4. *A natural and necessary affinity exists between the two "bodies" of law and moral order.*
5. *When there is a gap between the moral order of society and the law, some movement to close the gap is likely.* The law will move closer to the moral order of society, or the moral order will move closer to the law, or each will move toward the other. The likelihood of the movement to close the gap between law and moral order depends upon the size of the gap between the two bodies and the perceived significance of the subject matter concerning which the gap exists.[2]

Law and morality will not be identical in a pluralistic society, but there will also be attempts by dominant groups to insert their views of what is right into the legal code. The First Amendment prohibition against establishment of religion and the guarantee of freedom of religion are designed to protect those whose beliefs are different. Yet there have also been many historical examples of legal restrictions or limitations being imposed on minorities or of laws being ineffective because of the resistance of powerful groups. Prayers in the public schools, for example, which have been forbidden since the early 1960s, are still said in a few local communities.

Of the topics in this book, the insertion of morality into legal discussions has occurred most frequently in the abortion debate (Issue 5). It is probably fair to say that this issue remains high on the agenda of public debate because it involves strongly held values and beliefs. The nature of the debate is also colored by strong feelings that are held by the parties. Although empirical evidence about public health and abortion does exist, the debate is generally more emotional than objective.

Public Opinion and the Law

It is often claimed that the judicial process is insulated from public pressures. Judges are elected or appointed for long terms or for life, and the theory is that they will, therefore, be less subject to the force of public opinion. As a result, the law should be uniformly applied in different places, regardless of the nature of the community. It is fair to say that the judicial process is less responsive to public sentiment than is the political process, but that is not really saying much. What is important is that the legal process is not totally immune from public pressure. The force of public opinion is not applied directly through lobbying, but it would be naive to think that the force of what large numbers of people believe and desire never gets reflected in what happens in court. The most obvious examples are trials in which individuals are tried as much for their dissident beliefs as for their actions. Less obvious is the fact that the outcomes of cases may be determined in some measure by popular will. Judicial complicity in slavery or the internment of Japanese Americans during World War II are blatant examples of this.

Many of the issues selected for this volume are controversial because a large group is opposed to some practice sanctioned by the courts. Does this mean that the judges have taken a courageous stand and ignored public opinion? Not necessarily. Only in a few of the issues have courts adopted an uncompromising position. In most of the other issues, the trend of court decisions reflects a middle-of-the-road approach that could be interpreted as trying to satisfy everyone but those at the extremes. For example, in affirmative action (Issue 19), the *Bakke* decision, while generally approving of affirmative action, was actually won by Bakke and led to the abolition of all such programs that contained rigid quotas.

Assessing Influences on the Law

This summary of what can influence legal decisions is not meant to suggest that judges consciously ask what the public desires when interpretations of law are made. Rather, as members of society and as individuals who read newspapers and magazines and form opinions on political issues, there are subtle forces at work on judges that may not be obvious in any particular opinion but that can be discerned in a line of cases over a period of time. This may be explicitly denied by judges, such as in this statement by Justice Harry A. Blackmun in his majority opinion for the landmark *Roe v. Wade* abortion case: "Our task, of course, is to resolve the issue by constitutional measurement, free of emotion and predilection." However, a reading of that opinion raises the question of whether or not Blackmun succeeds in being totally objective in his interpretation of law and history.

Do these external and internal influences corrupt the system, create injustice, inject bias and discrimination, and pervert the law? Or do these influences enable judges to be flexible, to treat individual circumstances, and to fulfill the spirit of the law? Both of these ends are possible and do occur. What is important to realize is that there are so many points in the legal system where discretion is employed that it is hopeless to think that we could be governed by rules alone. "A government of laws, not men," aside from the sexism of the language, is not a realistic possibility, and it is not an alternative that many would find satisfying either.

On the other hand, it is also fair to say that the law, in striving to get the public to trust in it, must persuade citizens that it is more than the whim of those who are in power. While it cannot be denied that the law may be used in self-serving ways, there are also mechanisms at work that are designed to limit abuses of discretionary power. One quality of law that is relevant to this problem is that the legal process is fundamentally a conservative institution, which is, by nature, resistant to radical change. Lawyers are trained to give primary consideration in legal arguments to precedent—previous cases involving similar facts. As attention is focused on how the present case is similar to or different from past cases, some pressure is exerted on new decisions to be consistent with old ones and on the law to be stable. Thus, the way in which a legal argument is constructed tends to reduce the influence of currently popular psychological, sociological, philosophical, or anthropological theories. Prior decisions will reflect ideologies, economic considerations, and ethical values that were influential when these decisions were made, and, if no great change has occurred in the interim, the law will tend to preserve the status quo, both perpetuating old injustices and protecting traditional freedoms.

Legal Procedure

The law's great concern with the procedure of decision making is one of its more basic and important characteristics. Any discussion of the law that did not note the importance of procedure would be inadequate. Legal standards are often phrased not in terms of results but in terms of procedure. For example, it is not unlawful to convict the innocent if the right procedures are used (and it *is* unlawful to convict the guilty if the wrong procedures are followed). The law feels that it cannot guarantee that the right result will always be reached and that only the guilty will be caught, so it minimizes the risk of reaching the wrong result or convicting the innocent by specifying procedural steps to be followed. Lawyers, more than most people, are satisfied if the right procedures are followed even if there is something disturbing about the outcome. Law, therefore, has virtually eliminated the word *justice* from its vocabulary and has substituted the phrase *due process,* meaning that the proper procedures, such as right to counsel, right to a public trial, and right to cross-examine witnesses, have been followed. This concern with method is one of the pillars upon which law is based. It is one of the characteristics of law that distinguishes it from nonlegal methods of dispute resolution, where the atmosphere will be more informal and there may be no set procedures.

Conclusion

Law is a challenging area of study because many questions may not be amenable to simple solutions. The legal approach to problem solving is usually methodical and often slow. We frequently become frustrated with this process, and, in fact, it may be an inappropriate way to deal with some problems. For the issues in this book, however, an approach that pays careful attention to the many different aspects of these topics will be the most rewarding. Many of the readings provide historical, economic, and sociological data as well as information about law. The issues examined in *Taking Sides* involve basic cultural institutions such as religion, schools, and the family as well as basic cultural values such as privacy, individualism, and equality. While the law takes a narrow approach to problems, reading these issues should broaden your outlook on the problems discussed and, perhaps, encourage you to do further reading on those topics that are of particular interest to you.

For those who have not seen previous editions of this book, it should be noted that a new section has been added on Law and Terrorism. The events of September 11, 2001, have not only created new legal controversies but are forcing us to reconsider issues of privacy, security, and civil liberties in an emotionally charged environment. This book has always been about controversies and about how the law might respond to many different kinds of controversies. For the new issues, we hope that the reader will confront his or her own views and visions and participate in many debates that have only just begun.

Notes

1. Iredell Jenkins, *Social Order and the Limits of Law* (Princeton University Press, 1980), p. xi.
2. Lynn Wardle, "The Gap Between Law and Moral Order: An Examination of the Legitimacy of the Supreme Court Abortion Decisions," *Brigham Young University Law Review* (1980), pp. 811–835.

Internet References . . .

Findlaw Special Coverage "War on Terrorism"

http://news.findlaw.com/legalnews/us/terrorism/cases/index.html

Guide To Law Online: Terrorism Law

http://www.loc.gov/law/guide/terrorism.html

Congressional Research Service (CRS) Reports Regarding
the "War on Terrorism"

**http://digital.library.unt.edu/govdocs/crs/search.tkl?q=%22war+on+
terrorism%22&search_crit=fulltext&search=Search&date1=
Anytime&date2=Anytime&type=form**

DefendAmerica—U.S. Defense Dept.
War on Terror: 06/01/2007

DefendAmerica.mil is the United States Department of Defense Official Web site
on the War on Terrorism.

www.defendamerica.mil/

American Civil Liberties Union: National Security

http://www.aclu.org/natsec/index.html

Law and Terrorism

*T*he events of September 11, 2001 and the subsequent War on Terror have had a significant impact on the law. We are continuously being confronted with choices about what we want law to do and how we want law to do it. These choices touch many deeply held values, affect our identity as individuals and as a country, and pose questions that we are likely to visit and revisit for some time.

- Should Persons Who Are Declared to Be "Enemy Combatants" Be Able to Contest Their Detention Before a Judge?

- Does the President Possess Constitutional Authority to Order Wiretaps on U.S. Citizens?

- Is the Geneva Convention Irrelevant to Members of al Qaeda Who Are Held Prisoner at Guantanamo Bay?

- Should Someone Held by the CIA and Interrogated in a Foreign Country Be Allowed to Sue the U.S. Government?

ISSUE 1

Should Persons Who Are Declared to Be "Enemy Combatants" Be Able to Contest Their Detention Before a Judge?

YES: Sandra Day O'Connor, from Majority Opinion, *Hamdi, et al. v. Rumsfeld,* U.S. Supreme Court (June 28, 2004)

NO: Clarence Thomas, from Minority Opinion, *Hamdi, et al. v. Rumsfeld,* U.S. Supreme Court (June 28, 2004)

ISSUE SUMMARY

YES: Supreme Court Justice Sandra Day O'Connor finds that the Authorization for Use of Military Force passed by Congress does not authorize the indefinite detainment of a person found to be an "enemy combatant."

NO: Justice Clarence Thomas believes that the detention of an "enemy combatant" is permitted under the federal government's war powers.

T he factual background to this issue is well known. On September 11, 2001, the al Qaeda terrorist network launched a coordinated attack on the United States, striking the twin towers of the World Trade Center in New York City and the Pentagon. They failed to strike a third target in Washington, D.C., presumably the White House or the U.S. Capitol. Approximately 3,000 people were killed with thousands more injured. The attacks' immediate economic damages were calculated in the hundreds of millions of dollars. Their long-term effects, both human and economic, are still accumulating. It was the deadliest foreign attack on U.S. soil in this nation's history.

President George W. Bush took swift retaliatory action in response to the al Qaeda attacks. With the Authorization for Use of Military Force (AUMF), Pub. L. No. 107-40, secs. 1–2, 115 Stat. 224, Congress provided overwhelming bipartisan support for the president's use of "all necessary and appropriate force against those nations, organizations, or persons *he* determines planned, authorized, committed, or aided the terrorist attacks or harbored such organizations or person" (emphasis added). In addition to the power to commit military forces to battle, President Bush also claimed the authority to detain, indefinitely, those persons he designated as "enemy combatants"; a somewhat ambiguous term that includes suspected terrorists and their accomplices. Yaser Esam Hamdi was captured by Northern Alliance forces on the battlefields of Afghanistan in late 2001 and was eventually turned over to the American military. Hamdi was designated an "enemy combatant" and therefore subject to detention away from the battlefield for the duration of "hostilities."

Although he claimed to have been a noncombatant, Hamdi was held by the Department of Defense, without access to legal counsel for more than a year. Ultimately, Hamdi's father, acting as his "next friend," petitioned a federal district court for a writ of *habeas corpus*, alleging that his son had been wrongfully seized and was being unlawfully held by the U.S. government. In the course of the litigation, a central legal question that emerged was what level of review the courts should give to the government's determination of facts. In a time of war, should the courts simply defer to the executive branch because of national security concerns?

The legal challenge to Hamdi's detention moved back and forth between federal district court and the U.S. Court of Appeals. The U.S. government was ordered to grant a federal public defender's request to gain access to Hamdi in order to facilitate a due process challenge to his continued detention. Federal District Court Judge Robert Doumar characterized the government's factual declarations regarding Hamdi's original seizure as little more than their "say-so." He went on to insist that if the Court were to accept the government's factual claims alone as sufficient justification for Hamdi's continued detention, "it would in effect be abdicating any semblance of the most minimal level of judicial review. In effect, this Court would be acting as little more than a rubber-stamp." (*Hamdi v. Rumsfeld*, 243 F. Supp. 2d 527, 535 (E.D., Va. 2002)). On appeal, however, the Fourth Circuit Court of Appeals rejected the lower court's analysis, urging instead the need for limited judicial review during times of war. Fourth Circuit Judge J. Harvey Wilkinson, citing separation of powers concerns and the need to defer to the war-making powers of the executive and legislative branches, observed that, "[t]he safeguards that all Americans have come to expect in criminal prosecutions do not translate neatly to the arena of armed conflict. In fact, if deference to the executive branch is not exercised with respect to military judgments in the field, it is difficult to see where deference would ever obtain." (*Hamdi v. Rumsfeld*, 316 F.3d 450 (4th Cir. 2003)). With this decision, the Fourth Circuit Court denied further inquiry into the facts alleged by the U.S. government that justified Hamdi's status as an "enemy combatant." The U.S. Supreme Court granted review in this case, and the separation of powers question again would assume center stage. In a time of war, when an American citizen's individual liberties are in question, what role should the courts take in reviewing actions by the executive and legislative branches in their prosecution of that war?

YES ⟵

Sandra Day O'Connor

Majority Opinion, *Hamdi, et al. v. Rumsfeld*

JUSTICE O'CONNOR announced the judgment of the Court and delivered an opinion, in which the CHIEF JUSTICE, JUSTICE KENNEDY, and JUSTICE BREYER join.

At this difficult time in our Nation's history, we are called upon to consider the legality of the Government's detention of a United States citizen on United States soil as an "enemy combatant" and to address the process that is constitutionally owed to one who seeks to challenge his classification as such. The United States Court of Appeals for the Fourth Circuit held that petitioner's detention was legally authorized and that he was entitled to no further opportunity to challenge his enemy-combatant label. We now vacate and remand. We hold that although Congress authorized the detention of combatants in the narrow circumstances alleged here, due process demands that a citizen held in the United States as an enemy combatant be given a meaningful opportunity to contest the factual basis for that detention before a neutral decisionmaker.

I

... This case arises out of the detention of a man whom the Government alleges took up arms with the Taliban during this conflict. . . . The Government contends that Hamdi is an "enemy combatant," and that this status justifies holding him in the United States indefinitely—without formal charges or proceedings—unless and until it makes the determination that access to counsel or further process is warranted. . . .

The petition contends that Hamdi's detention was not legally authorized. *Id.*, at 105. It argues that, "[a]s an American citizen, . . . Hamdi enjoys the full protections of the Constitution," and that Hamdi's detention in the United States without charges, access to an impartial tribunal, or assistance of counsel "violated and continue[s] to violate the Fifth and Fourteenth Amendments to the United States Constitution. . . .

[The] District Court had failed to extend appropriate deference to the Government's security and intelligence interests. 296 F. 3d 278, 279, 283 (2002). It directed the District Court to consider "the most cautious procedures first," *id.*, at 284, and to conduct a deferential inquiry into Hamdi's status, . . .

Majority Opinion, Hamdi v. Rumsfeld, 542 U. S. 507 (2004). Some case citations omitted.

The Fourth Circuit emphasized that the "vital purposes" of the detention of uncharged enemy combatants—preventing those combatants from rejoining the enemy while relieving the military of the burden of litigating the circumstances of wartime captures halfway around the globe—were interests "directly derived from the war powers of Articles I and II." *Id.*, at 465–466. In that court's view, because "Article III contains nothing analogous to the specific powers of war so carefully enumerated in Articles I and II," *id.*, at 463, separation of powers principles prohibited a federal court from "delv[ing] further into Hamdi's status and capture," *id.*, at 473. Accordingly, the District Court's more vigorous inquiry "went far beyond the acceptable scope of review.". . .

II

The threshold question before us is whether the Executive has the authority to detain citizens who qualify as "enemy combatants." There is some debate as to the proper scope of this term, and the Government has never provided any court with the full criteria that it uses in classifying individuals as such. It has made clear, however, that, for purposes of this case, the "enemy combatant" that it is seeking to detain is an individual who, it alleges, was "'part of or supporting forces hostile to the United States or coalition partners'" in Afghanistan and who "'engaged in an armed conflict against the United States'" there. Brief for Respondents 3. We therefore answer only the narrow question before us: whether the detention of citizens falling within that definition is authorized.

The Government maintains that no explicit congressional authorization is required, because the Executive possesses plenary authority to detain pursuant to Article II of the Constitution. We do not reach the question whether Article II provides such authority, however, because we agree with the Government's alternative position, that Congress has in fact authorized Hamdi's detention, through the AUMF. . . .

The AUMF authorizes the President to use "all necessary and appropriate force" against "nations, organizations, or persons" associated with the September 11, 2001, terrorist attacks. 115 Stat. 224. There can be no doubt that individuals who fought against the United States in Afghanistan as part of the Taliban, an organization known to have supported the al Qaeda terrorist network responsible for those attacks, are individuals Congress sought to target in passing the AUMF. We conclude that detention of individuals falling into the limited category we are considering, for the duration of the particular conflict in which they were captured, is so fundamental and accepted an incident to war as to be an exercise of the "necessary and appropriate force" Congress has authorized the President to use.

The capture and detention of lawful combatants and the capture, detention, and trial of unlawful combatants, by "universal agreement and practice," are "important incident[s] of war.". . .

There is no bar to this Nation's holding one of its own citizens as an enemy combatant. . . .

Hamdi objects, nevertheless, that Congress has not authorized the *indefinite* detention to which he is now subject. . . . We take Hamdi's objection to be not to the lack of certainty regarding the date on which the conflict will end, but to the substantial prospect of perpetual detention. We recognize that the national security underpinnings of the "war on terror," although crucially important, are broad and malleable. As the Government concedes, "given its unconventional nature, the current conflict is unlikely to end with a formal cease-fire agreement." *Ibid.* The prospect Hamdi raises is therefore not far-fetched. If the Government does not consider this unconventional war won for two generations, and if it maintains during that time that Hamdi might, if released, rejoin forces fighting against the United States, then the position it has taken throughout the litigation of this case suggests that Hamdi's detention could last for the rest of his life. . . .

III

Even in cases in which the detention of enemy combatants is legally authorized, there remains the question of what process is constitutionally due to a citizen who disputes his enemy-combatant status. Hamdi argues that he is owed a meaningful and timely hearing and that "extra-judicial detention [that] begins and ends with the submission of an affidavit based on third-hand hearsay" does not comport with the Fifth and Fourteenth Amendments. . . .

A

. . . All agree that, absent suspension, the writ of habeas corpus remains available to every individual detained within the United States. U. S. Const., Art. I, §9, cl. 2. . . . Only in the rarest of circumstances has Congress seen fit to suspend the writ. . . . At all other times, it has remained a critical check on the Executive, ensuring that it does not detain individuals except in accordance with law. . . . All agree suspension of the writ has not occurred here. Thus, it is undisputed that Hamdi was properly before an Article III court to challenge his detention under 28 U. S. C. §2241. . . .

C

The Government's second argument requires closer consideration. This is the argument that further factual exploration is unwarranted and inappropriate in light of the extraordinary constitutional interests at stake. Under the Government's most extreme rendition of this argument, "[r]espect for separation of powers and the limited institutional capabilities of courts in matters of military decision-making in connection with an ongoing conflict" ought to eliminate entirely any individual process, restricting the courts to investigating only whether legal authorization exists for the broader detention scheme. At most, the Government argues, courts should review its determination that a citizen is an enemy combatant under a very deferential "some evidence" standard. *Id.,* at 34 ("Under the some evidence standard, the focus is exclusively on the factual basis supplied by the Executive to support its own determination.". . .

In response, Hamdi emphasizes that this Court consistently has recognized that an individual challenging his detention may not be held at the will of the Executive without recourse to some proceeding before a neutral tribunal to determine whether the Executive's asserted justifications for that detention have basis in fact and warrant in law. . . . He argues that the Fourth Circuit inappropriately "ceded power to the Executive during wartime to define the conduct for which a citizen may be detained, judge whether that citizen has engaged in the proscribed conduct, and imprison that citizen indefinitely," . . . and that due process demands that he receive a hearing in which he may challenge the Mobbs Declaration and adduce his own counter evidence. . . .

Both of these positions highlight legitimate concerns. And both emphasize the tension that often exists between the autonomy that the Government asserts is necessary in order to pursue effectively a particular goal and the process that a citizen contends he is due before he is deprived of a constitutional right. The ordinary mechanism that we use for balancing such serious competing interests, and for determining the procedures that are necessary to ensure that a citizen is not deprived of life, liberty, or property, . . .

1

It is beyond question that substantial interests lie on both sides of the scale in this case. Hamdi's "private interest . . . affected by the official action," *ibid.*, is the most elemental of liberty interests—the interest in being free from physical detention by one's own government. . . . "In our society liberty is the norm," and detention without trial "is the carefully limited exception.". . .

Nor is the weight on this side of the *Mathews* scale offset by the circumstances of war or the accusation of treasonous behavior, for "[i]t is clear that commitment for *any* purpose constitutes a significant deprivation of liberty that requires due process protection," . . . Indeed, as *amicus* briefs from media and relief organizations emphasize, the risk of erroneous deprivation of a citizen's liberty in the absence of sufficient process here is very real. . . . Moreover, as critical as the Government's interest may be in detaining those who actually pose an immediate threat to the national security of the United States during ongoing international conflict, history and common sense teach us that an unchecked system of detention carries the potential to become a means for oppression and abuse of others who do not present that sort of threat. . . . We reaffirm today the fundamental nature of a citizen's right to be free from involuntary confinement by his own government without due process of law, and we weigh the opposing governmental interests against the curtailment of liberty that such confinement entails.

2

On the other side of the scale are the weighty and sensitive governmental interests in ensuring that those who have in fact fought with the enemy during a war do not return to battle against the United States. . . . Without doubt, our Constitution recognizes that core strategic matters of warmaking belong in the hands of those who are best positioned and most politically accountable for making them. . . .

3

Striking the proper constitutional balance here is of great importance to the Nation during this period of ongoing combat. But it is equally vital that our calculus not give short shrift to the values that this country holds dear or to the privilege that is American citizenship. It is during our most challenging and uncertain moments that our Nation's commitment to due process is most severely tested; and it is in those times that we must preserve our commitment at home to the principles for which we fight abroad. . . .

With due recognition of these competing concerns, we believe that neither the process proposed by the Government nor the process apparently envisioned by the District Court below strikes the proper constitutional balance when a United States citizen is detained in the United States as an enemy combatant. That is, "the risk of erroneous deprivation" of a detainee's liberty interest is unacceptably high under the Government's proposed rule, while some of the "additional or substitute procedural safeguards" suggested by the District Court are unwarranted in light of their limited "probable value" and the burdens they may impose on the military in such cases. *Mathews*, 424 U. S., at 335.

We therefore hold that a citizen-detainee seeking to challenge his classi- fication as an enemy combatant must receive notice of the factual basis for his classification, and a fair opportunity to rebut the Government's factual assertions before a neutral decisionmaker. . . . "For more than a century the central meaning of procedural due process has been clear: 'Parties whose rights are to be affected are entitled to be heard; and in order that they may enjoy that right they must first be notified.' It is equally fundamental that the right to notice and an opportunity to be heard 'must be granted at a meaning- ful time and in a meaningful manner.'" . . . These essential constitutional promises may not be eroded.

At the same time, the exigencies of the circumstances may demand that, aside from these core elements, enemy combatant proceedings may be tai- lored to alleviate their uncommon potential to burden the Executive at a time of ongoing military conflict. . . .

We think it unlikely that this basic process will have the dire impact on the central functions of warmaking that the Government forecasts. . . .

In sum, while the full protections that accompany challenges to deten- tions in other settings may prove unworkable and inappropriate in the enemy- combatant setting, the threats to military operations posed by a basic system of independent review are not so weighty as to trump a citizen's core rights to challenge meaningfully the Government's case and to be heard by an impartial adjudicator.

D

In so holding, we necessarily reject the Government's assertion that separa- tion of powers principles mandate a heavily circumscribed role for the courts in such circumstances. . . . We have long since made clear that a state of war is not a blank check for the President when it comes to the rights of the Nation's citizens. . . . Whatever power the United States Constitution envisions for the

Executive in its exchanges with other nations or with enemy organizations in times of conflict, it most assuredly envisions a role for all three branches when individual liberties are at stake. . . . Likewise, we have made clear that, unless Congress acts to suspend it, the Great Writ of habeas corpus allows the Judicial Branch to play a necessary role in maintaining this delicate balance of governance, serving as an important judicial check on the Executive's discretion in the realm of detentions. . . .

Clarence Thomas

→ **NO**

Minority Opinion, *Hamdi, et al. v. Rumsfeld*

J USTICE THOMAS, dissenting.

The Executive Branch, acting pursuant to the powers vested in the President by the Constitution and with explicit congressional approval, has determined that Yaser Hamdi is an enemy combatant and should be detained. This detention falls squarely within the Federal Government's war powers, and we lack the expertise and capacity to second-guess that decision. As such, petitioners' habeas challenge should fail, and there is no reason to remand the case. The plurality reaches a contrary conclusion by failing adequately to consider basic principles of the constitutional structure as it relates to national security and foreign affairs and by using the balancing scheme of *Mathews* v. *Eldridge*, 424 U. S. 319 (1976). I do not think that the Federal Government's war powers can be balanced away by this Court. Arguably, Congress could provide for additional procedural protections, but until it does, we have no right to insist upon them. But even if I were to agree with the general approach the plurality takes, I could not accept the particulars. The plurality utterly fails to account for the Government's compelling interests and for our own institutional inability to weigh competing concerns correctly. I respectfully dissent.

I

"It is 'obvious and unarguable' that no governmental interest is more compelling than the security of the Nation." *Haig* v. *Agee*, 453 U. S. 280, 307 (1981). . . . The national security, after all, is the primary responsibility and purpose of the Federal Government. . . . But because the Founders understood that they could not foresee the myriad potential threats to national security that might later arise, they chose to create a Federal Government that necessarily possesses sufficient power to handle any threat to the security of the Nation. The power to protect the Nation

> "ought to exist without limitation . . . *[b]ecause it is impossible to foresee or define the extent and variety of national exigencies, or the correspondent extent & variety of the means which may be necessary to satisfy them.* The circumstances that endanger the safety of nations are infinite; and for this

Minority Opinion, Hamdi v. Rumsfeld, 542 U. S. 507 (2004). Some case citations omitted.

reason no constitutional shackles can wisely be imposed on the power to which the care of it is committed." *Id.,* at 147.

. . . The Founders intended that the President have primary responsibility—along with the necessary power—to protect the national security and to conduct the Nation's foreign relations. They did so principally because the structural advantages of a unitary Executive are essential in these domains. "Energy in the executive is a leading character in the definition of good government. It is essential to the protection of the community against foreign attacks." The Federalist No. 70. The principle "ingredien[t]" for "energy in the executive" is "unity.". . . This is because "[d]ecision, activity, secrecy, and dispatch will generally characterise the proceedings of one man, in a much more eminent degree, than the proceedings of any greater number."

These structural advantages are most important in the national-security and foreign-affairs contexts. "Of all the cares or concerns of government, the direction of war most peculiarly demands those qualities which distinguish the exercise of power by a single hand.". . . Also for these reasons, John Marshall explained that "[t]he President is the sole organ of the nation in its external relations, and its sole representative with foreign nations.". . . To this end, the Constitution vests in the President "[t]he executive Power," Art. II, §1, provides that he "shall be Commander in Chief of the" armed forces, §2, and places in him the power to recognize foreign governments, §3.

This Court has long recognized these features and has accordingly held that the President has *constitutional* authority to protect the national security and that this authority carries with it broad discretion. . . .

The Court has acknowledged that the President has the authority to "employ [the Nation's Armed Forces] in the manner he may deem most effectual to harass and conquer and subdue the enemy.". . . With respect to foreign affairs as well, the Court has recognized the President's independent authority and need to be free from interference. . . .

Congress, to be sure, has a substantial and essential role in both foreign affairs and national security. But it is crucial to recognize that *judicial* interference in these domains destroys the purpose of vesting primary responsibility in a unitary Executive. I cannot improve on Justice Jackson's words, speaking for the Court:

"The President, both as Commander-in-Chief and as the Nation's organ for foreign affairs, has available intelligence services whose reports are not and ought not to be published to the world. It would be intolerable that courts, without the relevant information, should review and perhaps nullify actions of the Executive taken on information properly held secret. Nor can courts sit *in camera* in order to be taken into executive confidences. But even if courts could require full disclosure, the very nature of executive decisions as to foreign policy is political, not judicial. Such decisions are wholly confided by our Constitution to the political departments of the government, Executive and Legislative. They are delicate, complex, and involve large elements of prophecy. They are and should be undertaken only by those directly responsible to the people whose welfare they advance or imperil. They are decisions of a kind for which the Judiciary has neither aptitude, facilities nor responsibility and which has long been held to belong in the domain of political power not subject to judicial intrusion or inquiry." *Ibid.*

Several points . . . are worth emphasizing. First, with respect to certain decisions relating to national security and foreign affairs, the courts simply lack the relevant information and expertise to second-guess determinations made by the President based on information properly withheld. Second, even if the courts could compel the Executive to produce the necessary information, such decisions are simply not amenable to judicial determination because "[t]hey are delicate, complex, and involve large elements of prophecy." Third, the Court . . . has correctly recognized the primacy of the political branches in the foreign-affairs and national-security contexts.

For these institutional reasons and because "Congress cannot anticipate and legislate with regard to every possible action the President may find it necessary to take or every possible situation in which he might act," it should come as no surprise that "[s]uch failure of Congress . . . does not, 'especially . . . in the areas of foreign policy and national security,' imply 'congressional disapproval' of action taken by the Executive." . . . Rather, in these domains, the fact that Congress has provided the President with broad authorities does not imply—and the Judicial Branch should not infer—that Congress intended to deprive him of particular powers not specifically enumerated. See *Dames & Moore*, 453 U. S., at 678. As far as the courts are concerned, "the enactment of legislation closely related to the question of the President's authority in a particular case which evinces legislative intent to accord the President broad discretion may be considered to 'invite' 'measures on independent presidential responsibility.'" *Ibid.* (quoting *Youngstown*, 343 U. S., at 637 (Jackson, J., concurring)). . . .

I acknowledge that the question whether Hamdi's executive detention is lawful is a question properly resolved by the Judicial Branch, though the question comes to the Court with the strongest presumptions in favor of the Government. The plurality agrees that Hamdi's detention is lawful if he is an enemy combatant. But the question whether Hamdi is actually an enemy combatant is "of a kind for which the Judiciary has neither aptitude, facilities nor responsibility and which has long been held to belong in the domain of political power not subject to judicial intrusion or inquiry." . . . That is, although it is appropriate for the Court to determine the judicial question whether the President has the asserted authority . . . we lack the information and expertise to question whether Hamdi is actually an enemy combatant, a question the resolution of which is committed to other branches.[1] . . .

II

"The war power of the national government is 'the power to wage war successfully.'" . . . The Authorization for Use of Military Force (AUMF), 115 Stat. 224, authorizes the President to "use all necessary and appropriate force against those nations, organizations, or persons he determines planned, authorized, committed, or aided the terrorist attacks" of September 11, 2001. Indeed, the Court has previously concluded that language materially identical to . . .

The plurality, however, qualifies its recognition of the President's authority to detain enemy combatants in the war on terrorism in ways that are at odds with our precedent. . . . [We] are bound by the political branches' determination that the United States is at war. . . . [The] power to detain does not end with the cessation of formal hostilities. . . .

Accordingly, the President's action here is "supported by the strongest of presumptions and the widest latitude of judicial interpretation.". . . The question becomes whether the Federal Government (rather than the President acting alone) has power to detain Hamdi as an enemy combatant. More precisely, we must determine whether the Government may detain Hamdi given the procedures that were used.

III

I agree with the plurality that the Federal Government has power to detain those that the Executive Branch determines to be enemy combatants. See *ante*, at 10. But I do not think that the plurality has adequately explained the breadth of the President's authority to detain enemy combatants, an authority that includes making virtually conclusive factual findings. In my view, the structural considerations discussed above, as recognized in our precedent, demonstrate that we lack the capacity and responsibility to second-guess this determination. . . .

The Court has held that an executive, acting pursuant to statutory and constitutional authority may, consistent with the Due Process Clause, unilaterally decide to detain an individual if the executive deems this necessary for the public safety *even if he is mistaken.*

. . . In *Luther* v. *Borden,* 7 How. 1 (1849), . . . the Court also addressed the natural concern that placing "this power in the President is dangerous to liberty, and may be abused." The Court noted that "[a]ll power may be abused if placed in unworthy hands," and explained that "it would be difficult . . . to point out any other hands in which this power would be more safe, and at the same time equally effectual." Putting that aside, the Court emphasized that this power "is conferred upon him by the Constitution and laws of the United States, and must therefore be respected and enforced in its judicial tribunals." Finally, the Court explained that if the President abused this power "it would be in the power of Congress to apply the proper remedy. But the courts must administer the law as they find it." *Id.,* at 45. . . .

The Government's asserted authority to detain an individual that the President has determined to be an enemy combatant, at least while hostilities continue, comports with the Due Process Clause. As these cases also show, the Executive's decision that a detention is necessary to protect the public need not and should not be subjected to judicial second-guessing. Indeed, at least in the context of enemy-combatant determinations, this would defeat the unity, secrecy, and dispatch that the Founders believed to be so important to the warmaking function. . . .

Accordingly, I conclude that the Government's detention of Hamdi as an enemy combatant does not violate the Constitution. By detaining Hamdi, the President, in the prosecution of a war and authorized by Congress, has acted well within his authority. Hamdi thereby received all the process to which he was due under the circumstances. I therefore believe that this is no occasion to balance the competing interests, as the plurality unconvincingly attempts to do.

IV

Although I do not agree with the plurality that the balancing approach of *Mathews* v. *Eldridge,* 424 U. S. 319 (1976), is the appropriate analytical tool with which to analyze this case,[2] I cannot help but explain that the plurality misapplies its chosen framework, one that if applied correctly would probably lead to the result I have reached. . . .

Undeniably, Hamdi has been deprived of a serious interest, one actually protected by the Due Process Clause. Against this, however, is the Government's overriding interest in protecting the Nation. If a deprivation of liberty can be justified by the need to protect a town, the protection of the Nation, *a fortiori*, justifies it.

I acknowledge that under the plurality's approach, it might, at times, be appropriate to give detainees access to counsel and notice of the factual basis for the Government's determination. See *ante*, at 25–27. But properly accounting for the Government's interests also requires concluding that access to counsel and to the factual basis would not always be warranted. . . .

Notes

1. Although I have emphasized national-security concerns, the President's foreign-affairs responsibilities are also squarely implicated by this case. The Government avers that Northern Alliance forces captured Hamdi, and the District Court demanded that the Government turn over information relating to statements made by members of the Northern Alliance. See 316 F. 3d 450, 462 (CA4 2003).
2. Evidently, neither do the parties, who do not cite *Mathews* even once.

POSTSCRIPT

Should Persons Who Are Declared to Be "Enemy Combatants" Be Able to Contest Their Detention Before a Judge?

Although the events of September 11th were unique in American history, many of the legal questions they entail are not. In a time of war, how do democracies erect and negotiate the difficult balance between the security of the many and protection of individual liberties? What should be the role of the courts in maintaining this balance? A look back in our own history is instructive.

On April 27, 1861, President Abraham Lincoln first suspended the writ of *habeas corpus*, nearly two weeks after Fort Sumpter fell to Confederate forces. He would do so again two more times before the end of the Civil War, in response to the profound nature of the threat posed to the nation's security by the war. Lambdin Milligan, Indiana lawyer and sympathizer of the Southern cause, was one of several thousand civilians arrested during this period. Sentenced to death for insurrectionary activities by a military commission, Milligan ultimately challenged his conviction before the U.S. Supreme Court. Rendering its decision after the war had come to an end, the Court overturned Milligan's conviction, holding that he had been denied his constitutional rights to a jury trial in a court of law (not the military tribunal that convicted him). Writing for the Court, Justice Davis observed: "During the late wicked Rebellion, the temper of the times did not allow that calmness in deliberation and discussion so necessary to a correct conclusion of a purely judicial question. *Then*, considerations of safety were mingled with the exercise of power; and feelings and interests prevailed which are happily terminated. *Now* that the public safety is assured, this question, as well as all others, can be discussed and decided without passion or the admixture of any element not required to form a legal judgment." (*Ex parte Milligan*, 24 Wall. [71 U.S.] 2, 1866).

Although Justice Davis would concede that constitutional protections of individual rights are "elastic," narrowing in a time of crisis, expanding in a time of calm, he would go on to insist on the absolute necessity for judicial review of executive action, even in time of war. The scope of such judicial review would remain in question. However, in one of the next great crises to confront this nation, World War II, a majority of the Supreme Court would uphold the constitutionality of the forced internment of innocent American citizens of Japanese descent (*Korematsu v. United States*, 323 U.S. 214, 1944). In doing so, the Court articulated the need on the part of the judiciary, in the

15

name of security, to defer to the military and the executive branch in times of national emergency. *Korematsu v. United States* was not a unanimous decision, however, and stinging dissents were written by Justices Murphy and Jackson. Justice Jackson just a few years later, would take leave from the Court to lead the U.S. prosecution team at the Nuremberg War Crimes Tribunal. Both Murphy and Jackson insisted that, in times of national crisis, it was especially important that not only there be judicial review of executive branch actions and the judiciary not adopt an overly deferential posture, but constitutional protections of individual rights remain continuous with their peacetime status. Although never reversed, the *Korematsu* decision was in later years repudiated. In 1998, Fred Korematsu was awarded the Presidential Medal of Freedom by President Clinton.

The literature dealing with this issue is enormous. One place to begin is with Michael Ignatieff's *The Lesser Evil: Political Ethics in an Age of Terror* (Princeton University Press, 2004), which provides a rich historical and comparative analysis of the unique problems democracies face when confronted by external military threats. Also valuable is the influential work of Louis Fisher; see *Military Tribunals and Presidential Power* (University Press of Kansas, 2005); and *Presidential War Power* (University Press of Kansas, 2004). In addition, current Supreme Court Chief Justice William Rehnquist has authored an interesting history of the issue; see *All the Laws but One: Civil Liberties in Wartime* (Vintage, 2000). Finally, for the Bush administration's current statement of its assessment of the nation's security concerns, see *The National Defense Strategy of the United States* (www.whitehouse.gov/nsc/nss.pdf).

ISSUE 2

Does the President Possess Constitutional Authority to Order Wiretaps on U.S. Citizens?

YES: U.S. Department of Justice, from "Legal Authorities Supporting the Activities of the National Security Agency Described by the President" (January 19, 2006)

NO: Letter to Congress, from 14 Law Professors and Former Government Attorneys to Congressional Leaders (January 2, 2006)

ISSUE SUMMARY

YES: The Department of Justice argues that the Constitution gives the president the right to engage in electronic surveillance, with or without congressional approval or judicial oversight. It further claims that the NSA wiretapping program ordered by President Bush does not violate federal law, specifically the Foreign Intelligent Surveillance Act (FISA), because such surveillance falls under the auspices of the military response to the 9/11 attacks that was authorized by Congress.

NO: Several lawyers with expertise in constitutional law or experience in the federal government argue that the NSA wiretapping program violates the Foreign Intelligence Surveillance Act (FISA) and the Fourth Amendment of the U.S. Constitution. They further argue that the president does not have any inherent ability either to engage in warrantless wiretapping or to violate federal law that limits such surveillance.

After discovering that President Nixon had used the FBI and other law enforcement mechanisms to spy on political opponents, the Senate voted in 1975 to establish a committee, chaired by Senator Frank Church, to investigate the government's recent intelligence gathering and whether it had involved any "illegal, improper, or unethical activities . . . by any agency of the Federal Government" (S. Res. 21, 1975). The Church Committee found, as many had speculated, that the FBI and CIA had engaged in massive spying on American citizens with little or no judicial oversight.

In issuing its numerous recommendations to Congress for how it should address the abuses that intelligence-gathering agencies had perpetrated, the Church Committee stated that it "believe[d] that there should be no electronic surveillance within the United States which is not subject to a judicial warrant procedure." The Supreme Court largely agreed: By the time of the Church Committee report, it had already ruled that most electronic surveillance, such as wiretapping phone calls, required a warrant. In *United States v. United States District Court* (1972), the majority declared that "Fourth Amendment freedoms cannot properly be guaranteed if domestic security surveillances may be conducted solely within the discretion of the Executive Branch . . . the Government's concerns do not justify departure in this case from the customary Fourth Amendment requirement of judicial approval prior to initiation of a search or surveillance."

However, in its decision in *United States v. U.S. District Court,* the Court was careful to disclaim that it was not passing judgment "on the scope of the President's surveillance power with respect to the activities of *foreign* powers, within or without this country" [emphasis added]. Congress similarly had avoided the subject of "foreign intelligence surveillance" in federal legislation on electronic surveillance. Thus, while there were constitutional and statutory restrictions on how law enforcement could conduct surveillance on criminal suspects and "domestic" national security threats, there were no guidelines on measures that the government undertook in the name of foreign intelligence surveillance.

To address this issue, Congress in 1978 passed FISA, the Foreign Intelligence Surveillance Act. FISA established a special court, the Foreign Intelligence Surveillance Court (FISC), that meets in secret to issue warrants for wiretapping and searches that relate to threats from "a foreign power or an agent of a foreign power," including potential acts of "sabotage and international terrorism" (FISA, codified as 50 USC 1801(e)(1)). FISA also established civil and criminal penalties for any government official who "engages in electronic surveillance under color of law except as authorized by statute" (50 USC 1809(a)(1). Congress believed that in passing FISA and in establishing a method whereby intelligence agencies could obtain warrants secretly and without any public record, it had balanced the Church Committee and the Supreme Court's concerns about civil liberties with the need of those agencies to collect information vital to national security.

In a 2002 presidential order, President Bush authorized the National Security Agency (NSA) to engage in warrantless wiretapping as part of its antiterrorism surveillance. Although, because of the secret nature of the program, its true extent is unknown, the *New York Times,* in breaking the story, reported that the NSA has monitored "the international telephone calls and international e-mail messages of hundreds, perhaps thousands, of people inside the United States." The president has since acknowledged the program's existence, and the Department of Justice released a memorandum, from which the attached "Yes" reading is excerpted, defending the legality of the program. In response, civil libertarians have criticized it as a dangerous invasion of the privacy of ordinary Americans, and many legal scholars, such as those who wrote this issue's "No" reading, have argued that it is both illegal and unconstitutional.

YES ⤶

Legal Authorities Supporting the Activities of the National Security Agency Described by the President

As the President has explained, since shortly after the attacks of September 11, 2001, he has authorized the National Security Agency ("NSA") to intercept international communications into and out of the United States of persons linked to al Qaeda or related terrorist organizations. The purpose of these intercepts is to establish an early warning system to detect and prevent another catastrophic terrorist attack on the United States. This paper addresses, in an unclassified form, the legal basis for the NSA activities described by the President ("NSA activities"). . . .

In its first legislative response to the terrorist attacks of September 11th, Congress authorized the President to "use all necessary and appropriate force against those nations, organizations, or persons he determines planned, authorized, committed, or aided the terrorist attacks" of September 11th in order to prevent "any future acts of international terrorism against the United States." Authorization for Use of Military Force, Pub. L. No. 107-40, § 2(a), 115 Stat. 224, 224 (Sept. 18, 2001) (reported as a note to 50 U.S.C.A. § 1541) ("AUMF"). History conclusively demonstrates that warrantless communications intelligence targeted at the enemy in time of armed conflict is a traditional and fundamental incident of the use of military force authorized by the AUMF. The Supreme Court's interpretation of the AUMF in *Hamdi v. Rumsfeld*, 542 U.S. 507 (2004), confirms that Congress in the AUMF gave its express approval to the military conflict against al Qaeda and its allies and thereby to the President's use of all traditional and accepted incidents of force in this current military conflict—including warrantless electronic surveillance to intercept enemy communications both at home and abroad. This understanding of the AUMF demonstrates Congress's support for the President's authority to protect the Nation and, at the same time, adheres to Justice O'Connor's admonition that "a state of war is not a blank check for the President," *Hamdi*, 542 U.S. at 536 (plurality opinion), particularly in view of the narrow scope of the NSA activities. . . .

Memorandum released by the U.S. Department of Justice, January 9, 2006.

Background

A. The Attacks of September 11, 2001

On September 14, 2001, the President declared a national emergency "by reason of the terrorist attacks at the World Trade Center, New York, New York, and the Pentagon, and the continuing and immediate threat of further attacks on the United States." Proclamation No. 7463, 66 Fed. Reg. 48,199 (Sept. 14, 2001). The same day, Congress passed a joint resolution authorizing the President "to use all necessary and appropriate force against those nations, organizations, or persons he determines planned, authorized, committed, or aided the terrorist attacks" of September 11th, which the President signed on September 18th. AUMF § 2(a). Congress also expressly acknowledged that the attacks rendered it "necessary and appropriate" for the United States to exercise its right "to protect United States citizens both at home and abroad," and in particular recognized that "the President has authority under the Constitution to take action to deter and prevent acts of international terrorism against the United States." *Id.* pmbl. Congress emphasized that the attacks "continue to pose an unusual and extraordinary threat to the national security and foreign policy of the United States." *Id.* The United States also launched a large-scale military response, both at home and abroad. In the United States, combat air patrols were immediately established over major metropolitan areas and were maintained 24 hours a day until April 2002. The United States also immediately began plans for a military response directed at al Qaeda's base of operations in Afghanistan. Acting under his constitutional authority as Commander in Chief, and with the support of Congress, the President dispatched forces to Afghanistan and, with the assistance of the Northern Alliance, toppled the Taliban regime.

As the President made explicit in his Military Order of November 13, 2001, authorizing the use of military commissions to try terrorists, the attacks of September 11th "created a state of armed conflict." Military Order § l(a), 66 Fed. Reg. 57,833 (Nov. 13, 2001). Indeed, shortly after the attacks, NATO—for the first time in its 46-year history—invoked article 5 of the North Atlantic Treaty, which provides that an "armed attack against one or more of [the parties] shall be considered an attack against them all." . . . The President also determined in his Military Order that al Qaeda and related terrorists organizations "possess both the capability and the intention to undertake further terrorist attacks against the United States that, if not detected and prevented, will cause mass deaths, mass injuries, and massive destruction of property, and may place at risk the continuity of the operations of the United States Government," and concluded that "an extraordinary emergency exists for national defense purposes." Military Order, § l(c), (g), 66 Fed. Reg. at 57,833-34.

B. The NSA Activities

Against this unfolding background of events in the fall of 2001, there was substantial concern that al Qaeda and its allies were preparing to carry out another attack within the United States. Al Qaeda had demonstrated its ability to introduce agents into the United States undetected and to perpetrate devastating attacks, and it was suspected that additional agents were likely already in position within the Nation's borders. As the President has explained, unlike a conventional enemy, al Qaeda has infiltrated "our cities and communities and communicated from here in America to plot and plan with bin Laden's lieutenants in Afghanistan, Pakistan and elsewhere." Press Conference of President Bush (Dec. 19, 2005). . . . To this day, finding al Qaeda sleeper agents in the United States remains one of the paramount concerns in the War on Terror. As the President has explained, "[t]he terrorists want to strike America again, and they hope to inflict even more damage than they did on September the 11th." *Id.*

The President has acknowledged that, to counter this threat, he has authorized the NSA to intercept international communications into and out of the United States of persons linked to al Qaeda or related terrorist organizations. The same day, the Attorney General elaborated and explained that in order to intercept a communication, there must be "a reasonable basis to conclude that one party to the communication is a member of al Qaeda, affiliated with al Qaeda, or a member of an organization affiliated with al Qaeda." Press Briefing by Attorney General Alberto Gonzales and General Michael Hayden, Principal Deputy Director for National Intelligence . . . (Dec. 19, 2005) (statement of Attorney General Gonzales). The purpose of these intercepts is to establish an early warning system to detect and prevent another catastrophic terrorist attack on the United States. The President has stated that the NSA activities "ha[ve] been effective in disrupting the enemy, while safeguarding our civil liberties." President's Press Conference. . . .

Analysis

I. The President Has Inherent Constitutional Authority to Order Warrantless Foreign Intelligence Surveillance

As Congress expressly recognized in the AUMF, "the President has authority under the Constitution to take action to deter and prevent acts of international terrorism against the United States," AUMF pmbl., especially in the context of the current conflict. Article II of the Constitution vests in the President all executive power of the United States, including the power to act as Commander in Chief of the Armed Forces, *see* U.S. Const. art. II, § 2, and authority over the conduct of the Nation's foreign affairs. . . .

To carry out these responsibilities, the President must have authority to gather information necessary for the execution of his office. The Founders, after all, intended the federal Government to be clothed with all authority necessary to protect the Nation. . . . Because of the structural advantages of the Executive Branch, the Founders also intended that the President would have the primary responsibility and necessary authority as Commander in Chief and Chief Executive to protect the Nation and to conduct the Nation's foreign affairs. . . . Thus, it has been long recognized that the President has the authority to use secretive means to collect intelligence necessary for the conduct of foreign affairs and military campaigns. . . .

In reliance on these principles, a consistent understanding has developed that the President has inherent constitutional authority to conduct warrantless searches and surveillance within the United States for foreign intelligence purposes. Wiretaps for such purposes thus have been authorized by Presidents at least since the administration of Franklin Roosevelt in 1940. *See, e.g., United States v. United States District Court,* 444 F.2d 651, 669-71 (6th Cir. 1971) (reproducing as an appendix memoranda from Presidents Roosevelt, Truman, and Johnson). In a Memorandum to Attorney General Jackson, President Roosevelt wrote on May 21, 1940:

> You are, therefore, authorized and directed in such cases as you may approve, after investigation of the need in each case, to authorize the necessary investigation agents that they are at liberty to secure information by listening devices directed to the conversation or other communications of persons suspected of subversive activities against the Government of the United States, including suspected spies. You are requested furthermore to limit these investigations so conducted to a minimum and limit them insofar as possible to aliens.

. . . In *United States v. United States District Court,* 407 U.S. 297 (1972) (the *"Keith"* case), the Supreme Court concluded that the Fourth Amendment's warrant requirement applies to investigations of wholly *domestic* threats to security—such as domestic political violence and other crimes. But the Court in the *Keith* case made clear that it was not addressing the President's authority to conduct *foreign* intelligence surveillance without a warrant and that it was expressly reserving that question: "[T]he instant case requires no judgment on the scope of the President's surveillance power with respect to the activities of foreign powers, within or without this country." *Id.* at 308; *see also id.* at 321-22 & n.20 ("We have not addressed, and express no opinion as to, the issues which may be involved with respect to activities of foreign powers or their agents."). That *Keith* does not apply in the context of protecting against a foreign attack has been confirmed by the lower courts. After *Keith,* each of the three courts of appeals that have squarely considered the question have concluded—expressly taking the Supreme Court's decision into account— that the President has inherent authority to conduct warrantless surveillance in the foreign intelligence context. *See, e.g., Truong Dinh Hung,* 629 F.2d at 913-14; *Butenko,* 494 F.2d at 603; *Brown,* 484 F.2d 425-26.

From a constitutional standpoint, foreign intelligence surveillance such as the NSA activities differs fundamentally from the domestic security surveillance at issue in *Keith.* As the Fourth Circuit observed, the President has uniquely strong constitutional powers in matters pertaining to foreign affairs and national security. "Perhaps most crucially, the executive branch not only has superior expertise in the area of foreign intelligence, it is also constitutionally designated as the pre-eminent authority in foreign affairs." *Truong,* 629 F.2d at 914. . . .

The present circumstances that support recognition of the President's inherent constitutional authority to conduct the NSA activities are considerably stronger than were the circumstances at issue in the earlier courts of appeals cases that recognized this power. All of the cases described above addressed inherent executive authority under the foreign affairs power to conduct surveillance in a peacetime context. The courts in these cases therefore had no occasion even to consider the fundamental authority of the President, as Commander in Chief, to gather intelligence in the context of an ongoing armed conflict in which the United States already had suffered massive civilian casualties and in which the intelligence gathering efforts at issue were specifically designed to thwart further armed attacks. Indeed, intelligence gathering is particularly important in the current conflict, in which the enemy attacks largely through clandestine activities and which, as Congress recognized, "pose[s] an unusual and extraordinary threat," AUMF pmbl. . . .

II. The AUMF Confirms and Supplements the President's Inherent Power to Use Warrantless Surveillance Against the Enemy in the Current Armed Conflict

In the Authorization for Use of Military Force enacted in the wake of September 11th, Congress confirms and supplements the President's constitutional authority to protect the Nation, including through electronic surveillance, in the context of the current post-September 11th armed conflict with al Qaeda and its allies. The broad language of the AUMF affords the President, at a minimum, discretion to employ the traditional incidents of the use of military force. The history of the President's use of warrantless surveillance during armed conflicts demonstrates that the NSA surveillance described by the President is a fundamental incident of the use of military force that is necessarily included in the AUMF. . . .

The AUMF passed by Congress on September 14, 2001, does not lend itself to a narrow reading. Its expansive language authorizes the President "to use *all necessary and appropriate force* against those nations, organizations, or persons *he determines* planned, authorized, committed, or aided the terrorist attacks that occurred on September 11, 2001." AUMF § 2(a) (emphases added). In the field of foreign affairs, and particularly that of war powers and national security, congressional enactments are to be broadly construed where they indicate support for authority long asserted and exercised by the Executive Branch. . . . Although Congress's war powers under Article I, Section 8 of the Constitution empower Congress to legislate regarding the raising, regulation, and material support of the Armed Forces and related matters, rather than the prosecution of military campaigns, the AUMF indicates Congress's endorsement of the President's use of his constitutional war powers. This authorization transforms the struggle against al Qaeda and related terrorist organizations from what Justice Jackson called "a zone of twilight," in which the President and the Congress may have concurrent powers whose "distribution is uncertain," *Youngstown Sheet & Tube Co. v. Sawyer*, 343 U.S. 579, 637 (1952) (Jackson, J., concurring), into a situation in which the President's authority is at is maximum because "it includes all that he possesses in his own right plus all that Congress can delegate," *id.* at 635. With regard to these fundamental tools of warfare—and, as demonstrated below, warrantless electronic surveillance against the declared enemy is one such tool—the AUMF places the President's authority at its zenith under *Youngstown*. . . .

Warrantless Electronic Surveillance Aimed at Intercepting Enemy
Communications Has Long Been Recognized as a Fundamental
Incident of the Use of Military Force

The history of warfare—including the consistent practice of Presidents since the earliest days of the Republic—demonstrates that warrantless intelligence surveillance against the enemy is a fundamental incident of the use of military force, and this history confirms the statutory authority provided by the AUMF. Electronic surveillance is a fundamental tool of war that must be included in any natural reading of the AUMF's authorization to use "all necessary and appropriate force."

As one author has explained:

> It is *essential* in warfare for a belligerent to be as fully informed as possible about the enemy—his strength, his weaknesses, measures taken by him and measures contemplated by him. This applies not only to military matters, but . . . anything which bears on and is material to his ability to wage the war in which he is engaged. *The laws of war recognize and sanction this aspect of warfare.*

Morris Greenspan, *The Modern Law of Land Warfare* 325 (1959) (emphases added). . . .

In accordance with these well-established principles, the Supreme Court has consistently recognized the President's authority to conduct intelligence activities. *See, e.g., Totten v. United States,* 92 U.S. 105, 106 (1876) (recognizing President's authority to hire spies); *Tenet v. Doe,* 544 U.S. 1 (2005) (reaffirming *Totten* and counseling against judicial interference with such matters); *see also Chicago & S. Air Lines v. Waterman S.S. Corp.,* 333 U.S. 103, 111 (1948) ("The President, both as Commander-in-Chief and as the Nation's organ for foreign affairs, has available intelligence services whose reports neither are not and ought not to be published to the world."); *United States v. Curtiss-Wright Export Corp.,* 299 U.S. 304, 320 (1936) (The President "has his confidential sources of information. He has his agents in the form of diplomatic, consular, and other officials."). Chief Justice John Marshall even described the gathering of intelligence as a military duty. *See Tatum v. Laird,* 444 F.2d 947, 952-53 (D.C. Cir. 1971) ("As Chief Justice John Marshall said of Washington, 'A general must be governed by his intelligence and must regulate his measures by his information. It is his duty to obtain correct information. . . .'") (quoting Foreword, U.S. Army Basic Field Manual, Vol. X, circa 1938), *rev'd on other grounds,* 408 U.S. 1 (1972). . . .

The interception of communications, in particular, has long been accepted as a fundamental method for conducting wartime surveillance. *See, e.g.,* Greenspan, *supra,* at 326 (accepted and customary means for gathering intelligence "include air reconnaissance and photography; ground reconnaissance; observation of enemy positions; *interception of enemy messages, wireless and other;* examination of captured documents; . . . and interrogation of prisoners and civilian inhabitants") (emphasis added). Indeed, since its independence, the United States has intercepted communications for wartime intelligence purposes and, if necessary, has done so within its own borders. During the Revolutionary War, for example, George Washington received and used to his advantage reports from American intelligence agents on British military strength, British strategic intentions, and British estimates of American strength.

More specifically, warrantless electronic surveillance of wartime communications has been conducted in the United States since electronic communications have existed, *i.e.,* since at least the Civil War, when "[t]elegraph wiretapping was common, and an important intelligence source for both sides." G.J.A. O'Toole, *The Encyclopedia of American Intelligence and Espionage* 498 (1988). Confederate General J.E.B. Stuart even "had his own personal wiretapper travel along with him in the field" to intercept military telegraphic communications. . . .

In light of the long history of prior wartime practice, the NSA activities fit squarely within the sweeping terms of the AUMF. The use of signals intelligence to identify and pinpoint the enemy is a traditional component of wartime military operations—or, to use the terminology of *Hamdi,* a "fundamental and accepted . . . incident to war," 542 U.S. at 518 (plurality opinion)—employed to defeat the enemy and to prevent enemy attacks in the United States. Here, as in other conflicts, the enemy may use public communications networks, and some of the enemy may already be in the United States. Although those factors may be present in this conflict to a greater degree than in the past, neither is novel. Certainly, both factors were well known at the time Congress enacted the AUMF. Wartime interception of international communications made by the enemy thus should be understood, no less than the wartime detention at issue in *Hamdi,* as one of the basic methods of engaging and defeating the enemy that Congress authorized in approving "*all* necessary and appropriate force" that the President would need to defend the Nation. AUMF § 2(a) (emphasis added).

⋅⊙⋅

III. The NSA Activities Are Consistent with the Foreign Intelligence Surveillance Act

The President's exercise of his constitutional authority to conduct warrantless wartime electronic surveillance of the enemy, as confirmed and supplemented by statute in the AUMF, is fully consistent with the requirements of the Foreign Intelligence Surveillance Act ("FISA").[1] FISA is a critically important tool in the War on Terror. The United States makes full use of the authorities available under FISA to gather foreign intelligence information, including authorities to intercept communications, conduct physical searches, and install and use pen registers and trap and trace devices. While FISA establishes certain procedures that must be followed for these authorities to be used (procedures that usually involve applying for and obtaining an order from a special court), FISA also expressly contemplates that a later legislative enactment could authorize electronic surveillance outside the procedures set forth in FISA itself. The AUMF constitutes precisely such an enactment. To the extent there is any ambiguity on this point, the canon of constitutional avoidance requires that such ambiguity be resolved in favor of the President's authority to conduct the communications intelligence activities he has described. Finally, if FISA could not be read to allow the President to authorize the NSA activities during the current congressionally authorized armed conflict with al Qaeda, FISA would be unconstitutional as applied in this narrow context.

A. The Requirements of FISA

FISA was enacted in 1978 to regulate "electronic surveillance," particularly when conducted to obtain "foreign intelligence information," as those terms are defined in section 101 of FISA, 50 U.S.C. § 1801. As a general matter, the statute requires that the Attorney General approve an application for an order from a special court composed of Article III judges and created by FISA—the Foreign Intelligence Surveillance Court ("FISC"). See 50 U.S.C. §§ 1803–1804. The application must demonstrate, among other things, that there is probable cause to believe that the target is a foreign power or an agent of a foreign power. See id. § 1805(a)(3)(A). It must also contain a certification from the Assistant to the President for National Security Affairs or an officer of the United States appointed by the President with the advice and consent of the Senate and having responsibilities in the area of national security or defense that the information sought is foreign intelligence information and cannot reasonably be obtained by normal investigative means. See id. § 1804(a)(7). FISA further requires the Government to state the means that it proposes to use to obtain the information and the basis for its belief that the facilities at which the surveillance will be directed are being used or are about to be used by a foreign power or an agent of a foreign power. See id. § 1804(a)(4), (a)(8).

FISA was the first congressional measure that sought to impose restrictions on the Executive Branch's authority to engage in electronic surveillance for foreign intelligence purposes, an authority that, as noted above, had been repeatedly recognized by the federal courts. . . .

In addition, Congress addressed, to some degree, the manner in which FISA might apply after a formal declaration of war by expressly allowing warrantless surveillance for a period of fifteen days following such a declaration. Section 111 of FISA allows the President to "authorize electronic surveillance without a court order under this subchapter to acquire foreign intelligence information for a period not to exceed fifteen calendar days following a declaration of war by the Congress." 50 U.S.C. § 1811.

The legislative history of FISA shows that Congress understood it was legislating on fragile constitutional ground and was pressing or even exceeding constitutional limits in regulating the President's authority in the field of foreign intelligence. The final House Conference Report, for example, recognized that the statute's restrictions might well impermissibly infringe on the President's constitutional powers. That report includes the extraordinary acknowledgment that "[t]he conferees agree that the establishment by this act of exclusive means by which the President may conduct electronic surveillance does not foreclose a different decision by the Supreme Court." H.R. Conf. Rep. No. 95-1720, at 35, reprinted in 1978 U.S.C.C.A.N. 4048, 4064. But, invoking Justice Jackson's concurrence in the Steel Seizure case, the Conference Report explained that Congress intended in FISA to exert whatever power Congress constitutionally had over the subject matter to restrict foreign intelligence surveillance and to leave the

President solely with whatever inherent constitutional authority he might be able to invoke against Congress's express wishes. . . .

B. FISA Contemplates and Allows Surveillance Authorized "by Statute"

Congress did not attempt through FISA to prohibit the Executive Branch from using electronic surveillance. Instead, Congress acted to bring the exercise of that power under more stringent congressional control. *See, e.g.,* H. Conf. Rep. No. 95-1720, at 32, *reprinted in* 1978 U.S.C.C.A.N. 4048, 4064. Congress therefore enacted a regime intended to supplant the President's reliance on his own constitutional authority. Consistent with this overriding purpose of bringing the use of electronic surveillance under *congressional* control and with the commonsense notion that the Congress that enacted FISA could not bind future Congresses, FISA expressly contemplates that the Executive Branch may conduct electronic surveillance outside FISA's express procedures if and when a subsequent statute authorizes such surveillance.

Thus, section 109 of FISA prohibits any person from intentionally "engag[ing] . . . in electronic surveillance under color of law *except as authorized by statute*." 50 U.S.C. § 1809(a)(1) (emphasis added). Because FISA's prohibitory provision broadly exempts surveillance "authorized by statute," the provision demonstrates that Congress did not attempt to regulate through FISA electronic surveillance authorized by Congress through a subsequent enactment. The use of the term "statute" here is significant because it strongly suggests that *any* subsequent authorizing statute, not merely one that amends FISA itself, could legitimately authorize surveillance outside FISA's standard procedural requirements. . . . In enacting FISA, therefore, Congress contemplated the possibility that the President might be permitted to conduct electronic surveillance pursuant to a later-enacted statute that did not incorporate all of the procedural requirements set forth in FISA or that did not expressly amend FISA itself. . . .

C. The AUMF Is a "Statute" Authorizing Surveillance Outside the Confines of FISA

The AUMF qualifies as a "statute" authorizing electronic surveillance within the meaning of section 109 of FISA.

First, because the term "statute" historically has been given broad meaning, the phrase "authorized by statute" in section 109 of FISA must be read to include joint resolutions such as the AUMF. . . .

Second, the longstanding history of communications intelligence as a fundamental incident of the use of force and the Supreme Court's decision in *Hamdi v. Rumsfeld* strongly suggest that the AUMF satisfies the requirement of section 109 of FISA for statutory authorization of electronic surveillance. As explained above, it is not necessary to demarcate the outer limits of the AUMF to conclude that it encompasses electronic surveillance targeted at the enemy. Just as a majority of the Court concluded in *Hamdi* that the AUMF authorizes detention of U.S. citizens who are enemy combatants without expressly mentioning the President's long-recognized power to detain, so too does it authorize the use of electronic surveillance without specifically mentioning the

President's equally long-recognized power to engage in communications intelligence targeted at the enemy. . . .

D. The Canon of Constitutional Avoidance Requires Resolving in Favor of the President's Authority any Ambiguity About Whether FISA Forbids the NSA Activities

As explained above, the AUMF fully authorizes the NSA activities. Because FISA contemplates the possibility that subsequent statutes could authorize electronic surveillance without requiring FISA's standard procedures, the NSA activities are also consistent with FISA and related provisions in title 18. Nevertheless, some might argue that sections 109 and 111 of FISA, along with section 2511(2)(f)'s "exclusivity" provision and section 2511(2)(e)'s liability exception for officers engaged in FISA-authorized surveillance, are best read to suggest that FISA requires that subsequent authorizing legislation specifically amend FISA in order to free the Executive from FISA's enumerated procedures. As detailed above, this is not the better reading of FISA. But even if these provisions were ambiguous, any doubt as to whether the AUMF and FISA should be understood to allow the President to make tactical military decisions to authorize surveillance outside the parameters of FISA must be resolved to avoid the serious constitutional questions that a contrary interpretation would raise.

It is well established that the first task of any interpreter faced with a statute that may present an unconstitutional infringement on the powers of the President is to determine whether the statute may be construed to avoid the constitutional difficulty. "[I]f an otherwise acceptable construction of a statute would raise serious constitutional problems, and where an alternative interpretation of the statute is 'fairly possible,' we are obligated to construe the statute to avoid such problems." *INS v. St. Cyr,* 533 U.S. 289, 299-300 (2001) (citations omitted); *Ashwander v. TVA,* 297 U.S. 288, 345-48 (1936) (Brandeis, J., concurring). Moreover, the canon of constitutional avoidance has particular importance in the realm of national security, where the President's constitutional authority is at its highest. . . . Thus, courts and the Executive Branch typically construe a general statute, even one that is written in unqualified terms, to be implicitly limited so as not to infringe on the President's Commander in Chief powers.

Reading FISA to prohibit the NSA activities would raise two serious constitutional questions, both of which must be avoided if possible: (1) whether the signals intelligence collection the President determined was necessary to undertake is such a core exercise of Commander in Chief control over the Armed Forces during armed conflict that Congress cannot interfere with it at all and (2) whether the particular restrictions imposed by FISA are such that their application would impermissibly impede the President's exercise of his constitutionally assigned duties as Commander in Chief. Constitutional avoidance principles require interpreting FISA, at least in the context of the military conflict authorized by the AUMF, to avoid these questions, if "fairly possible." Even if Congress intended FISA to use the full extent of its constitutional authority to "occupy the field" of "electronic surveillance," as FISA used that term, during peacetime, the legislative history indicates that Congress had not reached a definitive conclusion about its regulation during wartime. *See* H.R. Conf. Rep. No. 95-1720, at 34, *reprinted in* 1978 U.S.C.C.A.N. at 4063 (noting that the purpose of the fifteen-day period following a declaration of war in section 111 of FISA was to "allow time for consideration of any amendment to this act that may be appropriate during a wartime emergency"). Therefore, it is not clear that Congress, in fact, intended to test the limits of its constitutional authority in the context of wartime electronic surveillance.

Whether Congress may interfere with the President's constitutional authority to collect foreign intelligence information through interception of communications reasonably believed to be linked to the enemy poses a difficult constitutional question. As explained in Part I, it had long been accepted at the time of FISA's enactment that the President has inherent constitutional authority to conduct warrantless electronic surveillance for foreign intelligence purposes. Congress recognized at the time that the enactment of a statute purporting to eliminate the President's ability, even during peacetime, to conduct warrantless electronic surveillance to collect foreign intelligence was near or perhaps beyond the limit of Congress's Article I powers. The NSA activities, however, involve signals intelligence performed in the midst of a congressionally authorized armed conflict undertaken to prevent further hostile attacks on the United States. The NSA activities lie at the very core of the Commander in Chief power, especially in light of the AUMF's explicit authorization for the President to take *all* necessary and appropriate military action to stop al Qaeda from striking again. The constitutional principles at stake here thus involve not merely the President's well-established inherent authority to conduct warrantless surveillance for foreign intelligence purposes during peacetime, but also the powers and duties expressly conferred on him as Commander in Chief by Article II. . . .

IV. The NSA Activities Are Consistent with the Fourth Amendment

The Fourth Amendment prohibits "unreasonable searches and seizures" and directs that "no Warrants shall issue, but upon probable cause, supported by Oath or affirmation, and particularly describing the place to be searched, and the persons or things to be seized." U.S. Const. amend. IV. The touchstone for review of government action under the Fourth Amendment is whether the search is "reasonable." *See, e.g., Vernonia Sch. Dist. v. Acton,* 515 U.S. 646, 653 (1995).

As noted above, . . . all of the federal courts of appeals to have addressed the issue have affirmed the President's inherent constitutional authority to collect foreign intelligence without a warrant. *See In re Sealed Case,* 310 F.3d at 742. Properly understood, foreign intelligence collection in general, and the NSA activities in particular, fit within the "special needs" exception to the warrant requirement of the Fourth Amendment. Accordingly, the mere fact that no warrant is secured prior to the surveillance at issue in the NSA activities does not suffice to render the activities unreasonable. Instead, reasonableness in this context must be assessed under a general balancing approach, "'by assessing, on the one hand, the degree to which it intrudes upon an individual's privacy and, on the other, the degree to which it is needed for the promotion of legitimate governmental interests.'" *United States v. Knights*, 534 U.S. 112, 118-19 (2001) (quoting *Wyoming v. Houghton*, 526 U.S. 295, 300 (1999)). The NSA activities are reasonable because the Government's interest, defending the Nation from another foreign attack in time of armed conflict, outweighs the individual privacy interests at stake, and because they seek to intercept only international communications where one party is linked to al Qaeda or an affiliated terrorist organization.

A. The Warrant Requirement of the Fourth Amendment Does Not Apply to the NSA Activities

In "the criminal context," the Fourth Amendment reasonableness requirement "usually requires a showing of probable cause" and a warrant. *Board of Educ. v. Earls*, 536 U.S. 822, 828 (2002). The requirement of a warrant supported by probable cause, however, is not universal. Rather, the Fourth Amendment's "central requirement is one of reasonableness," and the rules the Court has developed to implement that requirement "[s]ometimes . . . require warrants." *Illinois v. McArthur*, 531 U.S. 326, 330 (2001). . . .

In particular, the Supreme Court repeatedly has made clear that in situations involving "special needs" that go beyond a routine interest in law enforcement, the warrant requirement is inapplicable. . . . It is difficult to encapsulate in a nutshell all of the different circumstances the Court has found to qualify as "special needs" justifying warrantless searches. But one application in which the Court has found the warrant requirement inapplicable is in circumstances in which the Government faces an increased need to be able to react swiftly and flexibly, or when there are at stake interests in public safety beyond the interests in ordinary law enforcement. One important factor in establishing "special needs" is whether the Government is responding to an emergency that goes beyond the need for general crime control. . . .

Thus, the Court has permitted warrantless searches of property of students in public schools, *see New Jersey v. T.L.O.*, 469 U.S. 325, 340 (1985) (noting that warrant requirement would "unduly interfere with the maintenance of the swift and informal disciplinary procedures needed in the schools"), to screen athletes and students involved in extracurricular activities at public schools for drug use, *see Vernonia*, 515 U.S. at 654-55; *Earls*, 536 U.S. at 829-38, to conduct drug testing of railroad personnel involved in train accidents, *see Skinner v. Railway Labor Executives' Ass'n*, 489 U.S. 602, 634 (1989), and to search probationers' homes, *see Griffin*, 483 U.S. 868. Many special needs doctrine and related cases have upheld *suspicionless* searches or seizures. *See, e.g., Illinois v. Lidster*, 540 U.S. 419, 427 (2004) (implicitly relying on special needs doctrine to uphold use of automobile checkpoint to obtain information about recent hit-and-run accident); *Earls*, 536 U.S. at 829-38 (suspicionless drug testing of public school students involved in extracurricular activities); *Michigan Dep't of State Police v. Sitz*, 496 U.S. 444, 449-55 (1990) (road block to check all motorists for signs of drunken driving); *United States v. Martinez-Fuerte*, 428 U.S. 543 (1976) (road block near the border to check vehicles for illegal immigrants); *cf. In re Sealed Case*, 310 F.3d at 745-46 (noting that suspicionless searches and seizures in one sense are a greater encroachment on privacy than electronic surveillance under FISA because they are not based on any particular suspicion, but "[o]n the other hand, wiretapping is a good deal more intrusive than an automobile stop accompanied by questioning"). To fall within the "special needs" exception to the warrant requirement, the purpose of the search must be distinguishable from ordinary general crime control. *See, e.g., Ferguson v. Charleston*, 532 U.S. 67 (2001); *City of Indianapolis v. Edmond*, 531 U.S. 32, 41 (2000).

Foreign intelligence collection, especially in the midst of an armed conflict in which the adversary has already launched catastrophic attacks within the United States, fits squarely within the area of "special needs, beyond the normal need for law enforcement" where the Fourth Amendment's touchstone of reasonableness can be satisfied without resort to a warrant. *Vernonia*, 515 U.S. at 653. The Executive Branch has long maintained that collecting foreign intelligence is far removed from the ordinary criminal law enforcement action to which the warrant requirement is particularly suited. . . .

In particular, the NSA activities are undertaken to prevent further devastating attacks on our Nation, and they serve the highest government purpose through means other than traditional law enforcement. The NSA activities are designed to enable the Government to act quickly and flexibly (and with secrecy) to find agents of al Qaeda and its affiliates—an international terrorist group which has already demonstrated a capability to infiltrate American communities without being detected—in time to disrupt future terrorist attacks against the United States. As explained by the Foreign Intelligence Surveillance Court of Review, the nature of the "emergency" posed by al Qaeda "takes the matter out of the realm of ordinary crime control." *In re Sealed Case*, 310 F.3d at 746. Thus, under the "special needs" doctrine, no warrant is required by the Fourth Amendment for the NSA activities.

B. The NSA Activities Are Reasonable

As the Supreme Court has emphasized repeatedly, "[t]he touchstone of the Fourth Amendment is reasonableness, and the reasonableness of a search is determined by assessing, on the one hand, the degree to which it intrudes upon an individual's privacy and, on the other, the degree to which it is needed for the promotion of legitimate governmental interests." . . . Under the standard balancing of interests analysis used for gauging reasonableness, the NSA activities are consistent with the Fourth Amendment.

With respect to the individual privacy interests at stake, there can be no doubt that, as a general matter, interception of telephone communications implicates a significant privacy interest of the individual whose conversation is intercepted. The Supreme Court has made clear at least since *Katz v. United States*, 389 U.S. 347 (1967), that individuals have a substantial and constitutionally protected reasonable expectation of privacy that their telephone conversations will not be subject to governmental eavesdropping. Although the individual privacy interests at stake may be substantial, it is well recognized that a variety of governmental interests—including routine law enforcement and foreign-intelligence gathering—can overcome those interests.

On the other side of the scale here, the Government's interest in engaging in the NSA activities is the most compelling interest possible—securing the Nation from foreign attack in the midst of an armed conflict. One attack already has taken thousands of lives and placed the Nation in state of armed conflict. Defending the Nation from attack is perhaps the most important function of the federal Government—and one of the few express obligations of the federal Government enshrined in the Constitution. *See* U.S. Const. art. IV, § 4 ("The United States shall guarantee to every State in this Union a Republican Form of Government, *and shall protect each of them against Invasion* . . . .") (emphasis added); *The Prize Cases,* 67 U.S. (2 Black) 635, 668 (1863) ("If war be made by invasion of a foreign nation, the President is not only authorized but bound to resist force by force."). As the Supreme Court has declared, "[i]t is 'obvious and unarguable' that no governmental interest is more compelling than the security of the Nation." *Haig v. Agee,* 453 U.S. 280, 307 (1981).

The Government's overwhelming interest in detecting and thwarting further al Qaeda attacks is easily sufficient to make reasonable the intrusion into privacy involved in intercepting one-end foreign communications where there is "a reasonable basis to conclude that one party to the communication is a member of al Qaeda, affiliated with al Qaeda, or a member of an organization affiliated with al Qaeda." Press Briefing by Attorney General Alberto Gonzales and General Michael Hayden, Principal Deputy Director for National Intelligence, *available at* http://www.whitehouse.gov/news/releases/2005/12/20051219-1.html (Dec. 19, 2005) (statement of Attorney General Gonzales). . . .

Conclusion

For the foregoing reasons, the President—in light of the broad authority to use military force in response to the attacks of September 11th and to prevent further catastrophic attack expressly conferred on the President by the Constitution and confirmed and supplemented by Congress in the AUMF—has legal authority to authorize the NSA to conduct the signals intelligence activities he has described. Those activities are authorized by the Constitution and by statute, and they violate neither FISA nor the Fourth Amendment.

Note

1. To avoid revealing details about the operation of the program, it is assumed for purposes of this paper that the activities described by the President constitute "electronic surveillance," as defined by FISA, 50 U.S.C. § 1801(f).

Letter to Congress from 14 Law Professors and Former Government Attorneys to Congressional Leaders

Dear Members of Congress:

We are scholars of constitutional law and former government officials. We write in our individual capacities as citizens concerned by the Bush Administration's National Security Agency domestic spying program, as reported in the New York Times, and in particular to respond to the Justice Department's December 22, 2005 letter to the majority and minority leaders of the House and Senate Intelligence Committees setting forth the administration's defense of the program. Although the program's secrecy prevents us from being privy to all of its details, the Justice Department's defense of what it concedes was secret and warrantless electronic surveillance of persons within the United States fails to identify any plausible legal authority for such surveillance. Accordingly the program appears on its face to violate existing law.

The basic legal question here is not new. In 1978, after an extensive investigation of the privacy violations associated with foreign intelligence surveillance programs, Congress and the President enacted the Foreign Intelligence Surveillance Act (FISA). Pub. L. 95-511, 92 Stat. 1783. FISA comprehensively regulates electronic surveillance within the United States, striking a careful balance between protecting civil liberties and preserving the "vitally important government purpose" of obtaining valuable intelligence in order to safeguard national security. S. Rep. No. 95-604, pt. 1, at 9 (1977).

With minor exceptions, FISA authorizes electronic surveillance only upon certain specified showings, and only if approved by a court. The statute specifically allows for warrantless *wartime* domestic electronic surveillance—but only for the first fifteen days of a war. 50 U.S.C. § 1811. It makes criminal any electronic surveillance not authorized by statute, *id.* § 1809; and it expressly establishes FISA and specified provisions of the federal criminal code (which govern wiretaps for criminal investigation) as the "*exclusive* means by which electronic surveillance . . . may be conducted," 18 U.S.C. § 2511(2)(f) (emphasis added).[1]

The Department of Justice concedes that the NSA program was not authorized by any of the above provisions. It maintains, however, that the program did

Letter to Congress from 14 Law Professors and Former Government Attorneys to Congressional Leaders (January 2, 2006).

not violate existing law because Congress implicitly authorized the NSA program when it enacted the Authorization for Use of Military Force (AUMF) against al Qaeda, Pub. L. No. 107-40, 115 Stat. 224 (2001). But the AUMF cannot reasonably be construed to implicitly authorize warrantless electronic surveillance in the United States during wartime, where Congress has expressly and specifically addressed that precise question in FISA and limited any such warrantless surveillance to the first fifteen days of war.

The DOJ also invokes the President's inherent constitutional authority as Commander in Chief to collect "signals intelligence" targeted at the enemy, and maintains that construing FISA to prohibit the President's actions would raise constitutional questions. But even conceding that the President in his role as Commander in Chief may generally collect signals intelligence on the enemy abroad, Congress indisputably has authority to regulate electronic surveillance within the United States, as it has done in FISA. Where Congress has so regulated, the President can act in contravention of statute only if his authority is *exclusive*, and not subject to the check of statutory regulation. The DOJ letter pointedly does not make that extraordinary claim.

Moreover, to construe the AUMF as the DOJ suggests would itself raise serious constitutional questions under the Fourth Amendment. The Supreme Court has never upheld warrantless wiretapping within the United States. Accordingly, the principle that statutes should be construed to avoid serious constitutional questions provides an additional reason for concluding that the AUMF does not authorize the President's actions here.

I. Congress Did Not Implicitly Authorize the NSA Domestic Spying Program in the AUMF, and in Fact Expressly Prohibited It in FISA

The DOJ concedes . . . that the NSA program involves "electronic surveillance," which is defined in FISA to mean the interception of the *contents* of telephone, wire, or email communications that occur, at least in part, in the United States. 50 U.S.C. §§ 1801(f)(1)-(2), 1801(n). NSA engages in such surveillance without judicial approval, and apparently without the substantive showings that FISA requires—e.g., that the subject is an "agent of a foreign power." *Id.* § 1805(a). The DOJ does not argue that FISA itself authorizes such electronic surveillance; and, as the DOJ letter acknowledges, 18 U.S.C. § 1809 makes criminal any electronic surveillance not authorized by statute.

The DOJ nevertheless contends that the surveillance is authorized by the AUMF, signed on September 18, 2001, which empowers the President to use "all necessary and appropriate force against" al Qaeda. According to the DOJ, collecting "signals intelligence" on the enemy, even if it involves tapping U.S. phones without court approval or probable cause, is a "fundamental incident of war" authorized by the AUMF. This argument fails for four reasons.

First, and most importantly, the DOJ's argument rests on an unstated general "implication" from the AUMF that directly contradicts *express* and *specific* language in FISA. Specific and "carefully drawn" statutes prevail over general statutes where there is a conflict. *Morales v. TWA, Inc.*, 504 U.S. 374, 384-85 (1992) (quoting *International Paper Co. v. Ouelette*, 479 U.S. 481, 494 (1987)). In FISA, Congress has directly and specifically spoken on the question of domestic warrantless wiretapping, including during wartime, and it could not have spoken more clearly.

As noted above, Congress has comprehensively regulated all electronic surveillance in the United States, and authorizes such surveillance only pursuant to specific statutes designated as the *"exclusive* means by which electronic surveillance . . . and the interception of domestic wire, oral, and electronic communications may be conducted." 18 U.S.C. § 2511(2)(f) (emphasis added). Moreover, FISA *specifically* addresses the question of domestic wiretapping during wartime. In a provision entitled "Authorization during time of war," FISA dictates that "[n]otwithstanding any other law, the President, through the Attorney General, may authorize electronic surveillance without a court order under this subchapter to acquire foreign intelligence information *for a period not to exceed fifteen calendar days following a declaration of war by the Congress."* 50 U.S.C. § 1811 (emphasis added). Thus, even where Congress has declared war—a more formal step than an authorization such as the AUMF—the law limits warrantless wiretapping to the first fifteen days of the conflict. Congress explained that if the President needed further warrantless surveillance during wartime, the fifteen days would be sufficient for Congress to consider and enact further authorization.[2] Rather than follow this course, the President acted unilaterally and secretly in contravention of FISA's terms. The DOJ letter remarkably does not even *mention* FISA's fifteen-day war provision, which directly refutes the President's asserted "implied" authority. . . .

Second, the DOJ's argument would require the conclusion that Congress implicitly and *sub silentio* repealed 18 U.S.C. § 2511(2)(f), the provision that identifies FISA and specific criminal code provisions as "the *exclusive* means by which electronic surveillance . . . may be conducted." Repeals by implication are strongly disfavored; they can be established only by "overwhelming evidence," *J.E.M. Ag. Supply, Inc. v. Pioneer Hi-Bred Int'l, Inc.*, 534 U.S. 124, 137 (2001), and "'the only permissible justification for a repeal by implication is when the earlier and later statutes are irreconcilable,'" *id.* at 141-142 (quoting *Morton v. Mancari*, 417 U.S. 535, 550 (1974)). The AUMF and § 2511(2)(f) are not irreconcilable, and there is *no* evidence, let alone overwhelming evidence, that Congress intended to repeal § 2511(2)(f).

Third, Attorney General Alberto Gonzales has admitted that the administration did not seek to amend FISA to authorize the NSA spying program because it was advised that Congress would reject such an amendment.[3] The administration cannot argue on the one hand that Congress authorized the NSA program in the AUMF, and at the same time that it did not ask Congress for such authorization because it feared Congress would say no.[4]

Finally, the DOJ's reliance upon *Hamdi v. Rumsfeld*, 542 U.S. 507 (2004), to support its reading of the AUMF, . . . is misplaced. A plurality of the Court in *Hamdi* held that the AUMF authorized military detention of enemy combatants captured on the battlefield abroad as a "fundamental incident of waging war." *Id.* at 519. The plurality expressly limited this holding to individuals who were "part of or supporting forces hostile to the United States or coalition partners *in Afghanistan and who engaged in an armed conflict against the United States there.*" *Id.* at 516 (emphasis added). It is one thing, however, to say that foreign battlefield capture of enemy combatants is an incident of waging war that Congress intended to authorize. It is another matter entirely to treat unchecked warrantless *domestic* spying as included in that authorization, especially where an existing statute specifies that other laws are the "exclusive means" by which electronic surveillance may be conducted and provides that even a declaration of war authorizes such spying only for a fifteen-day emergency period.

II. Construing FISA to Prohibit Warrantless Domestic Wiretapping Does Not Raise Any Serious Constitutional Question, Whereas Construing the AUMF to Authorize Such Wiretapping Would Raise Serious Questions Under the Fourth Amendment

The DOJ argues that FISA and the AUMF should be construed to permit the NSA program's domestic surveillance because otherwise there might be a "conflict between FISA and the President's Article II authority as Commander-in-Chief." DOJ Letter at 4. The statutory scheme described above is not ambiguous, and therefore the constitutional avoidance doctrine is not even implicated. *See United States v. Oakland Cannabis Buyers' Coop.,* 532 U.S. 483, 494 (2001) (the "canon of constitutional avoidance has no application in the absence of statutory ambiguity"). But were it implicated, it would work against the President, not in his favor. Construing FISA and the AUMF according to their plain meanings raises no serious constitutional questions regarding the President's duties under Article II. Construing the AUMF to *permit* unchecked warrantless wiretapping without probable cause, however, would raise serious questions under the Fourth Amendment.

A. FISA's Limitations Are Consistent with the President's Article II Role

We do not dispute that, absent congressional action, the President might have inherent constitutional authority to collect "signals intelligence" about the enemy abroad. Nor do we dispute that, had Congress taken no action in this area, the President might well be constitutionally empowered to conduct domestic surveillance directly tied and narrowly confined to that goal—subject, of course, to Fourth Amendment limits. Indeed, in the years before FISA was enacted, the federal law involving wiretapping specifically provided that "[n]othing contained in this chapter or in section 605 of the Communications Act of 1934 shall limit the constitutional power of the President . . . to obtain foreign intelligence information deemed essential to the security of the United States." 18 U.S.C. § 2511(3) (1976).

But FISA specifically *repealed* that provision. FISA § 201(c), 92 Stat. 1797, and replaced it with language dictating that FISA and the criminal code are the "exclusive means" of conducting electronic surveillance. In doing so, Congress did not deny that the President has constitutional power to conduct electronic surveillance for national security purposes; rather, Congress properly concluded that "even if the President has the inherent authority *in the absence of legislation* to authorize warrantless electronic surveillance for foreign intelligence purposes, Congress has the power to regulate the conduct of such surveillance by legislating a reasonable procedure, which then becomes the exclusive means by which such surveillance may be conducted." H.R. Rep. No. 95-1283, pt. 1, at 24 (1978) (emphasis added). This analysis, Congress noted, was "supported by two successive Attorneys General." *Id.*

To say that the President has inherent authority does not mean that his authority is exclusive, or that his conduct is not subject to statutory regulations enacted (as FISA was) pursuant to Congress's Article I powers. As Justice Jackson famously explained in his influential opinion in *Youngstown Sheet & Tube Co. v. Sawyer*, 343 U.S. at 635 (Jackson, J., concurring), the Constitution "enjoins upon its branches separateness but interdependence, autonomy but reciprocity. Presidential powers are not fixed but fluctuate, depending upon their disjunction or conjunction with those of Congress." For example, the President in his role as Commander in Chief directs military operations. But the Framers gave Congress the power to prescribe rules for the regulation of the armed and naval forces, Art. I, § 8, cl. 14, and if a duly enacted statute prohibits the military from engaging in torture or cruel, inhuman, and degrading treatment, the President must follow that dictate. As Justice Jackson wrote, when the President acts in defiance of "the expressed or implied will of Congress," his power is "at its lowest ebb." 343 U.S. at 637. In this setting, Jackson wrote, "Presidential power [is] most vulnerable to attack and in the least favorable of possible constitutional postures." *Id.* at 640.

Congress plainly has authority to regulate domestic wiretapping by federal agencies under its Article I powers, and the DOJ does not suggest otherwise. Indeed, when FISA was enacted, the Justice Department agreed that Congress had power to regulate such conduct, and could require judicial approval of foreign intelligence surveillance. FISA does not prohibit foreign intelligence surveillance, but merely imposes reasonable regulation to protect legitimate privacy rights. (For example, although FISA generally requires judicial approval for electronic surveillance of persons within the United States, it permits the executive branch to install a wiretap immediately so long as it obtains judicial approval within 72 hours. 50 U.S.C. § 1805(f).)

Just as the President is bound by the statutory prohibition on torture, he is bound by the statutory dictates of FISA. The DOJ once infamously argued that the President as Commander in Chief could ignore even the criminal prohibition on torture,[5] and, more broadly still, that statutes may not "place *any* limits on the President's determinations as to any terrorist threat, the amount of military force to be used in response, or the method, timing, and nature of the response."[6] But the administration withdrew the August 2002 torture memo after it was disclosed, and for good reason the DOJ does not advance these extreme arguments here. Absent a serious question about FISA's constitutionality, there is no reason even to consider construing the AUMF to have implicitly overturned the carefully designed regulatory regime that FISA establishes. *See, e.g., Reno v. Flores*, 507 U.S. 292, 314 n.9 (1993) (constitutional avoidance canon applicable only if the constitutional question to be avoided is a serious one, "not to eliminate all possible contentions that the statute *might* be unconstitutional") (emphasis in original; citation omitted).[7]

B. Construing the AUMF to Authorize Warrantless Domestic Wiretapping Would Raise Serious Constitutional Questions

The principle that ambiguous statutes should be construed to avoid serious constitutional questions works against the administration, not in its favor. Interpreting the AUMF and FISA to permit unchecked domestic wiretapping for the duration of the conflict with al Qaeda would certainly raise serious constitutional questions. The Supreme Court has never upheld such a sweeping power to invade the privacy of Americans at home without individualized suspicion or judicial oversight.

The NSA surveillance program permits wiretapping within the United States without *either* of the safeguards presumptively required by the Fourth Amendment for electronic surveillance—individualized probable cause and a warrant or other order issued by a judge or magistrate. The Court has long held that wiretaps generally require a warrant and probable cause. *Katz v. United States*, 389 U.S. 347 (1967). And the only time the Court considered the question of national security wiretaps, it held that the Fourth Amendment prohibits domestic security wiretaps without those safeguards. *United States v. United States Dist. Court*, 407 U.S. 297 (1972). Although the Court in that case left open the question of the Fourth Amendment validity of warrantless wiretaps for foreign intelligence purposes, its precedents raise serious constitutional questions about the kind of open-ended authority the President has asserted with respect to the NSA program. *See id.* at 316-18 (explaining difficulty of guaranteeing Fourth Amendment freedoms if domestic surveillance can be conducted solely in the discretion of the executive branch).

Indeed, serious Fourth Amendment questions about the validity of warrantless wiretapping led Congress to enact FISA, in order to "provide the secure framework by which the executive branch may conduct legitimate electronic surveillance for foreign intelligence purposes within the context of this nation's commitment to privacy and individual rights." S. Rep. No. 95-604, pt. 1, at 15 (1977) (citing, *inter alia, Zweibon v. Mitchell*, 516 F.2d 594 (D.C. Cir. 1975), in which "the court of appeals held that a warrant must be obtained before a wiretap is installed on a domestic organization that is neither the agent of, nor acting in collaboration with, a foreign power").

Relying on *In re Sealed Case No. 02-001*, the DOJ argues that the NSA program falls within an exception to the warrant and probable cause requirement for reasonable searches that serve "special needs" above and beyond ordinary law enforcement. But the existence of "special needs" has never been found to permit warrantless wiretapping. "Special needs" generally excuse the warrant and individualized suspicion requirements only where those requirements are impracticable and the intrusion on privacy is minimal. . . . Wiretapping is not a minimal intrusion on privacy, and the experience of FISA shows that foreign intelligence surveillance can be carried out through warrants based on individualized suspicion.

The court in *Sealed Case* upheld FISA itself, which requires warrants issued by Article III federal judges upon an individualized showing of probable cause that the subject is an "agent of a foreign power." The NSA domestic spying program, by contrast, includes none of these safeguards. It does not require individualized judicial approval, and it does not require a showing that the target is an "agent of a foreign power." According to Attorney General Gonzales, the NSA may wiretap any person in the United States who so much as receives a communication from anyone abroad, if the administration deems either of the parties to be affiliated with al Qaeda, a member of an organization affiliated with al Qaeda, "working in support of al Qaeda," or "part of" an organization or group "that is supportive of al Qaeda." Under this reasoning, a U.S. citizen living here who received a phone call from another U.S. citizen who attends a mosque that the administration believes is "supportive" of al Qaeda could be wiretapped without a warrant. The absence of meaningful safeguards on the NSA program at a minimum raises serious questions about the validity of the program under the Fourth Amendment, and therefore supports an interpretation of the AUMF that does not undercut FISA's regulation of such conduct.

✦

In conclusion, the DOJ letter fails to offer a plausible legal defense of the NSA domestic spying program. If the Administration felt that FISA was insufficient, the proper course was to seek legislative amendment, as it did with other aspects of FISA in the Patriot Act, and as Congress expressly contemplated when it enacted the wartime wiretap provision in FISA. One of the crucial features of a constitutional democracy is that it is always open to the President—or anyone else—to seek to change the law. But it is also beyond dispute that, in such a democracy, the President cannot simply violate criminal laws behind closed doors because he deems them obsolete or impracticable.[8]

We hope you find these views helpful to your consideration of the legality of the NSA domestic spying program.

Notes

1. More detail about the operation of FISA can be found in Congressional Research Service, "Presidential Authority to Conduct Warrantless Electronic Surveillance to Gather Foreign Intelligence Information" (Jan. 5, 2006). This letter was drafted prior to release of the CRS Report, which corroborates the conclusions drawn here.

2. "The Conferees intend that this [15-day] period will allow time for consideration of any amendment to this act that may be appropriate during a wartime emergency. . . . The conferees expect that such amendment would be reported with recommendations within 7 days and that each House would

vote on the amendment within 7 days thereafter." H.R. Conf. Rep. No. 95-1720, at 34 (1978).

3.   Attorney General Gonzales stated, "We have had discussions with Congress in the past—certain members of Congress—as to whether or not FISA could be amended to allow us to adequately deal with this kind of threat, and we were advised that that would be difficult, if not impossible." Press Briefing by Attorney General Alberto Gonzales and General Michael Hayden, Principal Deputy Director for National Intelligence (Dec. 19, 2005). . . .

4.   The administration had a convenient vehicle for seeking any such amendment in the USA PATRIOT Act of 2001, Pub. L. No. 107-56, 115 Stat. 272, enacted in October 2001. The Patriot Act amended FISA in several respects, including in sections 218 (allowing FISA wiretaps in criminal investigations) and 215 (popularly known as the "libraries provision"). Yet the administration did not ask Congress to amend FISA to authorize the warrantless electronic surveillance at issue here.

5.   *See* Memorandum from Jay S. Bybee, Assistant Attorney General, Department of Justice Office of Legal Counsel, to Alberto R. Gonzales, Counsel to the President, Re: *Standards of Conduct for Interrogation under 18 U.S.C. §§ 2340-2340A* (Aug. 1, 2002), at 31.

6.   Memorandum from John C. Yoo, Deputy Assistant Attorney General, Office of Legal Counsel, to the Deputy Counsel to the President, Re: *The President's Constitutional Authority To Conduct Military Operations Against Terrorists And Nations Supporting Them* (Sept. 25, 2001) . . . (emphasis added).

7.   Three years ago, the FISA Court of Review suggested in dictum that Congress cannot "encroach on the President's constitutional power" to conduct foreign intelligence surveillance. *In re Sealed Case No. 02-001*, 310 F.3d 717, 742 (FIS Ct. Rev. 2002) (per curiam). The FISA Court of Review, however, did not hold that FISA was unconstitutional, nor has any other court suggested that FISA's modest regulations constitute an impermissible encroachment on presidential authority. The FISA Court of Review relied upon *United States v. Truong Dihn Hung*, 629 F.2d 908 (4th Cir. 1980)—but that court did not suggest that the President's powers were beyond congressional control. To the contrary, the *Truong* court indicated that FISA's restrictions *were* constitutional. *See* 629 F.2d at 915 n.4 (noting that "the imposition of a warrant requirement, beyond the constitutional minimum described in this opinion, *should be left to the intricate balancing performed in the course of the legislative process by Congress and the President*") (emphasis added).

8.   During consideration of FISA, the House of Representatives noted that "the decision as to the standards governing when and how foreign intelligence electronic surveillance should be conducted is and should be a political decision, in the best sense of the term, because it involves the weighing of important public policy concerns–civil liberties and national security. Such a political decision is one properly made by the political branches of Government together, not adopted by one branch on its own and with no regard for the other. Under our Constitution legislation is the embodiment of just such political decisions." H. Rep. 95-1283, pt. I, at 21-22. Attorney General Griffin Bell supported FISA in part because "no matter how well intentioned or ingenious the persons in the Executive branch who formulate these measures, the crucible of the legislative process will ensure that the procedures will be affirmed by that branch of government which is more directly responsible to the electorate." Foreign Intelligence Surveillance Act of 1978: Hearings Before the Subcomm. on Intelligence and the Rights of Americans of the Senate Select Comm. On Intelligence, 95th Cong., 2d Sess. 12 (1977).

POSTSCRIPT

Does the President Possess Constitutional Authority to Order Wiretaps on U.S. Citizens?

The controversy surrounding the NSA wiretapping program has continued despite the Bush administration's claim that the warantless wiretapping has ceased. In January 2006, the American Civil Liberties Union (ACLU) filed a lawsuit in federal court against the National Security Agency, asking the court to shut down the program. The government responded by arguing that the case should be dismissed on the basis of the state secrets doctrine because it could not be litigated without publicly disclosing information about the NSA program that would be detrimental to national security. However, District Court Judge Anna Diggs Taylor denied the government's motion to dismiss, holding that the Bush administration's public acknowledgements of the program were sufficient to establish the facts in the case. She then concluded that the program violated both FISA and the Constitution. The government has appealed the decision and the case could very well reach the Supreme Court in the near future.

In the midst of this litigation, on January 17, 2007, Attorney General Alberto Gonzales sent a letter to the Senate Judiciary Committee stating that "the President has determined not to reauthorize the Terrorist Surveillance Program" because a judge on the court responsible for issuing warrants under FISA had "authoriz[ed] the Government to target for collection international communications into or out of the United States where there is probable cause to believe that one of the communicants is a member or agent of al Qaeda or an associated terrorist organization." However, the Bush administration has refused to release any of the details of the judge's order, which raises questions about whether it does, in fact, bring the program into compliance with FISA. Additionally, the Bush administration has continued to assert that it possesses the inherent constitutional authority to ignore FISA and order warrantless wiretapping, keeping open the possibility that it could decide to forego judicial scrutiny of its electronic surveillance in the future.

Interesting readings on this issue include "Symposium: 'Torture and the War on Terror': NSA Wiretapping Controversy: A Debate Between Professor David D. Cole and Professor Ruth Wedgwood," 37 *Case W. Res. J. Int'l L.* 509 (2006); Fletcher N. Baldwin, Jr., and Robert B. Shaw, "Down to the Wire: Assessing the Constitutionality of the National Security Agency's Warrantless Wiretapping Program: Exit the Rule of Law," 17 *J. Law. & Pub. Pol'y* 429 (2006); Peter P. Swire, "The System of Foreign Intelligence Surveillance Law," *George Washington Law Review,* Vol. 72 (2004) http://ssrn.com/abstract=586616.

ISSUE 3

Is the Geneva Convention Irrelevant to Members of al Qaeda Who Are Held Prisoner at Guantanamo Bay?

YES: John Yoo and Robert J. Delahunty, from "Application of Treaties and Laws to al Qaeda and Taliban Detainees," Memo to William Haynes II, General Counsel, U.S. Department of Defense (January 9, 2002)

NO: 271 United Kingdom and European Parliamentarians, from Brief of Amicus Curiae in Case of *Hamdan v. Rumsfeld* (September 29, 2004)

ISSUE SUMMARY

YES: In a memorandum prepared for the General Counsel of the Department of Defense, John Yoo and Robert Delahunty argue that the Geneva Convention only applies to states and that, as a result, captured members of al Qaeda are not covered by the Convention.

NO: In an amicus brief submitted by several human rights organizations, it is argued that the Geneva Convention creates individual rights that are enforceable in United States courts.

In the *Hamdi* case discussed in Issue 1, the Supreme Court made the observation that the "capture and detention of . . . combatants, by universal agreement and practice, are important incidents of waging war." The U.S. wars in Afghanistan and Iraq are no exception; in the process of invading Afghanistan and toppling the Taliban government in 2001, the U.S. government managed to capture numerous Taliban and al Qaeda fighters, some of whom were held abroad and many of whom were transferred to a detention facility at the U.S. naval base at Guantanamo Bay, Cuba. The Supreme Court's decision in *Hamdi* was predicated on the fact that Hamdi is a U.S. citizen, entitled to certain constitutional rights such as due process of law. But what about detainees who are foreign nationals, with no connection to the United States? The question eventually arose whether they are entitled to certain rights under international treaties such as the Geneva Conventions, to which the United States is a signatory.

The four Geneva Conventions are a series of international agreements that establish rules governing how wars are prosecuted. Specifically, each Convention outlines the protections that signatory countries must afford, during wartime, to specific groups of people who are not involved in the fighting, either because they are noncombatants (civilians) or because injury or capture has rendered them *hors de combat* ("out of the fight").

International law raises a host of legal and philosophical issues surrounding the extent to which the United States is, and should be, bound to follow agreements like the Geneva Conventions. Opponents have long argued that the idea of laws that transcend borders and purport to govern how sovereign countries act is an idealistic impracticality at best and a dangerous hindrance to U.S. interests at worst. John Bolton, the former Bush administration ambassador to the UN, once reflected this view in his claim that "[i]t is a big mistake for us to grant any validity to international law even when it may seem in our short-term interest to do so—because, over the long term, the goal of those who think that international law really means anything . . . [is] to constrict the United States."

In the first reading, two senior officials in the Bush administration elaborate on the view that the Geneva Conventions should no longer govern how the United States treats detainees captured during wartime.

The Geneva Conventions' applicability to the War on Terror became a key issue in a recent Supreme Court case, *Hamdan v. Rumsfeld*. Salim Ahmed Hamdan is a Yemeni national who, for several years, served as Osama bin Laden's driver. U.S. troops captured Hamdan in Afghanistan in 2001, and the Bush administration announced plans to try him, through a military commission, for crimes against the United States. Hamdan sued in federal court, claiming that the rules governing the military commissions violated his rights to a fair trial under both domestic law and the Geneva Conventions. Hamdan argued that he should be granted the protections afforded POWs under the Third Geneva Convention, but that, in the event he did not qualify for all such rights, he was still covered by common Article Three, which prohibits "the passing of sentences and the carrying out of executions without previous judgment pronounced by a regularly constituted court affording all the judicial guarantees which are recognized as indispensable by civilized peoples." Hamdan argued that the military commissions, which President Bush had established specifically for detainees in the War on Terror, failed to meet that standard.

The district court judge, James Robertson, agreed with Hamdan that he was entitled to certain protections under the Geneva Conventions, but an appeals court reversed this decision. The appeals court found that Hamdan did not qualify as a POW under the Third Geneva Convention. It also determined that Common Article Three did not apply to Hamdan because the War on Terror, which the United States was prosecuting in many countries, did not count as a "conflict not of an international character." In the second reading, which comes from an amicus curie ("friend of the court") brief in the *Hamdan* case, a group of European lawyers argue that the Geneva Conventions do apply to the War on Terror, providing an interpretation of common Article Three that is in marked contrast to the appeals court's view.

John Yoo and
Robert J. Delahunty

YES ⤶

Application of Treaties and Laws to al Qaeda and Taliban Detainees

You have asked for our Office's views concerning the effect of international treaties and federal laws on the treatment of individuals detained by the U.S. Armed Forces during the conflict in Afghanistan. In particular, you have asked whether the laws of armed conflict apply to the conditions of detention and the procedures for trial of members of al Qaeda and the Taliban militia. We conclude that these treaties do not protect members of the al Qaeda organization, which as a non-State actor cannot be a party to the international agreements governing war. We further conclude that these treaties do not apply to the Taliban militia. This memorandum expresses no view as to whether the President should decide, as a matter of policy, that the U.S. Armed Forces should adhere to the standards of conduct in those treaties with respect to the treatment of prisoners.

We believe it most useful to structure the analysis of these questions by focusing on the War Crimes Act, 18 U.S.C. § 2441 (Supp. III 1997) ("WCA"). The WCA directly incorporates several provisions of international treaties governing the laws of war into the federal criminal code. Part 1 of this memorandum describes the WCA and the most relevant treaties that it incorporates: the four 1949 Geneva Conventions, which generally regulate the treatment of non-combatants, such as prisoners of war ("POWs"), the injured and sick, and civilians.[1]

Part II examines whether al Qaeda detainees can claim the protection of these agreements. Al Qaeda is merely a violent political movement or organization and not a nation-state. As a result, it is ineligible to be a signatory to any treaty. Because of the novel nature of this conflict, moreover, we do not believe that al Qaeda would be included in non-international forms of armed conflict to which some provisions of the Geneva Conventions might apply. Therefore, neither the Geneva Conventions nor the WCA regulate the detention of al Qaeda prisoners captured during the Afghanistan conflict.

Part III discusses whether the same treaty provisions, as incorporated through the WCA, apply to the treatment of captured members of the Taliban militia. We believe that the Geneva Conventions do not apply for several reasons. First, the Taliban was not a government and Afghanistan was not—even

Memorandum for William J. Haynes II. General Counsel, Department of Defense, (January 9, 2002).

prior to the beginning of the present conflict—a functioning State during the period in which they engaged in hostilities against the United States and its allies. Afghanistan's status as a failed state is ground alone to find that members of the Taliban militia are not entitled to enemy POW status under the Geneva Conventions. Further, it is clear that the President has the constitutional authority to suspend our treaties with Afghanistan pending the restoration of a legitimate government capable of performing Afghanistan's treaty obligations. Second, it appears from the public evidence that the Taliban militia may have been so intertwined with al Qaeda as to be functionally indistinguishable from it. To the extent that the Taliban militia was more akin to a non-governmental organization that used military force to pursue its religious and political ideology than a functioning government, its members would be on the same legal footing as al Qaeda.

In Part IV, we address the question whether any customary international law of armed conflict might apply to the al Qaeda or Taliban militia members detained during the course of the Afghanistan conflict. We conclude that customary international law, whatever its source and content, does not bind the President, or restrict the actions of the United States military, because it does not constitute federal law recognized under the Supremacy Clause of the Constitution. The President, however, has the constitutional authority as Commander-in-Chief to interpret and apply the customary or common laws of war in such a way that they would extend to the conduct of members of both al Qaeda and the Taliban, and also to the conduct of the U.S. Armed Forces towards members of those groups taken as prisoners in Afghanistan.

I. Background and Overview of the War Crimes Act and the Geneva Conventions

It is our understanding that your Department is considering two basic plans regarding the treatment of members of al Qaeda and the Taliban militia detained during the Afghanistan conflict. First, the Defense Department intends to make available a facility at the U.S. Navy base at Guantanamo Bay, Cuba, for the long-term detention of these individuals, who have come under our control either through capture by our military or transfer from our allies in Afghanistan. We have discussed in a separate memorandum the federal jurisdiction issues that might arise concerning Guantanamo Bay.[2] Second, your Department is developing procedures to implement the President's Military Order of November 13, 2001, which establishes military commissions for the trial of violations of the laws of war committed by non-U.S. citizens.[3] The question has arisen whether the Geneva Conventions, or other relevant international treaties or federal laws, regulate these proposed policies.

We believe that the WCA provides a useful starting point for our analysis of the application of the Geneva Conventions to the treatment of detainees captured in the Afghanistan theater of operations.[4] Section 2441 of Title 18 renders certain acts punishable as "war crimes." The statute's definition of that term incorporates, by reference, certain treaties or treaty provisions relating to the laws of war, including the Geneva Conventions.

A. Section 2441: An Overview

Section 2441 reads in full as follows:
War crimes

1. Offense. —Whoever, whether inside or outside the United States, commits a war crime, in any of the circumstances described in subsection (b), shall be fined under this title or imprisoned for life or any term of years, or both, and if death results to the victim, shall also be subject to the penalty of death.
2. Circumstances. —The circumstances referred to in subsection (a) are that the person committing such war crime or the victim of such war crime is a member of the Armed Forces of the United States or a national of the United States (as defined in section 101 of the Immigration and Nationality Act).
3. Definition. —As used in this section the term "war crime" means any conduct—
   (1) defined as a grave breach in any of the international conventions signed at Geneva 12 August 1949, or any protocol to such convention to which the United States is a party;
   (2) prohibited by Article 23, 25, 27, or 28 of the Annex to the Hague Convention IV, Respecting the Laws and Customs of War on Land, signed 18 October 1907;
   (3) which constitutes a violation of common Article 3 of the international conventions signed at Geneva, 12 August 1949, or any protocol to such convention to which the United States is a party and which deals with non-international armed conflict; or
   (4) of a person who, in relation to an armed conflict and contrary to the provisions of the Protocol on Prohibitions or Restrictions on the Use of Mines, Booby-Traps and Other Devices as amended at Geneva on 3 May 1996 (Protocol II as amended on 3 May 1996), when the United States is a party to such Protocol, wilfully kills or causes serious injury to civilians.

18 U.S.C. § 2441

Section 2441 lists four categories of war crimes. First, it criminalizes "grave breaches" of the Geneva Conventions, which are defined by treaty and will be discussed below. Second, it makes illegal conduct prohibited by articles 23, 25, 27, and 28 of the Annex to the Hague Convention IV. Third, it criminalizes violations of what is known as "common" Article 3, which is an identical provision common to all four of the Geneva Conventions. Fourth, it criminalizes conduct prohibited by certain other laws of war treaties, once the United States joins them. A House Report states that the original legislation "carries out the international obligations of the United States under the Geneva Conventions of 1949 to provide criminal penalties for certain war crimes." H.R. Rep. No. 104–698 at 1 (1996), *reprinted in* 1996 U.S.C.C.A.N. 2166. 2166. Each of those four conventions includes a clause relating to legislative implementation and to criminal punishment.[5]

In enacting section 2441, Congress also sought to fill certain perceived gaps in the coverage of federal criminal law. The main gaps were thought to be of two kinds: subject matter jurisdiction and personal jurisdiction. First, Congress found that "[t]here are major gaps in the prosecutability of individuals under federal criminal law for war crimes committed against Americans." H.R. Rep. No. 104–698 at 6, *reprinted in* 1996 U.S.C.C.A.N. at 2171. For example, "the simple killing of a[n American] prisoner of war" was not covered by any existing Federal statute. *Id.* at 5, *reprinted in* 1996 U.S.C.C.A.N. at 2170.[6] Second, Congress found that "[t]he ability to court martial members of our armed services who commit war crimes ends when they leave military service. [Section 244] would allow for prosecution even after discharge." *Id.* at 7, *reprinted in* 1996 U.S.C.C.A.N. at 2172.[7] Congress considered it important to fill this gap, not only in the interest of the victims of war crimes, but also of the accused. "The Americans prosecuted would have available all the procedural protections of the American justice system. These might be lacking if the United States extradited the individuals to their victims' home countries for prosecution." *Id.*[8] Accordingly, Section 2441 criminalizes forms of conduct in which a U.S. national or a member of the Armed Forces may be either a victim or a perpetrator.

B. Grave Breaches of the Geneva Conventions

The Geneva Conventions were approved by a diplomatic conference on August 12, 1949, and remain the agreements to which more States have become parties than any other concerning the laws of war. Convention I deals with the treatment of wounded and sick in armed forces in the field; Convention II addresses treatment of the wounded, sick, and shipwrecked in armed forces at sea; Convention III regulates treatment of POWs; Convention IV addresses the treatment of citizens. While the Hague Convention IV establishes the rules of conduct against the enemy, the Geneva Conventions set the rules for the treatment of the victims of war.

The Geneva Conventions, like treaties generally, structure legal relationships between Nation States, not between Nation States and private, subnational groups or organizations.[9] All four Conventions share the same Article 2, known as "common Article 2." It states:

> In addition to the provisions which shall be implemented in peacetime, the present Convention shall apply to all cases of declared war or of any other armed conflict *which may arise between two or more of the High Contracting Parties,* even if the state of war is not recognized by one of them.
>
> The Convention shall also apply to all cases of partial or total occupation of the territory of a High Contracting Party, even if the said occupation meets with no armed resistance.
>
> Although one of the Powers in conflict may not be a party to the present Convention, the Powers who are parties thereto shall remain bound by it in their mutual relations. They shall furthermore be bound by the Convention in relation to the said Power, if the latter accepts and applies the provisions thereof.
>
> (Emphasis added)

As incorporated by § 2441(c)(1), the four Geneva Conventions similarly define "grave breaches." Geneva Convention III on POWs defines grave breach as:

> wilful killing, torture or inhuman treatment, including biological experiments, wilfully causing great suffering or serious injury to body or health, compelling a prisoner of war to serve in the forces of the hostile Power, or wilfully depriving a prisoner of war of the rights of fair and regular trial prescribed in this Convention.

Geneva Convention III art. 130. As mentioned before, the Geneva Conventions require the High Contracting Parties to enact penal legislation to punish anyone who commits or orders a grave breach. *See. e.g., id.* art. 129. Further, each State party has the obligation to search for and bring to justice (either before its courts or by delivering a suspect to another State party) anyone who commits a grave breach. No State party is permitted to absolve itself or any other nation of liability for committing a grave breach.

Thus, the WCA does not criminalize all breaches of the Geneva Conventions. Failure to follow some of the regulations regarding the treatment of POWs, such as difficulty in meeting all of the conditions set forth for POW camp conditions, does not constitute a grave breach within the meaning of Geneva Convention III, art. 130. Only by causing great suffering or serious bodily injury to POWs, killing or torturing them, depriving them of access to a fair trial, or forcing them to serve in the Armed Forces, could the United States actually commit a grave breach. Similarly, unintentional, isolated collateral damage on civilian targets would not constitute a grave breach within the meaning of Geneva Convention IV, art. 147. Article 147 requires that for a grave breach to have occurred, destruction of property must have been done "wantonly" and without military justification, while the killing of injury of civilians must have been "wilful."

D. Common Article 3 of the Geneva Conventions

Section 2441 (c)(3) also defines as a war crime conduct that "constitutes a violation of common Article 3" of the Geneva Conventions. Article 3 is a unique provision that governs the conduct of signatories to the Conventions in a particular kind of conflict that is *not* one between High Contracting Parties to the Conventions. Thus, common Article 3 may require the United States, as a High Contracting Party, to follow certain rules even if other parties to the conflict are not parties to the Conventions. On the other hand, Article 3 requires state parties to follow only certain minimum standards of treatment toward prisoners, civilians, or the sick and wounded, rather than the Conventions as a whole.

Common Article 3 reads in relevant part as follows:

> In the case of armed conflict not of an international character occurring in the territory of one of the High Contracting Parties, each Party to the conflict shall be bound to apply, as a minimum, the following provisions:

> (1) Persons taking no active part in the hostilities, including members of armed forces who have laid down their arms and those placed *hors de combat*

by sickness, wounds, detention, or any other cause, shall in all circumstances be treated humanely, without any adverse distinction founded on race, color, religion or faith, sex, birth, or wealth, or any other similar criteria.

To this end, the following acts are and shall remain prohibited at any time and in any place whatsoever with respect to the above-mentioned persons:

(a) violence to life and person, in particular murder of all kinds, mutilation, cruel treatment and torture;
(b) taking of hostages;
(c) outrages upon personal dignity, in particular, humiliating and degrading treatment;
(d) the passing of sentences and the carrying out of executions without previous judgment pronounced by a regularly constituted court, affording all the judicial guarantees which are recognized as indispensable by civilized peoples.

(2) The wounded and sick shall be collected and cared for. . . .

The application of the preceding provisions shall not affect the legal status of the Parties to the conflict.

Common Article 3 complements common Article 2. Article 2 applies to cases of declared war or of any other armed conflict that may arise between two or more of the High Contracting Parties, even if the state of war is not recognized by one of them.[10] Common Article 3, however, covers "armed conflict not of an international character"—a war that does not involve cross-border attacks—that occurs within the territory of one of the High Contracting Parties. There is substantial reason to think that this language refers specifically to a condition of civil war, or a large-scale armed conflict between a State and an armed movement within its own territory.

To begin with, Article 3's text strongly supports the interpretation that it applies to large-scale conflicts between a State and an insurgent group. First, the language at the end of Article 3 states that "[t]he application of the proceding provisions shall not affect the legal status of the Parties to the conflict." This provision was designed to ensure that a Party that observed Article 3 during a civil war would not be understood to have granted the "recognition of the insurgents as an adverse party." Frits Kalshoven, *Constraints on the Waging of War* 59 (1987). Second, Article 3 is in terms limited to "armed conflict . . . occurring *in the territory of one of the High Contracting Parties*" (emphasis added). This limitation makes perfect sense if the Article applies to civil wars, which are fought primarily or solely within the territory of a single state. The limitation makes little sense, however, as applied to a conflict between a State and a transitional terrorist group, which may operate from different territorial bases, some of which might be located in States that are parties to the Conventions and some of which might not be. In such a case, the Conventions would apply to a single armed conflict in some scenes of action but not in others—which seems inexplicable.

This interpretation is supported by commentators. One well-known commentary states that "a non-international armed conflict is distinct from an international armed conflict because of the legal status of the entities opposing each other the parties to the conflict are not sovereign States, but the government of a single State in conflict with one or more armed factions within its territory."[11] A legal scholar writing in the same year in which the Conventions were prepared stated that "a conflict not of an international character occurring in the territory of one of the High Contracting Parties . . . must normally mean a civil war."[12]

Analysis of the background to the adoption of the Geneva Conventions in 1949 confirms our understanding of common Article 3. It appears that the drafters of the Conventions had in mind only the two forms of armed conflict that were regarded as matters of general *international* concern at the time: armed conflict between Nation States (subject to Article 2), and large-scale civil war within a Nation State (subject to Article 3). To understand the context in which the Geneva Conventions were drafted, it will be helpful to identify three distinct phases in the development of the laws of war.

First, the traditional law of war was based on a stark dichotomy between "belligerency" and "insurgency." The category of "belligerency" applied to armed conflicts between sovereign States (unless there was recognition of belligerency in a civil war), while the category of "insurgency" applied to armed violence breaking out within the territory of a sovereign State.[13] Correspondingly, international law treated the two classes of conflict in different ways. Inter-state wars were regulated by a body of international legal rules governing both the conduct of hostilities and the protection of noncombatants. By contrast, there were very few international rules governing civil unrest, for States preferred to regard internal strife as rebellion, mutiny and treason coming within the purview of national criminal law, which precluded any possible intrusion by other States.[14] This was a "clearly sovereignty-oriented" phase of international law.[15]

The second phase began as early as the Spanish Civil War (1936–39) and extended through the time of the drafting of the Geneva Conventions until relatively recently. During this period, State practice began to apply certain general principles of humanitarian law beyond the traditional field of State-to-State conflict to "those internal conflicts that constituted large-scale civil wars."[16] In addition to the Spanish Civil War, events in 1947 during the Civil War between the Communists and the Nationalist regime in China illustrated this new tendency.[17] Common Article 3, which was prepared during this second phase, was apparently addressed to armed conflicts akin to the Chinese and Spanish civil wars. As one commentator has described it, Article 3 was designed to restrain governments "in the handling of armed violence directed against them for the express purpose of secession or at securing a change in the government of a State," but even after the adoption of the Conventions it remained "uncertain whether [Article 3] applied to full-scale civil war."[18]

The third phase represents a more complete break than the second with the traditional "State-sovereignty-oriented approach" of international law. This approach gives central place to individual human rights. As a consequence, it blurs the distinction between international and internal armed conflicts, and even that between civil wars and other forms of internal armed conflict. This approach is well illustrated by the ICTY's decision in *Tadic*, which appears to take the view that common Article 3 applies to non-international armed conflicts of *any* description, and is not limited to civil wars between a State and an insurgent group. In this conception, common Article 3 is not just a complement to common Article 2; rather, it is a catch-all that establishes standards for any and all armed conflicts not included in common Article 2.[19]

Nonetheless, despite this recent trend, we think that such an interpretation of common Article 3 fails to take into account, not only the language of the provision, but also its historical context. First, as we have described above, such a reading is inconsistent with the text of Article 3 itself, which applies only to "armed conflict not of an international character occurring in the territory of one of the High Contracting Parties." In conjunction with common Article 2, the text of Article 3 simply does not reach international conflicts where one of the parties is not a Nation State. If we were to read the Geneva Conventions as applying to all forms of armed conflict, we would expect the High Contracting Parties to have used broader language, which they easily could have done. To interpret common Article 3 by expanding its scope well beyond the meaning borne by the text is effectively to amend the Geneva Conventions without the approval of the State Parties to the agreements.

Second, as we have discussed, Article 3 was prepared during a period in which the traditional, State-centered view of international law was still dominant and was only just beginning to give way to a human-rights-based approach. Giving due weight to the State practice and doctrinal understanding of the time, it seems to us overwhelmingly likely that an armed conflict between a Nation State and a transnational terrorist organization, or between a Nation State and a failed State harboring and supporting a transnational terrorist organization, could not have been within the contemplation of the drafters of common Article 3. These would have been simply unforeseen and, therefore, not provided for. Indeed, it seems to have been uncertain even a decade after the Conventions were signed whether common Article 3 applied to armed conflicts that were neither international in character nor civil wars but anti-colonialist wars of independence such as those in Algeria and Kenya. *See* Gerald Irving Draper, *The Red Cross Conventions* 15 (1957). Further, it is telling that in order to address this unforeseen circumstance, the State Parties to the Geneva Conventions did not attempt to distort the terms of common Article 3 to apply it to cases that did not fit within its terms. Instead, they drafted two new protocols (neither of which the United States has ratified) to adapt the Conventions to the conditions of contemporary hostilities.[20] Accordingly, common Article 3 is best understood not to apply to such armed conflicts.

Third, it appears that in enacting the WCA, Congress did not understand the scope of Article 3 to extend beyond civil wars to all other types of internal armed conflict. As discussed in our review of the legislative history, when extending the WCA to cover violations of common Article 3, the House apparently understood that it was codifying treaty provisions that "forbid atrocities occurring in both civil wars and wars between nations."[21] If Congress had embraced a much broader view of common Article 3, and hence of 18 U.S.C. § 2441, we would expect both the statutory text and the legislative history to have included some type of clear statement of congressional intent. The WCA regulates the manner in which the U.S. Armed Forces may conduct military operations against the enemy; as such, it potentially comes into conflict with the President's Commander-in-Chief power under Article II of the Constitution. As we have advised others earlier in this conflict, the Commander-in-Chief power gives the President the plenary authority in determining how best to deploy troops in the field.[22] Any congressional effort to restrict presidential authority by subjecting the conduct of the U.S. Armed Forces to a broad construction of the Geneva Convention, one that is not clearly borne by its text, would represent a possible infringement on presidential discretion to direct the military. We believe that the Congress must state explicitly its intention to take the constitutionally dubious step of restricting the President's plenary power over military operations (including the treatment of prisoners), and that unless Congress clearly demonstrates such an intent, the WCA must be read to avoid such constitutional problems.[23] As Congress has not signaled such a clear intention in this case, we conclude that common Article 3, should not be read to include all forms of non-international armed conflict.

II. Application of WCA and Associated Treaties to al Qaeda

It is clear from the foregoing statements that members of the al Qaeda terrorist organization do not receive the protections of the laws of war. Therefore, neither their detention nor their trial by the U.S. Armed Forces is subject to the Geneva Conventions (or the WCA). Three reasons, examined in detail below, support this conclusion. First, al Qaeda's status as a non-State actor renders it ineligible to claim the protections of the Geneva Conventions. Second, the nature of the conflict precludes application of common Article 3 of the Geneva Conventions. Third, al Qaeda members fail to satisfy the eligibility requirements for treatment as POWs under Geneva Convention III.

Al Qaeda's status as a non-State actor renders it ineligible to claim the protections of the treaties specified by the WCA. Al Qaeda is not a State. It is a non-governmental terrorist organization composed of members from many nations, with ongoing operations in dozens of nations. Its members seem united in following a radical brand of Islam that seeks to attack Americans throughout the world. Non-governmental organizations cannot be parties to any of the international agreements here governing the laws of war. Al Qaeda is not eligible to sign the Geneva Conventions—and even if it were eligible, it has not done so. Common Article 2, which triggers the Geneva Convention provisions regulating detention conditions and procedures for trial of POWs, is limited only to cases of declared war or armed conflict "between two or more of the High Contracting Parties." Al Qaeda is not a High Contracting Party. As a result the U.S. military's treatment of al Qaeda members is not governed by the bulk of the Geneva Conventions, specifically those provisions concerning POWs. Conduct towards captured members of al Qaeda, therefore, also cannot constitute a violation of 18 U.S.C. § 2441(c)(1) or § 2441(c)(2).[24]

Second, the nature of the conflict precludes application of common Article 3 of the Geneva Conventions. Al Qaeda is not covered by common Article 3, because the current conflict is not covered by the Geneva Conventions. As discussed in Part I, the text of Article 3, when read in harmony with common Article 2, shows that the Geneva Conventions were intended to cover either: a) traditional wars between Nation States (Article 2), or non-international civil wars (Article 3). Our conflict with al Qaeda does not fit into either category. The current conflict is not an international war between Nation States, but rather a conflict between a Nation State and a non-governmental organization. At the same time, the current conflict is not a civil war under Article 3, because it is a conflict of "an international character," rather than an internal armed conflict between parties contending for control over a government or territory. Therefore, the military's treatment of al Qaeda members captured in that conflict is not limited either by common Article 3 of the Geneva Conventions or 18 U.S.C. § 2441(c)(3), the provision of the WCA incorporating that article.[25]

Third, al Qaeda members fail to satisfy the eligibility requirements for treatment as POWs under Geneva Convention III. It might be argued that, even though it is not a State party to the Geneva Convention, al Qaeda could be covered by some protections in Geneva Convention III on the treatment of POWs. Article 4(A)(2) of the Geneva Convention III defines prisoners of war as including not only captured members of the armed forces of a High Contracting Party, but also irregular forces such as "[m]embers of other militias and members of other volunteer corps, including those of organized resistance movements." Geneva Convention III, art. 4. Article 4(A)(3) also includes as POWs "[m]embers of regular armed forces who profess allegiance to a government or an authority not recognized by the Detaining Power." *Id.* art. 4(A)(3). It might be claimed that the broad terms of these provisions could be stretched to cover al Qaeda.

This view would be mistaken. Article 4 does not expand the application of the Convention beyond the circumstances expressly addressed in common Articles 2 and 3. Unless there is a conflict subject to Article 2 or 3 (the Convention's jurisdictional provisions), Article 4 simply does not apply. As we have argued with respect to Article 3, and shall further argue with respect to Article 2, the conflict in Afghanistan does not fall within either Articles 2 or 3. As a result, Article 4 has no application. In other words, Article 4 cannot be read as an alternative, and far more expansive, statement of the application of the Convention. It merely specifies, where there is a conflict covered by the Convention, who must be accorded POW status.

Even if Article 4, however, were considered somehow to be jurisdictional as well as substantive, captured members of al Qaeda still would not receive the protections accorded to POWs. Article 4(A)(2), for example, further requires that the militia or volunteers fulfill the conditions first established by the Hague Convention IV of 1907 for those who would receive that protections of the laws of war. Hague Convention IV declares that the "laws, rights and duties of war" only apply to armies, militia, and volunteer corps when they fulfill four conditions: command by responsible individuals, wearing insignia, carrying arms openly, and obeying the laws of war. Hague Convention IV, Respecting the Laws and Customs of War on Land, Oct. 18, 1907, 36 Stat. 2277. Al Qaeda members have clearly demonstrated that they will not follow these basic requirements of lawful warfare. They have attacked purely civilian targets of no military value; they refused to wear uniform or insignia or carry arms openly, but instead hijacked civilian airliners, took hostages, and killed them; they have deliberately targeted and killed thousands of civilians; and they themselves do not obey the laws of war concerning the protection of the lives of civilians or the means of legitimate combat. Thus, Article 4(A)(3) is inapt because al Qaeda do not qualify as "regular armed forces," and its members do not qualify for protection as lawful combatants under the laws of war. . . .

IV. The Customary International Laws of War

So far, this memorandum has addressed the issue whether the Geneva Conventions and the WCA, apply to the detention and trial of al Qaeda and Taliban militia members taken prisoner in Afghanistan. Having concluded that these laws do not apply, we turn to your question concerning the effect, if any, of customary international law. Some may take the view that even if the Geneva Conventions, by their terms, do not govern the conflict in Afghanistan, the substance of these agreements has received such universal approval that it has risen to the status of customary international law. Regardless of its substance, however, customary international law cannot bind the executive branch under the Constitution because it is not federal law. This is a view that this Office has expressed before,[26] and is one consistent with the views of the federal courts,[27] and with executive branch arguments in the courts.[28] As a result, any customary international law of armed conflict in no way binds, as a legal matter, the President or the U.S. Armed Forces concerning the detention or trial of members of al Qaeda and the Taliban.

A. Is Customary International Law Federal Law?

Under the view promoted by many international law academics, any presidential violation of customary international law is presumptively unconstitutional.[29] These scholars argue that customary international law is federal law, and that the President's Article II duty under the Take Care Clause requires him to execute customary international law as well as statutes lawfully enacted under the Constitution. A President may not violate customary international law, therefore, just as he cannot violate a statute, unless he believes it to be unconstitutional. Relying upon cases such as *The Paquete Habana,* 175 U.S. 677, 700 (1900), in which the Supreme Court observed that "international law is part of our law," this position often claims that the federal judiciary has the authority to invalidate executive action that runs counter to customary international law.[30]

This view of customary international law is seriously mistaken. The constitutional text nowhere brackets presidential or federal power within the confines of international law. When the Supremacy Clause discusses the sources of federal law, it enumerates only this Constitution, and the Laws of the United States which shall be made in Pursuance thereof and all Treaties made, or which shall be made, under the Authority of the United States." U.S. Constitution VI International law is nowhere mentioned in the Constitution as an independent source of federal law or as a constraint on the political branches of government. Indeed, if it were, there would have been no need to grant to Congress the power to "define and punish . . . Offenses against the Law of Nations."[31] It is also clear that the original understanding of the Framers was that "Laws of the United

States" did *not* include the law of nations, as international law was called in the late eighteenth century. In explaining the jurisdiction of the Article III courts to cases arising, "under the Constitution and the Laws of the United States," for the example, Alexander Hamilton did not include the law of nations as a source of jurisdiction.[32] Rather, Hamilton pointed out, claims involving the laws of nations would arise either in diversity cases or maritime cases, [33] which by definition do not involve "the Laws of the United States." Little evidence exists that those who attended the Philadelphia Convention in the summer of 1787 or the state ratifying conventions believed that federal law would have included customary international law, but rather that the law of nations was part of a general common law that was not true federal law.[34]

Indeed, allowing customary international law to rise to the level of federal law would create severe distortions in the structure of the Constitution. Incorporation of customary international law directly into federal law would bypass the delicate procedures, established by the Constitution for amending the Constitution or for enacting legislation.[35] Customary international law is not approved by two-thirds of Congress and three-quarters of the state legislatures, it has not been passed by both houses of Congress and signed by the President, nor is it made by the President with the advice and consent of two-thirds of the Senate. In other words, customary international law has not undergone the difficult hurdles that stand before enactment of constitutional amendments, statutes, or treaties. As such, it can have no legal effect on the government or on American citizens because it is not law.[36] Even the inclusion of treaties in the Supremacy Clause does not render treaties automatically self-executing in federal court, not to mention self-executing against the executive branch.[37] If even treaties that have undergone presidential signature and senatorial advice and consent can have no binding legal effect in the United States, then it certainly must be the case that a source of rules that never undergoes any process established by our Constitution cannot be law.[38] . . .

Indeed, proponents of the notion that customary international law is federal law can find little support in either history or Supreme Court case law. It is true that in some contexts mostly involving maritime, insurance, and commercial law, the federal courts in the nineteenth century looked to customary international law as a guide.[39] Upon closer examination of these cases, however, it is clear that customary international law had the status only of the general federal common law that was applied in federal diversity cases under *Swift v. Tyson,* 41 U.S. (16 Pet.) 1 (1842). As such it was not considered true federal law under the Supremacy Clause, it did not support Article III "arising under" jurisdiction; it did not pre-empt inconsistent state law; and it did not bind the executive branch. Indeed, even during this period the Supreme Court acknowledged that the laws of war did not qualify as true federal law and could not therefore serve as the basis for federal subject matter jurisdiction. In *New York Life Ins. Co v. Hendren*, 92 U.S. 286, for example, the Supreme Court declared that it had no jurisdiction to review the general laws of war, as recognized by the law of nations applicable to this case, because such laws do not involve the constitution, laws, treaties, or executive proclamations of the United States.[40] The spurious nature of this type of law led the Supreme

Court in the famous case of *Erie R.R. Co. v. Tompkins,* 304 U.S. 64, 78 (1938), to eliminate general federal common law. . . .

Constitutional text and Supreme Court decisions aside, allowing the federal courts to rely upon international law to restrict the President's discretion to conduct war would raise deep structural problems. First, if customary international law is indeed federal law, then it must receive all of the benefits of the Supremacy Clause. Therefore, customary international law would not only bind the President, but it also would pre-empt state law and even supersede inconsistent federal statutes and treaties that were enacted before the rule of customary international law came into being. This has never happened. Indeed, giving customary international law this power not only runs counter to the Supreme Court cases described above, but would have the effect of importing a body of law to restrain the three branches of American government that never underwent any approval by our democratic political process. If customary international law does not have these effects, as the constitutional text, practice and most sensible readings of the Constitution indicate, then it cannot be true federal law under the Supremacy Clause. As non-federal law, then, customary international law cannot bind the President or the executive branch, in any legally meaningful way, in its conduct of the war in Afghanistan. . . .

Conclusion

For the foregoing reasons, we conclude that neither the federal War Crimes Act nor the Geneva Conventions would apply to the detention condition in Guantanamo Bay, Cuba, or to trial by military commission of al Qaeda or Taliban prisoners. We also conclude that customary international law has no binding legal effect on either the President or the military because it is not federal law, as recognized by the Constitution. Nonetheless, we also believe that the President, as Commander-in-Chief, has the constitutional authority to impose the customary laws of war on both the al Qaeda and Taliban groups and the U.S. Armed Forces.

Please let us know if we can provide further assistance.

Notes

1. The four Geneva Conventions for the Protection of Victims of War, dated August 12, 1949, were ratified by the United States on July 14, 1955. These are the Convention for the Amelioration of the Condition of the Wounded and Sick in Armed Forces in the Field, 6 U.S.T. 3115 ("Geneva Convention I"); the Convention for the Amelioration of the Condition of Wounded, Sick and Shipwrecked Members of Armed Forces at Sea, 6 U.S.T. 3219 ("Geneva Convention II"); the Convention Relative to the Treatment of Prisoners of War, 6 U.S.T. 3517 ("Geneva Convention III"); and the Convention Relative to the Protection of Civilian Persons in Time of War, 6 U.S.T. 3317 ("Geneva Convention IV").

2. *See* Memorandum for William J. Haynes II, General Counsel, Department of Defense, from Patrick F. Philbin, Deputy Assistant Attorney General, and John Yoo, Deputy Assistant Attorney General, *Re: Possible Habeas Jurisdiction over Aliens Held in Guantanamo Bay, Cuba* (Dec. 28, 2001).

3. *See generally* Memorandum for Alberto R. Gonzales, Counsel to the President, from Patrick F. Philbin, Deputy Assistant Attorney General, Office of Legal Counsel, *Re: Legality of the Use of Military Commissions to Try Terrorists* (Nov. 6, 2001).

4. The rule of lenity requires that the WCA be read so as to ensure that prospective defendants have adequate notice of the nature of the acts that the statute condemns. *See, e.g., Castillo v. United States,* 530 U.S. 120, 131 (2000). In those cases in which the application of a treaty incorporated by the WCA is unclear, therefore, the rule of lenity requires that the interpretative issue be resolved in the defendant's favor.

5. That common clause reads as follows:

    > The [signatory Nations] undertake to enact any legislation necessary to provide effective penal sanctions for persons committing or ordering to be committed, any of the grave breaches of the present Convention. . . . Each [signatory nation] shall be under the obligation to search for persons alleged to have committed, or to have ordered to be committed, such grave breaches, and shall bring such persons, regardless of their nationality, before its own courts . . . It may also, if it prefers,. . . hand such persons over for trial to another [signatory nation], provided such [nation] has made out a *prima facie case.*

    Geneva Convention I, Article 49; Geneva Convention II, art. 50; Geneva Convention III, Article 129; Geneva Convention IV, Article 146.

6. In projecting our criminal law extraterritorially in order to protect victims who are United States nationals, Congress was apparently relying on the international law principle of passive personality. The passive personality principle "asserts that a state may apply law—particularly criminal law—to an act committed outside its territory by a person not its national where the victim of the act was its national" *United States v. Rezaq,* 134 F. 3d 1121, 1133 (D.C. Cir.), *cert. denied,* 525 U.S. 834 (1998). The principle marks recognition of the fact that "each nation has a legitimate interest that its nationals and permanent inhabitants not be maimed or disabled from self-support," or otherwise injured. *Lauritzen v. Larsen,* 345 U.S. 571, 586 (1953); *see also Hellenic Lines Ltd. v. Rhoditis,* 398 U.S. 306, 309 (1970).

7. United States *ex rel. Toth v. Quaries,* 350 U.S. 11 (1955), the Supreme Court had held that a former serviceman could not constitutionally be tried before a court martial under the Uniform Code for Military Justice (the UCMJ) for crimes he was alleged to have committed while in the armed services.

8. The principle of nationality in international law recognizes that (as Congress did here) a State may criminalize acts performed extraterritorially by its own nationals. *See, e.g., Skiriotes v. Florida,* 313 U.S. 69, 73 (1941); *Steele v. Bulova Watch Co.,* 344 U.S. 280, 282 (1952).

9. *See Trans World Airlines, Inc. v. Franklin Mint Corp.,* 466 U.S. 243, 253 (1984) ("A treaty is in the nature of a contract between nations."); *The Head Money Cases,* 112, U.S. 580, 598 (1884) ("A treaty is primarily a compact between independent nations."); *United States ex rel. Saroop v. Garcia,* 109 F.3d 165, 167 (3d Cir. 1997) ("[T]reaties are agreements between nations."); *Vienna Convention on the Law of Treaties,* May 23, 1969, art. 2. § 1(a). 1155 U.N.T.S. 331, 333 ("[T]reaty' means an international agreement concluded between States in written form and governed by international law. . . .") (the "Vienna Convention"); *see generally Banco Naçional de Cuba v. Sabbatino,* 376 U.S. 398, 422 (1964) ("The traditional view of international law is that it establishes substantive principles for determining whether one country has wronged another.").

10. Article 2's reference to a state of war "not recognized" by a belligerent was apparently intended to refer to conflicts such as the 1937 war between China and Japan. Both sides denied that a state of war existed. *See* Joyce A. C.

Gutteridge, *The Geneva Conventions of 1949,* 26 Brit. Y. B. Int'l L. 294, 298–99 (1949).

11. Commentary as the Additional Protocols of 8 June 1977 to the Geneva Conventions of 12 August 1949, at ¶ 4339 (Yves Sandoz et al. eds., 1987).

12. Gutteridge, *Supra* n.10, at 300.

13. *See* Joseph H. Beale, Jr., *The Recognition of Cuban Belligerency,* 9 Harv. L. Rev. 406, 406 n.1 (1896).

14. *See The Prosecutor v. Dusko Tadic (Jurisdiction* of *the Tribunal).* (Appeals Chamber of the International Criminal Tribunal for the Former Yugoslavia 1995) (the "ICTY"), 105 I.L.R. 453, 504–05 (E. Lauterpacht and C. J. Greenwood eds., 1997).

15. *Id.* at 505; *see also* Gerald Irving Draper, *Reflections of Law and Armed Conflicts* 107 (1998) ("Before 1949, in the absence of recognized belligerency accorded to the elements opposed to the government of a State, the law of war . . . had no application to internal armed conflicts . . . International law had little or nothing to say as to how the armed rebellion was crushed by the government concerned, for such matters fell within the domestic jurisdiction of States. Such conflicts were often waged with great lack of restraint and cruelty. Such conduct was a domestic matter.").

16. *Tadic,* 105 I.L.R. at 507. Indeed, the events of the Spanish Civil War, in which "both the republican Government [of Spain] and third States refused to recognize the [Nationalist] insurgents as belligerents," *id.* at 507, may be reflected in common Article 3's reference to "the legal status of the Parties to the conflict."

17. *See Id.* at 508.

18. *See* Draper, *Reflections on Law and Armed Conflicts, supra, at* 108.

19. An interpretation of common Article 3 that would apply it to all forms of non-international armed conflict accords better with some recent approaches to international humanitarian law. For example, *the Commentary on the Additional Protocols of 8 June 1977 to the Geneva Conventions of 12 August 1949, supra,* after first stating in the text that Article 3 applies when "the government of a single State [is] in conflict with one or more armed factions within its territory," thereafter suggests, in a footnote, that an armed conflict not of an international character "may also exist in which armed factions fight against each other without intervention by the armed forces of the established government." *Id.* ¶ 4339 at n. 2. A still broader interpretation appears to be supported by the language of the decision of the International Court of Justice (the "ICJ") in *Nicaragua v. United States*—which, it should be made clear, the United States refused to acknowledge by withdrawing from the compulsory jurisdiction of the ICJ:

> Article 3 which is common to all four Geneva Conventions of 12 August 1949 defines certain rules to be applied in *the armed conflicts of a non-international character.* There is no doubt that, in the event of international armed conflicts, these rules also constitute a minimum yardstick, in addition to the more elaborate rules which are also to apply to international conflicts; and they are rules which, in the Court's opinion, reflect what the Court in 1949 called "elementary considerations of humanity."

Military and Paramilitary Activities In and Against Nicaragua (Nicaragua v. United States), (International Court of Justice 1986), 76 I.L.R. 1, 448, ¶ 218 (E. Lauterpacht and C. J. Greenwood eds., 1988) (emphasis added). The ICJ's language is probably best read to suggest that all "armed conflicts" are either international or non-international, and that if they are non-international, they are governed by common Article 3. If that is the correct understanding of the quoted language, however, it should be noted that the result was merely stated as a conclusion, without taking account either of the precise language of Article 3 or of the background to its adoption. Moreover, while it was true that one of the conflicts to which the ICJ was addressing itself—"[t]he conflict between the *contras'* forces and those of the Government of Nicaragua"—"was an armed conflict which is 'not of an international character,'" *id.* at 448, ¶ 219, that conflict was recognizably a civil war between a State and an insurgent group, not a conflict between or among violent factions in a territory in which the State had collapsed. Thus there is substantial reason to question the logic and scope of the ICJ's interpretation of common Article 3.

20.   See, e.g., Protocol Additional to the Geneva Conventions of 12 August 1949, and Relating to the Protection of Victims of International Armed Conflicts (Protocol I), June 8, 1977, 1125 U.N.T.S. 4; Protocol Additional to the Geneva Conventions of 12 August 1949, and Relating to the Protection of Victims of Non-International Armed Conflicts (Protocol II), June 8 1977, 1125 U.N.T.S. 610.

21.   143 Cong. Rec. H5865–66 (daily ed. July 28, 1997) (remarks of Rep. Jenkins).

22.   Memorandum for Timothy E. Flanigan, Deputy Counsel to the President, from John C. Yoo, Deputy Assistant Attorney General, Office of Legal Counsel, *Re: The President's Constitutional Authority to Conduct Military Operations Against Terrorists and Nations Supporting them* (Sept. 25, 2001).

23.   *Cf. Public Citizen v. Department of Justice,* 491 U.S. 440, 466 (1989) (construing Federal Advisory Committee Act to avoid encroachment on presidential power); *Ashwander v. TVA.* 297 U.S. 288, 346–48 (1936) (Brandeis, J., concurring) (stating rule of avoidance); *Association of Am. Physicians & Surgeons, Inc. v. Clinton,* 997 F.2d 898, 906–11 (D.C. Cir. 1993) (same).

24.   Some difference in the language of the WCA might be thought to throw some doubt on the exact manner in which the statute incorporates these treaty norms. It might be argued, for example, with respect to the Hague Convention IV, that the WCA does not simply incorporate the terms of the treaty itself, with all of their limitations on application, but instead criminalizes the conduct described by that Convention. The argument starts from the fact that there is a textual difference in the way that the WCA references treaty provisions. Section 2441(c)(2) defines as a war crime conduct "prohibited" by the relevant sections of the Hague Convention IV. By contrast, §2441 (c)(1) makes a war crime any conduct that constitutes a "grave breach" of the Geneva Conventions, and § 2441(c)(3) prohibits conduct "which constitutes a violation" of common Article 3 of the Geneva Convention. It might be argued that this difference indicates that § 2441(c)(2) does not *incorporate* the treaty into federal law; rather, it prohibits the conduct *described by* the treaty. Section 2441(c)(3) prohibits conduct "which constitutes a *violation* of common Article 3" (emphasis added), and that can only be conduct which is a treaty violation. Likewise, § 2441(c)(1) only criminalizes conduct that is a "grave breach" of the Geneva Conventions—which, again, must be a treaty violation. In other words, § 2441 (c)(2) might be read to apply even when the Hague Convention IV, by its own terms, would not. On this interpretation, an act could violate § 2441(c)(2), whether or not the Hague Convention IV applied to the specific situation at issue.

We do not think that this interpretation is tenable. To begin with, § 2441(c)(2) makes clear that to be a war crime, conduct must be *"prohibited,"* by the Hague Convention IV (emphasis added). Use of the word "prohibited," rather than phrases such as "referred to" or "described," indicates that the treaty must, by its own operation, proscribe the conduct at issue. If the Hague Convention IV does not itself apply to a certain conflict, then it cannot itself proscribe any conduct undertaken as part of that conflict. Thus, the most natural reading of the statutory language is that an individual must violate the Hague Convention IV in order to violate Section 2441(c)(2). Had Congress intended broadly to criminalize the types of conduct proscribed by the relevant Hague Convention IV provisions as such, rather than as treaty violations, it could have done so more clearly. Furthermore, the basic purpose of § 2441 was to implement, by appropriate legislation, the United States' treaty obligations. That purpose would be accomplished by criminalizing acts that were also violations of certain key provisions of the Annex to Hague Convention IV. It would not be served by criminalizing acts *of the kind* condemned by those provisions, whether or not they were treaty violations.

Nothing in the legislative history supports the opposite result. To the contrary, the legislative history suggests an entirely different explanation for the minor variations in language between §§ 2441(c)(1) and 2441(c)(2). As originally enacted, the WCA criminalized violations of the Geneva Conventions. See Pub. L. No. 104–192, § 2(a), 110 Stat. 2104, § 2401 (1996). In signing the original legislation, President Clinton urged that it be expanded to include other serious war crimes involving violation of the Hague Conventions IV and the Amended Protocol II. *See* 2 Pub. Papers of William J. Clinton 1323 (1996). The Expanded War Crimes Act of 1997, introduced as H.R. 1348 in the 105th Congress, was designed to meet these requests. Thus, § 2441(c)(2) was added as an amendment at a later time, and was not drafted at the same time and in the same process as § 2441(c)(1).

25. This understanding is supported by the WCA's legislative history. When extending the WCA to cover violations of common Article 3, the House apparently understood that it was codifying treaty provisions that "forbid atrocities occurring in both civil wars and wars between nations." 143 Cong. Rec. H5865–66 (remarks of Rep. Jenkins). The Senate also understood that "[t]he inclusion of common Article 3 of the Geneva Conventions . . . expressly allows the United States to prosecute war crimes perpetrated in non-international conflicts, such as Bosnia and Rwanda." 143 Cong. Rec. S7544, S7589 (daily ed. July 16, 1997) (remarks of Sen. Leahy). In referring to Bosnia and Rwanda, both civil wars of a non-international character, Senator Leahy appears to have understood common Article 3 as covering only civil wars as well. Thus, Congress apparently believed that the WCA would apply only to traditional international wars between States, or purely internal civil wars.

26. *See Authority of the Federal Bureau of Investigation to Override International Law in Extraterritorial Law Enforcement Activities,* 13 Op. O.L.C. 163 (1989).

27. *See, e.g., United States v. Alvarez-Machain,* 504 U.S. 655 (1992).

28. See, id. at 669–70, *Committee of United States Citizens Living in Nicaragua v. Reagan,* 859 F.2d 929, 935–36 (D. C. Cir. 1988); *Garcia-Mir v. Meese,* 788 F.2d 1446, 1453–55 (11th Cir.), *cert. denied,* 479 U.S. 889 (1986).

29. See, e.g., Michael J. Glennon, Raising the Paquete Habana: Is Violation of Customary International Law by the Executive Unconstitutional?, 80 NW. U. L. Rev. 321, 325 (1985); Louis Henkin, International Law As Law in the United States, 82 MICH L. REV. 1555, 1567 (1984); Jules Lobel, The Limits of Constitutional Power. Conflicts Between Foreign Policy and International Law, 71 VA. L. REV. 1071, 1179 (1985); see also Jonathan R. Charney, Agora: May the President Violate Customary International Law?, 80 A M J. INTL L. 913 (1986).

30. Recently, the status of customary international law within the federal legal systems has been the subject of sustained debate with legal academia. The legitimacy of incorporating customary international law as federal law has been subjected in these exchanges to crippling doubts. See Curtis A. Bradley & Jack L. Goldsmith, Customary International Law As Federal Common Law: A Critique of the Modern Position, 110 Harv. L. Rev. 815, 817 (1997), see also Phillip R. Trimble, A Revisionist View of Customary International Law, 33 UCLA L. Rev.

665, 672–673 (1986), Arthur M. Weisburd, The Executive Branch and International Law, 41 Vand. L. Rev. 1205, 1269 (1988). These claims have not gone unchallenged. Harold H. Koh. Is International Law Really State Law?, 111 Harv. L. Rev. 1824, 1827 (1998); Gerald L. Neuman, Sense and Nonsense About Customary International Law: A Response to Professors Bradley and Goldsmith, 66 Fordham L. Rev. 371, 371 (1997), Beth Stephens, The Law of Our Land: Customary International Law As Federal Law After Erie, 66 Fordham L. Rev. 393, 396–97 (1997). Bradley and Goldsmith have responded to their critics several times. See Curtis A. Bradley & Jack L. Goldsmith, Federal Courts and the incorporation of International Law, 111 Harv. L. Rev. 2260 (1998); Curtis A. Bradley & Jack L. Goldsmith, The Current Illegitimacy of International Human Rights Litigation, 66 Fordham L. Rev. 319, 330 (1997).

31. U.S. Const art. 1, § 8.

32. *The Federalist No. 80,* at 447–49 (Alexander Hamilton) (Clinton Rossiter ed., 1999).

33. *Id.* at 444–46.

34. See, e.g., Stewart Jay, The Status of the Law of Nations in Early American Law, 42 Vand. L. Rev. 819, 830–37 (1989), Bradford R. Clark, Federal Common Law: A Structural Reinterpretation 144 U. Pa. L. Rev. 1245, 1306–12 (1996). Curtis A. Bradley & Jack L. Goldsmith, The Current Illegitimacy of International Human Rights Litigation, 66 Fordham L. Rev. 319, 333–36 (1997).

35. *Cf. INS v. Chadha,* 462 U.S. 919 (1983) (invalidating legislative veto for failure to undergo bicameralism and presentment as required by Article I, Section 8 for all legislation).

36. In fact, allowing customary international law to bear the force of federal law would create significant problems under the Appointments Clause and the non-delegation doctrine, as it would be law made completely outside the American legal system through a process of international practice, rather than either the legislative or officers of the United States authorized to do so.

37. *See, e.g., Foster v. Neilson,* 27 U.S. (2 Pet) 253, 314 (1829).

38. See John C. Yoo, Globalism and the Constitution: Treaties, Non-Self-Execution, and the Original Understanding, 99 Colum. L. Rev. 1955 (1999) (non-self-execution of treaties justified by the original understanding); John C. Yoo, Treaties and Public Lawmaking: A Textual and Structural Defense of Non-Self-Execution, 99 Colum. L. Rev. 2218 (1999) (demonstrating that constitutional text and structure require implementation of treaty obligations by federal statute).

39. See, e.g., Oliver Am. Trading Co. v. Mexico, 264 U.S. 440, 442–43 (1924); Huntington v. Attrill, 146, U.S. 657, 683 (1892); New York Life Ins. Co. v. Hendren, 92 U.S. 286, 286–287 (1875).

40. 92 U.S. 286, 286–87.

41. Two lines of cases are often cited for the proposition that the Supreme Court has found customary international law to be federal law. The first, which derives from Murray v. Schooner Charming Betsy, 6 U.S. (2 Cranch) 64 (1804). The "Charming Betsy" rule, as it is sometimes known, is a rule of construction that a statute should be construed when possible so as not to conflict with international law. This rule, however, does not apply international law of its own force, but instead can be seen as measure of judicial restraint that violating international law is a decision for the political branches to make, and that if they wish to do so, they should state clearly their intentions. The second, Banco Naçional de Cuba v. Sabbatino, 376 U.S. 398, applied the "act of state" doctrine, which generally precludes courts from examining the validity of the decisions of foreign governments taken on their own soil, as federal common law to a suit over expropriations by the Cuban government. As with Charming Betsy, however, the Court developed this rule as one of judicial self-restraint to

preserve the flexibility of the political branches to decide how to conduct foreign policy.

Some supporters of customary international law as federal law rely on a third line of cases, beginning with Filártiga v. Peña-Irala, 630 F.2d 876 (2d Cir. 1980). In Filártiga, the Second Circuit read the federal Alien Tort Statute, 28 U.S.C. § 1350 (1994), to allow a tort suit in federal court against the former official of a foreign government for violating norms of international human rights law, namely torture. Incorporation of customary international law via the Alien Tort Statute, while accepted by several circuit courts, has never received the blessings of the Supreme Court and has been sharply criticized by some circuits, see, e.g., Tel-Oren v. Libyan Arab Republic, 726 F.2d 774, 808–10 (D.C. Cir. 1984) (Bork, J., concurring), cert. denied, 470 U.S. 1003 (1985), as well as by academics, see Curtis A. Bradley & Jack L. Goldsmith, The Current Illegitimacy of International Human Rights Litigation, 66 Fordharm L. rev. 319, 330 (1997).

 **NO**

Brief of Amicus Curiae in Case of *Hamdan v. Rumsfield*

Identity and Interest of the *Amici Curiae*

The Identity of the *Amici*

The *amicus* group numbers 271, comprising 186 Members of the Houses of Parliament of the United Kingdom of Great Britain and Northern Ireland (the "UK Parliament") and 85 current or former Members of the European Parliament and a Vice President of the European Commission. The *amicus* group spans the political spectrum. It includes senior figures from all the major political parties in the United Kingdom, 5 retired Law Lords (judges in the highest court in the UK), including a former Lord Chancellor, other senior lawyers, some of whom have held high judicial office, 11 Bishops of the Church of England and former Cabinet ministers. . . .

The Interest of the *Amici*

Amici consider that aspects of the military commission system put the United States in breach of its international law obligations, a situation they consider to be deeply regrettable.

Now, more than ever, the international legal order needs to be strengthened by the world's most powerful nations transparently and effectively demonstrating their adherence to the rule of law and to the legally mandated protection of the due process rights of individuals, including those affected by the war on terror. These principles are fundamental and they can yield to no person and to no circumstances: "there are certain principles on which there can be no compromise. Fair trial is one of those."

Adherence to these principles inhibits neither the protection of U.S. citizens nor the effective defence of the United States. Rather, ensuring that those accused of terrorist acts receive a transparently fair trial that meets international minimum standards enhances the political capital of the United States: abrogation of those principles imperils its moral authority. Moreover, it risks a tragic descent from the high standards of behaviour to which civilised nations have committed themselves and undermines the hard won progress since World War II devastated the lives of so many citizens of both the United States and the nations of Europe.

Brief of Amicus Curiae in Case of Hamdan v. Rumsfeld, September 29, 2004.

Amici express no view on the guilt of any individual detainee generally and none on the position of Salim Ahmed Hamdan specifically. Equally, they do not express any view on the legitimacy of the military action in Afghanistan or Iraq, the politics or tactics of the "war on terror" in general, or against al Qaeda in particular, or on the decisions of any individual member of the U.S. administration. *Amici* hold different individual views on these issues. But *amici* share the view that, however horrific and barbaric the attacks on the United States on 11 September 2001, and whatever the continuing threat to world security posed by terrorism, these threats can and should be met without breach of the United States' international legal obligations.[1] The United States must ensure fair processes for the prosecution of those accused of terrorism-related crimes with the safeguard of independent judicial review. *Amici* there-fore urge this Court to allow the innocence or guilt of the accused to be deter-mined "after a hearing as dispassionate as the times and horrors we deal with will permit, and upon a record that will leave our reasons and motives clear."[2]

The Relevance of the *Amici*'s Views

Amici respect the independence of the judiciary in a friendly foreign state. Nevertheless, they hope that the views of leading parliamentarians in states with close legal, historical and political ties to the United States may be of assistance to the Court when it is weighing the arguments. They base that hope on the long tradition of shared policies, joint legal progress and mutual learning that have characterised the development of relevant domestic and international law in the United States of America and in other democracies governed by the rule of law. The United States has long been known as a nation "unwilling to witness or permit the slow undoing of those human rights to which this nation has always been committed."[3] It is right that the United States should strive to set the highest standards in this respect: the international legal principles upon which *amici* rely find eloquent expression in the Declaration of Independence and the Constitution of the United States, which themselves reflect principles in the Magna Carta and the English Bill of Rights and have in turn influenced the development of constitutional democ-racies the world over. Moreover, in the modern era, the United States and the nations of Europe, including the United Kingdom, have frequently cooperated in developing the international treaties, principles and institutions that create the public international law framework that nations share today. *Amici,* con-cerned that the United States should be seen clearly to respect its international legal obligations, submit their arguments in the light of the shared domestic and international legal experiences and commitments of both the United States and the jurisdictions of Europe, in particular the United Kingdom, which are relevant to those arguments. . . .

This Court can, and should, have regard to the United States' international legal obligations. Those obligations, which speak directly to the situation of individuals detained at Guantanamo Bay, are embodied in a number of treaties to which the United States is a party, including the 1949 Geneva Convention Rel-ative to the Treatment of Prisoners of War and the 1966 International Covenant on Civil and Political Rights, and are also embodied in customary international law. International law establishes certain minimum due process standards which the United States has legally bound itself to meet and which should therefore be observed.

The military commission process to which Hamdan and other detainees are subject does not satisfy these international legal standards in a number of respects.

First, the processes for prosecuting detainees for alleged terrorist acts are not sufficiently independent of executive influence to meet fair trial requirements, in particular in so far as: (a) the processes are closely intertwined with the executive power, leading to a decision by the President of the United States (or his appointee) on the conviction and sentence of the accused, when the President has not acted in a judicial capacity in so doing, has already made strong public statements on culpability, and has made the preliminary determination that the detainees are to be incarcerated; and/or (b) there is no independent appeal process from the military commissions.

Second, there has been inordinate delay in bringing detainees to trial with no objective review of the position of the individual or the justification for detention.

Third, the use of evidence obtained by torture is not excluded by the military commission process.

Fourth, in distinguishing between U.S. citizens and aliens accused of terrorist offences, the United States has failed to ensure that the fundamental rights afforded to U.S. citizens are also afforded to alien detainees. . . .

I. The Court Is Charged with Enforcing the United States' International Legal Obligations

A. International Law Is Part of the Law of the United States, and It Is to Be Ascertained and Applied by This Court

Amici note the well-established principle that international law is part of the law of the United States and that federal courts are to ascertain and apply it. See *Sosa* v. *Alvarez-Machain*, _U.S._, 124 S. Ct. 2739, 2764–5 (2004) ("For two centuries we have affirmed that the domestic law of the United States recognizes the law of nations. . . . It would take some explaining to say now that federal courts must avert their gaze entirely from any international norm intended to protect individuals.") (citations omitted); *The Paquete Habana*, 175 U.S. 677, 700 (1900) ("International law is part of our law, and must be ascertained and administered by the courts of justice of appropriate jurisdiction, as often as questions of right depending upon it are duly presented for their determination."). "Courts in the United States are bound to give effect to international law. . . ." Restatement (Third) of the Foreign Relations Law of the United States 1561 (1987).

The Constitution of the United States explicitly provides that "all Treaties made, or which shall be made, under the Authority of the United States, shall be the supreme Law of the land." U.S. Const., art. VI, cl. 2. It is equally well established that customary international law[4] also constitutes the law of the land. . . . Accordingly the international law that is to be ascertained and administered by the federal courts includes both the United States' commitments in treaties and customary international law. . . .

This petition is, in part, based on the 1949 Geneva Convention Relative to the Treatment of Prisoners of War, Aug. 12, 1949, . . . ("Third Geneva Convention"), a treaty that has been signed and ratified by the United States and incorporated into U.S. domestic law through military regulations, see, *e.g.,* Army Regulation 190–8, Enemy Prisoners of War, Retained Personnel, Civilian Internees and Other Detainees § 1-6(a) (1977). . . . In addressing Hamdan's claim under the Third Geneva Convention, this Court is therefore called upon to determine the applicability of the Convention. International law is also, equally importantly, relevant to the Court's consideration of Hamdan's claims under the Uniform Code of Military Justice and the United States Constitution in the indirect senses discussed above.

International law is of relevance in this case irrespective of whether or not a particular treaty is self-executing. Such issues affect only direct enforcement of international law by U.S. courts. The status of a treaty as non-self-executing does not reduce its binding force in international law. This is an implication of the well established principle of international law that a state "may not rely on the provisions of its internal law as justification for failure to comply with its obligations," United Nations International Law Commission's Articles on Responsibility of States for Internationally Wrongful Acts, art. 32, G.A. Res. 82, U.N. GAOR, 56th Sess., Supp. No. 10 and Corriegendum, U.N. Doc. A/56/83 (2001) ("Articles on State Responsibility"). . . . Because of this principle, the status and binding force of a treaty or customary rule as a matter of international law does not depend upon the provision made for domestic enforcement of that rule.

B. Respect for International Law Reflects the United States' Tradition and Serves the United States' Interests

Ascertaining and applying international law in this case is also in keeping with the United States' leadership in the development of international human rights norms and its longstanding tradition of respect for international law, and it moreover serves the United States' immediate interests.

The United States' historical leadership in the field of international human rights law is well established, and it is especially notable in respect of international humanitarian law, a branch of international law specifically applicable to armed conflict. "The first modern attempt to draw up a binding code for the conduct of an armed force in the field was that prepared by Professor Francis Lieber of the United States, promulgated as law by President Lincoln in 1863 during the American Civil War." Leslie C. Green, The Contemporary Law of Armed Conflict 29 (2d ed. 2000). The Lieber Code is widely recognized as having "had significant influence on the international debate regarding the further codification of the laws of war and is viewed as a starting point for subsequent international conventions." Brief of Human Rights Institute of the International Bar Association as *Amicus Curiae* in Support of Petitioners, at 23 n.16, *Rasul* v.

Bush, _U.S._, 124 S. Ct. 2686 (2004) (Nos. 03-334 and 03-343). Following World War Two, the United States supported the negotiation—and promptly ratified—the Geneva Conventions of 1949, widely regarded as the pillars of contemporary international humanitarian law and binding both as treaties and as a matter of customary international law.

When it disregards international law, the United States risks setting precedents that will adversely affect its own citizens abroad. With the "war on terror" now being fought on multiple fronts, the United States has a compelling interest in securing the fullest protection possible for individuals operating in zones of conflict, many of whom are American soldiers and civilians.

II. International Law Applies to the Conduct of the United States at Guantanamo Bay

Amici take no view on the application of domestic law, but emphasise that international law applies to the actions of the United States Government in respect of detainees at Guantanamo Bay.

A. International Law, Including International Human Rights Law, Applies to the Conduct of the United States Anywhere in the World

It is well established that state responsibility under international human rights treaties turns upon whether the respondent state exercises sufficient authority and control in the situation that the action can be said to have been taken under the jurisdiction of the state in question. Thus, for example, each State Party to the ICCPR (including the United States) expressly undertakes "to respect and ensure to all individuals within its territory and subject to its jurisdiction the rights recognized in the present Covenant." ICCPR, art. 2(1). The International Court of Justice ("ICJ") has recently reaffirmed that the effect of this provision is "that the International Covenant on Civil and Political Rights is applicable in respect of acts done by a State in the exercise of its jurisdiction outside its own territory." *Legal Consequences of the Construction of a Wall in the Occupied Palestinian Territories,* 2004 I.C.J., ¶ at 111 (Advisory Opinion of 9 July 2004). . . . In so holding, the ICJ considered the text of the treaty in the light of its object and purpose, "the constant practice of the Human Rights Committee" established under the auspices of the United Nations to monitor compliance with the ICCPR, and the fact that the *travaux préparatoires* (or "legislative history") of the ICCPR "show[ed] that in adopting the wording chosen, the drafters of the Covenant did not intend to allow States to escape from their obligations when they exercise jurisdiction outside their national territory." *Id.,* ¶ 109. . . .

It is therefore well established that the application of international human rights norms "turns not on the presumed victim's nationality or presence within a particular geographic area, but on whether, under the specific circumstances, the State observed the rights of a person subject to its authority and control," *Ibid.* Whatever the position in terms of ultimate sovereignty over Guantanamo Bay, the United States unquestionably exercises authority and control there. . . . To paraphrase the words of the Human Rights Committee, it would be "unconscionable to so interpret the responsibility" of the United States under international human rights treaties as to allow the U.S. "to perpetrate violations [of human rights norms] on the territory of another State, which violations it could not perpetrate on its own territory." *López Burgos, supra,* at ¶ 12.3. Accordingly, to comply with international law the treatment of the Guantanamo detainees must protect fundamental human rights. . . .

B. International Law Applies in Times of Armed Conflict and National Emergency

The United States has never declared war in the aftermath of the September 11 atrocities, however the "war on terror" has resulted at various times in a state of armed conflict. The existence of a state of war or armed conflict does not suspend the application of international law. Indeed, the norms of international humanitarian law, and especially the Geneva Conventions, apply in terms to situations of armed conflict. And whether or not specific instruments of international humanitarian law apply in a particular case, it has been recognized that "civilians and combatants remain under the protection and authority of the principles of international law derived from established custom, from the principles of humanity and from the dictates of public conscience." Protocol Additional to the Geneva Conventions of 12 August 1949, and relating to the Protection of Victims of International Armed Conflicts (Protocol 1), art. 1(2), *adopted* June 8,1977, 1125 U.N.T.S. 3.[5]

There is no tension between the application of international humanitarian law in time of war or armed conflict and the residual application of international human rights law at the same time. As the Inter-American Commission stated when considering the application of international human rights norms in a case arising out of the U.S. military engagement in Grenada:

> while international humanitarian law pertains primarily in time of war and the international law of human rights applies most fully in times of peace, the potential application of one does not necessarily exclude or displace the other. There is an integral linkage between the law of human rights and humanitarian law because they share a "common nucleus of non-derogable rights and a common purpose of protecting human life and dignity," and there may be a substantial overlap in the application of these bodies of law. Certain core guarantees apply in all circumstances, including situations of conflict, and this is reflected, inter alia, in the designation of certain protections pertaining to the person as peremptory norms (jus cogens) and obligations erga omnes, in a vast body of treaty law, in principles of customary international law, and in the doctrine and practice of international human rights bodies such as this Commission. Both normative systems may thus be applicable to the situation under study.

Coard, supra, ¶ 39 (footnotes omitted). Thus the non-derogable rules of international human rights law continue to operate even in times of war and armed conflict. The ICJ concurs, having repeatedly rejected the assertion that international human rights protections cease to apply at such times. In its opinion on the *Legal Consequences of the Construction of a Wall* the ICJ reaffirmed the determination in a previous Advisory Opinion that "the protection of the International Covenant of Civil and Political Rights does not cease in time of war, except by operation of Article 4 of the Covenant whereby certain provisions may be derogated from in a time of national emergency." 2004 I.C.J. at ¶ 105 (quoting *Legality of the Threat or Use of Nuclear Weapons,* 1996 I.C.J. 266, 240 (Advisory Opinion of 8 July)). Similar provisions for temporary derogations from particular human rights obligations in order to confront war or other public emergency are provided in other human rights treaties. . . . These provisions confirm that, absent such a derogation, international human rights norms are not generally suspended in the face of war. The United States has not entered a derogation from its obligations under the ICCPR in respect of Guantanamo Bay or the military action in Afghanistan.

Moreover, notwithstanding the provision for derogation from certain human rights protection, some obligations are in any event non-derogable. As the United Nations Human Rights Committee has ruled in respect of the ICCPR, these norms include "humanitarian law" and "peremptory norms of international law" such as those prohibiting hostage-taking, the imposition of collective punishments, "arbitrary deprivations of liberty" and "deviating from fundamental principles of fair trial, including the presumption of innocence." General Comment No. 29, States of Emergency (article 4), U.N. Doc. CCPR/C/21/Rev.1/Add.11, ¶ 11 (2001). Accordingly, this Court must consider the United States' obligations under both international humanitarian law and international human rights law.

C. International Law Applies in Respect of Alleged Al Qaeda Members

The characterization of a particular individual as an "al Qaeda detainee" or otherwise does not eliminate the protections afforded to that individual under international human rights law; those rights pertain to the individual, not to any state or sub-state entity. One of the principal achievements of international law in the decades following World War Two was the widespread recognition of individual rights and obligations under international law, which hitherto had generally addressed only the rights and duties of states. The legacy of the Nuremberg Trials was the imposition of individual responsibility for some violations of the international law governing armed conflict, while the legacy of the United Nations system and the Universal Declaration of Human Rights was the recognition of the inherent dignity of individuals and their enjoyment of fundamental rights protected by international law. As a result of these developments, international law governing armed conflict and international human rights law operate not exclusively on the plane of inter-state relations, but also, and most importantly, on the plane of relations between states and individuals subject to their authority. Therefore the status of al Qaeda as a non-state actor, or even as a terrorist organization, does not remove individuals alleged to be associated with al Qaeda from the realm of international human rights law. Indeed, that the United States plans to prosecute Hamdan and other detainees for alleged violations of the laws of war—that is to say, for violations of international law governing armed conflict—is an implicit recognition that these individuals, even if they are members or associates of al Qaeda (which Hamdan denies), remain subjects of international law. It is only just and proper that Hamdan and other detainees be subjected to international law equally with respect to its benefits—the protections of international humanitarian and human rights law—as with respect to its burdens. . . .

E. International Humanitarian Law and the Geneva Conventions Comprehensively Protect Individuals in Armed Conflict

Although *amici* have demonstrated above the relevance of a number of other international legal instruments to the Court's consideration of the issues arising in this case, the instant petition concerns the provisions of the Third Geneva Convention. As was noted above, this is one of four conventions negotiated following World War Two that govern the treatment of individuals in armed conflict and that form the central pillars of modern international humanitarian law. The object and purpose of international humanitarian law, including the Geneva Conventions, was to provide comprehensive protection to individuals caught up in armed conflict. Those who are deemed or alleged to be combatants come within the scope of the Third Geneva Convention, while non-combatants are covered by the Geneva Convention Relative to the Protection of Civilian Persons in Time of War, Aug. 12, 1949, 6 U.S.T. 3516, T.I.A.S. 3365 ("Fourth Geneva Convention"), to which the United States is also a party. The Geneva Conventions protect "intransgressible" rights; reflect customary international law, see *Legality of Threat or Use of Nuclear Weapons* (Advisory Opinion), *supra,* at 257; and parallel the numerous international legal instruments discussed above, which, of course, continue to apply regardless of the applicability of the Geneva Conventions in a particular case. Individuals may have slightly different rights and duties depending upon whether they are, e.g., combatants or civilians, but no one lies outside the protection of the law.

A key determinant of which provisions of the Geneva Conventions apply to a particular individual is characterization of the conflict in which he was involved (whether as a combatant or not). The majority of the specific provisions of the Geneva Conventions (including article 103 of the Third Geneva Convention relied upon by Petitioner) apply in cases of *international armed conflict*. Article 3, which is common to all four Geneva Conventions (and hence is known as "common article 3"), applies to *"armed conflict not of an international character,"* and provides baseline protection against, *inter alia,* "cruel treatment and torture," "humiliating and degrading treatment" and "the passing of sentences . . . without previous judgment pronounced by a regularly constituted court affording all the judicial guarantees which are recognized as indispensable by civilized people." Respondents would characterize some aspects of the conflict in Afghanistan as armed conflict that is neither international because, by assertion, it is not between states, nor armed conflict "not of an international character" because it occurs in the territory of more than one state. As a result of this characterization, according to the Respondents, the individuals detained at Guantanamo Bay, or some category of them that includes Hamdan, fall into an exceptional third category which is entirely outside the protections of the Geneva Conventions.

Not only is it difficult to accept that armed conflict could simultaneously not be international and also not be "armed conflict not of an international character," but this approach conflicts with recent authority on the scope of application of the Geneva Conventions. The United States Government has separately acknowledged authority directly undermining the Respondents' arguments: internal government documents (which have been made public) analyzing the application of international legal norms, including the Third Geneva Convention, to the detention of individuals at Guantanamo Bay and elsewhere take note of recent authority, including authority from the International Court of Justice, "that common Article 3 is better read as applying to all forms of non-international armed conflict" and "that all 'armed conflicts' are either international or non-international, and that if they are non-international, they are governed by common Article 3." See Memorandum for Alberto R. Gonzales, Counsel to the President, and William J. Haynes II, General Counsel of the Department of Defence from Office of Legal Counsel, U.S. Department of Justice, dated January 22, 2002, at 8 n.23 (citing Commentary on the Additional Protocols of 8 June 1977 to the Geneva Conventions of 12 August 1949 ¶ 4339 n.2 (Yves Sandoz et al. eds., 1987)); *Military and Paramilitary Activities in and against Nicaragua* (Nicaragua v. U.S.) 1986 I.C.J. 14, 114 (Judgment of June 27); see also *id.* at 8 (citing the decision of the International Criminal Tribunal for the Former Yugoslavia in *Prosecutor* v. *Tadic,* Case No. 160 (ICTY Appeals Chamber, Oct. 2, 199)).

In *Tadic,* the Appeals Chamber of the International Criminal Tribunal for the Former Yugoslavia emphasized the comprehensive scope of international humanitarian law, rejecting an argument that neither the branch of international humanitarian law applicable to non-international armed conflict (common article 3) nor that applicable to international armed conflict (the remaining provisions of the Geneva Conventions)—applied to one phase of the hostilities in the former Yugoslavia. See *Prosecutor* v. *Tadic,* Case No. 160, ¶¶ 66–70 (Decision on the Defence Motion for Interlocutory Appeal on Jurisdiction, 2 October 1995) available at http://www.un.org/icty/tadic/appeal/decision-e/51002.htm. The Appeals Chamber emphasized that "the temporal and geographical scope of both internal and international armed conflicts extends beyond the exact time and place of hostilities," *id.,* ¶ 67, to encompass "the entire territory of the Parties to the conflict," *id.,* ¶ 68. Accordingly, the Appeals Chamber concluded:

> an armed conflict exists whenever there is a resort to armed force between States or protracted armed violence between governmental authorities and organized armed groups or between such groups within a State. International

humanitarian law applies from the initiation of such armed conflicts and extends beyond the cessation of hostilities until a general conclusion of peace is reached; or, in the case of internal conflicts, a peaceful settlement is achieved. Until that moment, international humanitarian law continues to apply in the whole territory of the warring States or, in the case of internal conflicts the whole territory under the control of a party, whether or not actual combat takes place there.

Id., ¶ 70.

Thus international humanitarian law applies from the time of the initiation of hostilities until their conclusion and throughout the territory of the parties to the conflict. The "armed conflict with al Qaeda" began with an invasion of Afghanistan, which constituted "declared war or . . . any other armed conflict . . . between two or more of the High Contracting Parties"; Afghanistan like the United States is a party to the Geneva Conventions. The Geneva Conventions thus began to apply, and they persist in application throughout the territory of Afghanistan (or at the least throughout the "whole territory under the control of a party" to the hostilities) "until a general conclusion of peace is reached; or, in the case of internal conflicts, a peaceful settlement is achieved." *Tadic,* ¶ 70. Individuals detained prior to any such time—military actions in Afghanistan are ongoing and the United States has repeatedly indicated that the "war on terror" continues—are entitled to the basic protections of the Geneva Conventions.

Given the central importance of the Geneva Conventions to securing all individuals caught up in armed conflict against the barbarism of war, the Court must give full weight to the *Tadic* decision. The Court should evaluate the parties' arguments on the application of the Third Geneva Convention against the backdrop of the United States' commitment to international law; its obligations to perform treaties in good faith, see VCLOT, art. 26 ("Every treaty in force is binding upon the parties to it and must be performed by them in good faith."); the tradition of respect for the rule of law shared by the United States; and the tradition of leadership by the United States in the field of human rights and international law.

Notes

1. As was famously stated in a leading UK case, *Liversage v. Andersen* 1942 AC 206, "amid the clash of arms, the laws are not silent. They may be changed but they speak the same language in war as in peace."
2. Report on the forthcoming Nuremburg Trials by Robert H. Jackson to President Harry S.Truman, June 7, 1945, Dep't St. Bull., June 10, 1945, at 1071, 1073.
3. President Kennedy, Inaugural Address, 20 January 1961. . . .
4. This is defined as "international custom, as evidence of a general practice accepted as law." Statute of the International Court of Justice, art. 38(1)(b).
5. Although the United States is not a signatory to Protocol I, aspects of the treaty, including article 1(2), reflect customary international law, which is binding on the United States.

POSTSCRIPT

Is the Geneva Convention Irrelevant to Members of al Qaeda Who Are Held Prisoner at Guantanamo Bay?

The *Hamdan* case eventually reached the Supreme Court, which overturned the appeals court finding that Hamdan was not entitled to any protections under the Geneva Conventions. The Court stated that it did not need to address the question of whether Hamdan deserved the "full protections" of the Third Geneva Convention—which are reserved for POWs captured during conflicts between signatory nations— "because there is at least one provision of the Geneva Conventions that applies here even if the relevant conflict is not one between signatories . . . Common Article 3." The Supreme Court then went on to reject the appeals court's interpretation of common Article Three:

> The Court of Appeals thought . . . that Common Article 3 does not apply to Hamdan because the conflict with al Qaeda, being "international in scope," does not qualify as a "conflict not of an international character." That reasoning is erroneous. The term "conflict not of an international character" is used here in contradistinction to a conflict between nations. . . . [In contrast to Common Article 2,] Common Article 3 . . . affords some minimal protection, falling short of full protection under the Conventions, to individuals associated with neither a signatory nor even a nonsignatory "Power" who are involved in a conflict "in the territory of" a signatory. The latter kind of conflict is distinguishable from the conflict described in Common Article 2 chiefly because it does not involve a clash between nations (whether signatories or not). In context, then, the phrase "not of an international character" bears its literal meaning. See, *e.g.*, J. Bentham, *Introduction to the Principles of Morals and Legislation* 6, 296 (J. Burns & H. Hart eds. 1970) (using the term "international law" [to mean] "betwixt nation and nation"; defining "international" to include "mutual transactions between sovereigns as such"). . . . Common Article 3, then, is applicable here and . . . requires that Hamdan be tried by a "regularly constituted court affording all the judicial guarantees which are recognized as indispensable by civilized peoples. (*Hamdan v. Rumsfeld*, 126 S. Ct. 2749, 2006)
>
> Reflecting more broadly on U.S. obligations under international law, the Court also stated that Common Article 3 obviously tolerates a great degree of flexibility in trying individuals captured during armed conflict; its requirements are general ones, crafted to accommodate a wide variety of legal systems. But *requirements* they are nonetheless. The commission that the President has convened to try Hamdan does not meet those requirements.

One might think that this Supreme Court pronouncement would settle the question of whether the Geneva Conventions apply to the War on Terror.

However, in the aftermath of the Court's *Hamdan* decision, Congress passed legislation making it difficult for foreign nationals to sue in U.S. court to enforce their rights under the Geneva Conventions. As it currently stands, although the "law of the land" is that the detainees have rights under Common Article Three, it is unclear whether they have any means to vindicate those rights. Such a situation brings to mind the adage that a law without a mechanism to enforce it is merely a piece of advice.

Additionally, aside from whether the United States is currently legally bound to uphold the Geneva Conventions, there is always the normative question of whether the United States *should* agree to international accords that may limit its sovereignty. The Geneva Conventions provide that signatory countries are free to withdraw from the Conventions, and, though unlikely, Congress could pass legislation to that effect if it felt the War on Terror was being excessively hindered by the U.S. obligations under the Conventions. Concerns regarding U.S. sovereignty also arise whenever the United States is debating whether to agree to new international agreements. Recently, for instance, a controversy erupted regarding whether the United States should support the International Criminal Court (ICC) that was established to try war criminals. Although President Clinton signed the international legislation establishing the ICC, President Bush announced that his administration did not feel bound in any way by Clinton's signature, citing as his reason for opposing the ICC that it claimed jurisdiction over the United States and its leaders.

The text of the Geneva Conventions as well as links to other basic documents of international law can be found at http://www.ohchr.org/english/law/index.htm and http://www.genevaconventions.org/.

ISSUE 4

Should Someone Held by the CIA and Interrogated in a Foreign Country Be Allowed to Sue the U.S. Government?

YES: American Civil Liberties Union, from Brief for Plaintiff-Appellant *El Masri vs. United States of America, George Tenet, et al.,* U.S. Court of Appeals for the Fourth Circuit (September 25, 2006)

NO: Robert King, from Opinion, *El-Masri v. Tenet,* U.S. Court of Appeals for the Fourth Circuit (March 2, 2007)

ISSUE SUMMARY

YES: In a brief submitted to the Court of Appeals, the American Civil Liberties Union, representing Mr. El-Masri, argues that dismissing his case outright because the government claims state secrets might be revealed is both dangerous and unnecessary.

NO: In the decision handed down by the Court of Appeals, Judge Robert King rejects the ACLU position and argues that a plaintiff cannot bring a lawsuit against the government when the government claims that the case might reveal information that could endanger national security.

Supreme Court Justice Potter Stewart once wrote that

> it is elementary that . . . the maintenance of an effective national defense require[s] both confidentiality and secrecy. . . . [W]ithin our own executive departments, the development of considered and intelligent international policies would be impossible if those charged with their formulation could not communicate with each other freely, frankly, and in confidence. In the area of basic national defense, the frequent need for absolute secrecy is, of course, self-evident. (Concurring Opinion, *New York Times v. United States,* 1971)

Stewart went even further than to maintain that secrecy was sometimes the prerogative of the president; at times, he wrote, it is actually the president's "constitutional *duty*" [emphasis added]. After all, if a primary purpose of the federal government is to protect U.S. citizens and, in the words of the U.S. Constitution, "provide for the common defense," then in certain instances where national security is at stake, the protection of government secrets may actually be *required* in order for the president to carry out the responsibilities of the executive branch.

At the same time that secrecy can be essential for the president to protect national security, excessive government secrecy can be equally as dangerous. Former U.S. Senator Patrick Moynihan once wrote that secrecy can be "something more than inconveniencing to the citizen. At times, in the name of national security, secrecy has put that very security in harm's way." In his book *Secrecy: The American Experience*, Moynihan pointed out that secrecy often allows the government, especially the presidency, to abuse its power in ways that could be curtailed by public scrutiny. Furthermore, according to Moynihan, secrecy, by limiting debate and disagreement, often encourages the government to make ignorant decisions and engage in disastrous policies that could have been prevented if a greater diversity of viewpoints had been available.

The readings in this issue present a quintessential example of the inherent challenge that governmental secrecy poses in a democracy. Khaled El-Masri, a German citizen, was on vacation in Macedonia when, he alleges, he was kidnapped by CIA agents and transported to a prison in Afghanistan. For several months, he was held incommunicado, tortured, and interrogated about his supposed ties to Al Qaeda. According to his complaint, which has been largely corroborated by outside sources, El-Masri was a victim of "extraordinary rendition," a covert U.S. government program in which the CIA abducts suspected terrorists and transports them to be interrogated by foreign governments, many of which routinely use torture to extract confessions from prisoners. One former CIA official, who helped develop the program, described it as "the most successful . . . program that the United States has ever conducted" in its fight against terrorism; its critics, however, argue that it is illegal and makes a mockery of the U.S. commitment to due process and human rights. While the U.S. government has admitted to its use of "renditions"—that is, the seizure and international transport of suspected terrorists through means other than traditional extradition legal proceedings—officials such as Secretary of State Condoleezza Rice have asserted that it does so only to "take terrorists out of action" so "they can be questioned, held, or brought to justice. . . . The United States has not transported anyone, and will not transport anyone, to a country when we believe he will be tortured."

El-Masri filed suit against the CIA in federal court, arguing that it had violated his rights and should be held legally accountable for the torture and ill-treatment he experienced. However, rather than responding to the merits of his claim, the government argued that the case should be dismissed because it could not be litigated without the public disclosure of sensitive and classified national security information. The court agreed that the nature of the suit, and the details that would doubtlessly arise during discovery for the case, rendered this an appropriate instance for the government to invoke the "states secrets privilege." In the readings that follow, the appeals court outlines its reasoning for reaching this conclusion, while the American Civil Liberties Union, El-Masri's counsel in the case, argues that this sets a dangerous precedent for the government to escape accountability for illegal actions.

YES ⤶   American Civil Liberties Union

Reply Brief for Plaintiff-Appellant in Case of *El-Masri v. Tenet*

Introductory Statement

This case arrives in the court of appeals with a markedly altered factual and legal landscape. Since the district court's premature dismissal of this case, an eyewitness to Mr. El-Masri's detention in Afghanistan has emerged; an intergovernmental body representing forty-six European member states has issued a detailed public report concluding that Mr. El-Masri and others were abducted and detained by the CIA; and, most recently, the President of the United States has confirmed the widely known fact that the CIA has operated detention and interrogation facilities in other nations, as well as the identities of specific individuals who have been held. Of equal significance, three separate Article III courts have rejected sweeping assertions of the state secrets privilege nearly identical to the assertion at issue here, and have embraced a common-sense approach to accommodating the twin goals of security and accountability that is wholly at odds with the radical theory of executive power advanced by the United States here. Quite remarkably, the United States does not even cite—let alone attempt to distinguish—any of those cases.

The government's silence speaks volumes. Simply put, there is no way to reconcile the government's view that the executive branch is effectively the sole arbiter of the scope of its own immunity from suit, *see* Brief of the Appellee ("Govt. Br.") at 18–20, with the recent cases in which federal courts have assessed, with sensitivity and care, the government's claim that suits challenging various aspects of the National Security Agency's warrantless wiretapping of American citizens must be dismissed immediately on state secrets grounds. *See Al-Haramain Islamic Foundation, Inc. v. Bush,* —F. Supp. 2d—, 2006 WL 2583425 (D.Or., Sept. 7, 2006) (Slip Copy); *American Civil Liberties Union v. National Sec. Agency,* 438 F. Supp. 2d 754 (E.D.Mich., Aug. 17, 2006); *Hepting v. AT & T Corporation,* 439 F. Supp. 2d 974 (N.D.Cal., July 20 2006). As these cases and others cited in Mr. El-Masri's Opening Brief make clear, courts faced with state secrets claims must independently assess whether the information at issue is genuinely secret; whether disclosure of particular information will reasonably cause harm to national security; and whether, even if state secrets are legitimately implicated, dismissal of an entire suit at the pleading stage is

From Brief for El-Masri v. United States and Tenet, U.S. Court of Appeals for the Fourth Circuit, September 25, 2006.

warranted. There can be no doubt that federal courts are well equipped to do so. Were it otherwise, the Constitution's careful balancing of power between coequal branches of government would have little meaning, and the responsibility and authority of the judiciary to safeguard individual rights would be impermissibly "abdicated to the caprice of executive officers." *United States v. Reynolds,* 345 U.S. 1, 9–10 (1953).

Argument

1. *Three recent district court decisions have rejected the government's argument that the state secrets privilege justifies dismissal of a case at the outset.*

In three recent cases, Article III courts have reaffirmed that the government's legitimate security concerns may be accommodated without eliminating altogether the role of the judiciary in adjudicating claims of executive misconduct. In *Al-Haramain,* 2006 WL 2583425, the court declined to dismiss on state secrets grounds a challenge to the NSA's warrantless wiretapping program and its surveillance of plaintiffs—who alleged that they had seen evidence that they were monitored under that program—and permitted the suit to proceed through limited discovery and presentation of evidence *in camera.* Similarly, in *Hepting v. AT&T Corp.,* 439 F. Supp. 2d, the court denied the government's motion to dismiss a suit challenging AT&T's alleged participation in the NSA's warrantless wiretapping program, rejecting the government's contention that the very subject matter of the suit was a state secret and that AT&T's role in the program could be neither confirmed nor denied without harm to national security. Finally, in *ACLU v. NSA,* 438 F. Supp. 2d, the court declined to dismiss a challenge to the legality of the NSA's warrantless wiretapping program and determined, on the basis of non-privileged evidence, that the program violated the law and the Constitution. *Id.* at 771–82.

Collectively, these cases offer critical guidance about the proper role of courts in evaluating state secrets claims at the outset of litigation. In each case, for example, the court began its analysis by seeking to determine which allegedly privileged information actually "qualifie[d] as a secret." *Al-Haramain,* 2006 WL 2583425 at *5; *see also Hepting,* 439 F. Supp. 2d at 988; *ACLU v. NSA,* 438 F. Supp. 2d at 764. In *Hepting,* the court evaluated official public statements concerning the challenged program, as well as other "publicly reported information that possesse[d] substantial indicia of reliability," and concluded, after "assessing the value of the information" to actual terrorists, that not every detail of the program was a secret. *Hepting,* 439 F. Supp. 2d at 990. And in *Al-Haramain,* because government officials had confirmed the existence of the NSA's warrantless wiretapping program, publicly discussed the scope and operation of the program, and engaged in a vigorous public defense of the legality and efficacy of the program, the court concluded that "the existence of the Surveillance Program is not a secret, the subjects of the program are not a secret, and the general method of the program . . . is not a secret." *Al-Haramain,* 2006 WL 2583425 at *6; *see also ACLU v. NSA,* 438 F. Supp. 2d at 764–65.

The courts also embraced a common-sense approach to the question whether disclosure of allegedly privileged information would reasonably cause harm to national security. For example, in *Al-Haramain,* the court concluded that "no harm to the national security would occur if plaintiffs are able to prove the general point that they were subject to surveillance . . . without publicly disclosing any other information," because, to the extent that there was any risk that disclosure might lead a target to change his behavior or disclose "sources and methods," that harm had already occurred. *Al-Haramain,* 2006 WL 2583425 at *7–8. Similarly, in *Hepting,* the court rejected the government's contention that harm to national security would necessarily result from confirmation or denial of whether AT&T received a certification from the government that its participation in the program was legal. Because "the government [had] already opened the door for judicial inquiry by publicly confirming and denying information about its monitoring of communication content," confirmation of the existence of a certification would "not-reveal any new information that would assist a terrorist and adversely affect national security." *Hepting,* 439 F. Supp. 2d at 996. Rather, the court believed it possible that AT&T could later confirm or deny the existence of the certification in a general manner, and respond to relevant interrogatories *in camera,* if necessary. *Id.* at 996–97. . . .

Each court emphatically rejected the notion that simply because the case involved foreign intelligence gathering or because some aspects of the program remained secret, the case must be dismissed on the ground that the *very subject matter* was a state secret or that the suit was barred under the *Totten* doctrine. Thus, in *Hepting,* after considering that "AT&T and the government [had] for all practical purposes already disclosed that AT&T assists the government in monitoring communication content," the impossibility of conducting such a program without AT&T's cooperation, and "AT&T's history of cooperating with the government" in national security surveillance, the court held that "AT&T's assistance in national security surveillance [was] hardly the kind of 'secret' that the *Totten* bar and the state secrets privilege were intended to protect or that a potential terrorist would fail to anticipate." *Hepting,* 439 F. Supp. 2d at 992–93; *see also Al-Haramain,* 2006 WL 2583425 at *9 (refusing to find the very subject matter of the action a state secret where the government had already "lifted the veil of secrecy on the existence of the Surveillance Program and plaintiffs only [sought] to establish whether interception of their communications—an interception they purport to know about—was unlawful"); *ACLU v. NSA,* 438 F. Supp. 2d at 763–65. . . .

Finally, each court declined to adopt the government's unilateral pleading-stage assertion that the facts necessary to decide the legal issues were too sensitive to be revealed even to an Article III court. In *Al-Haramain,* for example, the court was simply "not yet convinced that [allegedly privileged] information [was] relevant to the case and [would] need to be revealed." *Al-Haramain,* 2006 WL 2583425 at *10. While the court acknowledged that after further discovery and *in camera* presentation of evidence it might well conclude that plaintiffs' claims must be dismissed, it was "not prepared to dismiss this case without first examining all available options and allowing plaintiffs their constitutional right to seek relief in this Court." *Id.* at *11. The *Hepting* court likewise concluded that it was "premature" to decide which facts were relevant and necessary to claims and defenses "at the present time," and held that plaintiffs were "entitled to at least some discovery," after which the privilege could be assessed "in light of the facts." *Hepting*, 439 F. Supp. 2d at 994; *see also* Opening Br. at 46–57. In *ACLU v. NSA*, because the government had already announced the facts necessary to decide the legality of the program, the court was capable of adjudicating the merits of a summary judgment motion notwithstanding the government's privilege claim. Even after reviewing the classified, *ex parte* evidence submitted by the government, the court held that plaintiffs were "able to establish a *prima facie* case based solely on Defendants' public admissions regarding the [warrantless wiretapping program]," *ACLU v. NSA*, 438 F. Supp. 2d at 765, and that privileged information was "not necessary to any viable defense" of the surveillance program. *Id.* at 766. Because the government had "repeatedly told the general public that there is a valid basis in law" for warrantless wiretapping, and the government had, supported its legal arguments without recourse to classified information, the court found defendants' contention that it could not defend the legality of its actions without state secrets "disingenuous and without merit." *Id.* at 765–66.

The approach adopted in these cases demonstrates the careful manner in which Article III courts can assess responsibly even the most sweeping state secrets assertions. Rather than accept the government's claim that the need for secrecy must automatically and prematurely extinguish any possibility for relief, these courts were able to accommodate the government's legitimate secrecy concerns without eliminating the plaintiffs' right of access to a forum for judicial redress. The district court below, in deferring entirely to the government's secrecy claims, erred in several respects: it failed to evaluate whether information necessary to proving or defending against Mr. El-Masri's claims could plausibly be characterized as "secret"; it failed to consider the actual rather than speculative impact of disclosure of information already known throughout the world in assessing whether such disclosure would reasonably cause harm to national security; it failed adequately to assess whether it was even possible at the pleading stage to determine the relevance of alleged secrets to the litigation; and it failed to use the requisite creativity and care to fashion appropriate and secure procedures that would permit the case to go forward.

In evaluating the government's assertion of the privilege in this case, this Court should be mindful of the broader context in which the government has sought to avoid accountability for alleged illegality and misconduct on grounds of secrecy. These cases concern more than the efforts of individual plaintiffs to obtain justice for alleged wrongdoing. Unless the government's premature and overbroad claims of secrecy are subjected to meaningful judicial scrutiny, the government will routinely deploy a common-law evidentiary privilege to shield even its most egregious conduct from accountability. As the *Hepting* court recognized, "even the state secrets privilege has its limits." *Hepting*, 439 F. Supp. 2d at 995.

> *2. This case can be litigated without disclosure of means, methods, and operational details of the CIA's clandestine activities.*

The United States contends here, as it did below, that Mr. El-Masri's suit must be terminated at its outset because further litigation would expose means, methods, and operational details of the CIA's overseas operations. Indeed, the district court conclusorily accepted that argument, without explanation as to why or how exposure of means and methods unknown to the public would inevitably occur were Mr. El-Masri's case to proceed beyond the pleading stage. . . . Mr. El-Masri does not dispute that the state secrets privilege may be legitimately invoked to block publication of details of clandestine operations, where such disclosures would educate enemy intelligence agencies as to the United States' efforts to defeat them. But the government's insistence that any judicial involvement, however cautious, will necessarily reveal such details need not—indeed, cannot—be accepted without scrutiny. Had this Court deferred to the government's similar claims in the *Moussaoui* litigation, there would have been no accommodation permitting Mr. Moussaoui's counsel to submit written questions to witnesses with potentially exculpatory evidence. . . . *United States v. Moussaoui*, 382 F. 3d 453 (4th Cir. 2004) (No. 03-4792), *available at* 2003 WL 22519704 (insisting that permitting any access to Al-Qaeda detainees "would irretrievably cripple painstaking efforts for securing the flow of information," and that "the courts [were] in no position to second guess such Executive Branch judgments"). There has been no discernable harm to the nation resulting from this Court's exercise of Article III independence, and Mr. Moussaoui was convicted by a jury without resort to the manifestly unfair process demanded by the government.

In this case, it is difficult to conceive how requiring the government to answer Mr. El-Masri's complaint would alert our terrorist enemies to anything that they do not already know. In fact, just as the President's confirmation that fourteen suspected terrorists had been detained and interrogated by the CIA did not reveal classified "means and methods" that were unknown to the public, it is highly likely that Mr. El-Masri would be able to establish defendants' liability without such revelations. Moreover, the manner in which the CIA operates its rendition program is by now widely known and has been publicly aired not only in the media, . . . but in the official reports of foreign governments.

For example, the Council of Europe, in a section of its report on rendition and secret detention entitled "CIA methodology—how a detainee is treated during a rendition," distills the testimony of several rendition victims, as well as other eyewitnesses, regarding the CIA's "method" of subduing and transporting rendition targets, and concludes that "[c]ollectively[,] the cases in the report testify as to the existence of an established *modus operandi* of rendition. . . ." Dick Marty, Committee on Legal Affairs and Human Rights, Council of Europe, *Alleged Secret Detentions and Unlawful Inter-State Transfers Involving Council of Europe Member States* § 2.7.1, ¶85 (draft report 2006), *available at* http:/news.bbc.co.uk/1/shared/bsp/hi/pdfs/07_06_06_renditions_draft.pdf. The report proceeds to describe that *modus operandi*, in part, as follows:

> i. it generally takes place in a small room (a locker room, a police reception area) at the airport, or at a transit facility nearby.
> ii. the man is sometimes already blindfolded when the operation begins, or will be blindfolded quickly and remain so through most of the operation.

iii. four to six CIA agents perform the operation in a highly-disciplined, consistent fashion—they are dressed in black (either civilian clothes or special 'uniforms'), wearing black gloves, with their full faces covered. Testimonies speak, variously, of *"big people in black balaclavas,"* people *"dressed in black like ninjas,"* or people wearing *"ordinary clothes, but hooded."*

iv. the CIA agents *"don't utter a word when they communicate with one another,"* using only hand signals or simply knowing their roles implicitly.

v. some men speak of being punched or shoved by the agents at the beginning of the operation in a rough and brutal fashion; others talked about being gripped firmly from several sides.

vi. the man's hands and feet are shackled.

vii. the man has all his clothes (including his underwear) cut from his body using knives or scissors in a careful, methodical fashion; an eyewitness described how *"someone was taking these clothes and feeling every part, you know, as if there was something inside the clothes, and then putting them in a bag."*

viii. the man is subjected to a full-body cavity search, which also entails a close examination of his hair, ears, mouth and lips.

ix. the man is photographed with a flash camera, including when he is nearly or totally naked; in some instances, the man's blindfold may be removed for the purpose of a photograph in which his face is also identifiable.

x. some accounts speak of a foreign object being forcibly inserted into the man's anus; some accounts speak more specifically of a tranquiliser or a suppository being administered *per rectum. . . .*

xi. the man is then dressed in a nappy or incontinence pad and a loose-fitting *"Jump-suit"* or set of overalls; *"they put diapers on him and then there is some handling with these handcuffs and foot chains, because first they put them on and then they are supposed to put him in overalls, so then they have to alternately unlock and relock them."*

xii. the man has his ears muffled, sometimes being made to wear a pair of *"headphones."*

xiii. finally a cloth bag is placed over the man's head, with no holes through which to breathe or detect light; they *"put a blindfold on him and after that a hood that apparently reaches far down on his body."*

xiv. the man is typically forced aboard a waiting aeroplane, where he may be *"placed on a stretcher, shackled,"* or strapped to a mattress or seat, or *"laid down on the floor of the plane and they bind him up in a very uncomfortable position that makes him hurt from moving."*

xv. in some cases the man is drugged and experiences little or nothing of the actual rendition flight; in other cases factors such as the pain of the shackles or the refusal to drink water or use the toilet make the flight unbearable: *"this was the hardest moment in my life."*

xvi. in most cases, the man has no notion of where he is going, nor the fate that awaits him upon arrival.

Id. at § 2.7.1, ¶85 (citations omitted) (emphasis in original). These facts are well known. Foreign terrorists surely are on notice that, should they be captured by or turned over to the CIA, these or similar methods will be employed against them. Confirming or denying that Mr. El-Masri was a victim of these practices will no more educate our enemies about clandestine anti-terror tactics than did President Bush's confirmation that fourteen specific individuals had been held in CIA custody.

Similarly, there is no danger whatsoever that litigation of this matter will disclose classified interrogation methods. Mr. El-Masri's complaint does not allege any such methods: he contends that he was repeatedly beaten, imprisoned incommunicado in a foul dungeon, and summoned for nighttime questioning, but makes no mention of so-called "alternative interrogation procedures," such as waterboarding, that have been reported by the media but not confirmed by the government. None of these allegations can plausibly be said to describe a state secret. As in *Al-Haramain*, "the existence of the . . . Program is not a secret, the subjects of the program are not a secret, and the general method of the program . . . is not a secret." *Al-Haramain*, 2006 WL 2583425 at *6.

That is not to say that there might not be specific details—such as, for example, the identities of covert operatives—that may be legitimately withheld on state secrets grounds. But it is precisely the role of the district court to ensure that such "sensitive information . . . [is] disentangled from nonsensitive information to allow for the release of the latter." *Ellsberg v. Mitchell*, 709 F.2d 51, 57 (D.C. Cir. 1983). The question is not whether the CIA Director has identified any classified facts in his affidavits; rather, the question is whether it can be determined with certainty at this stage of the litigation that those facts are absolutely *essential* either for Mr. El-Masri to prove his claims or for the government validly to defend against them. As explained here and in Mr. El-Masri's Opening Brief, such a determination would be premature. . . .

Conclusion

The arguments raised by the government in this case are not new ones. Indeed, more than three decades ago, in seeking to prevent the disclosure of information about its activities and misconduct during wartime, the government used similar language in insisting that courts were in no position to second guess the determination by executive officials that release of information would harm the nation:

> In the present cases high government officials have explained the reasons for their concern; that judgment is enough to support the Executive Branch's conclusion, reflected in the top secret classification of the documents and in the in camera evidence, that disclosure would pose the threat of serious injury to the national security.

That case was *New York Times v. United States,* and the documents at issue were the Pentagon Papers. *See* Brief for the United States at *18, *New York Times, Co. v. United States,* 403 U.S. 713 (1971), *available at* 1971 WL 167581. Some twenty years after the release of the papers, former Solicitor General Erwin Griswold, who had argued the case on behalf of the United States, conceded: "I have never seen any trace of a threat to the national security from the publication. Indeed, I have never seen it even suggested that there was such a threat."

Erwin N. Griswold, *Secrets Not Worth Keeping: The Courts and Classified Information,* Wash. Post, Feb. 15, 1989 at A25.

The stakes in this case are substantial. As *Amici* Former United States Diplomats make clear: "[D]enial of a judicial forum to Mr. El-Masri will affect not only his private interests but will damage vital public interests: our Nation's standing in the world community and our ability to obtain cooperation from foreign governments needed to combat international terrorism." Amicus Br. at 5. In these circumstances, it is all the more critical that this Court "not merely unthinkingly ratify the executive's assertion of absolute privilege, lest it inappropriately abandon its important judicial role." *In re United States,* 872 F.2d at 475.

For the foregoing reasons and for the reasons set forth in Mr. El-Masri's Opening Brief, this Court should reverse the judgment of the district court and remand for further proceedings.

Respectfully submitted,
ANN BEESON
BEN WIZNER
STEVEN WATT
MELISSA GOODMAN
American Civil Liberties Union Foundation
125 Broad Street, 18th Floor
New York, NY 10004
Ph: (212) 549-2500
Fax: (212) 549-2629

REBECCA K. GLENBERG
American Civil Liberties Union of
Virginia Foundation, Inc.
530 E. Main Street, Suite 310
Richmond, VA 23219
Ph: (804) 644-8080
Fax: (804) 649-2733

PAUL HOFFMAN
Schonbrun DeSimone Seplow Harris &
Hoffman LLP
723 Ocean Front Walk, Suite 100
Venice, CA 90291
Ph: (310) 396-0731, ext. 4
Fax: (310) 399-7040

VICTOR M. GLASBERG
Victor M. Glasberg & Associates
121 S. Columbus Street
Alexandria, VA 22314
Ph: (703) 684-1100
Fax: (703) 684-1104

Dated: September 25, 2006
New York, NY

Opinion in Case of *El-Masri v. Tenet*

Khaled El-Masri appeals from the dismissal of his civil action against former Director of Central Intelligence George Tenet, three corporate defendants, ten unnamed employees of the Central Intelligence Agency (the "CIA"), and ten unnamed employees of the defendant corporations. In his Complaint in the Eastern District of Virginia, El-Masri alleged that the defendants were involved in a CIA operation in which he was detained and interrogated in violation of his rights under the Constitution and international law. The United States intervened as a defendant in the district court, asserting that El-Masri's civil action could not proceed because it posed an unreasonable risk that privileged state secrets would be disclosed. By its Order of May 12, 2006, the district court agreed with the position of the United States and dismissed El-Masri's Complaint. *See El-Masri v. Tenet*, 437 F. Supp. 2d 530, 541 (E.D. Va. 2006) (the "Order"). On appeal, El-Masri contends that the district court misapplied the state secrets doctrine and erred in dismissing his Complaint. As explained below, we affirm. . . .

The Complaint alleged three separate causes of action. The first claim was against Director Tenet and the unknown CIA employees, pursuant to *Bivens v. Six Unknown Named Agents of Federal Bureau of Narcotics*, 403 U.S. 388 (1971), for violations of El-Masri's Fifth Amendment right to due process. Specifically, El-Masri contends that Tenet and the defendant CIA employees contravened the Due Process Clause's prohibition against subjecting anyone held in United States custody to treatment that shocks the conscience or depriving a person of liberty in the absence of legal process. El-Masri's second cause of action was initiated pursuant to the Alien Tort Statute (the "ATS"), and alleged that each of the defendants had contravened the international legal norm against prolonged arbitrary detention. The third cause of action was also asserted under the ATS, and maintained that each defendant had violated international legal norms prohibiting cruel, inhuman, or degrading treatment.

On March 8, 2006, the United States filed a Statement of Interest in the underlying proceedings, pursuant to 28 U.S.C. § 517, and interposed a claim of the state secrets privilege. The then Director of the CIA, Porter Goss, submitted two sworn declarations to the district court in support of the state secrets privilege claim. The first declaration was unclassified, and explained in general terms the reasons for the United States' assertion of privilege. The other declaration was classified; it detailed the information that the United States sought to protect, explained why further court proceedings would unreasonably risk that

El-Masri v. United States and Tenet, F.3d No. 06-1667, 2007 WL 625130 (4th Cir. March 2, 2007).

information's disclosure, and spelled out why such disclosure would be detrimental to the national security (the "Classified Declaration"). Along with its Statement of Interest, the United States filed a motion to stay the district court proceedings pending resolution of its privilege claim; the next day, March 9, 2006, the court granted the requested stay. On March 13, 2006, the United States formally moved to intervene as a defendant in the district court proceedings. Contemporaneous with seeking to intervene as a defendant, the United States moved to dismiss the Complaint, contending that its interposition of the state secrets privilege precluded the litigation of El-Masri's causes of action.

El-Masri responded that the state secrets doctrine did not necessitate dismissal of his Complaint, primarily because CIA rendition operations, including El-Masri's alleged rendition, had been widely discussed in public forums. In support of this contention, Steven Macpherson Watt, a human rights adviser to the American Civil Liberties Union, filed a sworn declaration in the district court, dated April 7, 2006, in which he asserted that United States officials—including Secretary of State Condoleezza Rice, White House Press Secretary Scott McClellan, and Directors Tenet and Goss—had publicly acknowledged that the United States had conducted renditions. Watt also observed that international human rights organizations had issued statements on various United States rendition operations, including El-Masri's alleged rendition, and that at least one such release had described the use of privately owned aircraft in the renditions of El-Masri and others. Additionally, according to Watt, the European Parliament and the Council of Europe had commenced investigations into possible European cooperation in United States renditions, and similar inquiries were pending in eighteen European countries.

Watt further asserted that "[m]edia reports on the rendition program generally, and Mr. El-Masri's rendition specifically, are too numerous to assemble." Watt Declaration ¶ 26. According to Watt, these media reports revealed the existence of secret CIA detention facilities where some rendition subjects were held, as well as the United States' "modus operandi" for conducting renditions: "masked men in an unmarked jet seize their target, cut off his clothes, put him in a blindfold and jumpsuit, tranquilize him and fly him away." *Id.* ¶ 26(vi). And, Watt represented, the news media had documented some of the details of El-Masri's alleged rendition, including the underlying "decision-making process" and the roles of the German and Macedonian governments. *Id.* ¶ 26(viii).

On May 12, 2006, after receiving the parties' memoranda and declarations, and after oral argument of the matter, the district court concluded that the claim of the state secrets privilege was valid, and that, "given the application of the privilege to this case, the United States' motion to dismiss must be . . . granted." *See* Order, 437 F. Supp. 2d at 541. El-Masri has appealed from the Order and corresponding judgment of dismissal, and we possess jurisdiction pursuant to 28 U.S.C. § 1291.

B.

We review de novo a district court's "legal determinations involving state secrets," including its decision to grant dismissal of a complaint on state secrets grounds. *Sterling v. Tenet*, 416 F.3d 338, 342 (4th Cir. 2005).

C.

In the period after the district court's dismissal of El-Masri's Complaint, his alleged rendition—and the rendition operations of the United States generally—have remained subjects of public discussion. In El-Masri's view, two additions to the body of public information on these topics are especially significant in this appeal. First, on June 7, 2006, the Council of Europe released a draft report on alleged United States renditions and detentions involving the Council's member countries. This report concluded that El-Masri's account of his rendition and confinement was substantially accurate. Second, on September 6, 2006, in a White House address, President Bush publicly disclosed the existence of a CIA program in which suspected terrorists are detained and interrogated at locations outside the United States. The President declined, however, to reveal any of this CIA program's operational details, including the locations or other circumstances of its detainees' confinement.

II.

El-Masri maintains on appeal that the district court misapplied the state secrets doctrine in dismissing his Complaint without requiring any responsive pleadings from the defendants or permitting any discovery to be conducted. Importantly, El-Masri does not contend that the state secrets privilege has no role in these proceedings. To the contrary, he acknowledges that at least some information important to his claims is likely to be privileged, and thus beyond his reach. But he challenges the court's determination that state secrets are so central to this matter that any attempt at further litigation would threaten their disclosure. As explained below, we conclude that the district court correctly assessed the centrality of state secrets in this dispute. We therefore affirm its Order and the dismissal of El-Masri's Complaint.

A.

1.

Under the state secrets doctrine, the United States may prevent the disclosure of information in a judicial proceeding if "there is a reasonable danger" that such disclosure "will expose military matters which, in the interest of national security, should not be divulged." *United States v. Reynolds*, 345 U.S. 1, 10 (1953). *Reynolds*, the Supreme Court's leading decision on the state secrets privilege, established the doctrine in its modern form. There, an Air Force B-29 bomber had crashed during testing of secret electronic equipment, killing three civilian observers who were on board. Their widows sued the United States under the Federal Tort Claims Act, and they sought discovery of certain Air Force documents relating to the crash. The Air Force refused to disclose the documents and filed a formal "Claim of Privilege," contending that the plane had been on "a highly secret mission of the Air Force," and that disclosure of the requested materials would "seriously hamper[] national security, flying safety and the development of highly technical and secret military equipment." *Id.* at 4-5.

The Court sustained the Air Force's refusal to disclose the documents sought by the plaintiffs, concluding that the officials involved had properly invoked the "privilege against revealing military secrets." 345 U.S. at 6-7. This state secrets privilege, the Court observed, was "well established in the law of evidence." *Id.* The Court relied in part on Greenleaf's classic evidence treatise, which traced the recognition of a privilege for state secrets to the 1807 treason trial of Aaron Burr. *See* I Simon Greenleaf & John Henry Wigmore, *A Treatise on the Law of Evidence* § 251 n.5 (16th ed. 1899); *United States v. Burr*, 25 F. Cas. 30, 37 (Marshall, Circuit Justice, C.C.D. Va. 1807) (No. 14,692D) (observing that, in appropriate circumstances, government may refuse to disclose confidential state matters in judicial proceedings). The *Reynolds* Court also reviewed a long line of decisions, both American and English, that had recognized and refined a privilege for state secrets. These included *Totten v. United States*, where, in 1875, the Supreme Court affirmed the dismissal of an action for breach of a secret espionage contract, concluding that "public policy forbids the maintenance of any suit in a court of justice, the trial of which would inevitably lead to the disclosure of matters which the law itself regards as confidential, and respecting which it will not allow the confidence to be violated." 92 U.S. 105, 107 (1875).

Although the state secrets privilege was developed at common law, it performs a function of constitutional significance, because it allows the executive branch to protect information whose secrecy is necessary to its military and foreign-affairs responsibilities. *Reynolds* itself suggested that the state secrets doctrine allowed the Court to avoid the constitutional conflict that might have arisen had the judiciary demanded that the Executive disclose highly sensitive military secrets. *See* 345 U.S. at 6. In *United States v. Nixon*, the Court further articulated the doctrine's constitutional dimension, observing that the state secrets privilege provides exceptionally strong protection because it concerns "areas of Art. II duties [in which] the courts have traditionally shown the utmost deference to Presidential responsibilities." 418 U.S. 683, 710 (1974). . . .

2.

A court faced with a state secrets privilege question is obliged to resolve the matter by use of a three-part analysis. At the outset, the court must ascertain that the procedural requirements for invoking the state secrets privilege have been satisfied. Second, the court must decide whether the information sought to be protected qualifies as privileged under the state secrets doctrine. Finally, if the subject information is determined to be privileged, the ultimate question to be resolved is how the matter should proceed in light of the successful privilege claim.

a.   The procedural requirements for invoking the state secrets privilege are set forth in *Reynolds*, which derived them largely from prior decisions on the subject. First, the state secrets privilege must be asserted by the United States. *See* 345 U.S. at 7. It "belongs to the Government and . . . can neither be claimed nor waived by a private party." *Id.* Second, "[t]here must be a formal claim of privilege, lodged by the head of the department which has control over the matter." *Id.* at 7–8. Third, the department head's formal privilege claim may be made only "after actual personal consideration by that officer." *Id.* at 8. *Reynolds* emphasized that the state secrets privilege "is not to be lightly invoked," and the foregoing constraints on its assertion give practical effect to that principle. *Id.* at 7.

b.   After a court has confirmed that the *Reynolds* procedural prerequisites are satisfied, it must determine whether the information that the United States seeks to shield is a state secret, and thus privileged from disclosure. This inquiry is a difficult one, for it pits the judiciary's search for truth against the Executive's duty to maintain the nation's security. The *Reynolds* Court recognized this tension, observing that "[j]udicial control over the evidence in a case cannot be abdicated to the caprice of executive officers"—no matter how great the interest in national security—but that the President's ability to preserve state secrets likewise cannot be placed entirely at the mercy of the courts. 345 U.S. at 9-10. Moreover, a court evaluating a claim of privilege must "do so without forcing a disclosure of the very thing the privilege is designed to protect."

The *Reynolds* Court balanced those concerns by leaving the judiciary firmly in control of deciding whether an executive assertion of the state secrets privilege is valid, but subject to a standard mandating restraint in the exercise of its authority. A court is obliged to honor the Executive's assertion of the privilege if it is satisfied, "from all the circumstances of the case, that there is a reasonable danger that compulsion of the evidence will expose military matters which, in the interest of national security, should not be divulged." *Reynolds*, 345 U.S. at 10. In assessing the risk that such a disclosure might pose to national security, a court is obliged to accord the "utmost deference" to the responsibilities of the executive branch. *Nixon*, 418 U.S. at 710. Such deference is appropriate not only for constitutional reasons, but also practical ones: the Executive and the intelligence agencies under his control occupy a position superior to that of the courts in evaluating the consequences of a release of sensitive information. In the related context of confidentiality classification decisions, we have observed that "[t]he courts, of course, are ill-equipped to become sufficiently steeped in foreign intelligence matters to serve effectively in the review of secrecy classifications in that area." *United States v. Marchetti*, 466 F.2d 1309, 1318 (4th Cir. 1972). The executive branch's expertise in predicting the potential consequences of intelligence disclosures is particularly important given the sophisticated nature of modern intelligence analysis, in which "[t]he significance of one item of information may frequently depend upon knowledge of many other items of information," and "[w]hat may seem trivial to the uninformed, may appear of great moment to one who has a broad view of the scene and may put the questioned item of information in its proper context." *Id.* In the same vein, in those situations where the state secrets privilege has been invoked because disclosure risks impairing our foreign relations, the President's assessment of the diplomatic situation is entitled to great weight. . . .

After information has been determined to be privileged under the state secrets doctrine, it is absolutely protected from disclosure—even for the purpose of in camera examination by the court. On this point, *Reynolds* could not be more specific: "When . . . the occasion for the privilege is appropriate, . . .

the court should not jeopardize the security which the privilege is meant to protect by insisting upon an examination of the evidence, even by the judge alone, in chambers." 345 U.S. at 10. Moreover, no attempt is made to balance the need for secrecy of the privileged information against a party's need for the information's disclosure; a court's determination that a piece of evidence is a privileged state secret removes it from the proceedings entirely. *See id.* at 11.

c.   The effect of a successful interposition of the state secrets privilege by the United States will vary from case to case. If a proceeding involving state secrets can be fairly litigated without resort to the privileged information, it may continue. But if "'the circumstances make clear that sensitive military secrets will be so central to the subject matter of the litigation that any attempt to proceed will threaten disclosure of the privileged matters,' dismissal is the proper remedy." *Sterling*, 416 F.3d at 348 (quoting *DTM Research, LLC v. AT & T Corp.*, 245 F.3d 327, 334 (4th Cir. 2001)). The Supreme Court has recognized that some matters are so pervaded by state secrets as to be incapable of judicial resolution once the privilege has been invoked. . . .

3.

To summarize, our analysis of the Executive's interposition of the state secrets privilege is governed primarily by two standards. First, evidence is privileged pursuant to the state secrets doctrine if, under all the circumstances of the case, there is a reasonable danger that its disclosure will expose military (or diplomatic or intelligence) matters which, in the interest of national security, should not be divulged. *See Reynolds*, 345 U.S. at 10. Second, a proceeding in which the state secrets privilege is successfully interposed must be dismissed if the circumstances make clear that privileged information will be so central to the litigation that any attempt to proceed will threaten that information's disclosure. *See Sterling*, 416 F.3d at 348; *see also Reynolds*, 345 U.S. at 11 n.26; *Totten*, 92 U.S. at 107. With these controlling principles in mind, and being cognizant of the delicate balance to be struck in applying the state secrets doctrine, we proceed to our analysis of El-Masri's contentions.

B.

1.

The question before us is whether the facts of this proceeding satisfy the governing standard for dismissal of an action on state secrets grounds, as the district court ruled. El-Masri essentially accepts the legal framework described above. He acknowledges that the state secrets doctrine protects sensitive military intelligence information from disclosure in court proceedings, and that dismissal at the pleading stage is appropriate if state secrets are so central to a proceeding that it cannot be litigated without threatening their disclosure. El-Masri contends, however, that the facts that are central to his claim are not state secrets, and that the district court thus erred in dismissing his Complaint.

a.   The heart of El-Masri's appeal is his assertion that the facts essential to his Complaint have largely been made public, either in statements by United

States officials or in reports by media outlets and foreign governmental entities. He maintains that the subject of this action is simply "a rendition and its consequences," and that its critical facts—the CIA's operation of a rendition program targeted at terrorism suspects, plus the tactics employed therein—have been so widely discussed that litigation concerning them could do no harm to national security. Appellant's Br. 38. As a result, El-Masri contends that the district court should have allowed his case to move forward with discovery, perhaps with special procedures imposed to protect sensitive information.

El-Masri's contention in that regard, however, misapprehends the nature of our assessment of a dismissal on state secrets grounds. The controlling inquiry is not whether the general subject matter of an action can be described without resort to state secrets. Rather, we must ascertain whether an action can be *litigated* without threatening the disclosure of such state secrets. Thus, for purposes of the state secrets analysis, the "central facts" and "very subject matter" of an action are those facts that are essential to prosecuting the action or defending against it.

El-Masri is therefore incorrect in contending that the central facts of this proceeding are his allegations that he was detained and interrogated under abusive conditions, or that the CIA conducted the rendition program that has been acknowledged by United States officials. Facts such as those furnish the general terms in which El-Masri has related his story to the press, but advancing a case in the court of public opinion, against the United States at large, is an undertaking quite different from prevailing against specific defendants in a court of law. If El-Masri's civil action were to proceed, the facts central to its resolution would be the roles, if any, that the defendants played in the events he alleges. To establish a prima facie case, he would be obliged to produce admissible evidence not only that he was detained and interrogated, but that the defendants were involved in his detention and interrogation in a manner that renders them personally liable to him. Such a showing could be made only with evidence that exposes how the CIA organizes, staffs, and supervises its most sensitive intelligence operations. With regard to Director Tenet, for example, El-Masri would be obliged to show in detail how the head of the CIA participates in such operations, and how information concerning their progress is relayed to him. With respect to the defendant corporations and their unnamed employees, El-Masri would have to demonstrate the existence and details of CIA espionage contracts, an endeavor practically indistinguishable from that categorically barred by *Totten* and *Tenet v. Doe*. See *Totten v. United States*, 92 U.S. 105, 107 (1875) (establishing absolute bar to enforcement of confidential agreements to conduct espionage, on ground that "public policy forbids the maintenance of any suit in a court of justice, the trial of which would inevitably lead to the disclosure of matters which the law itself regards as confidential"); *Tenet v. Doe*, 544 U.S. 1, 10-11 (2005) (reaffirming *Totten* in unanimous decision). Even marshalling the evidence necessary to make the requisite showings would implicate privileged state secrets, because El-Masri would need to rely on witnesses whose identities, and evidence the very existence of which, must remain confidential in the interest of national security. See *Sterling*, 416 F.3d at 347 ("[T]he very methods by which evidence would be gathered in this case are themselves problematic.").

b.   Furthermore, if El-Masri were somehow able to make out a prima facie case despite the unavailability of state secrets, the defendants could not properly defend themselves without using privileged evidence. The main avenues of defense available in this matter are to show that El-Masri was not subject to the treatment that he alleges; that, if he was subject to such treatment, the defendants were not involved in it; or that, if they were involved, the nature of their involvement does not give rise to liability. Any of those three showings would require disclosure of information regarding the means and methods by which the CIA gathers intelligence. If, for example, the truth is that El-Masri was detained by the CIA but his description of his treatment is inaccurate, that fact could be established only by disclosure of the actual circumstances of his detention, and its proof would require testimony by the personnel involved. Or, if El-Masri was in fact detained as he describes, but the operation was conducted by some governmental entity other than the CIA, or another government entirely, that information would be privileged. Alternatively, if the CIA detained El-Masri, but did so without Director Tenet's active involvement, effective proof thereof would require a detailed explanation of how CIA operations are supervised. Similarly, although an individual CIA officer might demonstrate his lack of involvement in a given operation by disclosing that he was actually performing some other function at the time in question, establishing his alibi would likely require him to reveal privileged information.

Moreover, proof of the involvement—or lack thereof—of particular CIA officers in a given operation would provide significant information on how the CIA makes its personnel assignments. Similar concerns would attach to evidence produced in defense of the corporate defendants and their unnamed employees. And, like El-Masri's prima facie case, any of the possible defenses suggested above would require the production of witnesses whose identities are confidential and evidence the very existence of which is a state secret. We do not, of course, mean to suggest that any of these hypothetical defenses represents the true state of affairs in this matter, but they illustrate that virtually any conceivable response to El-Masri's allegations would disclose privileged information.

c.   It is clear from precedent that the "central facts" or "very subject matter" of a civil proceeding, for purposes of our dismissal analysis, are those facts necessary to litigate it—not merely to discuss it in general terms. . . .

2.

El-Masri also contends that, instead of dismissing his Complaint, the district court should have employed some procedure under which state secrets would have been revealed to him, his counsel, and the court, but withheld from the public. Specifically, he suggests that the court ought to have received all the state secrets evidence in camera and under seal, provided his counsel access to it pursuant to a nondisclosure agreement (after arranging for necessary security clearances), and then conducted an in camera trial. We need not dwell long on El-Masri's proposal in this regard, for it is expressly foreclosed by *Reynolds*, the Supreme Court decision that controls this entire field of inquiry. *Reynolds* plainly held that when "the occasion for the privilege is appropriate, . . . the court should not jeopardize the security which the privilege is meant to protect by insisting upon an examination of the evidence, even by the judge alone, in chambers." 345 U.S. at 10. El-Masri's assertion that the district court erred in not compelling the disclosure of state secrets to him and his lawyers is thus without merit.

C.

In addition to his analysis under the controlling legal principles, El-Masri presents a sharp attack on what he views as the dire constitutional and policy consequences of dismissing his Complaint. He maintains that the district court's ruling, if affirmed, would enable the Executive to unilaterally avoid judicial scrutiny merely by asserting that state secrets are at stake in a given matter. More broadly, he questions the very application of the state secrets doctrine in matters where "egregious executive misconduct" is alleged, contending that, in such circumstances, the courts' "constitutional duty to review executive action" should trump the procedural protections traditionally accorded state secrets. . . .

Contrary to El-Masri's assertion, the state secrets doctrine does not represent a surrender of judicial control over access to the courts. As we have explained, it is the court, not the Executive, that determines whether the state secrets privilege has been properly invoked. In order to successfully claim the state secrets privilege, the Executive must satisfy the court that disclosure of the information sought to be protected would expose matters that, in the interest of national security, ought to remain secret. Similarly, in order to win dismissal of an action on state secrets grounds, the Executive must persuade the court that state secrets are so central to the action that it cannot be fairly litigated without threatening their disclosure. The state secrets privilege cannot be successfully interposed, nor can it lead to dismissal of an action, based merely on the Executive's assertion that the pertinent standard has been met.

In this matter, the reasons for the United States' claim of the state secrets privilege and its motion to dismiss were explained largely in the Classified Declaration, which sets forth in detail the nature of the information that the Executive seeks to protect and explains why its disclosure would be detrimental to national security. We have reviewed the Classified Declaration, as did the district court, and the extensive information it contains is crucial to our decision in this matter. El-Masri's contention that his Complaint was dismissed based on the Executive's "unilateral assert[ion] of a need for secrecy" is entirely unfounded. It is no doubt frustrating to El-Masri that many of the specific reasons for the dismissal of his Complaint are classified. An inherent feature of the state secrets privilege, however, is that the party against whom it is asserted will often not be privy to the information that the Executive seeks to protect. That El-Masri is unfamiliar with the Classified Declaration's explanation for the privilege claim does not imply, as he would have it, that no such explanation was required, or that the district court's ruling was simply an unthinking ratification of a conclusory demand by the executive branch. . . .

III.

Pursuant to the foregoing, we affirm the Order of the district court. *See El-Masri v. Tenet*, 437 F. Supp. 2d 530 (E.D. Va. 2006).

AFFIRMED

POSTSCRIPT

Should Someone Held by the CIA and Interrogated in a Foreign Country Be Allowed to Sue the U.S. Government?

In stressing the importance of the Constitution during wartime, former Supreme Court Justice David Davis wrote, in the court's decision in the *Milligan* case discussed in the postscript to Issue 1:

> The Constitution of the United States is a law for rulers and people, equally in war and in peace, and covers with the shield of its protection all classes of men, at all times and under all circumstances. No doctrine involving more pernicious consequences was ever invented by the wit of man than that any of its provisions can be suspended during any of the great exigencies of government. Such a doctrine leads directly to anarchy or despotism, but the theory of necessity on which it is based is false, for the government, within the Constitution, has all the powers granted to it which are necessary to preserve its existence, as has been happily proved by the result of the great effort to throw off its just authority. (71 US 2, 1866)

However, even if one assumes that an individual's constitutional protections should remain inviolable during wartime, there is still the question of whether the courts should intervene in national security matters to protect these rights—and as the readings in this issue illustrate, the need for the courts to exercise restraint when involving themselves in national security matters is especially important when dealing with confidential information that the executive branch is withholding from the public on national security grounds. The Supreme Court pointed out in *United States v. Reynolds*, where it first acknowledged the necessity of a "state secret privilege," that "[t]oo much judicial inquiry into the claim of privilege would force disclosure of the thing the privilege was meant to protect." Such a limitation immediately forecloses the ability of the courts to protect individual rights against governmental abuses, since it obviously cannot make a determination about the constitutionality or legality of the government's actions if the circumstances surrounding these actions are entirely unknown. In such cases, even if an individual's rights have been violated, it may well be that, unfortunately, they have no recourse to the judiciary to vindicate their rights. The District Court, in dismissing El-Masri's complaint, came to this very conclusion:

> In times of war, our country, chiefly through the Executive Branch, must often take exceptional steps to thwart the enemy. Of course, reasonable

and patriotic Americans are still free to disagree about the propriety and efficacy of those exceptional steps. But what this decision holds is that these steps are not proper grist for the judicial mill where, as here, state secrets are at the center of the suit and the privilege is validly invoked. If El-Masri's allegations are true or essentially true, then all fair-minded people, including those who believe that state secrets must be protected, that this lawsuit cannot proceed, and that renditions are a necessary step to take in this war, must also agree that El-Masri has suffered injuries as a result of our country's mistake and deserves a remedy. Yet, it is also clear from the result reached here that the only sources of that remedy must be the Executive Branch or the Legislative Branch, not the Judicial Branch. (*El-Masri v. Tenet*, 437 F.Supp.2d 530, 2006)

Interesting readings on the "extraordinary rendition" program are Jane Meyer, "Outsourcing Torture," *New Yorker Magazine,* February 14, 2005, http://www.newyorker.com/archive/2005/02/14/050214fa_fact6; John T. Parry, "The Shape of Modern Torture: Extraordinary Rendition and Ghost Detainees," http://mjil.law.unimelb.edu.au/issues/archive/2005(2)/11Parry.pdf. Links to various sources about torture are at http://jurist.law.pitt.edu/currentawareness/rendition.php.

Internet References . . .

Cornell Legal Information Institute

This is a reliable and useful site for primary legal information and documents.

http://www.law.cornell.edu

FindLaw

This is a good place to begin looking for court decisions, statutes, law reviews, and other primary legal resources.

http://www.findlaw.com

American Civil Liberties Union

The American Civil Liberties Union (ACLU) Web site is a significant repository of information related to individual rights.

http://www.aclu.org

Court TV's Choices and Consequences

This guide for parents, teachers, and community leaders provides resources and information for addressing issues that young people face today, including media literacy, self-esteem, diversity, teen violence, and peer pressure.

http://www.courttv.corn/choices/links.html

Law and the Individual

*T*he American legal and political systems are oriented around protection of the individual. The law does not provide absolute protection for the individual, however, because legitimate state interests are often recognized as being controlling. This unit examines issues that affect individual choice and the dignity of the individual.

- Is It Constitutional to Ban Partial-Birth Abortions Without Providing for an Exception to Protect the Health of the Mother?

- Are Restrictions on Physician-Assisted Suicide Constitutional?

- Does the Sharing of Music Files Through the Internet Violate Copyright Laws?

- Can the Police Require Individuals to Identify Themselves?

ISSUE 5

Is It Constitutional to Ban Partial-Birth Abortions Without Providing for an Exception to Protect the Health of the Mother?

YES: Anthony Kennedy, from Majority Opinion, *Gonzales v. Carhart*, U.S. Supreme Court (April 18, 2007)

NO: Ruth Bader Ginsburg, from Minority Opinion, *Gonzales v. Carhart*, U.S. Supreme Court (April 18, 2007)

ISSUE SUMMARY

YES: Justice Anthony Kennedy's rules that the federal Partial-Birth Abortion Ban Act of 2003 was constitutional even without a "health exception" for the woman.

NO: In dissent, Justice Ruth Bader Ginsburg argues that the law clearly contravenes the Court's holding in prior cases that any regulation limiting a woman's access to abortion, even post-viability, must include a health exception.

Abortion is an issue that has never left the spotlight, even though it has been more than three decades since the Supreme Court ruled, in *Roe v. Wade* (410 US 113, 1973), that laws banning the procedure violated the Constitution. The Supreme Court has repeatedly upheld and reaffirmed its decision in *Roe* that the Due Process Clause of the Fourteenth Amendment provides a right to privacy that encompasses a woman's right to choose whether to terminate a pregnancy. However, the Court did not say in *Roe* that this right was absolute.

The recognition in *Roe* and *Planned Parenthood v. Casey* (505 US 833, 1992) that the government has a "legitimate interest" in "protecting the potentiality of human life" has led to a considerable litigation surrounding the extent to which both state and federal legislatures can pass laws regulating abortion. The difficulty of deciding which types of laws cross the ill-defined line that separates legitimate governmental action from unconstitutional interference in a private decision is evident in the Supreme Court's mixed holdings in post-*Roe* abortion cases. For instance, can states mandate that doctors perform all second-trimester abortions in hospitals? No, according to the Court's decision in *Planned Parenthood of Kansas City, MO v. Ashcroft,* 462 US 476 (1983). Can states mandate that a second doctor be present at all late-term abortions? Yes, according to the same ruling.

Adding to this confusion was the Court's decision in *Planned Parenthood v. Casey* to reaffirm *Roe*'s "central holding" while modifying some of its methodology for determining which laws violate a woman's right to choose. In *Casey,* the Court stated that in many of its rulings since *Roe,* it had gone "too far" and "[struck] down . . . some abortion regulations which in no real sense deprived women of the ultimate decision." Part of the problem, according to the Court, was its use of *Roe*'s "trimester approach," under which "almost no regulation at all [wa]s permitted during the first trimester of pregnancy; regulations designed to protect the woman's health, but not to further the State's interest in potential life, [were] permitted during the second trimester; and during the third trimester, when the fetus is viable, prohibitions [were] permitted provided the life or health of the mother [wa]s not at stake." The Court announced in *Casey* that it would adopt a new standard to determine the constitutionality of abortion regulations—whether they posed an "undue burden" to a woman's exercise of her right to choose—and it overruled some of its previous abortion decisions, for example, its holding in two cases that states could not require doctors to provide certain information to all women seeking abortions.

In 2000, the Court faced one of its most significant post-*Casey* abortion cases, *Stenberg v. Carhart. Stenberg* required the Court to weigh in, using its "undue burden" standard, on the constitutionality of a Nebraska state law banning certain types of late-term abortions that critics have dubbed "partial-birth" abortions.

Nevertheless, the Court, in a 5-4 opinion, held the Nebraska law unconstitutional for two reasons. First, it lacked an exception, required by *Roe* and *Casey,* to allow for the banned procedure when necessary to safeguard the mother's health. Second, the language was so broad that it could be read to outlaw the most common types of second-trimester abortions, "thereby unduly burdening the right to choose abortion itself."

In 2007, the Court once again addressed the constitutionality of a law prohibiting partial-birth abortions. This time, however, the Court—again in a 5-4 decision—upheld the ban. According to Justice Anthony Kennedy's decision for the five-justice majority, the law at issue—the federal Partial-Birth Abortion Ban Act of 2003—was sufficiently different from the Nebraska statute in *Stenberg* that the Court could not conclude that it posed an "undue burden." However, in her dissent, Justice Ruth Bader Ginsburg argued that the law clearly contravenes the Court's holding, in both *Roe* and *Casey,* that any regulation limiting a woman's access to abortion, even post-viability, must include a health exception.

Majority Opinion,
Gonzales v. Carhart

J USTICE KENNEDY delivered the opinion of the Court.

These cases require us to consider the validity of the Partial-Birth Abortion Ban Act of 2003 (Act), 18 U. S. C. §1531 (2000 ed., Supp. IV), a federal statute regulating abortion procedures. In recitations preceding its operative provisions the Act refers to the Court's opinion in *Stenberg v. Carhart,* 530 U. S. 914 (2000), which also addressed the subject of abortion procedures used in the later stages of pregnancy. Compared to the state statute at issue in *Stenberg,* the Act is more specific concerning the instances to which it applies and in this respect more precise in its coverage. We conclude the Act should be sustained against the objections lodged by the broad, facial attack brought against it. . . .

In 2003, after this Court's decision in *Stenberg,* Congress passed the Act at issue here. H. R. Rep. No. 108–58, at 12–14. On November 5, 2003, President Bush signed the Act into law. It was to take effect the following day. 18 U. S. C. §1531(a) (2000 ed., Supp. IV).

The Act responded to *Stenberg* in two ways. First, Congress made factual findings. Congress determined that this Court in *Stenberg* "was required to accept the very questionable findings issued by the district court judge," . . . but that Congress was "not bound to accept the same factual findings," . . . Congress found, among other things, that "[a] moral, medical, and ethical consensus exists that the practice of performing a partial-birth abortion . . . is a gruesome and inhumane procedure that is never medically necessary and should be prohibited." . . .

Second, and more relevant here, the Act's language differs from that of the Nebraska statute struck down in *Stenberg.* . . .

C

The District Court in *Carhart* concluded the Act was unconstitutional for two reasons. First, it determined the Act was unconstitutional because it lacked an exception allowing the procedure where necessary for the health of the mother. 331 F. Supp. 2d, at 1004–1030. Second, the District Court found the Act deficient because it covered not merely intact D&E but also certain other D&Es. *Id.,* at 1030–1037.

From U.S. Supreme Court, April 18, 2007.

The Court of Appeals for the Eighth Circuit addressed only the lack of a health exception. 413 F. 3d, at 803–804. The court began its analysis with what it saw as the appropriate question—"whether 'substantial medical authority' supports the medical necessity of the banned procedure." *Id.*, at 796 (quoting *Stenberg*, 530 U. S., at 938). This was the proper framework, according to the Court of Appeals, because "when a lack of consensus exists in the medical community, the Constitution requires legislatures to err on the side of protecting women's health by including a health exception." 413 F. 3d, at 796. The court rejected the Attorney General's attempt to demonstrate changed evidentiary circumstances since *Stenberg* and considered itself bound by *Stenberg's* conclusion that a health exception was required. 413 F. 3d, at 803 (explaining "[t]he record in [the] case and the record in *Stenberg* [were] similar in all significant respects"). It invalidated the Act. *Ibid.* . . .

II

The principles set forth in the joint opinion in *Planned Parenthood of Southeastern Pa. v. Casey*, 505 U. S. 833 (1992), did not find support from all those who join the instant opinion. See *id.*, at 979–1002 (SCALIA, J., joined by THOMAS, J., *inter alios*, concurring in judgment in part and dissenting in part). Whatever one's views concerning the *Casey* joint opinion, it is evident a premise central to its conclusion—that the government has a legitimate and substantial interest in preserving and promoting fetal life—would be repudiated were the Court now to affirm the judgments of the Courts of Appeals.

Casey involved a challenge to *Roe v. Wade*, 410 U. S. 113 (1973). The opinion contains this summary:

> "It must be stated at the outset and with clarity that *Roe's* essential holding, the holding we reaffirm, has three parts. First is a recognition of the right of the woman to choose to have an abortion before viability and to obtain it without undue interference from the State. Before viability, the State's interests are not strong enough to support a prohibition of abortion or the imposition of a substantial obstacle to the woman's effective right to elect the procedure. Second is a confirmation of the State's power to restrict abortions after fetal viability, if the law contains exceptions for pregnancies which endanger the woman's life or health. And third is the principle that the State has legitimate interests from the outset of the pregnancy in protecting the health of the woman and the life of the fetus that may become a child. These principles do not contradict one another; and we adhere to each." 505 U. S., at 846 (opinion of the Court).

Though all three holdings are implicated in the instant cases, it is the third that requires the most extended discussion; for we must determine whether the Act furthers the legitimate interest of the Government in protecting the life of the fetus that may become a child.

To implement its holding, *Casey* rejected both *Roe's* rigid trimester framework and the interpretation of *Roe* that considered all previability regulations of abortion unwarranted. 505 U. S., at 875–876, 878 (plurality opinion). On this point *Casey* overruled the holdings in two cases because they undervalued the State's interest in potential life. See *id.*, at 881–883 (joint opinion) (overruling *Thornburgh v. American College of Obstetricians and Gynecologists*, 476 U. S. 747 (1986) and *Akron v. Akron Center for Reproductive Health, Inc.*, 462 U. S. 416 (1983)).

We assume the following principles for the purposes of this opinion. Before viability, a State "may not prohibit any woman from making the ultimate decision to terminate her pregnancy." 505 U. S., at 879 (plurality opinion). It also may not impose upon this right an undue burden, which exists if a regulation's "purpose or effect is to place a substantial obstacle in the path of a woman seeking an abortion before the fetus attains viability." *Id.*, at 878. On the other hand, "[r]egulations which do no more than create a structural mechanism by which the State, or the parent or guardian of a minor, may express profound respect for the life of the unborn are permitted, if they are not a substantial obstacle to the woman's exercise of the right to choose." *Id.*, at 877. *Casey*, in short, struck a balance. The balance was central to its holding. We now apply its standard to the cases at bar. . . .

IV

Under the principles accepted as controlling here, the Act, as we have interpreted it, would be unconstitutional "if its purpose or effect is to place a substantial obstacle in the path of a woman seeking an abortion before the fetus attains viability." *Casey*, 505 U. S., at 878 (plurality opinion). The abortions affected by the Act's regulations take place both previability and postviability; so the quoted language and the undue burden analysis it relies upon are applicable. The question is whether the Act, measured by its text in this facial attack, imposes a substantial obstacle to late-term, but previability, abortions. The Act does not on its face impose a substantial obstacle, and we reject this further facial challenge to its validity.

A

The Act's purposes are set forth in recitals preceding its operative provisions. A description of the prohibited abortion procedure demonstrates the rationale for the congressional enactment. The Act proscribes a method of abortion in which a fetus is killed just inches before completion of the birth process. Congress stated as follows: "Implicitly approving such a brutal and inhumane procedure by choosing not to prohibit it will further coarsen society to the humanity of not only newborns, but all vulnerable and innocent human life, making it increasingly difficult to protect such life." Congressional Findings (14)(N), in notes following 18 U. S. C. §1531 (2000 ed., Supp. IV), p. 769. The Act expresses respect for the dignity of human life.

Congress was concerned, furthermore, with the effects on the medical community and on its reputation caused by the practice of partial-birth abortion. The findings in the Act explain:

"Partial-birth abortion . . . confuses the medical, legal, and ethical duties of physicians to preserve and promote life, as the physician acts directly against the physical life of a child, whom he or she had just delivered, all but the head, out of the womb, in order to end that life." Congressional Findings (14)(J), *ibid.*

There can be no doubt the government "has an interest in protecting the integrity and ethics of the medical profession." *Washington* v. *Glucksberg*, 521 U. S. 702, 731 (1997); see also *Barsky* v. *Board of Regents of Univ. of N. Y.*, 347 U. S. 442, 451 (1954) (indicating the State has "legitimate concern for maintaining high standards of professional conduct" in the practice of medicine). Under our precedents it is clear the State has a significant role to play in regulating the medical profession.

Casey reaffirmed these governmental objectives. The government may use its voice and its regulatory authority to show its profound respect for the life within the woman. A central premise of the opinion was that the Court's precedents after *Roe* had "undervalue[d] the State's interest in potential life." 505 U. S., at 873 (plurality opinion); see also *id.*, at 871. The plurality opinion indicated "[t]he fact that a law which serves a valid purpose, one not designed to strike at the right itself, has the incidental effect of making it more difficult or more expensive to procure an abortion cannot be enough to invalidate it." *Id.*, at 874. This was not an idle assertion. The three premises of *Casey* must coexist. See *id.*, at 846 (opinion of the Court). The third premise, that the State, from the inception of the pregnancy, maintains its own regulatory interest in protecting the life of the fetus that may become a child, cannot be set at naught by interpreting *Casey's* requirement of a health exception so it becomes tantamount to allowing a doctor to choose the abortion method he or she might prefer. Where it has a rational basis to act, and it does not impose an undue burden, the State may use its regulatory power to bar certain procedures and substitute others, all in furtherance of its legitimate interests in regulating the medical profession in order to promote respect for life, including life of the unborn.

The Act's ban on abortions that involve partial delivery of a living fetus furthers the Government's objectives. No one would dispute that, for many, D&E is a procedure itself laden with the power to devalue human life. Congress could nonetheless conclude that the type of abortion proscribed by the Act requires specific regulation because it implicates additional ethical and moral concerns that justify a special prohibition. Congress determined that the abortion methods it proscribed had a "disturbing similarity to the killing of a newborn infant," Congressional Findings (14)(L), in notes following 18 U. S. C. §1531 (2000 ed., Supp. IV), p. 769, and thus it was concerned with "draw[ing] a bright line that clearly distinguishes abortion and infanticide." Congressional Findings (14)(G), *ibid.* The Court has in the past confirmed the validity of drawing boundaries to prevent certain practices that extinguish life and are close to actions that are condemned. *Glucksberg* found reasonable the State's "fear that permitting assisted suicide will start it down the path to voluntary and perhaps even involuntary euthanasia." 521 U. S., at 732–735, and n. 23. . . .

B

The Act's furtherance of legitimate government interests bears upon, but does not resolve, the next question: whether the Act has the effect of imposing an unconstitutional burden on the abortion right because it does not allow use of the barred procedure where " 'necessary, in appropriate medical judgment, for [the] preservation of the . . . health of the mother.' " *Ayotte*, 546 U. S., at 327– 328 (quoting *Casey, supra*, at 879 (plurality opinion)). The prohibition in the Act would be unconstitutional, under precedents we here assume to be controlling, if it "subject[ed] [women] to significant health risks." *Ayotte, supra*, at 328; see also *Casey, supra*, at 880 (opinion of the Court). In *Ayotte* the parties agreed a health exception to the challenged parental-involvement statute was necessary "to avert serious and often irreversible damage to [a pregnant minor's] health." 546 U. S., at 328. Here, by contrast, whether the Act creates significant health risks for women has been a contested factual question. The evidence presented in the trial courts and before Congress demonstrates both sides have medical support for their position.

Respondents presented evidence that intact D&E may be the safest method of abortion, for reasons similar to those adduced in *Stenberg*. See 530 U. S., at 932. Abortion doctors testified, for example, that intact D&E decreases the risk of cervical laceration or uterine perforation because it requires fewer passes into the uterus with surgical instruments and does not require the removal of bony fragments of the dismembered fetus, fragments that may be sharp. Respondents also presented evidence that intact D&E was safer both because it reduces the risks that fetal parts will remain in the uterus and because it takes less time to complete. Respondents, in addition, proffered evidence that intact D&E was safer for women with certain medical conditions or women with fetuses that had certain anomalies. . . .

These contentions were contradicted by other doctors who testified in the District Courts and before Congress. They concluded that the alleged health advantages were based on speculation without scientific studies to support them. They considered D&E always to be a safe alternative. See, *e.g., Carhart, supra*, at 930–940; *Nat. Abortion Federation*, 330 F. Supp. 2d, at 470–474; *Planned Parenthood*, 320 F. Supp. 2d, at 983.

There is documented medical disagreement whether the Act's prohibition would ever impose significant health risks on women. See, *e.g., id.*, at 1033 ("[T]here continues to be a division of opinion among highly qualified experts regarding the necessity or safety of intact D & E"); see also *Nat. Abortion Federation, supra*, at 482. The three District Courts that considered the Act's constitutionality appeared to be in some disagreement on this central factual question. The District Court for the District of Nebraska concluded "the banned procedure is, sometimes, the safest abortion procedure to preserve the health of women." *Carhart, supra,* at 1017. The District Court for the Northern District of California reached a similar conclusion. *Planned Parenthood, supra*, at 1002 (finding intact D&E was "under certain circumstances . . . significantly safer than D & E by disarticulation"). The District Court for the Southern District of New York was more skeptical of the purported health benefits of intact D&E. It found the Attorney General's "expert witnesses reasonably and effectively refuted [the plaintiffs'] proffered bases for the opinion that [intact D&E] has safety advantages over other second-trimester abortion procedures." *Nat. Abortion Federation*, 330 F. Supp. 2d, at 479. In addition it did "not believe that many of [the plaintiffs'] purported reasons for why [intact D&E] is medically necessary [were] credible; rather [it found them to be] theoretical or false." *Id.*, at 480. The court nonetheless invalidated the Act because it determined "a significant body of medical opinion . . . holds that D & E has safety advantages over induction and that [intact D&E] has some safety advantages (however hypothetical and unsubstantiated by scientific evidence) over D & E for some women in some circumstances." *Ibid.*

The question becomes whether the Act can stand when this medical uncertainty persists. The Court's precedents instruct that the Act can survive this facial attack. The Court has given state and federal legislatures wide discretion to pass legislation in areas where there is medical and scientific uncertainty. . . .

This traditional rule is consistent with *Casey*, which confirms the State's interest in promoting respect for human life at all stages in the pregnancy. Physicians are not entitled to ignore regulations that direct them to use reasonable alternative procedures. The law need not give abortion doctors unfettered choice in the course of their medical practice, nor should it elevate their status above other physicians in the medical community. In *Casey* the controlling opinion held an informed-consent requirement in the abortion context was "no different from a requirement that a doctor give certain specific information about any medical procedure." 505 U. S., at 884 (joint opinion). The opinion stated "the doctor-patient relation here is entitled to the same solicitude it receives in other contexts." *Ibid.*; see also *Webster* v. *Reproductive Health Services,* 492 U. S. 490, 518–519 (1989) (plurality opinion) (criticizing *Roe's* trimester framework because, *inter alia,* it "left this Court to serve as the country's *ex officio* medical board with powers to approve or disapprove medical and operative practices and standards throughout the United States" (internal quotation marks omitted)); *Mazurek* v. *Armstrong,* 520 U. S. 968, 973 (1997) (*per curiam*) (upholding a restriction on the performance of abortions to licensed physicians despite the respondents' contention "all health evidence contradicts the claim that there is any health basis for the law" (internal quotation marks omitted)).

Medical uncertainty does not foreclose the exercise of legislative power in the abortion context any more than it does in other contexts. . . . The medical uncertainty over whether the Act's prohibition creates significant health risks provides a sufficient basis to conclude in this facial attack that the Act does not impose an undue burden.

The conclusion that the Act does not impose an undue burden is supported by other considerations. Alternatives are available to the prohibited procedure. As we have noted, the Act does not proscribe D&E. One District Court found D&E to have extremely low rates of medical complications. *Planned Parenthood, supra,* at 1000. Another indicated D&E was "generally the safest method of abortion during the second trimester." *Carhart,* 331 F. Supp. 2d, at 1031; see also *Nat. Abortion Federation, supra,* at 467–468 (explaining that "[e]xperts testifying for both sides" agreed D&E was safe). In addition the Act's prohibition only applies to the delivery of "a living fetus." 18 U. S. C. §1531(b)(1)(A) (2000 ed., Supp. IV). If the intact D&E procedure is truly necessary in some circumstances, it appears likely an injection that kills the fetus is an alternative under the Act that allows the doctor to perform the procedure.

The instant cases, then, are different from *Planned Parenthood of Central Mo.* v. *Danforth,* 428 U. S. 52, 77– 79 (1976), in which the Court invalidated a ban on saline amniocentesis, the then-dominant second-trimester abortion method. The Court found the ban in *Danforth* to be "an unreasonable or arbitrary regulation designed to inhibit, and having the effect of inhibiting, the vast majority of abortions after the first 12 weeks." *Id.,* at 79. Here the Act allows, among other means, a commonly used and generally accepted method, so it does not construct a substantial obstacle to the abortion right.

In reaching the conclusion the Act does not require a health exception we reject certain arguments made by the parties on both sides of these cases. On the one hand, the Attorney General urges us to uphold the Act on the basis of the congressional findings alone. . . . Although we review congressional factfinding under a deferential standard, we do not in the circumstances here place dispositive weight on Congress' findings. The Court retains an independent constitutional duty to review factual findings where constitutional rights are at stake. . . .

As respondents have noted, and the District Courts recognized, some recitations in the Act are factually incorrect. . . . Whether or not accurate at the time, some of the important findings have been superseded. Two examples suffice. Congress determined no medical schools provide instruction on the prohibited procedure. Congressional Findings (14)(B), in notes following 18 U. S. C. §1531 (2000 ed., Supp. IV), p. 769. The testimony in the District Courts, however, demonstrated intact D&E is taught at medical schools. . . . Congress also found there existed a medical consensus that the prohibited procedure is never medically necessary. Congressional Findings (1), in notes following 18 U. S. C. §1531 (2000 ed., Supp. IV), p. 767. The evidence presented in the District Courts contradicts that conclusion. See, *e.g., Carhart, supra,* at 1012–1015; *Nat. Abortion Federation, supra,* at 488–489; *Planned Parenthood, supra,* at 1025–1026. Uncritical deference to Congress' factual findings in these cases is inappropriate.

On the other hand, relying on the Court's opinion in *Stenberg,* respondents contend that an abortion regulation must contain a health exception "if 'substantial medical authority supports the proposition that banning a particular procedure could endanger women's health.'" Brief for Respondents in No. 05–380, p. 19 (quoting 530 U. S., at 938); see also Brief for Respondent Planned Parenthood et al. in No. 05–1382, at 12 (same). As illustrated by respondents' arguments and the decisions of the Courts of Appeals, *Stenberg* has been interpreted to leave no margin of error for legislatures to act in the face of medical uncertainty. *Carhart,* 413 F. 3d, at 796; *Planned Parenthood,* 435 F. 3d, at 1173; see also *Nat. Abortion Federation,* 437 F. 3d, at 296 (Walker, C. J., concurring) (explaining the standard under *Stenberg* "is a virtually insurmountable evidentiary hurdle").

A zero tolerance policy would strike down legitimate abortion regulations, like the present one, if some part of the medical community were disinclined to follow the proscription. This is too exacting a standard to impose on the legislative power, exercised in this instance under the Commerce Clause, to regulate the medical profession. Considerations of marginal safety, including the balance of risks, are within the legislative competence when the regulation is rational and in pursuit of legitimate ends. When standard medical options are available, mere convenience does not suffice to displace them; and if some procedures have different risks than others, it does not follow that the State is altogether barred from imposing reasonable regulations. The Act is not invalid on its face where there is uncertainty over whether the barred procedure is ever necessary to preserve a woman's health, given the availability of other abortion procedures that are considered to be safe alternatives. . . .

❧❀❧

Respondents have not demonstrated that the Act, as a facial matter, is void for vagueness, or that it imposes an undue burden on a woman's right to abortion based on its overbreadth or lack of a health exception. For these reasons the judgments of the Courts of Appeals for the Eighth and Ninth Circuits are reversed.

It is so ordered.

Ruth Bader Ginsburg  **NO**

Minority Opinion,
Gonzales v. Carhart

JUSTICE GINSBURG, with whom JUSTICE STEVENS, JUSTICE SOUTER, and JUSTICE BREYER join, dissenting.

In *Planned Parenthood of Southeastern Pa.* v. *Casey,* 505 U. S. 833, 844 (1992), the Court declared that "[l]iberty finds no refuge in a jurisprudence of doubt." There was, the Court said, an "imperative" need to dispel doubt as to "the meaning and reach" of the Court's 7-to-2 judgment, rendered nearly two decades earlier in *Roe* v. *Wade,* 410 U. S. 113 (1973). Responsive to that need, the Court endeavored to provide secure guidance to "[s]tate and federal courts as well as legislatures throughout the Union," by defining "the rights of the woman and the legitimate authority of the State respecting the termination of pregnancies by abortion procedures." *Ibid.*

Taking care to speak plainly, the *Casey* Court restated and reaffirmed *Roe*'s essential holding. 505 U. S., at 845–846. First, the Court addressed the type of abortion regulation permissible prior to fetal viability. It recognized "the right of the woman to choose to have an abortion before viability and to obtain it without undue interference from the State." *Id.,* at 846. Second, the Court acknowledged "the State's power to restrict abortions *after fetal viability,* if the law contains exceptions for pregnancies which endanger the woman's life *or health.*" *Ibid.* (emphasis added). Third, the Court confirmed that "the State has legitimate interests from the outset of the pregnancy in protecting *the health of the woman* and the life of the fetus that may become a child." *Ibid.* (emphasis added).

In reaffirming *Roe,* the *Casey* Court described the centrality of "the decision whether to bear . . . a child," *Eisenstadt* v. *Baird,* 405 U. S. 438, 453 (1972), to a woman's "dignity and autonomy," her "personhood" and "destiny," her "conception of . . . her place in society." 505 U. S., at 851–852. Of signal importance here, the *Casey* Court stated with unmistakable clarity that state regulation of access to abortion procedures, even after viability, must protect "the health of the woman." *Id.,* at 846.

Seven years ago, in *Stenberg* v. *Carhart,* 530 U. S. 914 (2000), the Court invalidated a Nebraska statute criminalizing the performance of a medical procedure that, in the political arena, has been dubbed "partial-birth abortion."[1]

From Minority Opinion, Gonzales v. Carhart, U.S. Supreme Court, April 19, 2007.

With fidelity to the *Roe-Casey* line of precedent, the Court held the Nebraska statute unconstitutional in part because it lacked the requisite protection for the preservation of a woman's health. . . .

Today's decision is alarming. It refuses to take *Casey* and *Stenberg* seriously. It tolerates, indeed applauds, federal intervention to ban nationwide a procedure found necessary and proper in certain cases by the American College of Obstetricians and Gynecologists (ACOG). It blurs the line, firmly drawn in *Casey,* between previability and postviability abortions. And, for the first time since *Roe,* the Court blesses a prohibition with no exception safeguarding a woman's health.

I dissent from the Court's disposition. Retreating from prior rulings that abortion restrictions cannot be imposed absent an exception safeguarding a woman's health, the Court upholds an Act that surely would not survive under the close scrutiny that previously attended state-decreed limitations on a woman's reproductive choices.

I

A

As *Casey* comprehended, at stake in cases challenging abortion restrictions is a woman's "control over her [own] destiny." 505 U. S., at 869 (plurality opinion). . . . "There was a time, not so long ago," when women were "regarded as the center of home and family life, with attendant special responsibilities that precluded full and independent legal status under the Constitution." *Id.,* at 896–897 (quoting *Hoyt* v. *Florida,* 368 U. S. 57, 62 (1961)). Those views, this Court made clear in *Casey,* "are no longer consistent with our understanding of the family, the individual, or the Constitution." 505 U. S., at 897. Women, it is now acknowledged, have the talent, capacity, and right "to participate equally in the economic and social life of the Nation." *Id.,* at 856. Their ability to realize their full potential, the Court recognized, is intimately connected to "their ability to control their reproductive lives." *Ibid.* Thus, legal challenges to undue restrictions on abortion procedures do not seek to vindicate some generalized notion of privacy; rather, they center on a woman's autonomy to determine her life's course, and thus to enjoy equal citizenship stature. . . .

In keeping with this comprehension of the right to reproductive choice, the Court has consistently required that laws regulating abortion, at any stage of pregnancy and in all cases, safeguard a woman's health.

We have thus ruled that a State must avoid subjecting women to health risks not only where the pregnancy itself creates danger, but also where state regulation forces women to resort to less safe methods of abortion. See *Planned Parenthood of Central Mo.* v. *Danforth,* 428 U. S. 52, 79 (1976) (holding unconstitutional a ban on a method of abortion that "force[d] a woman . . . to terminate her pregnancy by methods more dangerous to her health"). See also *Stenberg,* 530 U. S., at 931 ("[Our cases] make clear that a risk to . . . women's health is the same whether it happens to arise from regulating a particular method of abortion, or from barring abortion entirely."). Indeed, we have applied the rule that abortion regulation must safeguard a woman's health to the particular procedure at issue here—intact dilation and evacuation (D&E).

In *Stenberg,* we expressly held that a statute banning intact D&E was unconstitutional in part because it lacked a health exception. We noted that there existed a "division of medical opinion" about the relative safety of intact D&E, but we made clear that as long as "substantial medical authority supports the proposition that banning a particular abortion procedure could endanger women's health," a health exception is required, *id.,* at 938. We explained:

> "The word 'necessary' in *Casey's* phrase 'necessary, in appropriate medical judgment, for the preservation of the life or health of the [pregnant woman],' cannot refer to an absolute necessity or to absolute proof. Medical treatments and procedures are often considered appropriate (or inappropriate) in light of estimated comparative health risks (and health benefits) in particular cases. Neither can that phrase require unanimity of medical opinion. Doctors often differ in their estimation of comparative health risks and appropriate treatment. And *Casey's* words 'appropriate medical judgment' must embody the judicial need to tolerate responsible differences of medical opinion . . . ." *Id.,* at 937 (citation omitted).

Thus, we reasoned, division in medical opinion "at most means uncertainty, a factor that signals the presence of risk, not its absence." *Ibid.* "[A] statute that altogether forbids [intact D&E]. . . . consequently must contain a health exception." *Id.,* at 938. . . .

B

In 2003, a few years after our ruling in *Stenberg,* Congress passed the Partial-Birth Abortion Ban Act—without an exception for women's health.[2] . . . The congressional findings on which the Partial-Birth Abortion Ban Act rests do not withstand inspection, as the lower courts have determined and this Court is obliged to concede. . . . See *National Abortion Federation* v. *Ashcroft,* 330 F. Supp. 2d 436, 482 (SDNY 2004) ("Congress did not . . . carefully consider the evidence before arriving at its findings."), aff'd *sub nom. National Abortion Federation* v. *Gonzales,* 437 F. 3d 278 (CA2 2006). See also *Planned Parenthood Federation of Am.* v. *Ashcroft,* 320 F. Supp. 2d 957, 1019 (ND Cal. 2004) ("[N]one of the six physicians who testified before Congress had ever performed an intact D&E. Several did not provide abortion services at all; and one was not even an obgyn. . . . [T]he oral testimony before Congress was not only unbalanced, but intentionally polemic."), aff'd, 435 F. 3d 1163 (CA9 2006); *Carhart* v. *Ashcroft,* 331 F. Supp. 2d 805, 1011 (Neb. 2004) ("Congress arbitrarily relied upon the opinions of doctors who claimed to have no (or very little) recent and relevant experience with surgical abortions, and disregarded the views of doctors who had significant and relevant experience with those procedures."), aff'd, 413 F. 3d 791 (CA8 2005).

Many of the Act's recitations are incorrect. . . . For example, Congress determined that no medical schools provide instruction on intact D&E. . . . But in fact, numerous leading medical schools teach the procedure. . . .

More important, Congress claimed there was a medical consensus that the banned procedure is never necessary. . . . But the evidence "very clearly demonstrate[d] the opposite." *Planned Parenthood,* 320 F. Supp. 2d, at 1025. See also *Carhart,* 331 F. Supp. 2d, at 1008–1009 ("[T]here was no evident consensus in the record that Congress compiled. There was, however, a substantial body of medical opinion presented to Congress in opposition. If anything . . . the congressional record establishes that there was a 'consensus' in favor of the banned procedure."); *National Abortion Federation,* 330 F. Supp. 2d, at 488 ("The congressional record itself undermines [Congress'] finding" that there is a medical consensus that intact D&E "is never medically necessary and should be prohibited." (internal quotation marks omitted)).

Similarly, Congress found that "[t]here is no credible medical evidence that partial-birth abortions are safe or are safer than other abortion procedures." Congressional Findings (14)(B), in notes following 18 U. S. C. §1531 (2000 ed., Supp. IV), p. 769. But the congressional record includes letters from numerous individual physicians stating that pregnant women's health would be jeopardized under the Act, as well as statements from nine professional associations, including ACOG, the American Public Health Association, and the California Medical Association, attesting that intact D&E carries meaningful safety advantages over other methods. See *National Abortion Federation,* 330 F. Supp. 2d, at 490. See also *Planned Parenthood,* 320 F. Supp. 2d, at 1021 ("Congress in its findings . . . chose to disregard the statements by ACOG and other medical organizations."). No comparable medical groups supported the ban. In fact, "all of the government's own witnesses disagreed with many of the specific congressional findings." *Id.,* at 1024.

C

In contrast to Congress, the District Courts made findings after full trials at which all parties had the opportunity to present their best evidence. The courts had the benefit of "much more extensive medical and scientific evidence . . . concerning the safety and necessity of intact D&Es." *Planned Parenthood,* 320 F. Supp. 2d, at 1014. . . .

During the District Court trials, "numerous" "extraordinarily accomplished" and "very experienced" medical experts explained that, in certain circumstances and for certain women, intact D&E is safer than alternative procedures and necessary to protect women's health. *Carhart,* 331 F. Supp. 2d, at 1024–1027; see *Planned Parenthood,* 320 F. Supp. 2d, at 1001 ("[A]ll of the doctors who actually perform intact D&Es concluded that in their opinion and clinical judgment, intact D&Es remain the safest option for certain individual women under certain individual health circumstances, and are significantly safer for these women than other abortion techniques, and are thus medically necessary."); cf. *ante,* at 31 ("Respondents presented evidence that intact D&E may be the safest method of abortion, for reasons similar to those adduced in *Stenberg*.").

According to the expert testimony plaintiffs introduced, the safety advantages of intact D&E are marked for women with certain medical conditions, for example, uterine scarring, bleeding disorders, heart disease, or compromised immune systems. . . . Further, plaintiffs' experts testified that intact D&E is significantly safer for women with certain pregnancy-related conditions, such as placenta previa and accreta, and for women carrying fetuses with certain abnormalities, such as severe hydrocephalus. . . .

Based on thoroughgoing review of the trial evidence and the congressional record, each of the District Courts to consider the issue rejected Congress' findings as unreasonable and not supported by the evidence. . . . The trial courts concluded, in contrast to Congress' findings, that "significant medical authority supports the proposition that in some circumstances, [intact D&E] is the safest procedure." *Id.*, at 1033. . . .

The District Courts' findings merit this Court's respect. Today's opinion supplies no reason to reject those findings. Nevertheless, despite the District Courts' appraisal of the weight of the evidence, and in undisguised conflict with *Stenberg,* the Court asserts that the Partial-Birth Abortion Ban Act can survive "when . . . medical uncertainty persists." *Ante,* at 33. This assertion is bewildering. Not only does it defy the Court's longstanding precedent affirming the necessity of a health exception, with no carve-out for circumstances of medical uncertainty, see *supra,* at 4–5; it gives short shrift to the records before us, carefully canvassed by the District Courts. Those records indicate that "the majority of highly-qualified experts on the subject believe intact D&E to be the safest, most appropriate procedure under certain circumstances." *Planned Parenthood,* 320 F. Supp. 2d, at 1034. . . .

The Court acknowledges some of this evidence, *ante,* at 31, but insists that, because some witnesses disagreed with the ACOG and other experts' assessment of risk, the Act can stand. . . . In this insistence, the Court brushes under the rug the District Courts' well-supported findings that the physicians who testified that intact D&E is never necessary to preserve the health of a woman had slim authority for their opinions. They had no training for, or personal experience with, the intact D&E procedure, and many performed abortions only on rare occasions. See *Planned Parenthood,* 320 F. Supp. 2d, at 980; *Carhart,* 331 F. Supp. 2d, at 1025; cf. *National Abortion Federation,* 330 F. Supp. 2d, at 462–464. Even indulging the assumption that the Government witnesses were equally qualified to evaluate the relative risks of abortion procedures, their testimony could not erase the "significant medical authority support[ing] the proposition that in some circumstances, [intact D&E] would be the safest procedure." *Stenberg,* 530 U. S., at 932.

II

A

The Court offers flimsy and transparent justifications for upholding a nationwide ban on intact D&E *sans* any exception to safeguard a women's health. Today's ruling, the Court declares, advances "a premise central to [*Casey*'s] conclusion"— *i.e.,* the Government's "legitimate and substantial interest in preserving and promoting fetal life." *Ante,* at 14. But the Act scarcely furthers that interest: The law saves not a single fetus from destruction, for it targets only a *method* of performing abortion. . . . In short, the Court upholds a law that, while doing nothing to "preserv[e] . . . fetal life," *ante,* at 14, bars a woman from choosing intact D&E although her doctor "reasonably believes [that procedure] will best protect [her]." *Stenberg,* 530 U. S., at 946 (STEVENS, J., concurring).

As another reason for upholding the ban, the Court emphasizes that the Act does not proscribe the nonintact D&E procedure. See *ante,* at 34. But why not, one might ask. Nonintact D&E could equally be characterized as "brutal," *ante,* at 26, involving as it does "tear[ing] [a fetus] apart" and "ripp[ing] off" its limbs, *ante,* at 4, 6. "[T]he notion that either of these two equally gruesome procedures . . . is more akin to infanticide than the other, or that the State furthers any legitimate interest by banning one but not the other, is simply irrational." *Stenberg,* 530 U. S., at 946–947 (STEVENS, J., concurring).

Delivery of an intact, albeit nonviable, fetus warrants special condemnation, the Court maintains, because a fetus that is not dismembered resembles an infant. . . . But so, too, does a fetus delivered intact after it is terminated by injection a day or two before the surgical evacuation, . . . or a fetus delivered through medical induction or cesarean. . . . Yet, the availability of those procedures—along with D&E by dismemberment—the Court says, saves the ban on intact D&E from a declaration of unconstitutionality. . . . Never mind that the procedures deemed acceptable might put a woman's health at greater risk. . . .

Ultimately, the Court admits that "moral concerns" are at work, concerns that could yield prohibitions on any abortion. . . . ("Congress could . . . conclude that the type of abortion proscribed by the Act requires specific regulation because it implicates additional ethical and moral concerns that justify a special prohibition."). Notably, the concerns expressed are untethered to any ground genuinely serving the Government's interest in preserving life. By allowing such concerns to carry the day and case, overriding fundamental rights, the Court dishonors our precedent. See, *e.g., Casey,* 505 U. S., at 850 ("Some of us as individuals find abortion offensive to our most basic principles of morality, but that cannot control our decision. Our obligation is to define the liberty of all, not to mandate our own moral code."); *Lawrence* v. *Texas,* 539 U. S. 558, 571 (2003) (Though "[f]or many persons [objections to homosexual conduct] are not trivial concerns but profound and deep convictions accepted as ethical and moral principles," the power of the State may not be used "to enforce these views on the whole society through operation of the criminal law." (citing *Casey,* 505 U. S., at 850)).

Revealing in this regard, the Court invokes an antiabortion shibboleth for which it concededly has no reliable evidence: Women who have abortions come to regret their choices, and consequently suffer from "[s]evere depression and loss of esteem." *Ante,* at 29.[3] Because of women's fragile emotional state and because of the "bond of love the mother has for her child," the Court worries, doctors may withhold information about the nature of the intact D&E procedure. *Ante,* at 28–29.[4] The solution the Court approves, then, is *not* to require doctors to inform women, accurately and adequately, of the different procedures and their attendant risks. Cf. *Casey,* 505 U. S., at 873 (plurality opinion) ("States are free to enact laws to provide a reasonable framework for a woman to make a decisison that has such profound and lasting meaning.").

Instead, the Court deprives women of the right to make an autonomous choice, even at the expense of their safety.[5]

This way of thinking reflects ancient notions about women's place in the family and under the Constitution—ideas that have long since been discredited. Compare, *e.g., Muller* v. *Oregon,* 208 U. S. 412, 422–423 (1908) ("protective" legislation imposing hours-of-work limitations on women only held permissible in view of women's "physical structure and a proper discharge of her maternal funct[ion]"); *Bradwell* v. *State,* 16 Wall. 130, 141 (1873) (Bradley, J., concurring) ("Man is, or should be, woman's protector and defender. The natural and proper timidity and delicacy which belongs to the female sex evidently unfits it for many of the occupations of civil life. . . . The paramount destiny and mission of woman are to fulfil[l] the noble and benign offices of wife and mother."), with *United States* v. *Virginia,* 518 U. S. 515, 533, 542, n. 12 (1996) (State may not rely on "overbroad generalizations" about the "talents, capacities, or preferences" of women; "[s]uch judgments have . . . impeded . . . women's progress toward full citizenship stature throughout our Nation's history"); *Califano* v. *Goldfarb,* 430 U. S. 199, 207 (1977) (gender-based Social Security classification rejected because it rested on "archaic and overbroad generalizations" "such as assumptions as to [women's] dependency" (internal quotation marks omitted)).

Though today's majority may regard women's feelings on the matter as "self-evident," *ante,* at 29, this Court has repeatedly confirmed that "[t]he destiny of the woman must be shaped . . . on her own conception of her spiritual imperatives and her place in society." *Casey,* 505 U. S., at 852. See also *id.,* at 877 (plurality opinion) ("[M]eans chosen by the State to further the interest in potential life must be calculated to inform the woman's free choice, not hinder it."); *supra,* at 3–4.

B

In cases on a "woman's liberty to determine whether to [continue] her pregnancy," this Court has identified viability as a critical consideration. See *Casey,* 505 U. S., at 869–870 (plurality opinion). "[T]here is no line [more workable] than viability," the Court explained in *Casey,* for viability is "the time at which there is a realistic possibility of maintaining and nourishing a life outside the womb, so that the independent existence of the second life can in reason and all fairness be the object of state protection that now overrides the rights of the woman. . . . In some broad sense it might be said that a woman who fails to act before viability has consented to the State's intervention on behalf of the developing child." *Id.,* at 870.

Today, the Court blurs that line, maintaining that "[t]he Act [legitimately] appl[ies] both previability and postviability because . . . a fetus is a living organism while within the womb, whether or not it is viable outside the womb." *Ante,* at 17. Instead of drawing the line at viability, the Court refers to Congress' purpose to differentiate "abortion and infanticide" based not on whether a fetus can survive outside the womb, but on where a fetus is anatomically located when a particular medical procedure is performed. . . .

One wonders how long a line that saves no fetus from destruction will hold in face of the Court's "moral concerns." . . . The Court's hostility to the right *Roe* and *Casey* secured is not concealed. Throughout, the opinion refers to obstetrician-gynecologists and surgeons who perform abortions not by the titles of their medical specialties, but by the pejorative label "abortion doctor." . . . A fetus is described as an "unborn child," and as a "baby," . . . second-trimester, previability abortions are referred to as "late-term," . . . and the reasoned medical judgments of highly trained doctors are dismissed as "preferences" motivated by "mere convenience." . . . Instead of the heightened scrutiny we have previously applied, the Court determines that a "rational" ground is enough to uphold the Act, *ante,* at 28, 37. And, most troubling, *Casey*'s principles, confirming the continuing vitality of "the essential holding of *Roe,*" are merely "assume[d]" for the moment, *ante,* at 15, 31, rather than "retained" or "reaffirmed," *Casey,* 505 U. S., at 846.

III

A

The Court further confuses our jurisprudence when it declares that "facial attacks" are not permissible in "these circumstances," *i.e.,* where medical uncertainty exists. *Ante,* at 37; see *ibid.* ("In an as-applied challenge the nature of the medical risk can be better quantified and balanced than in a facial attack."). This holding is perplexing given that, in materially identical circumstances we held that a statute lacking a health exception was unconstitutional on its face. *Stenberg,* 530 U. S., at 930; see *id.,* at 937 (in facial challenge, law held unconstitutional because "significant body of medical opinion believes [the] procedure may bring with it greater safety for *some patients*" (emphasis added)). . . .

Without attempting to distinguish *Stenberg* and earlier decisions, the majority asserts that the Act survives review because respondents have not shown that the ban on intact D&E would be unconstitutional "in a large fraction of relevant cases." *Ante,* at 38 (citing *Casey,* 505 U. S., at 895). But *Casey* makes clear that, in determining whether any restriction poses an undue burden on a "large fraction" of women, the relevant class is *not* "all women," nor "all pregnant women," nor even all women "seeking abortions." 505 U. S., at 895. Rather, a provision restricting access to abortion, "must be judged by reference to those [women] for whom it is an actual rather than an irrelevant restriction," *ibid.* Thus the absence of a health exception burdens *all* women for whom it is relevant—women who, in the judgment of their doctors, require an intact D&E because other procedures would place their health at risk. . . . It makes no sense to conclude that this facial challenge fails because respondents have not shown that a health exception is necessary for a large fraction of second-trimester abortions, including those for which a health exception is unnecessary: The very purpose of a health *exception* is to protect women in *exceptional* cases.

B

If there is anything at all redemptive to be said of today's opinion, it is that the Court is not willing to foreclose entirely a constitutional challenge to the Act. "The Act is open," the Court states, "to a proper as-applied challenge in a discrete case.". . . But the Court offers no clue on what a "proper" lawsuit might look like. . . . Nor does the Court explain why the injunctions ordered by the District Courts should not remain in place, trimmed only to exclude instances in which another procedure would safeguard a woman's health at least equally well. Surely the Court cannot mean that no suit may be brought until a woman's health is immediately jeopardized by the ban on intact D&E. A woman "suffer[ing] from medical complications," *ante,* at 38, needs access to the medical procedure at once and cannot wait for the judicial process to unfold. See *Ayotte,* 546 U. S., at 328.

The Court appears, then, to contemplate another lawsuit by the initiators of the instant actions. In such a second round, the Court suggests, the challengers could succeed upon demonstrating that "in discrete and well-defined instances a particular condition has or is likely to occur in which the procedure prohibited by the Act must be used." *Ante,* at 37. One may anticipate that such a preenforcement challenge will be mounted swiftly, to ward off serious, sometimes irremediable harm, to women whose health would be endangered by the intact D&E prohibition.

The Court envisions that in an as-applied challenge, "the nature of the medical risk can be better quantified and balanced." . . . But it should not escape notice that the record already includes hundreds and hundreds of pages of testimony identifying "discrete and well-defined instances" in which recourse to an intact D&E would better protect the health of women with particular conditions. . . . Record evidence also documents that medical exigencies, unpredictable in advance, may indicate to a well-trained doctor that intact D&E is the safest procedure. . . .

The Court's allowance only of an "as-applied challenge in a discrete case," *ante,* at 38—jeopardizes women's health and places doctors in an untenable position. Even if courts were able to carve-out exceptions through piecemeal litigation for "discrete and well-defined instances," *ante,* at 37, women whose circumstances have not been anticipated by prior litigation could well be left unprotected. In treating those women, physicians would risk criminal prosecution, conviction, and imprisonment if they exercise their best judgment as to the safest medical procedure for their patients. The Court is thus gravely mistaken to conclude that narrow as-applied challenges are "the proper manner to protect the health of the woman." . . .

IV

As the Court wrote in *Casey,* "overruling *Roe's* central holding would not only reach an unjustifiable result under principles of *stare decisis,* but would seriously weaken the Court's capacity to exercise the judicial power and to function as the Supreme Court of a Nation dedicated to the rule of law." 505 U. S., at 865. "[T]he very concept of the rule of law underlying our own Constitution requires such continuity over time that a respect for precedent is, by definition, indispensable." *Id.*, at 854. See also *id.*, at 867 ("[T]o overrule under fire in the absence of the most compelling reason to reexamine a watershed decision would subvert the Court's legitimacy beyond any serious question.").

Though today's opinion does not go so far as to discard *Roe* or *Casey*, the Court, differently composed than it was when we last considered a restrictive abortion regulation, is hardly faithful to our earlier invocations of "the rule of law" and the "principles of *stare decisis.*" Congress imposed a ban despite our clear prior holdings that the State cannot proscribe an abortion procedure when its use is necessary to protect a woman's health. . . . Although Congress' findings could not withstand the crucible of trial, the Court defers to the legislative override of our Constitution-based rulings. . . . A decision so at odds with our jurisprudence should not have staying power.

In sum, the notion that the Partial-Birth Abortion Ban Act furthers any legitimate governmental interest is, quite simply, irrational. The Court's defense of the statute provides no saving explanation. In candor, the Act, and the Court's defense of it, cannot be understood as anything other than an effort to chip away at a right declared again and again by this Court—and with increasing comprehension of its centrality to women's lives. . . . When "a statute burdens constitutional rights and all that can be said on its behalf is that it is the vehicle that legislators have chosen for expressing their hostility to those rights, the burden is undue." *Stenberg*, 530 U. S., at 952 (GINSBURG, J., concurring) (quoting *Hope Clinic* v. *Ryan*, 195 F. 3d 857, 881 (CA7 1999) (Posner, C. J., dissenting)).

⋅⟨⊙⟩⋅

For the reasons stated, I dissent from the Court's disposition and would affirm the judgments before us for review.

Notes

1. The term "partial-birth abortion" is neither recognized in the medical literature nor used by physicians who perform second-trimester abortions. See *Planned Parenthood Federation of Am.* v. *Ashcroft*, 320 F. Supp. 2d 957, 964 (ND Cal. 2004), aff'd, 435 F. 3d 1163 (CA9 2006). The medical community refers to the procedure as either dilation & extraction (D&X) or intact dilation and evacuation (intact D&E). See, *e.g., ante,* at 5; *Stenberg* v. *Carhart*, 530 U. S. 914, 927 (2000).

2. The Act's sponsors left no doubt that their intention was to nullify our ruling in *Stenberg*, 530 U. S. 914. See, *e.g.,* 149 Cong. Rec. 5731 (2003) (statement of Sen. Santorum) ("Why are we here? We are here because the Supreme Court defended the indefensible. . . . We have responded to the Supreme Court."). See also 148 Cong. Rec. 14273 (2002) (statement of Rep. Linder) (rejecting proposition that Congress has "no right to legislate a ban on this horrible practice because the Supreme Court says [it] cannot").

3. The Court is surely correct that, for most women, abortion is a painfully difficult decision. See *ante,* at 28. But "neither the weight of the scientific evidence to date nor the observable reality of 33 years of legal abortion in the United States comports with the idea that having an abortion is any more dangerous to a woman's long-term mental health than delivering and parenting a child that she did not intend to have . . . ." Cohen, Abortion and Mental Health: Myths and Realities, 9 Guttmacher Policy Rev. 8 (2006); see generally Bazelon, Is There a Post-Abortion Syndrome? N. Y. Times Magazine, Jan. 21, 2007, p. 40. See also, *e.g.,* American Psychological Association, APA Briefing Paper on the Impact of Abortion (2005) (rejecting theory of a post-abortion syndrome and stating that "[a]ccess to legal abortion to terminate an unwanted pregnancy is vital to safeguard both the physical and mental health of women"); Schmiege & Russo, Depression and Unwanted First Pregnancy: Longitudinal Cohort Study, 331 British Medical J. 1303 (2005) (finding no credible evidence that choosing to terminate an unwanted first pregnancy contributes to risk of subsequent depression); Gilchrist, Hannaford, Frank, & Kay, Termination of Pregnancy and Psychiatric Morbidity, 167 British J. of Psychiatry 243, 247–248 (1995) (finding, in a cohort of more than 13,000 women, that the rate of psychiatric disorder was no higher among women who terminated pregnancy than among those who carried pregnancy to term); Stodland, The Myth of the Abortion Trauma Syndrome, 268 JAMA 2078, 2079 (1992) ("Scientific studies indicate that legal abortion results in fewer deleterious sequelae for women compared with other possible outcomes of unwanted pregnancy. There is no evidence of an abortion trauma syndrome."); American Psychological Association, Council Policy Manual: (N)(I)(3), Public Interest (1989) (declaring assertions about widespread severe negative psychological effects of abortion to be "without fact"). But see Cougle, Reardon, & Coleman, Generalized Anxiety Following Unintended Pregnancies Resolved Through Childbirth and Abortion: A Cohort Study of the 1995 National Survey of Family Growth, 19 J. Anxiety Disorders 137, 142 (2005) (advancing theory of a postabortion syndrome but acknowledging that "no causal relationship between pregnancy outcome and anxiety could be determined" from study); Reardon et al., Psychiatric Admissions of Low-Income Women following Abortion and Childbirth, 168 Canadian Medical Assn. J. 1253, 1255–1256 (May 13, 2003) (concluding that psychiatric admission rates were higher for women who had an abortion compared with women who delivered); cf. Major, Psychological Implications of Abortion—Highly Charged and Rife with Misleading Research, 168 Canadian Medical Assn. J. 1257, 1258 (May 13, 2003) (critiquing Reardon study for failing to control for a host of differences between women in the delivery and abortion samples).

4. Notwithstanding the "bond of love" women often have with their children, see *ante,* at 28, not all pregnancies, this Court has recognized, are wanted, or even the product of consensual activity. See *Casey,* 505 U. S., at 891 ("[O]n an average day in the United States, nearly 11,000 women are severely assaulted by their male partners. Many of these incidents involve sexual assault."). See also Glander, Moore, Michielutte, & Parsons, The Prevalence of Domestic Violence Among Women Seeking Abortion, 91 Obstetrics & Gynecology 1002 (1998); Holmes, Resnick, Kilpatrick, & Best, Rape-Related Pregnancy; Estimates and Descriptive Characteristics from a National Sample of Women, 175 Am. J. Obstetrics & Gynecology 320 (Aug. 1996).

5. Eliminating or reducing women's reproductive choices is manifestly *not* a means of protecting them. When safe abortion procedures cease to be an option, many women seek other means to end unwanted or coerced pregnancies. See, *e.g.,* World Health Organization, Unsafe Abortion: Global and Regional Estimates of the Incidence of Unsafe Abortion and Associated Mortality in 2000, pp. 3, 16 (4th ed. 2004) ("Restrictive legislation is associated with a

high incidence of unsafe abortion" worldwide; unsafe abortion represents 13% of all "maternal" deaths); Henshaw, Unintended Pregnancy and Abortion: A Public Health Perspective, in A Clinician's Guide to Medical and Surgical Abortion 11, 19 (M. Paul, E. Lichtenberg, L. Borgatta, D. Grimes, & P. Stubblefield eds. 1999) ("Before legalization, large numbers of women in the United States died from unsafe abortions."); H. Boonstra, R. Gold, C. Richards, & L. Finer, Abortion in Women's Lives 13, and fig. 2.2 (2006) ("as late as 1965, illegal abortion still accounted for an estimated . . . 17% of all officially reported pregnancy-related deaths"; "[d]eaths from abortion declined dramatically after legalization").

POSTSCRIPT

Is It Constitutional to Ban Partial-Birth Abortions Without Providing for an Exception to Protect the Health of the Mother?

In claiming that the Court's decision in *Gonzales v. Carhart* is "in undisguised conflict with *Stenberg*" and "surely would not survive under the close scrutiny that previously attended state-decreed limitations on a woman's reproductive choices," Justice Bader Ginsburg hints at one factor that could explain the Court's divergent opinions in these two cases: the change in the composition of the Supreme Court between 2000 and 2007. In 2005, Justice Sandra Day O'Connor, who was generally pro-choice and even wrote the Court's decision in *Casey,* announced she was planning to retire. She was soon replaced by Justice Samuel Alito, who sided with the Court's majority in *Gonzales v. Carhart.* Former Justice Potter Stewart once lamented that a "basic change in the law upon a ground no firmer than a change in our membership invites the popular misconception that this institution is little different from the two political branches of the Government. No misconception could do more lasting injury to this Court and to the system of law which it is our abiding mission to serve" (Dissenting Opinion, *Michell v. W. T. Grant Co.,* 416 US 600, 1974). The need to maintain a consistent approach to legal issues and downplay the effect of justices' own value systems on its decision-making process is part of the reason the Supreme Court has adopted the principle of stare decisis as one of its central tenets.

Stare decisis, Latin for "to stand by decisions," is the concept that the Court will restrain itself when possible from overruling previous decisions that have set important legal precedents. As former Justice Byron White once described it, "The rule of stare decisis is essential if case-by-case judicial decisionmaking is to be reconciled with the principle of the rule of law, for when governing legal standards are open to revision in every case, deciding cases becomes a mere exercise of judicial will, with arbitrary and unpredictable results" (Dissenting Opinion, *Akron v. Akron Reproductive Health,* 462 US 416, 1983). According to Justice O'Connor in her *Casey* decision, stare decisis was a key reason why the Court should hesitate to overrule *Roe*:

> The obligation to follow precedent begins with necessity, and a contrary necessity marks its outer limit. . . . no judicial system could do society's work if it eyed each issue afresh in every case that raised it. . . . Indeed, the very concept of the rule of law underlying our own Constitution requires

such continuity over time that a respect for precedent is, by definition, indispensable.

Nevertheless, there are, of course, times when the Court has found it both prudent and necessary to overrule precedent, especially in constitutional cases. Whereas Congress can overcome the Court's judgments on statutory issues by passing new laws, the difficulty of amending the Constitution has made the Supreme Court more willing to review its constitutional holdings when previous decisions have proven difficult in practice or no longer seem defensible on principle. For instance, the Court has shown willingness to revisit periodically its decisions on what constitutes "cruel and unusual punishment" under the Eighth Amendment, citing as its justification former Chief Justice Warren's assertion that "the words of the Amendment are not precise. . . . their scope is not static. The Amendment must draw its meaning from the evolving standards of decency that mark the progress of a maturing society" (*Trop v. Dulles*, 356 US 86, 1958). Of course, one could make a similar pronouncement about many of the amendments to the Constitution, making the Supreme Court's determination of which of its decisions are worthy of adherence, and which should be overruled, an important part of its constitutional jurisprudence.

ISSUE 6

Are Restrictions on Physician-Assisted Suicide Constitutional?

YES: William H. Rehnquist, from Majority Opinion, *Washington et al. v. Glucksberg et al.,* U.S. Supreme Court (June 26, 1997)

NO: Stephen Reinhardt, from Majority Opinion, *Compassion in Dying v. State of Washington,* U.S. Supreme Court (1996)

ISSUE SUMMARY

YES: Supreme Court Chief Justice William H. Rehnquist rules that although patients have the right to refuse life-sustaining treatment, physician-assisted suicide is not constitutionally protected.

NO: Judge Stephen Reinhardt argues that forbidding physician-assisted suicide in the cases of competent, terminally ill patients violates the due process clause of the Constitution.

In 1990 the Supreme Court issued its landmark ruling in *Cruzan v. Director, Missouri Department of Health,* 497 U.S. 261 (1990). Nancy Beth Cruzan had sustained severe and irreversible injuries in an automobile accident; her condition was one commonly characterized as a "persistent vegetative state." She displayed no discernible cognitive functioning and was kept alive through the use of artificial hydration and feeding equipment. Four years after the accident, Nancy's parents began proceedings in a Missouri state trial court so that they could withdraw all artificial means of life support.

Cruzan was one of an estimated 10,000 persons in the United States in a vegetative state. She had left no explicit directions on whether or not she wanted to continue to be fed and receive treatment if she were ever to be in such a condition. Should her parents have been allowed to make life-and-death decisions under such circumstances? How clear should an incompetent person's wishes be before the parents are allowed to make a decision? The trial court granted the parents' request to withdraw life support. However, the State of Missouri intervened, claiming an "unqualified governmental interest in preserving the sanctity of human life." Although the state recognized the legal validity of "living wills," in which a person indicates what he or she would like done if the individual were no longer able to make treatment decisions, it argued that in the absence of a living will, "clear and convincing" evidence of the patient's wishes was required to authorize the removal of life-sustaining devices. Agreeing with the state, the Missouri Supreme Court reversed the trial court order directing the withdrawal of life-support equipment.

In *Cruzan* the U.S. Supreme Court granted *certiorari* to hear, for the first time, a constitutional question concerning a "right to die." Upholding the constitutionality of Missouri's evidentiary requirements, the decision of the Missouri Supreme Court was affirmed. Chief Justice William H. Rehnquist delivered the opinion of the Court and wrote that while a "right to die" might be exercised by an individual who was able to make his or her own decisions, "clear and convincing" evidence of the individual's wishes was needed before a court could allow parents or someone else to make a decision to stop treatment or care. The postscript to this issue describes what the consequences of this were for Cruzan and her parents.

The issues raised in the *Cruzan* case illustrate a basic distinction made by the law. The law prohibits active euthanasia, in which death results from some positive act, such as a lethal injection. "Mercy killings" fall into this category and can be prosecuted as acts of homicide. The law is more tolerant of passive euthanasia, in which death results from the failure to act or on the removal of life-saving equipment. This distinction is not always easy to apply, however.

YES

William H. Rehnquist

Majority Opinion

Washington *v.* Glucksberg

CHIEF JUSTICE REHNQUIST delivered the opinion of the Court.

The question presented in this case is whether Washington's prohibition against "causing" or "aiding" a suicide offends the Fourteenth Amendment to the United States Constitution. We hold that it does not.

It has always been a crime to assist a suicide in the State of Washington. In 1854, Washington's first Territorial Legislature outlawed "assisting another in the commission of self-murder." Today, Washington law provides: "A person is guilty of promoting a suicide attempt when he knowingly causes or aids another person to attempt suicide." Wash. Rev. Code 9A.36.060(1)(1994). "Promoting a suicide attempt" is a felony, punishable by up to five years' imprisonment and up to a $10,000 fine. §§ 9A.36.060(2) and 9A.20.021(1)(c). At the same time, Washington's Natural Death Act, enacted in 1979, states that the "withholding or withdrawal of life-sustaining treatment" at a patient's direction "shall not, for any purpose, constitute a suicide." Wash. Rev. Code § 70.122.070(1).[1]

Petitioners in this case are the State of Washington and its Attorney General. Respondents Harold Glucksberg, M.D., Abigail Halperin, M.D., Thomas A. Preston, M.D., and Peter Shalit, M.D., are physicians who practice in Washington. These doctors occasionally treat terminally ill, suffering patients, and declare that they would assist these patients in ending their lives if not for Washington's assisted-suicide ban. In January 1994, respondents, along with three gravely ill, pseudonymous plaintiffs who have since died and Compassion in Dying, a nonprofit organization that counsels people considering physician-assisted suicide, sued in the United States District Court, seeking a declaration that Wash. Rev. Code 9A.36.060(1) (1994) is, on its face, unconstitutional. *Compassion in Dying v. Washington, 850 F. Supp. 1454, 1459 (WD Wash. 1994).*

The plaintiffs asserted "the existence of a liberty interest protected by the Fourteenth Amendment which extends to a personal choice by a mentally competent, terminally ill adult to commit physician-assisted suicide." Relying primarily on *Planned Parenthood v. Casey, 505 U.S. 833 (1992),* and *Cruzan v. Director, Missouri Dept. of Health, 497 U.S. 261 (1990),* the District Court agreed, *850 F. Supp., at 1459–1462,* and concluded that Washington's assisted-suicide ban is unconstitutional because it "places an undue burden on the exercise of

---

From *Washington et al. v. Glucksberg et al.,* 117 S. Ct. 2258, 117 S. Ct. 2302, 1997 U.S. LEXIS 4039, 138 L. Ed. 2d 772 (1997). References, some notes, and some case citations omitted.

[that] constitutionally protected liberty interest." The District Court also decided that the Washington statute violated the Equal Protection Clause's requirement that "'all persons similarly situated . . . be treated alike.'"

A panel of the Court of Appeals for the Ninth Circuit reversed, emphasizing that "in the two hundred and five years of our existence no constitutional right to aid in killing oneself has ever been asserted and upheld by a court of final jurisdiction." *Compassion in Dying v. Washington, 49 F.3d 586, 591 (1995).* The Ninth Circuit reheard the case en banc, reversed the panel's decision, and affirmed the District Court. *Compassion in Dying v. Washington, 79 F.3d 790, 798 (1996).* Like the District Court, the en banc Court of Appeals emphasized our Casey and Cruzan decisions. The court also discussed what it described as "historical" and "current societal attitudes" toward suicide and assisted suicide, and concluded that "the Constitution encompasses a due process liberty interest in controlling the time and manner of one's death—that there is, in short, a constitutionally-recognized 'right to die.'" After "weighing and then balancing" this interest against Washington's various interests, the court held that the State's assisted-suicide ban was unconstitutional "as applied to terminally ill competent adults who wish to hasten their deaths with medication prescribed by their physicians." The court did not reach the District Court's equal-protection holding. We granted certiorari, and now reverse.

I

We begin, as we do in all due-process cases, by examining our Nation's history, legal traditions, and practices. In almost every State—indeed, in almost every western democracy—it is a crime to assist a suicide. The States' assisted-suicide bans are not innovations. Rather, they are longstanding expressions of the States' commitment to the protection and preservation of all human life.

More specifically, for over 700 years, the Anglo-American common-law tradition has punished or otherwise disapproved of both suicide and assisting suicide. In the 13th century, Henry de Bracton, one of the first legal-treatise writers, observed that "just as a man may commit felony by slaying another so may he do so by slaying himself." 2 Bracton on Laws and Customs of England 423 (f. 150) (G. Woodbine ed., S. Thorne transl., 1968). The real and personal property of one who killed himself to avoid conviction and punishment for a crime were forfeit to the king; however, thought Bracton, "if a man slays himself in weariness of life or because he is unwilling to endure further bodily pain . . . [only] his movable goods [were] confiscated." Thus, "the principle that suicide of a sane person, for whatever reason, was a punishable felony was . . . introduced into English common law."

For the most part, the early American colonies adopted the common-law approach. For example, the legislators of the Providence Plantations, which would later become Rhode Island, declared, in 1647, that "self-murder is by all agreed to be the most unnatural, and it is by this present Assembly declared, to be that, wherein he that doth it, kills himself out of a premeditated hatred against his own life or other humor: . . . his goods and chattels are the king's custom, but not his debts nor lands; but in case he be an infant, a lunatic, mad or distracted man, he forfeits nothing." The Earliest Acts and Laws of the Colony of Rhode Island and Providence Plantations 1647–1719, p. 19 (J. Cushing ed. 1977). Virginia also required ignominious burial for suicides, and their estates were forfeit to the crown. A. Scott, Criminal Law in Colonial Virginia 108, and n.93, 198, and n.15 (1930).

Over time, however, the American colonies abolished these harsh common-law penalties. William Penn abandoned the criminal-forfeiture sanction in Pennsylvania in 1701, and the other colonies (and later, the other States) eventually followed this example. *Cruzan, 497 U.S. at 294* (SCALIA, J., concurring). . . .

[T]he movement away from the common law's harsh sanctions did not represent an acceptance of suicide; rather, as Chief Justice Swift observed, this change reflected the growing consensus that it was unfair to punish the suicide's family for his wrongdoing. Nonetheless, although States moved away from Blackstone's treatment of suicide, courts continued to condemn it as a grave public wrong.

That suicide remained a grievous, though nonfelonious, wrong is confirmed by the fact that colonial and early state legislatures and courts did not retreat from prohibiting assisting suicide. Swift, in his early 19th century treatise on the laws of Connecticut, stated that "if one counsels another to commit suicide, and the other by reason of the advice kills himself, the advisor is guilty of murder as principal." 2 Z. Swift, A Digest of the Laws of the State of Connecticut 270 (1823). This was the well established common-law view.

And the prohibitions against assisting suicide never contained exceptions for those who were near death. Rather, "the life of those to whom life had become a burden—of those who [were] hopelessly diseased or fatally wounded—nay, even the lives of criminals condemned to death, [were] under the protection of law, equally as the lives of those who [were] in the full tide of life's enjoyment, and anxious to continue to live." *Blackburn v. State, 23 Ohio St. 146, 163 (1872).*

The earliest American statute explicitly to outlaw assisting suicide was enacted in New York in 1828, and many of the new States and Territories followed New York's example. Between 1857 and 1865, a New York commission led by Dudley Field drafted a criminal code that prohibited "aiding" a suicide and, specifically, "furnishing another person with any deadly weapon or poisonous drug, knowing that such person intends to use such weapon or drug in taking his own life." By the time the Fourteenth Amendment was ratified, it was a crime in most States to assist a suicide. The Field Penal Code was adopted in the Dakota Territory in 1877, in New York in 1881, and its language served as a model for several other western States' statutes in the late 19th and early 20th centuries. California, for example, codified its assisted-suicide prohibition in 1874, using language similar to the Field Code's. In this century, the Model Penal Code also prohibited "aiding" suicide, prompting many States to enact or revise their assisted-suicide bans. . . .

Though deeply rooted, the States' assisted-suicide bans have in recent years been reexamined and, generally, reaffirmed. Because of advances in medicine and technology, Americans today are increasingly likely to die in institutions, from chronic illnesses. Public concern and democratic action are therefore sharply focused on how best to protect dignity and independence at the end of life, with the result that there have been many significant changes in state laws and in the attitudes these laws reflect. Many States, for example, now permit "living wills," surrogate health-care decisionmaking, and the withdrawal or refusal of life-sustaining medical treatment. At the same time, however, voters and legislators continue for the most part to reaffirm their States' prohibitions on assisting suicide.

The Washington statute at issue in this case, Wash. Rev. Code § 9A.36.060 (1994), was enacted in 1975 as part of a revision of that State's criminal code. Four years later, Washington passed its Natural Death Act, which specifically stated that the "withholding or withdrawal of life-sustaining treatment . . . shall not, for any purpose, constitute a suicide" and that "nothing in this chapter shall be construed to condone, authorize, or approve mercy killing. . . ." In 1991, Washington voters rejected a ballot initiative which, had it passed, would have permitted a form of physician-assisted suicide. Washington then added a provision to the Natural Death Act expressly excluding physician-assisted suicide.

California voters rejected an assisted-suicide initiative similar to Washington's in 1993. On the other hand, in 1994, voters in Oregon enacted, also through ballot initiative, that State's "Death With Dignity Act," which legalized physician-assisted suicide for competent, terminally ill adults. Since the Oregon vote, many proposals to legalize assisted suicide have been and continue to be introduced in the States' legislatures, but none has been enacted. And just last year, Iowa and Rhode Island joined the overwhelming majority of States explicitly prohibiting assisted suicide. See Iowa Code Ann. §§ 707A.2, 707A.3 (Supp. 1997); R. I. Gen. Laws §§ 11-60-1, 11-60-3 (Supp. 1996). Also, on April 30, 1997, President Clinton signed the Federal Assisted Suicide Funding Restriction Act of 1997, which prohibits the use of federal funds in support of physician-assisted suicide. . . .

Attitudes toward suicide itself have changed since Bracton, but our laws have consistently condemned, and continue to prohibit, assisting suicide. Despite changes in medical technology and notwithstanding an increased emphasis on the importance of end-of-life decisionmaking, we have not retreated from this prohibition. Against this backdrop of history, tradition, and practice, we now turn to respondents' constitutional claim.

II

. . . In a long line of cases, we have held that, in addition to the specific freedoms protected by the Bill of Rights, the "liberty" specially protected by the Due Process Clause includes the rights to marry, *Loving v. Virginia, 388 U.S. 1 (1967);* to have children, *Skinner v. Oklahoma ex rel. Williamson, 316 U.S. 535 (1942);* to direct the education and upbringing of one's children, *Meyer v. Nebraska, 262 U.S. 390 (1923); Pierce v. Society of Sisters, 268 U.S. 510 (1925);* to marital privacy, *Griswold v. Connecticut, 381 U.S. 479 (1965);* to use contraception, ibid; *Eisenstadt v. Baird, 405 U.S. 438 (1972);* to bodily integrity, *Rochin v. California, 342 U.S. 165*

(1952), and to abortion, Casey, supra. We have also assumed, and strongly suggested, that the Due Process Clause protects the traditional right to refuse unwanted lifesaving medical treatment. *Cruzan, 497 U.S. at 278-279.*

But we "have always been reluctant to expand the concept of substantive due process because guideposts for responsible decisionmaking in this unchartered area are scarce and open-ended." *Collins, 503 U.S. at 125.* By extending constitutional protection to an asserted right or liberty interest, we, to a great extent, place the matter outside the arena of public debate and legislative action. We must therefore "exercise the utmost care whenever we are asked to break new ground in this field," ibid, lest the liberty protected by the Due Process Clause be subtly transformed into the policy preferences of the members of this Court, *Moore, 431 U.S. at 502* (plurality opinion).

Our established method of substantive-due-process analysis has two primary features: First, we have regularly observed that the Due Process Clause specially protects those fundamental rights and liberties which are, objectively, "deeply rooted in this Nation's history and tradition," *id., at 503* (plurality opinion); *Snyder v. Massachusetts, 291 U.S. 97, 105 (1934)* ("so rooted in the traditions and conscience of our people as to be ranked as fundamental"), and "implicit in the concept of ordered liberty," such that "neither liberty nor justice would exist if they were sacrificed," *Palko v. Connecticut, 302 U.S. 319, 325, 326 (1937).* Second, we have required in substantive-due-process cases a "careful description" of the asserted fundamental liberty interest. Our Nation's history, legal traditions, and practices thus provide the crucial "guideposts for responsible decisionmaking," that direct and restrain our exposition of the Due Process Clause. As we stated recently in Flores, the Fourteenth Amendment "forbids the government to infringe . . . 'fundamental' liberty interests at all, no matter what process is provided, unless the infringement is narrowly tailored to serve a compelling state interest." *507 U.S. at 302.*

JUSTICE SOUTER, relying on Justice Harlan's dissenting opinion in Poe v. Ullman, would largely abandon this restrained methodology, and instead ask "whether [Washington's] statute sets up one of those 'arbitrary impositions' or 'purposeless restraints' at odds with the Due Process Clause of the Fourteenth Amendment," post, at 1 (quoting *Poe, 367 U.S. 497, 543 (1961)* (Harlan, J., dissenting)). In our view, however, the development of this Court's substantive-due-process jurisprudence, described briefly above, has been a process whereby the outlines of the "liberty" specially protected by the Fourteenth Amendment— never fully clarified, to be sure, and perhaps not capable of being fully clarified— have at least been carefully refined by concrete examples involving fundamental rights found to be deeply rooted in our legal tradition. This approach tends to rein in the subjective elements that are necessarily present in due-process judicial review. In addition, by establishing a threshold requirement—that a challenged state action implicate a fundamental right—before requiring more than a reasonable relation to a legitimate state interest to justify the action, it avoids the need for complex balancing of competing interests in every case.

Turning to the claim at issue here, the Court of Appeals stated that "properly analyzed, the first issue to be resolved is whether there is a liberty interest in determining the time and manner of one's death," or, in other words, "is there a right to die?" Similarly, respondents assert a "liberty to choose how to die" and a right to "control of one's final days," and describe the asserted liberty as "the right to choose a humane, dignified death," and "the liberty to shape death." As noted above, we have a tradition of carefully formulating the interest at stake in substantive-due-process cases. For example, although Cruzan is often described as a "right to die" case, see *79 F.3d, at 799;* post, at 9 (STEVENS, J., concurring in judgment) (Cruzan recognized "the more specific interest in making decisions about how to confront an imminent death"), we were, in fact, more precise: we assumed that the Constitution granted competent persons a "constitutionally protected right to refuse lifesaving hydration and nutrition." *Cruzan, 497 U.S. at 279; id., at 287* (O'CONNOR, J., concurring) ("[A] liberty interest in refusing unwanted medical treatment may be inferred from our prior decisions"). The Washington statute at issue in this case prohibits "aiding another person to attempt suicide," Wash. Rev. Code § 9A.36.060(1) (1994), and, thus, the question before us is whether the "liberty" specially protected by the Due Process Clause includes a right to commit suicide which itself includes a right to assistance in doing so.

We now inquire whether this asserted right has any place in our Nation's traditions. Here, as discussed above, we are confronted with a consistent and almost universal tradition that has long rejected the asserted right, and continues explicitly to reject it today, even for terminally ill, mentally competent adults. To hold for respondents, we would have to reverse centuries of legal doctrine and practice, and strike down the considered policy choice of almost every State.

Respondents contend, however, that the liberty interest they assert is consistent with this Court's substantive-due-process line of cases, if not with this Nation's history and practice. Pointing to Casey and Cruzan, respondents read our jurisprudence in this area as reflecting a general tradition of "self-sovereignty," and as teaching that the "liberty" protected by the Due Process Clause includes "basic and intimate exercises of personal autonomy" ("It is a promise of the Constitution that there is a realm of personal liberty which the government may not enter"). According to respondents, our liberty jurisprudence, and the broad, individualistic principles it reflects, protects the "liberty of competent, terminally ill adults to make end-of-life decisions free of undue government interference." Brief for Respondents 10. The question presented in this case, however, is whether the protections of the Due Process Clause include a right to commit suicide with another's assistance. With this "careful description" of respondents' claim in mind, we turn to Casey and Cruzan.

In Cruzan, we considered whether Nancy Beth Cruzan, who had been severely injured in an automobile accident and was in a persistive vegetative state, "had a right under the United States Constitution which would require the hospital to withdraw life-sustaining treatment" at her parents' request. We began with the observation that "at common law, even the touching of one person by another without consent and without legal justification was a battery." We then discussed the related rule that "informed consent is generally required for medical treatment." After reviewing a long line of relevant state cases, we concluded that "the common-law doctrine of informed consent is viewed as generally encompassing the right of a competent individual to refuse medical treatment." Next, we reviewed our own cases on the subject, and stated that "the principle that a competent person has a constitutionally protected liberty interest in refusing unwanted medical treatment may be inferred from our prior decisions." Therefore, "for purposes of [that] case, we assumed that the United States Constitution would grant a competent person a constitutionally protected right to refuse lifesaving hydration and nutrition." We concluded that, notwithstanding this right, the Constitution permitted Missouri to require clear and convincing evidence of an incompetent patient's wishes concerning the withdrawal of life-sustaining treatment.

Respondents contend that in Cruzan we "acknowledged that competent, dying persons have the right to direct the removal of life-sustaining medical treatment and thus hasten death," Brief for Respondents 23, and that "the constitutional principle behind recognizing the patient's liberty to direct the withdrawal of artificial life support applies at least as strongly to the choice to hasten impending death by consuming lethal medication." Similarly, the Court of Appeals concluded that "Cruzan, by recognizing a liberty interest that includes the refusal of artificial provision of life-sustaining food and water, necessarily recognized a liberty interest in hastening one's own death." *79 F.3d, at 816.*

The right assumed in Cruzan, however, was not simply deduced from abstract concepts of personal autonomy. Given the common-law rule that forced medication was a battery, and the long legal tradition protecting the decision to refuse unwanted medical treatment, our assumption was entirely consistent with this Nation's history and constitutional traditions. The decision to commit suicide with the assistance of another may be just as personal and profound as the decision to refuse unwanted medical treatment, but it has never enjoyed similar legal protection. Indeed, the two acts are widely and reasonably regarded as quite distinct. In Cruzan itself, we recognized that most States outlawed assisted suicide—and even more do today—and we certainly gave no intimation that the right to refuse unwanted medical treatment could be somehow transmuted into a right to assistance in committing suicide.

Respondents also rely on Casey. There, the Court's opinion concluded that "the essential holding of Roe v. Wade should be retained and once again reaffirmed." *Casey, 505 U.S. at 846.* We held, first, that a woman has a right, before her fetus is viable, to an abortion "without undue interference from the State"; second, that States may restrict post-viability abortions, so long as exceptions are made to protect a woman's life and health; and third, that the State has legitimate interests throughout a pregnancy in protecting the health of the woman and the life of the unborn child. Ibid. In reaching this conclusion, the opinion discussed in some detail this Court's substantive-due-process tradition of interpreting the Due Process Clause to protect certain fundamental rights and "personal decisions relating to marriage, procreation, contraception, family relationships, child rearing, and education," and noted that many of those rights and liberties "involve the most intimate and personal choices a person may make in a lifetime."

The Court of Appeals, like the District Court, found Casey "'highly instructive'" and "'almost prescriptive'" for determining "'what liberty interest may inhere in a terminally ill person's choice to commit suicide'":

"Like the decision of whether or not to have an abortion, the decision how and when to die is one of 'the most intimate and personal choices a person may make in a lifetime,' a choice 'central to personal dignity and autonomy.'" *79 F.3d, at 813–814.*

Similarly, respondents emphasize the statement in Casey that:

"At the heart of liberty is the right to define one's own concept of existence, of meaning, of the universe, and of the mystery of human life. Beliefs about these matters could not define the attributes of personhood were they formed under compulsion of the State." *Casey, 505 U.S. at 851.*

. . . By choosing this language, the Court's opinion in Casey described, in a general way and in light of our prior cases, those personal activities and decisions that this Court has identified as so deeply rooted in our history and traditions, or so fundamental to our concept of constitutionally ordered liberty, that they are protected by the Fourteenth Amendment. The opinion moved from the recognition that liberty necessarily includes freedom of conscience and belief about ultimate considerations to the observation that "though the abortion decision may originate within the zone of conscience and belief, it is more than a philosophic exercise." *Casey, 505 U.S. at 852.* . . . That many of the rights and liberties protected by the Due Process Clause sound in personal autonomy does not warrant the sweeping conclusion that any and all important, intimate, and personal decisions are so protected, *San Antonio Independent School Dist. v. Rodriguez, 411 U.S. 1, 33–35 (1973),* and Casey did not suggest otherwise.

The history of the law's treatment of assisted suicide in this country has been and continues to be one of the rejection of nearly all efforts to permit it. That being the case, our decisions lead us to conclude that the asserted "right" to assistance in committing suicide is not a fundamental liberty interest protected by the Due Process Clause. The Constitution also requires, however, that Washington's assisted-suicide ban be rationally related to legitimate government interests. See *Heller v. Doe, 509 U.S. 312, 319–320 (1993); Flores, 507 U.S. at 305.* This requirement is unquestionably met here. As the court below recognized, Washington's assisted-suicide ban implicates a number of state interests.

First, Washington has an "unqualified interest in the preservation of human life." *Cruzan, 497 U.S. at 282.* The State's prohibition on assisted suicide, like all homicide laws, both reflects and advances its commitment to this interest. ("The interests in the sanctity of life that are represented by the criminal homicide laws are threatened by one who expresses a willingness to participate in taking the life of another"). This interest is symbolic and aspirational as well as practical:

"While suicide is no longer prohibited or penalized, the ban against assisted suicide and euthanasia shores up the notion of limits in human relationships. It reflects the gravity with which we view the decision to take one's own life or the life of another, and our reluctance to encourage or promote these decisions." New York Task Force 131–132.

Respondents admit that "the State has a real interest in preserving the lives of those who can still contribute to society and enjoy life." Brief for Respondents 35, n.23. The Court of Appeals also recognized Washington's interest in protecting life, but held that the "weight" of this interest depends on the "medical condition and the wishes of the person whose life is at stake." *79 F.3d, at 817.* Washington, however, has rejected this sliding-scale approach and, through its assisted-suicide ban, insists that all persons' lives, from beginning to end, regardless of physical or mental condition, are under the full protection of the law. See *United States v. Rutherford, 442, U.S. 544, 558 (1979)* (". . . Congress could reasonably have determined to protect the terminally ill, no less than other patients, from the vast range of self-styled panaceas that inventive minds can devise"). As we have previously affirmed, the States "may properly decline to make judgments about the 'quality' of life that a particular individual may enjoy," *Cruzan, 497 U.S. at 282.* This remains true, as Cruzan makes clear, even for those who are near death.

Relatedly, all admit that suicide is a serious public-health problem, especially among persons in otherwise vulnerable groups.

Those who attempt suicide—terminally ill or not—often suffer from depression or other mental disorders. Research indicates, however, that many people who request physician-assisted suicide withdraw that request if their depression and pain are treated. The New York Task Force, however, expressed its concern that, because depression is difficult to diagnose, physicians and medical professionals often fail to respond adequately to seriously ill patients' needs. Thus, legal physician-assisted suicide could make it more difficult for the State to protect depressed or mentally ill persons, or those who are suffering from untreated pain, from suicidal impulses.

The State also has an interest in protecting the integrity and ethics of the medical profession. In contrast to the Court of Appeals' conclusion that "the integrity of the medical profession would [not] be threatened in any way [by physician-assisted suicide]," *79 F.3d, at 827,* the American Medical Association, like many other medical and physicians' groups, has concluded that "physician-assisted suicide is fundamentally incompatible with the physician's role as healer." American Medical Association, Code of Ethics § 2.211 (1994); see Council on Ethical and Judicial Affairs, Decisions Near the End of Life, *267 JAMA 2229, 2233 (1992)* ("The societal risks of involving physicians in medical interventions to cause patients' deaths is too great"); New York Task Force 103–109 (discussing physicians' views). And physician-assisted suicide could, it is argued, undermine the trust that is essential to the doctor-patient relationship by blurring the time-honored line between healing and harming.

Next, the State has an interest in protecting vulnerable groups—including the poor, the elderly, and disabled persons—from abuse, neglect, and mistakes. The Court of Appeals dismissed the State's concern that disadvantaged persons might be pressured into physician-assisted suicide as "ludicrous on its face." *79 F.3d, at 825.* We have recognized, however, the real risk of subtle coercion and undue influence in end-of-life situations. *Cruzan, 497 U.S. at 281.* Similarly, the New York Task Force warned that "legalizing physician-assisted suicide would pose profound risks to many individuals who are ill and vulnerable. . . . The risk of harm is greatest for the many individuals in our society whose autonomy and well-being are already compromised by poverty, lack of access to good medical care, advanced age, or membership in a stigmatized social group." If physician-assisted suicide were permitted, many might resort to it to spare their families the substantial financial burden of end-of-life health-care costs.

The State's interest here goes beyond protecting the vulnerable from coercion; it extends to protecting disabled and terminally ill people from prejudice, negative and inaccurate stereotypes, and "societal indifference." *49 F.3d, at 592.* The state's assisted-suicide ban reflects and reinforces its policy that the lives of terminally ill, disabled, and elderly people must be no less valued than the lives of the young and healthy, and that a seriously disabled person's suicidal impulses should be interpreted and treated the same way as anyone else's.

Finally, the State may fear that permitting assisted suicide will start it down the path to voluntary and perhaps even involuntary euthanasia. The Court of Appeals struck down Washington's assisted-suicide ban only "as applied to competent, terminally ill adults who wish to hasten their deaths by obtaining medication prescribed by their doctors." *79 F.3d, at 838.* Washington insists, however, that the impact of the court's decision will not and cannot be so limited. If suicide is protected as a matter of constitutional right, it is argued, "every man and woman in the United States must enjoy it."

The Court of Appeals' decision, and its expansive reasoning, provide ample support for the State's concerns. The court noted, for example, that the "decision of a duly appointed surrogate decision maker is for all legal purposes the decision of the patient himself," *79 F.3d, at 832, n.120;* that "in some instances, the patient may be unable to self-administer the drugs and . . . administration by the physician . . . may be the only way the patient may be able to receive them," *id., at 831;* and that not only physicians, but also family members and loved ones, will inevitably participate in assisting suicide. *Id., at 838, n.140.* Thus, it turns out that what is couched as a limited right to "physician-assisted suicide" is likely, in effect, a much broader license, which could prove extremely difficult to police and contain. Washington's ban on assisting suicide prevents such erosion.

This concern is further supported by evidence about the practice of euthanasia in the Netherlands. The Dutch government's own study revealed that in 1990, there were 2,300 cases of voluntary euthanasia (defined as "the deliberate termination of another's life at his request"), 400 cases of assisted suicide, and more than 1,000 cases of euthanasia without an explicit request. In addition to these latter 1,000 cases, the study found an additional 4,941 cases where physicians administered lethal morphine overdoses without the patients' explicit consent. Physician-Assisted Suicide and Euthanasia in the Netherlands: A Report of Chairman Charles T. Canady, at 12–13 (citing Dutch study). This study suggests that, despite the existence of various reporting procedures, euthanasia in the Netherlands has not been limited to competent, terminally ill adults who are enduring physical suffering, and that regulation of the practice may not have prevented abuses in cases involving vulnerable persons, including severely disabled neonates and elderly persons suffering from dementia. The New York Task Force, citing the Dutch experience, observed that "assisted suicide and euthanasia are closely linked," New York Task Force 145, and concluded that the "risk of . . . abuse is neither speculative nor distant." Washington, like most other States, reasonably ensures against this risk by banning, rather than regulating, assisting suicide.

We need not weigh exactly the relative strengths of these various interests. They are unquestionably important and legitimate, and Washington's ban on assisted suicide is at least reasonably related to their promotion and protection. We therefore hold that Wash. Rev. Code § 9A.36.060(1)(1994) does not violate the Fourteenth Amendment, either on its face or "as applied to competent, terminally ill adults who wish to hasten their deaths by obtaining medication prescribed by their doctors." *79 F.3d, at 838.*

Throughout the Nation, Americans are engaged in an earnest and profound debate about the morality, legality, and practicality of physician-assisted suicide. Our holding permits this debate to continue, as it should in a democratic society. The decision of the en banc Court of Appeals is reversed, and the case is remanded for further proceedings consistent with this opinion.

Note

1. Under Washington's Natural Death Act, "adult persons have the fundamental right to control the decisions relating to the rendering of their own health care, including the decision to have life-sustaining treatment withheld or withdrawn in instances of a terminal condition or permanent unconscious condition." Wash. Rev. Code § 70.122.010 (1994). In Washington, "any adult person may execute a directive directing the withholding or withdrawal of life-sustaining treatment in a terminal condition or permanent unconscious condition," § 70.122.030, and a physician who, in accordance with such a directive, participates in the withholding or withdrawal of life-sustaining treatment is immune from civil, criminal, or professional liability. § 70.122.051.

Stephen Reinhardt   ➔ **NO**

Majority Opinion

Compassion in Dying *v.* State of Washington

I.

This case raises an extraordinarily important and difficult issue. It compels us to address questions to which there are no easy or simple answers, at law or otherwise. It requires us to confront the most basic of human concerns—the mortality of self and loved ones—and to balance the interest in preserving human life against the desire to die peacefully and with dignity. People of good will can and do passionately disagree about the proper result, perhaps even more intensely than they part ways over the constitutionality of restricting a woman's right to have an abortion. Heated though the debate may be, we must determine whether and how the United States Constitution applies to the controversy before us, a controversy that may touch more people more profoundly than any other issue the courts will face in the foreseeable future.

Today, we are required to decide whether a person who is terminally ill has a constitutionally-protected liberty interest in hastening what might otherwise be a protracted, undignified, and extremely painful death. If such an interest exists, we must next decide whether or not the state of Washington may constitutionally restrict its exercise by banning a form of medical assistance that is frequently requested by terminally ill people who wish to die. We first conclude that there is a constitutionally-protected liberty interest in determining the time and manner of one's own death, an interest that must be weighed against the state's legitimate and countervailing interests, especially those that relate to the preservation of human life. After balancing the competing interests, we conclude by answering the narrow question before us: We hold that insofar as the Washington statute prohibits physicians from prescribing life-ending medication for use by terminally ill, competent adults who wish to hasten their own deaths, it violates the Due Process Clause of the Fourteenth Amendment.

II. Preliminary Matters and History of the Case

. . . The plaintiffs do not challenge Washington statute RCW 9A.36.060 in its entirety. Specifically they do not object to the portion of the Washington statute that makes it unlawful for a person knowingly to cause another to commit

From *Compassion in Dying v. State of Washington,* 96 C.D.O.S. 1507 (1996).

suicide. Rather, they only challenge the statute's "or aids" provision. They challenge that provision both on its face and as applied to terminally ill, mentally competent adults who wish to hasten their own deaths with the help of medication prescribed by their doctors. The plaintiffs contend that the provision impermissibly prevents the exercise by terminally ill patients of a constitutionally-protected liberty interest in violation of the Due Process Clause of the Fourteenth Amendment, and also that it impermissibly distinguishes between similarly situated terminally ill patients in violation of the Equal Protection Clause. . . .

III. Overview of Legal Analysis: Is There a Due Process Violation?

In order to answer the question whether the Washington statute violates the Due Process Clause insofar as it prohibits the provision of certain medical assistance to terminally ill, competent adults who wish to hasten their own deaths, we first determine whether there is a liberty interest in choosing the time and manner of one's death—a question sometimes phrased in common parlance as: Is there a right to die? Because we hold that there is, we must then determine whether prohibiting physicians from prescribing life-ending medication for use by terminally ill patients who wish to die violates the patients' due process rights.

The mere recognition of a liberty interest does not mean that a state may not prohibit the exercise of that interest in particular circumstances, nor does it mean that a state may not adopt appropriate regulations governing its exercise. Rather, in cases like the one before us, the courts must apply a balancing test under which we weigh the individual's liberty interests against the relevant state interests in order to determine whether the state's actions are constitutionally permissible. . . .

Defining the Liberty Interest and Other Relevant Terms

. . . While some people refer to the liberty interest implicated in right-to-die cases as a liberty interest in committing suicide, we do not describe it that way. We use the broader and more accurate terms, "the right to die," "determining the time and manner of one's death," and "hastening one's death" for an important reason. The liberty interest we examine encompasses a whole range of acts that are generally not considered to constitute "suicide." Included within the liberty interest we examine, is for example, the act of refusing or terminating unwanted medical treatment . . . a competent adult has a liberty interest in refusing to be connected to a respirator or in being disconnected from one, even if he is terminally ill and cannot live without mechanical assistance. The law does not classify the death of a patient that results from the granting of his wish to decline or discontinue treatment as "suicide." Nor does the law label the acts of those who help the patient carry out that wish, whether by physically disconnecting the respirator or by removing an intravenous tube, as assistance in suicide. Accordingly, we believe that the broader terms—"the right to die," "controlling the time and manner of one's death," and "hastening one's death"—more accurately describe the liberty interest at issue here. . . .

Like the Court in *Roe [v. Wade]*, we begin with ancient attitudes. In Greek and Roman times, far from being universally prohibited, suicide was often considered commendable in literature, mythology, and practice. . . .

While Socrates counseled his disciples against committing suicide, he willingly drank the hemlock as he was condemned to do, and his example inspired others to end their lives. Plato, Socrates' most distinguished student, believed suicide was often justifiable.

He suggested that if life itself became immoderate, then suicide became a rational, justifiable act. Painful disease, or intolerable constraint were sufficient reasons to depart. And this when religious superstitions faded was philosophic justification enough.

Many contemporaries of Plato were even more inclined to find suicide a legitimate and acceptable act. In *Roe,* while surveying the attitudes of the Greeks toward abortion, the Court stated that "only the Pythagorean school of philosophers frowned on the related act of suicide," 410 U.S. at 131; it then noted that the Pythagorean school represented a distinctly minority view. *Id.*

The Stoics glorified suicide as an act of pure rational will. Cato, who killed himself to avoid dishonor when Ceasar crushed his military aspirations, was the most celebrated of the many suicides among the Stoics. Montaigne wrote of Cato: "This was a man chosen by nature to show the heights which can be attained by human steadfastness and constancy. . . . Such courage is above philosophy."

Like the Greeks, the Romans often considered suicide to be acceptable or even laudable.

To live nobly also meant to die nobly and at the right time. Everything depended on a dominant will and a rational choice. . . .

Suicide was a crime under the English common law, at least in limited circumstances, probably as early as the thirteenth century. Bracton, incorporating Roman Law as set forth in Justinian's Digest, declared that if someone commits suicide to avoid conviction of a felony, his property escheats to his lords. Bracton said "[i]t ought to be otherwise if he kills himself through madness or unwillingness to endure suffering." Despite his general fidelity to Roman law, Bracton did introduce a key innovation: "[I]f a man slays himself in weariness of life or because he is unwilling to endure further bodily pain . . . he may have a successor, but his movable goods [personal property] are confiscated. He does not lose his inheritance [real property], only his movable goods." Bracton's innovation was incorporated into English common law, which has thus treated suicides resulting from the inability to "endure further bodily pain" with compassion and understanding ever since a common law scheme was firmly established. . . .

English attitudes toward suicide, including the tradition of ignominious burial, carried over to America where they subsequently underwent a transformation. By 1798, six of the 13 original colonies had abolished all penalties for suicide either by statute or state constitution. There is no evidence that any court ever imposed a punishment for suicide or attempted suicide under common law in post-revolutionary America. By the time the Fourteenth Amendment was adopted in 1868, suicide was generally not punishable, and in only nine of the 37 states is it clear that there were statutes prohibiting assisting suicide.

The majority of states have not criminalized suicide or attempted suicide since the turn of the century. The New Jersey Supreme Court declared in 1901 that since suicide was not punishable it should not be considered a crime. "[A]ll will admit that in some cases it is ethically defensible," the court said, as when a woman kills herself to escape being raped or "when a man curtails weeks or months of agony of an incurable disease." *Campbell v. Supreme Conclave Improved Order Heptasophs,* 66 N.J.L. 274, 49 A. 550, 553 (1901). Today, no state has a statute prohibiting suicide or attempted suicide; nor has any state had such a statute for at least 10 years. A majority of states do, however, still have laws on the books against assisting suicide.

Current Societal Attitudes

Clearly the absence of a criminal sanction alone does not show societal approbation of a practice. Nor is there any evidence that Americans approve of suicide in general. In recent years, however, there has been increasingly widespread support for allowing the terminally ill to hasten their deaths and avoid painful, undignified, and inhumane endings to their lives. Most Americans simply do not appear to view such acts as constituting suicide, and there is much support in reason for that conclusion.

Polls have repeatedly shown that a large majority of Americans—sometimes nearing 90%—fully endorse recent legal changes granting terminally ill patients, and sometimes their families, the prerogative to accelerate their death by refusing or terminating treatment. Other polls indicate that a majority of Americans favor doctor-assisted suicide for the terminally ill. In April, 1990, the Roper Report found that 64% of Americans believed that the terminally ill should have the right to request and receive physician aid-in-dying. Another national poll, conducted in October 1991, shows that "nearly two out of three Americans favor doctor-assisted suicide and euthanasia for terminally ill patients who request it." A 1994 Harris poll found 73% of Americans favor legalizing physician-assisted suicide. Three states have held referenda on proposals to allow physicians to help terminally ill, competent adults commit suicide with somewhat mixed results. In Oregon, voters approved the carefully-crafted referendum by a margin of 51 to 49 percent in November of 1994. In Washington and California where the measures contained far fewer practical safeguards, they narrowly failed to pass. . . . Accounts of doctors who have helped their patients end their lives have appeared both in professional journals and in the daily press. . . .

Liberty Interest Under Casey

In *[Planned Parenthood v.] Casey,* the Court surveyed its prior decisions affording "constitutional protection to personal decisions relating to marriage, procreation, contraception, family relationships, child rearing, and education," *id.* at 2807 and then said:

> These matters, involving the most intimate and personal choices a person may make in a lifetime, choices central to personal dignity and autonomy, are central to the liberty protected by the Fourteenth Amendment. At the heart of liberty is the right to define one's own concept of existence, of meaning, of the universe, and of the mystery of human life. Beliefs about these matters could not define the attributes of personhood were they formed under compulsion of the State. The district judge in this case found the Court's reasoning in *Casey* "highly instructive" and "almost prescriptive" for determining "what liberty interest may inhere in a terminally ill person's choice to commit suicide." Compassion In Dying, 850 F. Supp. at 1459. We agree.

Like the decision of whether or not to have an abortion, the decision how and when to die is one of "the most intimate and personal choices a person may make in a lifetime," a choice "central to personal dignity and autonomy." A competent terminally ill adult, having lived nearly the full measure of his life, has a strong liberty interest in choosing a dignified and humane death rather than being reduced at the end of his existence to a childlike state of helplessness, diapered, sedated, incontinent. How a person dies not only determines the nature of the final period of his existence, but in many cases, the enduring memories held by those who love him.

Prohibiting a terminally ill patient from hastening his death may have an even more profound impact on that person's life than forcing a woman to carry a pregnancy to term. The case of an AIDS patient treated by Dr. Peter Shalit, one of the physician-plaintiffs in this case, provides a compelling illustration. In his declaration, Dr. Shalit described his patient's death this way:

> One patient of mine, whom I will call Smith, a fictitious name, lingered in the hospital for weeks, his lower body so swollen from oozing Kaposi's lesions that he could not walk, his genitals so swollen that he required a catheter to drain his bladder, his fingers gangrenous from clotted arteries. Patient Smith's friends stopped visiting him because it gave them nightmares. Patient Smith's agonies could not be relieved by medication or by the excellent nursing care he received. Patient Smith begged for assistance in hastening his death. As his treating doctor, it was my professional opinion that patient Smith was mentally competent to make a choice with respect to shortening his period of suffering before inevitable death. I felt that I should accommodate his request. However, because of the statute, I was unable to assist him and he died after having been tortured for weeks by the end-phase of his disease.

For such patients, wracked by pain and deprived of all pleasure, a state-enforced prohibition on hastening their deaths condemns them to unrelieved misery or torture. Surely, a person's decision whether to endure or avoid such an existence constitutes one of the most, if not the most, "intimate and personal choices a person may make in a life-time," a choice that is "central to personal dignity and autonomy." *Casey,* 112 S.Ct. at 2807. . . .

Cruzan stands for the proposition that there is a due process liberty interest in rejecting unwanted medical treatment, including the provision of food and water by artificial means. Moreover, the Court majority clearly recognized that granting the request to remove the tubes through which Cruzan received artificial nutrition and hydration would lead inexorably to her death. *Cruzan,* 497 U.S. at 267–68, 283. Accordingly, we conclude that *Cruzan,* by recognizing a liberty interest that includes the refusal of artificial provision of life-sustaining food and water, necessarily recognizes a liberty interest in hastening one's own death.

Summary

Casey and *Cruzan* provide persuasive evidence that the Constitution encompasses a due process liberty interest in controlling the time and manner of one's death—that there is, in short, a constitutionally recognized "right to die." Our conclusion is strongly influenced by, but not limited to, the plight of mentally competent, terminally ill adults. We are influenced as well by the plight of others, such as those whose existence is reduced to a vegetative state or a permanent and irreversible state of unconsciousness.

Our conclusion that there is a liberty interest in determining the time and manner of one's death does not mean that there is a concomitant right to exercise that interest in all circumstances or to do so free from state regulation. To the contrary, we explicitly recognize that some prohibitory and regulatory state action is fully consistent with constitutional principles.

In short, finding a liberty interest constitutes a critical first step toward answering the question before us. The determination that must now be made is whether the state's attempt to curtail the exercise of that interest is constitutionally justified.

V. Relevant Factors and Interests

To determine whether a state action that impairs a liberty interest violates an individual's substantive due process rights we must identify the factors relevant to the case at hand, assess the state's interests and the individual's liberty interest in light of those factors, and then weigh and balance the competing interests. The relevant factors generally include: 1) the importance of the various state interests, both in general and in the factual context of the case; 2) the manner in which those interests are furthered by the state law or regulation; 3) the importance of the liberty interest, both in itself and in the context in which it is being exercised; 4) the extent to which that interest is burdened by the challenged state action; and, 5) the consequences of upholding or overturning the statute or regulation. . . .

B. The Means by Which the State Furthers Its Interests

In applying the balancing test, we must take into account not only the strength of the state's interests but also the means by which the state has chosen to further those interests.

1. Prohibition—A Total Ban for the Terminally Ill

Washington's statute prohibiting assisted suicide has a drastic impact on the terminally ill. By prohibiting physician assistance, it bars what for many terminally ill patients is the only palatable, and only practical, way to end their lives. Physically frail, confined to wheelchairs or beds, many terminally ill patients do not have the means or ability to kill themselves in the multitude of ways that healthy individuals can. Often, for example, they cannot even secure the medication or devices they would need to carry out their wishes.

Some terminally ill patients stockpile prescription medicine, which they can use to end their lives when they decide the time is right. The successful use of the stockpile technique generally depends, however, on the assistance of a physician, whether tacit or unknowing (although it is possible to end one's life with over-the-counter medication). Even if the terminally ill patients are able to accumulate sufficient drugs, given the pain killers and other medication they are taking, most of them would lack the knowledge to determine what dose of any given drug or drugs they must take, or in what combination. Miscalculation can be tragic. It can lead to an even more painful and lingering death. Alternatively, if the medication reduces respiration enough to restrict the flow of oxygen to the brain but not enough to cause death, it can result in the patient's falling into a comatose or vegetative state.

Thus for many terminally ill patients, the Washington statute is effectively a prohibition. While technically it only prohibits one means of exercising a liberty interest, practically it prohibits the exercise of that interest as effectively as prohibiting doctors from performing abortions prevented women from having abortions in the days before *Roe*.

2. Regulation—A Permissible Means of Promoting State Interests

State laws or regulations governing physician-assisted suicide are both necessary and desirable to ensure against errors and abuse, and to protect legitimate state interests. Any of several model statutes might serve as an example of how these legitimate and important concerns can be addressed effectively.

By adopting appropriate, reasonable, and properly drawn safeguards Washington could ensure that people who choose to have their doctors prescribe lethal doses of medication are truly competent and meet all of the requisite standards. Without endorsing the constitutionality of any particular procedural safeguards, we note that the state might, for example, require: witnesses to ensure voluntariness; reasonable, though short, waiting periods to prevent rash decisions; second medical opinions to confirm a patient's terminal status and also to confirm that the patient has been receiving proper treatment, including adequate comfort care; psychological examinations to ensure that the patient is not suffering from momentary or treatable depression; reporting procedures that will aid in the avoidance of abuse. Alternatively, such safeguards could be adopted by interested medical associations and other organizations involved in the provision of health care, so long as they meet the state's needs and concerns. . . .

E. The Consequences of Upholding or Overturning the Statutory Provision

In various earlier sections of this opinion, we have discussed most of the consequences of upholding or overturning the Washington statutory provision at issue, because in this case those consequences are best considered as part of the discussion of the specific factors or interests. The one remaining consequence of significance is easy to identify: Whatever the outcome here, a host of painful and agonizing issues involving the right to die will continue to confront the courts. More important, these problems will continue to plague growing numbers of Americans of advanced age as well as their families, dependents, and loved ones. The issue is truly one which deserves the most thorough, careful, and objective attention from all segments of society.

VI. Application of the Balancing Test and Holding

Weighing and then balancing a constitutionally-protected interest against the state's countervailing interests, while bearing in mind the various consequences of the decision, is quintessentially a judicial role. Despite all of the efforts of generations of courts to categorize and objectify, to create multi-part tests and identify weights to be attached to the various factors, in the end balancing entails the exercise of judicial judgment rather than the application of scientific or mathematical formulae. No legislative body can perform the task for us. Nor can any computer. In the end, mindful of our constitutional obligations, including the limitations imposed on us by that document, we must rely on our judgment, guided by the facts and the law as we perceive them.

As we have explained, in this case neither the liberty interest in choosing the time and manner of death nor the state's countervailing interests are static. The magnitude of each depends on objective circumstances and generally varies inversely with the other. The liberty interest in hastening death is at its strongest when the state's interest in protecting life and preventing suicide is at its weakest, and vice-versa.

The liberty interest at issue here is an important one and, in the case of the terminally ill, is at its peak. Conversely, the state interests, while equally important in the abstract, are for the most part at a low point here. We recognize that in the case of life and death decisions the state has a particularly strong interest in avoiding undue influence and other forms of abuse. Here, that concern is ameliorated in large measure because of the mandatory involvement in the decision-making process of physicians, who have a strong bias in favor of preserving life, and because the process itself can be carefully regulated and rigorous safeguards adopted. Under these circumstances, we believe that the possibility of abuse, even when considered along with the other state interests, does not outweigh the liberty interest at issue.

The state has chosen to pursue its interests by means of what for terminally ill patients is effectively a total prohibition, even though its most important interests could be adequately served by a far less burdensome measure. The consequences of rejecting the as-applied challenge would be disastrous for the terminally ill, while the adverse consequences for the state would be of a far lesser order. This, too, weighs in favor of upholding the liberty interest.

We consider the state's interests in preventing assisted suicide as being different only in degree and not in kind from its interests in prohibiting a number of other medical practices that lead directly to a terminally ill patient's death. Moreover, we do not consider those interests to be significantly greater in the case of assisted suicide than they are in the case of those other medical practices, if indeed they are greater at all. However, even if the difference were one of kind and not degree, our result would be no different. For no matter how much weight we could legitimately afford the state's interest in preventing suicide, that weight, when combined with the weight we give all the other state's interests, is insufficient to outweigh the terminally ill individual's interest in deciding whether to end his agony and suffering by hastening the time of his death with medication prescribed by his physician. The individual's interest in making that vital decision is compelling indeed, for no decision is more painful, delicate, personal, important, or final than the decision how and when one's life shall end. If broad general state policies can be used to deprive a terminally ill individual of the right to make that choice, it is hard to envision where the exercise of arbitrary and intrusive power by the state can be halted. In this case, the state has wide power to regulate, but it may not ban the exercise of the liberty interest, and that is the practical effect of the program before us. Accordingly, after examining one final legal authority, we hold that the "or aids" provision of Washington statute RCW 9A.36.06 is unconstitutional as applied to terminally ill competent adults who wish to hasten their deaths with medication prescribed by their physicians. . . .

VII. Conclusion

We hold that a liberty interest exists in the choice of how and when one dies, and that the provision of the Washington statute banning assisted suicide, as applied to competent, terminally ill adults who wish to hasten their deaths by obtaining medication prescribed by their doctors, violates the Due Process Clause. We recognize that this decision is a most difficult and controversial one, and that it leaves unresolved a large number of equally troublesome issues that will require resolution in the years ahead. We also recognize that other able and dedicated jurists, construing the Constitution as they believe it must be construed, may disagree not only with the result we reach but with our method of constitutional analysis. Given the nature of the judicial process and the complexity of the task of determining the rights and interests comprehended by the Constitution, good faith disagreements within the judiciary should not surprise or disturb anyone who follows the development of the law. For these reasons, we express our hope that whatever debate may accompany the future exploration of the issues we have touched on today will be conducted in an objective, rational, and constructive manner that will increase, not diminish, respect for the Constitution.

There is one final point we must emphasize. Some argue strongly that decisions regarding matters affecting life or death should not be made by the courts. Essentially, we agree with that proposition. In this case, by permitting the individual to exercise the right to choose we are following the constitutional mandate to take such decisions out of the hands of the government, both state and federal, and to put them where they rightly belong, in the hands of the people. We are allowing individuals to make the decisions that so profoundly affect their very existence—and precluding the state from intruding excessively into that critical realm. The Constitution and the courts stand as a bulwark between individual freedom and arbitrary and intrusive governmental power. Under our constitutional system, neither the state nor the majority of the people in a state can impose its will upon the individual in a matter so highly "central to personal dignity and autonomy," *Casey,* 112 S.Ct. at 2807. Those who believe strongly that death must come without physician assistance are free to follow that creed, be they doctors or patients. They are not free, however, to force their views, their religious convictions, or their philosophies on all the other members of a democratic society, and to compel those whose values differ with theirs to die painful, protracted, and agonizing deaths.

Affirmed.

POSTSCRIPT

Are Restrictions on Physician-Assisted Suicide Constitutional?

Nancy Cruzan died six months after the U.S. Supreme Court's ruling on her right to die. Two months after the Court's decision, the Cruzans asked for a court hearing to present new evidence from three of their daughter's coworkers. At the hearing, the coworkers testified that they recalled her saying she would never want to live "like a vegetable." At the same hearing, Cruzan's doctor called her existence a "living hell" and recommended removal of the tube. Her court-appointed guardian concurred. The judge then ruled that there was clear evidence of Cruzan's wishes and gave permission for the feeding tube to be removed. She died on December 26, 1990.

The fundamental concern of courts in right-to-die cases—indeed in most civil liberties cases—is the fear of what will happen in the next case. In other words, a judge may avoid doing what seems reasonable in one case if his ruling could be used to reach a less desirable result in a future case with slightly different facts. Lawyers refer to this as the "slippery slope." If euthanasia is justified in a case where the patient is conscious and competent, it may be allowed in a later case where, perhaps due to the pain the patient is in, competency is not perfectly clear.

The most recent "right to die" case in the news involved Terry Schiavo, a severely brain-damaged forty-two-year-old woman. Schiavo's husband, Michael Schiavo, wanted the feeding tube removed from his wife, and the courts supported his right to make this decision. Schiavo's parents bitterly opposed Michael Schiavo's decision. On March 18, 2005, the feeding tube was removed, and Terry Schiavo passed away on March 30, 2005. Detailed information about the issues in the case can be found at http://www.miami.edu/ethics/schiavo_project.htm.

The legal issues involved in assisting suicide are covered in a symposium in the *Ohio Northern Law Review*, p. 559 (vol. 20, 1994). The case of Dr. Jack Kevorkian, who helped terminally ill patients to die from 1990 to 1998, is discussed by his attorney, Geoffrey Fieger, in "The Persecution and Prosecution of Dr. Death and His Mercy Machine," 20 *Ohio Northern Law Review* 659 (1994). Other interesting writings in this area include "Physician-Assisted Suicide and the Right to Die With Assistance," 105 *Harvard Law Review* 2021 (1992); Yale Kamisar, "When Is There a Constitutional 'Right to Die'? When Is There No Constitutional 'Right to Live'?" 25 *Georgia Law Review* 1203 (1991); John A. Robertson, "Assessing Quality of Life: A Response to Professor Kamisar," 25 *Georgia Law Review* 1243 (1991); and A. W. Alschuler, "The Right to Die," 141 *New Law Journal* 1637 (1991).

ISSUE 7

Does the Sharing of Music Files Through the Internet Violate Copyright Laws?

YES: Ruth Bader Ginsburg, from Concurring Opinion, *Metro-Goldwyn-Mayer Studios v. Grokster*, U.S. Supreme Court (June 27, 2005)

NO: Stephen Breyer, from Concurring Opinion, *Metro-Goldwyn-Mayer Studios v. Grokster*, U.S. Supreme Court (June 27, 2005)

ISSUE SUMMARY

YES: Justice Ginsburg believes that the copyright laws are violated by a company when its software is used primarily for illegal file sharing, and lawful uses in the future are unlikely.

NO: Justice Breyer does not want the copyright laws to hinder technological innovation and is more willing to take into account the potential use of the software for lawful file sharing.

When the first edition of *Taking Sides: Legal Issues* was published, it would have been impossible to think of a copyright issue that was controversial and newsworthy enough to include. Today, however, the issue of file sharing and copyright may be the issue in this book that most directly touches the daily activities of readers. Several decades ago, it would have been difficult for ordinary citizens to commit a copyright violation that would provoke a response from the copyright owner. Today, every person who downloads music from a free file-sharing site exposes himself or herself to some measure of risk.

On June 27, 2005, the final day of its 2004–2005 term, the U.S. Supreme Court issued its decision in the case of *MGM Studios v. Grokster*. Those awaiting the decision hoped that it would clarify an important question, namely whether software that allowed users to exchange music and other copyrighted files was a violation of the copyrighted laws. The producers of such software did not themselves copy anything, but they made it possible for many millions of users to copy and circulate copyrighted files.

The decision in *MGM Studios v. Grokster* was unanimous and held that Grokster could be held liable for violating the copyright laws. The Court did not, however, go so far as to state that all file-sharing programs would violate the copyright laws. The justices were willing to hold Grokster liable since Grokster, in addition to making its software available, encouraged users to copy copyrighted files. But what if a developer simply made software available online that could be used for file sharing but did not actively encourage file sharing of copyrighted works? What if a developer made available software that in fact was used by many to exchange copyrighted works but was also used to exchange non-protected works?

While *Grokster* was the first file-sharing case for the U.S. Supreme Court, it was not the first case involving a technology that made possible the copying of copyrighted works. The landmark case in this area is *Sony v. Universal City Studios,* 464 U.S. 417 (1984), a case questioning whether the VCR manufactured by Sony violated the copyrighted laws. The decision in that case was very close, 5–4, and held that machines that were being used to violate the copyright law but that also were being used in ways that didn't violate the copyright laws could not be banned.

In the *Sony* case, five of the justices felt that if that only 10 percent of the copying done with the VCR might be lawful, that was sufficient to keep the technology from being banned. But what if the lawful copying were less than 10 percent? The *Sony* court suggested that a technology that could be used both for lawful and unlawful copying does not violate the copyright laws if it is "capable of substantial non-infringing use." But how much use qualifies as being "substantial"? And is this an appropriate standard in a case where tens of millions of unlawful copies are being made, but the technology is still "capable" of broad lawful use?

On the above questions, the Court was not unanimous. The two concurring opinions differed greatly on what the standard should be for a company that produces software that is used unlawfully, an issue that the Court will have to decide in some future case. In the first reading, Justice Ruth Bader Ginsburg writes that without evidence of non-infringing uses, a company that distributes a product used to violate the copyright law should be held responsible, perhaps even that the Sony standard needs to be modified. Justice Stephen Breyer, on the other hand, emphasizes the need to encourage the development of new technologies, something that will not happen if creators are worried that their creations will be held to violate the copyright law. Thus, Justice Breyer believes that it is sufficient in a case like this merely to show a capability of future non-infringing use in order to escape liability under the copyright laws.

YES

Ruth Bader Ginsburg

Concurring Opinion

Metro-Goldwyn-Mayer Studios Inc., et al., Petitioners *v.* Grokster, Ltd., et al.

JUSTICE GINSBURG, with whom THE CHIEF JUSTICE AND JUSTICE KENNEDY join, concurring

I concur in the Court's decision, which vacates in full the judgment of the Court of Appeals for the Ninth Circuit, and write separately to clarify why I conclude that the Court of Appeals misperceived, and hence misapplied, our holding in *Sony Corp. of America* v. *Universal City Studios, Inc.,* 464 U. S. 417 (1984). There is here at least a "genuine issue as to [a] material fact," Fed. Rule Civ. Proc. 56(c), on the liability of Grokster or StreamCast, not only for actively inducing copyright infringement, but also or alternatively, based on the distribution of their software products, for contributory copyright infringement. On neither score was summary judgment for Grokster and StreamCast warranted.

At bottom, however labeled, the question in this case is whether Grokster and StreamCast are liable for the direct infringing acts of others. Liability under our jurisprudence may be predicated on actively encouraging (or inducing) infringement through specific acts (as the Court's opinion develops) or on distributing a product distributees use to infringe copyrights, if the product is not capable of "substantial" or "commercially significant" noninfringing uses. *Sony,* 464 U. S., at 442. While the two categories overlap, they capture different culpable behavior. Long coexisting, both are now codified in patent law. Compare 35 U. S. C. §271(b) (active inducement liability), with §271(c) (contributory liability for distribution of a product not "suitable for substantial noninfringing use").

In *Sony,* 464 U. S. 417, the Court considered Sony's liability for selling the Betamax video cassette recorder. It did so enlightened by a full trial record. Drawing an analogy to the staple article of commerce doctrine from patent law, the *Sony* Court observed that the "sale of an article . . . adapted to [a patent] infringing use" does not suffice "to make the seller a contributory infringer" if the article "is also adapted to other and lawful uses." *Id.,* at 441 (quoting *Henry* v. *A. B. Dick Co.,* 224 U. S. 1, 48 (1912), overruled on other grounds, *Motion Picture Patents Co.* v. *Universal Film Mfg. Co.,* 243 U. S. 502, 517 (1917)).

Concurring Opinion, Metro-Goldwyn-Mayer Studios Inc., et al., Petitioners v. Grokster, Ltd., et al. United States Court of Appeals for the Ninth Circuit Case Nos.: (03-55894, 03-55901, 03-56236). Decision Date: August 19, 2004. Some case citations omitted.

"The staple article of commerce doctrine" applied to copyright, the Court stated, "must strike a balance between a copyright holder's legitimate demand for effective—not merely symbolic—protection of the statutory monopoly, and the rights of others freely to engage in substantially unrelated areas of commerce." *Sony*, 464 U. S., at 442. "Accordingly," the Court held, "the sale of copying equipment, like the sale of other articles of commerce, does not constitute contributory infringement if the product is widely used for legitimate, unobjectionable purposes. Indeed, it need merely be capable of substantial noninfringing uses." Thus, to resolve the *Sony* case, the Court explained, it had to determine "whether the Betamax is capable of commercially significant noninfringing uses."

To answer that question, the Court considered whether "a significant number of [potential uses of the Betamax were] noninfringing." The Court homed in on one potential use—private, noncommercial time-shifting of television programs in the home (*i.e.*, recording a broadcast TV program for later personal viewing). Time-shifting was noninfringing, the Court concluded, because in some cases trial testimony showed it was authorized by the copyright holder, and in others it qualified as legitimate fair use. Most purchasers used the Betamax principally to engage in time-shifting, a use that "plainly satisfie[d]" the Court's standard. Thus, there was no need in *Sony* to "give precise content to the question of how much [actual or potential] use is commercially significant." *Ibid.*[1] Further development was left for later days and cases.

The Ninth Circuit went astray, I will endeavor to explain, when that court granted summary judgment to Grokster and StreamCast on the charge of contributory liability based on distribution of their software products. Relying on its earlier opinion in *A&M Records, Inc.* v. *Napster, Inc.*, 239 F. 3d 1004 (CA9 2001), the Court of Appeals held that "if substantial noninfringing use was shown, the copyright owner would be required to show that the defendant had reasonable knowledge of specific infringing files." 380 F. 3d 1154, 1161 (CA9 2004). "A careful examination of the record," the court concluded, "indicates that there is no genuine issue of material fact as to noninfringing use." The appeals court pointed to the band Wilco, which made one of its albums available for free downloading, to other recording artists who may have authorized free distribution of their music through the Internet, and to public domain literary works and films available through Grokster's and StreamCast's software. Although it acknowledged MGM's assertion that "the vast majority of the software use is for copyright infringement," the court concluded that Grokster's and StreamCast's proffered evidence met *Sony*'s requirement that "a product need only be *capable* of substantial noninfringing uses." 380 F. 3d, at 1162.[2]

This case differs markedly from *Sony*. Cf. Peters, Brace Memorial Lecture: Copyright Enters the Public Domain, 51 J. Copyright Soc. 701, 724 (2004) ("The *Grokster* panel's reading of *Sony* is the broadest that any court has given it. . . ."). Here, there has been no finding of any fair use and little beyond anecdotal evidence of noninfringing uses. In finding the Grokster and StreamCast software products capable of substantial noninfringing uses, the District Court and the Court of Appeals appear to have relied largely on declarations submitted by the defendants. These declarations include assertions (some of them hearsay) that a number of copyright owners authorize distribution of their works on the Internet and that some public domain material is available through peer-to-peer networks including those accessed through Grokster's and StreamCast's software. 380 F. 3d, at 1161; 259 F. Supp. 2d 1029, 1035–1036 (CD Cal. 2003); App. 125–171.

The District Court declared it "undisputed that there are substantial noninfringing uses for Defendants' software," thus obviating the need for further proceedings. 259 F. Supp. 2d, at 1035. This conclusion appears to rest almost entirely on the collection of declarations submitted by Grokster and StreamCast. Review of these declarations reveals mostly anecdotal evidence, sometimes obtained second-hand, of authorized copyrighted works or public domain works available online and shared through peer-to-peer networks, and general statements about the benefits of peer-to-peer technology. See, *e.g.,* Decl. of Janis Ian ¶13, App. 128 ("P2P technologies offer musicians an alternative channel for promotion and distribution."); Decl. of Gregory Newby ¶12, *id.,* at 136 ("Numerous authorized and public domain Project Gutenberg eBooks are made available on Morpheus, Kazaa, Gnutella, Grokster, and similar software products."); Decl. of Aram Sinnreich ¶6, *id.,* at 151 ("file sharing seems to have a net positive impact on music sales"); Decl. of John Busher ¶8, *id.,* at 166 ("I estimate that Acoustica generates sales of between $1,000 and $10,000 per month as a result of the distribution of its trialware software through the Gnutella and FastTrack Networks."); Decl. of Patricia D. Hoekman ¶¶3–4, *id.,* at 169–170 (search on Morpheus for "President Bush speeches" found several video recordings, searches for "Declaration of Independence" and "Bible" found various documents and declarant was able to download a copy of the Declaration); Decl. of Sean L. Mayers ¶11, *id.,* at 67 ("Existing open, decentralized peer-to-peer file-sharing networks . . . offer content owners distinct business advantages over alternate online distribution technologies."). Compare Decl. of Brewster Kahle ¶20, *id.,* at 142 ("Those who download the Prelinger films . . . are entitled to redistribute those files, and the Archive welcomes their redistribution by the Morpheus-Grokster-KaZaa community of users."), with Deposition of Brewster Kahle, *id.,* at 396–403 (Sept. 18, 2002) (testifying that he has no knowledge of any person downloading a Prelinger film using Morpheus, Grokster, or KaZaA). Compare also Decl. of Richard Prelinger ¶17, *id.,* at 147 ("[W]e welcome further redistribution of the Prelinger films . . . by individuals using peer-to-peer software products like Morpheus, KaZaA and Grokster."), with Deposition of Richard Prelinger, *id.,* at 410–411 (Oct. 1, 2002) ("Q. What is your understanding of Grokster? A. I have no understanding of Grokster. . . . Q. Do you know whether any user of the Grokster software has made available to share any Prelinger film? A. No."). See also Deposition of Aram Sinnreich, *id.,* at 390 (Sept. 25, 2002) (testimony about the band Wilco based on "[t]he press and industry news groups and scuttlebutt."). These declarations do not support summary judgment in the face of evidence, proffered by MGM, of overwhelming use of Grokster's and StreamCast's software for infringement.[3]

Even if the absolute number of noninfringing files copied using the Grokster and StreamCast software is large, it does not follow that the products are therefore put to substantial noninfringing uses and are thus immune from liability. The number of noninfringing copies may be reflective of, and dwarfed by, the huge total volume of files shared. Further, the District Court and the Court of Appeals did not sharply distinguish between uses of Grokster's and StreamCast's software products (which this case is about) and uses of peer-to-peer technology generally (which this case is not about).

In sum, when the record in this case was developed, there was evidence that Grokster's and StreamCast's products were, and had been for some time, overwhelmingly used to infringe, and that this infringement was the overwhelming source of revenue from the products. Fairly appraised, the evidence was insufficient to demonstrate, beyond genuine debate, a reasonable prospect that substantial or commercially significant noninfringing uses were likely to develop over time. On this record, the District Court should not have ruled dispositively on the contributory infringement charge by granting summary judgment to Grokster and StreamCast.[4]

If, on remand, the case is not resolved on summary judgment in favor of MGM based on Grokster and StreamCast actively inducing infringement, the Court of Appeals, I would emphasize, should reconsider, on a fuller record, its interpretation of *Sony*'s product distribution holding.

Notes

1. JUSTICE BREYER finds in *Sony Corp. of America* v. *Universal City Studios, Inc.*, 464 U. S. 417 (1984), a "clear" rule permitting contributory liability for copyright infringement based on distribution of a product only when the product "will be used *almost exclusively* to infringe copyrights." *Post*, at 9–10. But cf. *Sony*, 464 U. S., at 442 (recognizing "copyright holder's legitimate demand for effective—not merely symbolic—protection"). *Sony*, as I read it, contains no clear, near-exclusivity test. Nor have Courts of Appeals unanimously recognized JUSTICE BREYER'S clear rule. Compare *A&M Records, Inc.* v. *Napster, Inc.*, 239 F. 3d 1004, 1021 (CA9 2001) ("[E]vidence of actual knowledge of specific acts of infringement is required to hold a computer system operator liable for contributory copyright infringement."), with *In re Aimster Copyright Litigation*, 334 F. 3d 643, 649–650 (CA7 2003) ("[W]hen a supplier is offering a product or service that has noninfringing as well as infringing uses, some estimate of the respective magnitudes of these uses is necessary for a finding of contributory infringement. . . . But the balancing of costs and benefits is necessary only in a case in which substantial noninfringing uses, present or prospective, are demonstrated."). See also *Matthew Bender & Co., Inc.* v. *West Pub. Co.*, 158 F. 3d 693, 707 (CA2 1998) ("The Supreme Court applied [the *Sony*] test to prevent copyright holders from leveraging the copyrights in their original work to control distribution of . . . products that might be used incidentally for infringement, but that had substantial noninfringing uses. . . . The same rationale applies here [to products] that have substantial, predominant and noninfringing uses as tools for research and citation."). All Members of the Court agree, moreover, that "the Court of Appeals misapplied *Sony*," at least to the extent it read that decision to limit "secondary liability" to a hardly-ever category, "quite beyond the circumstances to which the case applied." *Ante*, at 16.

2. Grokster and StreamCast, in the Court of Appeals' view, would be entitled to summary judgment unless MGM could show that that the software companies had knowledge of specific acts of infringement and failed to act on that

knowledge—a standard the court held MGM could not meet. 380 F. 3d, at 1162–1163.

3.   JUSTICE BREYER finds support for summary judgment in this motley collection of declarations and in a survey conducted by an expert retained by MGM. *Post*, at 4–8. That survey identified 75% of the files available through Grokster as copyrighted works owned or controlled by the plaintiffs, and 15% of the files as works likely copyrighted. App. 439. As to the remaining 10% of the files, "there was not enough information to form reasonable conclusions either as to what those files even consisted of, and/or whether they were infringing or non-infringing." App. 479. Even assuming, as JUSTICE BREYER does, that the *Sony* Court would have absolved Sony of contributory liability solely on the basis of the use of the Betamax for authorized time-shifting, *post*, at 3–4, summary judgment is not inevitably appropriate here. *Sony* stressed that the plaintiffs there owned "well below 10%" of copyrighted television programming, 464 U. S., at 443, and found, based on trial testimony from representatives of the four major sports leagues and other individuals authorized to consent to home-recording of their copyrighted broadcasts, that a similar percentage of program copying was authorized, *id.*, at 424. Here, the plaintiffs allegedly control copyrights for 70% or 75% of the material exchanged through the Grokster and StreamCast software, 380 F. 3d, at 1158; App. 439, and the District Court does not appear to have relied on comparable testimony about authorized copying from copyright holders.

4.   The District Court's conclusion that "[p]laintiffs do not dispute that Defendants' software is being used, and could be used, for substantial noninfringing purposes," 259 F. Supp. 2d 1029, 1036 (CD Cal. 2003); accord 380 F. 3d, at 1161, is, to say the least, dubious. In the courts below and in this Court, MGM has continuously disputed any such conclusion. Brief for Motion Picture Studio and Recording Company Petitioners 30–38; Brief for MGM Plaintiffs-Appellants in No. 03– 55894, etc. (CA9), p. 41; App. 356–357, 361–365.

Concurring Opinion

Metro-Goldwyn-Mayer Studios Inc., et al., Petitioners *v.* Grokster, Ltd., et al.

JUSTICE BREYER, with whom JUSTICE STEVENS and JUSTICE O'CONNOR join, concurring.

I agree with the Court that the distributor of a dual-use technology may be liable for the infringing activities of third parties where he or she actively seeks to advance the infringement. I further agree that, in light of our holding today, we need not now "revisit" *Sony Corp. of America* v. *Universal City Studios, Inc.*, 464 U. S. 417 (1984). Other Members of the Court, however, take up the *Sony* question: whether Grokster's product is "capable of 'substantial' or 'commercially significant' noninfringing uses." (GINSBURG, J., concurring) (quoting *Sony, supra*, at 442). And they answer that question by stating that the Court of Appeals was wrong when it granted summary judgment on the issue in Grokster's favor. I write to explain why I disagree with them on this matter.

I

The Court's opinion in *Sony* and the record evidence (as described and analyzed in the many briefs before us) together convince me that the Court of Appeals' conclusion has adequate legal support.

A

I begin with *Sony*'s standard. In *Sony*, the Court considered the potential copyright liability of a company that did not itself illegally copy protected material, but rather sold a machine—a Video Cassette Recorder (VCR)—that could be used to do so. A buyer could use that machine for *non*infringing purposes, such as recording for later viewing (sometimes called "'time-shifting,'" *Sony*, 464 U. S., at 421) uncopyrighted television programs or copyrighted programs with a copyright holder's permission. The buyer could use the machine for infringing purposes as well, such as building libraries of taped copyrighted programs. Or, the buyer might use the machine to record copyrighted programs under circumstances in which the legal status of the act of recording was uncertain (*i.e.*, where

Concurring Opinion, Metro-Goldwyn-Mayer Studios Inc., et al., Petitioners v. Grokster, Ltd., et al. United States Court of Appeals for the Ninth Circuit Case Nos.: (03-55894, 03-55901, 03-56236). Decision Date: August 19, 2004. Some case citations omitted.

the copying may, or may not, have constituted a "fair use." Sony knew many customers would use its VCRs to engage in unauthorized copying and "'library-building.'" *Id.*, at 458–459 (Blackmun, J., dissenting). But that fact, said the Court, was insufficient to make Sony itself an infringer. And the Court ultimately held that Sony was not liable for its customers' acts of infringement.

In reaching this conclusion, the Court recognized the need for the law, in fixing *secondary* copyright liability, to "strike a balance between a copyright holder's legitimate demand for effective—not merely symbolic—protection of the statutory monopoly, and the rights of others freely to engage in substantially unrelated areas of commerce." *Id.*, at 442. It pointed to patent law's "staple article of commerce" doctrine, under which a distributor of a product is not liable for patent infringement by its customers unless that product is "unsuited for any commercial noninfringing use." *Dawson Chemical Co.* v. *Rohm & Haas Co.*, 448 U. S. 176, 198 (1980). The Court wrote that the sale of copying equipment, "like the sale of other articles of commerce, does not constitute contributory infringement if the product is widely used for legitimate, unobjectionable purposes. *Indeed, it need merely be capable of substantial noninfringing uses.*" *Sony*, 464 U. S., at 442 (emphasis added). The Court ultimately characterized the legal "question" in the particular case as "whether [Sony's VCR] is *capable of commercially significant noninfringing uses*" (while declining to give "precise content" to these terms). *Ibid.* (emphasis added).

It then applied this standard. The Court had before it a survey (commissioned by the District Court and then prepared by the respondents) showing that roughly 9% of all VCR recordings were of the type—namely, religious, educational, and sports programming—owned by producers and distributors testifying on Sony's behalf who did not object to time-shifting. See Brief for Respondent Universal Studios et al. O. T. 1983, No. 81–1687, pp. 52–53; see also *Sony, supra*, at 424 (7.3% of all Sony VCR use is to record sports programs; representatives of the sports leagues do not object). A much higher percentage of VCR *users* had at one point taped an authorized program, in addition to taping unauthorized programs. And the plaintiffs—not a large class of content providers as in this case—owned only a small percentage of the total available *un*authorized programming. See *ante*, at 6–7, and n. 3 (GINSBURG, J., concurring). But of all the taping actually done by Sony's customers, only around 9% was of the sort the Court referred to as authorized.

The Court found that the magnitude of authorized programming was "significant," and it also noted the "significant potential for future authorized copying." 464 U. S., at 444. The Court supported this conclusion by referencing the trial testimony of professional sports league officials and a religious broadcasting representative. It also discussed (1) a Los Angeles educational station affiliated with the Public Broadcasting Service that made many of its programs available for home taping, and (2) Mr. Rogers' Neighborhood, a widely watched children's program. On the basis of this testimony and other similar evidence, the Court determined that producers of this kind had authorized duplication of their copyrighted programs "in significant enough numbers to create a *substantial* market for a noninfringing use of the" VCR. *Id.*, at 447, n. 28 (emphasis added).

The Court, in using the key word "substantial," indicated that these circumstances alone constituted a sufficient basis for rejecting the imposition of secondary liability. See *id.*, at 456 ("Sony demonstrated a significant likelihood that *substantial* numbers of copyright holders" would not object to time-shifting (emphasis added)). Nonetheless, the Court buttressed its conclusion by finding separately that, in any event, *un*authorized time-shifting often constituted not infringement, but "fair use."

B

When measured against *Sony*'s underlying evidence and analysis, the evidence now before us shows that Grokster passes *Sony*'s test—that is, whether the company's product is capable of substantial or commercially significant noninfringing uses. For one thing, petitioners' (hereinafter MGM) own expert declared that 75% of current files available on Grokster are infringing and 15% are "likely infringing." See App. 436–439, ¶¶6–17 (Decl. of Dr. Ingram Olkin); cf. *ante*, at 4 (opinion of the Court). That leaves some number of files near 10% that apparently are noninfringing, a figure very similar to the 9% or so of authorized time-shifting uses of the VCR that the Court faced in *Sony*.

As in *Sony*, witnesses here explained the nature of the noninfringing files on Grokster's network without detailed quantification. Those files include:

- Authorized copies of music by artists such as Wilco, Janis Ian, Pearl Jam, Dave Matthews, John Mayer, and others. See App. at 152–153, ¶¶9–13 (Decl. of Aram Sinnreich) (Wilco's "lesson has already been adopted by artists still signed to their major labels"); *id.*, at 170, ¶¶5–7 (Decl. of Patricia D. Hoekman) (locating "numerous audio recordings" that were authorized for swapping); *id.*, at 74, ¶10 (Decl. of Daniel B. Rung) (describing Grokster's partnership with a company that hosts music from thousands of independent artists)
- Free electronic books and other works from various online publishers, including Project Gutenberg. See id., at 136, ¶12 (Decl. of Gregory B. Newby) ("Numerous authorized and public domain Project Gutenberg eBooks are made available" on Grokster. Project Gutenberg "welcomes this widespread sharing . . . using these software products[,] since they assist us in meeting our objectives"); id., at 159–160, ¶32 (Decl. of Sinnreich)
- Public domain and authorized software, such as WinZip 8.1. Id., at 170, ¶8 (Decl. of Hoekman); id., at 165, ¶¶4–7 (Decl. of John Busher)
- Licensed music videos and television and movie segments distributed via digital video packaging with the permission of the copyright holder. Id., at 70, ¶24 (Decl. of Sean L. Mayers)

The nature of these and other lawfully swapped files is such that it is reasonable to infer quantities of current lawful use roughly approximate to those at issue in *Sony*. At least, MGM has offered no evidence sufficient to survive summary judgment that could plausibly demonstrate a significant quantitative difference. See *ante*, at 4 (opinion of the Court); see also Brief for Motion Picture Studio and Recording Company Petitioners i (referring to "at least 90% of the total use of the services"); but see *ante*, at 6–7, n. 3 (GINSBURG, J., concurring). To be sure, in quantitative terms these uses account for only a small percentage of the total number of uses of Grokster's product. But the same was true in *Sony*, which characterized the relatively limited authorized copying market as "substantial." (The Court made clear as well in *Sony* that the amount of material then presently available for lawful copying—if not actually copied—was significant, see 464 U. S., at 444, and the same is certainly true in this case.)

Importantly, *Sony* also used the word "capable," asking whether the product is *"capable of"* substantial noninfringing uses. Its language and analysis suggest that a figure like 10%, if fixed for all time, might well prove insufficient, but that such a figure serves as an adequate foundation where there is a reasonable prospect of expanded legitimate uses over time. See *ibid.* (noting a "significant potential for future authorized copying"). And its language also indicates the appropriateness of looking to potential future uses of the product to determine its "capability."

Here the record reveals a significant future market for noninfringing uses of Grokster-type peer-to-peer software. Such software permits the exchange of *any* sort of digital file—whether that file does, or does not, contain copyrighted material. As more and more uncopyrighted information is stored in swappable form, it seems a likely inference that lawful peer-to-peer sharing will become increasingly prevalent. See, *e.g.*, App. 142, ¶20 (Decl. of Brewster Kahle) ("The [Internet Archive] welcomes [the] redistribution [of authorized films] by the Morpheus-Grokster-KaZaa community of users"); *id.*, at 166, ¶8 (Decl. of Busher) (sales figures of $1,000 to $10,000 per month through peer-to-peer networks "will increase in the future as Acoustica's trialware is more widely distributed through these networks"); *id.*, at 156–164, ¶¶21–40 (Decl. of Sinnreich).

And that is just what is happening. Such legitimate noninfringing uses are coming to include the swapping of: *research information* (the initial purpose of many peer-to-peer networks); *public domain films* (*e.g.*, those owned by the Prelinger Archive); *historical recordings and digital educational materials* (*e.g.*, those stored on the Internet Archive); *digital photos* (OurPictures, for example, is starting a P2P photo-swapping service); *"shareware" and "freeware"* (*e.g.*, Linux and certain Windows software); *secure licensed music and movie files* (Intent MediaWorks, for example, protects licensed content sent across P2P networks); *news broadcasts past and present* (the BBC Creative Archive lets users "rip, mix and share the BBC"); *user-created audio and video files* (including "podcasts" that may be distributed through P2P software); *and all manner of free "open content" works collected by Creative Commons* (one can search for Creative Commons material on StreamCast). See Brief for Distributed Computing Industry Association as *Amicus Curiae* 15–26; Merges, A New Dynamism in the Public Domain, 71 U. Chi. L. Rev. 183 (2004). I can find nothing in the record that suggests that this course of events will *not* continue to flow naturally as a consequence of the character of the software taken together with the foreseeable development of the Internet and of information technology. Cf. *ante*, at 1–2 (opinion of the Court) (discussing the significant benefits of peer-to-peer technology).

There may be other now-unforeseen noninfringing uses that develop for peer-to-peer software, just as the home-video rental industry (unmentioned in

Sony) developed for the VCR. But the foreseeable development of such uses, when taken together with an estimated 10% noninfringing material, is sufficient to meet *Sony*'s standard. And while *Sony* considered the record following a trial, there are no facts asserted by MGM in its summary judgment filings that lead me to believe the outcome after a trial here could be any different. The lower courts reached the same conclusion.

Of course, Grokster itself may not want to develop these other noninfringing uses. But *Sony*'s standard seeks to protect not the Groksters of this world (which in any event may well be liable under today's holding), but the development of technology more generally. And Grokster's desires in this respect are beside the point.

II

The real question here, I believe, is not whether the record evidence satisfies *Sony*. As I have interpreted the standard set forth in that case, it does. And of the Courts of Appeals that have considered the matter, only one has proposed interpreting *Sony* more strictly than I would do—in a case where the product might have failed under *any* standard. *In re Aimster Copyright Litigation*, 334 F. 3d 643, 653 (CA7 2003) (defendant "failed to show that its service is *ever* used for any purpose other than to infringe" copyrights (emphasis added)); see *Matthew Bender & Co., Inc.* v. *West Pub. Co.*, 158 F. 3d 693, 706–707 (CA2 1998) (court did not *require* that noninfringing uses be "predominant," it merely found that they *were* predominant, and therefore provided no analysis of *Sony*'s boundaries); but see *ante*, at 3 n. 1 (GINSBURG, J., concurring); see also *A&M Records* v. *Napster, Inc.*, 239 F. 3d 1004, 1020 (CA9 2001) (discussing *Sony*); *Cable/Home Communication Corp.* v. *Network Productions, Inc.*, 902 F. 2d 829, 842–847 (CA11 1990) (same); *Vault Corp.* v. *Quaid Software, Ltd.*, 847 F. 2d 255, 262 (CA5 1988) (same); cf. *Dynacore Holdings Corp.* v. *U. S. Philips Corp.*, 363 F. 3d 1263, 1275 (CA Fed. 2004) (same); see also *Doe* v. *GTE Corp.*, 347 F. 3d 655, 661 (CA7 2003) ("A person may be liable as a contributory infringer if the product or service it sells has no (or only slight) legal use").

Instead, the real question is whether we should modify the *Sony* standard, as MGM requests, or interpret *Sony* more strictly, as I believe JUSTICE GINSBURG's approach would do in practice. Compare *ante*, at 4–8 (concurring) (insufficient evidence in this case of both present lawful uses and of a reasonable prospect that substantial noninfringing uses would develop over time), with *Sony*, 464 U. S., at 442–447 (basing conclusion as to the likely existence of a substantial market for authorized copying upon general declarations, some survey data, and common sense).

As I have said, *Sony* itself sought to "strike a balance between a copyright holder's legitimate demand for effective—not merely symbolic—protection of the statutory monopoly, and the rights of others freely to engage in substantially unrelated areas of commerce." *Id.*, at 442. Thus, to determine whether modification, or a strict interpretation, of *Sony* is needed, I would ask whether MGM has shown that *Sony* incorrectly balanced copyright and new-technology interests. In particular: (1) Has *Sony* (as I interpret it) worked to protect new technology? (2) If so, would modification or strict interpretation significantly weaken that protection? (3) If so, would new or necessary copyright-related benefits outweigh any such weakening?

A

The first question is the easiest to answer. *Sony*'s rule, as I interpret it, has provided entrepreneurs with needed assurance that they will be shielded from copyright liability as they bring valuable new technologies to market.

Sony's rule is clear.   That clarity allows those who develop new products that are capable of substantial noninfringing uses to know, *ex ante*, that distribution of their product will not yield massive monetary liability. At the same time, it helps deter them from distributing products that have no other real function than—or that are specifically intended for—copyright infringement, deterrence that the Court's holding today reinforces (by adding a weapon to the copyright holder's legal arsenal).

Sony's rule is strongly technology protecting.   The rule deliberately makes it difficult for courts to find secondary liability where new technology is at issue. It establishes that the law will not impose copyright liability upon the distributors of dual-use technologies (who do not themselves engage in unauthorized copying) unless the product in question will be used *almost exclusively* to infringe copyrights (or unless they actively induce infringements as we today describe). *Sony* thereby recognizes that the copyright laws are not intended to discourage or to control the emergence of new technologies, including (perhaps especially) those that help disseminate information and ideas more broadly or more efficiently. Thus *Sony*'s rule shelters VCRs, typewriters, tape recorders, photocopiers, computers, cassette players, compact disc burners, digital video recorders, MP3 players, Internet search engines, and peer-to-peer software. But *Sony*'s rule does not shelter descramblers, even if one could *theoretically* use a descrambler in a noninfringing way. 464 U. S., at 441–442; Compare *Cable/Home Communication Corp., supra*, at 837–850 (developer liable for advertising television signal descrambler), with *Vault Corp., supra*, at 262 (primary use infringing but a substantial noninfringing use).

Sony's rule is forward looking.   It does not confine its scope to a static snapshot of a product's current uses (thereby threatening technologies that have undeveloped future markets). Rather, as the VCR example makes clear, a product's market can evolve dramatically over time. And *Sony*—by referring to a *capacity* for substantial noninfringing uses—recognizes that fact. *Sony*'s word "capable" refers to a plausible, not simply a theoretical, likelihood that such uses will come to pass, and that fact anchors *Sony* in practical reality.

Sony's rule is mindful of the limitations facing judges where matters of technology are concerned.   Judges have no specialized technical ability to answer questions about present or future technological feasibililiy or commercial viability where technology professionals, engineers, and venture capitalists themselves may radically disagree and where answers may differ depending upon whether one focuses upon the time of product development or the time of distribution. Consider, for example, the question whether devices can be added to Grokster's software that will filter out infringing files. MGM tells us this is easy enough to do, as do several *amici* that produce and sell the filtering technology. See, *e.g.*, Brief for Motion Picture Studio Petitioners 11; Brief for Audible Magic Corp. et al. as *Amicus Curiae* 3–10. Grokster says it is not at all easy to do, and not an efficient solution in any event, and several apparently disinterested computer science professors agree. See Brief for Respondents 31; Brief for Computer Science Professors as *Amicus Curiae* 6–10, 14–18. Which account should a judge credit? *Sony* says that the judge will not necessarily have to decide.

Given the nature of the *Sony* rule, it is not surprising that in the last 20 years, there have been relatively few contributory infringement suits—based on a product distribution theory—brought against technology providers (a small handful of federal appellate court cases and perhaps fewer than two dozen District Court cases in the last 20 years). I have found nothing in the briefs or the record that shows that *Sony* has failed to achieve its innovation-protecting objective.

B

The second, more difficult, question is whether a modified *Sony* rule (or a strict interpretation) would significantly weaken the law's ability to protect new technology. Justice Ginsburg's approach would require defendants to produce considerably more concrete evidence—more than was presented here—to earn *Sony*'s shelter. That heavier evidentiary demand, and especially the more dramatic (case-by-case balancing) modifications that MGM and the Government seek, would, I believe, undercut the protection that *Sony* now offers.

To require defendants to provide, for example, detailed evidence—say business plans, profitability estimates, projected technological modifications, and so forth—would doubtless make life easier for copyrightholder plaintiffs. But it would simultaneously increase the legal uncertainty that surrounds the creation or development of a new technology capable of being put to infringing uses. Inventors and entrepreneurs (in the garage, the dorm room, the corporate lab, or the boardroom) would have to fear (and in many cases endure) costly and extensive trials when they create, produce, or distribute the sort of information technology that can be used for copyright infringement. They would often be left guessing as to how a court, upon later review of the product and its uses, would decide when necessarily rough estimates amounted to sufficient evidence. They would have no way to predict how courts would weigh the respective values of infringing and noninfringing uses; determine the efficiency and advisability of technological changes; or assess a product's potential future markets. The price of a wrong guess—even if it involves a good-faith effort to assess technical and commercial viability—could be large statutory damages (not less than $750 and up to $30,000 *per infringed work*). 17 U. S. C. §504(c)(1). The additional risk and uncertainty would mean a consequent additional chill of technological development.

C

The third question—whether a positive copyright impact would outweigh any technology-related loss—I find the most difficult of the three. I do not doubt that a more intrusive *Sony* test would generally provide greater revenue security for copyright holders. But it is harder to conclude that the gains on the copyright swings would exceed the losses on the technology roundabouts.

For one thing, the law disfavors equating the two different kinds of gain and loss; rather, it leans in favor of protecting technology. As *Sony* itself makes clear, the producer of a technology which *permits* unlawful copying does not himself *engage* in unlawful copying—a fact that makes the attachment of copyright liability to the creation, production, or distribution of the technology an exceptional thing. See 464 U. S., at 431 (courts "must be circumspect" in construing the copyright laws to preclude distribution of new technologies). Moreover, *Sony* has been the law for some time. And that fact imposes a serious burden upon copyright holders like MGM to show a need for change in the current rules of the game, including a more strict interpretation of the test. See, *e.g.*, Brief for Motion Picture Studio Petitioners 31 (*Sony* should not protect products when the "primary or principal" use is infringing).

In any event, the evidence now available does not, in my view, make out a sufficiently strong case for change. To say this is not to doubt the basic need to protect copyrighted material from infringement. The Constitution itself stresses the vital role that copyright plays in advancing the "useful Arts." Art. I, §8, cl. 8. No one disputes that "reward to the author or artist serves to induce release to the public of the products of his creative genius." *United States* v. *Paramount Pictures, Inc.*, 334 U. S. 131, 158 (1948). And deliberate unlawful copying is no less an unlawful taking of property than garden-variety theft. See, *e.g.*, 18 U. S. C. §2319 (criminal copyright infringement); §1961(1)(B) (copyright infringement can be a predicate act under the Racketeer Influenced and Corrupt Organizations Act); §1956(c)(7)(D) (money laundering includes the receipt of proceeds from copyright infringement). But these highly general principles cannot by themselves tell us how to balance the interests at issue in *Sony* or whether *Sony*'s standard needs modification. And at certain key points, information is lacking.

Will an unmodified *Sony* lead to a significant diminution in the amount or quality of creative work produced? Since copyright's basic objective is creation and its revenue objectives but a means to that end, this is the underlying copyright question. See *Twentieth Century Music Corp.* v. *Aiken*, 422 U. S. 151, 156 (1975) ("Creative work is to be encouraged and rewarded, but private motivation must ultimately serve the cause of promoting broad public availability of literature, music, and the other arts"). And its answer is far from clear.

Unauthorized copying likely diminishes industry revenue, though it is not clear by how much. Compare S. Liebowitz, Will MP3 Downloads Annihilate the Record Industry? The Evidence So Far, p. 2 (June 2003), http://www.utdallas.edu/~liebowit/intprop/records.pdf (all Internet materials as visited June 24, 2005, and available in Clerk of Court's case file) (file sharing has caused a decline in music sales), and Press Release, Informa Media Group Report (citing

Music on the Internet (5th ed. 2004)) (estimating total lost sales to the music industry in the range of $2 billion annually), at http://www.informatm.com, with F. Oberholzer & K. Strumpf, The Effect of File Sharing on Record Sales: An Empirical Analysis, p. 24 (Mar. 2004), www.unc.edu/~cigar/papers/FileSharing_ March2004.pdf (academic study concluding that "file sharing has no statistically significant effect on purchases of the average album"), and McGuire, Study: File-Sharing No Threat to Music Sales (Mar. 29, 2004), http://www.washingtonpost.com/ ac2/wp-dyn/A34300-2004Mar29?language=printer (discussing mixed evidence).

The extent to which related production has actually and resultingly declined remains uncertain, though there is good reason to believe that the decline, if any, is not substantial. See, *e.g.*, M. Madden, Pew Internet & American Life Project, Artists, Musicians, and the Internet, p. 21, http://www. pewinternet.org/pdfs/PIP_Artists.Musicians_Report.pdf (nearly 70% of musicians believe that file sharing is a minor threat or no threat at all to creative industries); Benkler, Sharing Nicely: On Shareable Goods and the Emergence of Sharing as a Modality of Economic Production, 114 Yale L. J. 273, 351–352 (2004) ("Much of the actual flow of revenue to artists—from performances and other sources—is stable even assuming a complete displacement of the CD market by peer-to-peer distribution. . . . [I]t would be silly to think that music, a cultural form without which no human society has existed, will cease to be in our world [because of illegal file swapping]").

More importantly, copyright holders at least potentially have other tools available to reduce piracy and to abate whatever threat it poses to creative production. As today's opinion makes clear, a copyright holder may proceed against a technology provider where a provable specific intent to infringe (of the kind the Court describes) is present. *Ante*, at 24 (opinion of the Court). Services like Grokster may well be liable under an inducement theory.

In addition, a copyright holder has always had the legal authority to bring a traditional infringement suit against one who wrongfully copies. Indeed, since September 2003, the Recording Industry Association of America (RIAA) has filed "thousands of suits against people for sharing copyrighted material." Walker, New Movement Hits Universities: Get Legal Music, *Washington Post,* Mar. 17, 2005, p. E1. These suits have provided copyright holders with damages; have served as a teaching tool, making clear that much file sharing, if done without permission, is unlawful; and apparently have had a real and significant deterrent effect. See, *e.g.*, L. Rainie, M. Madden, D. Hess, & G. Mudd, Pew Internet Project and comScore Media Metrix Data Memo: The state of music downloading and file-sharing online, pp. 2, 4, 6, 10 (Apr. 2004), www. pewinternet.org/pdfs/PIP_Filesharing_April_04.pdf (number of people downloading files fell from a peak of roughly 35 million to roughly 23 million in the year following the first suits; 38% of current downloaders report downloading fewer files because of the suits); M. Madden & L. Rainie, Pew Internet Project Data Memo: Music and video downloading moves beyond P2P, p. 7 (March 2005), www.pewinternet.org/pdfs/PIP_Filesharing_March05.pdf (number of downloaders has "inched up" but "continues to rest well below the peak level"); Groennings, Note, Costs and Benefits of the Recording Industry's Litigation Against Individuals, 20 Berkeley Technology L. J. 571 (2005); but see Evangelista, Downloading

Music and Movie Files is as Popular as Ever, San Francisco Chronicle, Mar. 28, 2005, p. E1 (referring to the continuing "tide of rampant copyright infringement," while noting that the RIAA says it believes the "campaign of lawsuits and public education has at least contained the problem").

Further, copyright holders may develop new technological devices that will help curb unlawful infringement. Some new technology, called "digital 'watermarking'" and "digital fingerprint[ing]," can encode within the file information about the author and the copyright scope and date, which "fingerprints" can help to expose infringers. RIAA Reveals Method to Madness, Wired News, Aug. 28, 2003, http://www.wired.com/news/digiwood/0,1412,60222,00.html; Besek, Anti-Circumvention Laws and Copyright: A Report from the Kernochan Center for Law, Media and the Arts, 27 Colum. J. L. & Arts 385, 391, 451 (2004). Other technology can, through encryption, potentially restrict users' ability to make a digital copy. See J. Borland, Tripping the Rippers, C/net News.com (Sept. 28, 2001), http://news.com.com/Tripping+the+rippers/2009=1023_3=273619.html; but see Brief for Bridgemar Services Ltd. as *Amicus Curiae* 5–8 (arguing that peer-to-peer service providers can more easily block unlawful swapping).

At the same time, advances in technology have discouraged unlawful copying by making *lawful* copying (*e.g.*, downloading music with the copyright holder's permission) cheaper and easier to achieve. Several services now sell music for less than $1 per song. (Walmart.com, for example, charges $0.88 each). Consequently, many consumers initially attracted to the convenience and flexibility of services like Grokster are now migrating to lawful paid services (services with copying permission) where they can enjoy at little cost even greater convenience and flexibility without engaging in unlawful swapping. See Wu, When Code Isn't Law, 89 Va. L. Rev. 679, 731–735 (2003) (noting the prevalence of technological problems on unpaid swapping sites); K. Dean, P2P Tilts Toward Legitimacy, wired.com, Wired News (Nov. 24, 2004), http://www.wired.com/news/digiwood/0,1412,65836,00.html; M. Madden & L. Rainie, March 2005 Data Memo, *supra*, at 6–7 (percentage of current downloaders who have used paid services rose from 24% to 43% in a year; number using free services fell from 58% to 41%).

Thus, lawful music downloading services—those that charge the customer for downloading music and pay royalties to the copyright holder—have continued to grow and to produce substantial revenue. See Brief for Internet Law Faculty as *Amici Curiae* 5–20; Bruno, Digital Entertainment: Piracy Fight Shows Encouraging Signs (Mar. 5, 2005), available at LEXIS, News Library, Billboard File (in 2004, consumers worldwide purchased more than 10 times the number of digital tracks purchased in 2003; global digital music market of $330 million in 2004 expected to double in 2005); Press Release, Informa Media Report, *supra* (global digital revenues will likely exceed $3 billion in 2010); Ashton, [International Federation of the Phonographic Industry] Predicts Downloads Will Hit the Mainstream, Music Week, Jan. 29, 2005, p. 6 (legal music sites and portable MP3 players "are helping transform the digital music market" into "an everyday consumer experience"). And more advanced types of *non*-music-oriented P2P networks have also started to develop, drawing in part on the lessons of Grokster.

Finally, as *Sony* recognized, the legislative option remains available. Courts are less well suited than Congress to the task of "accommodat[ing] fully the varied permutations of competing interests that are inevitably implicated by such new technology." *Sony*, 464 U. S., at 431; see, *e.g.*, Audio Home Recording Act of 1992, 106 Stat. 4237 (adding 17 U. S. C., ch. 10); Protecting Innovation and Art While Preventing Piracy: Hearing Before the Senate Comm. on the Judiciary, 108th Cong., 2d Sess. (July 22, 2004).

I do not know whether these developments and similar alternatives will prove sufficient, but I am reasonably certain that, given their existence, a strong demonstrated need for modifying *Sony* (or for interpreting *Sony*'s standard more strictly) has not yet been shown. That fact, along with the added risks that modification (or strict interpretation) would impose upon technological innovation, leads me to the conclusion that we should maintain *Sony*, reading its standard as I have read it. As so read, it requires affirmance of the Ninth Circuit's determination of the relevant aspects of the *Sony* question.

✺

For these reasons, I disagree with JUSTICE GINSBURG, but I agree with the Court and join its opinion.

POSTSCRIPT

Does the Sharing of Music Files Through the Internet Violate Copyright Laws?

In 1983, Jack Valenti, the president of the Motion Picture Association of America (MPAA), appeared before a House of Representatives Committee and testified that "the VCR is to the motion picture industry and the American public what the Boston strangler is to the woman alone." He felt that if the Sony case were decided in favor of Sony, as it was, copying would be rampant, and the movie industry would suffer terribly. As it turned out, however, the VCR may have saved the movie industry by providing new outlets and new sources of revenue. Similarly dire predications are currently being made about the impact of file sharing on the music and film industry. Will more aggressive enforcement of the copyright laws encourage the investment of time and money and lead to more creative activity, or will it interfere with the process of creation and inhibit those trying to express themselves in new ways? Will tolerating file sharing lead to new outlets of expression and new models for creating value?

Copyright is mentioned in the U.S. Constitution. Article I, Section 8 states that the purpose of copyright is "To promote the progress of science and useful arts, by securing for limited times to authors and inventors the exclusive right to their respective writings and discoveries." Copyright, therefore, is for the benefit of society, and rewarding authors and creators is the means to do this. But it should be kept in mind that there will always be a tension between encouraging the use and processing of information, and discouraging it. If there is too little control, there may be a negative effect on creative activity. But if there is too much control and too many restrictions on copying, there will also be interference with creative activity.

Copyright questions are particularly important today because so much economic value and economic activity relates to information and communication. Thus, copyright law has the attention of both the legal community and the public at large. Yet, in addition to the question of whether stricter controls on copying are desirable, is the question of whether the law is capable of restricting copying when the technology is so widespread, when communication across borders is so easy, and when new applications which can be used for copying appear frequently. Copyright owners may have won the Grokster case but it is not certain that the cases will have a significant impact on the practice or volume of file sharing.

The first file-sharing challenge involved Napster, a Web site that allowed one to obtain copies of music that might have been stored on a machine in some distant country. Typically, when one "surfs" the Web, one is only able to look at files located on a machine called a *server.* If anyone has something they want to make available on the Web, they must find a server and then find a way to put the file containing the information on that server. Every server, in order to be reachable on the Web, has an address, such as www.mhcls.com or 128.119.199.27.

Napster and other "peer-to-peer" software (such as Kazaa and Grokster) made it possible to obtain files that were located on anyone's machine, located anywhere in the world, whether it was a server or not. Obviously, there are many more machines using the Web and connected to the Web than there are servers. Thus, Napster greatly increased the number of files available for download on the Web. Although Napster was put out of business and Grokster lost this case, file sharing and new patterns of file sharing can be expected, and there is little doubt that courts will be faced with more such cases.

Interesting readings about copyright in a digital age are Jessica Litman, *Digital Copyright: Protecting Intellectual Property on the Internet* (2001); Lawrence Lessig's two works, *The Future of Ideas* (2002) and *Free Culture* (2004); Robert P. Merges, Peter S. Menell, and Mark A. Lemley, *Intellectual Property in the New Technological Age,* 2d ed. (2000); and Paul Edward Geller, "Copyright's History and the Future: What's Culture Got To Do with It?", 47 J. Copyright Soc'y U.S.A. 209, 264 (2000). An interesting recent case about how "limited" the term of a copyright should be is *Eldred v. Ashcroft* (2003) http://supct.law .cornell.edu/ supct/html/01-618.ZS.html.

ISSUE 8

Can the Police Require Individuals to Identify Themselves?

YES: Anthony Kennedy, from Majority Opinion, *Larry D. Hiibel v. Sixth Judicial District Court of Nevada, Humboldt County,* U.S. Supreme Court (June 21, 2004)

NO: James P. Logan, Jr., Harriet E. Cummings, and Robert E. Dolan, from A Brief for the Petitioner, *Hiibel v. Sixth Judicial District Court* (2004)

ISSUE SUMMARY

YES: Supreme Court Justice Anthony Kennedy holds that requiring an individual to identify himself does not violate the right to remain silent and does not infringe rights guaranteed by the Fourth and Fifth Amendments.

NO: In a brief filed by the Office of the Nevada State Public Defender, the argument is put forward that when persons are detained on less than probable cause, it is unconstitutional for police to demand that such persons identify themselves and provide the police with their names.

On May 21, 2000, Larry Hiibel was approached by a sherriff's deputy while smoking a cigarette next to his truck at the side of a Nevada road. Giving no reason to the deputy other than, "I don't want to talk. I've done nothing. I've broken no laws," Hiibel refused to answer any of the police officers questions, including the request to provide his name. After asking 11 times and receiving no response, the deputy arrested Hiibel, charging him under a Nevada statute that declares failure to identify oneself to the police as a form of obstruction of justice.

Over a century ago, the Supreme Court established that the Fifth Amendment guarantees freedom not only from testifying against oneself but also from having to provide any self-incriminatory evidence (*Boyd v. US,* 1886). The *Hiibel* case was the first instance where the Supreme Court had to address whether one's name alone could constitute a form of incriminating evidence.

Unlike the Fifth Amendment, whose applicability would be to judge mostly on opinion and common sense, the Fourth Amendment had a rich history of case law dealing specifically with how the standards for warrantless searches and seizures applied to individuals outside their homes and in public arenas. In the 1968 case *Terry v. Ohio*, the Supreme Court addressed the concerns of law enforcement concerning the safety of police officers when stopping and questioning suspicious-acting individuals without a warrant. The Supreme Court responded by establishing the right to so-called Terry stops, during which police could briefly detain, question, and "frisk" the outer clothing of a suspect without probable cause. Arguing that such stops were of small enough consequence not to constitute custodial interference and thus the protections afforded to suspects who have been arrested, the Court established that the police could conduct "Terry stops" based on a "reasonable suspicion," a much lower threshold than the probable cause needed for official arrests.

While critics argued that the Court had given the police too much discretionary power, the Court argued that it was necessary to allow the police to investigate suspicious activity and to also protect themselves from criminals who might be carrying concealed weapons. Justice White in his concurring opinion argued, "the person may be briefly detained against his will while pertinent questions are directed to him [but] the person stopped is not obliged to answer, answers may not be compelled, and refusal to answer furnishes no basis for arrest." Under the *Terry* ruling, a suspect such as Hiibel was not required to answer police questions even though such questions are permissible under the Fourth Amendment. However, the *Terry* ruling did not address the legality or constitutionality of outside legislation, which does mandate answering certain police questions such as the Nevada statute, which made refusing to provide one's name to police an arrestable offense.

The constitutionality of such laws had been addressed in various state and federal appellate courts in the years preceding *Hiibel*. In the 1970 case of *East Brunswick v. Malfitano*, the appellate division of the New Jersey superior court upheld the conviction of a man who was arrested for refusing to provide his name to a police officer attempting to fill out paperwork for a civil grievance against him. The court specifically rejected the claim that forcing the defendant to provide his name violated his right to privacy under the Fourth Amendment, arguing, "The officer considered, and properly so, that his duty required him to obtain defendant's name and address for the purpose of preparing the necessary complaint and summons. In declining to comply with this reasonable request, the defendant interfered with the officer in the performance of his duty."

In a similar case three decades later, *State of West Virginia v. Srnsky* (2003), the supreme court of West Virginia argued that one could refuse to provide one's name to a police officer if the officer failed to provide a reason for the request, which was the same situation Hiibel had faced but not "when required to do so by express statutory direction or when the refusal occurs after a law enforcement officer has communicated the reason why the citizen's name is being sought in relation to the officer's official duties" (*W. V. v. Srnsky*). The West Virginia supreme court believed this struck a balance between the needs of law enforcement for basic identificatory information and the fear that police could arbitrarily use such authority against random individuals who the police had no legitimate need to identify. When the issue finally reached the U.S. Supreme Court in the Hiibel case, the Court voted to give even more expansive authority to the police.

YES ⤶ **Anthony Kennedy**

Majority Opinion

Larry D. Hiibel *v.* Sixth Judicial District Court of Nevada, Humboldt County

JUSTICE KENNEDY delivered the opinion of the Court.

The petitioner was arrested and convicted for refusing to identify himself during a stop allowed by *Terry* v. *Ohio*, 392 U. S. 1 (1968). He challenges his conviction under the Fourth and Fifth Amendments to the United States Constitution, applicable to the States through the Fourteenth Amendment.

I

The sheriff's department in Humboldt County, Nevada, received an afternoon telephone call reporting an assault. The caller reported seeing a man assault a woman in a red and silver GMC truck on Grass Valley Road. Deputy Sheriff Lee Dove was dispatched to investigate. When the officer arrived at the scene, he found the truck parked on the side of the road. A man was standing by the truck, and a young woman was sitting inside it. The officer observed skid marks in the gravel behind the vehicle, leading him to believe it had come to a sudden stop.

The officer approached the man and explained that he was investigating a report of a fight. The man appeared to be intoxicated. The officer asked him if he had "any identification on [him]," which we understand as a request to produce a driver's license or some other form of written identification. The man refused and asked why the officer wanted to see identification. The officer responded that he was conducting an investigation and needed to see some identification. The unidentified man became agitated and insisted he had done nothing wrong. The officer explained that he wanted to find out who the man was and what he was doing there. After continued refusals to comply with the officer's request for identification, the man began to taunt the officer by placing his hands behind his back and telling the officer to arrest him and take him to jail. This routine kept up for several minutes: the officer asked for identification 11 times and was refused each time. After warning the man that he would be arrested if he continued to refuse to comply, the officer placed him under arrest.

Majority Opinion, Hiibel v. Sixth Judicial Dist. Court of Nev., Humboldt Cty., 542 U. S. 177 (2004). Some case citations omitted.

We now know that the man arrested on Grass Valley Road is Larry Dudley Hiibel. Hiibel was charged with "willfully resist[ing], delay[ing], or obstruct[ing] a public officer in discharging or attempting to discharge any legal duty of his office" in violation of Nev. Rev. Stat. (NRS) §199.280 (2003). The government reasoned that Hiibel had obstructed the officer in carrying out his duties under §171.123, a Nevada statute that defines the legal rights and duties of a police officer in the context of an investigative stop. Section 171.123 provides in relevant part:

> "1. Any peace officer may detain any person whom the officer encounters under circumstances which reasonably indicate that the person has committed, is committing or is about to commit a crime.

> "3. The officer may detain the person pursuant to this section only to ascertain his identity and the suspicious circumstances surrounding his presence abroad. Any person so detained shall identify himself, but may not be compelled to answer any other inquiry of any peace officer."

Hiibel was tried in the Justice Court of Union Township. The court agreed that Hiibel's refusal to identify himself as required by §171.123 "obstructed and delayed Dove as a public officer in attempting to discharge his duty" in violation of §199.280. Hiibel was convicted and fined $250. The Sixth Judicial District Court affirmed, rejecting Hiibel's argument that the application of §171.123 to his case violated the Fourth and Fifth Amendments. On review the Supreme Court of Nevada rejected the Fourth Amendment challenge in a divided opinion. Hiibel petitioned for rehearing, seeking explicit resolution of his Fifth Amendment challenge. The petition was denied without opinion. We granted certiorari.

II

NRS §171.123(3) is an enactment sometimes referred to as a "stop and identify" statute. . . .

Stop and identify statutes often combine elements of traditional vagrancy laws with provisions intended to regulate police behavior in the course of investigatory stops. The statutes vary from State to State, but all permit an officer to ask or require a suspect to disclose his identity. A few States model their statutes on the Uniform Arrest Act, a model code that permits an officer to stop a person reasonably suspected of committing a crime and "demand of him his name, address, business abroad and whither he is going." Other statutes are based on the text proposed by the American Law Institute as part of the Institute's Model Penal Code. The provision, originally designated §250.12, provides that a person who is loitering "under circumstances which justify suspicion that he may be engaged or about to engage in crime commits a violation if he refuses the request of a peace officer that he identify himself and give a reasonably credible account of the lawfulness of his conduct and purposes." In some States, a suspect's refusal to identify himself is a misdemeanor offense or civil violation; in others, it is a factor to be considered in whether the suspect has violated loitering laws. In other States, a suspect may decline to identify himself without penalty.

Stop and identify statutes have their roots in early English vagrancy laws that required suspected vagrants to face arrest unless they gave "a good Account of themselves," a power that itself reflected common-law rights of private persons to "arrest any suspicious night-walker, and detain him till he give a good account of himself. . . ." In recent decades, the Court has found constitutional infirmity in traditional vagrancy laws. In *Papachristou* v. *Jacksonville,* the Court held that a traditional vagrancy law was void for vagueness. Its broad scope and imprecise terms denied proper notice to potential offenders and permitted police officers to exercise unfettered discretion in the enforcement of the law.

The Court has recognized similar constitutional limitations on the scope and operation of stop and identify statutes. In *Brown* v. *Texas,* the Court invalidated a conviction for violating a Texas stop and identify statute on Fourth Amendment grounds. The Court ruled that the initial stop was not based on specific, objective facts establishing reasonable suspicion to believe the suspect was involved in criminal activity. Absent that factual basis for detaining the defendant, the Court held, the risk of "arbitrary and abusive police practices" was too great and the stop was impermissible. Four Terms later, the Court invalidated a modified stop and identify statute on vagueness grounds. The California law in *Kolender* required a suspect to give an officer "credible and reliable" identification when asked to identify himself. The Court held that the statute was void because it provided no standard for determining what a suspect must do to comply with it, resulting in "virtually unrestrained power to arrest and charge persons with a violation."

The present case begins where our prior cases left off. Here there is no question that the initial stop was based on reasonable suspicion, satisfying the Fourth Amendment requirements noted in *Brown.* Further, the petitioner has not alleged that the statute is unconstitutionally vague, as in *Kolender.* Here the Nevada statute is narrower and more precise. The statute in *Kolender* had been interpreted to require a suspect to give the officer "credible and reliable" identification. In contrast, the Nevada Supreme Court has interpreted NRS §171.123(3) to require only that a suspect disclose his name. As we understand it, the statute does not require a suspect to give the officer a driver's license or any other document. Provided that the suspect either states his name or communicates it to the officer by other means—a choice, we assume, that the suspect may make—the statute is satisfied and no violation occurs.

III

Hiibel argues that his conviction cannot stand because the officer's conduct violated his Fourth Amendment rights. We disagree.

Asking questions is an essential part of police investigations. In the ordinary course a police officer is free to ask a person for identification without implicating the Fourth Amendment. "[I]nterrogation relating to one's identity or a request for identification by the police does not, by itself, constitute a

Fourth Amendment seizure." Beginning with *Terry* v. *Ohio,* the Court has recognized that a law enforcement officer's reasonable suspicion that a person may be involved in criminal activity permits the officer to stop the person for a brief time and take additional steps to investigate further. To ensure that the resulting seizure is constitutionally reasonable, a *Terry* stop must be limited. The officer's action must be "justified at its inception, and . . . reasonably related in scope to the circumstances which justified the interference in the first place." For example, the seizure cannot continue for an excessive period of time, or resemble a traditional arrest.

Our decisions make clear that questions concerning a suspect's identity are a routine and accepted part of many *Terry* stops. . . .

Obtaining a suspect's name in the course of a *Terry* stop serves important government interests. Knowledge of identity may inform an officer that a suspect is wanted for another offense, or has a record of violence or mental disorder. On the other hand, knowing identity may help clear a suspect and allow the police to concentrate their efforts elsewhere. Identity may prove particularly important in cases such as this, where the police are investigating what appears to be a domestic assault. Officers called to investigate domestic disputes need to know whom they are dealing with in order to assess the situation, the threat to their own safety, and possible danger to the potential victim.

Although it is well established that an officer may ask a suspect to identify himself in the course of a *Terry* stop, it has been an open question whether the suspect can be arrested and prosecuted for refusal to answer. Petitioner draws our attention to statements in prior opinions that, according to him, answer the question in his favor. In *Terry,* Justice White stated in a concurring opinion that a person detained in an investigative stop can be questioned but is "not obliged to answer, answers may not be compelled, and refusal to answer furnishes no basis for an arrest." The Court cited this opinion in dicta in *Berkemer* v. *McCarty,* a decision holding that a routine traffic stop is not a custodial stop requiring the protections of *Miranda* v. *Arizona.* In the course of explaining why *Terry* stops have not been subject to *Miranda,* the Court suggested reasons why *Terry* stops have a "nonthreatening character," among them the fact that a suspect detained during a *Terry* stop "is not obliged to respond" to questions. According to petitioner, these statements establish a right to refuse to answer questions during a *Terry* stop.

We do not read these statements as controlling. The passages recognize that the Fourth Amendment does not impose obligations on the citizen but instead provides rights against the government. As a result, the Fourth Amendment itself cannot require a suspect to answer questions. This case concerns a different issue, however. Here, the source of the legal obligation arises from Nevada state law, not the Fourth Amendment. Further, the statutory obligation does not go beyond answering an officer's request to disclose a name. As a result, we cannot view the dicta in *Berkemer* or Justice White's concurrence in *Terry* as answering the question whether a State can compel a suspect to disclose his name during a *Terry* stop.

The principles of *Terry* permit a State to require a suspect to disclose his name in the course of a *Terry* stop. The reasonableness of a seizure under the

Fourth Amendment is determined "by balancing its intrusion on the individual's Fourth Amendment interests against its promotion of legitimate government interests." The Nevada statute satisfies that standard. The request for identity has an immediate relation to the purpose, rationale, and practical demands of a *Terry* stop. The threat of criminal sanction helps ensure that the request for identity does not become a legal nullity. On the other hand, the Nevada statute does not alter the nature of the stop itself: it does not change its duration, or its location. A state law requiring a suspect to disclose his name in the course of a valid *Terry* stop is consistent with Fourth Amendment prohibitions against unreasonable searches and seizures.

Petitioner argues that the Nevada statute circumvents the probable cause requirement, in effect allowing an officer to arrest a person for being suspicious. According to petitioner, this creates a risk of arbitrary police conduct that the Fourth Amendment does not permit. These are familiar concerns; they were central to the opinion in *Papachristou,* and also to the decisions limiting the operation of stop and identify statutes in *Kolender* and *Brown.* Petitioner's concerns are met by the requirement that a *Terry* stop must be justified at its inception and "reasonably related in scope to the circumstances which justified" the initial stop. Under these principles, an officer may not arrest a suspect for failure to identify himself if the request for identification is not reasonably related to the circumstances justifying the stop. The Court noted a similar limitation in *Hayes*, where it suggested that *Terry* may permit an officer to determine a suspect's identity by compelling the suspect to submit to fingerprinting only if there is "a reasonable basis for believing that fingerprinting will establish or negate the suspect's connection with that crime." It is clear in this case that the request for identification was "reasonably related in scope to the circumstances which justified" the stop. The officer's request was a commonsense inquiry, not an effort to obtain an arrest for failure to identify after a *Terry* stop yielded insufficient evidence. The stop, the request, and the State's requirement of a response did not contravene the guarantees of the Fourth Amendment.

IV

Petitioner further contends that his conviction violates the Fifth Amendment's prohibition on compelled self-incrimination. The Fifth Amendment states that "[n]o person . . . shall be compelled in any criminal case to be a witness against himself." To qualify for the Fifth Amendment privilege, a communication must be testimonial, incriminating, and compelled.

Respondents urge us to hold that the statements NRS §171.123(3) requires are nontestimonial, and so outside the Clause's scope. We decline to resolve the case on that basis. "[T]o be testimonial, an accused's communication must itself, explicitly or implicitly, relate a factual assertion or disclose information." Stating one's name may qualify as an assertion of fact relating to identity. Production of identity documents might meet the definition as well. As we noted in *Hubbell*, acts of production may yield testimony establishing "the existence, authenticity, and custody of items [the police seek]." Even if these required actions are testimonial, however, petitioner's challenge must fail because in this case disclosure of his name presented no reasonable danger of incrimination.

The Fifth Amendment prohibits only compelled testimony that is incriminating. . . .

In this case petitioner's refusal to disclose his name was not based on any articulated real and appreciable fear that his name would be used to incriminate him, or that it "would furnish a link in the chain of evidence needed to prosecute" him. As best we can tell, petitioner refused to identify himself only because he thought his name was none of the officer's business. Even today, petitioner does not explain how the disclosure of his name could have been used against him in a criminal case. While we recognize petitioner's strong belief that he should not have to disclose his identity, the Fifth Amendment does not override the Nevada Legislature's judgment to the contrary absent a reasonable belief that the disclosure would tend to incriminate him.

The narrow scope of the disclosure requirement is also important. One's identity is, by definition, unique; yet it is, in another sense, a universal characteristic. Answering a request to disclose a name is likely to be so insignificant in the scheme of things as to be incriminating only in unusual circumstances. . . . Even witnesses who plan to invoke the Fifth Amendment privilege answer when their names are called to take the stand. Still, a case may arise where there is a substantial allegation that furnishing identity at the time of a stop would have given the police a link in the chain of evidence needed to convict the individual of a separate offense. In that case, the court can then consider whether the privilege applies, and, if the Fifth Amendment has been violated, what remedy must follow. We need not resolve those questions here.

The judgment of the Nevada Supreme Court is

Affirmed.

James P. Logan, Jr., Harriet E. Cummings, and Robert E. Dolan

→ **NO**

A Brief for the Petitioner

. . . Under current Nevada law, persons may be compelled to identify themselves to peace officers acting under reasonable suspicion of criminal activity, and if they refuse, such persons can be convicted of a misdemeanor and punished by up to six months in jail. The question the Court must answer in this case is as follows: When persons are being lawfully detained upon less than probable cause, may the government constitutionally require them, under threat of imprisonment, to identify themselves?

Petitioner submits that such a government practice is abhorrent to the Constitution. A brief review of the case law leading up to the issue in this case suggests that this Court agrees. . . .

This Court has held that seemingly innocent conduct can be the basis for reasonable suspicion justifying a *Terry* stop. Moreover, this Court recently acknowledged that "the concept of reasonable suspicion is somewhat abstract," and that "the cause 'sufficient to authorize police to stop a person' is an 'elusive concept.'". . . Officers are thus left to rely on their own subjective judgment when deciding who should be *Terry* stopped. By deliberately avoiding reducing that cause to "'a neat set of legal rules,'" the Court has necessarily muddied what, in Nevada, an officer must observe before he may stop, and demand identification from, a person. In essence, police officers proceed with neither guidance nor limitations in assessing what behavior qualifies as suspicious.

Thus, under the current state of the law in Nevada, a person can be stopped by the police for engaging in perfectly innocent yet "suspicious" behavior, asked to identify himself, and if he declines, be arrested and hauled off to jail. This is frighteningly reminiscent of Nazi Germany, where people lived in fear of being approached by the Gestapo and commanded to turn over "Your papers, please.". . .

At this juncture it is important to note that Mr. Hiibel is not claiming that police authorities do not have the right to ask any questions reasonably related to the purpose of the seizure. . . . Moreover, although certainly a strong argument can be made that the Nevada statute is unconstitutionally vague, it is Mr. Hiibel's contention that even if the statute could be rewritten in such a way that it would not be vague, it would nevertheless be unconstitutional as violative of the Fifth and Fourth Amendments.

Minority Opinion, Hiibel v. Sixth Judicial Dist. Court of Nev., Humboldt Cty., 542 U. S. 177 (2004). Some case citations omitted.

Mr. Hiibel is, however, asserting that although the police authorities have the right to ask questions, he is not required to answer those questions, in particular questions regarding his identity, and that his failure to do so should not result in criminal sanctions which can include arrest, a fine, and jail.[1] For the reasons that follow, Nev. Rev. Stat. 171.123(3) is violative of the Fifth and Fourth Amendments to the United States Constitution.

The Requirement of Nev. Rev. Stat. 171.123(3) Which Compels a Person Detained Upon Reasonable Suspicion to Identify Himself to the Police Violates the Fifth Amendment Privilege Against Compulsory Self-Incrimination

The Fifth Amendment to the United States Constitution provides, in pertinent part: "No person . . . shall be compelled in any criminal case to be a witness against himself, nor be deprived of life, liberty, or property, without due process of law. . . ."

The requirement of Nev. Rev. Stat. 171.123(3) that an individual disclose his identity or suffer a criminal conviction frustrates this important Fifth Amendment protection, which is designed to "prevent the use of legal process to force from the lips of the accused individual the evidence necessary to convict him. . . ." The Fifth Amendment requires prosecutors "to search for independent evidence instead of relying upon proof extracted from individuals by force of law. The immediate and potential evils of compulsory self-disclosure transcend any difficulties that the exercise of the privilege may impose on society in the detection and prosecution of crime." As this Court has noted, the privilege "is firmly embedded in our constitutional and legal frameworks as a bulwark against iniquitous methods of prosecution."

The Fifth Amendment safeguards the "right of a person to remain silent unless he chooses to speak in the unfettered exercise of his own will, and to suffer no penalty . . . for such silence." Our accusatorial system of criminal justice "demands that the government seeking to punish an individual produce the evidence against him by its own independent labors, rather than by the cruel, simple expedient of compelling it from his own mouth." In short, the proposition *Miranda* has become known for—the right to remain silent—is a bulwark of our legal system.

In speaking of testimony given in response to a grant of legislative immunity this Court has recognized that such statements compelled by law are:

> [T]he essence of coerced testimony. In such cases there is no question whether physical or psychological pressures overrode the defendant's will; the witness is told to talk or face the government's coercive sanctions, notably, a conviction for contempt. The information given in response to a grant of immunity may well be more reliable than information beaten from a helpless defendant, but it is no less compelled. The Fifth and Fourteenth

Amendments provide a privilege against *compelled* self-incrimination, not merely against unreliable self-incrimination.

As noted by Justice Powell, joined in concurrence by Justice Rehnquist, "the Fifth Amendment . . . prohibits a State from using compulsion to extract truthful information from a defendant, when that information is to be used later in obtaining the individual's conviction." Accordingly, it is plain that the government is prohibited from requiring a person to identify himself to the police under threat of criminal prosecution because to do so violates the Fifth Amendment privilege against compulsory self-incrimination.

Here too, moreso even than if the police resorted to sophisticated techniques of custodial interrogation, it is the force of the law that extracts proof of identity from the suspect under a *Terry* detention. If the suspect exercises his Fifth Amendment right to remain silent, he is punished as a criminal. There is no right to remain silent if silence receives a criminal sanction. To hold otherwise would render the protections of the Fifth Amendment meaningless.

Being Compelled to Identify Oneself to the Police Is a Testimonial Communication Protected by the Fifth Amendment

The Fifth Amendment protects persons from being compelled to testify against themselves or to otherwise provide the state with evidence of a testimonial or communicative nature. It does not protect a person from being compelled to disclose real or physical evidence. . . . Being compelled to identify oneself to an inquiring officer is not evidence of real or physical evidence in the nature of physical characteristics such as blood or handwriting exemplars; rather, it is evidence of a testimonial or communicative nature that, upon disclosure, can itself be incriminating or lead to incriminating evidence. If it did not, the police would have little interest in asking persons their names or identities. Consciousness of who we are goes to the very essence of our being, and being commanded to reveal our identity and hence face the "trilemma" of truth, falsity, or silence, causes us to reveal evidence which is testimonial at its core.

Significantly, in *Lefkowitz v. Turley*, 414 U.S. 70 (1973), this Court said of the Fifth Amendment privilege against compelled self-incrimination:

The Amendment not only protects the individual against being involuntarily called as a witness against himself in a criminal prosecution but also privileges him not to answer official questions put to him in any other proceeding, civil or criminal, formal or informal, where the answers might incriminate him in future criminal proceedings.

Thus, it does not matter that Mr. Hiibel was asked to identify himself in the context of a *Terry* stop rather than in a formal judicial proceeding. In fact, it appears that this Court and various of its members have assumed that the Fifth Amendment's prohibition against compulsory self-incrimination applies to *Terry* stops. Following the dictates of *Lefkowitz*, this assumption is plainly correct. Compulsory identification for purposes of permitting an officer "to ascertain his identity and the suspicious circumstances surrounding his presence abroad," Nev. Rev. Stat. 171.123(3), is inherently testimonial and falls within the purview of the Fifth Amendment. By itself, the identification process can be incriminating or lead to evidence which might incriminate the person in future criminal proceedings. It is therefore the type of testimonial or communicative evidence which the Fifth Amendment is designed to protect against being compelled. . . .

⋰⊙⋱

The request for identification takes place during a valid Fourth Amendment seizure when there is an articulable suspicion that criminal activity is afoot. Therefore, the only time the request for identification takes place is during an actual criminal investigation. [Under Nevada law], failure to identify oneself can be the basis for the crime of resisting a public officer, a misdemeanor punishable by up to six months in jail. Unmistakably, then, this is an area of activity "permeated with criminal statutes." Moreover, the statute is directed at a "highly selective" group of persons "inherently suspect of criminal activities," as it is limited to persons whom the officer believes "has committed, is committing or is about to commit a crime," and the officer is limited to inquiring about the person's identity and "suspicious circumstances surrounding his presence abroad." Nev. Rev. Stat. 171.123(1), (3). . . . The circumstances of this case demonstrate how there is a direct likelihood that being compelled to identify oneself can be incriminating by providing testimonial information in one's name that could be used as evidence against a suspect otherwise lacking probable cause for arrest.

In this case the officer, having been advised that someone was seen striking a female passenger inside a pickup truck, was investigating a possible battery or domestic battery. The same last name can be evidence of a relationship which triggers the domestic battery laws. The alleged victim of the battery was Mr. Hiibel's daughter. Thus, one's name can in itself be incriminating. . . .

The prior record of the offender is discoverable through sophisticated electronic databases indexed by name among other ways. It is clear that at this time in our criminal justice, a person's name can be used to enforce a harsher penalty. While the police can obtain this information through other sources (e.g., fingerprints), the Fifth Amendment protects individuals from being compelled to provide information which tends to incriminate them. Nev. Rev. Stat. 171.123's requirement that a detained person identify himself plainly violates this important constitutional safeguard.

Additionally, little imagination is required to devise scenarios in which compelled identification can be incriminating. For example, in *Kirby v. Illinois*, a lawfully stopped suspect produced the credentials of a mugging victim upon an officer's demand for identification. In another case, *United States v. Purry*, officers requested identification from a suspect whose wallet they had discovered at the scene of a crime. In each of these cases, the proof of identity provided evidence supporting an eventual conviction. Therefore, in both of these cases a statutory requirement of self-identification would have constituted compelled self-incrimination in violation of the Fifth Amendment.

As can be readily seen from the above discussion, compelled identification during a *Terry* stop is a testimonial communication which gives police authorities information that can be later used in a subsequent criminal proceeding. The Nevada statute applies to an area of activity that is permeated with criminal statutes, is directed at a highly selective group of persons who are inherently suspect of criminal activities, and poses a substantial hazard of self-incrimination. Because this statute directly contravenes the protections preserved by the Fifth Amendment, it must be held unconstitutional.

Nev. Rev. Stat. 171.123(3) Requiring Individuals Who Are the Subject of a *Terry* Stop to Identify Themselves Violates the Fourth Amendment Prohibition Against Unreasonable Searches and Seizures

. . . Imposition of criminal sanctions for the refusal to produce identification, when the demand for identification is made without probable cause to believe an offense has been committed, violates the Fourth Amendment rights of individuals: "The right of the people to be secure in their persons, houses, papers and effects, against unreasonable searches and seizures, shall not be violated, and no warrants shall issue, but upon probable cause. . . ."

Over a period of decades this Court has stressed many times the central importance of the probable cause requirement to the protection of a person's privacy afforded by the guarantees of the Fourth Amendment. As stated, for example, in *Dunaway v. New York,* "The long-prevailing standards of probable cause embodied the best compromise that has been found for accommodating the often opposing interests in safeguarding citizens from rash and unreasonable interferences with privacy and in seeking to give fair leeway for enforcing the law in the community's protection."

The Fourth Amendment's protection of the right to privacy and its safeguards against unreasonable searches and seizures are not shed simply because an individual leaves his home to walk or drive the streets. . . .

Although the Court in *Terry* created an exception to the principle that seizures of the individual must be based on probable cause, the standard of probable cause continues to govern. "Because *Terry* involved an exception to the general rule requiring probable cause, this Court has been careful to maintain its narrow scope." . . .

The test of reasonableness under the Fourth Amendment requires a balancing of the need for the particular search or seizure "against the invasion of personal rights that the search [or seizure] entails." Balancing those competing interests in this case reveals that the scales tip heavily in favor of protecting individual rights. . . .

◦◦◦

The requirement of Nev. Rev. Stat. 171.123(3) that proof of identity be disclosed upon no more than satisfaction of the *Terry* criteria of reasonable suspicion represents an unwarranted departure from the probable cause standard so essential to Fourth

Amendment freedoms. The statute effectively undermines the probable cause standard by sanctioning an arrest where there are insufficient grounds to arrest the suspect for the underlying offense that was the predicate to the initial stop. When a suspect refuses to provide proof of identity under Nev. Rev. Stat. 171.123(3), the officer is justified in arresting the suspect for violating Nev. Rev. Stat. 199.280. Thus, Nevada law impermissibly allows an officer to conduct a complete search incident to arrest even though he has only a suspicion of underlying criminal activity.

Accordingly, Nevada's statutory scheme violates the Fourth Amendment because, as a result of the demand for identification, "the statutes bootstrap the authority to arrest on less than probable cause." In addition, the serious intrusion on personal security, privacy and mobility that results from enforcement of the statute "outweighs the mere possibility that identification might provide a link leading to arrest." . . .

If, as this Court has unanimously held, "[a] direction by a legislature to the police to arrest all 'suspicious' persons would not pass constitutional muster," then a blanket direction to arrest all "suspicious" persons who refuse or are unable to dispel the suspicions officially perceived as to their activities should be similarly unconstitutional. For persons who refuse to identify themselves, the police still lack more than just reasonable suspicion, "a particularized and objective basis for suspecting the particular person stopped of criminal activity." Certainly, the mere refusal to identify oneself does not add enough to a *Terry*-based suspicion to give rise to probable cause to arrest for the underlying activity that prompted the stop.

Nev. Rev. Stat. 171.123(3), at its core, makes criminal an individual's refusal to identify himself. The sole intent of the law's identification requirement is to find out who the person under detention is—to increase police knowledge about that individual in order to create a case against him. The statute is otherwise useless: surely once the person provides identification to the police, without more facts brought to the attention of the officer to establish probable cause to arrest or arouse reasonable suspicion warranting further investigation, the person is free to go. The statute therefore creates "a crime out of what under the Constitution cannot be a crime.". . .

Nev. Rev. Stat. 171.123(3) Authorizes Significant Intrusion on the Individual's Constitutionally Protected First, Fourth, and Fifth Amendment Liberty Interests Even Though These Important Interests in Personal Security, Mobility and Privacy Greatly Outweigh the Intrusion's Speculative Law Enforcement Value

The enforcement of Nev. Rev. Stat. 171.123(3)'s identification requirement significantly impairs the exercise of constitutionally protected interests in personal security, mobility and privacy. "In the absence of any basis for suspecting [an individual] of misconduct, the balance between the public interest [in preventing crime] and [the individual's] right to personal security and privacy tilts in favor of freedom from police interference."

The balance between constitutional rights and crime prevention does not shift by conditioning the demand for proof of identity upon the police first establishing a *Terry* basis for detention. As already noted, although the police have the right to request persons to answer voluntarily questions concerning unsolved crimes, they have no right to compel their answers. In balancing the need for the particular seizure against the invasion of personal rights that it entails, it is apparent that Nev. Rev. Stat. 171.123(3) authorizes a significant intrusion on constitutionally protected liberty interests. . . .

❦

In parting, petitioner will conclude with a quote from the dissenting opinion of the Chief Justice of the Nevada Supreme Court:

> . . . Now is precisely the time when our duty to vigilantly guard the rights enumerated in the Constitution becomes most important. To ease our guard now, in the wake of fear of unknown perpetrators who may still seek to harm the United States and its people, would sound the call of retreat and begin the erosion of civil liberties. . . . The majority, by its decision today, has allowed the first layer of our civil liberties to be whittled away. The holding weakens the democratic principles upon which this great nation was founded. . . . At this time, this extraordinary time, the true test of our national courage is not our necessary and steadfast resolve to defend ourselves against terrorist activity. The true test is our necessary and steadfast resolve to protect and safeguard the rights and principles upon which our nation was founded, our constitution and our personal liberties.

For the reasons stated above, Nev. Rev. Stat. 171.123(3) violates the Fourth and Fifth Amendments to the United States Constitution because it compels people to identify themselves during a police investigation when they are seized upon less than probable cause. Accordingly, the judgment of the Nevada Supreme Court should be reversed.

Note

1. *Cf. Coates v. Cincinnati*, 402 U.S. 611, 616 (1971) (the state may not "make[ ] a crime out of what under the Constitution cannot be a crime.")

POSTSCRIPT

Can the Police Require Individuals to Identify Themselves?

Though there is no explicit statement of a right to privacy in the Constitution, the Supreme Court has long interpreted the various guarantees of the Bill of Rights, especially the Fourth Amendment prohibition against "unreasonable searches and seizures," as establishing a bulwark against government intrusion into the private affairs of individuals. As Justice Louis Brandeis once explained,

> The makers of our Constitution undertook to secure conditions favorable to the pursuit of happiness. They recognized the significance of man's spiritual nature, of his feelings and of his intellect. They knew that only a part of the pain, pleasure and satisfactions of life are to be found in material things. They sought to protect Americans in their beliefs, their thoughts, their emotions and their sensations. They conferred, as against the government, the right to be let alone—the most comprehensive of rights and the right most valued by civilized men. To protect that right, every unjustifiable intrusion by the government upon the privacy of the individual, whatever the means employed, must be deemed a violation of the Fourth Amendment. (*Olmstead v. United States,* dissenting opinion)

If privacy requirements impede the investigative work of law enforcement, the constitutional guarantees against self-incrimination provide an even greater burden. The Fifth Amendment merely states that no one "shall be compelled in any criminal case to be a witness against himself." However, in *Miranda v. Arizona,* the Supreme Court vastly expanded such protections to include the right of all criminal suspects to refuse to answer any questions once taken into custody. The Court even mandated that arresting officers inform criminal suspects that they have such "a right to remain silent" while taking them into custody.

The Court has often faced criticism for such decisions that made it more difficult for police to obtain confessions, conduct surveillance, or question suspects. Public furor over *Miranda* included the frequent charge that the Supreme Court was ignoring the reality of crime prevention by "coddling criminals." However, in other cases, such as *Terry v. Ohio* and the *Hiibel* decision, civil libertarian critics have argued exactly opposite, proclaiming that the court has focused too much on the demands of law enforcement and its concerns with maintaining law and order while neglecting the rights of citizens to be free from governmental surveillance and intrusion into their daily lives. Maintaining the delicate balance between individual rights on the one hand and the needs of law enforcement to protect public safety on the other, will no doubt remain a central concern of the Supreme Court in the twenty-first century.

For more analysis of police stops, one might usefully consult the following: Angela J. Davis, "Race, Cops, and Traffic Stops," *University of Miami Law Review* (51: 425, 1997); David A. Harris, "Car Wars: The Fourth Amendment's Death on the Highway," *George Washington Law Review* (66: 556, 1998); Tracey Maclin, "Race and the Fourth Amendment," *Vanderbilt Law Review* (51: 333, 1998); and David Slansky, "Traffic Stops, Minority Motorists, and the Future of the Fourth Amendment," *Supreme Court Review* (1997: 271). New technologies and the war on terror are raising additional concerns about revealing information about oneself. See Eric P. Haas, "Back To The Future? The Use of Biometrics, Its Impact on Airport Security, and How This Technology Should Be Governed," 69 *J. Air L. & Com.* 459 (2004).

Internet References . . .

Thomas: Legislative Information on the Internet

This site of the Library of Congress provides access to federal statutes, pending legislation, and other legal material.

http://thomas.loc.gov

FedWorld

FedWorld is a highly comprehensive site with links to federal agencies and to the reports and information produced by those agencies.

http://www.fedworld.gov/

FedNet

FedNet allows you to listen in on congressional hearings and events and also provides links to archives of previously recorded material.

http://www.fednet.net

Death Penalty Information Center

The Death Penalty Information Center provides a wealth of information on a variety of topics related to capital punishment, including a history of the death penalty, race issues, and mental retardation and the death penalty.

http://www.deathpenaltyinfo.org/index.html

Law and the State

*T*he use of state power can be seen in various ways, including in the promotion of patriotic and moral values, in efforts to deal with crime, in responses to public opinion, and in choices of policies to be implemented. The majority is not always allowed to rule, and determining when state interests are compelling and legitimate is often difficult. The issues in this section confront some of these challenges.

- Do Religious Groups Have a Right to Use Public School Facilities After Hours?

- Does the Use of High-Technology Thermal Imaging Devices Violate the Fourth Amendment Search and Seizure Guarantee?

- Are Laws Requiring Schools and Public Libraries to Filter Internet Access Constitutional?

- Does the "Cruel and Unusual Punishment" Clause of the Eighth Amendment Bar the Imposition of the Death Penalty on Juveniles?

- Is a Sentence of Life in Prison for Stealing $150 Worth of Videotapes Constitutional?

- Is Drug Use Testing of Students Who Participate in Extracurricular Activities Permitted Under the Fourth Amendment?

ISSUE 9

Do Religious Groups Have a Right to Use Public School Facilities After Hours?

YES: Clarence Thomas, from Majority Opinion, *Good News Club et al. v. Milford Central School*, U.S. Supreme Court (June 11, 2001)

NO: David Souter, from Dissenting Opinion, *Good News Club et al. v. Milford Central School*, U.S. Supreme Court (June 11, 2001)

ISSUE SUMMARY

YES: Supreme Court Justice Clarence Thomas affirms the right of religious groups to use school facilities after the school day ends, maintaining that restricting such use is a violation of free speech rights.

NO: Supreme Court Justice David Souter, dissenting from the Court's opinion, contends that the use of school facilities by religious groups blurs the line between public classroom instruction and private religious indoctrination and therefore violates the establishment clause of the Constitution.

An Easter egg hunt on the White House lawn. Christmas as a national holiday. Prayers opening legislative sessions of state legislatures. If you were a judge and the above practices were challenged as being unconstitutional, how would you rule?

The First Amendment to the Constitution states that "Congress shall make no law respecting an establishment of religion, or prohibiting the free exercise thereof." Interpreting these words and applying them in particular cases has been exceedingly difficult for the courts. What, for example, does "respecting an establishment of religion" mean? Is any governmental involvement or support for religion, direct or indirect, small or great, barred by this phrase?

While the courts have struggled to keep church and state separate, they have also recognized that it would be impossible to have an absolute prohibition on the celebration of religious values and holidays. Therefore, cases continue to be brought, challenging the courts to determine how the words of the Constitution and the standards of prior cases should be applied to the facts of each new case.

The clearest and most well known of the establishment of religion cases are the school prayer decisions. In 1963, in *School District of Abington Township, Pennsylvania v. Schempp*, 374 U.S. 203, the Supreme Court ruled that it was unconstitutional to require students to open the school day by reading biblical passages and reciting the Lord's Prayer. A year earlier, in *Engel v. Vitale*, 370 U.S. 421 (1962), the Supreme Court had ruled that recitation of the New York Regent's Prayer was unconstitutional. This prayer read, "Almighty God, we acknowledge our dependence upon Thee, and we beg thy blessings upon us, our parents, our teachers, and our country."

While banning prayer in the schools, the courts have upheld some questionable practices, such as Sunday closing laws and the loaning of secular textbooks to parochial schools. Yet they have struck down other statutes, such as the Kentucky law that required posting the Ten Commandments in the classroom (see *Stone v. Graham*, 101 S. Ct. 192 [1980]). More generally, the Court has upheld prayers at the beginning of legislative sessions and tuition tax credits for parochial schools. Yet it held unconstitutional a statute requiring a moment of silence in public schools, remedial programs for parochial schools, and a law requiring the teaching of "creation science" whenever evolution is taught.

The many cases involving religion that have been considered by the Supreme Court in the past 30 years indicate that the task of defining precisely what role religion should have in government-sponsored activities is extraordinarily difficult. Religion has not been banned from public life. "In God We Trust" appears on U.S. coins, prayers are said at presidential inaugurations, Christmas is a national holiday, the lighting of the national Christmas tree at the White House is a newsworthy event, and tax exemptions are given to religious institutions. It is probably still accurate, as Supreme Court justice William O. Douglas once wrote, that "we are a religious people whose institutions presuppose a Supreme Being." It is also true, however, that many religious activities may not be sponsored by the government.

The following case is one of the most recent Supreme Court decisions to consider the intersection between the free exercise of religion and the establishment of religion. Justice Clarence Thomas finds that the plaintiff, the Good News Club, has as much a right as anyone else to use school grounds. Justice David Souter dissents.

YES ⬅

Clarence Thomas

Majority Opinion

Good News Club *v.* Milford Central School

JUSTICE THOMAS delivered the opinion of the Court.

This case presents two questions. The first question is whether Milford Central School violated the free speech rights of the Good News Club when it excluded the Club from meeting after hours at the school. The second question is whether any such violation is justified by Milford's concern that permitting the Club's activities would violate the Establishment Clause. We conclude that Milford's restriction violates the Club's free speech rights and that no Establishment Clause concern justifies that violation.

I

The State of New York authorizes local school boards to adopt regulations governing the use of their school facilities. In particular, N. Y. Educ. Law §414 (McKinney 2000) enumerates several purposes for which local boards may open their schools to public use. In 1992, respondent Milford Central School (Milford) enacted a community use policy adopting seven of §414's purposes for which its building could be used after school. Two of the stated purposes are relevant here. First, district residents may use the school for "instruction in any branch of education, learning or the arts." Second, the school is available for "social, civic and recreational meetings and entertainment events, and other uses pertaining to the welfare of the community, provided that such uses shall be nonexclusive and shall be opened to the general public."

Stephen and Darleen Fournier reside within Milford's district and therefore are eligible to use the school's facilities as long as their proposed use is approved by the school. Together they are sponsors of the local Good News Club, a private Christian organization for children ages 6 to 12. Pursuant to Milford's policy, in September 1996 the Fourniers submitted a request to Dr. Robert McGruder, interim superintendent of the district, in which they sought permission to hold the Club's weekly afterschool meetings in the school cafeteria. The next month, McGruder formally denied the Fourniers' request on the ground that the proposed use—to have "a fun time of singing songs, hearing a Bible lesson and memorizing scripture,"—was "the equivalent of religious worship." According to McGruder, the community use policy,

From *Good News Club et al. v. Milford Central School,* 533 U.S. (2001). Some notes and case citations omitted.

which prohibits use "by any individual or organization for religious purposes," foreclosed the Club's activities.

In response to a letter submitted by the Club's counsel, Milford's attorney requested information to clarify the nature of the Club's activities. The Club sent a set of materials used or distributed at the meetings and the following description of its meeting:

> "The Club opens its session with Ms. Fournier taking attendance. As she calls a child's name, if the child recites a Bible verse the child receives a treat. After attendance, the Club sings songs. Next Club members engage in games that involve, *inter alia,* learning Bible verses. Ms. Fournier then relates a Bible story and explains how it applies to Club members' lives. The Club closes with prayer. Finally, Ms. Fournier distributes treats and the Bible verses for memorization."

McGruder and Milford's attorney reviewed the materials and concluded that "the kinds of activities proposed to be engaged in by the Good News Club were not a discussion of secular subjects such as child rearing, development of character and development of morals from a religious perspective, but were in fact the equivalent of religious instruction itself." In February 1997, the Milford Board of Education adopted a resolution rejecting the Club's request to use Milford's facilities "for the purpose of conducting religious instruction and Bible study."

In March 1997, petitioners, the Good News Club, Ms. Fournier, and her daughter Andrea Fournier (collectively, the Club), filed an action under 42 U.S.C. §1983 against Milford in the United States District Court for the Northern District of New York. The Club alleged that Milford's denial of its application violated its free speech rights under the First and Fourteenth Amendments, its right to equal protection under the Fourteenth Amendment, and its right to religious freedom under the Religious Freedom Restoration Act of 1993, 107 Stat. 1488, 42 U.S.C. §2000bb *et seq.*

The Club moved for a preliminary injunction to prevent the school from enforcing its religious exclusion policy against the Club and thereby to permit the Club's use of the school facilities. On April 14, 1997, the District Court granted the injunction. The Club then held its weekly afterschool meetings from April 1997 until June 1998 in a high school resource and middle school special education room.

In August 1998, the District Court vacated the preliminary injunction and granted Milford's motion for summary judgment. 21 F. Supp. 2d 147 (NDNY 1998). The court found that the Club's "subject matter is decidedly religious in nature, and not merely a discussion of secular matters from a religious perspective that is otherwise permitted under [Milford's] use policies." Because the school had not permitted other groups that provided religious instruction to use its limited public forum, the court held that the school could deny access to the Club without engaging in unconstitutional viewpoint discrimination. The court also rejected the Club's equal protection claim.

The Club appealed, and a divided panel of the United States Court of Appeals for the Second Circuit affirmed. 202 F. 3d 502 (2000). First, the court rejected the Club's contention that Milford's restriction against allowing religious instruction in its facilities is unreasonable. Second, it held that, because the subject matter of the Club's activities is "quintessentially religious," and the activities "fall outside the bounds of pure 'moral and character development,'" Milford's policy of excluding the Club's meetings was constitutional subject discrimination, not unconstitutional viewpoint discrimination. Judge Jacobs filed a dissenting opinion in which he concluded that the school's restriction did constitute viewpoint discrimination under *Lamb's Chapel v. Center Moriches Union Free School Dist.,* 508 U.S. 384 (1993).

There is a conflict among the Courts of Appeals on the question whether speech can be excluded from a limited public forum on the basis of the religious nature of the speech. Compare *Gentala v. Tucson,* 244 F. 3d 1065 (CA9 2001) (en banc) (holding that a city properly refused National Day of Prayer organizers' application to the city's civic events fund for coverage of costs for city services); *Campbell v. St. Tammany's School Bd.,* 206 F. 3d 482 (CA5 2000) (holding that a school's policy against permitting religious instruction in its limited public forum did not constitute viewpoint discrimination), cert. pending, No. 00–1194; *Bronx Household of Faith v. Community School Dist. No. 10,* 127 F. 3d 207 (CA2 1997) (concluding that a ban on religious services and instruction in the limited public forum was constitutional), with *Church on the Rock v. Albuquerque,* 84 F. 3d 1273 (CA10 1996) (holding that a city's denial of permission to show the film Jesus in a senior center was unconstitutional viewpoint discrimination); and *Good News/Good Sports Club v. School Dist. of Ladue,* 28 F. 3d 1501 (CA8 1994) (holding unconstitutional a school use policy that prohibited Good News Club from meeting during times when the Boy Scouts could meet). We granted certiorari to resolve this conflict. 531 U.S. 923 (2000).

II

The standards that we apply to determine whether a State has unconstitutionally excluded a private speaker from use of a public forum depend on the nature of the forum. See *Perry Ed. Assn. v. Perry Local Educators' Assn.,* 460 U.S. 37, 44 (1983). If the forum is a traditional or open public forum, the State's restrictions on speech are subject to stricter scrutiny than are restrictions in a limited public forum. *Id.,* at 45–46. We have previously declined to decide whether a school district's opening of its facilities pursuant to N. Y. Educ. Law §414 creates a limited or a traditional public forum. See *Lamb's Chapel, supra,* at 391–392. Because the parties have agreed that Milford created a limited public forum when it opened its facilities in 1992, we need not resolve the issue here. Instead, we simply will assume that Milford operates a limited public forum.

When the State establishes a limited public forum, the State is not required to and does not allow persons to engage in every type of speech. The State may be justified "in reserving [its forum] for certain groups or for the discussion of certain topics." *Rosenberger v. Rector and Visitors of Univ. of Va.,* 515 U.S. 819, 829 (1995); see also *Lamb's Chapel, supra,* at 392–393. The State's power to restrict speech, however, is not without limits. The restriction must not discriminate against speech on the basis of viewpoint, *Rosenberger, supra,* at 829, and the restriction must be "reasonable in light of the purpose served by the forum," *Cornelius v. NAACP Legal Defense & Ed. Fund, Inc.,* 473 U.S. 788, 806 (1985).

III

Applying this test, we first address whether the exclusion constituted viewpoint discrimination. We are guided in our analysis by two of our prior opinions, *Lamb's Chapel* and *Rosenberger.* In *Lamb's Chapel,* we held that a school district violated the Free Speech Clause of the First Amendment when it excluded a private group from presenting films at the school based solely on the films' discussions of family values from a religious perspective. Likewise, in *Rosenberger,* we held that a university's refusal to fund a student publication because the publication addressed issues from a religious perspective violated the Free Speech Clause. Concluding that Milford's exclusion of the Good News Club based on its religious nature is indistinguishable from the exclusions in these cases, we hold that the exclusion constitutes viewpoint discrimination. Because the restriction is viewpoint discriminatory, we need not decide whether it is unreasonable in light of the purposes served by the forum.

Milford has opened its limited public forum to activities that serve a variety of purposes, including events "pertaining to the welfare of the community." Milford interprets its policy to permit discussions of subjects such as child rearing, and of "the development of character and morals from a religious perspective." Brief for Appellee in No. 98–9494 (CA2), p. 6. For example, this policy would allow someone to use Aesop's Fables to teach children moral values. Additionally, a group could sponsor a debate on whether there should be a constitutional amendment to permit prayer in public schools, and the Boy Scouts could meet "to influence a boy's character, development and spiritual growth." In short, any group that "promote[s] the moral and character development of children" is eligible to use the school building.

Just as there is no question that teaching morals and character development to children is a permissible purpose under Milford's policy, it is clear that the Club teaches morals and character development to children. For example, no one disputes that the Club instructs children to overcome feelings of jealousy, to treat others well regardless of how they treat the children, and to be obedient, even if it does so in a nonsecular way. Nonetheless, because Milford found the Club's activities to be religious in nature—"the equivalent of religious instruction itself," 202 F. 3d, at 507—it excluded the Club from use of its facilities.

Applying *Lamb's Chapel,*[1] we find it quite clear that Milford engaged in viewpoint discrimination when it excluded the Club from the afterschool forum. In *Lamb's Chapel,* the local New York school district similarly had adopted §414's "social, civic or recreational use" category as a permitted use in its limited public forum. The district also prohibited use "by any group for religious purposes." 508 U.S., at 387. Citing this prohibition, the school district excluded a church that wanted to present films teaching family values from a Christian perspective. We held that, because the films "no doubt dealt with a subject otherwise permissible" under the rule, the teaching of family values, the district's exclusion of the church was unconstitutional viewpoint discrimination. *Id.,* at 394.

Like the church in *Lamb's Chapel* the Club seeks to address a subject otherwise permitted under the rule, the teaching of morals and character, from a religious standpoint. Certainly, one could have characterized the film presentations in *Lamb's Chapel* as a religious use, as the Court of Appeals did, *Lamb's Chapel v. Center Moriches Union Free School Dist.,* 959 F. 2d 381, 388–389 (CA2 1992). And one easily could conclude that the films' purpose to instruct that "'society's slide toward humanism . . . can only be counterbalanced by a loving home where Christian values are instilled from an early age,'" *id.,* at 384, was "quintessentially religious," 202 F. 3d, at 510. The only apparent difference between the activity of Lamb's Chapel and the activities of the Good News Club is that the Club chooses to teach moral lessons from a Christian perspective through live storytelling and prayer, whereas Lamb's Chapel taught lessons through films. This distinction is inconsequential. Both modes of speech use a religious viewpoint. Thus, the exclusion of the Good News Club's activities, like the exclusion of Lamb's Chapel's films, constitutes unconstitutional viewpoint discrimination.

Our opinion in *Rosenberger* also is dispositive. In *Rosenberger,* a student organization at the University of Virginia was denied funding for printing expenses because its publication, Wide Awake, offered a Christian viewpoint. Just as the Club emphasizes the role of Christianity in students' morals and character, Wide Awake "'challenge[d] Christians to live, in word and deed, according to the faith they proclaim and . . . encourage[d] students to consider what a personal relationship with Jesus Christ means.'" 515 U.S., at 826. Because the university "select[ed] for disfavored treatment those student journalistic efforts with religious editorial viewpoints," we held that the denial of funding was unconstitutional. *Id.,* at 831. Although in *Rosenberger* there was no prohibition on religion as a subject matter, our holding did not rely on this factor. Instead, we concluded simply that the university's denial of funding to print Wide Awake was viewpoint discrimination, just as the school district's refusal to allow Lamb's Chapel to show its films was viewpoint discrimination. Given the obvious religious content of Wide Awake, we cannot say that the Club's activities are any more "religious" or deserve any less First Amendment protection than did the publication of Wide Awake in *Rosenberger.*

Despite our holdings in *Lamb's Chapel* and *Rosenberger,* the Court of Appeals, like Milford, believed that its characterization of the Club's activities as religious in nature warranted treating the Club's activities as different in kind from the other activities permitted by the school. See 202 F. 3d, at 510 (the Club "is doing something other than simply teaching moral values"). The "Christian viewpoint" is unique, according to the court, because it contains an "additional layer" that other kinds of viewpoints do not. *Id.,* at 509. That is, the Club "is focused on teaching children how to cultivate their relationship with God through Jesus Christ," which it characterized as "quintessentially religious." *Id.,* at 510. With these observations, the court concluded that, because the Club's activities "fall outside the bounds of pure 'moral and character development,'" the exclusion did not constitute viewpoint discrimination. *Id.,* at 511.

We disagree that something that is "quintessentially religious" or "decidedly religious in nature" cannot also be characterized properly as the teaching of morals and character development from a particular viewpoint. See 202 F. 3d, at 512 (Jacobs, J., dissenting) ("[W]hen the subject matter is morals and character, it is quixotic to attempt a distinction between religious viewpoints and religious subject matters"). What matters for purposes of the Free Speech Clause is that we can see no logical difference in kind between the invocation of Christianity by the Club and the invocation of teamwork, loyalty, or patriotism by other associations to provide a foundation for their lessons. It is apparent that the unstated principle of the Court of Appeals' reasoning is its conclusion that any time religious instruction and prayer are used to discuss morals and character, the discussion is simply not a "pure" discussion of those issues. According to the Court of Appeals, reliance on Christian principles taints moral and character instruction in a way that other foundations for thought or viewpoints do not. We, however, have never reached such a conclusion. Instead, we reaffirm our holdings in *Lamb's Chapel* and *Rosenberger* that speech discussing otherwise permissible subjects cannot be excluded from a limited public forum on the ground that the subject is discussed from a religious viewpoint. Thus, we conclude that Milford's exclusion of the Club from use of the school, pursuant to its community use policy, constitutes impermissible viewpoint discrimination.

IV

Milford argues that, even if its restriction constitutes viewpoint discrimination, its interest in not violating the Establishment Clause outweighs the Club's interest in gaining equal access to the school's facilities. In other words, according to Milford, its restriction was required to avoid violating the Establishment Clause. We disagree.

We have said that a state interest in avoiding an Establishment Clause violation "may be characterized as compelling," and therefore may justify content-based discrimination. *Widmar* v. *Vincent,* 454 U.S. 263, 271 (1981). However, it is not clear whether a State's interest in avoiding an Establishment Clause violation would justify viewpoint discrimination. See *Lamb's Chapel,* 508 U.S., at 394–395 (noting the suggestion in *Widmar* but ultimately not finding an Establishment Clause problem). We need not, however, confront the issue in this case, because we conclude that the school has no valid Establishment Clause interest.

We rejected Establishment Clause defenses similar to Milford's in two previous free speech cases, *Lamb's Chapel* and *Widmar.* In particular, in *Lamb's Chapel,* we explained that "[t]he showing of th[e] film series would not have been during school hours, would not have been sponsored by the school, and would have been open to the public, not just to church members." 508 U.S., at 395. Accordingly, we found that "there would have been no realistic danger that the community would think that the District was endorsing religion or any particular creed." *Ibid.* Likewise, in *Widmar,* where the university's forum was already available to other groups, this Court concluded that there was no Establishment Clause problem. 454 U.S., at 272–273, and n. 13.

The Establishment Clause defense fares no better in this case. As in *Lamb's Chapel,* the Club's meetings were held after school hours, not sponsored by the school, and open to any student who obtained parental consent, not just to Club members. As in *Widmar,* Milford made its forum available to other organizations. The Club's activities are materially indistinguishable from those in *Lamb's Chapel* and *Widmar.* Thus, Milford's reliance on the Establishment Clause is unavailing.

Milford attempts to distinguish *Lamb's Chapel* and *Widmar* by emphasizing that Milford's policy involves elementary school children. According to Milford, children will perceive that the school is endorsing the Club and will feel coercive pressure to participate, because the Club's activities take place on school grounds, even though they occur during nonschool hours. This argument is unpersuasive.

First, we have held that "a significant factor in upholding governmental programs in the face of Establishment Clause attack is their *neutrality* towards religion." *Rosenberger,* 515 U.S., at 839 (emphasis added). See also *Mitchell v. Helms,* 530 U.S. 793 (2000) (slip op., at 10) (plurality opinion) ("In distinguishing between indoctrination that is attributable to the State and indoctrination that is not, [the Court has] consistently turned to the principle of neutrality, upholding aid that is offered to a broad range of groups or persons without regard to their religion" (emphasis added)); (O'CONNOR, J., concurring in judgment) ("[N]eutrality is an important reason for upholding government-aid programs against Establishment Clause challenges"). Milford's implication that granting access to the Club would do damage to the neutrality principle defies logic. For the "guarantee of neutrality is respected, not offended, when the government, following neutral criteria and evenhanded policies, extends benefits to recipients whose ideologies and viewpoints, including religious ones, are broad and diverse." *Rosenberger, supra,* at 839. The Good News Club seeks nothing more than to be treated neutrally and given access to speak about the same topics as are other groups. Because allowing the Club to speak on school grounds would ensure neutrality, not threaten it, Milford faces an uphill battle in arguing that the Establishment Clause compels it to exclude the Good News Club.

Second, to the extent we consider whether the community would feel coercive pressure to engage in the Club's activities, cf. *Lee v. Weisman,* 505 U.S. 577, 592–593 (1992), the relevant community would be the parents, not the elementary school children. It is the parents who choose whether their children will attend the Good News Club meetings. Because the children cannot attend without their parents' permission, they cannot be coerced into engaging in the Good News Club's religious activities. Milford does not suggest that the parents of elementary school children would be confused about whether the school was endorsing religion. Nor do we believe that such an argument could be reasonably advanced.

Third, whatever significance we may have assigned in the Establishment Clause context to the suggestion that elementary school children are more impressionable than adults, cf., *e.g., Lee, supra,* at 592; *School Dist. of Grand Rapids v. Ball,* 473 U.S. 373, 390 (1985) (stating that "symbolism of a union between church and state is most likely to influence children of tender years, whose experience is limited and whose beliefs consequently are the function of environment as much as of free and voluntary choice"), we have never extended our Establishment Clause jurisprudence to foreclose private religious conduct during nonschool hours merely because it takes place on school premises where elementary school children may be present.

None of the cases discussed by Milford persuades us that our Establishment Clause jurisprudence has gone this far. For example, Milford cites *Lee* v. *Weisman* for the proposition that "there are heightened concerns with protecting freedom of conscience from subtle coercive pressure in the elementary and secondary public schools," 505 U.S., at 592. In *Lee,* however, we concluded that attendance at the graduation exercise was obligatory. *Id.,* at 586. See also *Santa Fe Independent School Dist. v. Doe,* 530 U.S. 290 (2000) (holding the school's policy of permitting prayer at football games unconstitutional where the activity took place during a school-sponsored event and not in a public forum). We did not place independent significance on the fact that the graduation exercise might take place on school premises, *Lee, supra,* at 583. Here, where the school facilities are being used for a nonschool function and there is no government sponsorship of the Club's activities, *Lee* is inapposite.

Equally unsupportive is *Edwards* v. *Aguillard,* 482 U.S. 578 (1987), in which we held that a Louisiana law that proscribed the teaching of evolution as part of the public school curriculum, unless accompanied by a lesson on creationism, violated the Establishment Clause. In *Edwards,* we mentioned that students are susceptible to pressure in the classroom, particularly given their possible reliance on teachers as role models. See *id.,* at 584. But we did not discuss this concern in our application of the law to the facts. Moreover, we did note that mandatory attendance requirements meant that State advancement of religion in a school would be particularly harshly felt by impressionable students. But we did not suggest that, when the school was not actually advancing religion, the impressionability of students would be relevant to the Establishment Clause issue. Even if *Edwards* had articulated the principle Milford believes it did, the facts in *Edwards* are simply too remote from those here to give the principle any weight. *Edwards* involved the content of the curriculum taught by state teachers during the schoolday to children required to attend. Obviously, when individuals who are not schoolteachers are giving lessons after school to children permitted to attend only with parental consent, the concerns expressed in *Edwards* are not present.

Fourth, even if we were to consider the possible misperceptions by schoolchildren in deciding whether Milford's permitting the Club's activities would violate the Establishment Clause, the facts of this case simply do not support Milford's conclusion. There is no evidence that young children are permitted to loiter outside classrooms after the schoolday has ended. Surely even young children are aware of events for which their parents must sign permission forms. The meetings were held in a combined high school resource room and middle school special education room, not in an elementary school classroom. The instructors are not schoolteachers. And the children in the group are not all the same age as in the normal classroom setting; their ages range from 6 to 12. In sum, these circumstances simply do not support the theory that small children would perceive endorsement here.

Finally, even if we were to inquire into the minds of schoolchildren in this case, we cannot say the danger that children would misperceive the endorsement of religion is any greater than the danger that they would perceive a hostility toward the religious viewpoint if the Club were excluded from the public forum. This concern is particularly acute given the reality that Milford's building is not used only for elementary school children. Students, from kindergarten through the 12th grade, all attend school in the same building. There may be as many, if not more, upperclassmen than elementary school children who occupy the school after hours. For that matter, members of the public writ large are permitted in the school after hours pursuant to the community use policy. Any bystander could conceivably be aware of the school's use policy and its exclusion of the Good News Club, and could suffer as much from viewpoint discrimination as elementary school children could suffer from perceived endorsement. Cf. *Rosenberger,* 515 U.S., at 835–836 (expressing the concern that viewpoint discrimination can chill individual thought and expression).

We cannot operate, as Milford would have us do, under the assumption that any risk that small children would perceive endorsement should counsel in favor of excluding the Club's religious activity. We decline to employ Establishment Clause jurisprudence using a modified heckler's veto, in which a group's religious activity can be proscribed on the basis of what the youngest members of the audience might misperceive. Cf. *Capitol Square Review and Advisory Bd. v. Pinette,* 515 U.S. 753, 779–780 (1995) (O'CONNOR, J., concurring in part and concurring in judgment) ("[B]ecause our concern is with the political community writ large, the endorsement inquiry is *not about the perceptions of particular individuals* or saving isolated nonadherents from . . . discomfort. . . . It is for this reason that the reasonable observer in the endorsement inquiry must be deemed aware of the history and context of the community and forum in which the religious [speech takes place]" (emphasis added)). There are countervailing constitutional concerns related to rights of other individuals in the community. In this case, those countervailing concerns are the free speech rights of the Club and its members. Cf. *Rosenberger, supra,* at 835 ("Vital First Amendment speech principles are at stake here"). And, we have already found that those rights have been violated, not merely perceived to have been violated, by the school's actions toward the Club.

We are not convinced that there is any significance in this case to the possibility that elementary school children may witness the Good News Club's activities on school premises, and therefore we can find no reason to depart from our holdings in *Lamb's Chapel* and *Widmar.* Accordingly, we conclude that permitting the Club to meet on the school's premises would not have violated the Establishment Clause.

V

When Milford denied the Good News Club access to the school's limited public forum on the ground that the Club was religious in nature, it discriminated against the Club because of its religious viewpoint in violation of the Free Speech Clause of the First Amendment. Because Milford has not raised a valid Establishment Clause claim, we do not address the question whether such a claim could excuse Milford's viewpoint discrimination.

❧

The judgment of the Court of Appeals is reversed, and the case is remanded for further proceedings consistent with this opinion.

It is so ordered.

Note

1. We find it remarkable that the Court of Appeals majority did not cite *Lamb's Chapel,* despite its obvious relevance to the case. We do not necessarily expect a court of appeals to catalog every opinion that reverses one of its precedents. Nonetheless, this oversight is particularly incredible because the majority's attention was directed to it at every turn. See, *e.g.,* 202 F. 3d 502, 513 (CA2 2000) (Jacobs, J., dissenting) ("I cannot square the majority's analysis in this case with *Lamb's Chapel*"); 21 F. Supp. 2d, at 150; App. O9–O11 (District Court stating "that *Lamb's Chapel* and Rosenberger pinpoint the critical issue in this case"); Brief for Appellee in No. 98–9494 (CA2) at 36–39; Brief for Appellants in No. 98–9494 (CA2), pp. 15, 36.

Dissenting Opinion of David Souter

JUSTICE SOUTER, with whom JUSTICE GINSBURG joins, dissenting.

The majority rules on two issues. First, it decides that the Court of Appeals failed to apply the rule in *Lambs's Chapel v. Center Moriches Union Free School Dist.*, 508 U.S. 384 (1993), which held that the government may not discriminate on the basis of viewpoint in operating a limited public forum. The majority applies that rule and concludes that Milford violated *Lambs's Chapel* in denying Good News the use of the school. The majority then goes on to determine that it would not violate the Establishment Clause of the First Amendment for the Milford School District to allow the Good News Club to hold its intended gatherings of public school children in Milford's elementary school. The majority is mistaken on both points. The Court of Appeals unmistakably distinguished this case from *Lamb's Chapel*, though not by name, and accordingly affirmed the application of a policy, unchallenged in the District Court, that Milford's public schools may not be used for religious purposes. As for the applicability of the Establishment Clause to the Good News Club's intended use of Milford's school, the majority commits error even in reaching the issue, which was addressed neither by the Court of Appeals nor by the District Court. I respectfully dissent.

I

Lamb's Chapel, a case that arose (as this one does) from application of N.Y. Educ. Law §414 (McKinney 2000) and local policy implementing it, built on the accepted rule that a government body may designate a public forum subject to a reasonable limitation on the scope of permitted subject matter and activity, so long as the government does not use the forum-defining restrictions to deny expression to a particular viewpoint on subjects open to discussion. Specifically, *Lamb's Chapel* held that the government could not "permit school property to be used for the presentation of all views about family issues and child rearing except those dealing with the subject matter from a religious standpoint." 508 U.S., at 393–394.

This case, like *Lamb's Chapel,* properly raises no issue about the reasonableness of Milford's criteria for restricting the scope of its designated public forum. Milford has opened school property for, among other things, "instruction in any branch of education, learning or the arts" and for "social, civic and recreational

From *Good News Club et al. v. Milford Central School,* 533 U.S. (2001). Some notes and case citations omitted.

meetings and entertainment events and other uses pertaining to the welfare of the community, provided that such uses shall be nonexclusive and shall be opened to the general public." App. to Pet. for Cert. D1–D3. But Milford has done this subject to the restriction that "[s]chool premises shall not be used . . . for religious purposes." As the District Court stated, Good News did "not object to the reasonableness of [Milford]'s policy that prohibits the use of [its] facilities for religious purposes."

The sole question before the District Court was, therefore, whether, in refusing to allow Good News's intended use, Milford was misapplying its unchallenged restriction in a way that amounted to imposing a viewpoint-based restriction on what could be said or done by a group entitled to use the forum for an educational, civic, or other permitted purpose. The question was whether Good News was being disqualified when it merely sought to use the school property the same way that the Milford Boy and Girl Scouts and the 4-H Club did. The District Court held on the basis of undisputed facts that Good News's activity was essentially unlike the presentation of views on secular issues from a religious standpoint held to be protected in *Lamb's Chapel,* see App. to Pet. for Cert. C29–C31, and was instead activity precluded by Milford's unchallenged policy against religious use, even under the narrowest definition of that term.

The Court of Appeals understood the issue the same way. See 202 F. 3d 502, 508 (CA2 2000) (Good News argues that "to exclude the Club because it teaches morals and values from a Christian perspective constitutes unconstitutional viewpoint discrimination"); *id.,* at 509 ("The crux of the Good News Club's argument is that the Milford school's application of the Community Use Policy to exclude the Club from its facilities is not viewpoint neutral"). The Court of Appeals also realized that the *Lamb's Chapel* criterion was the appropriate measure: "The activities of the Good News Club do not involve merely a religious perspective on the secular subject of morality." 202 F. 3d, at 510. Cf. *Lamb's Chapel, supra,* at 393 (district could not exclude "religious standpoint" in discussion on childrearing and family values, an undisputed "use for social or civic purposes otherwise permitted" under the use policy).[1] The appeals court agreed with the District Court that the undisputed facts in this case differ from those in *Lamb's Chapel,* as night from day. A sampling of those facts shows why both courts were correct.

Good News's classes open and close with prayer. In a sample lesson considered by the District Court, children are instructed that "[t]he Bible tells us how we can have our sins forgiven by receiving the Lord Jesus Christ. It tells us how to live to please Him. . . . If you have received the Lord Jesus as your Saviour from sin, you belong to God's special group—His family." The lesson plan instructs the teacher to "lead a child to Christ," and, when reading a Bible verse, to "[e]mphasize that this verse is from the Bible, God's Word" and is "important—and true—because God said it." The lesson further exhorts the teacher to "[b]e sure to give an opportunity for the 'unsaved' children in your class to respond to the Gospel" and cautions against "neglect[ing] this responsibility."

While Good News's program utilizes songs and games, the heart of the meeting is the "challenge" and "invitation," which are repeated at various times throughout the lesson. During the challenge, "saved" children who "already believe in the Lord Jesus as their Savior" are challenged to "'stop and ask God for the strength and the "want" . . . to obey Him.'" *Ibid.* They are instructed that

> "[i]f you know Jesus as your Savior, you need to place God first in your life. And if you don't know Jesus as Savior and if you would like to, then we will—we will pray with you separately, individually. . . . And the challenge would be, those of you who know Jesus as Savior, you can rely on God's strength to obey Him." *Ibid.*

During the invitation, the teacher "invites" the "unsaved" children "'to trust the Lord Jesus to be your Savior from sin,'" and "'receiv[e] [him] as your Savior from sin.'" *Id.*, at C21. The children are then instructed that

> "[i]f you believe what God's Word says about your sin and how Jesus died and rose again for you, you can have His forever life today. Please bow your heads and close your eyes. If you have never believed on the Lord Jesus as your Savior and would like to do that, please show me by raising your hand. If you raised your hand to show me you want to believe on the Lord Jesus, please meet me so I can show you from God's Word how you can receive His everlasting life." *Ibid.*

It is beyond question that Good News intends to use the public school premises not for the mere discussion of a subject from a particular, Christian point of view, but for an evangelical service of worship calling children to commit themselves in an act of Christian conversion.[2] The majority avoids this reality only by resorting to the bland and general characterization of Good News's activity as "teaching of morals and character, from a religious standpoint." See *ante,* at 9. If the majority's statement ignores reality, as it surely does, then today's holding may be understood only in equally generic terms. Otherwise, indeed, this case would stand for the remarkable proposition that any public school opened for civic meetings must be opened for use as a church, synagogue, or mosque. . . .

This Court has accepted the independent obligation to obey the Establishment Clause as sufficiently compelling to satisfy strict scrutiny under the First Amendment. See *id.*, at 271 ("[T]he interest of the [government] in complying with its constitutional obligations may be characterized as compelling"); *Lamb's Chapel,* 508 U.S., at 394. Milford's actions would offend the Establishment Clause if they carried the message of endorsing religion under the circumstances, as viewed by a reasonable observer. See *Capitol Square Review and Advisory Bd. v. Pinette,* 515 U.S. 753, 777 (1995) (O'CONNOR, J., concurring). The majority concludes that such an endorsement effect is out of the question in Milford's case, because the context here is "materially indistinguishable" from the facts in *Lamb's Chapel* and *Widmar. Ante,* at 13. In fact, the majority is in no position to say that, for the principal grounds on which we based our Establishment Clause holdings in those cases are clearly absent here.

In *Widmar,* we held that the Establishment Clause did not bar a religious student group from using a public university's meeting space for worship as well as discussion. As for the reasonable observers who might perceive government endorsement of religion, we pointed out that the forum was used by university students, who "are, of course, young adults," and, as such, "are less impressionable than younger students and should be able to appreciate that the University's policy is one of neutrality toward religion." 454 U.S., at 274, n. 14. To the same effect, we remarked that the "large number of groups meeting on campus" negated "any reasonable inference of University support from the mere fact of a campus meeting place." *Ibid.* Not only was the forum "available to a broad class of nonreligious as well as religious speakers," but there were, in fact, over 100 recognized student groups at the University, and an "absence of empirical evidence that religious groups [would] dominate [the University's] open forum." *Id.,* at 274–275; see also *id.,* at 274 ("The provision of benefits to so broad a spectrum of groups is an important index of secular effect"). And if all that had not been enough to show that the university-student use would probably create no impression of religious endorsement, we pointed out that the university in that case had issued a student handbook with the explicit disclaimer that "the University's name will not 'be identified in any way with the aims, policies, programs, products, or opinions of any organization or its members.'" *Id.,* at 274, n. 14.

Lamb's Chapel involved an evening film series on childrearing open to the general public (and, given the subject matter, directed at an adult audience). See 508 U.S., at 387, 395. There, school property "had repeatedly been used by a wide variety of private organizations," and we could say with some assurance that "[u]nder these circumstances . . . there would have been no realistic danger that the community would think that the District was endorsing religion or any particular creed. . . ." *Id.,* at 395.

What we know about this case looks very little like *Widmar* or *Lamb's Chapel.* The cohort addressed by Good News is not university students with relative maturity, or even high school pupils, but elementary school children as young as six.[3] The Establishment Clause cases have consistently recognized the particular impressionability of schoolchildren, see *Edwards v. Aguillard,* 482 U.S. 578, 583–584 (1987), and the special protection required for those in the elementary grades in the school forum, see *County of Allegheny v. American Civil Liberties Union, Greater Pittsburgh Chapter,* 492 U.S. 573, 620, n. 69 (1989). We have held the difference between college students and grade school pupils to be a "distinction [that] warrants a difference in constitutional results," *Edwards v. Aguillard, supra,* at 584, n. 5 (internal quotation marks and citation omitted).

Nor is Milford's limited forum anything like the sites for wide-ranging intellectual exchange that were home to the challenged activities in *Widmar* and *Lamb's Chapel.* See also *Rosenberger,* 515 U.S., at 850, 836–837. In Widmar, the nature of the university campus and the sheer number of activities offered precluded the reasonable college observer from seeing government endorsement in any one of them, and so did the time and variety of community use in the *Lamb's Chapel* case. See also *Rosenberger,* 515 U.S., at 850 ("Given this wide array of nonreligious, antireligious and competing religious viewpoints in the forum supported by the University, any perception that the

University endorses one particular viewpoint would be illogical"); *id.,* at 836–837, 850 (emphasizing the array of university-funded magazines containing "widely divergent viewpoints" and the fact that believers in Christian evangelism competed on equal footing in the University forum with aficionados of "Plato, Spinoza, and Descartes," as well as "Karl Marx, Bertrand Russell, and Jean-Paul Sartre"); *Board of Ed. of Westside Community Schools (Dist. 66) v. Mergens,* 496 U.S. 226, 252 (1990) (plurality opinion) ("To the extent that a religious club is merely one of many different student-initiated voluntary clubs, students should perceive no message of government endorsement of religion").

The timing and format of Good News's gatherings, on the other hand, may well affirmatively suggest the *imprimatur* of officialdom in the minds of the young children. The club is open solely to elementary students (not the entire community, as in *Lamb's Chapel*), only four outside groups have been identified as meeting in the school, and Good News is, seemingly, the only one whose instruction follows immediately on the conclusion of the official school day. See Brief for National School Boards Association et al. as *Amici Curiae* 6. Although school is out at 2:56 p.m., Good News apparently requested use of the school beginning at 2:30 on Tuesdays "during the school year," so that instruction could begin promptly at 3:00, at which time children who are compelled by law to attend school surely remain in the building. Good News's religious meeting follows regular school activities so closely that the Good News instructor must wait to begin until "the room is clear," and "people are out of the room," before starting proceedings in the classroom located next to the regular third- and fourth-grade rooms. In fact, the temporal and physical continuity of Good News's meetings with the regular school routine seems to be the whole point of using the school. When meetings were held in a community church, 8 or 10 children attended; after the school became the site, the number went up three-fold.

Even on the summary judgment record, then, a record lacking whatever supplementation the trial process might have led to, and devoid of such insight as the trial and appellate judges might have contributed in addressing the Establishment Clause, we can say this: there is a good case that Good News's exercises blur the line between public classroom instruction and private religious indoctrination, leaving a reasonable elementary school pupil unable to appreciate that the former instruction is the business of the school while the latter evangelism is not. Thus, the facts we know (or think we know) point away from the majority's conclusion, and while the consolation may be that nothing really gets resolved when the judicial process is so truncated, that is not much to recommend today's result.

Notes

1. It is true, as the majority notes, *ante,* at 8, n. 3, that the Court of Appeals did not cite *Lamb's Chapel* by name. But it followed it in substance, and it did cite an earlier opinion written by the author of the panel opinion here, *Bronx Household of Faith v. Community School Dist. No. 10,* 127 F. 3d 207 (CA2 1997), which discussed *Lamb's Chapel* at length.

2. The majority rejects Milford's contention that Good News's activities fall outside the purview of the limited forum because they constitute "religious worship" on the ground that the Court of Appeals made no such determination regarding the character of the club's program, see *ante,* at 11, n. 4. This distinction is merely semantic, in light of the Court of Appeals's conclusion that "[i]t is difficult to see how the Club's activities differ materially from the 'religious worship' described" in other case law, 202 F. 3d, at 510, and the record below.

JUSTICE STEVENS distinguishes between proselytizing and worship, *ante,* at 1 (dissenting opinion), and distinguishes each from discussion reflecting a religious point of view. I agree with JUSTICE STEVENS that Good News's activities may be characterized as proselytizing and therefore as outside the purpose of Milford's limited forum, *ante,* at 5. Like the Court of Appeals, I also believe Good News's meetings have elements of worship that put the club's activities further afield of Milford's limited forum policy, the legitimacy of which was unchallenged in the summary judgment proceeding.

3. It is certainly correct that parents are required to give permission for their children to attend Good News's classes, see *ante,* at 14, (as parents are often required to do for a host of official school extracurricular activities), and correct that those parents would likely not be confused as to the sponsorship of Good News's classes. But the proper focus of concern in assessing effects includes the elementary school pupils who are invited to meetings, Lodging, Exh. X2, who see peers heading into classrooms for religious instruction as other classes end, and who are addressed by the "challenge" and "invitation."

The fact that there may be no evidence in the record that individual students were confused during the time the Good News Club met on school premises pursuant to the District Court's preliminary injunction is immaterial, cf. Brief for Petitioners 38. As JUSTICE O'CONNOR explained in *Capitol Square Review and Advisory Bd. v. Pinette,* 515 U.S. 753 (1995), the endorsement test does not focus "on the actual perception of individual observers, who naturally have differing degrees of knowledge," but on "the perspective of a hypothetical observer." *Id.,* at 779–780 (opinion concurring in part and concurring in judgment).

POSTSCRIPT

Do Religious Groups Have a Right to Use Public School Facilities After Hours?

Why should church and state be separate? Is there any danger to be feared from public religious displays? It is probably fair to say that behind the debates over this issue and the ongoing controversy over prayer in the schools are differing interpretations of the history of religion. Does religion bring us to a higher level of existence, or is it a system that will oppress dissidents, nonbelievers, and members of minority faiths? Almost everyone has an opinion on this question, and most can find some historical support for their positions. Ironically, the same historical circumstance may even be used to support opposing points of view. For example, at a congressional hearing on school prayer, the following testimony was introduced:

> *When I was educated in German public schools, they provided as part of the regular curriculum separate religious instruction for children of the three major faiths. At that time, all children in public schools from the ages of 6 to 18 were required not merely to recite a prayer at the beginning of each school session but to receive religious instruction twice a week. That system continued in the following decades.*

> —Statement by Joachim Prinz, quoted in testimony of Nathan Dershowitz, Hearings on Prayer in Public Schools and Buildings, Committee on the Judiciary, House of Representatives, August 19, 1980

Did that program effectively teach morality to the German people? If it did, it would be difficult to explain the rise of Hitler and the total moral collapse and even depravity of many German people, which resulted in the torture and death of millions of Jews and Christians.

Another witness, however, testifying in support of prayer in the schools, quoted the report of the President's Commission on the Holocaust, which stated,

> *The Holocaust could not have occurred without the collapse of certain religious norms; increasing secularity fueled a devaluation of the image of the human being created in the likeness of God.*

> —Statement of Judah Glasner, Hearings on Prayer in Public Schools and Buildings, Committee on the Judiciary, House of Representatives, July 30, 1980

Relevant cases concerning religion in the public schools are *McCollum v. Board of Education,* 333 U.S. 203 (1948), about religious instruction on school property; *Zorach v. Clauson,* 343 U.S. 306 (1952), regarding free time from school for religious instruction off school property; and *Board of Education of the Westside Community Schools v. Mergens,* 110 S. Ct. 2356 (1990), regarding the use of school premises for an after-school religious club. *Rosenberger v. University of Virginia,* 115 S. Ct. 2510 (1995) involved funding of a student newspaper by a religious group. The pro-prayer lobby has had its greatest failure in cases involving schools or children, the area where it would probably most like to see change. See, for example, *Wallace v. Jaffree,* 105 S. Ct. 2479 (1985), which ruled that the Alabama moment of silence statute was unconstitutional, or *Edwards v. Aquillard,* 107 S. Ct. 2573 (1987), which prohibited the teaching of "creation science." Recent cases involving the constitutionality of the pledge of allegiance are discussed by Steven G. Gey in "'Under God,' the Pledge of Allegiance, and Other Constitutional Trivia," 81 *North Carolina Law Review* 1865 (2003). In June 2005, the Supreme Court decided two cases involving the placing of the Ten Commandments in public places. In a Kentucky case, *McReary County, Kentucky v. ACLU,* the Court found the purpose for the display to be religious and prohibited it. In a Texas case, *Van Orden v. Perry,* the Court found a secular purpose to the display and allowed it. Both decisions were by a 5–4 vote, indicating a significant difference of opinion among the justices and the possibility for further cases involving this issue in the future.

ISSUE 10

Does the Use of High-Technology Thermal Imaging Devices Violate the Fourth Amendment Search and Seizure Guarantee?

YES: Antonin Scalia, from Majority Opinion, *Danny Lee Kyllo v. United States*, U.S. Supreme Court (June 11, 2001)

NO: John Paul Stevens, from Dissenting Opinion, *Danny Lee Kyllo v. United States*, U.S. Supreme Court (June 11, 2001)

ISSUE SUMMARY

YES: Supreme Court Justice Antonin Scalia maintains that thermal imaging devices reveal information "that would previously have been unknowable without physical intrusion" and that using such devices for surveillance without a warrant constitutes a violation of the Fourth Amendment.

NO: Supreme Court Justice John Paul Stevens asserts that the Court's application of search and seizure rules to new technology is too broad and that collecting thermal imaging data from outside the home is not a violation of privacy rights.

In 1991 agent William Elliott of the U.S. Department of the Interior became suspicious that marijuana was being grown in the home of Danny Kyllo. Indoor marijuana growth typically requires high-intensity lamps, and at 3:20 a.m. on January 16, 1992, Elliott scanned Kyllo's home with a thermal imaging device. Such devices can detect infrared radiation, which virtually all objects emit but which is not visible to the naked eye. The imager converts radiation into images based on relative warmth—black is cool, white is hot, and shades of gray connote relative differences.

The scan of Kyllo's home took only a few minutes. It showed that the roof over the garage and a side wall of the home were relatively hot compared to the rest of the home and substantially warmer than neighboring homes. Elliott concluded that Kyllo was using special lamps to grow marijuana in his house. Based on tips from informants, utility bills, and the thermal imaging, a warrant was issued authorizing a search of Kyllo's home, where the agents found more than 100 plants being grown. Kyllo was indicted on one count of manufacturing marijuana. He unsuccessfully moved to suppress the evidence seized from his home and then entered a conditional guilty plea.

The Fourth Amendment to the Constitution requires authorities to obtain a search warrant before conducting a search. In order to do this, they must first persuade a judge that probable cause exists that a crime has been committed and that the evidence sought will be found in the place to be searched. The warrant requirement is the key constitutional element restricting the power of the police to decide unilaterally to invade the privacy of someone's home.

There are exceptions to this requirement. The Court has held that search warrants are not required for school officials to search school lockers if there are reasonable grounds for believing that the search will reveal evidence of criminal behavior (*New Jersey v. T. L. O., A Juvenile,* 105 S. Ct. 733, [1985]). Nor are search warrants required when a person is searched after an arrest or when the object seized is in plain view. Technological advances, however, are posing new challenges. We are developing technological capabilities to do things at a distance and to obtain information that previously would have required entering a physical location. The *Kyllo* case is a perfect example of this.

The lower court ruled against Kyllo and found that the thermal imager "is a non-intrusive device which emits no rays or beams and shows a crude visual image of the heat being radiated from the outside of the house"; it "did not show any people or activity within the walls of the structure"; "the device used cannot penetrate walls or windows to reveal conversations or human activities"; and "no intimate details of the home were observed." Kyllo appealed to the Court of Appeals and then to the U.S. Supreme Court, which ruled in his favor. The following selections are from the majority and dissenting opinions in the case, as delivered by Justice Antonin Scalia and Justice John Paul Stevens, respectively.

Thermal imaging is only the latest technological challenge to the Fourth Amendment. In *Katz v. United States,* 389 U.S. 347 (1967), the Court held that wiretapping without a warrant could violate the search and seizure clause. It was not necessary for the police to enter someone's property physically to "search" something. Rather, "once it is recognized that the Fourth Amendment protects people—and not simply 'areas'—against unreasonable searches and seizures, it becomes clear that the reach of [the Fourth] Amendment cannot turn upon the presence or absence of a physical intrusion into any given enclosure."

Thermal imaging has been used by law enforcement authorities for some time, and *Kyllo* was not the first case in which a lower court ruled on its use. As it often does, the Supreme Court agreed to hear the *Kyllo* case because various lower courts had come to different conclusions about the constitutionality of using this technology without first obtaining a warrant. As new technological applications that assist law enforcement but also invade privacy are perfected, the opinions covered by the following selections are likely to be referred to often.

YES ⤶

Antonin Scalia

Majority Opinion

Kyllo *v.* United States

JUSTICE SCALIA delivered the opinion of the Court. . . .

I

In 1991 Agent William Elliott of the United States Department of the Interior came to suspect that marijuana was being grown in the home belonging to petitioner Danny Kyllo, part of a triplex on Rhododendron Drive in Florence, Oregon. Indoor marijuana growth typically requires high-intensity lamps. In order to determine whether an amount of heat was emanating from petitioner's home consistent with the use of such lamps, at 3:20 a.m. on January 16, 1992, Agent Elliott and Dan Haas used an Agema Thermovision 210 thermal imager to scan the triplex. . . .

II

The Fourth Amendment provides that "[t]he right of the people to be secure in their persons, houses, papers, and effects, against unreasonable searches and seizures, shall not be violated." "At the very core" of the Fourth Amendment "stands the right of a man to retreat into his own home and there be free from unreasonable governmental intrusion." *Silverman v. United States,* 365 U.S. 505, 511 (1961). With few exceptions, the question whether a warrantless search of a home is reasonable and hence constitutional must be answered no. See *Illinois v. Rodriguez,* 497 U.S. 177, 181 (1990); *Payton v. New York,* 445 U.S. 573, 586 (1980).

On the other hand, the antecedent question of whether or not a Fourth Amendment "search" has occurred is not so simple under our precedent. The permissibility of ordinary visual surveillance of a home used to be clear because, well into the 20th century, our Fourth Amendment jurisprudence was tied to common-law trespass. . . . Visual surveillance was unquestionably lawful because "'the eye cannot by the laws of England be guilty of a trespass.'" *Boyd v. United States,* 116 U.S. 616, 628 (1886) (quoting *Entick v. Carrington,* 19 How. St. Tr. 1029, 95 Eng. Rep. 807 (K. B. 1765)). We have since decoupled violation of a person's Fourth Amendment rights from trespassory violation of his property, see *Rakas v. Illinois,* 439 U.S. 128, 143 (1978), but the lawfulness of warrantless visual surveillance of a home has still been preserved. As we observed in *California v. Ciraolo,*

From *Danny Lee Kyllo v. United States,* 533 U.S. 210 (2001). Some notes and case citations omitted.

476 U.S. 207, 213 (1986), "[t]he Fourth Amendment protection of the home has never been extended to require law enforcement officers to shield their eyes when passing by a home on public thoroughfares."

One might think that the new validating rationale would be that examining the portion of a house that is in plain public view, while it is a "search" despite the absence of trespass, is not an "unreasonable" one under the Fourth Amendment. See *Minnesota v. Carter,* 525 U.S. 83, 104 (1998) (BREYER, J., concurring in judgment). But in fact we have held that visual observation is no "search" at all—perhaps in order to preserve somewhat more intact our doctrine that warrantless searches are presumptively unconstitutional. See *Dow Chemical Co. v. United States,* 476 U.S. 227, 234-235, 239 (1986). In assessing when a search is not a search, we have applied somewhat in reverse the principle first enunciated in *Katz v. United States,* 389 U.S. 347 (1967). *Katz* involved eavesdropping by means of an electronic listening device placed on the outside of a telephone booth—a location not within the catalog ("persons, houses, papers, and effects") that the Fourth Amendment protects against unreasonable searches. We held that the Fourth Amendment nonetheless protected Katz from the warrantless eavesdropping because he "justifiably relied" upon the privacy of the telephone booth. *Id.,* at 353. As Justice Harlan's oft-quoted concurrence described it, a Fourth Amendment search occurs when the government violates a subjective expectation of privacy that society recognizes as reasonable. See *id.,* at 361. We have subsequently applied this principle to hold that a Fourth Amendment search does *not* occur—even when the explicitly protected location of a *house* is concerned—unless "the individual manifested a subjective expectation of privacy in the object of the challenged search," and "society [is] willing to recognize that expectation as reasonable." *Ciraolo, supra,* at 211. We have applied this test in holding that it is not a search for the police to use a pen register at the phone company to determine what numbers were dialed in a private home, *Smith v. Maryland,* 442 U.S. 735, 743-744 (1979), and we have applied the test on two different occasions in holding that aerial surveillance of private homes and surrounding areas does not constitute a search, *Ciraolo, supra; Florida v. Riley,* 488 U.S. 445 (1989).

The present case involves officers on a public street engaged in more than naked-eye surveillance of a home. We have previously reserved judgment as to how much technological enhancement of ordinary perception from such a vantage point, if any, is too much. While we upheld enhanced aerial photography of an industrial complex in *Dow Chemical,* we noted that we found "it important that this is *not* an area immediately adjacent to a private home, where privacy expectations are most heightened," 476 U.S., at 237, n. 4 (emphasis in original).

III

It would be foolish to contend that the degree of privacy secured to citizens by the Fourth Amendment has been entirely unaffected by the advance of technology. For example, as the cases discussed above make clear, the technology enabling human flight has exposed to public view (and hence, we have said, to official observation) uncovered portions of the house and its curtilage that once were private. See *Ciraolo, supra,* at 215. The question we confront today is what limits there are upon this power of technology to shrink the realm of guaranteed privacy.

The *Katz* test—whether the individual has an expectation of privacy that society is prepared to recognize as reasonable—has often been criticized as circular, and hence subjective and unpredictable. See 1 W. LaFave, Search and Seizure §2.1(d), pp. 393–394 (3d ed. 1996); Posner, The Uncertain Protection of Privacy by the Supreme Court, 1979 S. Ct. Rev. 173, 188; *Carter, supra,* at 97 (SCALIA, J., concurring). But see *Rakas, supra,* at 143–144, n. 12. While it may be difficult to refine Katz when the search of areas such as telephone booths, automobiles, or even the curtilage and uncovered portions of residences are at issue, in the case of the search of the interior of homes—the prototypical and hence most commonly litigated area of protected privacy—there is a ready criterion, with roots deep in the common law, of the minimal expectation of privacy that *exists,* and that is acknowledged to be *reasonable.* To withdraw protection of this minimum expectation would be to permit police technology to erode the privacy guaranteed by the Fourth Amendment. We think that obtaining by sense-enhancing technology any information regarding the interior of the home that could not otherwise have been obtained without physical "intrusion into a constitutionally protected area," *Silverman,* 365 U.S., at 512, constitutes a search—at least where (as here) the technology in question is not in general public use. This assures preservation of that degree of privacy against government that existed when the Fourth Amendment was adopted. On the basis of this criterion, the information obtained by the thermal imager in this case was the product of a search.[1]

The Government maintains, however, that the thermal imaging must be upheld because it detected "only heat radiating from the external surface of the house," Brief for United States 26. The dissent makes this its leading point, see *post,* at 1, contending that there is a fundamental difference between what it calls "off-the-wall" observations and "through-the-wall surveillance." But just as a thermal imager captures only heat emanating from a house, so also a powerful directional microphone picks up only sound emanating from a house—and a satellite capable of scanning from many miles away would pick up only visible light emanating from a house. We rejected such a mechanical interpretation of the Fourth Amendment in *Katz,* where the eavesdropping device picked up only sound waves that reached the exterior of the phone booth. Reversing that approach would leave the homeowner at the mercy of advancing technology—including imaging technology that could discern all human activity in the home. While the technology used in the present case was relatively crude, the rule we adopt must take account of more sophisticated systems that are already in use or in development.[2] The dissent's reliance on the distinction between "off-the-wall" and "through-the-wall" observation is entirely incompatible with the dissent's belief, which we discuss below, that thermal-imaging observations of the intimate details of a home are impermissible. The most sophisticated thermal imaging devices continue to measure heat "off-the-wall" rather than "through-the-wall"; the dissent's disapproval of those more sophisticated thermal-imaging devices, see *post,* at 10, is an acknowledgement that there is no substance to this distinction. As for the dissent's extraordinary assertion that anything learned through "an inference" cannot be a search, see *post,* at 4–5, that would validate even the "through-the-wall" technologies that the dissent purports to disapprove. Surely the dissent does not believe that the through-the-wall radar or ultrasound technology produces an 8-by-10 Kodak glossy that needs no analysis (*i.e.,* the making of inferences). And, of course, the novel proposition that inference insulates a search is blatantly contrary to *United States v. Karo,* 468 U.S. 705 (1984), where the police "inferred" from the activation of a beeper that a certain can of ether was in the home. The police activity was held to be a search, and the search was held unlawful.[3]

The Government also contends that the thermal imaging was constitutional because it did not "detect private activities occurring in private areas," Brief for United States 22. It points out that in *Dow Chemical* we observed that the enhanced aerial photography did not reveal any "intimate details." 476 U.S., at 238. *Dow Chemical,* however, involved enhanced aerial photography of an industrial complex, which does not share the Fourth Amendment sanctity of the home. The Fourth Amendment's protection of the home has never been tied to measurement of the quality or quantity of information obtained. In *Silverman,* for example, we made clear that any physical invasion of the structure of the home, "by even a fraction of an inch," was too much, 365 U.S., at 512, and there is certainly no exception to the warrant requirement for the officer who barely cracks open the front door and sees nothing but the nonintimate rug on the vestibule floor. In the home, our cases show, *all* details are intimate details, because the entire area is held safe from prying government eyes. Thus, in *Karo, supra,* the only thing detected was a can of ether in the home; and in *Arizona v. Hicks,* 480 U.S. 321 (1987), the only thing detected by a physical search that went beyond what officers lawfully present could observe in "plain view" was the registration number of a phonograph turntable. These were intimate details because they were details of the home, just as was the detail of how warm—or even how relatively warm—Kyllo was heating his residence.[4]

Limiting the prohibition of thermal imaging to "intimate details" would not only be wrong in principle; it would be impractical in application, failing to provide "a workable accommodation between the needs of law enforcement and the interests protected by the Fourth Amendment," *Oliver v. United States,* 466 U.S. 170, 181 (1984). To begin with, there is no necessary connection between the sophistication of the surveillance equipment and the "intimacy" of the details that it observes—which means that one cannot say (and the police cannot be assured) that use of the relatively crude equipment at issue here will always be lawful. The Agema Thermovision 210 might disclose, for example, at what hour each night the lady of the house takes her daily sauna and bath—a detail that many would consider "intimate"; and a much more sophisticated system might detect nothing more intimate than the fact that someone left a closet light on. We could not, in other words, develop a rule approving only that through-the-wall surveillance which identifies objects no smaller than 36 by 36 inches, but would have to develop a jurisprudence specifying which home activities are "intimate" and which are not. And even when (if ever) that jurisprudence were fully developed, no police officer would be able to know in *advance* whether his through-the-wall surveillance picks up "intimate" details—and thus would be unable to know in advance whether it is constitutional.

The dissent's proposed standard—whether the technology offers the "functional equivalent of actual presence in the area being searched," *post,* at 7—would seem quite similar to our own at first blush. The dissent concludes that *Katz* was such a case, but then inexplicably asserts that if the same listening device only revealed the volume of the conversation, the surveillance would be permissible, *post,* at 10. Yet if, without technology, the police could not discern volume without being actually present in the phone booth, JUSTICE STEVENS should conclude a search has occurred. Cf. *Karo, supra,* at 735 (STEVENS, J., concurring in part and dissenting in part) ("I find little comfort in the Court's notion that no invasion of privacy occurs until a listener obtains some significant information by use of the device. . . . A bathtub is a less private area when the plumber is present even if his back is turned"). The same should hold for the interior heat of the home if only a person present in the home could discern the heat. Thus the driving force of the dissent, despite its recitation of the above standard, appears to be a distinction among different types of information—whether the "homeowner would even care if anybody noticed," *post,* at 10. The dissent offers no practical guidance for the application of this standard, and for reasons already discussed, we believe there can be none. The people in their houses, as well as the police, deserve more precision.[5]

We have said that the Fourth Amendment draws "a firm line at the entrance to the house," *Payton,* 445 U.S., at 590. That line, we think, must be not only firm but also bright—which requires clear specification of those methods of surveillance that require a warrant. While it is certainly possible to conclude from the videotape of the thermal imaging that occurred in this case that no "significant" compromise of the homeowner's privacy has occurred, we must take the long view, from the original meaning of the Fourth Amendment forward.

> "The Fourth Amendment is to be construed in the light of what was deemed an unreasonable search and seizure when it was adopted, and in a manner which will conserve public interests as well as the interests and rights of individual citizens." *Carroll v. United States,* 267 U.S. 132, 149 (1925).

Where, as here, the Government uses a device that is not in general public use, to explore details of the home that would previously have been unknowable without physical intrusion, the surveillance is a "search" and is presumptively unreasonable without a warrant.

Since we hold the Thermovision imaging to have been an unlawful search, it will remain for the District Court to determine whether, without the evidence it provided, the search warrant issued in this case was supported by probable cause—and if not, whether there is any other basis for supporting admission of the evidence that the search pursuant to the warrant produced.

⋘◉⋙

The judgment of the Court of Appeals is reversed; the case is remanded for further proceedings consistent with this opinion.

It is so ordered.

Notes

1. The dissent's repeated assertion that the thermal imaging did not obtain information regarding the interior of the home, *post,* at 3, 4 (opinion of STEVENS, J.), is simply inaccurate. A thermal imager reveals the relative heat of various rooms in the home. The dissent may not find that information particularly private or important, see *post,* at 4, 5, 10, but there is no basis for saying it is not information regarding the interior of the home. The dissent's comparison of the thermal imaging to various circumstances in which outside observers might be able to perceive, without technology, the heat of the home—for example, by observing snowmelt on the roof, *post,* at 3—is quite irrelevant. The fact that equivalent information could sometimes be obtained by other means does not make lawful the use of means that violate the Fourth Amendment. The police might, for example, learn how many people are in a particular house by setting up year-round surveillance; but that does not make breaking and entering to find out the same information lawful. In any event, on the night of January 16, 1992, no outside observer could have discerned the relative heat of Kyllo's home without thermal imaging.

2. The ability to "see" through walls and other opaque barriers is a clear, and scientifically feasible, goal of law enforcement research and development. The National Law Enforcement and Corrections Technology Center, a program within the United States Department of Justice, features on its Internet Website projects that include a "Radar-Based Through-the-Wall Surveillance System," "Handheld Ultrasound Through the Wall Surveillance," and a "Radar Flashlight" that "will enable law officers to detect individuals through interior building walls." www.nlectc.org/techproj/ (visited May 3, 2001). Some devices may emit low levels of radiation that travel "through-the-wall," but others, such as more sophisticated thermal imaging devices, are entirely passive, or "off-the-wall" as the dissent puts it.

3. The dissent asserts, *post,* at 5, n. 3, that we have misunderstood its point, which is not that inference *insulates* a search, but that inference alone is *not* a search. If we misunderstood the point, it was only in a good-faith effort to render the point germane to the case at hand. The issue in this case is not the police's allegedly unlawful inferencing, but their allegedly unlawful thermal-imaging measurement of the emanations from a house. We say such measurement is a search; the dissent says it is not, because an inference is not a search. We took that to mean that, since the technologically enhanced emanations had to be the basis of inferences before anything inside the house could be known, the use of the emanations could not be a search. But the dissent certainly knows better than we what it intends. And if it means only that an inference is not a search, we certainly agree. That has no bearing, however, upon whether hi-tech measurement of emanations from a house is a search.

4. The Government cites our statement in *California v. Ciraolo,* 476 U.S. 207 (1986), noting apparent agreement with the State of California that aerial surveillance of a house's curtilage could become "'invasive'" if "'modern technology'" revealed "'those intimate associations, objects or activities otherwise imperceptible to police or fellow citizens.'" *Id.,* at 215, n. 3 (quoting brief of

the State of California). We think the Court's focus in this second-hand dictum was not upon intimacy but upon otherwise-imperceptibility, which is precisely the principle we vindicate today.

5. The dissent argues that we have injected potential uncertainty into the constitutional analysis by noting that whether or not the technology is in general public use may be a factor. See *post,* at 7–8. That quarrel, however, is not with us but with this Court's precedent. See *Ciraolo, supra,* at 215 ("In an age where private and commercial flight in the public airways is routine, it is unreasonable for respondent to expect that his marijuana plants were constitutionally protected from being observed with the naked eye from an altitude of 1,000 feet"). Given that we can quite confidently say that thermal imaging is not "routine," we decline in this case to reexamine that factor.

➡ **NO**

Dissenting Opinion of
John Paul Stevens

J USTICE STEVENS, with whom THE CHIEF JUSTICE, JUSTICE O'CONNOR, and JUSTICE KENNEDY join, dissenting.

There is, in my judgment, a distinction of constitutional magnitude between "through-the-wall surveillance" that gives the observer or listener direct access to information in a private area, on the one hand, and the thought processes used to draw inferences from information in the public domain, on the other hand. The Court has crafted a rule that purports to deal with direct observations of the inside of the home, but the case before us merely involves indirect deductions from "off-the-wall" surveillance, that is, observations of the exterior of the home. Those observations were made with a fairly primitive thermal imager that gathered data exposed on the outside of petitioner's home but did not invade any constitutionally protected interest in privacy.[1] Moreover, I believe that the supposedly "bright-line" rule the Court has created in response to its concerns about future technological developments is unnecessary, unwise, and inconsistent with the Fourth Amendment.

I

There is no need for the Court to craft a new rule to decide this case, as it is controlled by established principles from our Fourth Amendment jurisprudence. One of those core principles, of course, is that "searches and seizures *inside a home* without a warrant are presumptively unreasonable." *Payton v. New York,* 445 U.S. 573, 586 (1980) (emphasis added). But it is equally well settled that searches and seizures of property in plain view are presumptively reasonable. See *id.,* at 586–587.[2] Whether that property is residential or commercial, the basic principle is the same: "'What a person knowingly exposes to the public, even in his own home or office, is not a subject of Fourth Amendment protection.'" *California v. Ciraolo,* 476 U.S. 207, 213 (1986) (quoting *Katz v. United States,* 389 U.S. 347, 351 (1967)); see *Florida v. Riley,* 488 U.S. 445, 449–450 (1989); *California v. Greenwood,* 486 U.S. 35, 40–41 (1988); *Dow Chemical Co. v. United States,* 476 U.S. 227, 235–236 (1986); *Air Pollution Variance Bd. of Colo. v. Western Alfalfa Corp.,* 416 U.S. 861, 865 (1974). That is the principle implicated here.

From *Danny Lee Kyllo v. United States,* 533 U.S. (2001). Some notes and case citations omitted.

While the Court "take[s] the long view" and decides this case based largely on the potential of yet-to-be-developed technology that might allow "through-the-wall surveillance," this case involves nothing more than off-the-wall surveillance by law enforcement officers to gather information exposed to the general public from the outside of petitioner's home. All that the infra-red camera did in this case was passively measure heat emitted from the exterior surfaces of petitioner's home; all that those measurements showed were relative differences in emission levels, vaguely indicating that some areas of the roof and outside walls were warmer than others. As still images from the infrared scans show, no details regarding the interior of petitioner's home were revealed. Unlike an x-ray scan, or other possible "through-the-wall" techniques, the detection of infrared radiation emanating from the home did not accomplish "an unauthorized physical penetration into the premises," *Silverman v. United States,* 365 U.S. 505, 509 (1961), nor did it "obtain information that it could not have obtained by observation from outside the curtilage of the house," *United States v. Karo,* 468 U.S. 705, 715 (1984).

Indeed, the ordinary use of the senses might enable a neighbor or passerby to notice the heat emanating from a building, particularly if it is vented, as was the case here. Additionally, any member of the public might notice that one part of a house is warmer than another part or a nearby building if, for example, rainwater evaporates or snow melts at different rates across its surfaces. Such use of the senses would not convert into an unreasonable search if, instead, an adjoining neighbor allowed an officer onto her property to verify her perceptions with a sensitive thermometer. Nor, in my view, does such observation become an unreasonable search if made from a distance with the aid of a device that merely discloses that the exterior of one house, or one area of the house, is much warmer than another. Nothing more occurred in this case.

Thus, the notion that heat emissions from the outside of a dwelling is a private matter implicating the protections of the Fourth Amendment (the text of which guarantees the right of people "to be secure *in* their... houses" against unreasonable searches and seizures (emphasis added)) is not only unprecedented but also quite difficult to take seriously. Heat waves, like aromas that are generated in a kitchen, or in a laboratory or opium den, enter the public domain if and when they leave a building. A subjective expectation that they would remain private is not only implausible but also surely not "one that society is prepared to recognize as 'reasonable.'" *Katz,* 389 U.S., at 361 (Harlan, J., concurring).

To be sure, the homeowner has a reasonable expectation of privacy concerning what takes place within the home, and the Fourth Amendment's protection against physical invasions of the home should apply to their functional equivalent. But the equipment in this case did not penetrate the walls of petitioner's home, and while it did pick up "details of the home" that were exposed to the public, *ante,* at 10, it did not obtain "any information regarding the *interior* of the home," *ante,* at 6 (emphasis added). In the Court's own words, based on what the thermal imager "showed" regarding the outside of petitioner's home, the officers "concluded" that petitioner was engaging in illegal activity inside the home. It would be quite absurd to characterize their thought processes as "searches," regardless of whether they inferred (rightly) that petitioner was growing marijuana in his house, or (wrongly) that "the lady of the house [was taking] her daily sauna and bath." In either case, the only conclusions the officers reached concerning the interior of the home were at least as indirect as those that might have been inferred from the contents of discarded garbage, see *California v. Greenwood,* 486 U.S. 35 (1988), or pen register data, see *Smith v. Maryland,* 442 U.S. 735 (1979), or, as in this case, subpoenaed utility records, see 190 F. 3d 1041, 1043 (CA9 1999). For the first time in its history, the Court assumes that an inference can amount to a Fourth Amendment violation.

Notwithstanding the implications of today's decision, there is a strong public interest in avoiding constitutional litigation over the monitoring of emissions from homes, and over the inferences drawn from such monitoring. Just as "the police cannot reasonably be expected to avert their eyes from evidence of criminal activity that could have been observed by any member of the public," *Greenwood,* 486 U.S., at 41, so too public officials should not have to avert their senses or their equipment from detecting emissions in the public domain such as excessive heat, traces of smoke, suspicious odors, odorless gases, airborne particulates, or radioactive emissions, any of which could identify hazards to the community. In my judgment, monitoring such emissions with "sense-enhancing technology," and drawing useful conclusions from such monitoring, is an entirely reasonable public service.

On the other hand, the countervailing privacy interest is at best trivial. After all, homes generally are insulated to keep heat in, rather than to prevent the detection of heat going out, and it does not seem to me that society will suffer from a rule requiring the rare homeowner who both intends to engage in uncommon activities that produce extraordinary amounts of heat, and wishes to conceal that production from outsiders, to make sure that the surrounding area is well insulated. Cf. *United States v. Jacobsen,* 466 U.S. 109, 122 (1984) ("The concept of an interest in privacy that society is prepared to recognize as reasonable is, by its very nature, critically different from the mere expectation, however well justified, that certain facts will not come to the attention of the authorities"). The interest in concealing the heat escaping from one's house pales in significance to the "chief evil against which the wording of the Fourth Amendment is directed," the "physical entry of the home," *United States v. United States Dist. Court for Eastern Dist. of Mich.,* 407 U.S. 297, 313 (1972), and it is hard to believe that it is an interest the Framers sought to protect in our Constitution.

Since what was involved in this case was nothing more than drawing inferences from off-the-wall surveillance, rather than any "through-the-wall" surveillance, the officers' conduct did not amount to a search and was perfectly reasonable.[3]

II

Instead of trying to answer the question whether the use of the thermal imager in this case was even arguably unreasonable, the Court has fashioned a rule that is intended to provide essential guidance for the day when "more sophisticated systems" gain the "ability to 'see' through walls and other opaque barriers." The newly minted rule encompasses "obtaining [1] by sense-enhancing technology [2] any information regarding the interior of the home [3] that could not otherwise have been obtained without physical intrusion into a constitutionally protected area . . . [4] at least where (as here) the technology in question is not in general public use." In my judgment, the Court's new rule is at once too broad and too narrow, and is not justified by the Court's explanation for its adoption. As I have suggested, I would not erect a constitutional impediment to the use of sense-enhancing technology unless it provides its user with the functional equivalent of actual presence in the area being searched.

Despite the Court's attempt to draw a line that is "not only firm but also bright," the contours of its new rule are uncertain because its protection apparently dissipates as soon as the relevant technology is "in general public use." Yet how much use is general public use is not even hinted at by the Court's opinion, which makes the somewhat doubtful assumption that the thermal imager used in this case does not satisfy that criterion.[4] In any event, putting aside its lack of clarity, this criterion is somewhat perverse because it seems likely that the threat to privacy will grow, rather than recede, as the use of intrusive equipment becomes more readily available.

It is clear, however, that the category of "sense-enhancing technology" covered by the new rule is far too broad. It would, for example, embrace potential mechanical substitutes for dogs trained to react when they sniff narcotics. But in *United States v. Place,* 462 U.S. 696, 707 (1983), we held that a dog sniff that "discloses only the presence or absence of narcotics" does "not constitute a 'search' within the meaning of the Fourth Amendment," and it must follow that sense-enhancing equipment that identifies nothing but illegal activity is not a search either. Nevertheless, the use of such a device would be unconstitutional under the Court's rule, as would the use of other new devices that might detect the odor of deadly bacteria or chemicals for making a new type of high explosive, even if the devices (like the dog sniffs) are "so limited in both the manner in which" they obtain information and "in the content of the information" they reveal. If nothing more than that sort of information could be obtained by using the devices in a public place to monitor emissions from a house, then their use would be no more objectionable than the use of the thermal imager in this case.

The application of the Court's new rule to "any information regarding the interior of the home," is also unnecessarily broad. If it takes sensitive equipment to detect an odor that identifies criminal conduct and nothing else, the fact that the odor emanates from the interior of a home should not provide it with constitutional protection. The criterion, moreover, is too sweeping in that information "regarding" the interior of a home apparently is not just information obtained through its walls, but also information concerning the outside of the building that could lead to (however many) inferences "regarding" what might be inside. Under that expansive view, I suppose, an officer using an infrared camera to observe a man silently entering the side door of a house at night carrying a pizza might conclude that its interior is now occupied by someone who likes pizza, and by doing so the officer would be guilty of conducting an unconstitutional "search" of the home.

Because the new rule applies to information regarding the "interior" of the home, it is too narrow as well as too broad. Clearly, a rule that is designed to protect individuals from the overly intrusive use of sense-enhancing equipment should not be limited to a home. If such equipment did provide its user with the functional equivalent of access to a private place—such as, for example, the telephone booth involved in *Katz,* or an office building—then the rule should apply to such an area as well as to a home. See *Katz,* 389 U.S., at 351 ("[T]he Fourth Amendment protects people, not places").

The final requirement of the Court's new rule, that the information "could not otherwise have been obtained without physical intrusion into a constitutionally protected area," *ante,* at 6 (internal quotation marks omitted), also extends too far as the Court applies it. As noted, the Court effectively treats the mental process of analyzing data obtained from external sources as the equivalent of a physical intrusion into the home. As I have explained, however, the process of drawing inferences from data in the public domain should not be characterized as a search.

The two reasons advanced by the Court as justifications for the adoption of its new rule are both unpersuasive. First, the Court suggests that its rule is compelled by our holding in *Katz,* because in that case, as in this, the surveillance consisted of nothing more than the monitoring of waves emanating from a private area into the public domain. Yet there are critical differences between the cases. In *Katz,* the electronic listening device attached to the outside of the phone booth allowed the officers to pick up the content of the conversation inside the booth, making them the functional equivalent of intruders because they gathered information that was otherwise available only to someone inside the private area; it would be as if, in this case, the thermal imager presented a view of the heat-generating activity inside petitioner's home. By contrast, the thermal imager here disclosed only the relative amounts of heat radiating from the house; it would be as if, in Katz, the listening device disclosed only the relative volume of sound leaving the booth, which presumably was discernible in the public domain.[5] Surely, there is a significant difference between the general and well-settled expectation that strangers will not have direct access to the contents of private communications, on the one hand, and the rather theoretical expectation that an occasional homeowner would even care if anybody noticed the relative amounts of heat emanating from the walls of his house, on the other. It is pure hyperbole for the Court to suggest that refusing to extend the holding of *Katz* to this case would leave the homeowner at the mercy of "technology that could discern all human activity in the home." *Ante,* at 8.

Second, the Court argues that the permissibility of "through-the-wall surveillance" cannot depend on a distinction between observing "intimate details" such as "the lady of the house [taking] her daily sauna and bath," and noticing only "the nonintimate rug on the vestibule floor" or "objects no smaller than 36 by 36 inches." *Ante,* at 10–11. This entire argument assumes, of course, that the thermal imager in this case could or did perform "through-the-wall surveillance" that could identify any detail "that would previously have been unknowable without physical intrusion." In fact, the device could not, and did not, enable its user to identify either the lady of the house, the rug on the vestibule floor, or anything else inside the house, whether smaller or larger than 36 by 36 inches. Indeed, the vague thermal images of petitioner's home that are reproduced in the Appendix were submitted by him to the District Court as part of an expert report raising the question whether the device could even take "accurate, consistent infrared images" of the *outside* of his house. Defendant's Exhibit 107, p. 4. But even if the device could reliably show extraordinary differences in the amounts of heat leaving his home, drawing the inference that there was something suspicious occurring inside the residence—a conclusion that officers far less gifted than Sherlock Holmes would readily draw—does not qualify as "through-the-wall surveillance," much less a Fourth Amendment violation.

III

Although the Court is properly and commendably concerned about the threats to privacy that may flow from advances in the technology available to the law enforcement profession, it has unfortunately failed to heed the tried and true counsel of judicial restraint. Instead of concentrating on the rather mundane issue that is actually presented by the case before it, the Court has endeavored to craft an all-encompassing rule for the future. It would be far wiser to give legislators an unimpeded opportunity to grapple with these emerging issues rather than to shackle them with prematurely devised constitutional constraints.

I respectfully dissent.

Notes

1. After an evidentiary hearing, the District Court found:

    "[T]he use of the thermal imaging device here was not an intrusion into Kyllo's home. No intimate details of the home were observed, and there was no intrusion upon the privacy of the individuals within the home. The device used cannot penetrate walls or windows to reveal conversations or human activities. The device recorded only the heat being emitted from the home." Supp. App. to Pet. for Cert. 40.

2. Thus, for example, we have found consistent with the Fourth Amendment, even absent a warrant, the search and seizure of garbage left for collection outside the curtilage of a home, *California v. Greenwood,* 486 U.S. 35 (1988); the aerial surveillance of a fenced-in backyard from an altitude of 1,000 feet, *California v. Ciraolo,* 476 U.S. 207 (1986); the aerial observation of a partially exposed interior of a residential greenhouse from 400 feet above, *Florida v. Riley,* 488 U.S. 445 (1989); the aerial photography of an industrial complex from several thousand feet above, *Dow Chemical Co. v. United States,* 476 U.S. 227 (1986); and the observation of smoke emanating from chimney stacks, *Air Pollution Variance Bd. of Colo. v. Western Alfalfa Corp.,* 416 U.S. 861 (1974).

3. This view comports with that of all the Courts of Appeals that have resolved the issue. See 190 F. 3d 1041 (CA9 1999); *United States v. Robinson,* 62 F. 3d 1325 (CA11 1995) (upholding warrantless use of thermal imager); *United States v. Myers,* 46 F. 3d 668 (CA7 1995) (same); *United States v. Ishmael,* 48 F. 3d 850 (CA5 1995) (same); *United States v. Pinson,* 24 F. 3d 1056 (CA8 1994) (same).

But see *United States v. Cusumano,* 67 F. 3d 1497 (CA10 1995) (warrantless use of thermal imager violated Fourth Amendment), vacated and decided on other grounds, 83 F. 3d 1247 (CA10 1996) (en banc).

4. The record describes a device that numbers close to a thousand manufactured units; that has a predecessor numbering in the neighborhood of 4,000 to 5,000 units; that competes with a similar product numbering from 5,000 to 6,000 units; and that is "readily available to the public" for commercial, personal, or law enforcement purposes, and is just an 800-number away from being rented from "half a dozen national companies" by anyone who wants one. App. 18. Since, by virtue of the Court's new rule, the issue is one of first impression, perhaps it should order an evidentiary hearing to determine whether these facts suffice to establish "general public use."

5. The use of the latter device would be constitutional given *Smith v. Maryland,* 442 U.S. 735, 741 (1979), which upheld the use of pen registers to record numbers dialed on a phone because, unlike "the listening device employed in *Katz* . . . pen registers do not acquire the *contents* of communications."

POSTSCRIPT

Does the Use of High-Technology Thermal Imaging Devices Violate the Fourth Amendment Search and Seizure Guarantee?

Even though Scalia's opinion is a strong statement about the need for protecting privacy in a technological era, there will certainly be more cases in which challenging issues will be presented. Law enforcement's ability to invade privacy at a distance is increasing, and the Supreme Court has not, as it did in this case, always sided with the individual. Indeed, the Court has upheld various novel search techniques in other Fourth Amendment cases. Consider the following:

- *Dow Chemical v. United States,* 476 U.S. 227 (1986)—The Court allowed aerial pictures taken by the Environmental Protection Agency (EPA) even though the company had refused to allow inspectors to enter.
- *Florida v. Riley,* 488 U.S. 445, 450 (1989)—The Court allowed a search in which a police officer in a helicopter looked into a greenhouse from a height of 400 feet and observed through openings in the roof what he thought was marijuana.
- *California v. Ciraolo,* 476 U.S. 207, 213–214 (1986)—The Court held that police officers were not "searching" when they flew over the defendant's property and observed marijuana growing.
- *Smith v. Maryland,* 442 U.S. 735, 742–744 (1979)—The Court allowed the authorities to look at "pen registers," or records of telephone numbers dialed, without a warrant.

Scalia does not mention the use of trained dogs to sniff out the presence of drugs at airports and other public places. The Court, in *United States v. Place,* 462 U.S. 696 (1983), allowed the use of dogs when the sniff "discloses only the presence or absence of narcotics." Stevens raises the interesting question of whether or not "mechanical substitutes for dogs trained to react when they sniff narcotics" would be lawful. Since technology allows information to be obtained at a distance, often without a person feeling that his or her privacy has been invaded, we can expect additional cases in which the lawful use of "mechanical substitutes" is the main issue.

Background information on law enforcement and the drug problem can be found on the Web site of the Drug Enforcement Administration of the U.S. Department of Justice at http://www.usdoj.gov/dea/. Readings on the thermal imaging issue are Kathleen A. Lomas, "Bad Physics and Bad Law: A Review of the Constitutionality of Thermal Imagery Surveillance After *United States v. Elkins,*" 34 *University of San Francisco Law Review* 799 (2000); Jennifer Murphy, "Trash, Thermal Imagers, and the Fourth Amendment: The New Search and Seizure," 53 *Southern Methodist University Law Review* 1645 (2000); and Jeffrey P. Campisi, "The Fourth Amendment and New Technologies: The Constitutionality of Thermal Imaging," 46 *Villanova Law Review* 241 (2001).

ISSUE 11

Are Laws Requiring Schools and Public Libraries to Filter Internet Access Constitutional?

YES: William H. Rehnquist, from Majority Opinion, *United States et al. v. American Library Association, Inc. et al.*, U.S. Supreme Court (June 23, 2003)

NO: John Paul Stevens, from Dissenting Opinion, *United States et al. v. American Library Association, Inc. et al.*, U.S. Supreme Court (June 23, 2003)

ISSUE SUMMARY

YES: Supreme Court Chief Justice William H. Rehnquist rules that a federal law withholding funds from public libraries that fail to install filters on computers that are connected to the Internet does not violate the First Amendment.

NO: Supreme Court Justice John Paul Stevens argues that filters on computers that are connected to the Internet are flawed and that the Children's Internet Protection Act violates the First Amendment.

The growth of the Internet and the World Wide Web is, perhaps, the most significant economic and cultural development of the last decade. Cyberspace is increasingly the "place" where people shop, relax, socialize, learn, etc. It has been equated with such physical places as a library, a shopping mall, a school, a conference center, an arcade, and a casino because we can read, buy, learn, converse, play games, and gamble online. Looked at most simply, cyberspace allows information to be distributed and exchanged extremely quickly and at much lower costs than before. As a result, its continuing growth in our lives should not be surprising.

Cyberspace may be a creative, lucrative, and interesting place, but it is not a harmonious place or a problem-free environment. This, too, should not be surprising. Since there is an enormous amount of activity in cyberspace, a great deal of money is being spent there, and numerous relationships are

226

being formed there. When so much is happening so fast, regulatory controls and the need for law need to be considered.

Is there a need for new rules, new frameworks for thinking about traditional rules, and new processes for dealing with disputes that arise online? If so, how can the flow of information online be regulated without interfering with traditional freedoms for receiving and communicating information? These are difficult questions because it is not yet clear what the truly new features of cyberspace are. What we do know is that we can do more things at a distance than ever before, that we can do them faster than ever before, and that, as a result, it is harder for the state and other previously powerful entities to exercise control over some online activities. The problem of control is significant to law because of the issue of enforcement. Even if a law seems desirable as a matter of substance, it is not desirable to have a law that is not enforceable.

One area of law that has attracted a great deal of attention involves pornography and obscenity. Early on, Congress recognized that there were pornographic and obscene sites on the Web and passed legislation called the Communications Decency Act (CDA) to try to respond to the amount of sexually oriented material on the Web. It was not particularly careful, however, in drafting the legislation, and in *Reno v. American Civil Liberties Union* (http://laws.findlaw.com/US/000/96-511.html), the Supreme Court found that the statute violated First Amendment standards of free speech.

More recently, the Court was faced with the issue of whether "virtual child pornography"—pornographic images of children that are digital creations rather than pictures of actual children—should be banned in the same way that pornographic images of real children are. In *Ashcroft v. Free Speech Coalition*, 122 S. Ct. 1389 (2002), the Court ruled that existing child pornography laws would have to be redrafted in order for such regulation to be constitutional.

The following case concerns legislation proposed not to outlaw certain Web sites but to prevent public school students and public library patrons to access sites containing pornographic images. Under the 1996 Telecommunications Act, the federal government offers discounted Internet access to schools and libraries. The program is called E-rate access, and the legislation in question would require recipients of E-rate funds to put a filter on computers that provide access to the Internet. What is problematic about filters is the fact that control over what one has access to is delegated to a piece of software. The District Court for the Eastern District of Pennsylvania found that basing federal funding on such a filtering scheme is unconstitutional. A majority of the Supreme Court came to a different conclusion.

YES

William H. Rehnquist

Majority Opinion

United States *v.* American Library Association, Inc.

CHIEF JUSTICE REHNQUIST announced the judgment of the Court. . . .

To address the problems associated with the availability of Internet pornography in public libraries, Congress enacted the Children's Internet Protection Act (CIPA), 114 Stat. 2763A–335. Under CIPA, a public library may not receive federal assistance to provide Internet access unless it installs software to block images that constitute obscenity or child pornography, and to prevent minors from obtaining access to material that is harmful to them. The District Court held these provisions facially invalid on the ground that they induce public libraries to violate patrons' First Amendment rights. We now reverse.

To help public libraries provide their patrons with Internet access, Congress offers two forms of federal assistance. First, the E-rate program established by the Telecommunications Act of 1996 entitles qualifying libraries to buy Internet access at a discount. 110 Stat. 71, 47 U.S.C. §254(h)(1)(B). In the year ending June 30, 2002, libraries received $58.5 million in such discounts. Second, pursuant to the Library Services and Technology Act (LSTA), 110 Stat. 3009–295, as amended, 20 U.S.C. §9101 *et seq.,* the Institute of Museum and Library Services makes grants to state library administrative agencies to "electronically lin[k] libraries with educational, social, or information services," "assis[t] libraries in accessing information through electronic networks," and "pa[y] costs for libraries to acquire or share computer systems and telecommunications technologies." §§9141(a)(1)(B), (C), (E). In fiscal year 2002, Congress appropriated more than $149 million in LSTA grants. These programs have succeeded greatly in bringing Internet access to public libraries: By 2000, 95% of the Nation's libraries provided public Internet access. J. Bertot & C. McClure, Public Libraries and the Internet 2000: Summary Findings and Data Tables, p. 3 (Sept. 7, 2000), http://www.nclis.gov/statsuru/2000plo.pdf .

By connecting to the Internet, public libraries provide patrons with a vast amount of valuable information. But there is also an enormous amount of pornography on the Internet, much of which is easily obtained. 201 F. Supp. 2d 401, 419 (ED Pa. 2002). The accessibility of this material has created serious

From *United States et al. v. American Library Association, Inc. et al.,* 539 U.S. ___ (2003). Some notes and case citations omitted.

problems for libraries, which have found that patrons of all ages, including minors, regularly search for online pornography. *Id.,* at 406. Some patrons also expose others to pornographic images by leaving them displayed on Internet terminals or printed at library printers. *Id.,* at 423.

Upon discovering these problems, Congress became concerned that the E-rate and LSTA programs were facilitating access to illegal and harmful pornography. S. Rep. No. 105–226, p. 5 (1998). Congress learned that adults "us[e] library computers to access pornography that is then exposed to staff, passers-by, and children," and that "minors acces[s] child and adult pornography in libraries."

But Congress also learned that filtering software that blocks access to pornographic Web sites could provide a reasonably effective way to prevent such uses of library resources. *Id.,* at 20–26. By 2000, before Congress enacted CIPA, almost 17% of public libraries used such software on at least some of their Internet terminals, and 7% had filters on all of them. Library Research Center of U. Ill., Survey of Internet Access Management in Public Libraries 8, http://alexia. lis.uiuc.edu/gslis/research/internet.pdf. A library can set such software to block categories of material, such as "Pornography" or "Violence." 201 F. Supp. 2d, at 428. When a patron tries to view a site that falls within such a category, a screen appears indicating that the site is blocked. *Id.,* at 429. But a filter set to block pornography may sometimes block other sites that present neither obscene nor pornographic material, but that nevertheless trigger the filter. To minimize this problem, a library can set its software to prevent the blocking of material that falls into categories like "Education," "History," and "Medical." *Id.,* at 428–429. A library may also add or delete specific sites from a blocking category, *id.,* at 429, and anyone can ask companies that furnish filtering software to unblock particular sites, *id.,* at 430.

Responding to this information, Congress enacted CIPA. It provides that a library may not receive E-rate or LSTA assistance unless it has "a policy of Internet safety for minors that includes the operation of a technology protection measure . . . that protects against access" by all persons to "visual depictions" that constitute "obscen[ity]" or "child pornography," and that protects against access by minors to "visual depictions" that are "harmful to minors." 20 U.S.C. §§9134(f)(1)(A)(i) and (B)(i); 47 U.S.C. §§254(h)(6)(B)(i) and (C)(i). The statute defines a "[t]echnology protection measure" as "a specific technology that blocks or filters Internet access to material covered by" CIPA. §254(h)(7)(I). CIPA also permits the library to "disable" the filter "to enable access for bona fide research or other lawful purposes." 20 U.S.C. §9134(f)(3); 47 U.S.C. §254(h)(6)(D). Under the E-rate program, disabling is permitted "during use by an adult." §254(h)(6)(D). Under the LSTA program, disabling is permitted during use by any person. 20 U.S.C. §9134(f)(3).

Appellees are a group of libraries, library associations, library patrons, and Web site publishers, including the American Library Association (ALA) and the Multnomah County Public Library in Portland, Oregon (Multnomah). They sued the United States and the Government agencies and officials responsible for administering the E-rate and LSTA programs in District Court, challenging the constitutionality of CIPA's filtering provisions. A three-judge District Court convened pursuant to §1741(a) of CIPA, 114 Stat. 2763A–351, note following 20 U.S.C. §7001.

After a trial, the District Court ruled that CIPA was facially unconstitutional and enjoined the relevant agencies and officials from withholding federal assistance for failure to comply with CIPA. The District Court held that Congress had exceeded its authority under the Spending Clause, U.S. Const., Art. I, §8, cl. 1, because, in the court's view, "any public library that complies with CIPA's conditions will necessarily violate the First Amendment." 201 F. Supp. 2d, at 453. The court acknowledged that "generally the First Amendment subjects libraries' content-based decisions about which print materials to acquire for their collections to only rational [basis] review." *Id.*, at 462. But it distinguished libraries' decisions to make certain Internet material inaccessible. "The central difference," the court stated, "is that by providing patrons with even filtered Internet access, the library permits patrons to receive speech on a virtually unlimited number of topics, from a virtually unlimited number of speakers, without attempting to restrict patrons' access to speech that the library, in the exercise of its professional judgment, determines to be particularly valuable." *Ibid.* Reasoning that "the provision of Internet access within a public library . . . is for use by the public . . . for expressive activity," the court analyzed such access as a "designated public forum." *Id.*, at 457 (citation and internal quotation marks omitted). The District Court also likened Internet access in libraries to "traditional public fora . . . such as sidewalks and parks" because it "promotes First Amendment values in an analogous manner." *Id.*, at 466.

Based on both of these grounds, the court held that the filtering software contemplated by CIPA was a content-based restriction on access to a public forum, and was therefore subject to strict scrutiny. Applying this standard, the District Court held that, although the Government has a compelling interest "in preventing the dissemination of obscenity, child pornography, or, in the case of minors, material harmful to minors," *id.*, at 471, the use of software filters is not narrowly tailored to further those interests, *id.*, at 479. We noted probable jurisdiction, 537 U.S. 1017 (2002), and now reverse.

Congress has wide latitude to attach conditions to the receipt of federal assistance in order to further its policy objectives. *South Dakota* v. *Dole*, 483 U.S. 203, 206 (1987). But Congress may not "induce" the recipient "to engage in activities that would themselves be unconstitutional." *Id.*, at 210. To determine whether libraries would violate the First Amendment by employing the filtering software that CIPA requires,[1] we must first examine the role of libraries in our society.

Public libraries pursue the worthy missions of facilitating learning and cultural enrichment. Appellee ALA's Library Bill of Rights states that libraries should provide "[b]ooks and other . . . resources . . . for the interest, information, and enlightenment of all people of the community the library serves." 201 F. Supp. 2d, at 420 (internal quotation marks omitted). To fulfill their traditional missions, public libraries must have broad discretion to decide what material to provide to their patrons. Although they seek to provide a wide array of information, their goal has never been to provide "universal coverage." *Id.*, at 421. Instead, public libraries seek to provide materials "that would be of the greatest direct benefit or interest to the community." To this end, libraries collect only those materials deemed to have "requisite and appropriate quality." *Ibid.* See W. Katz, Collection Development: The Selection of Materials for Libraries 6 (1980) ("The librarian's responsibility . . . is to separate out the gold from the garbage, not to preserve everything"); F. Drury, Book Selection xi (1930) ("[I]t is the aim of the selector to give the public, not everything it wants, but the best that it will read or use to advantage"); App. 636 (Rebuttal Expert Report of Donald G. Davis, Jr.) ("A hypothetical collection of everything that has been produced is not only of dubious value, but actually detrimental to users trying to find what they want to find and really need").

We have held in two analogous contexts that the government has broad discretion to make content-based judgments in deciding what private speech to make available to the public. In *Arkansas Ed. Television Comm'n* v. *Forbes,* 523 U.S. 666, 672–673 (1998), we held that public forum principles do not generally apply to a public television station's editorial judgments regarding the private speech it presents to its viewers. "[B]road rights of access for outside speakers would be antithetical, as a general rule, to the discretion that stations and their editorial staff must exercise to fulfill their journalistic purpose and statutory obligations." *Id.,* at 673. Recognizing a broad right of public access "would [also] risk implicating the courts in judgments that should be left to the exercise of journalistic discretion." *Id.,* at 674.

Similarly, in *National Endowment for Arts* v. *Finley,* 524 U.S. 569 (1998), we upheld an art funding program that required the National Endowment for the Arts (NEA) to use content-based criteria in making funding decisions. We explained that "[a]ny content-based considerations that may be taken into account in the grant-making process are a consequence of the nature of arts funding." *Id.,* at 585. In particular, "[t]he very assumption of the NEA is that grants will be awarded according to the 'artistic worth of competing applicants,' and absolute neutrality is simply inconceivable." *Ibid.* (some internal quotation marks omitted). We expressly declined to apply forum analysis, reasoning that it would conflict with "NEA's mandate . . . to make esthetic judgments, and the inherently content-based 'excellence' threshold for NEA support." *Id.,* at 586.

The principles underlying *Forbes* and *Finley* also apply to a public library's exercise of judgment in selecting the material it provides to its patrons. Just as forum analysis and heightened judicial scrutiny are incompatible with the role of public television stations and the role of the NEA, they are also incompatible with the discretion that public libraries must have to fulfill their traditional missions. Public library staffs necessarily consider content in making collection decisions and enjoy broad discretion in making them.

The public forum principles on which the District Court relied, 201 F. Supp. 2d, at 457–470, are out of place in the context of this case. Internet access in public libraries is neither a "traditional" nor a "designated" public forum. See *Cornelius* v. *NAACP Legal Defense & Ed. Fund, Inc.,* 473 U.S. 788, 802 (1985) (describing types of forums). First, this resource—which did not exist until quite recently— has not "immemorially been held in trust for the use of the public and, time out of mind, . . . been used for purposes of assembly, communication of thoughts between citizens, and discussing public questions." *International Soc. for Krishna*

Consciousness, Inc. v. *Lee,* 505 U.S. 672, 679 (1992) (internal quotation marks omitted). We have "rejected the view that traditional public forum status extends beyond its historic confines." *Forbes, supra,* at 678. The doctrines surrounding traditional public forums may not be extended to situations where such history is lacking.

Nor does Internet access in a public library satisfy our definition of a "designated public forum." To create such a forum, the government must make an affirmative choice to open up its property for use as a public forum. *Cornelius, supra,* at 802–803; *Perry Ed. Assn.* v. *Perry Local Educators' Assn.,* 460 U.S. 37, 45 (1983). "The government does not create a public forum by inaction or by permitting limited discourse, but only by intentionally opening a nontraditional forum for public discourse." *Cornelius, supra,* at 802. The District Court likened public libraries' Internet terminals to the forum at issue in *Rosenberger* v. *Rector and Visitors of Univ. of Va.,* 515 U.S. 819 (1995). 201 F. Supp. 2d, at 465. In *Rosenberger,* we considered the "Student Activity Fund" established by the University of Virginia that subsidized all manner of student publications except those based on religion. We held that the fund had created a limited public forum by giving public money to student groups who wished to publish, and therefore could not discriminate on the basis of viewpoint.

The situation here is very different. A public library does not acquire Internet terminals in order to create a public forum for Web publishers to express themselves, any more than it collects books in order to provide a public forum for the authors of books to speak. It provides Internet access, not to "encourage a diversity of views from private speakers," *Rosenberger, supra,* at 834, but for the same reasons it offers other library resources: to facilitate research, learning, and recreational pursuits by furnishing materials of requisite and appropriate quality. See *Cornelius, supra,* at 805 (noting, in upholding limits on participation in the Combined Federal Campaign (CFC), that "[t]he Government did not create the CFC for purposes of providing a forum for expressive activity"). As Congress recognized, "[t]he Internet is simply another method for making information available in a school or library." S. Rep. No. 106–141, p. 7 (1999). It is "no more than a technological extension of the book stack." *Ibid.*[2]

The District Court disagreed because, whereas a library reviews and affirmatively chooses to acquire every book in its collection, it does not review every Web site that it makes available. 201 F. Supp. 2d, at 462–463. Based on this distinction, the court reasoned that a public library enjoys less discretion in deciding which Internet materials to make available than in making book selections. *Ibid.* We do not find this distinction constitutionally relevant. A library's failure to make quality-based judgments about all the material it furnishes from the Web does not somehow taint the judgments it does make. A library's need to exercise judgment in making collection decisions depends on its traditional role in identifying suitable and worthwhile material; it is no less entitled to play that role when it collects material from the Internet than when it collects material from any other source. Most libraries already exclude pornography from their print collections because they deem it inappropriate for inclusion. We do not subject these decisions to heightened scrutiny; it would make little sense to treat libraries' judgments to block online pornography any differently, when these judgments are made for just the same reason.

Moreover, because of the vast quantity of material on the Internet and the rapid pace at which it changes, libraries cannot possibly segregate, item by item, all the Internet material that is appropriate for inclusion from all that is not. While a library could limit its Internet collection to just those sites it found worthwhile, it could do so only at the cost of excluding an enormous amount of valuable information that it lacks the capacity to review. Given that tradeoff, it is entirely reasonable for public libraries to reject that approach and instead exclude certain categories of content, without making individualized judgments that everything they do make available has requisite and appropriate quality.

Like the District Court, the dissents fault the tendency of filtering software to "overblock"—that is, to erroneously block access to constitutionally protected speech that falls outside the categories that software users intend to block. See *post,* at 1–3 (opinion of STEVENS, J.); *post,* at 3–4 (opinion of SOUTER, J.). Due to the software's limitations, "[m]any erroneously blocked [Web] pages contain content that is completely innocuous for both adults and minors, and that no rational person could conclude matches the filtering companies' category definitions, such as 'pornography' or 'sex.'" 201 F. Supp. 2d, at 449. Assuming that such erroneous blocking presents constitutional difficulties, any such concerns are dispelled by the ease with which patrons may have the filtering software disabled. When a patron encounters a blocked site, he need only ask a librarian to unblock it or (at least in the case of adults) disable the filter. As the District Court found, libraries have the capacity to permanently unblock any erroneously blocked site, *id.,* at 429, and the Solicitor General stated at oral argument that a "library may . . . eliminate the filtering with respect to specific sites . . . at the request of a patron." Tr. of Oral Arg. 4. With respect to adults, CIPA also expressly authorizes library officials to "disable" a filter altogether "to enable access for bona fide research or other lawful purposes." 20 U.S.C. §9134(f)(3) (disabling permitted for both adults and minors); 47 U.S.C. §254(h)(6)(D) (disabling permitted for adults). The Solicitor General confirmed that a "librarian can, in response to a request from a patron, unblock the filtering mechanism altogether," Tr. of Oral Arg. 11, and further explained that a patron would not "have to explain . . . why he was asking a site to be unblocked or the filtering to be disabled," *id.,* at 4. The District Court viewed unblocking and disabling as inadequate because some patrons may be too embarrassed to request them. 201 F. Supp. 2d, at 411. But the Constitution does not guarantee the right to acquire information at a public library without any risk of embarrassment.[3]

Appellees urge us to affirm the District Court's judgment on the alternative ground that CIPA imposes an unconstitutional condition on the receipt of federal assistance. Under this doctrine, "the government 'may not deny a benefit to a person on a basis that infringes his constitutionally protected . . . freedom of speech' even if he has no entitlement to that benefit." *Board of Comm'rs, Wabaunsee Cty.* v. *Umbehr,* 518 U.S. 668, 674 (1996) (quoting *Perry* v. *Sindermann,* 408 U.S. 593, 597 (1972)). Appellees argue that CIPA imposes an unconstitutional condition on libraries that receive E-rate and LSTA subsidies by requiring them, as a condition on their receipt of federal funds, to surrender their First Amendment right to provide the public with access to constitutionally protected speech. The Government counters that this claim fails because Government entities do not have First Amendment rights.

We need not decide this question because, even assuming that appellees may assert an "unconstitutional conditions" claim, this claim would fail on the merits. Within broad limits, "when the Government appropriates public funds to establish a program it is entitled to define the limits of that program." *Rust* v. *Sullivan,* 500 U.S. 173, 194 (1991). In *Rust,* Congress had appropriated federal funding for family planning services and forbidden the use of such funds in programs that provided abortion counseling. *Id.,* at 178. Recipients of these funds challenged this restriction, arguing that it impermissibly conditioned the receipt of a benefit on the relinquishment of their constitutional right to engage in abortion counseling. *Id.,* at 196. We rejected that claim, recognizing that "the Government [was] not denying a benefit to anyone, but [was] instead simply insisting that public funds be spent for the purposes for which they were authorized." *Ibid.*

The same is true here. The E-rate and LSTA programs were intended to help public libraries fulfill their traditional role of obtaining material of requisite and appropriate quality for educational and informational purposes.[4] Congress may certainly insist that these "public funds be spent for the purposes for which they were authorized." Especially because public libraries have traditionally excluded pornographic material from their other collections, Congress could reasonably impose a parallel limitation on its Internet assistance programs. As the use of filtering software helps to carry out these programs, it is a permissible condition under *Rust.*

JUSTICE STEVENS asserts the premise that "[a] federal statute penalizing a library for failing to install filtering software on every one of its Internet-accessible computers would unquestionably violate [the First] Amendment." But—assuming again that public libraries have First Amendment rights—CIPA does not "penalize" libraries that choose not to install such software, or deny them the right to provide their patrons with unfiltered Internet access. Rather, CIPA simply reflects Congress' decision not to subsidize their doing so. To the extent that libraries wish to offer unfiltered access, they are free to do so without federal assistance. "'A refusal to fund protected activity, without more, cannot be equated with the imposition of a 'penalty' on that activity.'" *Rust,* *supra,* at 193 (quoting *Harris* v. *McRae,* 448 U.S. 297, 317, n. 19 (1980)). "'[A] legislature's decision not to subsidize the exercise of a fundamental right does not infringe the right. *Rust, supra,* at 193 (quoting *Regan* v. *Taxation With Representation of Wash.,* 461 U.S. 540, 549 (1983)).[5]

Appellees mistakenly contend, in reliance on *Legal Services Corporation* v. *Velazquez,* 531 U.S. 533 (2001), that CIPA's filtering conditions "[d]istor[t] the [u]sual [f]unctioning of [p]ublic [l]ibraries." Brief for Appellees ALA et al. 40 (citing *Velazquez, supra,* at 543); Brief for Appellees Multnomah et al. 47–48 (same). In *Velazquez,* the Court concluded that a Government program of furnishing legal aid to the indigent differed from the program in *Rust* "[i]n th[e] vital respect" that the role of lawyers who represent clients in welfare disputes is to advocate *against* the Government, and there was thus an assumption that counsel would be free of state control. 531 U.S., at 542–543. The Court concluded that the restriction on advocacy in such welfare disputes would distort the usual functioning of the legal profession and the federal and state courts before which the lawyers appeared. Public libraries, by contrast, have no comparable role that pits them against the Government, and there is no comparable assumption that they must be free of any conditions that their benefactors might attach to the use of donated funds or other assistance.[6]

Because public libraries' use of Internet filtering software does not violate their patrons' First Amendment rights, CIPA does not induce libraries to violate the Constitution, and is a valid exercise of Congress' spending power. Nor does CIPA impose an unconstitutional condition on public libraries. Therefore, the judgment of the District Court for the Eastern District of Pennsylvania is

Reversed.

Notes

1. JUSTICE STEVENS misapprehends the analysis we must perform to determine whether CIPA exceeds Congress' authority under the Spending Clause. He asks and answers whether it is constitutional for Congress to "impose [CIPA's filtering] requirement" on public libraries, instead of "allowing local decision-makers to tailor their responses to local problems." *Post,* at 1 (dissenting opinion). But under our well-established Spending Clause precedent, that is not the proper inquiry. Rather, as the District Court correctly recognized, 201 F. Supp. 2d 401, 453 (ED Pa. 2002), we must ask whether the condition that Congress requires "would . . . be unconstitutional" if performed by the library itself. *Dole,* 830 U.S., at 210.

   CIPA does not directly regulate private conduct; rather, Congress has exercised its Spending Power by specifying conditions on the receipt of federal funds. Therefore, *Dole* provides the appropriate framework for assessing CIPA's constitutionality.

2. Even if appellees had proffered more persuasive evidence that public libraries intended to create a forum for speech by connecting to the Internet, we would hesitate to import "the public forum doctrine . . . wholesale into" the context of the Internet. *Denver Area Ed. Telecommunications Consortium, Inc.* v. *FCC,* 518 U.S. 727, 749 (1996) (opinion of BREYER, J.). "[W]e are wary of the notion that a partial analogy in one context, for which we have developed doctrines, can compel a full range of decisions in such a new and changing area." *Ibid.*

   The dissents agree with the District Court that less restrictive alternatives to filtering software would suffice to meet Congress' goals. Post, at 4 (opinion of STEVENS, J.) (quoting 201 F. Supp. 2d, at 410); *post,* at 4 (opinion of SOUTER, J.) (quoting 201 F. Supp. 2d, at 422–427). But we require the Government to employ the least restrictive means only when the forum is a public one and strict scrutiny applies. For the reasons stated above, see *supra,* at 8–10, such is not the case here. In deciding not to collect pornographic material from the Internet, a public library need not satisfy a court that it has pursued the least restrictive means of implementing that decision.

   In any case, the suggested alternatives have their own drawbacks. Close monitoring of computer users would be far more intrusive than the use of filtering software, and would risk transforming the role of a librarian from a professional to whom patrons turn for assistance into a compliance officer whom many patrons might wish to avoid. Moving terminals to places where their displays cannot easily be seen by other patrons, or installing privacy screens or recessed monitors, would not address a library's interest in preventing patrons from deliberately using its computers to view online pornography. To the contrary, these alternatives would make it *easier* for patrons to do so.

3. The dissents argue that overblocking will "'reduce the adult population . . . to reading only what is fit for children.'" *Post,* at 3, n. 2 (opinion of STEVENS, J.) (quoting *Butler* v. *Michigan,* 352 U.S. 380, 383 (1957)). See also *post,* at 3, and n. 2 (citing *Ashcroft* v. *Free Speech Coalition,* 535 U.S. 234, 252 (2002); *United States* v. *Playboy Entertainment Group, Inc.,* 529 U.S. 803, 814 (2000); and *Reno* v. *American Civil Liberties Union,* 521 U.S. 844, 875 (1997)); see *post,* at 7–8 (opinion of SOUTER, J.). But these cases are inapposite because they addressed Congress' direct regulation of private conduct, not exercises of its Spending Power.

    The dissents also argue that because some library patrons would not make specific unblocking requests, the interest of authors of blocked Internet material "in reaching the widest possible audience would be abridged." *Post,* at 6 (opinion of STEVENS, J.); see *post,* at 13, n. 8 (opinion of Souter, J.). But this mistakes a public library's purpose for acquiring Internet terminals: A library does so to provide its patrons with materials of requisite and appropriate quality, not to create a public forum for Web publishers to express themselves. See *supra,* at 9–10.

    JUSTICE STEVENS further argues that, because some libraries' procedures will make it difficult for patrons to have blocked material unblocked, CIPA "will create a significant prior restraint on adult access to protected speech." *Post,* at 6. But this argument, which the District Court did not address, mistakenly extends prior restraint doctrine to the context of public libraries' collection decisions. A library's decision to use filtering software is a collection decision, not a restraint on private speech. Contrary to JUSTICE STEVENS' belief, a public library does not have an obligation to add material to its collection simply because the material is constitutionally protected.

4. See 20 U.S.C. §9121 ("It is the purpose of [LSTA] (2) to stimulate excellence and promote access to learning and information resources in all types of libraries for individuals of all ages"); S. Conf. Rep. No. 104–230, p. 132 (1996) (The E-rate program "will help open new worlds of knowledge, learning and education to all Americans . . . . [It is] intended, for example, to provide the ability to browse library collections, review the collections of museums, or find new information on the treatment of an illness, to Americans everywhere via . . . libraries").

5. These holdings, which JUSTICE STEVENS ignores, also make clear that his reliance on *Rutan* v. *Republican Party of Ill.,* 497 U.S. 62 (1990), *Elrod* v. *Burns,* 427 U.S. 347 (1976), and *Wieman* v. *Updegraff,* 344 U.S. 183 (1952), is misplaced. See *post,* at 8. The invalidated state action in those cases involved true penalties, such as denial of a promotion or outright discharge from employment, not nonsubsidies.

6. Relying on *Velazquez,* JUSTICE STEVENS argues mistakenly that *Rust* is inapposite because that case "only involved and only applies to . . . situations in which the government seeks to communicate a specific message," *post,* at 9, and unlike the Title X program in *Rust,* the E-rate and LSTA programs "are not designed to foster or transmit any particular governmental message." *Post,* at 10. But he misreads our cases discussing *Rust,* and again misapprehends the purpose of providing Internet terminals in public libraries. *Velazquez* held only that viewpoint-based restrictions are improper "'when the [government] does not itself speak or subsidize transmittal of a message it favors *but instead expends funds to encourage a diversity of views from private speakers.'*" 531 U.S., at 542

(quoting *Rosenberger* v. *Rector and Visitors of Univ. of Va.,* 515 U.S. 819, 834 (1995) (emphasis added)). See also 531 U.S., at 542 ("[T]he salient point is that, like the program in *Rosenberger,* the LSC [Legal Services Corporation] program was designed to *facilitate private speech . . . "* (emphasis added)); *Board of Regents of Univ. of Wis. System* v. *Southworth,* 529 U.S. 217, 229 (2000) ("The University of Wisconsin exacts the fee at issue for the sole purpose of facilitating the free and open exchange of ideas"); *Rosenberger, supra,* at 830, 834 ("The [Student Activities Fund] is a forum"; "[T]he University . . . expends funds to encourage a diversity of views from private speakers"). Indeed, this very distinction led us to state in *Southworth* that that case did not implicate our unconstitutional conditions jurisprudence. 529 U.S., at 229 ("The case we decide here . . . does not raise the issue of the government's right . . . to use its own funds to advance a particular message"). As we have stated above, *supra,* at 9–10, public libraries do not install Internet terminals to provide a forum for Web publishers to express themselves, but rather to provide patrons with online material of requisite and appropriate quality.

Dissenting Opinion of John Paul Stevens

J USTICE STEVENS, dissenting.

"To fulfill their traditional missions, public libraries must have broad discretion to decide what material to provide their patrons." *Ante,* at 6. Accordingly, I agree with the plurality that it is neither inappropriate nor unconstitutional for a local library to experiment with filtering software as a means of curtailing children's access to Internet Web sites displaying sexually explicit images. I also agree with the plurality that the 7% of public libraries that decided to use such software on *all* of their Internet terminals in 2000 did not act unlawfully. *Ante,* at 3. Whether it is constitutional for the Congress of the United States to impose that requirement on the other 93%, however, raises a vastly different question. Rather than allowing local decisionmakers to tailor their responses to local problems, the Children's Internet Protection Act (CIPA) operates as a blunt nationwide restraint on adult access to "an enormous amount of valuable information" that individual librarians cannot possibly review. *Ante,* at 11. Most of that information is constitutionally protected speech. In my view, this restraint is unconstitutional.

I

The unchallenged findings of fact made by the District Court reveal fundamental defects in the filtering software that is now available or that will be available in the foreseeable future. Because the software relies on key words or phrases to block undesirable sites, it does not have the capacity to exclude a precisely defined category of images. As the District Court explained:

> "[T]he search engines that software companies use for harvesting are able to search text only, not images. This is of critical importance, because CIPA, by its own terms, covers only 'visual depictions.' 20 U.S.C. §9134(f)(1)(A)(i); 47 U.S.C. §254(h)(5)(B)(i). Image recognition technology is immature, ineffective, and unlikely to improve substantially in the near future. None of the filtering software companies deposed in this case employs image recognition technology when harvesting or categorizing URLs. Due to the reliance on automated text analysis and the absence of image recognition technology, a Web page with sexually explicit images

From *United States et al. v. American Library Association, Inc. et al.,* 539 U.S. ____ (2003). Some notes and case citations omitted.

and no text cannot be harvested using a search engine. This problem is complicated by the fact that Web site publishers may use image files rather than text to represent words, i.e., they may use a file that computers understand to be a picture, like a photograph of a printed word, rather than regular text, making automated review of their textual content impossible. For example, if the Playboy Web site displays its name using a logo rather than regular text, a search engine would not see or recognize the Playboy name in that logo." 201 F. Supp. 2d 401, 431–432 (ED Pa. 2002).

Given the quantity and ever-changing character of Web sites offering free sexually explicit material,[1] it is inevitable that a substantial amount of such material will never be blocked. Because of this "underblocking," the statute will provide parents with a false sense of security without really solving the problem that motivated its enactment. Conversely, the software's reliance on words to identify undesirable sites necessarily results in the blocking of thousands of pages that "contain content that is completely innocuous for both adults and minors, and that no rational person could conclude matches the filtering companies' category definitions, such as 'pornography' or 'sex.'" *Id.*, at 449. In my judgment, a statutory blunderbuss that mandates this vast amount of "overblocking" abridges the freedom of speech protected by the First Amendment.

The effect of the overblocking is the functional equivalent of a host of individual decisions excluding hundreds of thousands of individual constitutionally protected messages from Internet terminals located in public libraries throughout the Nation. Neither the interest in suppressing unlawful speech nor the interest in protecting children from access to harmful materials justifies this overly broad restriction on adult access to protected speech. "The Government may not suppress lawful speech as the means to suppress unlawful speech." *Ashcroft* v. *Free Speech Coalition*, 535 U.S. 234, 255 (2002).[2]

Although CIPA does not permit any experimentation, the District Court expressly found that a variety of alternatives less restrictive are available at the local level:

> "[L]ess restrictive alternatives exist that further the government's legitimate interest in preventing the dissemination of obscenity, child pornography, and material harmful to minors, and in preventing patrons from being unwillingly exposed to patently offensive, sexually explicit content. To prevent patrons from accessing visual depictions that are obscene and child pornography, public libraries may enforce Internet use policies that make clear to patrons that the library's Internet terminals may not be used to access illegal speech. Libraries may then impose penalties on patrons who violate these policies, ranging from a warning to notification of law enforcement, in the appropriate case. Less restrictive alternatives to filtering that further libraries' interest in preventing minors from exposure to visual depictions that are harmful to minors include requiring parental consent to or presence during unfiltered access, or restricting minors' unfiltered access to terminals within view of library staff. Finally, optional filtering, privacy screens, recessed monitors, and placement of unfiltered Internet terminals outside of sight-lines provide less restrictive alternatives

for libraries to prevent patrons from being unwillingly exposed to sexually explicit content on the Internet." 201 F. Supp. 2d, at 410.

Those findings are consistent with scholarly comment on the issue arguing that local decisions tailored to local circumstances are more appropriate than a mandate from Congress.[3] The plurality does not reject any of those findings. Instead, "[a]ssuming that such erroneous blocking presents constitutional difficulties," it relies on the Solicitor General's assurance that the statute permits individual librarians to disable filtering mechanisms whenever a patron so requests. *Ante,* at 12. In my judgment, that assurance does not cure the constitutional infirmity in the statute.

Until a blocked site or group of sites is unblocked, a patron is unlikely to know what is being hidden and therefore whether there is any point in asking for the filter to be removed. It is as though the statute required a significant part of every library's reading materials to be kept in unmarked, locked rooms or cabinets, which could be opened only in response to specific requests. Some curious readers would in time obtain access to the hidden materials, but many would not. Inevitably, the interest of the authors of those works in reaching the widest possible audience would be abridged. Moreover, because the procedures that different libraries are likely to adopt to respond to unblocking requests will no doubt vary, it is impossible to measure the aggregate effect of the statute on patrons' access to blocked sites. Unless we assume that the statute is a mere symbolic gesture, we must conclude that it will create a significant prior restraint on adult access to protected speech. A law that prohibits reading without official consent, like a law that prohibits speaking without consent, "constitutes a dramatic departure from our national heritage and constitutional tradition." *Watchtower Bible & Tract Soc. of N. Y., Inc.* v. *Village of Stratton,* 536 U.S. 150, 166 (2002).

II

The plurality incorrectly argues that the statute does not impose "an unconstitutional condition on public libraries." *Ante,* at 17. On the contrary, it impermissibly conditions the receipt of Government funding on the restriction of significant First Amendment rights.

The plurality explains the "worthy missions" of the public library in facilitating "learning and cultural enrichment." *Ante,* at 6. It then asserts that in order to fulfill these missions, "libraries must have broad discretion to decide what material to provide to their patrons." *Ibid.* Thus the selection decision is the province of the librarians, a province into which we have hesitated to enter:

> "A library's need to exercise judgment in making collection decisions depends on its traditional role in identifying suitable and worthwhile material; it is no less entitled to play that role when it collects material from the Internet than when it collects material from any other source. Most libraries already exclude pornography from their print collections because they deem it inappropriate for inclusion. We do not subject these

decisions to heightened scrutiny; it would make little sense to treat libraries' judgments to block online pornography any differently, when these
judgments are made for just the same reason." *Ante,* at 11.

As the plurality recognizes, we have always assumed that libraries have
discretion when making decisions regarding what to include in, and exclude
from, their collections. That discretion is comparable to the "'business of a
university . . . to determine for itself on academic grounds who may teach, what
may be taught, how it shall be taught, and who may be admitted to study.'"
Sweezy v. *New Hampshire,* 354 U.S. 234, 263 (1957) (Frankfurter, J., concurring in
result) (citation omitted).[4] As the District Court found, one of the central purposes of a library is to provide information for educational purposes: "'Books
and other library resources should be provided for the interest, information,
and enlightenment of all people of the community the library serves.'" 201 F.
Supp. 2d, at 420 (quoting the American Library Association's Library Bill of
Rights). Given our Nation's deep commitment "to safeguarding academic freedom" and to the "robust exchange of ideas," *Keyishian* v. *Board of Regents of
Univ. of State of N. Y.,* 385 U.S. 589, 603 (1967), a library's exercise of judgment
with respect to its collection is entitled to First Amendment protection.

A federal statute penalizing a library for failing to install filtering software on every one of its Internet-accessible computers would unquestionably
violate that Amendment. Cf. *Reno* v. *American Civil Liberties Union,* 521 U.S.
844 (1997). I think it equally clear that the First Amendment protects libraries
from being denied funds for refusing to comply with an identical rule. An
abridgment of speech by means of a threatened denial of benefits can be just
as pernicious as an abridgment by means of a threatened penalty. . . .

The issue in this case does not involve governmental attempts to control
the speech or views of its employees. It involves the use of its treasury to
impose controls on an important medium of expression. In an analogous situation, we specifically held that when "the Government seeks to use an existing medium of expression and to control it, in a class of cases, in ways which
distort its usual functioning," the distorting restriction must be struck down
under the First Amendment. *Legal Services Corporation* v. *Velazquez,* 531 U.S.
533, 543 (2001). The question, then, is whether requiring the filtering software on all
Internet-accessible computers distorts that medium. As I have discussed above, the
over- and underblocking of the software does just that.

The plurality argues that the controversial decision in *Rust* v. *Sullivan,*
500 U.S. 173 (1991), requires rejection of appellees' unconstitutional conditions
claim. But, as subsequent cases have explained, *Rust* only involved and only
applies to instances of governmental speech—that is, situations in which the
government seeks to communicate a specific message. The discounts under the
E-rate program and funding under the Library Services and Technology Act
(LSTA) program involved in this case do not subsidize any message favored by
the Government. As Congress made clear, these programs were designed "[t]o
help public libraries provide their patrons with Internet access," which in turn
"provide[s] patrons with a vast amount of valuable information." These programs thus are designed to provide access, particularly for individuals in low-
income communities, see 47 U.S.C. §254(h)(1), to a vast amount and wide

variety of private speech. They are not designed to foster or transmit any particular governmental message.

Even if we were to construe the passage of CIPA as modifying the E-rate and LSTA programs such that they now convey a governmental message that no "'visual depictions' that are 'obscene,' 'child pornography,' or in the case of minors, 'harmful to minors,'" 201 F. Supp. 2d, at 407, should be expressed or viewed, the use of filtering software does not promote that message. As described above, all filtering software erroneously blocks access to a substantial number of Web sites that contain constitutionally protected speech on a wide variety of topics. Moreover, there are "frequent instances of underblocking," that is, instances in which filtering software did not prevent access to Web sites with depictions that fall within what CIPA seeks to block access to. In short, the message conveyed by the use of filtering software is not that all speech except that which is prohibited by CIPA is supported by the Government, but rather that all speech that gets through the software is supported by the Government. And the items that get through the software include some visual depictions that are obscene, some that are child pornography, and some that are harmful to minors, while at the same time the software blocks an enormous amount of speech that is not sexually explicit and certainly does not meet CIPA's definitions of prohibited content. As such, since the message conveyed is far from the message the Government purports to promote—indeed, the material permitted past the filtering software does not seem to have any coherent message—*Rust* is inapposite.

The plurality's reliance on *National Endowment for Arts* v. *Finley*, 524 U.S. 569 (1998), is also misplaced. That case involved a challenge to a statute setting forth the criteria used by a federal panel of experts administering a federal grant program. Unlike this case, the Federal Government was not seeking to impose restrictions on the administration of a nonfederal program. As explained *supra*, at 9–10 *Rust* would appear to permit restrictions on a federal program such as the NEA arts grant program at issue in *Finley*.

Further, like a library, the NEA experts in *Finley* had a great deal of discretion to make judgments as to what projects to fund. But unlike this case, *Finley* did not involve a challenge by the NEA to a governmental restriction on its ability to award grants. Instead, the respondents were performance artists who had applied for NEA grants but were denied funding. If this were a case in which library patrons had challenged a library's decision to install and use filtering software, it would be in the same posture as *Finley*. Because it is not, *Finley* does not control this case.

Also unlike *Finley*, the Government does not merely seek to control a library's discretion with respect to computers purchased with Government funds or those computers with Government-discounted Internet access. CIPA requires libraries to install filtering software on *every* computer with Internet access if the library receives *any* discount from the E-rate program or *any* funds from the LSTA program. See 20 U.S.C. §9134(f)(1); 47 U.S.C. §§254(h)(6)(B) and (C). If a library has 10 computers paid for by nonfederal funds and has Internet service for those computers also paid for by nonfederal funds, the library may choose not to put filtering software on any of those 10 computers.

Or a library may decide to put filtering software on the 5 computers in its children's section. Or a library in an elementary school might choose to put filters on every single one of its 10 computers. But under this statute, if a library attempts to provide Internet service for even *one* computer through an E-rate discount, that library must put filtering software on *all* of its computers with Internet access, not just the one computer with E-rate discount.

This Court should not permit federal funds to be used to enforce this kind of broad restriction of First Amendment rights, particularly when such a restriction is unnecessary to accomplish Congress' stated goal. See *supra*, at 4 (discussing less restrictive alternatives). The abridgment of speech is equally obnoxious whether a rule like this one is enforced by a threat of penalties or by a threat to withhold a benefit.

I would affirm the judgment of the District Court.

Notes

1. "The percentage of Web pages on the indexed Web containing sexually explicit content is relatively small. Recent estimates indicate that no more than 1–2% of the content on the Web is pornographic or sexually explicit. However, the absolute number of Web sites offering free sexually explicit material is extremely large, approximately 100,000 sites." 201 F. Supp. 2d. 401, 419 (ED Pa. 2002).

2. We have repeatedly reaffirmed the holding in *Butler* v. *Michigan*, 352 U.S. 380, 383 (1957), that the State may not "reduce the adult population . . . to reading only what is fit for children." See *Ashcroft* v. *Free Speech Coalition*, 535 U.S., at 252; *United States* v. *Playboy Entertainment Group, Inc.*, 529 U.S. 803, 814 (2000) ("[T]he objective of shielding children does not suffice to support a blanket ban if the protection can be accomplished by a less restrictive alternative"); *Reno* v. *American Civil Liberties Union*, 521 U.S. 844, 875 (1997) ("[T]he governmental interest in protecting children from harmful materials . . . does not justify an unnecessarily broad suppression of speech addressed to adults").

3. "Indeed, federal or state mandates in this area are unnecessary and unwise. Locally designed solutions are likely to best meet local circumstances. Local decision makers and library boards, responding to local concerns and the prevalence of the problem in their own libraries, should decide if minors' Internet access requires filters. They are the persons in the best position to judge local community standards for what is and is not obscene, as required by the *Miller* [v. *California*, 413 U.S. 15 (1973)] test. Indeed, one nationwide solution is not needed, as the problems are local and, to some extent, uniquely so. Libraries in rural communities, for instance, have reported much less of a problem than libraries in urban areas. A library in a rural community with only one or two computers with Internet access may find that even the limited filtering advocated here provides little or no additional benefit. Further, by allowing the nation's public libraries to develop their own approaches, they may be able to develop a better understanding of what methods work well and what methods add little or nothing, or are even counter-productive. Imposing a mandatory nationwide solution may well impede developing truly effective approaches that do not violate the First Amendment. The federal and state governments can best assist this effort by providing libraries with sufficient funding to experiment with a variety of constitutionally permissible approaches." Laughlin, Sex, Lies, and Library Cards: The First Amendment Implications of

the Use of Software Filters to Control Access to Internet Pornography in Public Libraries, 51 Drake L. Rev. 213, 279 (2003).

4. See also J. Boyer, Academic Freedom and the Modern University: The Experience of the University of Chicago 95 (2002) ("The right to speak, to write, and to teach freely is a precious right, one that the American research universities over the course of the twentieth century have slowly but surely made central to the very identity of the university in the modern world").

POSTSCRIPT

Are Laws Requiring Schools and Public Libraries to Filter Internet Access Constitutional?

The existing legal model for regulating obscenity and pornography is often misunderstood. These terms are often used synonymously by lay people, but the courts distinguish between them and, as a consequence, obscenity can be punished in any medium, while pornographic communications, no matter how offensive they may be to some people, may not be barred. When the issue involves material that is pornographic or indecent but not obscene, what becomes significant is whether or not the court will recognize an exception to the First Amendment. The First Amendment does not provide absolute protection to everything that is spoken or printed. The most common example of unprotected speech is obscenity. Obscene publications have been deemed to contribute so little to society that the courts have held the First Amendment to be essentially irrelevant to obscene publications. Similarly, "fighting words," in which someone advocates illegal acts "where such advocacy is directed to inciting or producing imminent lawless action and is likely to incite or produce such action," can sometimes be punished. In general, however, constitutional theory holds that the solution to speech that someone does not like is more speech.

Writings on the problem of pornography include Catharine A. MacKinnon, *Only Words* (Harvard University Press, 1993); Dany Lacombe, *Blue Politics: Pornography and the Law in the Age of Feminism* (University of Toronto Press, 1994); and Nadine Strossen, "A Feminist Critique of 'the' Feminist Critique of Pornography," 79 *Virginia Law Review* 1099 (1993). Child pornography was dealt with by the Supreme Court in *New York v. Ferber,* 458 U.S. 747 (1982). The most relevant obscenity case is *Miller v. California,* 413 U.S. 15 (1974).

The impact of computers and electronic communication on the First Amendment is discussed in Andrew L. Shapiro, *The Control Revolution: How the Internet Is Putting Individuals in Charge and Changing the World We Know* (PublicAffairs, 1999); Stuart Biegel, *Beyond Our Control? Confronting the Limits of Our Legal System in Cyberspace* (MIT Press, 2001); and Dawn C. Nunziato, *Toward a Constitutional Regulation of Minors' Access to Harmful Internet Speech,* 79 Chi.-Kent. L. Rev. 121 (2004). On the Internet itself, information about government regulation can be found at the Web sites of the American Civil Liberties Union (http://www.aclu.org) and the American Center for Law and Justice (http://www.aclj.org).

ISSUE 12

Does the "Cruel and Unusual Punishment" Clause of the Eighth Amendment Bar the Imposition of the Death Penalty on Juveniles?

YES: Anthony Kennedy, from Majority Opinion, *Donald P. Roper, Superintendent, Potosi Correctional Center, Petitioner v. Christopher Simmons*, U.S. Supreme Court (March 1, 2005)

NO: Antonin Scalia, from Minority Opinion, *Donald P. Roper, Superintendent, Potosi Correctional Center, Petitioner v. Christopher Simmons*, U.S. Supreme Court (March 1, 2005)

ISSUE SUMMARY

YES: Supreme Court Justice Anthony Kennedy holds that the Constitution prohibits the execution of a person who was under the age of eighteen at the time of the offense.

NO: Supreme Court Justice Antonin Scalia believes that the Constitution does not preclude the execution of a juvenile.

The questions of how a society punishes its wrongdoers, and to what extent it does so, are central to the very structure of social organization. These questions are particularly complex in democratic societies. Modern states, democratic or not, claim a monopoly over the use of violence. When democratic states punish, they do so in the name of its citizens. Such questions are particularly urgent when they deal with capital punishment. Death, it is often said, is different. If someone takes a life, should the state take his or hers in return? These questions are informed by centuries of debate. For example, in 428 B.C.E., Thucydides recorded the following arguments by Cleon in support of the death penalty:

> Punish them as they deserve, and teach your other allies by a striking example that the penalty of rebellion is death. Let them once understand this and you will not so often have to neglect your enemies while you are fighting with your confederates.

In response, Diodotus wrote:

All states and individuals are alike prone to err, and there is no law that will prevent them, or why should men have exhausted the list of punishments in search of enactments to protect them from evil doers? It is probable that in early times the penalties for the greatest offenses were less severe, and that as these were disregarded, the penalty of death has been by degrees in most cases arrived at, which is itself disregarded in like manner. Either some means of terror more terrible than this must be discovered, or it must be owned that this restraint is useless. . . . We must make up our minds to look for our protection not to legal terrors but to careful administration.

During the last four decades, the United States Supreme Court has been confronted with death penalty cases almost every term. The most significant was that of *Furman v. Georgia*, 408 U.S. 238 (1972). Furman, a 26-year-old African American, had killed a homeowner during a break-in and was sentenced to death. In a 5-4 decision, the Court overturned the sentence. It held that the procedure used by Georgia (and most other states at the time) was "cruel and unusual" and, therefore, a violation of the Eighth Amendment of the Constitution. At the heart of the case was the fact that Georgia law left it to the discretion of the jury to decide whether or not the death penalty was appropriate in a particular case. Two justices, Thurgood Marshall and William Brennan, believed that at that point in the development of American civilization, infliction of the death penalty under any circumstances violated the cruel and unusual punishments clause of the Eighth Amendment. The three other justices in the *Furman* majority, however, held that the death penalty was not, in itself, unconstitutional but that the procedures by which it was applied in this case were unlawful. *Furman* resulted in a nationwide moratorium on capital punishment that lasted until the Supreme Court revisited the issue in 1976 with its decision in *Gregg v. Georgia*, 428 U.S. 153. In *Gregg*, the Court upheld a revised Georgia death penalty statute that, in keeping with the *Furman* guidelines, was intended to limit the capital jury's discretion. The process effected a bifurcated trial—divided into a "guilt phase" and a "penalty phase"—that aimed at greater equalization of punishment, while, at the same time, remaining sensitive to the unique characteristics of the individual defendant and the circumstances of the crime.

Since 1972, 38 states have enacted new death penalty statutes, with actual executions resuming in 1977. From the 1970s to the present, the United States Supreme Court has continued to examine various aspects of the administration of capital punishment, but a majority of the Court has continued to find that the death penalty, in itself, is consistent with the requirements of the Eighth Amendment. A majority of the Court has also held, however, that the meaning of the Eighth Amendment is not fixed, but continues to evolve. Accordingly, in 2002, the Court found in *Atkins v. Virginia*, 536 U.S. 304, that a "national consensus" had evolved against the execution of the mentally retarded and held that such punishment now violates the Eighth Amendment's prohibition of cruel and unusual punishment.

YES ⤶

Majority Opinion

Donald P. Roper Superintendent, Potosi Correctional Center, Petitioner *v.* Christopher Simmons

JUSTICE KENNEDY delivered the opinion of the Court.

This case requires us to address, for the second time in a decade and a half, whether it is permissible under the Eighth and Fourteenth Amendments to the Constitution of the United States to execute a juvenile offender who was older than 15 but younger than 18 when he committed a capital crime. In *Stanford v. Kentucky*, 492 U.S. 361 (1989), a divided Court rejected the proposition that the Constitution bars capital punishment for juvenile offenders in this age group. We reconsider the question. . . .

⋅◉⋅

After these proceedings in Simmons' case had run their course, this Court held that the Eighth and Fourteenth Amendments prohibit the execution of a mentally retarded person. *Atkins* v. *Virginia,* 536 U.S. 304 (2002). Simmons filed a new petition for state postconviction relief, arguing that the reasoning of *Atkins* established that the Constitution prohibits the execution of a juvenile who was under 18 when the crime was committed.

The Missouri Supreme Court agreed. *State ex rel. Simmons* v. *Roper,* 112 S. W. 3d 397 (2003) (en banc). It held that since *Stanford*,

> "a national consensus has developed against the execution of juvenile offenders, as demonstrated by the fact that eighteen states now bar such executions for juveniles, that twelve other states bar executions altogether, that no state has lowered its age of execution below 18 since *Stanford*, that five states have legislatively or by case law raised or established the minimum age at 18, and that the imposition of the juvenile death penalty has become truly unusual over the last decade." 112 S. W. 3d, at 399.

On this reasoning it set aside Simmons' death sentence and resentenced him to "life imprisonment without eligibility for probation, parole, or release except by act of the Governor." *Id.,* at 413.

Majority Opinion, Roper v. Simmons, 543 U. S. 177 (2005). Some case citations omitted.

We granted certiorari, 540 U.S. 1160 (2004), and now affirm.

❦

The Eighth Amendment provides: "Excessive bail shall not be required, nor excessive fines imposed, nor cruel and unusual punishments inflicted." The provision is applicable to the States through the Fourteenth Amendment. As the Court explained in *Atkins*, the Eighth Amendment guarantees individuals the right not to be subjected to excessive sanctions. The right flows from the basic "'precept of justice that punishment for crime should be graduated and proportioned to [the] offense.'" By protecting even those convicted of heinous crimes, the Eighth Amendment reaffirms the duty of the government to respect the dignity of all persons.

The prohibition against "cruel and unusual punishments," like other expansive language in the Constitution, must be interpreted according to its text, by considering history, tradition, and precedent, and with due regard for its purpose and function in the constitutional design. To implement this framework we have established the propriety and affirmed the necessity of referring to "the evolving standards of decency that mark the progress of a maturing society" to determine which punishments are so disproportionate as to be cruel and unusual.

In *Thompson* v. *Oklahoma*, 487 U.S. 815 (1988), a plurality of the Court determined that our standards of decency do not permit the execution of any offender under the age of 16 at the time of the crime. *Id.,* at 818–838. The plurality opinion explained that no death penalty State that had given express consideration to a minimum age for the death penalty had set the age lower than 16. *Id.,* at 826–829. The plurality also observed that "[t]he conclusion that it would offend civilized standards of decency to execute a person who was less than 16 years old at the time of his or her offense is consistent with the views that have been expressed by respected professional organizations, by other nations that share our Anglo-American heritage, and by the leading members of the Western European community." *Id.,* at 830. . . .

The next year, in *Stanford* v. *Kentucky*, the Court, . . . referred to contemporary standards of decency in this country and concluded the Eighth and Fourteenth Amendments did not proscribe the execution of juvenile offenders over 15 but under 18. . . . A plurality of the Court also "emphatically reject[ed]" the suggestion that the Court should bring its own judgment to bear on the acceptability of the juvenile death penalty.

The same day the Court decided *Stanford*, it held that the Eighth Amendment did not mandate a categorical exemption from the death penalty for the mentally retarded. *Penry* v. *Lynaugh*, 492 U.S. 302 (1989). In reaching this conclusion it stressed that only two States had enacted laws banning the imposition of the death penalty on a mentally retarded person convicted of a capital offense. *Id.,* at 334. According to the Court, "the two state statutes prohibiting execution of the mentally retarded, even when added to the 14 States that have rejected capital punishment completely, [did] not provide sufficient evidence at present of a national consensus." *Ibid.*

Three Terms ago the subject was reconsidered in *Atkins*. We held that standards of decency have evolved since *Penry* and now demonstrate that the execution of the mentally retarded is cruel and unusual punishment. The Court noted objective indicia of society's standards, as expressed in legislative enactments and state practice with respect to executions of the mentally retarded. When *Atkins* was decided only a minority of States permitted the practice, and even in those States it was rare. 536 U.S., at 314–315. On the basis of these indicia the Court determined that executing mentally retarded offenders "has become truly unusual, and it is fair to say that a national consensus has developed against it." *Id.*, at 316. . . .

The *Atkins* Court neither repeated nor relied upon the statement in *Stanford* that the Court's independent judgment has no bearing on the acceptability of a particular punishment under the Eighth Amendment. Instead we returned to the rule, established in decisions predating *Stanford*, that "'the Constitution contemplates that in the end our own judgment will be brought to bear on the question of the acceptability of the death penalty under the Eighth Amendment.'" . . . Based on these considerations and on the finding of national consensus against executing the mentally retarded, the Court ruled that the death penalty constitutes an excessive sanction for the entire category of mentally retarded offenders, and that the Eighth Amendment "'places a substantive restriction on the State's power to take the life' of a mentally retarded offender."

Just as the *Atkins* Court reconsidered the issue decided in *Penry*, we now reconsider the issue decided in *Stanford*. The beginning point is a review of objective indicia of consensus, as expressed in particular by the enactments of legislatures that have addressed the question. This data gives us essential instruction. We then must determine, in the exercise of our own independent judgment, whether the death penalty is a disproportionate punishment for juveniles.

❧

The evidence of national consensus against the death penalty for juveniles is similar, and in some respects parallel, to the evidence *Atkins* held sufficient to demonstrate a national consensus against the death penalty for the mentally retarded. . . .

Though less dramatic than the change from *Penry* to *Atkins* . . . we still consider the change from *Stanford* to this case to be significant. . . . The number of States that have abandoned capital punishment for juvenile offenders since *Stanford* is smaller than the number of States that abandoned capital punishment for the mentally retarded after *Penry*; yet we think the same consistency of direction of change has been demonstrated. Since *Stanford*, no State that previously prohibited capital punishment for juveniles has reinstated it. This fact, coupled with the trend toward abolition of the juvenile death penalty, carries special force in light of the general popularity of anti-crime legislation, and in light of the particular trend in recent years toward cracking down on juvenile crime in other respects, . . .

As in *Atkins*, the objective indicia of consensus in this case—the rejection of the juvenile death penalty in the majority of States; the infrequency of its use even where it remains on the books; and the consistency in the trend toward abolition of the practice—provide sufficient evidence that today our society views juveniles, in the words *Atkins* used respecting the mentally retarded, as "categorically less culpable than the average criminal." 536 U.S., at 316.

·◆·

A majority of States have rejected the imposition of the death penalty on juvenile offenders under 18, and we now hold this is required by the Eighth Amendment.

Because the death penalty is the most severe punishment, the Eighth Amendment applies to it with special force. Capital punishment must be limited to those offenders who commit "a narrow category of the most serious crimes" and whose extreme culpability makes them "the most deserving of execution." . . .

Three general differences between juveniles under 18 and adults demonstrate that juvenile offenders cannot with reliability be classified among the worst offenders. First, . . .

The second area of difference . . .

The third broad difference . . .

These differences render suspect any conclusion that a juvenile falls among the worst offenders. The susceptibility of juveniles to immature and irresponsible behavior means "their irresponsible conduct is not as morally reprehensible as that of an adult." *Thompson, supra,* at 835 (plurality opinion). Their own vulnerability and comparative lack of control over their immediate surroundings mean juveniles have a greater claim than adults to be forgiven for failing to escape negative influences in their whole environment. See *Stanford*, 492 U.S., at 395 (Brennan, J., dissenting). The reality that juveniles still struggle to define their identity means it is less supportable to conclude that even a heinous crime committed by a juvenile is evidence of irretrievably depraved character. From a moral standpoint it would be misguided to equate the failings of a minor with those of an adult, for a greater possibility exists that a minor's character deficiencies will be reformed. Indeed, "[t]he relevance of youth as a mitigating factor derives from the fact that the signature qualities of youth are transient; as individuals mature, the impetuousness and recklessness that may dominate in younger years can subside." *Johnson, supra,* at 368; see also Steinberg & Scott 1014 ("For most teens, [risky or antisocial] behaviors are fleeting; they cease with maturity as individual identity becomes settled. Only a relatively small proportion of adolescents who experiment in risky or illegal activities develop entrenched patterns of problem behavior that persist into adulthood"). . . .

Once the diminished culpability of juveniles is recognized, it is evident that the penological justifications for the death penalty apply to them with lesser force than to adults. We have held there are two distinct social purposes served by the death penalty: "'retribution and deterrence of capital crimes by prospective offenders.'" As for retribution, we remarked in *Atkins* that "[i]f the culpability of the average murderer is insufficient to justify the most extreme sanction available to the State, the lesser culpability of the mentally retarded offender surely does not merit that form of retribution." The same conclusions follow from the lesser culpability of the juvenile offender. Whether viewed as an attempt to express the community's moral outrage or as an attempt to right the balance for the wrong to the victim, the case for retribution is not as strong with a minor as with an adult. Retribution is not proportional if the law's most severe penalty is imposed on one whose culpability or blameworthiness is diminished, to a substantial degree, by reason of youth and immaturity.

As for deterrence, it is unclear whether the death penalty has a significant or even measurable deterrent effect on juveniles, as counsel for the petitioner acknowledged at oral argument. . . .

In concluding that neither retribution nor deterrence provides adequate justification for imposing the death penalty on juvenile offenders, we cannot deny or overlook the brutal crimes too many juvenile offenders have committed. . . .

Drawing the line at 18 years of age is subject, of course, to the objections always raised against categorical rules. The qualities that distinguish juveniles from adults do not disappear when an individual turns 18. By the same token, some under 18 have already attained a level of maturity some adults will never reach. For the reasons we have discussed, however, a line must be drawn. The plurality opinion in *Thompson* drew the line at 16. In the intervening years the *Thompson* plurality's conclusion that offenders under 16 may not be executed has not been challenged. The logic of *Thompson* extends to those who are under 18. The age of 18 is the point where society draws the line for many purposes between childhood and adulthood. It is, we conclude, the age at which the line for death eligibility ought to rest. . . .

✦

Our determination that the death penalty is disproportionate punishment for offenders under 18 finds confirmation in the stark reality that the United States is the only country in the world that continues to give official sanction to the juvenile death penalty. This reality does not become controlling, for the task of interpreting the Eighth Amendment remains our responsibility. Yet at least from the time of the Court's decision in *Trop*, the Court has referred to the laws of other countries and to international authorities as instructive for its interpretation of the Eighth Amendment's prohibition of "cruel and unusual punishments." . . .

As respondent and a number of *amici* emphasize, Article 37 of the United Nations Convention on the Rights of the Child, which every country in the world has ratified save for the United States and Somalia, contains an express prohibition on capital punishment for crimes committed by juveniles under 18. . . .

Respondent and his *amici* have submitted, and petitioner does not contest, that only seven countries other than the United States have executed juvenile offenders since 1990: Iran, Pakistan, Saudi Arabia, Yemen, Nigeria, the Democratic Republic of Congo, and China. Since then each of these countries has either abolished capital punishment for juveniles or made public disavowal of the practice. Brief for Respondent 49–50. In sum, it is fair to say that the United States now stands alone in a world that has turned its face against the juvenile death penalty. . . .

It is proper that we acknowledge the overwhelming weight of international opinion against the juvenile death penalty, resting in large part on the understanding that the instability and emotional imbalance of young people may often be a factor in the crime. See Brief for Human Rights Committee of the Bar of England and Wales et al. as *Amici Curiae* 10–11. The opinion of the world community, while not controlling our outcome, does provide respected and significant confirmation for our own conclusions.

Over time, from one generation to the next, the Constitution has come to earn the high respect and even, as Madison dared to hope, the veneration of the American people. See The Federalist No. 49, p. 314 (C. Rossiter ed. 1961). The document sets forth, and rests upon, innovative principles original to the American experience, such as federalism; a proven balance in political mechanisms through separation of powers; specific guarantees for the accused in criminal cases; and broad provisions to secure individual freedom and preserve human dignity. These doctrines and guarantees are central to the American experience and remain essential to our present-day self-definition and national identity. Not the least of the reasons we honor the Constitution, then, is because we know it to be our own. It does not lessen our fidelity to the Constitution or our pride in its origins to acknowledge that the express affirmation of certain fundamental rights by other nations and peoples simply underscores the centrality of those same rights within our own heritage of freedom.

❧❦❧

The Eighth and Fourteenth Amendments forbid imposition of the death penalty on offenders who were under the age of 18 when their crimes were committed. The judgment of the Missouri Supreme Court setting aside the sentence of death imposed upon Christopher Simmons is affirmed.

It is so ordered.

Antonin Scalia

NO

Minority Opinion

Donald P. Roper, Superintendent, Potosi Correctional Center, Petitioner
v. Christopher Simmons

JUSTICE SCALIA, with whom THE CHIEF JUSTICE and JUSTICE THOMAS join, dissenting.

In urging approval of a constitution that gave life-tenured judges the power to nullify laws enacted by the people's representatives, Alexander Hamilton assured the citizens of New York that there was little risk in this, since "[t]he judiciary . . . ha[s] neither FORCE nor WILL but merely judgment." The Federalist No. 78, p. 465 (C. Rossiter ed. 1961). But Hamilton had in mind a traditional judiciary, "bound down by strict rules and precedents which serve to define and point out their duty in every particular case that comes before them." *Id.,* at 471. Bound down, indeed. What a mockery today's opinion makes of Hamilton's expectation, announcing the Court's conclusion that the meaning of our Constitution has changed over the past 15 years—not, mind you, that this Court's decision 15 years ago was *wrong*, but that the Constitution *has changed*. The Court reaches this implausible result by purporting to advert, not to the original meaning of the Eighth Amendment, but to "the evolving standards of decency," *ante*, at 6 (internal quotation marks omitted), of our national society. It then finds, on the flimsiest of grounds, that a national consensus which could not be perceived in our people's laws barely 15 years ago now solidly exists. Worse still, the Court says in so many words that what our people's laws say about the issue does not, in the last analysis, matter: "[I]n the end our own judgment will be brought to bear on the question of the acceptability of the death penalty under the Eighth Amendment." *Ante*, at 9 (internal quotation marks omitted). The Court thus proclaims itself sole arbiter of our Nation's moral standards—and in the course of discharging that awesome responsibility purports to take guidance from the views of foreign courts and legislatures. Because I do not believe that the meaning of our Eighth Amendment, any more than the meaning of other provisions of our Constitution, should be determined by the subjective views of five Members of this Court and like-minded foreigners, I dissent. . . .

Minority Opinion, Roper v. Simmons, 543 U. S. 177 (2005). Some case citations omitted.

We have held that this determination should be based on "objective indicia that reflect the public attitude toward a given sanction"—namely, "statutes passed by society's elected representatives." As in *Atkins* v. *Virginia,* 536 U.S. 304, 312 (2002), the Court dutifully recites this test and claims half-heartedly that a national consensus has emerged since our decision in *Stanford,* because 18 States—or 47% of States that permit capital punishment—now have legislation prohibiting the execution of offenders under 18, and because all of four States have adopted such legislation since *Stanford.*

Words have no meaning if the views of less than 50% of death penalty States can constitute a national consensus. Our previous cases have required overwhelming opposition to a challenged practice, generally over a long period of time. . . .

In an attempt to keep afloat its implausible assertion of national consensus, the Court throws overboard a proposition well established in our Eighth Amendment jurisprudence. "It should be observed," the Court says, "that the *Stanford* Court should have considered those States that had abandoned the death penalty altogether as part of the consensus against the juvenile death penalty. . .; a State's decision to bar the death penalty altogether of necessity demonstrates a judgment that the death penalty is inappropriate for all offenders, including juveniles." The insinuation that the Court's new method of counting contradicts only "the *Stanford* Court" is misleading. *None* of our cases dealing with an alleged constitutional limitation upon the death penalty has counted, as States supporting a consensus in favor of that limitation, States that have eliminated the death penalty entirely. And with good reason. Consulting States that bar the death penalty concerning the necessity of making an exception to the penalty for offenders under 18 is rather like including old-order Amishmen in a consumer-preference poll on the electric car. Of *course* they don't like it, but that sheds no light whatever on the point at issue. That 12 States favor *no* executions says something about consensus against the death penalty, but nothing—absolutely nothing—about consensus that offenders under 18 deserve special immunity from such a penalty. In repealing the death penalty, those 12 States considered *none* of the factors that the Court puts forth as determinative of the issue before us today—lower culpability of the young, inherent recklessness, lack of capacity for considered judgment, etc. What might be relevant, perhaps, is how many of those States permit 16- and 17-year-old offenders to be treated as adults with respect to non-capital offenses. (They all do;[1] indeed, some even *require* that juveniles as young as 14 be tried as adults if they are charged with murder.[2]) The attempt by the Court to turn its remarkable minority consensus into a faux majority by counting Amishmen is an act of nomological desperation. . . .

The Court's reliance on the infrequency of executions, for under-18 murderers, *ante,* at 10–11, 13, credits an argument that this Court considered and explicitly rejected in *Stanford.* That infrequency is explained, we accurately said, both by "the undisputed fact that a far smaller percentage of capital crimes are committed by persons under 18 than over 18," 492 U.S., at 374, and by the fact that juries are required at sentencing to consider the offender's youth as a mitigating factor. Thus, "it is not only possible, but overwhelmingly probable, that the very considerations which induce [respondent] and [his] supporters to believe that death should *never* be imposed on offenders under 18 cause prosecutors and juries to believe that it should *rarely* be imposed." *Stanford, supra,* at 374. . . .

✦

Of course, the real force driving today's decision is not the actions of four state legislatures, but the Court's "' "own judgment" ' " that murderers younger than 18 can never be as morally culpable as older counterparts. The Court claims that this usurpation of the role of moral arbiter is simply a "retur[n] to the rul[e] established in decisions predating *Stanford.*" That supposed rule—which is reflected solely in dicta and never once in a *holding* that purports to supplant the consensus of the American people with the Justices' views[3]—was repudiated in *Stanford* for the very good reason that it has no foundation in law or logic. If the Eighth Amendment set forth an ordinary rule of law, it would indeed be the role of this Court to say what the law is. But the Court having pronounced that the Eighth Amendment is an ever-changing reflection of "the evolving standards of decency" of our society, it makes no sense for the Justices then to *prescribe* those standards rather than discern them from the practices of our people. On the evolving-standards hypothesis, the only legitimate function of this Court is to identify a moral consensus of the American people. By what conceivable warrant can nine lawyers presume to be the authoritative conscience of the Nation?[4]

The reason for insistence on legislative primacy is obvious and fundamental: "'[I]n a democratic society legislatures, not courts, are constituted to respond to the will and consequently the moral values of the people.'" *Gregg* v. *Georgia,* 428 U.S. 153, 175–176 (1976) (joint opinion of Stewart, Powell, and STEVENS, JJ.) (quoting *Furman* v. *Georgia,* 408 U.S. 238, 383 (1972) (Burger, C. J., dissenting)). For a similar reason we have, in our determination of society's moral standards, consulted the practices of sentencing juries: Juries "'maintain a link between contemporary community values and the penal system'" that this Court cannot claim for itself. *Gregg, supra,* at 181 (quoting *Witherspoon* v. *Illinois,* 391 U.S. 510, 519, n. 15 (1968)).

Today's opinion provides a perfect example of why judges are ill equipped to make the type of legislative judgments the Court insists on making here. To support its opinion that States should be prohibited from imposing the death penalty on anyone who committed murder before age 18, the Court looks to scientific and sociological studies, picking and choosing those that support its position. It never explains why those particular studies are methodologically sound; none was ever entered into evidence or tested in an adversarial proceeding. . . .

In other words, all the Court has done today, to borrow from another context, is to look over the heads of the crowd and pick out its friends. . . .

That "almost every State prohibits those under 18 years of age from voting, serving on juries, or marrying without parental consent," *ante,* at 15, is patently irrelevant—and is yet another resurrection of an argument that this Court gave a decent burial in *Stanford*. . . . As we explained in *Stanford*, it is "absurd to think that one must be mature enough to drive carefully, to drink responsibly, or to vote intelligently, in order to be mature enough to understand that murdering another human being is profoundly wrong, and to conform one's conduct to that most minimal of all civilized standards." Serving on a jury or entering into marriage also involve decisions far more sophisticated than the simple decision not to take another's life. . . .

The Court's contention that the goals of retribution and deterrence are not served by executing murderers under 18 is also transparently false. The argument that "[r]etribution is not proportional if the law's most severe penalty is imposed on one whose culpability or blameworthiness is diminished," is simply an extension of the earlier, false generalization that youth *always* defeats culpability. The Court claims that "juveniles will be less susceptible to deterrence," *ante,* at 18, because "'[t]he likelihood that the teenage offender has made the kind of cost-benefit analysis that attaches any weight to the possibility of execution is so remote as to be virtually nonexistent.'" The Court unsurprisingly finds no support for this astounding proposition, save its own case law. The facts of this very case show the proposition to be false. Before committing the crime, Simmons encouraged his friends to join him by assuring them that they could "get away with it" because they were minors. This fact may have influenced the jury's decision to impose capital punishment despite Simmons' age. Because the Court refuses to entertain the possibility that its own unsubstantiated generalization about juveniles could be wrong, it ignores this evidence entirely.

✎

Though the views of our own citizens are essentially irrelevant to the Court's decision today, the views of other countries and the so-called international community take center stage.

The Court begins by noting that "Article 37 of the United Nations Convention on the Rights of the Child, entered into force Sept. 2, 1990], which every country in the world has ratified *save for the United States* and Somalia, contains an express prohibition on capital punishment for crimes committed by juveniles under 18.". . .

Unless the Court has added to its arsenal the power to join and ratify treaties on behalf of the United States, I cannot see how this evidence favors, rather than refutes, its position. That the Senate and the President—those actors our Constitution empowers to enter into treaties, see Art. II, §2—have declined to join and ratify treaties prohibiting execution of under-18 offenders can only suggest that *our country* has either not reached a national consensus on the question, or has reached a consensus contrary to what the Court announces. . . .

More fundamentally, however, the basic premise of the Court's argument—that American law should conform to the laws of the rest of the world—ought to be rejected out of hand. In fact the Court itself does not believe it. In many significant respects the laws of most other countries differ from our law—including not only such explicit provisions of our Constitution as the right to jury trial and grand jury indictment, but even many interpretations of the Constitution prescribed by this Court itself. The Court-pronounced exclusionary rule, for example, is distinctively American. . . .

The Court has been oblivious to the views of other countries when deciding how to interpret our Constitution's requirement that "Congress shall make no law respecting an establishment of religion. . . ." . . .

And let us not forget the Court's abortion jurisprudence, which makes us one of only six countries that allow abortion on demand until the point of viability. . . .

The Court should either profess its willingness to reconsider all these matters in light of the views of foreigners, or else it should cease putting forth foreigners' views as part of the *reasoned basis* of its decisions. To invoke alien law when it agrees with one's own thinking, and ignore it otherwise, is not reasoned decisionmaking, but sophistry.[5]

⋅⁂⋅

To add insult to injury, the Court affirms the Missouri Supreme Court without even admonishing that court for its flagrant disregard of our precedent in *Stanford*. Until today, we have always held that "it is this Court's prerogative alone to overrule one of its precedents." . . . Today, however, the Court silently approves a state-court decision that blatantly rejected controlling precedent.

One must admit that the Missouri Supreme Court's action, and this Court's indulgent reaction, are, in a way, understandable. In a system based upon constitutional and statutory text democratically adopted, the concept of "law" ordinarily signifies that particular words have a fixed meaning. Such law does not change, and this Court's pronouncement of it therefore remains authoritative until (confessing our prior error) we overrule. The Court has purported to make of the Eighth Amendment, however, a mirror of the passing and changing sentiment of American society regarding penology. The lower courts can look into that mirror as well as we can; and what we saw 15 years ago bears no necessary relationship to what they see today. Since they are not looking at the same text, but at a different scene, why should our earlier decision control their judgment?

However sound philosophically, this is no way to run a legal system. We must disregard the new reality that, to the extent our Eighth Amendment decisions constitute something more than a show of hands on the current Justices' current personal views about penology, they purport to be nothing more than a snapshot of American public opinion at a particular point in time (with the timeframes now shortened to a mere 15 years). We must treat these decisions just as though they represented *real* law, *real* prescriptions democratically adopted by the American people, as conclusively (rather than sequentially) construed by this Court. Allowing lower courts to reinterpret the Eighth Amendment whenever they decide enough time has passed for a new snapshot leaves this Court's decisions without any force—especially since the "evolution" of our Eighth Amendment is no longer determined by objective criteria. To allow lower courts to behave as we do, "updating" the Eighth Amendment as needed, destroys stability and makes our case law an unreliable basis for the designing of laws by citizens and their representatives, and for action by public officials. The result will be to crown arbitrariness with chaos.

Notes

1. See Alaska Stat. §47.12.030 (Lexis 2002); Haw. Rev. Stat. §571–22 (1999); Iowa Code §232.45 (2003); Me. Rev. Stat. Ann., Tit. 15, §3101(4) (West 2003); Mass. Gen. Laws Ann., ch. 119, §74 (West 2003); Mich. Comp. Laws Ann. §764.27 (West 2000); Minn. Stat. §260B.125 (2002); N. D. Cent. Code §27–20–34 (Lexis Supp. 2003); R. I. Gen. Laws §14–1–7 (Lexis 2002); Vt. Stat. Ann., Tit. 33, §5516 (Lexis 2001); W. Va. Code §49–5–10 (Lexis 2004); Wis. Stat. §938.18 (2003–2004); see also National Center for Juvenile Justice, Trying and Sentencing Juveniles as Adults: An Analysis of State Transfer and Blended Sentencing Laws 1 (Oct. 2003). The District of Columbia is the only jurisdiction without a death penalty that specifically exempts under-18 offenders from its harshest sanction—life imprisonment without parole. See D. C. Code §22–2104 (West 2001).

2. See Mass. Gen. Laws Ann., ch. 119, §74 (West 2003); N. D. Cent. Code §27–20–34 (Lexis Supp. 2003); W. Va. Code §49–5–10 (Lexis 2004).

3. See, *e.g.*, *Enmund* v. *Florida*, 458 U.S. 782, 801 (1982) ("[W]e have no reason to disagree with th[e] judgment [of the state legislatures] for purposes of construing and applying the Eighth Amendment"); *Coker* v. *Georgia*, 433 U.S. 584, 597 (1977) (plurality opinion) ("[T]he legislative rejection of capital punishment for rape strongly confirms our own judgment").

4. JUSTICE O'CONNOR agrees with our analysis that no national consensus exists here, *ante*, at 8–12 (dissenting opinion). She is nonetheless prepared (like the majority) to override the judgment of America's legislatures if it contradicts her own assessment of "moral proportionality," *ante*, at 12. She dissents here only because it does not. The votes in today's case demonstrate that the offending of selected lawyers' moral sentiments is not a predictable basis for law—much less a democratic one.

5. JUSTICE O'CONNOR asserts that the Eighth Amendment has a "special character," in that it "draws its meaning directly from the maturing values of civilized society." *Ante*, at 19. Nothing in the text reflects such a distinctive character—and we have certainly applied the "maturing values" rationale to give brave new meaning to other provisions of the Constitution, such as the Due Process Clause and the Equal Protection Clause. See, *e.g.*, *Lawrence* v. *Texas*, 539 U.S. 558, 571–573 (2003); *United States* v. *Virginia*, 518 U.S. 515, 532–534 (1996); *Planned Parenthood of Southeastern Pa.* v. *Casey*, 505 U.S. 833, 847–850 (1992). Justice O'Connor asserts that an international consensus can at least "serve to confirm the reasonableness of a consonant and genuine American consensus." *Ante*, at 19. Surely not unless it can also demonstrate the *un*reasonableness of such a consensus. Either America's principles are its own, or they follow the world; one cannot have it both ways. Finally, Justice O'Connor finds it unnecessary to consult foreign law in the present case because there is "no . . . domestic consensus" to be confirmed. *Ibid.* But since she believes that the Justices can announce their own requirements of "moral proportionality" despite the absence of consensus, why would foreign law not be relevant to *that* judgment? If foreign law is powerful enough to supplant the judgment of the American people, surely it is powerful enough to change a personal assessment of moral proportionality.

POSTSCRIPT

Does the "Cruel and Unusual Punishment" Clause of the Eighth Amendment Bar the Imposition of the Death Penalty on Juveniles?

*R*oper v. *Simmons* presented the United States Supreme Court with the question of whether or not the execution of someone who was sixteen or seventeen at the time of their capital offense is "cruel and unusual." Clearly, the Eighth Amendment contemplates and allows for capital punishment. What is far less clear is what the language of that amendment *means* when we attempt to apply it under ever-changing historical and cultural conditions. Does the language of the Eighth Amendment mean today what it meant at the end of the eighteenth century when it was written? If not, what is the proper mechanism for its changed meaning? And, who shall be the authoritative agent of this change? Congress? the Courts? the people themselves?

The interpretive problems that attend the meaning of the Eighth Amendment are, of course, one manifestation of more general problems of constitutional interpretation. Justice Kennedy assumes a central role for the courts—the Supreme Court in particular—in determining the meaning of the Eighth Amendment. To fix that meaning, Kennedy's interpretive approach requires the courts to "read" public opinion, to comprehend dominant trends in state legislative enactments, and to be aware of comparative legal developments in the international arena. Justice Scalia, however, believes each of these moves is but a part of a more general problem of misunderstanding the proper nature of the judicial role, a misunderstanding that risks the legitimacy of the court itself. Who is correct? How do we adjudicate the different approaches to determining what the Constitution—here, the Eighth Amendment—means?

The literature on capital punishment is enormous. Perhaps one of the best places to begin is with Stuart Banner's recent history of capital punishment, *The Death Penalty: An American History* (Harvard, 2003). Hugo Adam Bedau, a long-time opponent of capital punishment, has recently published two useful collections. The first, *Debating the Death Penalty* (Oxford, 2003), provides a collection of recent arguments for and against capital punishment. The second, *The Death Penalty in America* (Oxford, 1998), provides a comprehensive overview of the subject.

One of the central points contested by Justices Kennedy and Scalia is the proper place of foreign legal developments in our understanding of the death penalty in the United States. In an important and widely cited new book, James Q. Whitman addresses the differences in approach to capital punishment between the United States and selected European nations. See *Harsh Justice: Capital Punishment and the Widening Divide Between America and Europe* (Oxford, 2003). Additionally, there are two recent books of note that deal with the question of capital punishment from slightly different yet equally challenging perspectives. The first, by Timothy Kaufman-Osborn, *From Noose to Needle: Capital Punishment and the Late Liberal State* (Michigan, 2002), approaches the subject from the perspective of a critique of liberal political thought. The second, by Austin Sarat, *When the State Kills: Capital Punishment and the American Condition* (Princeton, 2002), provides an analysis of the reciprocal relationship between capital punishment and American culture. Finally, for some useful basic information on capital punishment in the United States, one should consult the Web site of the Death Penalty Information Center at www.deathpenaltyinfo.org.

ISSUE 13

Is a Sentence of Life in Prison for Stealing $150 Worth of Videotapes Constitutional?

YES: Sandra Day O'Connor, from Majority Opinion, *Bill Lockyer, Attorney General of California, v. Leandro Andrade*, U.S. Supreme Court (March 5, 2003)

NO: David Souter, from Dissenting Opinion, *Bill Lockyer, Attorney General of California, v. Leandro Andrade*, U.S. Supreme Court (March 5, 2003)

ISSUE SUMMARY

YES: Supreme Court Justice Sandra Day O'Connor rules that a decision in a case involving the theft of $150 worth of merchandise that resulted in two consecutive terms of 25 years to life in prison for a "third strike" conviction was not "grossly disproportional" to the crime nor "contrary to, or an unreasonable application of, clearly established federal law."

NO: Supreme Court Justice David Souter argues that, under several prior Supreme Court decisions, the "third strike" punishment in this case was grossly disproportional to the crime committed.

> My object all sublime
> I shall achieve in time—
> To let the punishment fit the crime—
> The punishment fit the crime.
>
> —William S. Gilbert and Arthur Sullivan, *The Mikado*

Should the punishment fit the crime, so that all persons who commit the same crime receive comparable sentences? Or should the punishment fit the criminal by taking into account such factors as likelihood of rehabilitation and prior record? Focusing on the offense is generally thought to lead to more consistent sentencing. This goal is important, considering that discrimination in sentencing has occurred in the past. On the other hand, focusing on the person who has committed the crime allows some flexibility in considering the likely impact of incarceration on that person.

The practice in most of the United States is to try to achieve a balance between letting the punishment fit the crime and letting it fit the criminal. Thus, many states establish guidelines and formulas for sentencing while, at the same time, allowing judges to individualize a sentence if clear and public reasons are given. The three-strikes laws that are of concern in the following case are unusual in that they shift the balance over to a "punishment fit the criminal" model but take away discretion to consider individual circumstances.

Three-strikes laws typically provide for much more severe penalties if the offender has several prior convictions. Therefore, when a convicted person is a recidivist, he or she might receive a very different sentence than someone who has committed the same offense but who has no prior convictions. In some instances the differences in sentencing may be quite extreme.

In 1980 the Supreme Court decided that the Eighth Amendment prohibition against cruel and unusual punishment was not violated when a third felony led to a sentence of life imprisonment with the possibility of parole. In that case, *Rummel v. Estelle,* 445 U.S. 263 (1980), the defendant had been sentenced to life imprisonment because he had been convicted once for fraudulent use of a credit card to obtain $80 worth of goods or services, once for passing a forged check in the amount of $28.36, and a third time for obtaining $120.75 by false pretenses.

In *Solem v. Helm* 463 U.S. 277 (1983), the Supreme Court decided by a 5–4 vote that a life sentence without possibility of parole for a seventh nonviolent felony violated the Eighth Amendment prohibition against cruel and unusual punishment. The defendant, Jerry Helm, had previously been convicted of six nonviolent felonies—three third-degree burglaries, grand larceny, driving while intoxicated, and obtaining money under false pretenses. The final crime was bouncing a check, a crime that normally would have had a maximum penalty of five years' imprisonment in the state penitentiary and a $5,000 fine. Unlike in *Rummel,* the Court found the life sentence to be "grossly disproportionate to the nature of the offense."

Seven years later, in *Harmelin v. Michigan,* 501 U.S. 957 (1991), the Court upheld a life sentence for a defendant convicted of possession of more than 650 grams of cocaine. Justice Anthony Kennedy wrote that sentences may be evaluated as to whether they are "grossly disproportionate" to the crime, but, given the seriousness of the defendant's crime, the sentence was not disproportionate.

In the following case, *Lockyer v. Andrade,* the defendant was convicted of stealing videotapes worth approximately $150, and he received a sentence of two consecutive terms of 25 years to life. To which of the previous cases is this fact pattern most similar? Can there be any formula to determine whether or not a sentence is "grossly disproportionate"?

YES ⬋

Sandra Day O'Connor

Majority Opinion

Lockyer *v.* Andrade

JUSTICE O'CONNOR delivered the opinion of the Court.

This case raises the issue whether the United States Court of Appeals for the Ninth Circuit erred in ruling that the California Court of Appeal's decision affirming Leandro Andrade's two consecutive terms of 25 years to life in prison for a "third strike" conviction is contrary to, or an unreasonable application of, clearly established federal law as determined by this Court within the meaning of 28 U.S.C. §2254(d)(1).

I

A

On November 4, 1995, Leandro Andrade stole five videotapes worth $84.70 from a Kmart store in Ontario, California. Security personnel detained Andrade as he was leaving the store. On November 18, 1995, Andrade entered a different Kmart store in Montclair, California, and placed four videotapes worth $68.84 in the rear waistband of his pants. Again, security guards apprehended Andrade as he was exiting the premises. Police subsequently arrested Andrade for these crimes.

These two incidents were not Andrade's first or only encounters with law enforcement. According to the state probation officer's presentence report, Andrade has been in and out of state and federal prison since 1982. In January 1982, he was convicted of a misdemeanor theft offense and was sentenced to 6 days in jail with 12 months' probation. Andrade was arrested again in November 1982 for multiple counts of first-degree residential burglary. He pleaded guilty to at least three of those counts, and in April of the following year he was sentenced to 120 months in prison. In 1988, Andrade was convicted in federal court of "[t]ransportation of [m]arijuana," App. 24, and was sentenced to eight years in federal prison. In 1990, he was convicted in state court for a misdemeanor petty theft offense and was ordered to serve 180 days in jail. In September 1990, Andrade was convicted again in federal court for the same felony of "[t]ransportation of [m]arijuana," and was sentenced to

From *Bill Lockyer, Attorney General of California, v. Leandro Andrade,* 538 U.S. ____ (2003). Some case citations omitted.

2,191 days in federal prison. And in 1991, Andrade was arrested for a state parole violation—escape from federal prison. He was paroled from the state penitentiary system in 1993.

A state probation officer interviewed Andrade after his arrest in this case. The presentence report notes:

> "The defendant admitted committing the offense. The defendant further stated he went into the K-Mart Store to steal videos. He took four of them to sell so he could buy heroin. He has been a heroin addict since 1977. He says when he gets out of jail or prison he always does something stupid. He admits his addiction controls his life and he steals for his habit."

Because of his 1990 misdemeanor conviction, the State charged Andrade in this case with two counts of petty theft with a prior conviction, in violation of Cal. Penal Code Ann. §666 (West Supp. 2002). Under California law, petty theft with a prior conviction is a so-called "wobbler" offense because it is punishable either as a misdemeanor or as a felony. The decision to prosecute petty theft with a prior conviction as a misdemeanor or as a felony is in the discretion of the prosecutor. The trial court also has discretion to reduce the charge to a misdemeanor at the time of sentencing.

Under California's three strikes law, any felony can constitute the third strike, and thus can subject a defendant to a term of 25 years to life in prison. See Cal. Penal Code Ann. §667(e)(2)(A) (West 1999). In this case, the prosecutor decided to charge the two counts of theft as felonies rather than misdemeanors. The trial court denied Andrade's motion to reduce the offenses to misdemeanors, both before the jury verdict and again in state habeas proceedings.

A jury found Andrade guilty of two counts of petty theft with a prior conviction. According to California law, a jury must also find that a defendant has been convicted of at least two serious or violent felonies that serve as qualifying offenses under the three strikes regime. In this case, the jury made a special finding that Andrade was convicted of three counts of first-degree residential burglary. A conviction for first-degree residential burglary qualifies as a serious or violent felony for the purposes of the three strikes law. As a consequence, each of Andrade's convictions for theft under Cal. Penal Code Ann. §666 (West Supp. 2002) triggered a separate application of the three strikes law. Pursuant to California law, the judge sentenced Andrade to two consecutive terms of 25 years to life in prison. See §§667(c)(6), 667(e)(2)(B). The State stated at oral argument that under the decision announced by the Supreme Court of California in *People v. Garcia,* 20 Cal. 4th 490, 976 P.2d 831 (1999)—a decision that postdates his conviction and sentence—it remains "available" for Andrade to "file another State habeas corpus petition" arguing that he should serve only one term of 25 years to life in prison because "sentencing courts have a right to dismiss strikes on a count-by-count basis." Tr. of Oral Arg. 24.

B

On direct appeal in 1997, the California Court of Appeal affirmed Andrade's sentence of two consecutive terms of 25 years to life in prison. It rejected

Andrade's claim that his sentence violates the constitutional prohibition against cruel and unusual punishment. The court stated that "the proportionality analysis" of *Solem* v. *Helm,* 463 U.S. 277 (1983), "is questionable in light of" *Harmelin* v. *Michigan,* 501 U.S. 957 (1991). App. to Pet. for Cert. 76. The court then applied our decision in *Rummel* v. *Estelle,* 445 U.S. 263 (1980), where we rejected the defendant's claim that a life sentence was "'grossly disproportionate' to the three felonies that formed the predicate for his sentence." *Id.,* at 265. The California Court of Appeal then examined Andrade's claim in light of the facts in *Rummel:* "Comparing [Andrade's] crimes and criminal history with that of defendant Rummel, we cannot say the sentence of 50 years to life at issue in this case is disproportionate and constitutes cruel and unusual punishment under the United States Constitution." App. to Pet. for Cert. 76–77.

After the Supreme Court of California denied discretionary review, Andrade filed a petition for a writ of habeas corpus in Federal District Court. The District Court denied his petition. The Ninth Circuit granted Andrade a certificate of appealability as to his claim that his sentence violated the Eighth Amendment, and subsequently reversed the judgment of the District Court. 270 F. 3d 743 (2001).

The Ninth Circuit first noted that it was reviewing Andrade's petition under the Antiterrorism and Effective Death Penalty Act of 1996 (AEDPA), 110 Stat. 1214. Applying its own precedent, the Ninth Circuit held that an unreasonable application of clearly established federal law occurs "when our independent review of the legal question 'leaves us with a "firm conviction" that one answer, the one rejected by the [state] court, was correct and the other, the application of the federal law that the [state] court adopted, was erroneous—in other words that clear error occurred.'" 270 F. 3d, at 753 (alteration in original) (quoting *Van Tran* v. *Lindsey,* 212 F. 3d 1143, 1153–1154 (CA9 2000)).

The court then reviewed our three most recent major precedents in this area—*Rummel* v. *Estelle, supra, Solem* v. *Helm, supra,* and *Harmelin* v. *Michigan, supra.* The Ninth Circuit "follow[ed] the test prescribed by Justice Kennedy in *Harmelin,*" concluding that "both *Rummel* and *Solem* remain good law and are instructive in *Harmelin*'s application." 270 F. 3d, at 766. It then noted that the California Court of Appeal compared the facts of Andrade's case to the facts of *Rummel,* but not *Solem.* 270 F. 3d, at 766. The Ninth Circuit concluded that it should grant the writ of habeas corpus because the state court's "disregard for *Solem* results in an unreasonable application of clearly established Supreme Court law," and "is irreconcilable with . . . *Solem,*" thus constituting "clear error." *Id.,* at 766–767.

Judge Sneed dissented in relevant part. He wrote that "[t]he sentence imposed in this case is not one of the 'exceedingly rare' terms of imprisonment prohibited by the Eighth Amendment's proscription against cruel and unusual punishment." *Id.,* at 767 (quoting *Harmelin* v. *Michigan, supra,* at 1001 (KENNEDY, J., concurring in part and concurring in judgment)). Under his view, the state court decision upholding Andrade's sentence was thus "not an unreasonable application of clearly established federal law." 270 F. 3d, at 772. We granted certiorari, 535 U.S. 969 (2002), and now reverse.

II

Andrade's argument in this Court is that two consecutive terms of 25 years to life for stealing approximately $150 in videotapes is grossly disproportionate in violation of the Eighth Amendment. Andrade similarly maintains that the state court decision affirming his sentence is "contrary to, or involved an unreasonable application of, clearly established Federal law, as determined by the Supreme Court of the United States." 28 U.S.C. §2254(d)(1).

AEDPA circumscribes a federal habeas court's review of a state-court decision. Section 2254 provides:

> "(d) An application for a writ of habeas corpus on behalf of a person in custody pursuant to the judgment of a State court shall not be granted with respect to any claim that was adjudicated on the merits in State court proceedings unless the adjudication of the claim—
>
> "(1) resulted in a decision that was contrary to, or involved an unreasonable application of, clearly established Federal law, as determined by the Supreme Court of the United States."

The Ninth Circuit requires federal habeas courts to review the state court decision *de novo* before applying the AEDPA standard of review. See, e.g., *Van Tran* v. *Lindsey, supra,* at 1154–1155; *Clark* v. *Murphy,* 317 F. 3d 1038, 1044, n. 3 (CA9 2003). We disagree with this approach. AEDPA does not require a federal habeas court to adopt any one methodology in deciding the only question that matters under §2254(d)(1)—whether a state court decision is contrary to, or involved an unreasonable application of, clearly established Federal law. In this case, we do not reach the question whether the state court erred and instead focus solely on whether §2254(d) forecloses habeas relief on Andrade's Eighth Amendment claim.

III

A

As a threshold matter here, we first decide what constitutes "clearly established Federal law, as determined by the Supreme Court of the United States." §2254(d)(1). Andrade relies upon a series of precedents from this Court—*Rummel* v. *Estelle,* 445 U.S. 263 (1980), *Solem* v. *Helm,* 463 U.S. 277 (1983), and *Harmelin* v. *Michigan,* 501 U.S. 957 (1991)—that he claims clearly establish a principle that his sentence is so grossly disproportionate that it violates the Eighth Amendment. Section 2254(d)(1)'s "clearly established" phrase "refers to the holdings, as opposed to the dicta, of this Court's decisions as of the time of the relevant state-court decision." *Williams* v. *Taylor,* 529 U.S. 362, 412 (2000). In other words, "clearly established Federal law" under §2254(d)(1) is the governing legal principle or principles set forth by the Supreme Court at the time the state court renders its decision. In most situations, the task of determining what we have clearly established will be straightforward. The difficulty with

Andrade's position, however, is that our precedents in this area have not been a model of clarity. See *Harmelin* v. *Michigan,* 501 U.S., at 965 (opinion of SCALIA, J.); *id.,* at 996, 998 (KENNEDY, J., concurring in part and concurring in judgment). Indeed, in determining whether a particular sentence for a term of years can violate the Eighth Amendment, we have not established a clear or consistent path for courts to follow.

B

Through this thicket of Eighth Amendment jurisprudence, one governing legal principle emerges as "clearly established" under §2254(d)(1): A gross disproportionality principle is applicable to sentences for terms of years.

Our cases exhibit a lack of clarity regarding what factors may indicate gross disproportionality. In *Solem* (the case upon which Andrade relies most heavily), we stated: "It is clear that a 25-year sentence generally is more severe than a 15-year sentence, but in most cases it would be difficult to decide that the former violates the Eighth Amendment while the latter does not." 463 U.S., at 294 (footnote omitted). And in *Harmelin,* both JUSTICE KENNEDY and JUSTICE SCALIA repeatedly emphasized this lack of clarity: that "*Solem* was scarcely the expression of clear . . . constitutional law," 501 U.S., at 965 (opinion of SCALIA, J.), that in "adher[ing] to the narrow proportionality principle . . . our proportionality decisions have not been clear or consistent in all respects," *id.,* at 996 (KENNEDY, J., concurring in part and concurring in judgment), that "we lack clear objective standards to distinguish between sentences for different terms of years," *id.,* at 1001 (KENNEDY, J., concurring in part and concurring in judgment), and that the "precise contours" of the proportionality principle "are unclear," *id.,* at 998 (KENNEDY, J., concurring in part and concurring in judgment).

Thus, in this case, the only relevant clearly established law amenable to the "contrary to" or "unreasonable application of" framework is the gross disproportionality principle, the precise contours of which are unclear, applicable only in the "exceedingly rare" and "extreme" case. *Id.,* at 1001 (KENNEDY, J., concurring in part and concurring in judgment) (internal quotation marks omitted); see also *Solem* v. *Helm, supra,* at 290; *Rummel* v. *Estelle, supra,* at 272.

IV

The final question is whether the California Court of Appeal's decision affirming Andrade's sentence is "contrary to, or involved an unreasonable application of," this clearly established gross disproportionality principle.

First, a state court decision is "contrary to our clearly established precedent if the state court applies a rule that contradicts the governing law set forth in our cases" or "if the state court confronts a set of facts that are materially indistinguishable from a decision of this Court and nevertheless arrives at a result different from our precedent." *Williams* v. *Taylor, supra,* at 405–406; see also *Bell* v. *Cone, supra,* at 694. In terms of length of sentence and availability of parole, severity of the underlying offense, and the impact of recidivism,

Andrade's sentence implicates factors relevant in both *Rummel* and *Solem*. Because *Harmelin* and *Solem* specifically stated that they did not overrule *Rummel,* it was not contrary to our clearly established law for the California Court of Appeal to turn to *Rummel* in deciding whether a sentence is grossly disproportionate. See *Harmelin, supra,* at 998 (KENNEDY, J., concurring in part and concurring in judgment); *Solem, supra,* at 288, n. 13, 303–304, n. 32. Indeed, *Harmelin* allows a state court to reasonably rely on *Rummel* in determining whether a sentence is grossly disproportionate. The California Court of Appeal's decision was therefore not "contrary to" the governing legal principles set forth in our cases.

Andrade's sentence also was not materially indistinguishable from the facts in *Solem.* The facts here fall in between the facts in *Rummel* and the facts in *Solem. Solem* involved a sentence of life in prison without the possibility of parole. 463 U.S., at 279. The defendant in *Rummel* was sentenced to life in prison with the possibility of parole. 445 U.S., at 267. Here, Andrade retains the possibility of parole. *Solem* acknowledged that *Rummel* would apply in a "similar factual situation." 463 U.S., at 304, n. 32. And while this case resembles to some degree both *Rummel* and *Solem,* it is not materially indistinguishable from either. Cf. *Ewing* v. *California, ante,* at ＿ (slip op., at 6) (BREYER, J., dissenting) (recognizing a "twilight zone between *Solem* and *Rummel*"). Consequently, the state court did not "confron[t] a set of facts that are materially indistinguishable from a decision of this Court and nevertheless arriv[e] at a result different from our precedent." *Williams* v. *Taylor,* 529 U.S., at 406.[1]

Second, "[u]nder the 'unreasonable application' clause, a federal habeas court may grant the writ if the state court identifies the correct governing legal principle from this Court's decisions but unreasonably applies that principle to the facts of the prisoner's case." *Id.,* at 413. The "unreasonable application" clause requires the state court decision to be more than incorrect or erroneous. *Id.,* at 410, 412. The state court's application of clearly established law must be objectively unreasonable. *Id.,* at 409.

The Ninth Circuit made an initial error in its "unreasonable application" analysis. In *Van Tran* v. *Lindsey,* 212 F. 3d, at 1152–1154, the Ninth Circuit defined "objectively unreasonable" to mean "clear error." These two standards, however, are not the same. The gloss of clear error fails to give proper deference to state courts by conflating error (even clear error) with unreasonableness. See *Williams* v. *Taylor, supra,* at 410; *Bell* v. *Cone,* 535 U.S., at 699.

It is not enough that a federal habeas court, in its "independent review of the legal question" is left with a "'firm conviction'" that the state court was "'erroneous'" 270 F. 3d, at 753 (quoting *Van Tran* v. *Lindsey, supra,* at 1153–1154). We have held precisely the opposite: "Under §2254(d)(1)'s 'unreasonable application' clause, then, a federal habeas court may not issue the writ simply because that court concludes in its independent judgment that the relevant state-court decision applied clearly established federal law erroneously or incorrectly." *Williams* v. *Taylor,* 529 U.S., at 411. Rather, that application must be objectively unreasonable. *Id.,* at 409; *Bell* v. *Cone, supra,* at 699; *Woodford* v. *Visciotti,* 537 U.S. ＿, ＿ (2002) (*per curiam*) (slip op., at 6).

Section 2254(d)(1) permits a federal court to grant habeas relief based on the application of a governing legal principle to a set of facts different from those of the case in which the principle was announced. See, *e.g., Williams* v. *Taylor, supra,* at 407 (noting that it is "an unreasonable application of this Court's precedent if the state court identifies the correct governing legal rule from this Court's cases but unreasonably applies it to the facts of the particular state prisoner's case"). Here, however, the governing legal principle gives legislatures broad discretion to fashion a sentence that fits within the scope of the proportionality principle—the "precise contours" of which "are unclear." *Harmelin* v. *Michigan,* 501 U.S., at 998 (KENNEDY, J., concurring in part and concurring in judgment). And it was not objectively unreasonable for the California Court of Appeal to conclude that these "contours" permitted an affirmance of Andrade's sentence.

Indeed, since *Harmelin,* several Members of this Court have expressed "uncertainty" regarding the application of the proportionality principle to the California three strikes law. *Riggs* v. *California,* 525 U.S. 1114, 1115 (1999) (STEVENS, J., joined by SOUTER and GINSBURG, JJ., respecting denial of certiorari) ("[T]here is some uncertainty about how our cases dealing with the punishment of recidivists should apply"); see also *id.,* at 1116 ("It is thus unclear how, if at all, a defendant's criminal record beyond the requisite two prior 'strikes' . . . affects the constitutionality of his sentence"); cf. *Durden* v. *California,* 531 U.S. 1184 (2001) (SOUTER, J., joined by BREYER, J., dissenting from denial of certiorari) (arguing that the Court should hear the three strikes gross disproportionality issue on direct review because of the "potential for disagreement over application of" AEDPA).[2]

The gross disproportionality principle reserves a constitutional violation for only the extraordinary case. In applying this principle for §2254(d)(1) purposes, it was not an unreasonable application of our clearly established law for the California Court of Appeal to affirm Andrade's sentence of two consecutive terms of 25 years to life in prison.

V

The judgment of the United States Court of Appeals for the Ninth Circuit, accordingly, is reversed.

It is so ordered.

Notes

1. JUSTICE SOUTER argues that the possibility of Andrade's receiving parole in 50 years makes this case similar to the facts in *Solem* v. *Helm,* 463 U.S. 227 (1983). *Post,* at 2 (dissenting opinion). Andrade's sentence, however, is also similar to the facts in *Rummel* v. *Estelle,* 445 U.S. 263 (1980), a case that is also "controlling." *Post,* at 2. Given the lack of clarity of our precedents in *Solem, Rummel,* and *Harmelin* v. *Michigan,* 501 U.S. 957 (1991), we cannot say that the state court's affirmance of two sentences of 25 years to life in prison was contrary to our clearly established precedent. And to the extent that JUSTICE SOUTER

is arguing that the similarity of *Solem* to this case entitles Andrade to relief under the unreasonable application prong of §2254(d), we reject his analysis for the reasons given *infra,* at 11–12. Moreover, it is not true that Andrade's "sentence can only be understood as punishment for the total amount he stole." *Post,* at 2. To the contrary, California law specifically provides that *each* violation of Cal. Penal Code Ann. §666 (West Supp. 2002) triggers a separate application of the three strikes law, if the different felony counts are "not arising from the same set of operative facts." §667(c)(6); see also §667(e)(2)(B). Here, Andrade was sentenced to two consecutive terms under California law precisely because the two thefts of two different Kmart stores occurring two weeks apart were two distinct crimes.

JUSTICE SOUTER, relying on *Robinson* v. *California,* 370 U.S. 660 (1962), also argues that in this case, it is "unrealistic" to think that a sentence of 50 years to life for Andrade is not equivalent to life in prison without parole. *Post,* at 3. This argument, however, misses the point. Based on our precedents, the state court decision was not contrary to, or an unreasonable application of, our clearly established law. Moreover, JUSTICE SOUTER's position would treat a sentence of life without parole for the 77-year-old person convicted of murder as equivalent to a sentence of life with the possibility of parole in 10 years for the same person convicted of the same crime. Two different sentences do not become materially indistinguishable based solely upon the age of the persons sentenced.

2. JUSTICE SOUTER would hold that Andrade's sentence also violates the unreasonable application prong of §2254(d)(1). *Post,* at 3–6. His reasons, however, do not change the "uncertainty" of the scope of the proportionality principle. We cannot say that the state court decision was an unreasonable application of this principle.

Dissenting Opinion of David Souter

Justice SOUTER, with whom JUSTICE STEVENS, JUSTICE GINSBURG, and JUSTICE BREYER join, dissenting.

The application of the Eighth Amendment prohibition against cruel and unusual punishment to terms of years is articulated in the "clearly established" principle acknowledged by the Court: a sentence grossly disproportionate to the offense for which it is imposed is unconstitutional. See *ante,* at 4; *Harmelin* v. *Michigan,* 501 U.S. 957 (1991); *Solem* v. *Helm,* 463 U.S. 277 (1983); *Rummel* v. *Estelle,* 445 U.S. 263 (1980). For the reasons set forth in JUSTICE BREYER's dissent in *Ewing* v. *California, ante,* at ___, which I joined, Andrade's sentence cannot survive Eighth Amendment review. His criminal history is less grave than Ewing's, and yet he received a prison term twice as long for a less serious triggering offense. To be sure, this is a habeas case and a prohibition couched in terms as general as gross disproportion necessarily leaves state courts with much leeway under the statutory criterion that conditions federal relief upon finding that a state court unreasonably applied clear law, see 28 U.S.C. §2254(d). This case nonetheless presents two independent reasons for holding that the disproportionality review by the state court was not only erroneous but unreasonable, entitling Andrade to relief. I respectfully dissent accordingly.

The first reason is the holding in *Solem,* which happens to be our most recent effort at proportionality review of recidivist sentencing, the authority of which was not left in doubt by *Harmelin,* see 501 U.S., at 998. Although *Solem* is important for its instructions about applying objective proportionality analysis, see 463 U.S., at 290–292, the case is controlling here because it established a benchmark in applying the general principle. We specifically held that a sentence of life imprisonment without parole for uttering a $100 "no account" check was disproportionate to the crime, even though the defendant had committed six prior nonviolent felonies. In explaining our proportionality review, we contrasted the result with *Rummel*'s on the ground that the life sentence there had included parole eligibility after 12 years, *Solem,* 463 U.S., at 297.

The facts here are on all fours with those of *Solem* and point to the same result. Andrade, like the defendant in *Solem,* was a repeat offender who committed theft of fairly trifling value, some $150, and their criminal records are comparable, including burglary (though Andrade's were residential), with no violent crimes or crimes against the person. The respective sentences, too, are

From *Bill Lockyer, Attorney General of California, v. Leandro Andrade,* 538 U.S. ____ (2003). Some notes and case citations omitted.

strikingly alike. Although Andrade's petty thefts occurred on two separate occasions, his sentence can only be understood as punishment for the total amount he stole. The two thefts were separated by only two weeks; they involved the same victim; they apparently constituted parts of a single, continuing effort to finance drug sales; their seriousness is measured by the dollar value of the things taken; and the government charged both thefts in a single indictment. Cf. United States Sentencing Commission, Guidelines Manual §3D1.2 (Nov. 2002) (grouping temporally separated counts as one offense for sentencing purposes). The state court accordingly spoke of his punishment collectively as well, carrying a 50-year minimum before parole eligibility, see App. to Pet. for Cert. 77 ("[W]e cannot say the sentence of 50 years to life at issue in this case is disproportionate"), and because Andrade was 37 years old when sentenced, the substantial 50-year period amounts to life without parole. *Solem, supra,* at 287 (quoting *Robinson* v. *California,* 370 U.S. 660, 667 (1962) (when considering whether a punishment is cruel or unusual "'the questions cannot be considered in the abstract'")); cf. *Rummel, supra,* at 280–281 (defendant's eligibility for parole in 12 years informs a proper assessment of his cruel and unusual punishment claim). The results under the Eighth Amendment should therefore be the same in each case. The only ways to reach a different conclusion are to reject the practical equivalence of a life sentence without parole and one with parole eligibility at 87, see *ante,* at 9, ("Andrade retains the possibility of parole"), or to discount the continuing authority of *Solem*'s example, as the California court did, see App. to Pet. for Cert. 76 ("[T]he current validity of the Solem proportionality analysis is questionable.") The former is unrealistic; an 87-year-old man released after 50 years behind bars will have no real life left, if he survives to be released at all. And the latter, disparaging *Solem* as a point of reference on Eighth Amendment analysis, is wrong as a matter of law.

The second reason that relief is required even under the §2254(d) unreasonable application standard rests on the alternative way of looking at Andrade's 50-year sentence as two separate 25-year applications of the three-strikes law, and construing the challenge here as going to the second, consecutive 25-year minimum term triggered by a petty theft. To understand why it is revealing to look at the sentence this way, it helps to recall the basic difficulty inherent in proportionality review. We require the comparison of offense and penalty to disclose a truly gross disproportionality before the constitutional limit is passed, in large part because we believe that legislatures are institutionally equipped with better judgment than courts in deciding what penalty is merited by particular behavior. In this case, however, a court is substantially aided in its reviewing function by two determinations made by the State itself.

The first is the State's adoption of a particular penalogical theory as its principal reason for shutting a three-strikes defendant away for at least 25 years. Although the State alludes in passing to retribution or deterrence (see Brief for Petitioner 16, 24; Reply Brief for Petitioner 10), its only serious justification for the 25-year minimum treats the sentence as a way to incapacitate a given defendant from further crime; the underlying theory is the need to protect the public from a danger demonstrated by the prior record of violent and serious crime. See Brief for Petitioner 17 ("significant danger to society such that [defendant] must be imprisoned for no less than twenty-five years to life"); *id.*, at 21 ("statute carefully tailored to address . . . defendants that pose the greatest danger"); *id.*, at 23 ("isolating such a defendant for a substantial period of time"); Reply Brief for Petitioner 11 ("If Andrade's reasoning were accepted, however, California would be precluded from incapacitating him"). See also *Rummel*, 445 U.S., at 284 ("purpose of a recidivist statute . . . [is] to segregate").[1] The State, in other words has not chosen 25 to life because of the inherent moral or social reprehensibility of the triggering offense in isolation; the triggering offense is treated so seriously, rather, because of its confirmation of the defendant's danger to society and the need to counter his threat with incapacitation. As to the length of incapacitation, the State has made a second helpful determination, that the public risk or danger posed by someone with the specified predicate record is generally addressed by incapacitation for 25 years before parole eligibility. Cal. Penal Code Ann. §667(e)(2) (A)(ii) (West 1999). The three-strikes law, in sum, responds to a condition of the defendant shown by his prior felony record, his danger to society, and it reflects a judgment that 25 years of incapacitation prior to parole eligibility is appropriate when a defendant exhibiting such a condition commits another felony.

Whether or not one accepts the State's choice of penological policy as constitutionally sound, that policy cannot reasonably justify the imposition of a consecutive 25-year minimum for a second minor felony committed soon after the first triggering offense. Andrade did not somehow become twice as dangerous to society when he stole the second handful of videotapes; his dangerousness may justify treating one minor felony as serious and warranting long incapacitation, but a second such felony does not disclose greater danger warranting substantially longer incapacitation. Since the defendant's condition has not changed between the two closely related thefts, the incapacitation penalty is not open to the simple arithmetic of multiplying the punishment by two, without resulting in gross disproportion even under the State's chosen benchmark. Far from attempting a novel penal theory to justify doubling the sentence, the California Court of Appeal offered no comment at all as to the particular penal theory supporting such a punishment. Perhaps even more tellingly, no one could seriously argue that the second theft of videotapes provided any basis to think that Andrade would be so dangerous after 25 years, the date on which the consecutive sentence would begin to run, as to require at least 25 years more. I know of no jurisdiction that would add 25 years of imprisonment simply to reflect the fact that the two temporally related thefts took place on two separate occasions, and I am not surprised that California has found no such case, not even under its three-strikes law. In sum, the argument that repeating a trivial crime justifies doubling a 25-year minimum incapacitation sentence based on a threat to the public does not raise a seriously debatable point on which judgments might reasonably differ. The argument is irrational, and the state court's acceptance of it in response to a facially gross disproportion between triggering offense and penalty was unreasonable within the meaning of §2254(d).

This is the rare sentence of demonstrable gross disproportionality, as the California Legislature may well have recognized when it specifically provided that a prosecutor may move to dismiss or strike a prior felony conviction "in the furtherance of justice." Cal. Penal Code Ann. §667(f) (2) (West 1999). In this case, the statutory safeguard failed, and the state court was left to ensure that the Eighth Amendment prohibition on grossly disproportionate sentences was met. If Andrade's sentence is not grossly disproportionate, the principle has no meaning. The California court's holding was an unreasonable application of clearly established precedent.

Note

1. Implicit in the distinction between future dangerousness and repunishment for prior crimes is the notion that the triggering offense must, within some degree, be substantial enough to bear the weight of the sentence it elicits. As triggering offenses become increasingly minor and recidivist sentences grow, the sentences advance toward double jeopardy violations. When defendants are parking violators or slow readers of borrowed library books, there is not much room for belief, even in light of a past criminal record, that the State is permanently incapacitating the defendant because of future dangerousness rather than resentencing for past offenses.

    That said, I do not question the legitimacy of repeatedly sentencing a defendant in light of his criminal record: the Federal Sentencing Guidelines provide a prime example of how a sentencing scheme may take into account a defendant's criminal history without resentencing a defendant for past convictions, *Witte* v. *United States,* 515 U.S. 389, 403 (1995) (the triggering offense determines the range of possible sentences, and the past criminal record affects an enhancement of that sentence). The point is merely that the triggering offense must reasonably support the weight of even the harshest possible sentences.

POSTSCRIPT

Is a Sentence of Life in Prison for Stealing $150 Worth of Videotapes Constitutional?

According to law professor Bernard E. Harcourt, in "The Shaping of Chance: Actuarial Models and Criminal Profiling at the Turn of the Twenty-First Century," 70 *University of Chicago Law Review* 105 (2003),

> The turn of the twentieth century marked a new era of individualization in the field of criminal law. Drawing on the new science of positivist criminology, legal scholars called for diagnosis of the causes of delinquence and for imposition of individualized courses of remedial treatment specifically adapted to these individual diagnoses. . . . At the close of the century, the contrast could hardly have been greater. The rehabilitative project had been largely displaced by a model of criminal law enforcement that emphasized mandatory sentences, fixed guidelines, and sentencing enhancements for designated classes of crimes. The focus of criminal sentencing had become the category of crime, rather than the individual characteristics and history of the convicted person, with one major exception for prior criminal conduct. Incapacitation theory—the idea that incarcerating serious and repeat criminal offenders for lengthy sentences will significantly impact crime rates—had replaced the rehabilitative model. In the area of policing, the dominant strategy shifted from the model of the professional police force rapidly responding to 911 emergency calls to a more forward-looking crime prevention model that relied heavily on criminal profiling.

Along with a shift in sentencing practices, there has been enormous growth in the prison population in the United States. This did not happen immediately or quickly. Incarceration rates averaged 110 state and federal prisoners per 100,000 people until 1970. Between 1970 and 2001, however, federal and state prison populations nationwide grew from less than 200,000 to more than 1,300,000, with another 630,000 persons being held in local jails. The current rate of incarceration in prison is 478 per 100,000; if jailed inmates are included, the rate jumps to 699 per 100,000. This is six to ten times the incarceration rate of the Western European countries, and it means that a higher proportion of the adult population of America is incarcerated than that of any other country in the world except Russia. The United States, with 5 percent of the world's population, has 25 percent of its prisoners.

It is not clear that the three-strikes movement has had any significant impact on crime rates. Such rates did decline in the 1990s, but they had already begun declining before any of the three-strikes laws were enacted. The only jurisdiction in which three strikes has involved significant numbers is California. The federal government and many other states require that the third strike involve a violent or serious felony. As *Lockyer v. Andrade* illustrates, in California third-strike sentences can be applied even if the third felony conviction is for a relatively minor crime, such as petty theft. As a result, California has generated more than 40,000 three-strikes sentences. No other state has yet to generate 1,000, and the federal government has generated just 35 such sentences nationwide.

Some recommended additional readings are Franklin E. Zimring, Gordon Hawkins, and Sam Kamin, *Punishment and Democracy: Three Strikes and You're Out in California* (Oxford University Press, 2003); Marie Gottschalk, "Black Flower: Prisons and the Future of Incarceration," 582 *Annals of the American Academy of Political and Social Science* 195, 197 (2002); Randal S. Jeffrey, "Restricting Prisoners' Equal Access to the Federal Courts: The Three Strikes Provision of the Prison Litigation Reform Act and Substantive Equal Protection," 49 *Buffalo Law Review* 1099 (2001); and James Q. Whitman, *Harsh Justice: Criminal Punishment and the Widening Divide Between America and Europe* (New York: Oxford University Press, 2003).

ISSUE 14

Is Drug Use Testing of Students Who Participate in Extracurricular Activities Permitted Under the Fourth Amendment?

YES: Clarence Thomas, from Majority Opinion, *Board of Education of Independent School District No. 92 of Pottawatomie County et al. v. Lindsay Earls et al.,* U.S. Supreme Court (June 27, 2002)

NO: Ruth Bader Ginsburg, from Dissenting Opinion, *Board of Education of Independent School District No. 92 of Pottawatomie County et al. v. Lindsay Earls et al.,* U.S. Supreme Court (June 27, 2002)

ISSUE SUMMARY

YES: Supreme Court Justice Clarence Thomas finds that a school policy requiring all middle and high school students to consent to drug testing in order to participate in any extracurricular activity does not violate the Fourth Amendment.

NO: Supreme Court Justice Ruth Bader Ginsburg dissents, arguing that while testing student athletes may be justifiable, there is no justification for invading the privacy of students who participate in other extracurricular activities.

Illegal drug use among high school students has been a concern of parents, educators, and policymakers for some time. In response to a perceived crisis of drug abuse, many states and localities have recognized that their responsibility to educate also requires a meaningful attempt to reduce or eliminate altogether the use of illegal drugs, alcohol, tobacco, and even performance-enhancing drugs by students. In addition to educational initiatives, many states have assumed an even more aggressive proactive posture by adopting the use of random, suspicionless drug-testing programs for students.

Not surprisingly, the constitutionality of such programs was immediately challenged when they were first introduced. One of the first cases to address the Fourth Amendment implications of random, suspicionless drug tests was *Schaill v. Tippecanoe County School Corporation,* 864 F. 2d 1309 (1988).

In *Schaill,* the question before the Court of Appeals for the Seventh Circuit involved the drug testing of high school athletes. Upholding the constitutionality of the school's policy requiring student participation in the testing process prior to continued involvement in any athletic program, the court found that a student athlete's exposure to communal undress in the locker room suggested that student athletes already had a diminished expectation of privacy—an essential element in Fourth Amendment analysis.

In *Vernonia School District 47J v. Acton,* 115 S. Ct. 2386 (1995), the U.S. Supreme Court directly addressed the question of the appropriate standard to be used by the lower courts in their determination of the reasonableness of searches in the form of random, suspicionless drug tests. The Fourth Amendment provides that "the right of the people to be secure in their persons, houses, papers, and effects, against *unreasonable* searches and seizures, shall not be violated, and no Warrants shall issue, but upon probable cause, supported by Oath or affirmation, and particularly describing the place to be searched, and the persons or things to be seized" (emphasis added). The basis of the challenge in these cases has turned on the lack of *individualized* suspicion. That is, the courts have traditionally required the government, when conducting searches and seizures, to provide articulable, reasonable suspicion that an identified (or identifiable) *individual* has engaged or is about to engage in some form of criminal behavior. There are, of course, numerous exceptions to this general rule, and in *Vernonia*, the Supreme Court adopted a "special needs" exception to the warrant and probable cause requirements of the Fourth Amendment. According to the Court, this exception renders traditional Fourth Amendment requirements unnecessary "in those exceptional circumstances in which special needs, beyond the normal need for law enforcement" make them impracticable.

Writing for the Court and relying on the special needs exception, Justice Antonin Scalia held that random, suspicionless drug testing of students participating in the Vernonia school system's athletic programs did not violate the Fourth Amendment. He also determined that the school system's interests in addressing the drug problem in its high school combined with the relatively unobtrusive means of testing outweighed the student athletes' limited privacy interests.

Justice Sandra Day O'Connor, joined by Justices John Paul Stevens and David Souter, wrote a vigorous dissent, challenging the Court's retreat from the normal Fourth Amendment requirement of individualized suspicion. Nonetheless, the *Vernonia* decision clearly approved the use of random, suspicionless drug-testing programs for members of schools' athletic teams. Yet the scope of such programs and whether or not drug testing of nonathletes would be constitutional was left in doubt.

The following case, *Board of Education of Independent School District No. 92 of Pottawatomie County v. Earls,* involved a policy in which any student who participated in a competitive extracurricular activity, including band, choir, cheerleading, Future Farmers of America, and Future Homemakers of America, could be tested. *Vernonia* was decided by a 6–3 margin. *Earls* was decided by a 5–4 margin, with Justice Ruth Bader Ginsburg, a member of the majority in *Vernonia*, writing the dissenting opinion in this case.

YES ↵

Majority Opinion

Board of Education of Independent School District No. 92 of Pottawatomie County *v.* Earls

JUSTICE THOMAS delivered the opinion of the Court.

The Student Activities Drug Testing Policy implemented by the Board of Education of Independent School District No. 92 of Pottawatomie County (School District) requires all students who participate in competitive extra-curricular activities to submit to drug testing. Because this Policy reasonably serves the School District's important interest in detecting and preventing drug use among its students, we hold that it is constitutional.

I

The city of Tecumseh, Oklahoma, is a rural community located approximately 40 miles southeast of Oklahoma City. The School District administers all Tecumseh public schools. In the fall of 1998, the School District adopted the Student Activities Drug Testing Policy (Policy), which requires all middle and high school students to consent to drug testing in order to participate in any extracurricular activity. In practice, the Policy has been applied only to competitive extracurricular activities sanctioned by the Oklahoma Secondary Schools Activities Association, such as the Academic Team, Future Farmers of America, Future Homemakers of America, band, choir, pom pon, cheerleading, and athletics. Under the Policy, students are required to take a drug test before participating in an extracurricular activity, must submit to random drug testing while participating in that activity, and must agree to be tested at any time upon reasonable suspicion. The urinalysis tests are designed to detect only the use of illegal drugs, including amphetamines, marijuana, cocaine, opiates, and barbituates, not medical conditions or the presence of authorized prescription medications.

At the time of their suit, both respondents attended Tecumseh High School. Respondent Lindsay Earls was a member of the show choir, the marching band, the Academic Team, and the National Honor Society. Respondent Daniel James sought to participate in the Academic Team. Together with their

From *Board of Education of Independent School District No. 92 of Pottawatomie County et al. v. Lindsay Earls et al.*, 536 U.S.___(2002). Some notes and case citations omitted.

parents, Earls and James brought a 42 U.S.C. §1983 action against the School District, challenging the Policy both on its face and as applied to their participation in extracurricular activities. They alleged that the Policy violates the Fourth Amendment as incorporated by the Fourteenth Amendment and requested injunctive and declarative relief. They also argued that the School District failed to identify a special need for testing students who participate in extracurricular activities, and that the "Drug Testing Policy neither addresses a proven problem nor promises to bring any benefit to students or the school."

Applying the principles articulated in *Vernonia School Dist. 47J v. Acton,* 515 U.S. 646 (1995), in which we upheld the suspicionless drug testing of school athletes, the United States District Court for the Western District of Oklahoma rejected respondents' claim that the Policy was unconstitutional and granted summary judgment to the School District. The court noted that "special needs" exist in the public school context and that, although the School District did "not show a drug problem of epidemic proportions," there was a history of drug abuse starting in 1970 that presented "legitimate cause for concern." 115 F. Supp. 2d 1281, 1287 (2000). The District Court also held that the Policy was effective because "[i]t can scarcely be disputed that the drug problem among the student body is effectively addressed by making sure that the large number of students participating in competitive, extracurricular activities do not use drugs." *Id.,* at 1295.

The United States Court of Appeals for the Tenth Circuit reversed, holding that the Policy violated the Fourth Amendment. The Court of Appeals agreed with the District Court that the Policy must be evaluated in the "unique environment of the school setting," but reached a different conclusion as to the Policy's constitutionality. 242 F. 3d 1264, 1270 (2001). Before imposing a suspicionless drug testing program, the Court of Appeals concluded that a school "must demonstrate that there is some identifiable drug abuse problem among a sufficient number of those subject to the testing, such that testing that group of students will actually redress its drug problem." *Id.,* at 1278. The Court of Appeals then held that because the School District failed to demonstrate such a problem existed among Tecumseh students participating in competitive extracurricular activities, the Policy was unconstitutional. We granted certiorari, 534 U.S. 1015 (2001), and now reverse.

II

The Fourth Amendment to the United States Constitution protects "[t]he right of the people to be secure in their persons, houses, papers, and effects, against unreasonable searches and seizures." Searches by public school officials, such as the collection of urine samples, implicate Fourth Amendment interests. We must therefore review the School District's Policy for "reasonableness," which is the touchstone of the constitutionality of a governmental search.

In the criminal context, reasonableness usually requires a showing of probable cause. The probable-cause standard, however, "is peculiarly related to criminal investigations" and may be unsuited to determining the reasonableness of administrative searches where the "Government seeks to prevent the development of hazardous conditions." *Treasury Employees* v. *Von Raab*, 489 U.S. 656, 667–668 (1989). The Court has also held that a warrant and finding of probable cause are unnecessary in the public school context because such requirements "'would unduly interfere with the maintenance of the swift and informal disciplinary procedures [that are] needed.'"

Given that the School District's Policy is not in any way related to the conduct of criminal investigations, respondents do not contend that the School District requires probable cause before testing students for drug use. Respondents instead argue that drug testing must be based at least on some level of individualized suspicion. It is true that we generally determine the reasonableness of a search by balancing the nature of the intrusion on the individual's privacy against the promotion of legitimate governmental interests. See *Delaware* v. *Prouse*, 440 U.S. 648, 654 (1979). But we have long held that "the Fourth Amendment imposes no irreducible requirement of [individualized] suspicion." *United States* v. *Martinez-Fuerte*, 428 U.S. 543, 561 (1976). "[I]n certain limited circumstances, the Government's need to discover such latent or hidden conditions, or to prevent their development, is sufficiently compelling to justify the intrusion on privacy entailed by conducting such searches without any measure of individualized suspicion." Therefore, in the context of safety and administrative regulations, a search unsupported by probable cause may be reasonable "when 'special needs, beyond the normal need for law enforcement, make the warrant and probable-cause requirement impracticable.'"

Significantly, this Court has previously held that "special needs" inhere in the public school context. See *Vernonia, supra,* at 653; *T. L. O., supra,* at 339–340. While schoolchildren do not shed their constitutional rights when they enter the schoolhouse, see *Tinker* v. *Des Moines Independent Community School Dist.,* 393 U.S. 503, 506 (1969), "Fourth Amendment rights . . . are different in public schools than elsewhere; the 'reasonableness' inquiry cannot disregard the schools' custodial and tutelary responsibility for children." *Vernonia, supra,* at 656. In particular, a finding of individualized suspicion may not be necessary when a school conducts drug testing.

In *Vernonia,* this Court held that the suspicionless drug testing of athletes was constitutional. The Court, however, did not simply authorize all school drug testing, but rather conducted a fact-specific balancing of the intrusion on the children's Fourth Amendment rights against the promotion of legitimate governmental interests. Applying the principles of *Vernonia* to the somewhat different facts of this case, we conclude that Tecumseh's Policy is also constitutional.

A

We first consider the nature of the privacy interest allegedly compromised by the drug testing. As in *Vernonia,* the context of the public school environment serves as the backdrop for the analysis of the privacy interest at stake and the reasonableness of the drug testing policy in general. ("Central . . . is the fact that the subjects of the Policy are (1) children, who (2) have been committed to the temporary custody of the State as schoolmaster"); ("The most significant element in this case is the first we discussed: that the Policy was undertaken in furtherance of the government's responsibilities, under a public school system, as guardian and tutor of children entrusted to its care"); ("[W]hen the government acts as guardian and tutor the relevant question is whether the search is one that a reasonable guardian and tutor might undertake").

A student's privacy interest is limited in a public school environment where the State is responsible for maintaining discipline, health, and safety. Schoolchildren are routinely required to submit to physical examinations and vaccinations against disease. Securing order in the school environment sometimes requires that students be subjected to greater controls than those appropriate for adults. See *T. L. O., supra,* at 350 (Powell, J., concurring) ("Without first establishing discipline and maintaining order, teachers cannot begin to educate their students. And apart from education, the school has the obligation to protect pupils from mistreatment by other children, and also to protect teachers themselves from violence by the few students whose conduct in recent years has prompted national concern").

Respondents argue that because children participating in nonathletic extracurricular activities are not subject to regular physicals and communal undress, they have a stronger expectation of privacy than the athletes tested in *Vernonia.* This distinction, however, was not essential to our decision in *Vernonia,* which depended primarily upon the school's custodial responsibility and authority.[1]

In any event, students who participate in competitive extracurricular activities voluntarily subject themselves to many of the same intrusions on their privacy as do athletes.[2] Some of these clubs and activities require occasional off-campus travel and communal undress. All of them have their own rules and requirements for participating students that do not apply to the student body as a whole. For example, each of the competitive extracurricular activities governed by the Policy must abide by the rules of the Oklahoma Secondary Schools Activities Association, and a faculty sponsor monitors the students for compliance with the various rules dictated by the clubs and activities. This regulation of extracurricular activities further diminishes the expectation of privacy among schoolchildren. Cf. *Vernonia, supra,* at 657 ("Somewhat like adults who choose to participate in a closely regulated industry, students who voluntarily participate in school athletics have reason to expect intrusions upon normal rights and privileges, including privacy" (internal quotation marks omitted)). We therefore conclude that the students affected by this Policy have a limited expectation of privacy.

B

Next, we consider the character of the intrusion imposed by the Policy. Urination is "an excretory function traditionally shielded by great privacy." *Skinner,* 489 U.S., at 626. But the "degree of intrusion" on one's privacy caused by collecting a urine sample "depends upon the manner in which production of the urine sample is monitored." *Vernonia, supra,* at 658.

Under the Policy, a faculty monitor waits outside the closed restroom stall for the student to produce a sample and must "listen for the normal sounds of urination in order to guard against tampered specimens and to insure an accurate chain of custody." The monitor then pours the sample into two bottles that are sealed and placed into a mailing pouch along with a consent form signed by the student. This procedure is virtually identical to that reviewed in *Vernonia,* except that it additionally protects privacy by allowing male students to produce their samples behind a closed stall. Given that we considered the method of collection in *Vernonia* a "negligible" intrusion, 515 U.S., at 658, the method here is even less problematic.

In addition, the Policy clearly requires that the test results be kept in confidential files separate from a student's other educational records and released to school personnel only on a "need to know" basis. Respondents nonetheless contend that the intrusion on students' privacy is significant because the Policy fails to protect effectively against the disclosure of confidential information and, specifically, that the school "has been careless in protecting that information: for example, the Choir teacher looked at students' prescription drug lists and left them where other students could see them." Brief for Respondents 24. But the choir teacher is someone with a "need to know," because during off-campus trips she needs to know what medications are taken by her students. Even before the Policy was enacted the choir teacher had access to this information. See App. 132. In any event, there is no allegation that any other student did see such information. This one example of alleged carelessness hardly increases the character of the intrusion.

Moreover, the test results are not turned over to any law enforcement authority. Nor do the test results here lead to the imposition of discipline or have any academic consequences. Rather, the only consequence of a failed drug test is to limit the student's privilege of participating in extracurricular activities. Indeed, a student may test positive for drugs twice and still be allowed to participate in extracurricular activities. After the first positive test, the school contacts the student's parent or guardian for a meeting. The student may continue to participate in the activity if within five days of the meeting the student shows proof of receiving drug counseling and submits to a second drug test in two weeks. For the second positive test, the student is suspended from participation in all extracurricular activities for 14 days, must complete four hours of substance abuse counseling, and must submit to monthly drug tests. Only after a third positive test will the student be suspended from participating in any extracurricular activity for the remainder of the school year, or 88 school days, whichever is longer.

Given the minimally intrusive nature of the sample collection and the limited uses to which the test results are put, we conclude that the invasion of students' privacy is not significant.

C

Finally, this Court must consider the nature and immediacy of the government's concerns and the efficacy of the Policy in meeting them. *See Vernonia,*

515 U.S., at 660. This Court has already articulated in detail the importance of the governmental concern in preventing drug use by schoolchildren. The drug abuse problem among our Nation's youth has hardly abated since *Vernonia* was decided in 1995. In fact, evidence suggests that it has only grown worse.[3] As in *Vernonia*, "the necessity for the State to act is magnified by the fact that this evil is being visited not just upon individuals at large, but upon children for whom it has undertaken a special responsibility of care and direction." *Id.*, at 662. The health and safety risks identified in *Vernonia* apply with equal force to Tecumseh's children. Indeed, the nationwide drug epidemic makes the war against drugs a pressing concern in every school.

Additionally, the School District in this case has presented specific evidence of drug use at Tecumseh schools. Teachers testified that they had seen students who appeared to be under the influence of drugs and that they had heard students speaking openly about using drugs. See, *e.g.*, App. 72 (deposition of Dean Rogers); *id.*, at 115 (deposition of Sheila Evans). A drug dog found marijuana cigarettes near the school parking lot. Police officers once found drugs or drug paraphernalia in a car driven by a Future Farmers of America member. And the school board president reported that people in the community were calling the board to discuss the "drug situation." See 115 F. Supp. 2d, at 1285–1286. We decline to second-guess the finding of the District Court that "[v]iewing the evidence as a whole, it cannot be reasonably disputed that the [School District] was faced with a 'drug problem' when it adopted the Policy." *Id.*, at 1287.

Respondents consider the proffered evidence insufficient and argue that there is no "real and immediate interest" to justify a policy of drug testing nonathletes. Brief for Respondents 32. We have recognized, however, that "[a] demonstrated problem of drug abuse . . . [is] not in all cases necessary to the validity of a testing regime," but that some showing does "shore up an assertion of special need for a suspicionless general search program." *Chandler* v. *Miller*, 520 U.S. 305, 319 (1997). The School District has provided sufficient evidence to shore up the need for its drug testing program.

Furthermore, this Court has not required a particularized or pervasive drug problem before allowing the government to conduct suspicionless drug testing. For instance, in *Von Raab* the Court upheld the drug testing of customs officials on a purely preventive basis, without any documented history of drug use by such officials. See 489 U.S., at 673. In response to the lack of evidence relating to drug use, the Court noted generally that "drug abuse is one of the most serious problems confronting our society today," and that programs to prevent and detect drug use among customs officials could not be deemed unreasonable. *Id.*, at 674; cf. *Skinner*, 489 U.S., at 607, and n. 1 (noting nationwide studies that identified on-the-job alcohol and drug use by railroad employees). Likewise, the need to prevent and deter the substantial harm of childhood drug use provides the necessary immediacy for a school testing policy. Indeed, it would make little sense to require a school district to wait for a substantial portion of its students to begin using drugs before it was allowed to institute a drug testing program designed to deter drug use.

Given the nationwide epidemic of drug use, and the evidence of increased drug use in Tecumseh schools, it was entirely reasonable for the School District to enact this particular drug testing policy. We reject the Court of Appeals' novel test that "any district seeking to impose a random suspicionless drug testing policy as a condition to participation in a school activity must demonstrate that there is some identifiable drug abuse problem among a sufficient number of those subject to the testing, such that testing that group of students will actually redress its drug problem." 242 F. 3d, at 1278. Among other problems, it would be difficult to administer such a test. As we cannot articulate a threshold level of drug use that would suffice to justify a drug testing program for schoolchildren, we refuse to fashion what would in effect be a constitutional quantum of drug use necessary to show a "drug problem."

Respondents also argue that the testing of nonathletes does not implicate any safety concerns, and that safety is a "crucial factor" in applying the special needs framework. Brief for Respondents 25–27. They contend that there must be "surpassing safety interests," *Skinner, supra,* at 634, or "extraordinary safety and national security hazards," *Von Raab, supra,* at 674, in order to override the usual protections of the Fourth Amendment. See Brief for Respondents 25–26. Respondents are correct that safety factors into the special needs analysis, but the safety interest furthered by drug testing is undoubtedly substantial for all children, athletes and nonathletes alike. We know all too well that drug use carries a variety of health risks for children, including death from overdose.

We also reject respondents' argument that drug testing must presumptively be based upon an individualized reasonable suspicion of wrongdoing because such a testing regime would be less intrusive. In this context, the Fourth Amendment does not require a finding of individualized suspicion, and we decline to impose such a requirement on schools attempting to prevent and detect drug use by students. Moreover, we question whether testing based on individualized suspicion in fact would be less intrusive. Such a regime would place an additional burden on public school teachers who are already tasked with the difficult job of maintaining order and discipline. A program of individualized suspicion might unfairly target members of unpopular groups. The fear of lawsuits resulting from such targeted searches may chill enforcement of the program, rendering it ineffective in combating drug use. See *Vernonia,* 515 U.S., at 663–664 (offering similar reasons for why "testing based on 'suspicion' of drug use would not be better, but worse"). In any case, this Court has repeatedly stated that reasonableness under the Fourth Amendment does not require employing the least intrusive means, because "[t]he logic of such elaborate less-restrictive-alternative arguments could raise insuperable barriers to the exercise of virtually all search-and-seizure powers." *Martinez-Fuerte,* 428 U.S., at 556–557, n. 12; see also *Skinner, supra,* at 624 ("[A] showing of individualized suspicion is not a constitutional floor, below which a search must be presumed unreasonable").

Finally, we find that testing students who participate in extracurricular activities is a reasonably effective means of addressing the School District's legitimate concerns in preventing, deterring, and detecting drug use. While in *Vernonia* there might have been a closer fit between the testing of athletes and the trial court's finding that the drug problem was "fueled by the 'role model' effect of athletes' drug use," such a finding was not essential to the holding. 515 U.S., at 663; cf. *id.,* at 684–685 (O'CONNOR, J., dissenting) (questioning the extent of the drug problem, especially as applied to athletes). *Vernonia* did not require the school to test the group of students most likely to use drugs, but rather considered the constitutionality of the program in the context of the public school's custodial responsibilities. Evaluating the Policy in this context, we conclude that the drug testing of Tecumseh students who participate in extracurricular activities effectively serves the School District's interest in protecting the safety and health of its students.

III

Within the limits of the Fourth Amendment, local school boards must assess the desirability of drug testing schoolchildren. In upholding the constitutionality of the Policy, we express no opinion as to its wisdom. Rather, we hold only that Tecumseh's Policy is a reasonable means of furthering the School District's important interest in preventing and deterring drug use among its schoolchildren. Accordingly, we reverse the judgment of the Court of Appeals.

It is so ordered.

Notes

1. JUSTICE GINSBURG argues that *Vernonia School Dist. 47J* v. *Acton,* 515 U.S. 646 (1995), depended on the fact that the drug testing program applied only to student athletes. But even the passage cited by the dissent manifests the supplemental nature of this factor, as the Court in *Vernonia* stated that "[l]egitimate privacy expectations are *even less* with regard to student athletes." See *post,* at 5 (citing *Vernonia,* 515 U.S., at 657) (emphasis added). In upholding the drug testing program in *Vernonia,* we considered the school context "[c]entral" and "[t]he most significant element." 515 U.S., at 654, 665. This hefty weight on the side of the school's balance applies with similar force in this case even though we undertake a separate balancing with regard to this particular program.

2. JUSTICE GINSBURG's observations with regard to extracurricular activities apply with equal force to athletics. See *post,* at 4 ("Participation in such [extracurricular] activities is a key component of school life, essential in reality for students applying to college, and, for all participants, a significant contributor to the breadth and quality of the educational experience").

3. For instance, the number of 12th graders using any illicit drug increased from 48.4 percent in 1995 to 53.9 percent in 2001. The number of 12th graders reporting they had used marijuana jumped from 41.7 percent to 49.0 percent during that same period. See Department of Health and Human Services, Monitoring the Future: National Results on Adolescent Drug Use, Overview of Key Findings (2001) (Table 1).

➡ NO

Dissenting Opinion of Ruth Bader Ginsburg

J USTICE GINSBURG, with whom JUSTICE STEVENS, JUSTICE O'CONNOR, and JUSTICE SOUTER join, dissenting.

Seven years ago, in *Vernonia School Dist. 47J* v. *Acton,* 515 U.S. 646 (1995), this Court determined that a school district's policy of randomly testing the urine of its student athletes for illicit drugs did not violate the Fourth Amendment. In so ruling, the Court emphasized that drug use "increase[d] the risk of sports-related injury" and that Vernonia's athletes were the "leaders" of an aggressive local "drug culture" that had reached "'epidemic proportions.'" *Id.,* at 649. Today, the Court relies upon *Vernonia* to permit a school district with a drug problem its superintendent repeatedly described as "not . . . major" to test the urine of an academic team member solely by reason of her participation in a nonathletic, competitive extracurricular activity–participation associated with neither special dangers from, nor particular predilections for, drug use.

"[T]he legality of a search of a student," this Court has instructed, "should depend simply on the reasonableness, under all the circumstances, of the search." *New Jersey* v. *T. L. O.,* 469 U.S. 325, 341 (1985). Although "'special needs' inhere in the public school context," see *ante,* at 5 (quoting *Vernonia,* 515 U.S., at 653), those needs are not so expansive or malleable as to render reasonable any program of student drug testing a school district elects to install. The particular testing program upheld today is not reasonable, it is capricious, even perverse: Petitioners' policy targets for testing a student population least likely to be at risk from illicit drugs and their damaging effects. I therefore dissent.

I

A

A search unsupported by probable cause nevertheless may be consistent with the Fourth Amendment "when special needs, beyond the normal need for law

From *Board of Education of Independent School District No. 92 of Pottawatomie County et al. v. Lindsay Earls et al.,* 536 U.S. ____ (2002). Some case citations omitted.

enforcement, make the warrant and probable-cause requirement impracticable." *Griffin* v. *Wisconsin,* 483 U.S. 868, 873 (1987) (internal quotation marks omitted). In *Vernonia,* this Court made clear that "such 'special needs' . . . exist in the public school context." 515 U.S., at 653 (quoting *Griffin,* 483 U.S., at 873). The Court observed:

> "[W]hile children assuredly do not 'shed their constitutional rights . . . at the schoolhouse gate,' *Tinker* v. *Des Moines Independent Community School Dist.,* 393 U.S. 503, 506 (1969), the nature of those rights is what is appropriate for children in school. . . . Fourth Amendment rights, no less than First and Fourteenth Amendment rights, are different in public schools than elsewhere; the 'reasonableness' inquiry cannot disregard the schools' custodial and tutelary responsibility for children." 515 U.S., at 655–656 (other citations omitted).

The *Vernonia* Court concluded that a public school district facing a disruptive and explosive drug abuse problem sparked by members of its athletic teams had "special needs" that justified suspicionless testing of district athletes as a condition of their athletic participation.

This case presents circumstances dispositively different from those of *Vernonia.* True, as the Court stresses, Tecumseh students participating in competitive extracurricular activities other than athletics share two relevant characteristics with the athletes of *Vernonia.* First, both groups attend public schools. "[O]ur decision in *Vernonia,*" the Court states, "depended primarily upon the school's custodial responsibility and authority." *Ante,* at 7; see also *ante,* at 3 (BREYER, J., concurring) (school districts act *in loco parentis*). Concern for student health and safety is basic to the school's caretaking, and it is undeniable that "drug use carries a variety of health risks for children, including death from overdose." *Ante,* at 13 (majority opinion).

Those risks, however, are present for *all* schoolchildren. *Vernonia* cannot be read to endorse invasive and suspicionless drug testing of all students upon any evidence of drug use, solely because drugs jeopardize the life and health of those who use them. Many children, like many adults, engage in dangerous activities on their own time; that the children are enrolled in school scarcely allows government to monitor all such activities. If a student has a reasonable subjective expectation of privacy in the personal items she brings to school, see *T. L. O.,* 469 U.S., at 338–339, surely she has a similar expectation regarding the chemical composition of her urine. Had the *Vernonia* Court agreed that public school attendance, in and of itself, permitted the State to test each student's blood or urine for drugs, the opinion in *Vernonia* could have saved many words. See, *e.g.,* 515 U.S., at 662 ("[I]t must not be lost sight of that [the Vernonia School District] program is directed . . . to drug use by school athletes, where the risk of immediate physical harm to the drug user or those with whom he is playing his sport is particularly high.").

The second commonality to which the Court points is the voluntary character of both interscholastic athletics and other competitive extracurricular activities. "By choosing to 'go out for the team,' [school athletes] voluntarily subject themselves to a degree of regulation even higher than that imposed on students generally." *Id.,* at 657. Comparably, the Court today observes, "students who participate in competitive extracurricular activities voluntarily subject themselves to" additional rules not applicable to other students. *Ante,* at 7.

The comparison is enlightening. While extracurricular activities are "voluntary" in the sense that they are not required for graduation, they are part of the school's educational program; for that reason, the petitioner (hereinafter School District) is justified in expending public resources to make them available. Participation in such activities is a key component of school life, essential in reality for students applying to college, and, for all participants, a significant contributor to the breadth and quality of the educational experience. Students "volunteer" for extracurricular pursuits in the same way they might volunteer for honors classes: They subject themselves to additional requirements, but they do so in order to take full advantage of the education offered them. Cf. *Lee* v. *Weisman,* 505 U.S. 577, 595 (1992) ("Attendance may not be required by official decree, yet it is apparent that a student is not free to absent herself from the graduation exercise in any real sense of the term 'voluntary,' for absence would require forfeiture of those intangible benefits which have motivated the student through youth and all her high school years.").

Voluntary participation in athletics has a distinctly different dimension: Schools regulate student athletes discretely because competitive school sports by their nature require communal undress and, more important, expose students to physical risks that schools have a duty to mitigate. For the very reason that schools cannot offer a program of competitive athletics without intimately affecting the privacy of students, *Vernonia* reasonably analogized school athletes to "adults who choose to participate in a closely regulated industry." 515 U.S., at 657 (internal quotation marks omitted). Industries fall within the closely regulated category when the nature of their activities requires substantial government oversight. See, *e.g., United States* v. *Biswell,* 406 U.S. 311, 315–316 (1972). Interscholastic athletics similarly require close safety and health regulation; a school's choir, band, and academic team do not.

In short, *Vernonia* applied, it did not repudiate, the principle that "the legality of a search of a student should depend simply on the reasonableness, *under all the circumstances,* of the search." *T. L. O.,* 469 U.S., at 341 (emphasis added). Enrollment in a public school, and election to participate in school activities beyond the bare minimum that the curriculum requires, are indeed factors relevant to reasonableness, but they do not on their own justify intrusive, suspicionless searches. *Vernonia,* accordingly, did not rest upon these factors; instead, the Court performed what today's majority aptly describes as a "fact-specific balancing," *ante,* at 6. Balancing of that order, applied to the facts now before the Court, should yield a result other than the one the Court announces today.

B

Vernonia initially considered "the nature of the privacy interest upon which the search [there] at issue intrude[d]." 515 U.S., at 654. The Court emphasized that student athletes' expectations of privacy are necessarily attenuated:

> "Legitimate privacy expectations are even less with regard to student ath-
> letes. School sports are not for the bashful. They require 'suiting up' before
> each practice or event, and showering and changing afterwards. Public
> school locker rooms, the usual sites for these activities, are not notable for
> the privacy they afford. The locker rooms in Vernonia are typical: No indi-
> vidual dressing rooms are provided; shower heads are lined up along a wall,
> unseparated by any sort of partition or curtain; not even all the toilet stalls
> have doors. . . . [T]here is an element of communal undress inherent in ath-
> letic participation." *Id.,* at 657 (internal quotation marks omitted).

Competitive extracurricular activities other than athletics, however, serve students of all manner: the modest and shy along with the bold and uninhibited.
Activities of the kind plaintiff-respondent Lindsay Earls pursued—choir, show
choir, marching band, and academic team—afford opportunities to gain self-
assurance, to "come to know faculty members in a less formal setting than the
typical classroom," and to acquire "positive social supports and networks
[that] play a critical role in periods of heightened stress." Brief for American
Academy of Pediatrics et al. as *Amici Curiae* 13.

On "occasional out-of-town trips," students like Lindsay Earls "must
sleep together in communal settings and use communal bathrooms." 242 F.
3d 1264, 1275 (CA10 2001). But those situations are hardly equivalent to the
routine communal undress associated with athletics; the School District itself
admits that when such trips occur, "public-like restroom facilities," which presumably include enclosed stalls, are ordinarily available for changing, and that
"more modest students" find other ways to maintain their privacy. Brief for
Petitioners 34.[1]

After describing school athletes' reduced expectation of privacy, the
Vernonia Court turned to "the character of the intrusion . . . complained of." 515
U.S., at 658. Observing that students produce urine samples in a bathroom stall
with a coach or teacher outside, *Vernonia* typed the privacy interests compromised by the process of obtaining samples "negligible." *Ibid.* As to the required
pretest disclosure of prescription medications taken, the Court assumed that "the
School District would have permitted [a student] to provide the requested information in a confidential manner—for example, in a sealed envelope delivered to
the testing lab." *Id.,* at 660. On that assumption, the Court concluded that
Vernonia's athletes faced no significant invasion of privacy.

In this case, however, Lindsay Earls and her parents allege that the School
District handled personal information collected under the policy carelessly, with
little regard for its confidentiality. Information about students' prescription
drug use, they assert, was routinely viewed by Lindsay's choir teacher, who left
files containing the information unlocked and unsealed, where others, including students, could see them; and test results were given out to all activity sponsors
whether or not they had a clear "need to know." See Brief for Respondents 6,
24; App. 105–106, 131. But see *id.,* at 199 (policy requires that "[t]he medication list shall be submitted to the lab in a sealed and confidential envelope
and shall not be viewed by district employees").

In granting summary judgment to the School District, the District Court observed that the District's "Policy expressly provides for confidentiality of test results, and the Court must assume that the confidentiality provisions will be honored." 115 F. Supp. 2d 1281, 1293 (WD Okla. 2000). The assumption is unwarranted. Unlike *Vernonia,* where the District Court held a bench trial before ruling in the School District's favor, this case was decided by the District Court on summary judgment. At that stage, doubtful matters should not have been resolved in favor of the judgment seeker. See *United States* v. *Diebold, Inc.,* 369 U.S. 654, 655 (1962) (*per curiam*) ("On summary judgment the inferences to be drawn from the underlying facts contained in [affidavits, attached exhibits, and depositions] must be viewed in the light most favorable to the party opposing the motion."); see also 10A C. Wright, A. Miller, & M. Kane, Federal Practice and Procedure §2716, pp. 274–277 (3d ed. 1998).

Finally, the "nature and immediacy of the governmental concern," *Vernonia,* 515 U.S., at 660, faced by the Vernonia School District dwarfed that confronting Tecumseh administrators. Vernonia initiated its drug testing policy in response to an alarming situation: "[A] large segment of the student body, particularly those involved in interscholastic athletics, was in a state of rebellion . . . fueled by alcohol and drug abuse as well as the student[s'] misperceptions about the drug culture." *Id.,* at 649 (internal quotation marks omitted). Tecumseh, by contrast, repeatedly reported to the Federal Government during the period leading up to the adoption of the policy that "types of drugs [other than alcohol and tobacco] including controlled dangerous substances, are present [in the schools] but have not identified themselves as major problems at this time." 1998–1999 Tecumseh School's Application for Funds under the Safe and Drug-Free Schools and Communities Program, reprinted at App. 191; accord, 1996–1997 Application, reprinted at App. 186; 1995–1996 Application, reprinted at App. 180.[2] As the Tenth Circuit observed, "without a demonstrated drug abuse problem among the group being tested, the efficacy of the District's solution to its perceived problem is . . . greatly diminished." 242 F. 3d, at 1277.

The School District cites *Treasury Employees* v. *Von Raab,* 489 U.S. 656, 673–674 (1989), in which this Court permitted random drug testing of customs agents absent "any perceived drug problem among Customs employees," given that "drug abuse is one of the most serious problems confronting our society today." See also *Skinner* v. *Railway Labor Executives' Assn.,* 489 U.S. 602, 607, and n. 1 (1989) (upholding random drug and alcohol testing of railway employees based upon industry-wide, rather than railway-specific, evidence of drug and alcohol problems). The tests in *Von Raab* and *Railway Labor Executives,* however, were installed to avoid enormous risks to the lives and limbs of others, not dominantly in response to the health risks to users invariably present in any case of drug use. See *Von Raab,* 489 U.S., at 674 (drug use by customs agents involved in drug interdiction creates "extraordinary safety and national security hazards"); *Railway Labor Executives,* 489 U.S., at 628 (railway operators "discharge duties fraught with such risks of injury to others that even a momentary lapse of attention can have disastrous consequences"); see also *Chandler* v. *Miller,* 520 U.S. 305, 321 (1997) ("*Von Raab* must be read in its unique context").

Not only did the Vernonia and Tecumseh districts confront drug problems of distinctly different magnitudes, they also chose different solutions: Vernonia limited its policy to athletes; Tecumseh indiscriminately subjected to testing all participants in competitive extracurricular activities. Urging that "the safety interest furthered by drug testing is undoubtedly substantial for all children, athletes and nonathletes alike," *ante,* at 13, the Court cuts out an element essential to the *Vernonia* judgment. Citing medical literature on the effects of combining illicit drug use with physical exertion, the *Vernonia* Court emphasized that "the particular drugs screened by [Vernonia's] Policy have been demonstrated to pose substantial physical risks to athletes." 515 U.S., at 662; see also *id.,* at 666 (GINSBURG, J., concurring) (*Vernonia* limited to "those seeking to engage with others in team sports"). We have since confirmed that these special risks were necessary to our decision in *Vernonia.* See *Chandler,* 520 U.S., at 317 (*Vernonia* "emphasized the importance of deterring drug use by schoolchildren and the risk of injury a drug-using student athlete cast on himself and those engaged with him on the playing field"); see also *Ferguson* v. *Charleston,* 532 U.S. 67, 87 (2001) (KENNEDY, J., concurring) (Vernonia's policy had goal of "'[d]eterring drug use by our Nation's school-children,' and particularly by student-athletes, because 'the risk of immediate physical harm to the drug user or those with whom he is playing his sport is particularly high'") (quoting *Vernonia,* 515 U.S., at 661–662).

At the margins, of course, no policy of *random* drug testing is perfectly tailored to the harms it seeks to address. The School District cites the dangers faced by members of the band, who must "perform extremely precise routines with heavy equipment and instruments in close proximity to other students," and by Future Farmers of America, who "are required to individually control and restrain animals as large as 1500 pounds." Brief for Petitioners 43. For its part, the United States acknowledges that "the linebacker faces a greater risk of serious injury if he takes the field under the influence of drugs than the drummer in the halftime band," but parries that "the risk of injury to a student who is under the influence of drugs while playing golf, cross country, or volleyball (sports covered by the policy in *Vernonia*) is scarcely any greater than the risk of injury to a student . . . handling a 1500-pound steer (as [Future Farmers of America] members do) or working with cutlery or other sharp instruments (as [Future Home-makers of America] members do)." Brief for United States as *Amicus Curiae* 18. One can demur to the Government's view of the risks drug use poses to golfers, cf. *PGA TOUR, Inc.* v. *Martin,* 532 U.S. 661, 687 (2001) ("golf is a low intensity activity"), for golfers were surely as marginal among the linebackers, sprinters, and basketball players targeted for testing in Vernonia as steer-handlers are among the choristers, musicians, and academic-team members subject to urinalysis in Tecumseh.[3] Notwithstanding nightmarish images of out-of-control flatware, livestock run amok, and colliding tubas disturbing the peace and quiet of Tecumseh, the great majority of students the School District seeks to test in truth are engaged in activities that are not safety sensitive to an unusual degree. There is a difference between imperfect tailoring and no tailoring at all.

The Vernonia district, in sum, had two good reasons for testing athletes: Sports team members faced special health risks and they "were the leaders of the drug culture." *Vernonia,* 515 U.S., at 649. No similar reason, and no other tenable justification, explains Tecumseh's decision to target for testing all participants in every competitive extracurricular activity. See *Chandler,* 520 U.S., at 319 (drug testing candidates for office held incompatible with Fourth Amendment because program was "not well designed to identify candidates who violate antidrug laws").

Nationwide, students who participate in extracurricular activities are significantly less likely to develop substance abuse problems than are their less-involved peers. See, *e.g.,* N. Zill, C. Nord, & L. Loomis, Adolescent Time Use, Risky Behavior, and Outcomes 52 (1995) (tenth graders "who reported spending no time in school-sponsored activities were . . . 49 percent more likely to have used drugs" than those who spent 1–4 hours per week in such activities). Even if students might be deterred from drug use in order to preserve their extracurricular eligibility, it is at least as likely that other students might forgo their extracurricular involvement in order to avoid detection of their drug use. Tecumseh's policy thus falls short doubly if deterrence is its aim: It invades the privacy of students who need deterrence least, and risks steering students at greatest risk for substance abuse away from extracurricular involvement that potentially may palliate drug problems.[4]

To summarize, this case resembles *Vernonia* only in that the School Districts in both cases conditioned engagement in activities outside the obligatory curriculum on random subjection to urinalysis. The defining characteristics of the two programs, however, are entirely dissimilar. The Vernonia district sought to test a subpopulation of students distinguished by their reduced expectation of privacy, their special susceptibility to drug-related injury, and their heavy involvement with drug use. The Tecumseh district seeks to test a much larger population associated with none of these factors. It does so, moreover, without carefully safeguarding student confidentiality and without regard to the program's untoward effects. A program so sweeping is not sheltered by *Vernonia;* its unreasonable reach renders it impermissible under the Fourth Amendment.

II

In *Chandler,* this Court inspected "Georgia's requirement that candidates for state office pass a drug test"; we held that the requirement "d[id] not fit within the closely guarded category of constitutionally permissible suspicion-less searches." 520 U.S., at 309. Georgia's testing prescription, the record showed, responded to no "concrete danger," *id.,* at 319, was supported by no evidence of a particular problem, and targeted a group not involved in "high-risk, safety-sensitive tasks," *id.,* at 321–322. We concluded:

> "What is left, after close review of Georgia's scheme, is the image the State seeks to project. By requiring candidates for public office to submit to drug testing, Georgia displays its commitment to the struggle against drug abuse. . . . The need revealed, in short, is symbolic, not 'special,' as that term draws meaning from our case law." *Ibid.*

Close review of Tecumseh's policy compels a similar conclusion. That policy was not shown to advance the "'special needs' [existing] in the public school context [to maintain] . . . swift and informal disciplinary procedures . . . [and] order in the schools," *Vernonia*, 515 U.S., at 653 (internal quotation marks omitted). See *supra*, at 5–6, 8–11. What is left is the School District's undoubted purpose to heighten awareness of its abhorrence of, and strong stand against, drug abuse. But the desire to augment communication of this message does not trump the right of persons—even of children within the schoolhouse gate—to be "secure in their persons . . . against unreasonable searches and seizures." U.S. Const., Amdt. 4.

In *Chandler*, the Court referred to a pathmarking dissenting opinion in which "Justice Brandeis recognized the importance of teaching by example: 'Our Government is the potent, the omnipresent teacher. For good or for ill, it teaches the whole people by its example.'" 520 U.S., at 322 (quoting *Olmstead* v. *United States*, 277 U.S. 438, 485 (1928)). That wisdom should guide decision-makers in the instant case: The government is nowhere more a teacher than when it runs a public school.

It is a sad irony that the petitioning School District seeks to justify its edict here by trumpeting "the schools' custodial and tutelary responsibility for children." *Vernonia*, 515 U.S., at 656. In regulating an athletic program or endeavoring to combat an exploding drug epidemic, a school's custodial obligations may permit searches that would otherwise unacceptably abridge students' rights. When custodial duties are not ascendant, however, schools' tutelary obligations to their students require them to "teach by example" by avoiding symbolic measures that diminish constitutional protections. "That [schools] are educating the young for citizenship is reason for scrupulous protection of Constitutional freedoms of the individual, if we are not to strangle the free mind at its source and teach youth to discount important principles of our government as mere platitudes." *West Virginia Bd. of Ed.* v. *Barnette*, 319 U.S. 624, 637 (1943).

⌾

For the reasons stated, I would affirm the judgment of the Tenth Circuit declaring the testing policy at issue unconstitutional.

Notes

1. According to Tecumseh's choir teacher, choir participants who chose not to wear their choir uniforms to school on the days of competitions could change either in "a rest room in a building" or on the bus, where "[m]any of them have figured out how to [change] without having [anyone] . . . see anything." 2 Appellants' App. in No. 00–6128 (CA10), p. 296.

2. The Court finds it sufficient that there be evidence of *some* drug use in Tecumseh's schools: "As we cannot articulate a threshold level of drug use that would suffice to justify a drug testing program for schoolchildren, we refuse to fashion what would in effect be a constitutional quantum of drug use necessary to show a 'drug problem.'" *Ante*, at 12. One need not establish a bright-line "constitutional quantum of drug use" to recognize the relevance of the superintendent's reports characterizing drug use among Tecumseh's students as "not . . . [a] major proble[m]," App. 180, 186, 191.

3.   Cross-country runners and volleyball players, by contrast, engage in substantial physical exertion. See *Vernonia School Dist. 47J* v. *Acton* 515 U.S. 646, 663 (1995) (describing special dangers of combining drug use with athletics generally).

4.   The Court notes that programs of individualized suspicion, unlike those using random testing, "might unfairly target members of unpopular groups." *Ante,* at 13; see also *ante,* at 4 (BREYER, J., concurring). Assuming, *arguendo,* that this is so, the School District here has not exchanged individualized suspicion for random testing. It has installed random testing in addition to, rather than in lieu of, testing "at any time when there is reasonable suspicion." App. 197.

POSTSCRIPT

Is Drug Use Testing of Students Who Participate in Extracurricular Activities Permitted Under the Fourth Amendment?

In a concurring opinion in the case of *New Jersey v. T.L.O.*, 469 U.S. 325, 350 (1985), the late justice Lewis Powell observed that "the primary duty of school officials and teachers . . . is the education and training of young people. A state has a compelling interest in assuring that schools meet this responsibility. Without first establishing discipline and maintaining order, teachers cannot begin to educate their students." Drug abuse among students obviously threatens the maintenance of discipline in the schools and, as a result, the successful completion of the mission identified by Justice Powell. The U.S. Supreme Court's decision in *Vernonia* seemed to have established a reasonably clear framework to guide other school districts that wished to implement suspicionless drug-testing programs that would withstand challenges under the Fourth Amendment. The uncertainty that remained, however, concerned the question of whether such a drug-testing program must be limited to student athletes or whether the program could target the entire student population. The decision in this case extends the boundary but leaves open the question of whether a future case might extend the boundary even further.

Those who wish to read further in this area should begin with John Gilliom's *Surveillance, Privacy, and the Law: Employee Drug Testing and the Politics of Social Control* (University of Michigan Press, 1994). Although Gilliom addresses the question of employee drug testing in the workplace, he introduces the reader to the legal, political, and philosophical issues involved in drug testing more generally. For more specific treatments of the issue of student drug testing, see Caroline Slater Burnette, "Making Specimen Cups as Normal as Prom Night: The Implications of Board of Education v. Earls on Public Schools Across The Nation," 25 *Campbell Law Review* 71 (2002) and M. Casey Kucharson, "Please Report to the Principal's Office, Urine Trouble: The Effect of *Board of Education* v. *Earls* on America's Schoolchildren," 37 *Akron Law Rev.* 131 (2004). Steroids have been in the news because of its use by professional athletes and an article co-authored by the commissioner of baseball, Allan H. "Bud" Selig and Robert D. Manfred, Jr., "The Regulation of Nutritional Supplements in Professional Sports," 15 *Stan. L. & Pol'y Rev* 35 (2004). For a pro-drug-testing perspective, read the Federal Office of National Drug Control Policy report "What You Need to Know About Drug Testing in Schools" at http://www.whitehousedrugpolicy.gov/publications/drug_testing/. For information on issues relating to privacy rights, consult the Privacy Rights Clearinghouse at http://www.privacyrights.org and the Electronic Privacy Information Center at http://www.epic.org.

Internet References . . .

Organized Crime: A Crime Statistics Site

This is one of the best sites for finding out about crime statistics, where they come from, and how reliable they are.

http://www.crime.org

Politics1.com

This site links to organizations—representing the Left, the Right, and the middle— that are working on many controversial legal issues.

http://www.politics1.com/issues.htm

Law.com

At Law.com you can read about recent cases as well as current legal issues in the news.

http://www.lawnewsnetwork.com

Law and the Community

*W*hile we are all citizens of a state, we are also participants in various communities whose members generally hold shared values and hope to satisfy shared goals. The challenge of finding appropriate relationships between the individual, the state, and the community is examined in this section.

- Should the United States Require a Secure Identification System for Citizens?

- Are Blanket Prohibitions on Cross Burnings Unconstitutional?

- Should Same-Sex Couples Receive Constitutional Protection?

- Should Children with Disabilities Be Provided with Extraordinary Care in Order to Attend Regular Classes in Public Schools?

- Do Race-Conscious Programs in Public University Admissions Policies Violate the Fourteenth Amendment's Guarantee of Equal Protection Under the Law?

ISSUE 15

Should the United States Require a Secure Identification System for Citizens?

YES: Richard C. Barth, "On Understanding the Realities of REAL ID: A Review of Efforts to Secure Driver's Licenses and Identification Cards," from Testimony Before the Senate Committee on Homeland Security and Governmental Affairs (March 26, 2007)

NO: Timothy D. Sparapani, "The Real ID Act: An Unprecedented Threat to Privacy and Constitutional Rights," from Testimony Before the Senate Committee on Homeland Security and Government Affairs (March 26, 2007)

ISSUE SUMMARY

YES: Richard C. Barth, an assistant secretary for Policy Development in the Department of Homeland Security, argues that secure methods for identifying citizens is a necessary part of the War on Terror and will also reduce identity theft.

NO: Timothy D. Sparapani, legislative counsel for the American Civil Liberties Union, argues that the proposed system will require all citizens to carry a national identity card and that such a system will not deter terrorists but will invade privacy.

Consider the following two points of view about a federal law whose goal is for all states to issue driver's licenses that meet a set of specific conditions.

> The Real ID Act of 2005 is an $11 billion unfunded mandate on the states. The Real ID Act of 2005 is a backdoor attempt to institute a national ID card as more overt attempts to create a national ID card have always failed in the past. The Real ID Act of 2005 has serious constitutional and privacy problems. By requiring all states to issue driver's licenses to this new standard, the Federal Government is attempting to force the states to become part of a national database with 50,000 access points to sensitive data on every American Citizen. The opportunities for identity theft will multiply exponentially.

—Idaho Joint Memorial, March 12, 2007

On September 9, 2001, two days before 9/11 pilot Ziad Jarrah crashed a plane nose-first into a field in Pennsylvania, Jarrah was stopped for speeding. This could have led to trouble for him, and trouble for the entire 9/11 operation, but it did not. Instead, Jarrah simply drove away with a $270 speeding ticket. This would likely be the case today as well.

Why? Jarrah had obtained two driver licenses from the state of Florida—one on May 2 and the other on May 24, 2001. In addition, he fraudulently obtained a state-issued ID from Virginia on August 29. When he was stopped for speeding, we don't know which Florida license he presented to the officer.

Had REAL ID been in effect, Jarrah would have been limited to one active license and the officer could have checked for other violations. The officer could have checked an immigration database, which could have shown he had entered the U.S. illegally at least five times. Instead, the officer had none of this information. Jarrah got away with a ticket and he still had in his pocket the Virginia ID that he might need for the 9/11 operation. The operation remained unscathed.

—Janice L. Kephart, Former Counsel to the 9/11 Commission

This issue could have been placed in the first section of this book concerning law and the War on Terror since it is unlikely that the Real ID Act would have been passed if the events of September 11, 2001 had not occurred. It could also, quite reasonably, have been placed in the section on law and the individual since it touches on the issue of identity, perhaps the most fundamental of issues related to our individuality. It has been placed in this section because, as the introduction to this section of the book states, it is a pressing contemporary "challenge of finding appropriate relationships between the individual, the state, and the community."

The Real ID Act was an unusual piece of legislation. In February 2005, Congressman James Sensenbrenner of Wisconsin attached the Real ID Act to a defense appropriations bill. It was passed without any congressional hearings or debate and required state-issued driver's licenses to conform to a set of standards. If a state's licenses did not meet the standards, the licenses could not be used to board airplanes, enter federal buildings, or obtain other benefits for which proof of identity is required.

Congress did not provide any funding to states to carry out the process of issuing new licenses and the original date for implementing the act has been delayed until the end of 2009. Several states are resisting issuing the new licenses and the debate about them is likely to continue. The reasons for the controversy are represented in the following readings and relate not only to cost but to whether such licenses can effectively deter terrorism and how much of an invasion of privacy they are likely to be.

YES ←

Richard C. Barth

On Understanding the Realities of REAL ID: A Review of Efforts to Secure Driver's Licenses and Identification Cards

Chairman Akaka, Senator Voinovich and distinguished Members of the subcommittee, thank you for the opportunity to appear before you today to discuss REAL ID.

As you know, REAL ID is based on a recommendation of the 9/11 Commission. It is a recommendation to deter future terrorist acts that the Department of Homeland Security (DHS) strongly supports. Versions of this Act have passed Congress, twice: first, as part of the Intelligence Reform and Terrorism Prevention Act of 2004; and then, as the REAL ID Act of 2005.

On page 390 of its final report, the 9/11 Commission stated:

> "Secure identification should begin in the United States. The federal government should set standards for the issuance of birth certificates and sources of identification, such as driver's licenses. Fraud in identification documents is no longer just a problem of theft. At many entry points to vulnerable facilities, including gates for boarding aircraft, sources of identification are the last opportunity to ensure that people are who they say they are and to check whether they are terrorists."

All but one of the 9/11 hijackers acquired some form of U.S. identification document (ID). The remaining 18 hijackers fraudulently obtained 17 drivers licenses and 13 state issued identifications, and some even possessed duplicate driver's licenses. The pilot who crashed American Airlines Flight 77 into the Pentagon, Hani Hanjour, had ID cards from three states. The driver's licenses and state IDs enabled the hijackers to maneuver throughout the United States in order to plan and execute critical elements of their mission. Using these documents, they were able to rent cars, travel, take flying lessons and board airplanes. The 9/11 hijackers evidently believed that holding driver's licenses and ID cards would allow them to operate freely in our country. And they were right. The hijackers viewed U.S. driver's licenses and ID cards as easy and convenient ways to become "Americanized."

From Testimony before the Senate Committee on Homeland Security and Governmental Affairs, March 26, 2007.

The 9/11 hijackers are not the only terrorists operating inside the U.S. to have used fraudulently obtained IDs. The terrorist who killed two employees outside CIA headquarters in 1993, Mir Aimal Kansi, also exploited the loopholes in getting a driver's license. He was present illegally as a visa overstay, but was still able to obtain a valid driver's license.

Congress's recognition of the significant vulnerabilities in our current state systems of issuing driver's licenses led to the passage of the REAL ID Act.

The Department believes that the 9/11 Commission's REAL ID recommendation is one of the linchpins of our entire national security strategy. Counsel to the 9/11 Commission, Janice Kephart, said the recommendation was "perhaps the single most effective measure the United States can accomplish to lay the necessary framework for sustainable national and economic security and public safety" *(Identity and Security,* February 2007, page 1). Said another way, identity document security is a foundational layer for security in the United States. If we cannot verify that people are who they say they are and if we allow loopholes in obtaining driver's licenses and IDs to exist, DHS's job and that of law enforcement becomes exponentially more difficult. We know of instances where law enforcement pulled over one or more of the terrorists, then let them go. Sadly, four of the hijackers had been stopped for traffic violations in various States while out of legal immigration status.

As required by statute, DHS proposed for public comment REAL ID regulations that would create minimum standards for State driver's licenses and identification cards issued on or after May 11, 2008. Under this proposal, States must certify that they are in compliance with these requirements, and DHS must concur, before the driver's licenses and identification cards that the States issue may be accepted by Federal agencies for specified official purposes. Because DHS recognizes that not all driver's licenses and identification cards can be reissued by May 11, 2008, the proposal provides a five-year phase-in period for driver's license or identification card renewals. The proposed rule also includes an extension through December 31, 2009, for States requesting it. Therefore, all driver's licenses and identification cards that are intended to be accepted for official purposes as defined in these regulations must be REAL ID licenses and identification cards by May 11, 2013.

Key features of the proposed rule include the following:

- *Applicant documentation.* States would require individuals obtaining driver's licenses or personal identification cards to present documentation to establish identity—U.S. nationality or lawful immigration status as defined by the Act, date of birth, social security number (SSN) or ineligibility for SSN, and principal residence. States may establish an exceptions process for the documentation requirement, provided that each such exception is fully detailed in the applicant's motor vehicle record.
- *Verification requirements.* States would verify the issuance, validity, and completeness of a document presented. This proposal specifies electronic verification methods depending on the category of the documents.
- *Information on driver's licenses and identification cards.* The following information would be required to appear on State-issued driver's licenses and identification cards: full legal name, date of birth, gender, a unique

driver's license or identification card number (not the SSN), a full facial digital photograph, address of principal residence (with certain exceptions), issue and expiration dates, signature, physical security features and a common machine-readable technology (MRT).

- *Security features on the card.* The proposal contains standards for physical security features on the card designed to prevent tampering, counterfeiting or duplication for a fraudulent purpose, and a common MRT with defined data elements.
- *Physical security/security plans.* Each State must prepare a comprehensive security plan for all state Department of Motor Vehicle (DMV) offices and driver's license/identification card storage and production facilities, databases and systems and submit these plans to DHS as part of its certification package.
- *Employee background checks.* States would conduct name-based and fingerprint-based criminal history records checks against State criminal records and the FBI's National Crime information Center and Integrated Automated Fingerprint Identification System, respectively, on employees working in State DMVs who have the ability to affect the identity information that appears on the driver's license or identification card, who have access to the production process, or who are involved in the manufacture of the driver's licenses and identification cards. States would pay a fee to the FBI to cover the cost of each check. States would also conduct a financial history check on these employees.
- *State certification process.* Similar to Department of Transportation regulations governing State administration of commercial driver's licenses, States will be required to submit a certification and specified documents to DHS to demonstrate compliance with these regulations and demonstrate continued compliance annually.
- *Database connectivity.* States would be required to provide all other States with electronic access to specific information contained in the motor vehicle database of the State. States would have to verify with all other States that an applicant does not already hold a valid REAL ID in another State.

As demonstrated by the details of the proposed rule, REAL ID is not a national identification card and it does not create a national database. It is, however, a network-of-networks. All 50 States and U.S. territories are asked to meet a minimum standard of security for issuing state drivers licenses and IDs. Some States may opt to do more to enhance security. They will be given the flexibility to do that. And it is the States, not the Federal government, that will collect and store the information submitted to support issuance of the card as is the current practice. Furthermore, States will have the option of issuing non-REAL ID drivers' licenses if they choose.

REAL ID is a collaborative process with the States and territories. The NPRM reflects input from States and territories, including the extension for States which was previously touched upon. Secretary Chertoff announced on March 1st that States may use up to 20% of their Homeland Security Grant Program funds to comply with REAL ID. Again, here the Department is flexible and eagerly awaits further input by the States and territories during the comment period.

REAL ID is technically feasible. . . . [T]here is already widespread activity being undertaken throughout the country by States to improve their standards for issuing ID cards. In accordance with the proposed rule, States would be required to do checks against four databases before issuing a REAL ID license or identification card. Some States are already beginning to do checks against these databases. Forty-eight of the fifty States and the District of Columbia are connected to the SSOLV (Social Security On-Line Verification) database operated by the Social Security Administration. Twenty States are using the SAVE (Systematic Alien Verification for Entitlements) database operated by DHS, and the vast majority of the remainder have entered into memoranda of understanding to work with DHS toward SAVE participation on or before May 11, 2008. In FY06, participating State DMVs ran 1.2 million queries against the SAVE System. Three States are involved in a pilot with National Association for Public Health Statistics and Information Systems (NAPHSIS) to check birth certificates via the EVVE (Electronic Verification of Vital Events) database and seven States already are responding to EVVE requests. Finally, the State Department will be developing the system to permit DMVs to check electronically that a passport an individual presents to the DMV has been lawfully issued. Work here is still ongoing, but we have been fully engaging with State on this important matter.

Returning to the issue of Social Security number verification, a recent state audit report showed 27,000 people in North Carolina used bogus Social Security numbers when applying for a driver's license or state ID. About half of these belong to persons that are shown as deceased in SSA records. This report highlights the security need for crosschecking the databases required under REAL ID.

At the end of the day, what does all this look like? While the rule is still pending, there is no definitive answer quite yet. However, the final answer is that the REAL ID standards will likely draw from all the best and most secure State practices already in place. Critics have charged that there are privacy issues connected with the requirement to verify an individual's data. However, three of the four systems are already used by the States. In addition, the NPRM only requires State-to-State data exchange for those who possess a REAL ID license. This mandate simply extends data exchange requirements already successfully implemented in the Commercial Driver's License Information System (CDLIS). Decades ago, Congress enacted the Commercial Motor Vehicle Safety Act of 1986 to improve highway safety because prior to the Act, commercial drivers were able to obtain multiple licenses from different States, allowing persons to hide convictions and unqualified applicants to get licensed. CDLIS has eliminated this security problem successfully and has not had any privacy breaches since it began. In fact, once the program was up and running—during a four-year period from 1992 to 1996—an estimated 871,000 commercial motor vehicle operators were disqualified. With the potential of multiple licenses hiding convictions, etc. many of these drivers could have continued driving "under the radar screen" of law enforcement and escaped detection by States.

If the system the Department of Homeland Security proposes with REAL ID denies just a few bad actors, from hiding behind fraudulent identities, what a boon to national security that would be. And, at a minimum, it makes it tougher for terrorists to do their job. It destabilizes a sure-fire method employed by the 9/11 hijackers as well as other terrorists to become, as they perceived, "Americanized" simply by holding a license that grants broad entry and unlocks many doors in our society.

The 1986 Act also prompted motor carriers all across the country to strengthen safety departments and employee training programs. Much the same is true of REAL ID, which requires DMVs to train their employees to spot faulty documentation and stop terrorists or other criminals from exploiting loopholes that currently exist in obtaining a driver's license or state ID.

There have been concerns voiced about REAL ID creating a national identification card and national database. These concerns are simply not true. The proposed rule maintains the existing practices of how information is stored, collected and disseminated at the State and local level. The fact remains that REAL ID does not give the Federal government any greater access to the information than it had before.

States and territories would be required to include a Comprehensive Security Plan to show how information will be safeguarded, including procedures to prevent unauthorized access or use, and procedures for document retention and destruction. Additionally, DHS would require each state to submit a privacy policy.

Contrary to some press reports, DMV employees would not be able to "fish" around through other State or territory databases for personal information. Nor does the proposed rule require radio frequency identification (RFID).

Another aspect of privacy is encryption of data in the networks and of data on the cards. Since most States and territories do not encrypt information contained in their 2D barcodes, the Department does not require it in the proposed rule. DHS is seeking recommendations from the States, territories, and privacy community regarding the need for encryption as well as cost-effective ways to deploy it while still providing access to critical information to law enforcement. We do favor encryption of data flowing over the networks. We will be working with our partners, the States, to deploy the right solution that protects privacy while avoiding heavy costs on the States. Good encryption protection generally requires frequent re-keying of the encryption codes. While this is feasible for the networks carrying data between various Federal and State agencies, it appears to us at this time to be infeasible for the data stored on that cards that must be accessible to law enforcement officials.

The Department has been working with the privacy community on areas of common interest to protect personal information. Corruption within DMVs can sometimes be a problem. To give you a few examples, two DMV employees in Connecticut were charged in December of 2004 with stealing licensed drivers' identities in order to issue fake driver's licenses to illegal immigrants. In the same case, the identities of two males were stolen to commit credit card and bank account fraud in the amount of $15,000. At that same time, a New York ring was uncovered where five DMV employees were selling fake IDs for up to $4,000 apiece. Three buyers were illegal immigrants from Pakistan.

We believe REAL ID has benefits beyond national security. One such benefit is the prevention of identity theft. The system of gathering and verifying information and issuing REAL ID cards will make it much more difficult for document counterfeiters and identity thieves to steal identity from unsuspecting citizens and obtain a valid REAL ID card. A more stringent process in place for obtaining a driver's license will add a layer of defense in the fight against identity theft. Currently, it's all too easy to perpetrate identity theft and cross-checking vital documents prior to issuing a license will help crack down on this behavior.

There are many ways for a resourceful thief to commit identity theft. Some common forms of identity theft that could include use of a fraudulent driver's license are: bank fraud, employment-related fraud, evasion of legal sanctions, medical fraud, insurance fraud, and house and apartment rental fraud. These types of identity theft accounted for a significant percentage of all reported incidents in 2005. The total U.S. cost of identity theft in 2005 was $64 billion, of which $18.1 billion was for theft involving a license, as we document in the economic impact analysis published with the proposed rule. A more recent survey by the Council of Better Business Bureaus *(2006 Identity Fraud Survey Report, Javelin Strategy & Research)* found that roughly 8.9 million U.S. adults were victims of identity theft in 2006. Just resolving the theft cost for the average victim was approximately $422 and took 40 hours. Applying the average wage rate at that t time (i.e., $17 per hour), the economic value of the time victims spent just resolving identity theft has been nearly $10 billion. These figures were used by the Department in the Economic Analysis for REAL ID. But don't just take our word for it. A study by the Identity Theft Resource Center *(Identity Theft: The Aftermath 2004)* found that victims spent an average of 330 hours to recover from identity theft. Forty percent of the victims reported losses greater than $15,000. Regardless of which way you slice it, the loss of time and money is significant. These studies do not even include the mental duress victims go through, which must be significant.

Widespread acceptance of REAL ID as required identification could have other benefits as well, such as reducing unlawful employment, voter fraud, and underage drinking.

Initial issuance of REAL IDs will present challenges. However, for people who are organized and have their birth certificate, social security card and marriage certificate all in one place, it will not be unduly inconvenient. And, to be frank, we think spending a little more time at the DMV is a price worth paying to enhance our security. As Americans, we've made sacrifices every day since 9/11.

Any State or territory that does not comply increases the risk for the rest of the Nation. A State or territory identified as being the weak-link in the chain will draw terrorists and other bad actors to its territory, resulting in less security for all of us. While REAL ID does not create a national database or ID card, it addresses a national problem, the same problem recognized by the 9/11 Commission.

The 9/11 attacks cost 3,000 lives and $64 billion in immediate losses followed by longer-term financial losses of $375 billion. The potential for further loss of life and property far outweighs the financial burdens to States and territories in implementing REAL ID.

The Department has tried to address the financial burden on some stake-holders and we will continue to do that with the authority we have from our grant program. We have also sought to alleviate the time burden on some States and territories by announcing our extension policies in advance. However, these measures do not eliminate the security need for REAL ID to be implemented.

The Fraternal Order of Police supports implementation of the REAL ID Act, calling it "a common sense system that takes the right approach to ensuring the security and authenticity of the most commonly used identity document in the United States—a drivers' license."

To echo the words of the 9/11 Commission, "For terrorists, travel documents are as important as weapons." Our security as a nation is at stake, and I hope you will support the full implementation of REAL ID.

Thank you, Mr. Chairman, for the opportunity to appear before the Committee today. I would be delighted to answer any questions that the Committee may have.

Timothy D. Sparapani

➡ **NO**

The Real ID Act:
An Unprecedented Threat to
Privacy and Constitutional Rights

Subcommittee Chairman Akaka, Ranking Member Voinovich, and Subcommittee Members, on behalf of the American Civil Liberties Union ("ACLU"), America's oldest and largest civil liberties union, its 53 affiliates and hundreds of thousands of members, we recommend that this Subcommittee mark up legislation, such as S. 717, the Identification Security Enhancement Act of 2007, to replace Title II of the unworkable, Real ID Act of 2005, Pub. L. 109-13 (hereinafter "Real ID Act" or "Act."

As we approach the two-year anniversary of the Act's enactment on May 11, 2005, and rapidly approach the end of the statutorily mandated three-year-long period given to states to implement the Act, one thing has become clear—states and the public are moving en masse to reject the Real ID Act and calling for Congress to repeal it *in toto*. Diverse organizations such as the American Association of Retired Persons ("AARP"), the National Network to End Domestic Violence, and firearms owners and enthusiasts, have called for a repeal of the unworkable Real ID Act. In response, state governments are rapidly moving to opt out of this unfunded mandate altogether.

The impending deadline and recent action by the Department of Homeland Security ("DHS") have made three things abundantly clear.

- First, the minor delay offered to states is not sufficient; states will never be able to implement the Act within the timeline provided.
- Second, the entire Real ID Act scheme is collapsing as states recognize the unprecedented burdens on taxpayers' privacy and civil liberties imposed by this unfunded mandate, and as states—such as Maine and Idaho—opt out of participation.
- Third, Congress cannot sit idly by. Rather, Congress must repeal this Act and, if need be, replace it with a workable, achievable statute to improve licensing security devoid of the privacy and civil liberties infirmities that hamstring the Real ID Act, and which is agreed upon by all interested stakeholders.

This testimony will discuss each of these three realizations briefly. Further, it will elaborate on the four types of privacy concerns raised by the Act and the

From Testimony before the Senate Committee on Homeland Security and Government Affairs, March 26, 2007.

regulations promulgated by DHS to implement the Act, which are concerns regarding:

   (i) data on the face of the ID card;
  (ii) data in the machine readable zone on the back of the ID card;
 (iii) data in the interlinked national ID database supporting the cards; and,
  (iv) transmissions of data between users of the data.

Finally, this testimony will identify how the Real ID Act and the regulations promulgated to respond to it suffer from Constitutional infirmities that are intrinsic to the poorly drafted Real ID Act. Specifically, this testimony will briefly discuss how the Real ID Act potentially implicates (i) four separate First Amendment rights; (ii) gun owners' privacy rights, (iii) could cause derivative problems to citizens' Sixth Amendment rights; and (iv) threatens Due Process Clause rights in multiple ways. Any of these Constitutional infirmities could cause the Act and/or regulations to be struck down by a court in whole or in part. . . .

III. The Public and States Are Rebelling Against the Real ID Act and Calling for Its Repeal

Driven equally by the extraordinary threat the Act poses to personal privacy and civil liberties and its prohibitively expensive cost, now anticipated to be at least $23.1 billion according to DHS' own estimate, states are telling Congress that, no matter the consequences they will not participate. Already two states, Maine and Idaho have enacted legislation expressly stating that they will not implement the Real ID Act's mandates. The legislation Maine adopted states in part that the "Maine State Legislature refuses to implement the REAL ID Act and thereby protests the treatment by Congress and the President of the states as agents of the federal government." S.P. 113, 123 Leg. (Me. 2007). More significantly, just 7 days after DHS issued its Notice of Proposed Rulemaking that begins to set the contours for how states must implement the Act, the Idaho legislature voted to opt out of the Act with legislation stating that "the Idaho Legislature shall enact no legislation nor authorize an appropriation to implement the provisions of the REAL ID Act in Idaho, unless such appropriation is used exclusively for the purpose of undertaking a comprehensive analysis of the costs of implementing the REAL ID Act or to mount a constitutional challenge to the act by the state Attorney General." H.J.M. 3, 59th Leg. (Idaho 2007).

The Real ID rebellion in the states is spreading rapidly, and its pace is accelerating. Thirty states have introduced legislation opposing the Real ID Act,[1] and 13 states—Arizona, Arkansas, Georgia, Hawaii, Missouri, Montana, New Mexico, Oklahoma, Utah, Vermont, Washington, West Virginia and Wyoming—have had legislation passed by at least one of their legislative bodies. More significantly, many of these states have taken significant legislative action since DHS made public its draft Notice of Proposed Rulemaking on March 1, 2007. **Thus, after** reviewing DHS' proposed regulations states immediately moved to reject them. Since publication of the proposed regulations, legislators in Arkansas, Nevada, Pennsylvania and Texas have introduced anti-Real ID legislation, legislative bodies in Arizona, Arkansas (a different bill from the one introduced the same week), Hawaii, Missouri, Oklahoma, and Washington have passed bills rejecting the Real ID Act, and, as mentioned above, the State of Idaho formally opted out of the Real ID scheme altogether and called on Congress to repeal the Act.

The Real ID Act arguably violates the constitutional principles of federalism by usurping state authority. This usurpation, coupled with federal mandates requiring state employees to effectively serve as federal immigration officers, is compounded by the fact Congress has, to date, only appropriated $6 million of the estimated $23.1 billion cost of compliance. States are refusing to be required to raise the $22,994,000,000 for an Act that imposes substantial, rigid mandates on their licensing systems and their licensees. . . .

IV. Senators Never Voted to Support the Real ID Act and Should Repeal the Act

Today is a noteworthy day. One year, 10 months and 15 days after its enactment into law, the Real ID Act of 2005 is receiving its very first actual consideration by the U.S. Senate. Attached to H.R. 1268, in an extra-procedural manner by its House of Representative sponsor, Rep. James Sensenbrenner (R-WI), the Real ID Act never received a single hearing or any floor debate in the U.S. Senate. Rather than being considered by a Senate Committee or moved for consideration on the Senate Floor as a stand-alone measure, or even as an amendment to an authorizing bill, the Act was attached to the "Emergency Supplemental" appropriations bill providing funding for the war effort in Afghanistan and Iraq and humanitarian flood aid for the tsunami victims of southeast Asia. As a consequence, Senators were left with an impossible choice of either opposing emergency funding for troops in an active combat theatre and desperately needed humanitarian assistance, or pass H.R. 1268 with the unrelated Real ID Act attached. Because Senators never considered the Real ID Act, they should be free to vote to repeal it and replace it with a statutory licensing scheme that is both achievable and free of privacy and civil liberties concerns.

V. The Act Raises Unprecedented Privacy and Constitutional Threats and DHS' Proposed Regulations Do Not Resolve These Threats

Even if DHS proposed more complete regulations, which answered all the questions, raised by the Real ID Act that DHS was empowered to consider under the Real ID Act, Congress would still need to revisit Title II of that Act because it is a fatally flawed statute and its flaws cannot be addressed through regulations. Compounding this problem is the substantial failure of DHS to either answer central implementation questions or to mitigate some of the privacy and constitutional concerns. Thus, the regulations fail to resolve the glaring privacy and civil liberties problems created by the Real ID Act.

A) Regulations Proposed by DHS Ignore Substantial Threats to Personal Privacy Posed by Real ID

1) The Act and Regulations Establish the First National ID Card System Eroding Personal Privacy

By enacting the REAL ID Act, Congress set in place the first true National ID Card System. The Act mandates a National ID System by requiring the standardization of state license design and minimum data elements to be collected and stored about each licensee. Thus, although we will continue to have 56 state license issuers with 56 cosmetically different designs, the IDs will essentially be the same. More importantly, the National ID System is created by the mandate that all states make their databases of licensee information interoperable and that they engage in unprecedented data sharing about licensees. Finally, and most importantly, the Real ID licenses will become the de facto National ID as the federal, state and local governments and private sector entities begin to require a Real ID license to exercise rights and privileges and obtain goods and services.

Already, since the Act's passage, Members of Congress have proposed legislation requiring that every adult in America present a Real ID-compliant license to vote, receive authorization to obtain every new job, obtain benefits such as Medicaid, and travel on interstate buses, trains and planes. Thus, if the Act and the regulations are implemented, Senators should expect that no person would be able to function in our society without providing a Real ID-compliant license.

In addition to these burdens from ubiquitous future demands, the machine readable zone on each Real ID license will provide a digital trail everywhere it is read. The Act, therefore, makes possible the mapping of a person's movements throughout our society and eliminates the anonymity that has protected our privacy since the founding of our country.

2) Privacy Concerns Arising from Data on the ID Card's Face

In addition to the fact that the Act and the Regulations establish the first true National ID Card System, threats to personal privacy caused by the Act and the Regulations arise from four areas:

- (i) data on the face of the ID card;
- (ii) data in the machine readable zone on the back of the ID card;
- (iii) data in the interlinked national ID database supporting the cards; and,
- (iv) transmissions of data between users of the data.

Data on the face of the ID card raises substantial privacy concerns. First, it threatens the personal security of numerous classes of licensees by requiring that an individual's principal address be stated on the face of the license.

Consequently, police officers, elected officials, and judges will have their home address readily available to all who view their licenses. Address confidentiality laws in dozens of states to protect these government employees are completely overridden by this mandate putting these individuals at risk. Perhaps more importantly, victims of domestic violence and sexual assault who flee their abusers will be stripped of the power to list a Post Office Box as their address on the face of the license. They too will be easier to find by stalkers and abusers.

DHS's proposed solution in its regulations does not resolve this concern adequately. It is unclear how people without such an address or who live in different places—such as students, those who live in recreational vehicles ("RVs") and other mobile homes, and the homeless—will solve this issue. The regulations attempt to address this issue by defining principal address as the place where an individual has his "true, fixed and principal home" (72 Fed. Reg. at 10,851), and stating that DMVs can make exemptions for the homeless (72 Fed. Reg. at 10,803 and 10,836). There is still some concern regarding whether all states will be able and willing to create workable methods for utilizing these exemptions.

Second, Congress failed to prohibit states from noting a licensee's citizenship status on the license. Some have suggested pilot projects to denote citizenship on the face of a license. The ACLU believes that such a "reverse scarlet letter" provision could lead to innumerable discriminatory interactions between police and/or bigoted private citizens and individuals who appear or sound foreign and who do not have such a citizenship sticker on their license every time that license is demanded for presentation. Congress should expressly prohibit any such proposal.

3) Privacy Concerns Arising from Data Contained in the Machine Readable Zone

The Real ID Act created an enormous threat of private sector, third-party skimming and resale of data contained in the "machine readable" zone ("MRZ") on each card. DHS's proposed regulations failed to close the loophole because they do not require encryption of the data in the MRZ.

Because both the type of MRZ and the minimum data elements it must contain are standardized under the Real ID Act, it will become increasingly profitable for private sector retailers to skim a copy of that data from each customer. As states add additional data elements to the machine readable zone, such skimming will become even more valuable. Because the Act does not prohibit skimming, in the near future we can expect retailers to demand that customers produce their licenses for "anti-fraud" or "customer loyalty card" purposes and retailers will routinely retain all the data from the MRZ, combined with a record of each licensee's purchases. The retailers will have two ready markets to profit off such skimming:

(i) using the data to engage in highly-targeted direct marketing back to their customers thereby producing significant amounts of unwanted solicitations, and

(ii) reselling the data to data brokers such as Axciom, ChoicePoint and Lexis-Nexis who will share the information with other companies and federal, state and local governments. The result will be that data brokers and the government will know when and what each customer purchased including items such as the books and magazines we read, what types of birth control we use, and the prescriptions we obtain.

The result will be a substantial erosion of personal privacy.

DHS's proposed regulations failed to close this loophole because they refused to mandate encryption for this data and to place meaningful limits on what data can be harvested from the card and how it can be used. While DHS acknowledges the danger of license data being scanned by third parties, it fails to take action to stop the problem, and merely encourages the states to come up with a solution. DHS says it "leans toward" requiring that data be encrypted but opts not to mandate encryption due to "practical concerns." 72 Fed. Reg. 10819, at 10838. This proposed regulation flies in the face of DHS's own Privacy Office, which believes "there is a strong privacy rationale for cryptographic protections to safeguard the personal information stored digitally in the machine-readable zone (MRZ) on the credentials." Privacy Impact Assessment for the Real ID Act, March 1, 2007, pg. 3. Congress must revisit the Act, if for no other reason, than to expressly mandate encryption of the data provided.

This provision undercuts the Congress' earlier effort to protect driver's information, which considered by many to be of higher quality than commercial data amassed from warranty cards and the like. In 1994 the Congress in response to the murder of Amy Boyer, by a man who obtained her address from the NH DMV, passed the Drivers' Personal Privacy Act ("DPPA"), Pub. L. 103-322, 18 U.S.C. § 2721, *et seq.,* which requires the data to be kept confidentially. Every state has passed legislation to implement the DPPA. Many of these state statutes, like California's go beyond the original act.

The DPPA would be completely undercut if Congress allows for the easy harvesting of data from both the printed information and the MRZ on the license. How long will it be before another Amy Boyer?

4) Privacy Concerns Arising from Data Amassed by the States

The data storage and aggregation requirements imposed by the Act will lead to massive, and more serious cases of identity theft, which could lead to terrorists and sophisticated criminals impersonating innocent Americans, and will permit unlimited data mining by federal government agencies.

Contrary to DHS's assertions, the unprecedented data aggregation imposed by the Act will make us more vulnerable as a nation, not safer, primarily because it will facilitate massive identity theft and identity fraud, and make these cases more significant. The Act requires, *at a minimum,* that all source documents for licenses be retained either electronically or in storage at the DMV, along with additional biometric information and a driving history. Identity thieves will quickly recognize that the DMVs' records are a central location for obtaining all the documents and personally identifiable information they need to commit fraud.[2] Insider fraud, where state licensing officials sell IDs and information, will be impossible to stop and become even more profitable.

Further, identity theft and document fraud stemming from thefts from the Real ID databases will be far more significant than the troubling but garden variety identity theft that victims are currently experience. Instead of obtaining just one password to a bank account or one unique identifier, data thieves who access the Real ID database system will be able to obtain data on millions of individuals and obtain all at once a rich trove of information because DHS failed to require basic computer network data security be built into these databases. Thus, the data contained within the system will not be segmented or compartmentalized, with the result that any hacking event of the Real ID databases by an ID thief will provide access to all available documents and information. In short, the Real ID databases are destined to be the ID thieves' bank of choice to rob.

Further, the privacy invasion for those unfortunate ID theft victims will be more pronounced than current ID theft. The victims of Real ID database ID theft will encounter tremendous difficulty in obtaining new documents and recovering their identity because the ID thieves will have real copies—easily printed on a standard color printer—of the victim's Social Security Card and birth certificate.

The seriousness of this ID theft and document fraud will also make it easier for sophisticated criminals, immigrant smugglers and terrorists to obtain the identity of another person and pass themselves off as that person. **The aggregation of the data and the source documents thus opens a substantial security loophole.** This loophole is exactly contrary to the intent of the 9/11 Commission. Because of the rigidity of the Real ID Act's language, DHS had little flexibility to resolve this concern. **As a result, unless Congress revisits this portion of the Real ID Act, we will be weaker, not safer, due to the Real ID Act.**[3]

The Real ID database will also lead to significant privacy invasions by government snooping through data mining. Despite calls to expressly forbid data mining of the information aggregated in the Real ID database, to date, DHS refuses to promise not to data mine this interlinked data set or that to prohibit data mining by other federal anti-crime or anti-terror agencies. Senators should, therefore, expect that DHS would grant unfettered access to untested data mining programs that will search through millions of innocent licensees' most-sensitive personal information. Until these databases were linked under Real ID, such data mining was impractical or impossible. By linking these databases under Real ID, it will become possible for the government to conduct data mining on an unprecedented scale.

Unfortunately, the DPPA will not provide protections against this data mining. While the DPPA does prohibit DMVs from reselling data about licensees, it does not prohibit other agencies from accessing each DMVs databases. Congress should consider closing this loophole.

5) Privacy Concerns Regarding Data Transmissions
Mandated data sharing of licensees' information leads to what is referred to as a "false positive" problem in which the sharing of false or erroneous information

leads to significant problems for licensees with the same or similar names as people who have lost their driving privileges, criminals or suspected terrorists. Because many licensees have common names, states will certainly mistakenly confuse licensees with each other. Undoubtedly, this "false positive" problem will lead to innocent Americans being improperly labeled as criminals or worse because the data from one state database transmitted to another state is erroneous. No easy fix exists for this false positive problem. If states send too little personally identifiable information to each other, innocent people will not be distinguishable from similarly named problem drivers, criminals or terrorists.

VI. DHS Proposed Regulations Fail to Resolve Significant Constitutional and Civil Liberties Problems Caused by the Real ID Act

The Constitutional and civil liberties infirmities caused by the Real ID Act are unprecedented and are not resolved by DHS' Proposed Regulations. The Act could burden individuals' privacy rights and rights provided by the First and Sixth Amendments to the Constitution and its Due Process Clause. The Act arguable burdens the states in violation of the Tenth Amendment to the Constitution.

The Act unquestionably burdens the First Amendment guarantees of Freedom of Religion. The Act requires that all licensees be photographed and that all licenses contain on their face a digital photograph. As a result, Amish and Mennonite Christians whose religious beliefs forbid their images from being photographed face a clear burden on the practice of their religion. See, Alan Scher Zegeir, *Mennonites Leaving Mo. Over Photo Law,* Associated Press, Mar. 21, 2007 ("members of a [Missouri town's] Mennonite community are planning to move to Arkansas over a Missouri requirement that all drivers be photographed if they want a license. . . .because the law conflicts with the Biblical prohibition against the making of 'graven images.'"). Still other evangelical Christians believe the Real ID Act will enumerate them in a manner contrary to their religious beliefs. Most states currently grant practitioners of these faiths and others license exceptions and states issue more than 260,000 licenses without pictures every year. DHS Real ID Impacts, Survey One. The Real ID Act's rigid mandates eliminate such state flexibility. Therefore, Congress must revisit the Act to provide for exceptions for First Amendment-protected religious practice.

Should an individual be unable to obtain a Real ID-compliant license for any number of reasons, or should DHS follow through on its threat to prohibit the citizens of states that are not complying with the Act from using their licenses for any "federal purpose" or to travel on planes, additional First Amendment and Sixth Amendment protected rights would be implicated. For example, if individuals from those states do not have the proper IDs to enter a federal agency, their ability to petition their government for redress of their grievances is compromised, as is their right to peaceably assemble in a public venue or meeting place. Both such applications of DHS' authority would impermissibly burden First Amendment protected rights. Similarly, if a federal criminal defendant lacked proper ID, the defendant might not be able to enter a federal court house to confront his accusers. Should DHS block residents of non-Real ID compliant states from flying on planes, those residents First Amendment-protected, U.S. Supreme Court-confirmed, Right to Travel would be impermissibly burdened. See, e.g., Saenz v. Roe, 526 U.S. 489 (1999). For residents of Hawaii, Alaska and Puerto Rico, a burden on the Right to Travel would have substantial economic and practical consequences. Congress must revisit the Real ID Act because these burdens are written into the statute and may only be resolved through legislative amendments.

Firearms owners are also concerned that the information sharing mandated by the Real ID Act could lead to a backdoor creation of a federal gun owners' registry. Many believe this would burden the gun owners' privacy interests. Although federal statutes contain two prohibitions on the creation of such a registry, many states do not have similar registry prohibitions. Thus, if a state were to begin to encode gun ownership information in the machine readable zone and/or in the database supporting the ID card, other states would rapidly gain access to a list of the firearm owners of other states. The Real ID Act and the proposed regulations could, therefore, circumvent these two statutory prohibitions.

The Real ID Act and the DHS proposed regulations also raise certain Due Process Clause burdens. First, as noted above, if people cannot obtain Real ID-compliant licenses—because they lack proper documentation, they cannot afford vastly more expensive licenses, or due to bureaucratic bungling—similar burdens, will certainly arise for those unable to obtain licenses who need to visit a Social Security Administration office, federal prison, court house or any other federal agency. Congress must ask, because DHS did not: how will these people gain access to basic federal government services? If these burdens become substantial, Due Process Clause violations could result. Already, similar ID requirements have wrongly forced tens of thousands of individuals off the Medicaid roles. Robert Pear, *Lacking Papers, Citizens are Cut from Medicaid,* N.Y. Times, Mar. 12, 2007, at A1. Senators should expect to see their constituent case work rise exponentially with the implementation of the Act and corresponding license requirements to obtain government services and benefits.

Second, Due Process Clause concerns could arise for lawfully present immigrants. The Real ID Act's drafters failed to list numerous categories of lawful immigrants in the statutory list of those who could obtain a Real ID license or temporary license, such as parolees, persons under order of supervision, applicants for victim or witness visas, and applicants for cancellation of removal. Additionally, many lawfully present immigrants will be unable to prove their identity or immigration status. The proposed regulations unwisely limited the list of documents that immigrants could provide to prove identity and immigration status to a green card, employment authorization document, or current passport accompanied by a valid visa. Unfortunately, all too many lawfully present immigrants, such as many asylum applicants, will not likely possess these documents.

Third, Due Process Clause concerns will arise for the mass of citizens and lawfully present immigrants who find they need to challenge erroneous or incomplete information contained in state databases that wrongly prevents them from obtaining a license. The proposed regulations fail to provide an administrative or judicial process accessible as of right for would-be licensees to efficiently resolve data problems. Similarly, all too many lawfully present immigrants will suffer from an inability to see or correct immigration records. The proposed regulations do not provide a process for those immigrants whose status cannot be verified through DHS's Systematic Alien Verification for Entitlements ("SAVE") system. Nor do the regulations provide a process for those whose status was incorrectly reported to obtain their immigration records and correct them. DHS's only suggestion in its proposed regulations is for burdened immigrants to make an appointment with DHS or visit a local Citizenship and Immigration Service office. To obtain the documents, DHS recommends that immigrants file a Freedom of Information Act request, which could take years to be answered given current backlogs. For all aggrieved citizens and immigrants, DHS's failure to provide a process to challenge and correct such errors efficiently and speedily condemns them to a second-class existence. Congress should revisit the Act to create true due process safeguards.

If Congress fails to revisit the Real ID Act and eliminate these Constitutional infirmities, the implementation of the Act and the proposed regulations could be delayed years as provisions are tied up in litigation.

VII. Conclusion: Congress Should Repeal Title II of the Real ID Act and Replace It with an Achievable Licensing Scheme That Does Not Threaten Personal Privacy and Civil Liberties

Congress cannot fix Title II of the Real ID Act; therefore, Congress must repeal the Act. And, if Congress wishes to move forward with a federal standardization of state-based licensing, Congress should replace Title II with legislation—such as S. 717—creating a flexible, negotiated rulemaking as provided for in the Administrative Procedures Act 5 U.S.C. § 561, *et. seq.* (2007) that brings all interested parties to the negotiating table and grants them equal bargaining power.

S. 717, would eliminate the inflexible sections of the Real ID Act that drive up costs and do not allow for regulatory flexibility to protect privacy and constitutional rights. Without sufficient flexibility, DMVs will struggle to implement any licensing scheme. Further, S. 717 would put in place a negotiated rulemaking comprised of interested stakeholders and experts in various field, including privacy protection and civil liberties, to ensure that the final licensing scheme is workable while also respectful of our norms and values. The ACLU urges Congress to rapidly enact S. 717 to more rapidly produce counter- and tamper-resistant licenses in a statutory and regulatory framework devoid of privacy and civil liberties detriments.

Notes

1. States with pending anti-Real ID legislation (does not include states that have already passed legislation): Arizona, Arkansas, Georgia, Hawaii, Illinois, Kentucky, Maryland, Massachusetts, Michigan, Minnesota, Missouri, Montana, Nebraska,

Nevada, New Hampshire, Oklahoma, Oregon, Pennsylvania, Rhode Island, South Carolina, Texas, Vermont, and Washington.

2. DHS actually exacerbates the identity theft problems in its regulations, suggesting that individuals can prove their principal address with a *bank statement.* 72 Fed. Reg. 10831.

3. For example, see the statement by the Privacy Rights Clearinghouse, a nationally recognized resource center for the victim of ID theft, which states that "[i]f you think identity theft is bad now, wait until something called the Real ID Act goes into effect." . . .

POSTSCRIPT

Should the United States Require a Secure Identification System for Citizens?

It is clear that the 9/11 hijackers exploited our current system of issuing driver's licenses. As was stated at a forum on the Real ID Act at MIT, "the 9/11 hijackers knew well that having a license in this country was the key to operating just under the radar screen, which is why they sought as few as 38 licenses (official number) and state-issued IDs between them, and as many as 63 (unconfirmed number). Not only did those licenses allow them to board airplanes that fateful morning, but more importantly, they allowed the hijackers to operate inside our borders plotting, scheming and executing important parts of their attacks for months and years before the September 11th attack."

On the other hand, it is not clear that if the Real ID Act had been in place, September 11th would not have occurred. As privacy and security expert Bruce Schmeir has written:

> When most people think of ID cards, they think of a small plastic card with their name and photograph. This isn't wrong, but it's only a small piece of any ID program. What starts out as a seemingly simple security device—a card that binds a photograph with a name—rapidly becomes a complex security system. It doesn't really matter how well a Real ID works when used by the hundreds of millions of honest people who would carry it. What matters is how the system might fail when used by someone intent on subverting that system: how it fails naturally, how it can be made to fail, and how failures might be exploited. The first problem is the card itself. No matter how unforgeable we make it, it will be forged. We can raise the price of forgery, but we can't make it impossible. Real IDs will be forged.
>
> Even worse, people will get legitimate cards in fraudulent names. Two of the 9/11 terrorists had valid Virginia driver's licenses in fake names. And even if we could guarantee that everyone who issued national ID cards couldn't be bribed, cards are issued based on other identity documents—all of which are easier to forge. And we can't assume that everyone will always have a Real ID. Currently about 20% of all identity documents are lost per year. An entirely separate security system would have to be developed for people who lost their card, a system that itself would be susceptible to abuse. (Real-ID: Costs and Benefits, http://www.schneier.com/blog/archives/2007/ 01 /realid_costs_an.html)

Additional recommended readings on Real ID and national identity cards are the following: A. Michael Froomkin, "Creating a Viral Federal Privacy

Standard," *Boston College Law Review* (2007) http://www.bc.edu/schools/law/lawreviews/bclawreview/Past_Issues/48_1/48_1.html; Serge Egelman and Lorrie Faith Cranor, "The Real ID Act: Fixing Identity Documents with Duct Tape," *I/S: A Journal of Law and Policy for the Information Society* (2005) http://www.is-journal.org/V02I01/2ISJLP149.pdf; Department of Homeland Security Privacy Impact Assessment for the REAL ID Act (March 1, 2007) http://www.dhs.gov/xlibrary/assets/privacy/privacy_pia_ realid.pdf; Daniel J. Solove, *The Digital Person: Technology and Privacy in the Information Age* (2006); Robert O'Harrow, *No Place to Hide: Behind the Scenes of Our Emerging Surveillance Society* (2005).

ISSUE 16

Are Blanket Prohibitions on Cross Burnings Unconstitutional?

YES: Sandra Day O'Connor, from Majority Opinion, *Virginia v. Barry Elton Black, Richard J. Elliott, and Jonathan O'Mara,* U.S. Supreme Court (April 7, 2003)

NO: Clarence Thomas, from Dissenting Opinion, *Virginia v. Barry Elton Black, Richard J. Elliott, and Jonathan O'Mara,* U.S. Supreme Court (April 7, 2003)

ISSUE SUMMARY

YES: Supreme Court Justice Sandra Day O'Connor argues that a Virginia statute proscribing all forms of cross burning is unconstitutional because symbolic speech can only be prohibited when done with the intent to intimidate, and such an intent cannot be inferred solely from the type of symbolic speech used.

NO: Supreme Court Justice Clarence Thomas argues that the history and nature of cross burning in the United States inextricably links the act to threatening and menacing violence and that the intent to intimidate can therefore be inferred solely from the act of cross burning itself.

We do not live in tranquil, quiet, and harmonious times. Terrorism, as a domestic threat, is a fairly new challenge for the United States. Hate crimes, however, have occurred throughout the nation's history. The Community Relations Service of the U.S. Department of Justice has defined hate crime as "the violence of intolerance and bigotry, intended to hurt and intimidate someone because of their race, ethnicity, national origin, religion, sexual orientation, or disability."

Since 1991 the Hate Crimes Statistics Act has required the FBI to keep statistics on hate crimes, http://www.fbi.gov/ucr/hc2005/incidentsoffenses.htm. In general, these crimes are not separate, distinct crimes but traditional offenses, such as assault, that are motivated by the offender's bias. The following readings, which are from a case involving cross burning, focus on a criminal statute that explicitly targets bias activities.

In the United States, among the few categories of speech that can be constitutionally prohibited are "fighting words," which are defined by the Supreme Court as statements "which by their very utterance inflict injury or tend to incite an immediate breach of the peace" (see *Chaplinsky v. New Hampshire,* 315 U.S. 568, 1942). The "fighting words" prohibition has been narrowly construed throughout its history; the legislature can only prohibit speech that constitutes an immediate threat, and even calls for violence may be permissible if they are rhetorical in nature and will probably not incite any actual violence. In *R. A. V. v. City of St. Paul,* 505 U.S. 377 (1992), the Supreme Court even extended free speech protections to symbolic speech—actions that are not speech per se but that convey certain messages—as long as it does not violate the "fighting words" prohibition. In other words, an action like a Ku Klux Klan cross burning is legal if it merely conveys the Klan's political beliefs; on the other hand, it can be outlawed if it constitutes a threat to others.

In the *R. A. V.* case, the Supreme Court struck down a city ordinance in St. Paul, Minnesota, that outlawed cross burning not on the grounds that such an act would provoke violence but because cross burnings convey racist messages. The Court ruled that, to be constitutionally permissible, speech codes must address the *outcome* of the speech—whether it is foreseeable that the speech would encourage physical violence—and not the subjects that the speech addresses. According to the majority opinion in *R. A. V.,* the problem with the St. Paul ordinance was that it focused only on speech that "insult[s] or provoke[s] violence, 'on the basis of race, color, creed, religion, or gender.'" To fulfill the demands of content neutrality, however, the ordinance would have to outlaw *all* speech that provoked violence; the ordinance could not specify which subject matter, such as race or gender, was prohibited while ignoring, in the words of the Court, "those who wish to use 'fighting words' in connection with other ideas—to express hostility, for example, on the basis of political affiliation, union membership, or homosexuality."

In the case that follows, the Supreme Court once again addresses the limitations that legislatures can place on symbolic speech—specifically, cross burnings. The outcome of *R. A. V.* was to allow legislatures to outlaw symbolic speech, such as cross burnings, only insofar as such prohibitions are content-neutral and apply only to speech that constitutes "fighting words" (or one of the other limited categories of speech that fall outside constitutional protection). In *Virginia v. Black,* the Court addresses the question of whether the intent to intimidate—a prerequisite for establishing "fighting words" status—can be inferred from the nature of the act itself. In so doing, the Court tackles not only the philosophical nature of symbolic actions but also the social history of such acts as cross burning that help define what they stand for in the specific context of twenty-first-century America.

YES ⬅

Sandra Day O'Connor

Majority Opinion

Virginia *v.* Black

In this case we consider whether the Commonwealth of Virginia's statute banning cross burning with "an intent to intimidate a person or group of persons" violates the First Amendment. We conclude that while a State, consistent with the First Amendment, may ban cross burning carried out with the intent to intimidate, the provision in the Virginia statute treating any cross burning as prima facie evidence of intent to intimidate renders the statute unconstitutional in its current form.

I

Respondents Barry Black, Richard Elliott, and Jonathan O'Mara were convicted separately of violating Virginia's cross-burning statute, §18.2-423. That statute provides:

> "It shall be unlawful for any person or persons, with the intent of intimidating any person or group of persons, to burn, or cause to be burned, a cross on the property of another, a highway or other public place. Any person who shall violate any provision of this section shall be guilty of a Class 6 felony.
>
> "Any such burning of a cross shall be prima facie evidence of an intent to intimidate a person or group of persons."

On August 22, 1998, Barry Black led a Ku Klux Klan rally in Carroll County, Virginia. Twenty-five to thirty people attended this gathering, which occurred on private property with the permission of the owner, who was in attendance. The property was located on an open field just off Brushy Fork Road (State Highway 690) in Cana, Virginia.

When the sheriff of Carroll County learned that a Klan rally was occurring in his county, he went to observe it from the side of the road. During the approximately one hour that the sheriff was present, about 40 to 50 cars passed the site, a "few" of which stopped to ask the sheriff what was happening on the property. Eight to ten houses were located in the vicinity of the rally. Rebecca

From *Virginia v. Barry Elton Black, Richard J. Elliott, and Jonathan O'Mara*, 538 U.S. ____ (2003). References and some notes and case citations omitted.

Sechrist, who was related to the owner of the property where the rally took place, "sat and watched to see wha[t] [was] going on" from the lawn of her in-laws' house. She looked on as the Klan prepared for the gathering and subsequently conducted the rally itself.

During the rally, Sechrist heard Klan members speak about "what they were" and "what they believed in." The speakers "talked real bad about the blacks and the Mexicans." One speaker told the assembled gathering that "he would love to take a .30/.30 and just random[ly] shoot the blacks." The speakers also talked about "President Clinton and Hillary Clinton," and about how their tax money "goes to . . . the black people." Sechrist testified that this language made her "very . . . scared."

At the conclusion of the rally, the crowd circled around a 25- to 30-foot cross. The cross was between 300 and 350 yards away from the road. According to the sheriff, the cross "then all of a sudden . . . went up in a flame." As the cross burned, the Klan played Amazing Grace over the loudspeakers. Sechrist stated that the cross burning made her feel "awful" and "terrible."

When the sheriff observed the cross burning, he informed his deputy that they needed to "find out who's responsible and explain to them that they cannot do this in the State of Virginia." The sheriff then went down the driveway, entered the rally, and asked "who was responsible for burning the cross." Black responded, "I guess I am because I'm the head of the rally." The sheriff then told Black, "[T]here's a law in the State of Virginia that you cannot burn a cross and I'll have to place you under arrest for this."

Black was charged with burning a cross with the intent of intimidating a person or group of persons, in violation of §18.2-423. At his trial, the jury was instructed that "intent to intimidate means the motivation to intentionally put a person or a group of persons in fear of bodily harm. Such fear must arise from the willful conduct of the accused rather than from some mere temperamental timidity of the victim." The trial court also instructed the jury that "the burning of a cross by itself is sufficient evidence from which you may infer the required intent." When Black objected to this last instruction on First Amendment grounds, the prosecutor responded that the instruction was "taken straight out of the [Virginia] Model Instructions." The jury found Black guilty, and fined him $2,500. The Court of Appeals of Virginia affirmed Black's conviction.

On May 2, 1998, respondents Richard Elliott and Jonathan O'Mara, as well as a third individual, attempted to burn a cross on the yard of James Jubilee. Jubilee, an African-American, was Elliott's next-door neighbor in Virginia Beach, Virginia. Four months prior to the incident, Jubilee and his family had moved from California to Virginia Beach. Before the cross burning, Jubilee spoke to Elliott's mother to inquire about shots being fired from behind the Elliott home. Elliott's mother explained to Jubilee that her son shot firearms as a hobby, and that he used the backyard as a firing range.

On the night of May 2, respondents drove a truck onto Jubilee's property, planted a cross, and set it on fire. Their apparent motive was to "get back" at Jubilee for complaining about the shooting in the backyard. Respondents were not affiliated with the Klan. The next morning, as Jubilee was pulling his car out of the driveway, he noticed the partially burned cross approximately

20 feet from his house. After seeing the cross, Jubilee was "very nervous" because he "didn't know what would be the next phase," and because "a cross burned in your yard . . . tells you that it's just the first round."

Elliott and O'Mara were charged with attempted cross burning and conspiracy to commit cross burning. O'Mara pleaded guilty to both counts, reserving the right to challenge the constitutionality of the cross-burning statute. The judge sentenced O'Mara to 90 days in jail and fined him $2,500. The judge also suspended 45 days of the sentence and $1,000 of the fine.

At Elliott's trial, the judge originally ruled that the jury would be instructed "that the burning of a cross by itself is sufficient evidence from which you may infer the required intent." At trial, however, the court instructed the jury that the Commonwealth must prove that "the defendant intended to commit cross burning," that "the defendant did a direct act toward the commission of the cross burning," and that "the defendant had the intent of intimidating any person or group of persons." The court did not instruct the jury on the meaning of the word "intimidate," nor on the prima facie evidence provision of §18.2–423. The jury found Elliott guilty of attempted cross burning and acquitted him of conspiracy to commit cross burning. It sentenced Elliott to 90 days in jail and a $2,500 fine. The Court of Appeals of Virginia affirmed the convictions of both Elliott and O'Mara.

Each respondent appealed to the Supreme Court of Virginia, arguing that §18.2–423 is facially unconstitutional. The Supreme Court of Virginia consolidated all three cases, and held that the statute is unconstitutional on its face. It held that the Virginia cross-burning statute "is analytically indistinguishable from the ordinance found unconstitutional in *R. A. V.* [v. *St. Paul*]. The Virginia statute, the court held, discriminates on the basis of content since it "selectively chooses only cross burning because of its distinctive message." The court also held that the prima facie evidence provision renders the statute overbroad because "[t]he enhanced probability of prosecution under the statute chills the expression of protected speech."

Three justices dissented, concluding that the Virginia cross-burning statute passes constitutional muster because it proscribes only conduct that constitutes a true threat. The justices noted that unlike the ordinance found unconstitutional in *R. A. V.* v. *St. Paul,* the Virginia statute does not just target cross burning "on the basis of race, color, creed, religion or gender." Rather, "the Virginia statute applies to any individual who burns a cross for any reason provided the cross is burned with the intent to intimidate." The dissenters also disagreed with the majority's analysis of the prima facie provision because the inference alone "is clearly insufficient to establish beyond a reasonable doubt that a defendant burned a cross with the intent to intimidate." The dissent noted that the burden of proof still remains on the Commonwealth to prove intent to intimidate. We granted certiorari.

II

Cross burning originated in the 14th century as a means for Scottish tribes to signal each other. . . . Cross burning in this country, however, long ago became unmoored from its Scottish ancestry. Burning a cross in the United States is inextricably intertwined with the history of the Ku Klux Klan.

The first Ku Klux Klan began in Pulaski, Tennessee, in the spring of 1866. Although the Ku Klux Klan started as a social club, it soon changed into something far different. The Klan fought Reconstruction and the corresponding drive to allow freed blacks to participate in the political process. Soon the Klan imposed "a veritable reign of terror" throughout the South. The Klan employed tactics such as whipping, threatening to burn people at the stake, and murder. The Klan's victims included blacks, southern whites who disagreed with the Klan, and "carpetbagger" northern whites.

The activities of the Ku Klux Klan prompted legislative action at the national level. In 1871, "President Grant sent a message to Congress indicating that the Klan's reign of terror in the Southern States had rendered life and property insecure." In response, Congress passed what is now known as the Ku Klux Klan Act. President Grant used these new powers to suppress the Klan in South Carolina, the effect of which severely curtailed the Klan in other States as well. By the end of Reconstruction in 1877, the first Klan no longer existed.

The genesis of the second Klan began in 1905, with the publication of Thomas Dixon's The Clansmen: An Historical Romance of the Ku Klux Klan. Dixon's book was a sympathetic portrait of the first Klan, depicting the Klan as a group of heroes "saving" the South from blacks and the "horrors" of Reconstruction. Although the first Klan never actually practiced cross burning, Dixon's book depicted the Klan burning crosses to celebrate the execution of former slaves. Cross burning thereby became associated with the first Ku Klux Klan. When D. W. Griffith turned Dixon's book into the movie The Birth of a Nation in 1915, the association between cross burning and the Klan became indelible. In addition to the cross burnings in the movie, a poster advertising the film displayed a hooded Klansman riding a hooded horse, with his left hand holding the reins of the horse and his right hand holding a burning cross above his head. Soon thereafter, in November 1915, the second Klan began.

From the inception of the second Klan, cross burnings have been used to communicate both threats of violence and messages of shared ideology. The first initiation ceremony occurred on Stone Mountain near Atlanta, Georgia. While a 40-foot cross burned on the mountain, the Klan members took their oaths of loyalty. This cross burning was the second recorded instance in the United States. The first known cross burning in the country had occurred a little over one month before the Klan initiation, when a Georgia mob celebrated the lynching of Leo Frank by burning a "gigantic cross" on Stone Mountain that was "visible throughout" Atlanta.

The new Klan's ideology did not differ much from that of the first Klan. As one Klan publication emphasized, "We avow the distinction between [the] races, . . . and we shall ever be true to the faithful maintenance of White Supremacy and will strenuously oppose any compromise thereof in any and all things." Violence was also an elemental part of this new Klan. By September 1921, the New York World newspaper documented 152 acts of Klan violence, including 4 murders, 41 floggings, and 27 tar-and-featherings.

Often, the Klan used cross burnings as a tool of intimidation and a threat of impending violence. For example, in 1939 and 1940, the Klan burned crosses in front of synagogues and churches. After one cross burning at a synagogue, a Klan member noted that if the cross burning did not "shut the Jews up, we'll cut a few throats and see what happens." In Miami in 1941, the Klan burned four crosses in front of a proposed housing project, declaring, "We are here to keep niggers out of your town. . . . When the law fails you, call on us." And in Alabama in 1942, in "a whirlwind climax to weeks of flogging and terror," the Klan burned crosses in front of a union hall and in front of a union leader's home on the eve of a labor election. These cross burnings embodied threats to people whom the Klan deemed antithetical to its goals. And these threats had special force given the long history of Klan violence.

The Klan continued to use cross burnings to intimidate after World War II. In one incident, an African-American "school teacher who recently moved his family into a block formerly occupied only by whites asked the protection of city police . . . after the burning of a cross in his front yard." And after a cross burning in Suffolk, Virginia during the late 1940's, the Virginia Governor stated that he would "not allow any of our people of any race to be subjected to terrorism or intimidation in any form by the Klan or any other organization." These incidents of cross burning, among others, helped prompt Virginia to enact its first version of the cross-burning statute in 1950.

The decision of this Court in *Brown* v. *Board of Education,* 347 U.S. 483 (1954), along with the civil rights movement of the 1950's and 1960's, sparked another outbreak of Klan violence. These acts of violence included bombings, beatings, shootings, stabbings, and mutilations. Members of the Klan burned crosses on the lawns of those associated with the civil rights movement, assaulted the Freedom Riders, bombed churches, and murdered blacks as well as whites whom the Klan viewed as sympathetic toward the civil rights movement.

Throughout the history of the Klan, cross burnings have also remained potent symbols of shared group identity and ideology. The burning cross became a symbol of the Klan itself and a central feature of Klan gatherings. According to the Klan constitution (called the kloran), the "fiery cross" was the "emblem of that sincere, unselfish devotedness of all klansmen to the sacred purpose and principles we have espoused." And the Klan has often published its newsletters and magazines under the name The Fiery Cross.

At Klan gatherings across the country, cross burning became the climax of the rally or the initiation. Posters advertising an upcoming Klan rally often featured a Klan member holding a cross. Typically, a cross burning would start with a prayer by the "Klavern" minister, followed by the singing of Onward Christian Soldiers. The Klan would then light the cross on fire, as the members raised their left arm toward the burning cross and sang The Old Rugged Cross. Throughout the Klan's history, the Klan continued to use the burning cross in their ritual ceremonies.

For its own members, the cross was a sign of celebration and ceremony. During a joint Nazi-Klan rally in 1940, the proceeding concluded with the wedding of two Klan members who "were married in full Klan regalia beneath a blazing cross." In response to antimasking bills introduced in state legislatures after World

War II, the Klan burned crosses in protest. On March 26, 1960, the Klan engaged in rallies and cross burnings throughout the South in an attempt to recruit 10 million members. Later in 1960, the Klan became an issue in the third debate between Richard Nixon and John Kennedy, with both candidates renouncing the Klan. After this debate, the Klan reiterated its support for Nixon by burning crosses. And cross burnings featured prominently in Klan rallies when the Klan attempted to move toward more nonviolent tactics to stop integration. In short, a burning cross has remained a symbol of Klan ideology and of Klan unity.

To this day, regardless of whether the message is a political one or whether the message is also meant to intimidate, the burning of a cross is a "symbol of hate." And while cross burning sometimes carries no intimidating message, at other times the intimidating message is the *only* message conveyed. For example, when a cross burning is directed at a particular person not affiliated with the Klan, the burning cross often serves as a message of intimidation, designed to inspire in the victim a fear of bodily harm. Moreover, the history of violence associated with the Klan shows that the possibility of injury or death is not just hypothetical. The person who burns a cross directed at a particular person often is making a serious threat, meant to coerce the victim to comply with the Klan's wishes unless the victim is willing to risk the wrath of the Klan. Indeed, as the cases of respondents Elliott and O'Mara indicate, individuals without Klan affiliation who wish to threaten or menace another person sometimes use cross burning because of this association between a burning cross and violence.

In sum, while a burning cross does not inevitably convey a message of intimidation, often the cross burner intends that the recipients of the message fear for their lives. And when a cross burning is used to intimidate, few if any messages are more powerful.

III

A

The First Amendment, applicable to the States through the Fourteenth Amendment, provides that "Congress shall make no law . . . abridging the freedom of speech." The hallmark of the protection of free speech is to allow "free trade in ideas"—even ideas that the overwhelming majority of people might find distasteful or discomforting. Thus, the First Amendment "ordinarily" denies a State "the power to prohibit dissemination of social, economic and political doctrine which a vast majority of its citizens believes to be false and fraught with evil consequence." The First Amendment affords protection to symbolic or expressive conduct as well as to actual speech.

The protections afforded by the First Amendment, however, are not absolute, and we have long recognized that the government may regulate certain categories of expression consistent with the Constitution. The First Amendment permits "restrictions upon the content of speech in a few limited areas, which are 'of such slight social value as a step to truth that any benefit that may be derived from them is clearly outweighed by the social interest in order and morality.'"

Thus, for example, a State may punish those words "which by their very utterance inflict injury or tend to incite an immediate breach of the peace." We have consequently held that fighting words—"those personally abusive epithets which, when addressed to the ordinary citizen, are, as a matter of common knowledge, inherently likely to provoke violent reaction"—are generally proscribable under the First Amendment. Furthermore, "the constitutional guarantees of free speech and free press do not permit a State to forbid or proscribe advocacy of the use of force or of law violation except where such advocacy is directed to inciting or producing imminent lawless action and is likely to incite or produce such action." And the First Amendment also permits a State to ban a "true threat."

"True threats" encompass those statements where the speaker means to communicate a serious expression of an intent to commit an act of unlawful violence to a particular individual or group of individuals. The speaker need not actually intend to carry out the threat. Rather, a prohibition on true threats "protect[s] individuals from the fear of violence" and "from the disruption that fear engenders," in addition to protecting people "from the possibility that the threatened violence will occur." Intimidation in the constitutionally proscribable sense of the word is a type of true threat, where a speaker directs a threat to a person or group of persons with the intent of placing the victim in fear of bodily harm or death. Respondents do not contest that some cross burnings fit within this meaning of intimidating speech, and rightly so. As noted in Part II, *supra,* the history of cross burning in this country shows that cross burning is often intimidating, intended to create a pervasive fear in victims that they are a target of violence.

B

The Supreme Court of Virginia ruled that in light of *R. A. V. v. City of St. Paul,* even if it is constitutional to ban cross burning in a content-neutral manner, the Virginia cross-burning statute is unconstitutional because it discriminates on the basis of content and viewpoint. It is true, as the Supreme Court of Virginia held, that the burning of a cross is symbolic expression. The reason why the Klan burns a cross at its rallies, or individuals place a burning cross on someone else's lawn, is that the burning cross represents the message that the speaker wishes to communicate. Individuals burn crosses as opposed to other means of communication because cross burning carries a message in an effective and dramatic manner.[1]

The fact that cross burning is symbolic expression, however, does not resolve the constitutional question. The Supreme Court of Virginia relied upon *R. A. V. v. City of St. Paul* to conclude that once a statute discriminates on the basis of this type of content, the law is unconstitutional. We disagree.

In *R. A. V.,* we held that a local ordinance that banned certain symbolic conduct, including cross burning, when done with the knowledge that such conduct would "'arouse anger, alarm or resentment in others on the basis of race, color, creed, religion or gender'" was unconstitutional. We held that the ordinance did not pass constitutional muster because it discriminated on the basis of content by targeting only those individuals who "provoke violence" on a basis specified in the law. The ordinance did not cover "[t]hose who wish to use 'fighting words' in connection with other ideas—to express hostility, for example, on the basis of political affiliation, union membership, or homosexuality." This content-based discrimination was unconstitutional because it allowed the city "to impose special prohibitions on those speakers who express views on disfavored subjects."

We did not hold in *R. A. V.* that the First Amendment prohibits *all* forms of content-based discrimination within a proscribable area of speech. Rather, we specifically stated that some types of content discrimination did not violate the First Amendment:

> "When the basis for the content discrimination consists entirely of the very reason the entire class of speech at issue is proscribable, no significant danger of idea or viewpoint discrimination exists. Such a reason, having been adjudged neutral enough to support exclusion of the entire class of speech from First Amendment protection, is also neutral enough to form the basis of distinction within the class."

Indeed, we noted that it would be constitutional to ban only a particular type of threat: "[T]he Federal Government can criminalize only those threats of violence that are directed against the President . . . since the reasons why threats of violence are outside the First Amendment . . . have special force when applied to the person of the President." And a State may "choose to prohibit only that obscenity which is the most patently offensive *in its prurience—i.e.,* that which involves the most lascivious displays of sexual activity." Consequently, while the holding of *R. A. V.* does not permit a State to ban only obscenity based on "offensive *political* messages" or "only those threats against the President that mention his policy on aid to inner cities," the First Amendment permits content discrimination "based on the very reasons why the particular class of speech at issue . . . is proscribable."

Similarly, Virginia's statute does not run afoul of the First Amendment insofar as it bans cross burning with intent to intimidate. Unlike the statute at issue in *R. A. V.,* the Virginia statute does not single out for opprobrium only that speech directed toward "one of the specified disfavored topics." It does not matter whether an individual burns a cross with intent to intimidate because of the victim's race, gender, or religion, or because of the victim's "political affiliation, union membership, or homosexuality." Moreover, as a factual matter it is not true that cross burners direct their intimidating conduct solely to racial or religious minorities. Indeed, in the case of Elliott and O'Mara, it is at least unclear whether the respondents burned a cross due to racial animus.

The First Amendment permits Virginia to outlaw cross burnings done with the intent to intimidate because burning a cross is a particularly virulent form of intimidation. Instead of prohibiting all intimidating messages, Virginia may choose to regulate this subset of intimidating messages in light of cross burning's long and pernicious history as a signal of impending violence. Thus, just as a State may regulate only that obscenity which is the most obscene due to its prurient content, so too may a State choose to prohibit only those forms of intimidation that are most likely to inspire fear of bodily harm. A ban on cross burning carried out with the intent to intimidate is fully consistent with our holding in *R. A. V.* and is proscribable under the First Amendment.

IV

The Supreme Court of Virginia ruled in the alternative that Virginia's cross-burning statute was unconstitutionally overbroad due to its provision stating that "[a]ny such burning of a cross shall be prima facie evidence of an intent to intimidate a person or group of persons." The Commonwealth added the prima facie provision to the statute in 1968. The court below did not reach whether this provision is severable from the rest of the cross-burning statute under Virginia law. In this Court, as in the Supreme Court of Virginia, respondents do not argue that the prima facie evidence provision is unconstitutional as applied to any one of them. Rather, they contend that the provision is unconstitutional on its face.

The Supreme Court of Virginia has not ruled on the meaning of the prima facie evidence provision. It has, however, stated that "the act of burning a cross alone, with no evidence of intent to intimidate, will nonetheless suffice for arrest and prosecution and will insulate the Commonwealth from a motion to strike the evidence at the end of its case-in-chief." The jury in the case of Richard Elliott did not receive any instruction on the prima facie evidence provision, and the provision was not an issue in the case of Jonathan O'Mara because he pleaded guilty. The court in Barry Black's case, however, instructed the jury that the provision means: "The burning of a cross, by itself, is sufficient evidence from which you may infer the required intent."

The prima facie evidence provision, as interpreted by the jury instruction, renders the statute unconstitutional. Because this jury instruction is the Model Jury Instruction, and because the Supreme Court of Virginia had the opportunity to expressly disavow the jury instruction, the jury instruction's construction of the prima facie provision "is a ruling on a question of state law that is as binding on us as though the precise words had been written into" the statute. As construed by the jury instruction, the prima facie provision strips away the very reason why a State may ban cross burning with the intent to intimidate. The prima facie evidence provision permits a jury to convict in every cross-burning case in which defendants exercise their constitutional right not to put on a defense. And even where a defendant like Black presents a defense, the prima facie evidence provision makes it more likely that the jury will find an intent to intimidate regardless of the particular facts of the case. The provision permits the Commonwealth to arrest, prosecute, and convict a person based solely on the fact of cross burning itself.

It is apparent that the provision as so interpreted "'would create an unacceptable risk of the suppression of ideas.'" The act of burning a cross may mean that a person is engaging in constitutionally proscribable intimidation. But that same act may mean only that the person is engaged in core political speech. The prima facie evidence provision in this statute blurs the line between these two meanings of a burning cross. As interpreted by the jury instruction, the provision chills constitutionally protected political speech because of the possibility that a State will prosecute—and potentially convict— somebody engaging only in lawful political speech at the core of what the First Amendment is designed to protect.

As the history of cross burning indicates, a burning cross is not always intended to intimidate. Rather, sometimes the cross burning is a statement of ideology, a symbol of group solidarity. It is a ritual used at Klan gatherings, and it is used to represent the Klan itself. Thus, "[b]urning a cross at a political rally would almost certainly be protected expression." Indeed, occasionally a person who burns a cross does not intend to express either a statement of ideology or intimidation. Cross burnings have appeared in movies such as Mississippi Burning, and in plays such as the stage adaptation of Sir Walter Scott's The Lady of the Lake.

The prima facie provision makes no effort to distinguish among these different types of cross burnings. It does not distinguish between a cross burning done with the purpose of creating anger or resentment and a cross burning done with the purpose of threatening or intimidating a victim. It does not distinguish between a cross burning at a public rally or a cross burning on a neighbor's lawn. It does not treat the cross burning directed at an individual differently from the cross burning directed at a group of like-minded believers. It allows a jury to treat a cross burning on the property of another with the owner's acquiescence in the same manner as a cross burning on the property of another without the owner's permission. To this extent I agree with Justice Souter that the prima facie evidence provision can "skew jury deliberations toward conviction in cases where the evidence of intent to intimidate is relatively weak and arguably consistent with a solely ideological reason for burning."

It may be true that a cross burning, even at a political rally, arouses a sense of anger or hatred among the vast majority of citizens who see a burning cross. But this sense of anger or hatred is not sufficient to ban all cross burnings. As Gerald Gunther has stated, "The lesson I have drawn from my childhood in Nazi Germany and my happier adult life in this country is the need to walk the sometimes difficult path of denouncing the bigot's hateful ideas with all my power, yet at the same time challenging any community's attempt to suppress hateful ideas by force of law." The prima facie evidence provision in this case ignores all of the contextual factors that are necessary to decide whether a particular cross burning is intended to intimidate. The First Amendment does not permit such a shortcut.

For these reasons, the prima facie evidence provision, as interpreted through the jury instruction and as applied in Barry Black's case, is unconstitutional on its face. We recognize that the Supreme Court of Virginia has not authoritatively interpreted the meaning of the prima facie evidence provision. Unlike Justice Scalia, we refuse to speculate on whether any interpretation of the prima facie evidence provision would satisfy the First Amendment. Rather, all we hold is that because of the interpretation of the prima facie evidence provision given by the jury instruction, the provision makes the statute facially invalid at this point. We also recognize the theoretical possibility that the court, on remand, could interpret the provision in a manner different from that so far set forth in order to avoid the constitutional objections we have described. We leave open that possibility. We also leave open the possibility that the provision is severable, and if so, whether Elliott and O'Mara could be retried under §18.2-423.

V

With respect to Barry Black, we agree with the Supreme Court of Virginia that his conviction cannot stand, and we affirm the judgment of the Supreme Court of Virginia. With respect to Elliott and O'Mara, we vacate the judgment of the Supreme Court of Virginia, and remand the case for further proceedings.

It is so ordered.

Note

1. Justice Thomas argues in dissent that cross burning is "conduct, not expression." While it is of course true that burning a cross is conduct, it is equally true that the First Amendment protects symbolic conduct as well as pure speech. As Justice Thomas has previously recognized, a burning cross is a "symbol of hate," and a "a symbol of white supremacy."

➡ **NO**

Dissenting Opinion of Clarence Thomas

Justice Thomas, dissenting.

In every culture, certain things acquire meaning well beyond what outsiders can comprehend. That goes for both the sacred and the profane. I believe that cross burning is the paradigmatic example of the latter.

I

Although I agree with the majority's conclusion that it is constitutionally permissible to "ban . . . cross burning carried out with intent to intimidate," I believe that the majority errs in imputing an expressive component to the activity in question (relying on one of the exceptions to the First Amendment's prohibition on content-based discrimination outlined in *R. A. V. v. St. Paul*). In my view, whatever expressive value cross burning has, the legislature simply wrote it out by banning only intimidating conduct undertaken by a particular means. A conclusion that the statute prohibiting cross burning with intent to intimidate sweeps beyond a prohibition on certain conduct into the zone of expression overlooks not only the words of the statute but also reality.

A

"In holding [the ban on cross burning with intent to intimidate] unconstitutional, the Court ignores Justice Holmes' familiar aphorism that 'a page of history is worth a volume of logic.'"

To me, the majority's brief history of the Ku Klux Klan only reinforces [the] common understanding of the Klan as a terrorist organization, which, in its endeavor to intimidate, or even eliminate those it dislikes, uses the most brutal of methods.

Such methods typically include cross burning—"a tool for the intimidation and harassment of racial minorities, Catholics, Jews, Communists, and any other groups hated by the Klan." For those not easily frightened, cross burning has been followed by more extreme measures, such as beatings and murder. As the Solicitor General points out, the association between acts of intimidating cross burning and violence is well documented in recent American history.

From *Virginia v. Barry Elton Black, Richard J. Elliott, and Jonathan O'Mara*, 538 U.S. ___ (2003). References and some notes and case citations omitted.

Indeed, the connection between cross burning and violence is well ingrained, and lower courts have so recognized. . . .

But the perception that a burning cross is a threat and a precursor of worse things to come is not limited to blacks. Because the modern Klan expanded the list of its enemies beyond blacks and "radical[s]," to include Catholics, Jews, most immigrants, and labor unions, a burning cross is now widely viewed as a signal of impending terror and lawlessness. I wholeheartedly agree with the observation made by the Commonwealth of Virginia that

> "A white, conservative, middle-class Protestant, waking up at night to find a burning cross outside his home, will reasonably understand that someone is threatening him. His reaction is likely to be very different than if he were to find, say, a burning circle or square. In the latter case, he may call the fire department. In the former, he will probably call the police." Brief of Petitioner, at 26.

In our culture, cross burning has almost invariably meant lawlessness and understandably instills in its victims well-grounded fear of physical violence.

B

Virginia's experience has been no exception. In Virginia, though facing widespread opposition in 1920s, the KKK developed localized strength in the southeastern part of the State, where there were reports of scattered raids and floggings. Although the KKK was disbanded at the national level in 1944, a series of cross burnings in Virginia took place between 1949 and 1952.

Most of the crosses were burned on the lawns of black families, who either were business owners or lived in predominantly white neighborhoods. At least one of the cross burnings was accompanied by a shooting. The crosses burned near residences were about five to six feet tall; while a "huge cross reminiscent of the Ku Klux Klan days" burned "atop a hill" as part of the initiation ceremony of the secret organization of the Knights of Kavaliers, was twelve feet tall. These incidents were, in the words of the time, "*terroristic* [sic] . . . un-American act[s], designed to *intimidate* Negroes from seeking their rights as citizens."

In February 1952, in light of this series of cross burnings and attendant reports that the Klan, "long considered dead in Virginia, is being revitalized in Richmond," Governor Battle announced that "Virginia 'might well consider passing legislation' to restrict the activities of the Ku Klux Klan." As newspapers reported at the time, the bill was "to ban the burning of crosses and other similar evidences of *terrorism*." The bill was presented to the House of Delegates by a former FBI agent and future two-term Governor, Delegate Mills E. Godwin, Jr. "Godwin said law and order in the State were impossible if organized groups could *create fear by intimidation.*"

That in the early 1950s the people of Virginia viewed cross burning as creating an intolerable atmosphere of terror is not surprising: Although the cross took on some religious significance in the 1920's when the Klan became connected with certain southern white clergy, by the postwar period it had reverted to its original function "as an instrument of intimidation."

Strengthening Delegate Godwin's explanation, as well as my conclusion, that the legislature sought to criminalize terrorizing *conduct* is the fact that at the time the statute was enacted, racial segregation was not only the prevailing practice, but also the law in Virginia. And, just two years after the enactment of this statute, Virginia's General Assembly embarked on a campaign of "massive resistance" in response to *Brown* v. *Board of Education.*

It strains credulity to suggest that a state legislature that adopted a litany of segregationist laws self-contradictorily intended to squelch the segregationist message. Even for segregationists, violent and terroristic conduct, the Siamese twin of cross burning, was intolerable. The ban on cross burning with intent to intimidate demonstrates that even segregationists understood the difference between intimidating and terroristic conduct and racist expression. It is simply beyond belief that, in passing the statute now under review, the Virginia legislature was concerned with anything but penalizing conduct it must have viewed as particularly vicious.

Accordingly, this statute prohibits only conduct, not expression. And, just as one cannot burn down someone's house to make a political point and then seek refuge in the First Amendment, those who hate cannot terrorize and intimidate to make their point. In light of my conclusion that the statute here addresses only conduct, there is no need to analyze it under any of our First Amendment tests.

II

Even assuming that the statute implicates the First Amendment, in my view, the fact that the statute permits a jury to draw an inference of intent to intimidate from the cross burning itself presents no constitutional problems. Therein lies my primary disagreement with the plurality.

A

"The threshold inquiry is ascertaining the constitutional analysis applicable to [a jury instruction involving a presumption] is to determine the nature of the presumption it describes." We have categorized the presumptions as either permissive inferences or mandatory presumptions.

To the extent we do have a construction of this statute by the Virginia Supreme Court, we know that both the majority and the dissent agreed that the presumption was "a statutorily supplied *inference.*" Under Virginia law, the term "inference" has a well-defined meaning and is distinct from the term "presumption."

> A presumption is a rule of law that compels the fact finder to draw a certain conclusion or a certain inference from a given set of facts. [FN1: In contrast, *an inference,* sometimes loosely referred to as a presumption of fact, *does not compel a specific conclusion. An inference merely applies to the*

rational potency or probative value of an evidentiary fact to which the fact finder may attach whatever force or weight it deems best.] The primary significance of a presumption is that it operates to shift to the opposing party the burden of producing evidence tending to rebut the presumption. [FN2: *An inference, on the other hand, does not invoke this procedural consequence of shifting the burden of production.*] No presumption, however, can operate to shift the ultimate burden of persuasion from the party upon whom it was originally cast.

Both the majority and the dissent below classified the clause in question as an "inference," and I see no reason to disagree, particularly in light of the instructions given to the jury in Black's case, requiring it to find guilt beyond a reasonable doubt both as to the fact that "the defendant burned or caused to burn a cross in a public place," and that "he did so with the intent to intimidate any person or persons."

Even though under Virginia law the statutory provision at issue here is characterized as an "inference," the Court must still inquire whether the label Virginia attaches corresponds to the categorization our cases have given such clauses. In this respect, it is crucial to observe that what Virginia law calls an "inference" is what our cases have termed "a permissive inference or presumption."[1] Given that this Court's definitions of a "permissive inference" and a "mandatory presumption" track Virginia's definitions of "inference" and "presumption," the Court should judge the Virginia statute based on the constitutional analysis applicable to "inferences:" they raise no constitutional flags unless "no rational trier could make a connection permitted by the inference." As explained in Part I, *not* making a connection between cross burning and intimidation would be irrational.

But even with respect to statutes containing a mandatory irrebuttable presumption as to intent, the Court has not shown much concern. For instance, there is no scienter requirement for statutory rape. That is, a person can be arrested, prosecuted, and convicted for having sex with a minor, without the government ever producing any evidence, let alone proving beyond a reasonable doubt, that a minor did not consent. In fact, "[f]or purposes of the child molesting statute . . . consent is irrelevant. The legislature has determined in such cases that children under the age of sixteen (16) cannot, as a matter of law, consent to have sexual acts performed upon them, or consent to engage in a sexual act with someone over the age of sixteen (16)." The legislature finds the behavior so reprehensible that the intent is satisfied by the mere act committed by a perpetrator. Considering the horrific effect cross burning has on its victims, it is also reasonable to presume intent to intimidate from the act itself.

Statutes prohibiting possession of drugs with intent to distribute operate much the same way as statutory rape laws. Under these statutes, the intent to distribute is effectively satisfied by possession of some threshold amount of drugs. As with statutory rape, the presumption of intent in such statutes is irrebuttable—not only can a person be arrested for the crime of possession with intent to distribute (or "trafficking") without any evidence of intent beyond quantity of drugs, but such person cannot even mount a defense to the element of intent. However, as with statutory rape statutes, our cases do not reveal any controversy with respect to the presumption of intent in these drug statutes.

Because the prima facie clause here is an inference, not an irrebuttable presumption, there is all the more basis under our Due Process precedents to sustain this statute.

B

The plurality, however, is troubled by the presumption because this is a First Amendment case. The plurality laments the fate of an innocent cross-burner who burns a cross, but does so without an intent to intimidate. The plurality fears the chill on expression because, according to the plurality, the inference permits "the Commonwealth to arrest, prosecute and convict a person based solely on the fact of cross burning itself." First, it is, at the very least, unclear that the inference comes into play during arrest and initiation of a prosecution, that is, prior to the instructions stage of an actual trial. Second, as I explained above, the inference is rebuttable and, as the jury instructions given in this case demonstrate, Virginia law still requires the jury to find the existence of each element, including intent to intimidate, beyond a reasonable doubt.

Moreover, even in the First Amendment context, the Court has upheld such regulations where conduct that initially appears culpable, ultimately results in dismissed charges. A regulation of pornography is one such example. While possession of child pornography is illegal, possession of adult pornography, as long as it is not obscene, is allowed. As a result, those pornographers trafficking in images of adults who look like minors, may be not only deterred but also arrested and prosecuted for possessing what a jury might find to be legal materials. This "chilling" effect has not, however, been a cause for grave concern with respect to overbreadth of such statutes among the members of this Court.

That the First Amendment gives way to other interests is not a remarkable proposition. What is remarkable is that, under the plurality's analysis, the determination of whether an interest is sufficiently compelling depends not on the harm a regulation in question seeks to prevent, but on the area of society at which it aims. For instance, in *Hill* v. *Colorado,* the Court upheld a restriction on protests near abortion clinics, explaining that the State had a legitimate interest, which was sufficiently narrowly tailored, in protecting those seeking services of such establishments "from unwanted advice" and "unwanted communication." In so concluding, the Court placed heavy reliance on the "vulnerable physical and emotional conditions" of patients. Thus, when it came to the rights of those seeking abortions, the Court deemed restrictions on "unwanted advice," which, notably, can be given only from a distance of at least 8 feet from a prospective patient, justified by the countervailing interest in obtaining abortion. Yet, here, the plurality strikes down the statute because one day an individual might wish to burn a cross, but might do so without an intent to intimidate anyone. That cross burning subjects its targets, and, sometimes, an unintended audience, to extreme emotional distress, and is virtually never viewed merely as "unwanted communication," but rather, as a physical threat, is of no concern to the plurality. Henceforth, under the plurality's view, physical safety will be valued less than the right to be free from unwanted communications.

III

Because I would uphold the validity of this statute, I respectfully dissent.

Note

1.   As the Court explained in [*County Court of Ulster City* v.] *Allen,* a permissive inference or presumption "allows—but does not require—the trier of fact to infer the elemental fact from proof by the prosecutor of the basic one and which places no burden of any kind on the defendant. In that situation the basic fact may constitute prima facie evidence of the elemental fact. . . . Because this permissive presumption leaves the trier of fact free to credit or reject the inference and does not shift the burden of proof, it affects the application of the 'beyond a reasonable doubt' standard only if, under the facts of the case, there is no rational way the trier could make the connection permitted by the inference." *Id.* at 157 (internal citations omitted). By contrast, "a mandatory presumption . . . may affect not only the strength of the 'no reasonable doubt' burden but also the placement of that burden; it tells the trier that he or they *must* find the elemental fact upon proof of the basic fact, at least unless the defendant has come forward with some evidence to rebut the presumed connection between the two facts." *Id.*

POSTSCRIPT

Are Blanket Prohibitions on Cross Burnings Unconstitutional?

Cross burning and other acts of "symbolic speech" straddle the poorly defined line that distinguishes speech from conduct. In the history of the Supreme Court, this distinction has been a central cause of controversy surrounding what does and does not deserve First Amendment protection. According to Justice Thomas, the distinction between conduct and speech is one of the key issues in *Virginia v. Black*; he asserts that the majority reaches the wrong conclusion because it refuses to recognize cross burning as "conduct" that the state may constitutionally outlaw. "A conclusion," he writes, "that the statute prohibiting cross burning with intent to intimidate sweeps beyond a prohibition on certain conduct into the zone of expression overlooks not only the words of the statute but also reality."

In deciding what constituted "conduct" and "speech" in cases involving controversial actions, the Supreme Court had to consider a number of issues: whether the symbolic speech was likely to provoke "imminent lawless action" (*Brandenburg v. Ohio*, 89 S. Ct. 1827, 1969), whether the government regulations were content-neutral or discriminating based on popular beliefs and values, and whether "the State has a justifiable interest in regulating speech" (*Cohen v. California*, 91 S. Ct. 1780, 1971). Adding to the confusion, the Court has also stated that the presence of "expressive content" is not sufficient to mandate constitutional protection. In *Dallas v. Stanglin*, 109 S. Ct. 1591 (1989), the Court argued, "It is possible to find some kernel of expression in almost every activity a person undertakes—for example, walking down the street or meeting one's friends at a shopping mall—but such a kernel is not sufficient to bring the activity within the protection of the First Amendment." The issue of symbolic speech, and what actions fall under its special constitutional status, continues to provoke fierce debate in the Supreme Court.

Recommended readings include Wyn Craig Wade, *The Fiery Cross: The Ku Klux Klan in America* (Simon & Schuster, 1987); David M. Chalmers, *Hooded Americanism: The History of the Ku Klux Klan* (Duke University Press, 1987); Frederick Schauer, *Free Speech: A Philosophical Enquiry* (Cambridge University Press, 1982); Randall P. Bezanson, *Speech Stories: How Free Can Speech Be?* (New York University Press, 1998); Edward J. Cleary, *Beyond the Burning Cross: The First Amendment and the Landmark R. A. V. Case* (Random House, 1994); and Steven Gey, "The Nuremberg Files and the First Amendment Value of Threats," 78 *Texas Law Review* 541 (2000). Finally, an interesting case concerning speech, threats, and the Internet is *Planned Parenthood v. American Coalition of Life Activists*, 290 F.3d 1058 (9th Cir. 2002).

ISSUE 17

Should Same-Sex Couples Receive Constitutional Protection?

YES: **Margaret Marshall**, from Majority Opinion, *Goodridge et al., v. Department of Public Health*, Massachusetts Supreme Court (2003)

NO: **Robert Cordy**, from Minority Opinion, *Goodridge et al., v. Department of Public Health*, Massachusetts Supreme Court (2003)

ISSUE SUMMARY

YES: Massachusetts Supreme Court Justice Margaret Marshall rules that banning marriage to same-sex couples causes hardship to a segment of the population for no rational reason.

NO: Massachusetts Supreme Court Justice Robert Cordy, in dissent, holds that a statute banning same-sex marriage is a valid exercise of the state's police power.

In spring 2001, seven same-sex couples in Massachusetts unsuccessfully applied for marriage licenses from their respective town clerks. The clerks all denied the requests because the applicants were same-sex couples. As a result, the couples filed suit in the Massachusetts Superior Court (trial court), claiming that the clerks' actions violated the equal protection clause of the Massachusetts Constitution. That clause provides, "All people are born free and equal and have certain natural, essential and unalienable rights; among which may be reckoned the right of enjoying and defending their lives and liberties; that of acquiring, possessing and protecting property; in fine, that of seeking and obtaining their safety and happiness. Equality under the law shall not be denied or abridged because of sex, race, color, creed or national origin (Mass. Const. Pt. 1, Art. 1). The trial court rejected the same-sex couples' claims, and held that the state's prohibition of same-sex marriages was constitutionally permissible because it advanced the state's interest in protecting the primary purpose of the institution of marriage: procreation.

All sides agreed that the issue's importance was of sufficient magnitude to warrant bypassing the intermediate appellate court and, instead, called for direct appeal to the Massachusetts Supreme Judicial Court. There, in a sharply divided four to three decision, the Supreme Judicial Court vacated the trial court's ruling, holding that the prohibition of same-sex marriages was unconstitutional. The high court did not, however, order the state to begin to issue marriage licenses to the same sex applicants but, instead, remanded the case back to the Superior Court with a stay for 180 days to allow the Massachusetts legislature to take appropriate action.

The Massachusetts Court was immediately caught up in the political storm surrounding the question of gay rights in particular, and the question of "moral values" and contemporary society more generally. The Court was both reviled and praised. Little more than a year away from the presidential elections, the Court and its decision were pulled into the national political debates. Was this decision the fair and just thing to do, treating all, regardless of their sexual orientation, to the benefits of the institution of marriage? Or, is marriage an historically unique social institution, intended to recognize only the union between a man and a woman? With upwards of 50 percent of all marriages in the United States ending in divorce, would this decision further contribute to the fragility of a social institution that, historically, has been central to the organization and stability of society? Or, would it have the opposite effect: reaffirming the centrality of marriage, whether it be formed by same or opposite sex couples? Finally, was this decision yet one more example of a highly politicized, "activist" judiciary, usurping the law-making function and "legislating" from the bench? Or, was this a situation where the judiciary properly used its power of judicial review to protect the rights of a traditionally marginalized minority group? These issues are contested in the following opinions by Justices Marshall and Cordy from the *Goodridge* decision.

YES ⤶

Majority Opinion

Marriage is a vital social institution. The exclusive commitment of two individuals to each other nurtures love and mutual support; it brings stability to our society. For those who choose to marry, and for their children, marriage provides an abundance of legal, financial, and social benefits. In return it imposes weighty legal, financial, and social obligations. The question before us is whether, consistent with the Massachusetts Constitution, the Commonwealth may deny the protections, benefits, and obligations conferred by civil marriage to two individuals of the same sex who wish to marry. We conclude that it may not. The Massachusetts Constitution affirms the dignity and equality of all individuals. It forbids the creation of second-class citizens. In reaching our conclusion we have given full deference to the arguments made by the Commonwealth. But it has failed to identify any constitutionally adequate reason for denying civil marriage to same-sex couples.

We are mindful that our decision marks a change in the history of our marriage law. Many people hold deep-seated religious, moral, and ethical convictions that marriage should be limited to the union of one man and one woman, and that homosexual conduct is immoral. Many hold equally strong religious, moral, and ethical convictions that same-sex couples are entitled to be married, and that homosexual persons should be treated no differently than their heterosexual neighbors. Neither view answers the question before us. Our concern is with the Massachusetts Constitution as a charter of governance for every person properly within its reach. "Our obligation is to define the liberty of all, not to mandate our own moral code." *Lawrence v. Texas,* 123 S.Ct. 2472, 2480 (2003) (*Lawrence*), quoting *Planned Parenthood of Southeastern Pa. v. Casey,* 505 U.S. 833, 850 (1992).

Whether the Commonwealth may use its formidable regulatory authority to bar same-sex couples from civil marriage is a question not previously addressed by a Massachusetts appellate court. It is a question the United States Supreme Court left open as a matter of Federal law in *Lawrence, supra* at 2484, where it was not an issue. There, the Court affirmed that the core concept of common human dignity protected by the Fourteenth Amendment to the United States Constitution precludes government intrusion into the deeply personal realms of consensual adult expressions of intimacy and one's choice of an intimate partner. The Court also reaffirmed the central role that decisions whether to marry or have children bear in shaping one's identity. *Id.* at

Majority Opinion, Hillary Goodridge & others vs. Department Of Public Health & another. SJC-08860, March 4, 2003.–November 18, 2003. Some case citations omitted. Notes omitted.

2481. The Massachusetts Constitution is, if anything, more protective of individual liberty and equality than the Federal Constitution; it may demand broader protection for fundamental rights; and it is less tolerant of government intrusion into the protected spheres of private life. . . .

Barred access to the protections, benefits, and obligations of civil marriage, a person who enters into an intimate, exclusive union with another of the same sex is arbitrarily deprived of membership in one of our community's most rewarding and cherished institutions. That exclusion is incompatible with the constitutional principles of respect for individual autonomy and equality under law. . . .

The plaintiffs include business executives, lawyers, an investment banker, educators, therapists, and a computer engineer. Many are active in church, community, and school groups. They have employed such legal means as are available to them—for example, joint adoption, powers of attorney, and joint ownership of real property—to secure aspects of their relationships. Each plaintiff attests a desire to marry his or her partner in order to affirm publicly their commitment to each other and to secure the legal protections and benefits afforded to married couples and their children. . . .

The department, represented by the Attorney General, admitted to a policy and practice of denying marriage licenses to same-sex couples. It denied that its actions violated any law or that the plaintiffs were entitled to relief. The parties filed cross motions for summary judgment.

A Superior Court judge ruled for the department. In a memorandum of decision and order dated May 7, 2002, he dismissed the plaintiffs' claim that the marriage statutes should be construed to permit marriage between persons of the same sex, holding that the plain wording of G.L. c. 207, as well as the wording of other marriage statutes, precluded that interpretation. Turning to the constitutional claims, he held that the marriage exclusion does not offend the liberty, freedom, equality, or due process provisions of the Massachusetts Constitution, and that the Massachusetts Declaration of Rights does not guarantee "the fundamental right to marry a person of the same sex." He concluded that prohibiting same-sex marriage rationally furthers the Legislature's legitimate interest in safeguarding the "primary purpose" of marriage, "procreation." The Legislature may rationally limit marriage to opposite-sex couples, he concluded, because those couples are "theoretically . . . capable of procreation," they do not rely on "inherently more cumbersome" noncoital means of reproduction, and they are more likely than same-sex couples to have children, or more children. . . .

In short, for all the joy and solemnity that normally attend a marriage, G.L. c. 207, governing entrance to marriage, is a licensing law. The plaintiffs argue that because nothing in that licensing law specifically prohibits marriages between persons of the same sex, we may interpret the statute to permit "qualified same sex couples" to obtain marriage licenses, thereby avoiding the question whether the law is constitutional. . . . This claim lacks merit. . . .

∙◦∙

The larger question is whether, as the department claims, government action that bars same-sex couples from civil marriage constitutes a legitimate exercise of the State's authority to regulate conduct, or whether, as the plaintiffs claim, this categorical marriage exclusion violates the Massachusetts Constitution. We have recognized the long-standing statutory understanding, derived from the common law, that "marriage" means the lawful union of a woman and a man. But that history cannot and does not foreclose the constitutional question.

The plaintiffs' claim that the marriage restriction violates the Massachusetts Constitution can be analyzed in two ways. Does it offend the Constitution's guarantees of equality before the law? Or do the liberty and due process provisions of the Massachusetts Constitution secure the plaintiffs' right to marry their chosen partner? In matters implicating marriage, family life, and the upbringing of children, the two constitutional concepts frequently overlap, as they do here. . . .

We begin by considering the nature of civil marriage itself. Simply put, the government creates civil marriage. In Massachusetts, civil marriage is, and since pre-Colonial days has been, precisely what its name implies: a wholly secular institution. . . . No religious ceremony has ever been required to validate a Massachusetts marriage.

In a real sense, there are three partners to every civil marriage: two willing spouses and an approving State. . . . While only the parties can mutually assent to marriage, the terms of the marriage—who may marry and what obligations, benefits, and liabilities attach to civil marriage—are set by the Commonwealth. Conversely, while only the parties can agree to end the marriage (absent the death of one of them or a marriage void ab initio), the Commonwealth defines the exit terms.

Civil marriage is created and regulated through exercise of the police power. . . . "Police power" (now more commonly termed the State's regulatory authority) is an old-fashioned term for the Commonwealth's lawmaking authority, as bounded by the liberty and equality guarantees of the Massachusetts Constitution and its express delegation of power from the people to their government. In broad terms, it is the Legislature's power to enact rules to regulate conduct, to the extent that such laws are "necessary to secure the health, safety, good order, comfort, or general welfare of the community." . . .

Without question, civil marriage enhances the "welfare of the community." It is a "social institution of the highest importance." Civil marriage anchors an ordered society by encouraging stable relationships over transient ones. It is central to the way the Commonwealth identifies individuals, provides for the orderly distribution of property, ensures that children and adults are cared for and supported whenever possible from private rather than public funds, and tracks important epidemiological and demographic data.

Marriage also bestows enormous private and social advantages on those who choose to marry. Civil marriage is at once a deeply personal commitment to another human being and a highly public celebration of the ideals of mutuality, companionship, intimacy, fidelity, and family. "It is an association that promotes a way of life, not causes; a harmony in living, not political faiths; a bilateral loyalty, not commercial or social projects." *Griswold v. Connecticut,* 381 U.S. 479, 486 (1965). Because it fulfils yearnings for security, safe haven, and connection that express our common humanity, civil marriage is an esteemed institution, and the decision whether and whom to marry is among life's momentous acts of self-definition.

Tangible as well as intangible benefits flow from marriage. The marriage license grants valuable property rights to those who meet the entry requirements, and who agree to what might otherwise be a burdensome degree of government regulation of their activities. . . . The Legislature has conferred on "each party [in a civil marriage] substantial rights concerning the assets of the other which unmarried cohabitants do not have." . . .

꿏ꙮꙭ

For decades, indeed centuries, in much of this country (including Massachusetts) no lawful marriage was possible between white and black Americans. That long history availed not when the Supreme Court of California held in 1948 that a legislative prohibition against interracial marriage violated the due process and equality guarantees of the Fourteenth Amendment, *Perez v. Sharp,* 32 Cal.2d 711, 728 (1948), or when, nineteen years later, the United States Supreme Court also held that a statutory bar to interracial marriage violated the Fourteenth Amendment, *Loving v. Virginia,* 388 U.S. 1 (1967). As both *Perez* and *Loving* make clear, the right to marry means little if it does not include the right to marry the person of one's choice, subject to appropriate government restrictions in the interests of public health, safety, and welfare. See *Perez v. Sharp, supra* at 717 ("the essence of the right to marry is freedom to join in marriage with the person of one's choice"). See also *Loving v. Virginia, supra* at 12. In this case, as in *Perez* and *Loving,* a statute deprives individuals of access to an institution of fundamental legal, personal, and social significance—the institution of marriage—because of a single trait: skin color in *Perez* and *Loving,* sexual orientation here. As it did in *Perez* and *Loving,* history must yield to a more fully developed understanding of the invidious quality of the discrimination.

The Massachusetts Constitution protects matters of personal liberty against government incursion as zealously, and often more so, than does the Federal Constitution, even where both Constitutions employ essentially the same language. See *Planned Parenthood League of Mass., Inc. v. Attorney Gen.,* 424 Mass. 586, 590 (1997); *Corning Glass Works v. Ann & Hope, Inc. of Danvers,* 363 Mass. 409, 416 (1973). That the Massachusetts Constitution is in some instances more protective of individual liberty interests than is the Federal Constitution is not surprising. Fundamental to the vigor of our Federal system of government is that "state courts are absolutely free to interpret state constitutional provisions to accord greater protection to individual rights than do similar provisions of the United States Constitution." *Arizona v. Evans,* 514 U.S. 1, 8 (1995).

The individual liberty and equality safeguards of the Massachusetts Constitution protect both "freedom from" unwarranted government intrusion into protected spheres of life and "freedom to" partake in benefits created by the State for the common good. See *Bachrach v. Secretary of the Commonwealth,* 382 Mass. 268, 273 (1981); *Dalli v. Board of Educ.,* 358 Mass. 753, 759 (1971). Both freedoms are involved here. Whether and whom to marry, how to express sexual intimacy, and whether and how to establish a family—these are among the most basic of every individual's liberty and due process rights. See, e.g., *Lawrence, supra* at 2481; *Planned Parenthood of Southeastern Pa. v. Casey,* 505 U.S. 833, 851 (1992); *Zablocki v. Redhail,* 434 U.S. 374, 384 (1978); *Roe v. Wade,* 410 U.S. 113, 152–153 (1973); *Eisenstadt v. Baird,* 405 U.S. 438, 453 (1972); *Loving v. Virginia, supra.* And central to personal freedom and security is the assurance that the laws will apply equally to persons in similar situations. "Absolute equality before the law is a fundamental principle of our own Constitution." *Opinion of the Justices,* 211 Mass. 618, 619 (1912). The liberty interest in choosing whether and whom to marry would be hollow if the Commonwealth could, without sufficient justification, foreclose an individual from freely choosing the person with whom to share an exclusive commitment in the unique institution of civil marriage. . . .

The plaintiffs challenge the marriage statute on both equal protection and due process grounds. With respect to each such claim, we must first determine the appropriate standard of review. Where a statute implicates a fundamental right or uses a suspect classification, we employ "strict judicial scrutiny." *Lowell v. Kowalski,* 380 Mass. 663, 666 (1980). For all other statutes, we employ the "'rational basis' test." *English v. New England Med. Ctr.,* 405 Mass. 423, 428 (1989). For due process claims, rational basis analysis requires that statutes "bear[ ] a real and substantial relation to the public health, safety, morals, or some other phase of the general welfare." *Coffee-Rich, Inc. v. Commissioner of Pub. Health, supra,* quoting *Sperry & Hutchinson Co. v. Director of the Div. on the Necessaries of Life,* 307 Mass. 408, 418 (1940). For equal protection challenges, the rational basis test requires that "an impartial lawmaker could logically believe that the classification would serve a legitimate public purpose that transcends the harm to the members of the disadvantaged class." *English v. New England Med. Ctr., supra* at 429, quoting *Cleburne v. Cleburne Living Ctr., Inc.,* 473 U.S. 432, 452 (1985) (Stevens, J., concurring).

The department argues that no fundamental right or "suspect" class is at issue here, and rational basis is the appropriate standard of review. For the reasons we explain below, we conclude that the marriage ban does not meet the rational basis test for either due process or equal protection. Because the statute does not survive rational basis review, we do not consider the plaintiffs' arguments that this case merits strict judicial scrutiny.

The department posits three legislative rationales for prohibiting same-sex couples from marrying: (1) providing a "favorable setting for procreation"; (2) ensuring the optimal setting for child rearing, which the department defines as "a two-parent family with one parent of each sex"; and (3) preserving scarce State and private financial resources. We consider each in turn. . . .

Our laws of civil marriage do not privilege procreative heterosexual intercourse between married people above every other form of adult intimacy and every other means of creating a family. General Laws c. 207 contains no requirement that the applicants for a marriage license attest to their ability or intention to conceive children by coitus. Fertility is not a condition of marriage, nor is it grounds for divorce. People who have never consummated their marriage, and never plan to, may be and stay married. . . . People who cannot stir from their deathbed may marry. See G.L. c. 207, § 28A. While it is certainly true that many, perhaps most, married couples have children together (assisted or unassisted), it is the exclusive and permanent commitment of the marriage partners to one another, not the begetting of children, that is the sine qua non of civil marriage.

Moreover, the Commonwealth affirmatively facilitates bringing children into a family regardless of whether the intended parent is married or unmarried, whether the child is adopted or born into a family, whether assistive technology was used to conceive the child, and whether the parent or her partner is heterosexual, homosexual, or bisexual. If procreation were a necessary component of civil marriage, our statutes would draw a tighter circle around the permissible bounds of nonmarital child bearing and the creation of families by noncoital means. The attempt to isolate procreation as "the source of a fundamental right to marry," *post* at (Cordy, J., dissenting), overlooks the integrated way in which courts have examined the complex and overlapping realms of personal autonomy, marriage, family life, and child rearing. Our jurisprudence recognizes that, in these nuanced and fundamentally private areas of life, such a narrow focus is inappropriate.

The "marriage is procreation" argument singles out the one unbridgeable difference between same-sex and opposite-sex couples, and transforms that difference into the essence of legal marriage . . . and full access to the political process, the marriage restriction impermissibly "identifies persons by a single trait and then denies them protection across the board." *Romer v. Evans,* 517 U.S. 620, 633 (1996). In so doing, the State's action confers an official stamp of approval on the destructive stereotype that same-sex relationships are inherently unstable and inferior to opposite-sex relationships and are not worthy of respect.

The department's first stated rationale, equating marriage with unassisted heterosexual procreation, shades imperceptibly into its second: that confining marriage to opposite-sex couples ensures that children are raised in the "optimal" setting. Protecting the welfare of children is a paramount State policy. Restricting marriage to opposite-sex couples, however, cannot plausibly further this policy. . . .

The department has offered no evidence that forbidding marriage to people of the same sex will increase the number of couples choosing to enter into opposite-sex marriages in order to have and raise children. There is thus no rational relationship between the marriage statute and the Commonwealth's proffered goal of protecting the "optimal" child rearing unit. Moreover, the department readily concedes that people in same-sex couples may be "excellent" parents. These couples (including four of the plaintiff couples) have children for the reasons others do—to love them, to care for them, to nurture them. But the task of child rearing for same-sex couples is made infinitely harder by their status as outliers to the marriage laws. . . . Given the wide range of public benefits reserved only for married couples, we do not credit the department's contention that the absence of access to civil marriage amounts to little more than an inconvenience to same-sex couples and their children. Excluding same-sex couples from civil marriage will not make children of opposite-sex marriages more secure, but it does prevent children of same-sex couples from enjoying the immeasurable advantages that flow from the assurance of "a stable family structure in which children will be reared, educated, and socialized." . . .

In this case, we are confronted with an entire, sizeable class of parents raising children who have absolutely no access to civil marriage and its protections because they are forbidden from procuring a marriage license. It cannot be rational under our laws, and indeed it is not permitted, to penalize children by depriving them of State benefits because the State disapproves of their parents' sexual orientation.

The third rationale advanced by the department is that limiting marriage to opposite-sex couples furthers the Legislature's interest in conserving scarce State and private financial resources. The marriage restriction is rational, it argues, because the General Court logically could assume that same-sex couples are more financially independent than married couples and thus less needy of public marital benefits, such as tax advantages, or private marital benefits, such as employer-financed health plans that include spouses in their coverage.

An absolute statutory ban on same-sex marriage bears no rational relationship to the goal of economy. First, the department's conclusory generalization—that same-sex couples are less financially dependent on each other than opposite-sex couples—ignores that many same-sex couples, such as many of the plaintiffs in this case, have children and other dependents (here, aged parents) in their care. The department does not contend, nor could it, that these dependents are less needy or deserving than the dependents of married couples. Second, Massachusetts marriage laws do not condition receipt of public and private financial benefits to married individuals on a demonstration of financial dependence on each other; the benefits are available to married couples regardless of whether they mingle their finances or actually depend on each other for support. . . .

Here, the plaintiffs seek only to be married, not to undermine the institution of civil marriage. They do not want marriage abolished. They do not attack the binary nature of marriage, the consanguinity provisions, or any of the other gate-keeping provisions of the marriage licensing law. Recognizing the right of an individual to marry a person of the same sex will not diminish the validity or dignity of opposite-sex marriage, any more than recognizing the right of an individual to marry a person of a different race devalues the marriage of a person who marries someone of her own race. If anything, extending civil marriage to same-sex couples reinforces the importance of marriage to individuals and communities. That same-sex couples are willing to embrace marriage's solemn obligations of exclusivity, mutual support, and commitment to one another is a testament to the enduring place of marriage in our laws and in the human spirit. . . .

The marriage ban works a deep and scarring hardship on a very real segment of the community for no rational reason. The absence of any reasonable relationship between, on the one hand, an absolute disqualification of same-sex couples who wish to enter into civil marriage and, on the other, protection of public health, safety, or general welfare, suggests that the marriage restriction is rooted in persistent prejudices against persons who are (or who are believed to be) homosexual. "The Constitution cannot control such prejudices but neither can it tolerate them. Private biases may be outside the reach of the law, but the law cannot, directly or indirectly, give them effect." Limiting the protections, benefits, and obligations of civil marriage to opposite-sex couples violates the basic premises of individual liberty and equality under law protected by the Massachusetts Constitution.

⋅⋖❂⋗⋅

We consider next the plaintiffs' request for relief. We preserve as much of the statute as may be preserved in the face of the successful constitutional challenge. . . .

Here, no one argues that striking down the marriage laws is an appropriate form of relief. Eliminating civil marriage would be wholly inconsistent with the Legislature's deep commitment to fostering stable families and would dismantle a vital organizing principle of our society. . . .

We construe civil marriage to mean the voluntary union of two persons as spouses, to the exclusion of all others. This reformulation redresses the plaintiffs' constitutional injury and furthers the aim of marriage to promote stable, exclusive relationships. It advances the two legitimate State interests the department has identified: providing a stable setting for child rearing and conserving State resources. It leaves intact the Legislature's broad discretion to regulate marriage. . . .

So ordered. . . . .

Robert Cordy ➡ **NO**

Minority Opinion

. . . The court's opinion concludes that the Department of Public Health has failed to identify any "constitutionally adequate reason" for limiting civil marriage to opposite-sex unions, and that there is no "reasonable relationship" between a disqualification of same-sex couples who wish to enter into a civil marriage and the protection of public health, safety, or general welfare. Consequently, it holds that the marriage statute cannot withstand scrutiny under the Massachusetts Constitution. Because I find these conclusions to be unsupportable in light of the nature of the rights and regulations at issue, the presumption of constitutional validity and significant deference afforded to legislative enactments, and the "undesirability of the judiciary substituting its notions of correct policy for that of a popularly elected Legislature" responsible for making such policy, *Zayre Corp. v. Attorney Gen.,* 372 Mass. 423, 433 (1977), I respectfully dissent. Although it may be desirable for many reasons to extend to same-sex couples the benefits and burdens of civil marriage (and the plaintiffs have made a powerfully reasoned case for that extension), that decision must be made by the Legislature, not the court. . . .

A. *Limiting marriage to the union of one man and one woman does not impair the exercise of a fundamental right.* Civil marriage is an institution created by the State. In Massachusetts, the marriage statutes are derived from English common law. . . . They were enacted to secure public interests and not for religious purposes or to promote personal interests or aspirations. As the court notes in its opinion, the institution of marriage is "the legal union of a man and woman as husband and wife," *ante* at, and it has always been so under Massachusetts law, colonial or otherwise.

The plaintiffs contend that because the right to choose to marry is a "fundamental" right, the right to marry the person of one's choice, including a member of the same sex, must also be a "fundamental" right. While the court stops short of deciding that the right to marry someone of the same sex is "fundamental" such that strict scrutiny must be applied to any statute that impairs it, it nevertheless agrees with the plaintiffs that the right to choose to marry is of fundamental importance . . . and would be "hollow" if an individual was foreclosed from "freely choosing the person with whom to share . . . the . . . institution of civil marriage." Hence, it concludes that a marriage license cannot be denied to an individual who wishes to marry someone of the same sex. In

Minority Opinion, Hillary Goodridge & others vs. Department Of Public Health & another. SJC-08860, March 4, 2003.—November 18, 2003. Some case citations omitted. Notes omitted.

reaching this result the court has transmuted the "right" to marry into a right to change the institution of marriage itself. This feat of reasoning succeeds only if one accepts the proposition that the definition of the institution of marriage as a union between a man and a woman is merely "conclusory," rather than the basis on which the "right" to partake in it has been deemed to be of fundamental importance. In other words, only by assuming that "marriage" includes the union of two persons of the same sex does the court conclude that restricting marriage to opposite-sex couples infringes on the "right" of same-sex couples to "marry."

The plaintiffs ground their contention that they have a fundamental right to marry a person of the same sex in a long line of Supreme Court decisions that discuss the importance of marriage. In context, all of these decisions and their discussions are about the "fundamental" nature of the institution of marriage as it has existed and been understood in this country, not as the court has redefined it today. Even in that context, its "fundamental" nature is derivative of the nature of the interests that underlie or are associated with it. An examination of those interests reveals that they are either not shared by same-sex couples or not implicated by the marriage statutes.

Supreme Court cases that have described marriage or the right to marry as "fundamental" have focused primarily on the underlying interest of every individual in procreation, which, historically, could only legally occur within the construct of marriage because sexual intercourse outside of marriage was a criminal act. . . . Because same-sex couples are unable to procreate on their own, any right to marriage they may possess cannot be based on their interest in procreation, which has been essential to the Supreme Court's denomination of the right to marry as fundamental.

Supreme Court cases recognizing a right to privacy in intimate decision-making . . . have also focused primarily on sexual relations and the decision whether or not to procreate, and have refused to recognize an "unlimited right" to privacy. . . .

What the *Griswold* Court found "repulsive to the notions of privacy surrounding the marriage relationship" was the prospect of "allow[ing] the police to search the sacred precincts of marital bedrooms for telltale signs of the use of contraceptives." . . . When Justice Goldberg spoke of "marital relations" in the context of finding it "difficult to imagine what is more private or more intimate than a husband and wife's marital relations[hip]," he was obviously referring to sexual relations. Similarly, in *Lawrence v. Texas,* 123 S.Ct. 2472 (2003), it was the criminalization of private sexual behavior that the Court found violative of the petitioners' liberty interest. . . .

The marriage statute, which regulates only the act of obtaining a marriage license, does not implicate privacy in the sense that it has found constitutional protection under Massachusetts and Federal law. . . . It does not intrude on any right that the plaintiffs have to privacy in their choices regarding procreation, an intimate partner or sexual relations. The plaintiffs' right to privacy in such matters does not require that the State officially endorse their choices in order for the right to be constitutionally vindicated.

Although some of the privacy cases also speak in terms of personal autonomy, no court has ever recognized such an open-ended right. "That many of the rights and liberties protected by the Due Process Clause sound in personal autonomy does not warrant the sweeping conclusion that any and all important, intimate, and personal decisions are so protected. . . ." *Washington v. Glucksberg,* 521 U.S. 702, 727 (1997). Such decisions are protected not because they are important, intimate, and personal, but because the right or liberty at stake is "so deeply rooted in our history and traditions, or so fundamental to our concept of constitutionally ordered liberty" that it is protected by due process. *Id.* Accordingly, the Supreme Court has concluded that while the decision to refuse unwanted medical treatment is fundamental, *Cruzan v. Director, Mo. Dep't of Health,* 497 U.S. 261, 278 (1990), because it is deeply rooted in our nation's history and tradition, the equally personal and profound decision to commit suicide is not because of the absence of such roots. *Washington v. Glucksberg, supra.*

While the institution of marriage is deeply rooted in the history and traditions of our country and our State, the right to marry someone of the same sex is not. No matter how personal or intimate a decision to marry someone of the same sex might be, the right to make it is not guaranteed by the right of personal autonomy. . . .

Unlike opposite-sex marriages, which have deep historic roots, or the parent-child relationship, which reflects a "strong tradition" founded on "the history and culture of Western civilization" and "is now established beyond debate as an enduring American tradition," or extended family relationships, which have been "honored throughout our history," same-sex relationships, although becoming more accepted, are certainly not so "deeply rooted in this Nation's history and tradition" as to warrant such enhanced constitutional protection.

Although "expressions of emotional support and public commitment" have been recognized as among the attributes of marriage, which, "*[t]aken together . . .* form a constitutionally protected marital relationship," those interests, standing alone, are not the source of a fundamental right to marry. . . .

Finally, the constitutionally protected interest in child rearing, . . . is not implicated or infringed by the marriage statute here. The fact that the plaintiffs cannot marry has no bearing on their independently protected constitutional rights as parents which, as with opposite-sex parents, are limited only by their continued fitness and the best interests of their children. . . .

Because the rights and interests discussed above do not afford the plaintiffs any fundamental right that would be impaired by a statute limiting marriage to members of the opposite sex, they have no fundamental right to be declared "married" by the State.

Insofar as the right to marry someone of the same sex is neither found in the unique historical context of our Constitution nor compelled by the meaning ascribed by this court to the liberty and due process protections contained within it, should the court nevertheless recognize it as a fundamental right? The consequences of deeming a right to be "fundamental" are profound, and this court, as well as the Supreme Court, has been very cautious in recognizing them.

Such caution is required by separation of powers principles. If a right is found to be "fundamental," it is, to a great extent, removed from "the arena of public debate and legislative action"; utmost care must be taken when breaking new ground in this field "lest the liberty protected by the Due Process Clause be subtly transformed into the policy preferences of [judges]." . . .

Although public attitudes toward marriage in general and same-sex marriage in particular have changed and are still evolving, "the asserted contemporary concept of marriage and societal interests for which [plaintiffs] contend" are "manifestly [less] deeply founded" than the "historic institution" of marriage. . . .

Given this history and the current state of public opinion, as reflected in the actions of the people's elected representatives, it cannot be said that "a right to same-sex marriage is so rooted in the traditions and collective conscience of our people that failure to recognize it would violate the fundamental principles of liberty and justice that lie at the base of all our civil and political institutions. . . .

"[I]t is not the court's function to launch an inquiry to resolve a debate which has already been settled in the legislative forum. '[I]t [is] the judge's duty . . . to give effect to the will of the people as expressed in the statute by their representative body. It is in this way . . . that the doctrine of separation of powers is given meaning.' . . .

The court's opinion concedes that the civil marriage statute serves legitimate State . . .

Civil marriage is the institutional mechanism by which societies have sanctioned and recognized particular family structures, and the institution of marriage has existed as one of the fundamental organizing principles of human society. . . . Marriage has not been merely a contractual arrangement for legally defining the private relationship between two individuals (although that is certainly part of any marriage). Rather, on an institutional level, marriage is the "very basis of the whole fabric of civilized society," . . . and it serves many important political, economic, social, educational, procreational, and personal functions.

Paramount among its many important functions, the institution of marriage has systematically provided for the regulation of heterosexual behavior, brought order to the resulting procreation, and ensured a stable family structure in which children will be reared, educated, and socialized. Admittedly, heterosexual intercourse, procreation, and child care are not necessarily conjoined (particularly in the modern age of widespread effective contraception and supportive social welfare programs), but an orderly society requires some mechanism for coping with the fact that sexual intercourse commonly results in pregnancy and childbirth. The institution of marriage is that mechanism.

The institution of marriage provides the important legal and normative link between heterosexual intercourse and procreation on the one hand and family responsibilities on the other. The partners in a marriage are expected to engage in exclusive sexual relations, with children the probable result and paternity presumed. . . . Whereas the relationship between mother and child is demonstrably and predictably created and recognizable through the biological process of pregnancy and childbirth, there is no corresponding process for creating a relationship between father and child. Similarly, aside from an act of heterosexual intercourse nine months prior to childbirth, there is no process for creating a relationship between a man and a woman as the parents of a particular child. The institution of marriage fills this void by formally binding the husband-father to his wife and child, and imposing on him the responsibilities of fatherhood. . . . The alternative, a society without the institution of marriage, in which heterosexual intercourse, procreation, and child care are largely disconnected processes, would be chaotic.

The marital family is also the foremost setting for the education and socialization of children. Children learn about the world and their place in it primarily from those who raise them, and those children eventually grow up to exert some influence, great or small, positive or negative, on society. The institution of marriage encourages parents to remain committed to each other and to their children as they grow, thereby encouraging a stable venue for the education and socialization of children. See P. Blumstein & P. Schwartz, *supra* at 26; C.N. Degler, *supra* at 61; S.L. Nock, *supra* at 2–3; C. Lasch, *supra* at 81; M.A. Schwartz & B.M. Scott, *supra* at 6–7. More macroscopically, construction of a family through marriage also formalizes the bonds between people in an ordered and institutional manner, thereby facilitating a foundation of interconnectedness and interdependency on which more intricate stabilizing social structures might be built. See M. Grossberg, Governing the Hearth: Law and Family in Nineteenth-Century America 10 (1985); C. Lasch, *supra;* L. Saxton, *supra* at 260; J.Q. Wilson, *supra* at 221. . . .

It is undeniably true that dramatic historical shifts in our cultural, political, and economic landscape have altered some of our traditional notions about marriage, including the interpersonal dynamics within it, the range of responsibilities required of it as an institution, and the legal environment in which it exists. Nevertheless, the institution of marriage remains the principal weave of our social fabric. . . .

It is difficult to imagine a State purpose more important and legitimate than ensuring, promoting, and supporting an optimal social structure within which to bear and raise children. At the very least, the marriage statute continues to serve this important State purpose.

. . . The question we must turn to next is whether the statute, construed as limiting marriage to couples of the opposite sex, remains a rational way to further that purpose. Stated differently, we ask whether a conceivable rational basis exists on which the Legislature could conclude that continuing to limit the institution of civil marriage to members of the opposite sex furthers the legitimate purpose of ensuring, promoting, and supporting an optimal social structure for the bearing and raising of children.

In considering whether such a rational basis exists, we defer to the decision-making process of the Legislature, and must make deferential assumptions about the information that it might consider and on which it may rely. . . .

There is no reason to believe that legislative processes are inadequate to effectuate legal changes in response to evolving evidence, social values, and views of fairness on the subject of same-sex relationships. Deliberate consideration of, and incremental responses to rapidly evolving scientific and social understanding is the norm of the political process—that it may seem painfully slow to those who are already persuaded by the arguments in favor of change is not a sufficient basis to conclude that the processes are constitutionally infirm. . . . The Legislature is the appropriate branch, both constitutionally and practically, to consider and respond to it. It is not enough that we as Justices might be personally of the view that we have learned enough to decide what is best. So long as the question is at all debatable, it must be the Legislature that decides. The marriage statute thus meets the requirements of the rational basis test. . . .

POSTSCRIPT

Should Same-Sex Couples Receive Constitutional Protection?

After the Massachusetts Supreme Judicial Court decided *Goodridge*, the state senate requested an advisory opinion from the Court as to whether a pending "civil union" bill would satisfy the requirements of the Massachusetts Constitution. The bill would provide same-sex couples with the same benefits, protections, and responsibilities that a traditional marriage then provided to opposite sex couples. In response, the Court held that only the recognition of same-sex marriages would prove constitutionally satisfactory. In March 2004, the Massachusetts Constitutional Convention approved the language of a proposed constitutional amendment that would outlaw same-sex *marriages*, but allow for the recognition of same-sex *civil unions*. For such an amendment to become effective, it must be passed by a separate session of the Convention. It would then have to be approved by a ballot initiative. By law, this could not occur until the November elections of 2006.

Beyond the borders of Massachusetts, the *Goodridge* decision generated a wave of legal and political activity, much of it timed to the 2004 presidential election. Both major candidates, Bush and Kerry, voiced their opposition to same-sex marriage. Although the Massachusetts senator moderated his opposition by supporting the notion of same-sex civil unions, he insisted that a "marriage" must remain between a man and a woman. President Bush pushed the point further and, during the later phases of the campaign, called for a constitutional amendment (one that would seem to "constitutionalize" the basic points of the federal Defense of Marriage Act, 28 U.S.C. 1738C (2004)) declaring that a "marriage" was the union between a man and a woman. It was suggested that Bush's harder line was calculated for political appeal to an important part of his political base. Whether this issue played a decisive role in the election is much more difficult to determine. What we do know is that the November 2004 election saw eleven states (Arkansas, Georgia, Kentucky, Michigan, Mississippi, Montana, North Dakota, Oklahoma, Oregon, Ohio, and Utah) overwhelmingly pass ballot initiatives that contained same-sex marriage bans. After the intensity of a hotly contested presidential election has subsided, it is difficult to assess the legal and political implications of such developments.

This is a complex issue that is still very much in flux. A recent symposium on the issue is a good place to begin to understand some of the implications of these developments. See, Gary M. Segura, et al., "A Symposium on the Politics of Same-Sex Marriage," *PS: Political Science and Politics* (vol. 38, no. 2, April 2005). One should also consult Evan Gerstmann's *Same-Sex Marriage and the Constitution* (Cambridge, 2003), for a comprehensive overview of the subject. For an analysis of the virtues of marriage for both same and opposite-sex couples, see Jonathan Rauch, *Gay Marriage: Why It Is Good for Gays, Good for Straights, and Good for America* (Times Books, 2004). A counterpoint from the conservative perspective is offered by Maggie George, "What Marriage Is For," *Weekly Standard* (August 4–11), and Stanley Kurtz, "The End of Marriage in Scandinavia," *Weekly Standard* (February 2). For an example of one state's approach to the issue, see Vermont's attempt to craft a "civil union" alternative to same-sex marriages. See, State of Vermont, "Vermont Guide to Civil Unions," Office of the Secretary of State at http://www.sec.state.vt.us/otherprg/civilunions/civilunions.html.

ISSUE 18

Should Children with Disabilities Be Provided with Extraordinary Care in Order to Attend Regular Classes in Public Schools?

YES: John Paul Stevens, from Majority Opinion, *Cedar Rapids Community School District v. Garret F.,* U.S. Supreme Court (March 3, 1999)

NO: Clarence Thomas, from Dissenting Opinion, *Cedar Rapids Community School District v. Garret F.,* U.S. Supreme Court (March 3, 1999)

ISSUE SUMMARY

YES: Supreme Court Justice John Paul Stevens interprets the Individuals with Disabilities Education Act as requiring public school districts to provide students who have severe physical disabilities with individualized and continuous nursing services during school hours.

NO: Supreme Court Justice Clarence Thomas argues that such an interpretation will impose serious and unanticipated financial obligations on the states.

More and more children with "special needs" are now enrolled in public schools and attend classes with nondisabled students. This is due in large part to the recognition that such students are perfectly capable of pursuing and achieving the same educational goals as their nondisabled counterparts if they are provided with the required medical care. Federal legislation such as the Americans with Disabilities Act (ADA) and the Individuals with Disabilities Education Act (IDEA) have played a large role in establishing regulatory guidelines as well as educating the general public on this matter. Accordingly, school districts have been required to hire school nurses and other educational support personnel to dispense or administer a variety of medications, to help with the insertion of catheters or breathing tubes, and to assist in a variety of other tasks.

Although the IDEA provides federal money to states that agree to "provide disabled children with special education and related services," cash-strapped local school districts have been concerned about the level of support they might receive and the scope of their responsibilities to the targeted student population. Potentially, the financial burden some school districts face is significant. Indeed, these are the issues raised in the readings that follow—the majority and dissenting opinions in *Cedar Rapids Community School District v. Garret F.*, a 1999 decision that has clarified the scope of coverage of "related services" under the IDEA. According to the language of the statute, the legislation was passed "to assure that all children with disabilities have available to them . . . a free appropriate public education which emphasizes special education and related services designed to meet their unique needs." 20 U.S.C. sec. 1400(c). By the terms of the statute, the phrase "related services" means

> transportation, and such developmental, corrective, and other supportive services (including speech pathology and audiology, psychological services, physical and occupational therapy, recreation, including therapeutic recreation, social work services, counseling services, including rehabilitation counseling, and medical services, except that such medical services shall be for diagnostic and evaluation purposes only) as may be required to assist a child with a disability to benefit from special education, and includes the early identification and assessment of disabling conditions in children. 20 U.S.C. sec. 1401(a)(17)

The relevant facts of the case are set forth in Justice John Paul Stevens's opinion for the Court. Justice Clarence Thomas was joined in his dissent by Justice Anthony Kennedy.

YES

John Paul Stevens

Majority Opinion

Cedar Rapids Community School District *v.* Garret F.

The question presented in this case is whether the definition of "related services" in § 1401(a)(17) requires a public school district in a participating State to provide a ventilator-dependent student with certain nursing services during school hours.

I

Respondent Garret F. is a friendly, creative, and intelligent young man. When Garret was four years old, his spinal column was severed in a motorcycle accident. Though paralyzed from the neck down, his mental capacities were unaffected. He is able to speak, to control his motorized wheelchair through use of a puff and suck straw, and to operate a computer with a device that responds to head movements. Garret is currently a student in the Cedar Rapids Community School District (District), he attends regular classes in a typical school program, and his academic performance has been a success. Garret is, however, ventilator dependent, and therefore requires a responsible individual nearby to attend to certain physical needs while he is in school.

During Garret's early years at school his family provided for his physical care during the school day. When he was in kindergarten, his 18-year-old aunt attended him; in the next four years, his family used settlement proceeds they received after the accident, their insurance, and other resources to employ a licensed practical nurse. In 1993, Garret's mother requested the District to accept financial responsibility for the health care services that Garret requires during the school day. The District denied the request, believing that it was not legally obligated to provide continuous one-on-one nursing services.

Relying on both the IDEA and Iowa law, Garret's mother requested a hearing before the Iowa Department of Education. An Administrative Law Judge (ALJ) received extensive evidence concerning Garret's special needs, the District's treatment of other disabled students, and the assistance provided to other ventilator-dependent children in other parts of the country. In his 47-page report, the ALJ found that the District has about 17,500 students, of

From *Cedar Rapids Community School District v. Garret F.*, 119 S. Ct. 992 (1999). Notes omitted.

whom approximately 2,200 need some form of special education or special services. Although Garret is the only ventilator-dependent student in the District, most of the health care services that he needs are already provided for some other students. "The primary difference between Garret's situation and that of other students is his dependency on his ventilator for life support." The ALJ noted that the parties disagreed over the training or licensure required for the care and supervision of such students, and that those providing such care in other parts of the country ranged from nonlicensed personnel to registered nurses. However, the District did not contend that only a licensed physician could provide the services in question.

The ALJ explained that federal law requires that children with a variety of health impairments be provided with "special education and related services" when their disabilities adversely affect their academic performance, and that such children should be educated to the maximum extent appropriate with children who are not disabled. In addition, the ALJ explained that applicable federal regulations distinguish between "school health services," which are provided by a "qualified school nurse or other qualified person," and "medical services," which are provided by a licensed physician. See 34 CFR §§ 300.16(a), (b)(4), (b)(11) (1998). The District must provide the former, but need not provide the latter (except, of course, those "medical services" that are for diagnostic or evaluation purposes, § 1401(a)(17)). According to the ALJ, the distinction in the regulations does not just depend on "the title of the person providing the service"; instead, the "medical services" exclusion is limited to services that are "in the special training, knowledge, and judgment of a physician to carry out." The ALJ thus concluded that the IDEA required the District to bear financial responsibility for all of the services in dispute, including continuous nursing services.

The District challenged the ALJ's decision in Federal District Court, but that Court approved the ALJ's IDEA ruling and granted summary judgment against the District. The Court of Appeals affirmed. It noted that, as a recipient of federal funds under the IDEA, Iowa has a statutory duty to provide all disabled children a "free appropriate public education," which includes "related services." The Court of Appeals read our opinion in *Irving Independent School Dist. v. Tatro*, 468 U.S. 883 (1984), to provide a two-step analysis of the "related services" definition in § 1401(a)(17)—asking first, whether the requested services are included within the phrase "supportive services"; and second, whether the services are excluded as "medical services." The Court of Appeals succinctly answered both questions in Garret's favor. The Court found the first step plainly satisfied, since Garret cannot attend school unless the requested services are available during the school day. As to the second step, the Court reasoned that *Tatro* "established a bright-line test: the services of a physician (other than for diagnostic and evaluation purposes) are subject to the medical services exclusion, but services that can be provided in the school setting by a nurse or qualified layperson are not."

In its petition for certiorari, the District challenged only the second step of the Court of Appeals' analysis. The District pointed out that some federal courts have not asked whether the requested health services must be delivered by a physician, but instead have applied a multi-factor test that considers, generally speaking, the nature and extent of the services at issue. . . .

II

The District contends that § 1401(a)(17) does not require it to provide Garret with "continuous one-on-one nursing services" during the school day, even though Garret cannot remain in school without such care. However, the IDEA's definition of "related services," our decision in *Irving Independent School Dist. v. Tatro,* 468 U.S. 883 (1984), and the overall statutory scheme all support the decision of the Court of Appeals.

The text of the "related services" definition broadly encompasses those supportive services that "may be required to assist a child with a disability to benefit from special education." As we have already noted, the District does not challenge the Court of Appeals' conclusion that the in-school services at issue are within the covered category of "supportive services." As a general matter, services that enable a disabled child to remain in school during the day provide the student with "the meaningful access to education that Congress envisioned." *Tatro,* 468 U.S. at 891.

This general definition of "related services" is illuminated by a parenthetical phrase listing examples of particular services that are included within the statute's coverage. § 1401(a)(17). "Medical services" are enumerated in this list, but such services are limited to those that are "for diagnostic and evaluation purposes." *Ibid.* The statute does not contain a more specific definition of the "medical services" that are excepted from the coverage of § 1401(a)(17).

The scope of the "medical services" exclusion is not a matter of first impression in this Court. In *Tatro* we concluded that the Secretary of Education had reasonably determined that the term "medical services" referred only to services that must be performed by a physician, and not to school health services. 468 U.S. at 892–894. Accordingly, we held that a specific form of health care (clean intermittent catheterization) that is often, though not always, performed by a nurse is not an excluded medical service. We referenced the likely cost of the services and the competence of school staff as justifications for drawing a line between physician and other services, but our endorsement of that line was unmistakable. It is thus settled that the phrase "medical services" in § 1401(a)(17) does not embrace all forms of care that might loosely be described as "medical" in other contexts, such as a claim for an income tax deduction. See 26 U.S.C. § 213(d)(1) (1994 ed. and Supp. II) (defining "medical care").

The District does not ask us to define the term so broadly. Indeed, the District does not argue that any of the items of care that Garret needs, considered individually, could be excluded from the scope of § 1401(a)(17). It could not make such an argument, considering that one of the services Garret needs (catheterization) was at issue in *Tatro,* and the others may be provided competently by a school nurse or other trained personnel. As the ALJ concluded, most of the requested services are already provided by the District to other students, and the in-school care necessitated by Garret's ventilator dependency does not demand the training, knowledge, and judgment of a licensed physician. While more extensive, the in-school services Garret needs are no more "medical" than was the care sought in *Tatro*.

Instead, the District points to the combined and continuous character of the required care, and proposes a test under which the outcome in any particular case would "depend upon a series of factors, such as [1] whether the care is continuous or intermittent, [2] whether existing school health personnel can provide the service, [3] the cost of the service, and [4] the potential consequences if the service is not properly performed." The District's multi-factor test is not supported by any recognized source of legal authority. The proposed factors can be found in neither the text of the statute nor the regulations that we upheld in *Tatro*. Moreover, the District offers no explanation why these characteristics make one service any more "medical" than another. The continuous character of certain services associated with Garret's ventilator dependency has no apparent relationship to "medical" services, much less a relationship of equivalence. Continuous services may be more costly and may require additional school personnel, but they are not thereby more "medical." Whatever its imperfections, a rule that limits the medical services exemption to physician services is unquestionably a reasonable and generally workable interpretation of the statute. Absent an elaboration of the statutory terms plainly more convincing than that which we reviewed in *Tatro*, there is no good reason to depart from settled law.

Finally, the District raises broader concerns about the financial burden that it must bear to provide the services that Garret needs to stay in school. The problem for the District in providing these services is not that its staff cannot be trained to deliver them; the problem, the District contends, is that the existing school health staff cannot meet all of their responsibilities and provide for Garret at the same time. Through its multi-factor test, the District seeks to establish a kind of undue-burden exemption primarily based on the cost of the requested services. The first two factors can be seen as examples of cost-based distinctions: intermittent care is often less expensive than continuous care, and the use of existing personnel is cheaper than hiring additional employees. The third factor—the cost of the service—would then encompass the first two. The relevance of the fourth factor is likewise related to cost because extra care may be necessary if potential consequences are especially serious.

The District may have legitimate financial concerns, but our role in this dispute is to interpret existing law. Defining "related services" in a manner that accommodates the cost concerns Congress may have had, cf. *Tatro*, 468 U.S. at 892, is altogether different from using cost itself as the definition. Given that § 1401(a)(17) does not employ cost in its definition of "related services" or excluded "medical services," accepting the District's cost-based standard as the sole test for determining the scope of the provision would require us to engage in judicial lawmaking without any guidance from Congress. It would also create some tension with the purposes of the IDEA. The statute may not require public schools to maximize the potential of disabled students commensurate with the opportunities provided to other children, see *[Board of Education of the Hendrick Hudson Central School District v.] Rowley,* 458 U.S. at 200; and the potential financial burdens imposed on participating States may be relevant to arriving at a sensible construction of the IDEA, see *Tatro,* 468 U.S. at 892. But Congress intended "to open the door of public education" to all qualified children and "required participating States to educate handicapped children with nonhandicapped children whenever possible."

This case is about whether meaningful access to the public schools will be assured, not the level of education that a school must finance once access is attained. It is undisputed that the services at issue must be provided if Garret is to remain in school. Under the statute, our precedent, and the purposes of the IDEA, the District must fund such "related services" in order to help guarantee that students like Garret are integrated into the public schools.

The judgment of the Court of Appeals is accordingly Affirmed.

➡ **NO**

Dissenting Opinion
of Clarence Thomas

T he majority, relying heavily on our decision in *Irving Independent School Dist. v. Tatro,* 468 U.S. 883 (1984), concludes that the Individuals with Disabilities Education Act (IDEA), 20 U.S.C. § 1400 *et seq.,* requires a public school district to fund continuous, one-on-one nursing care for disabled children. Because *Tatro* cannot be squared with the text of IDEA, the Court should not adhere to it in this case. Even assuming that *Tatro* was correct in the first instance, the majority's extension of it is unwarranted and ignores the constitutionally mandated rules of construction applicable to legislation enacted pursuant to Congress' spending power.

I

As the majority recounts, IDEA authorizes the provision of federal financial assistance to States that agree to provide, inter alia, "special education and related services" for disabled children. § 1401(a)(18). In *Tatro, supra,* we held that this provision of IDEA required a school district to provide clean intermittent catheterization to a disabled child several times a day. In so holding, we relied on Department of Education regulations, which we concluded had reasonably interpreted IDEA's definition of "related services" to require school districts in participating States to provide "school nursing services" (of which we assumed catheterization was a subcategory) but not "services of a physician." This holding is contrary to the plain text of IDEA and its reliance on the Department of Education's regulations was misplaced.

A

Before we consider whether deference to an agency regulation is appropriate, "we first ask whether Congress has 'directly spoken to the precise question at issue. If the intent of Congress is clear, that is the end of the matter; for the court, as well as the agency, must give effect to the unambiguously expressed intent of Congress.'"

From *Cedar Rapids Community School District v. Garret F.,* 119 S. Ct. 992 (1999). Notes omitted.

Unfortunately, the Court in *Tatro* failed to consider this necessary antecedent question before turning to the Department of Education's regulations implementing IDEA's related services provision. The Court instead began "with the regulations of the Department of Education, which," it said, "are entitled to deference." The Court need not have looked beyond the text of IDEA, which expressly indicates that school districts are not required to provide medical services, except for diagnostic and evaluation purposes. 20 U.S.C. § 1401(a)(17). The majority asserts that *Tatro* precludes reading the term "medical services" to include "all forms of care that might loosely be described as 'medical.'" The majority does not explain, however, why "services" that are "medical" in nature are not "medical services." Not only is the definition that the majority rejects consistent with other uses of the term in federal law, it also avoids the anomalous result of holding that the services at issue in *Tatro* (as well as in this case), while not "medical services," would nonetheless qualify as medical care for federal income tax purposes.

The primary problem with *Tatro,* and the majority's reliance on it today, is that the Court focused on the provider of the services rather than the services themselves. We do not typically think that automotive services are limited to those provided by a mechanic, for example. Rather, anything done to repair or service a car, no matter who does the work, is thought to fall into that category. Similarly, the term "food service" is not generally thought to be limited to work performed by a chef. The term "medical" similarly does not support *Tatro's* provider-specific approach, but encompasses services that are "of, *relating to, or concerned with* physicians *or* the practice of medicine." See Webster's Third New International Dictionary 1402 (1986) (emphasis added). . . .

IDEA's structure and purpose reinforce this textual interpretation. Congress enacted IDEA to increase the educational opportunities available to disabled children, not to provide medical care for them. . . . As such, where Congress decided to require a supportive service—including speech pathology, occupational therapy, and audiology—that appears "medical" in nature, it took care to do so explicitly. See § 1401(a)(17). Congress specified these services precisely because it recognized that they would otherwise fall under the broad "medical services" exclusion. Indeed, when it crafted the definition of related services, Congress could have, but chose not to, include "nursing services" in this list.

B

Tatro was wrongly decided even if the phrase "medical services" was subject to multiple constructions, and therefore, deference to any reasonable Department of Education regulation was appropriate. The Department of Education has never promulgated regulations defining the scope of IDEA's "medical services" exclusion. One year before *Tatro* was decided, the Secretary of Education issued proposed regulations that defined excluded medical services as "services relating to the practice of medicine." 47 Fed. Reg. 33838 (1982). These regulations, which represent the Department's only attempt to define the disputed term, were never adopted. Instead, "the regulations actually define only those 'medical services' that *are* owed to handicapped children," . . . not those that *are not*. Now, as when *Tatro* was decided, the regulations require districts to provide services performed "by a licensed physician to determine a child's medically related handicapping condition which results in the child's need for special education and related services."

Extrapolating from this regulation, the *Tatro* Court presumed that this meant "that 'medical services' not owed under the statute are those 'services by a licensed physician' that serve other purposes." The Court, therefore, did not defer to the regulation itself, but rather relied on an inference drawn from it to speculate about how a regulation might read if the Department of Education promulgated one. Deference in those circumstances is impermissible. We cannot defer to a regulation that does not exist.

II

Assuming that *Tatro* was correctly decided in the first instance, it does not control the outcome of this case. Because IDEA was enacted pursuant to Congress' spending power, our analysis of the statute in this case is governed by special rules of construction. We have repeatedly emphasized that, when Congress places conditions on the receipt of federal funds, "it must do so unambiguously." *Pennhurst State School and Hospital v. Halderman*, 451 U.S. 1, 17 (1981). This is because a law that "conditions an offer of federal funding on a promise by the recipient . . . amounts essentially to a contract between the Government and the recipient of funds." *Gebser v. Lago Vista Independent School Dist.*, 524 U.S. 274, 276 (1998). As such, "the legitimacy of Congress' power to legislate under the spending power . . . rests on whether the State voluntarily and knowingly accepts the terms of the 'contract.' There can, of course, be no knowing acceptance if a State is unaware of the conditions or is unable to ascertain what is expected of it." It follows that we must interpret Spending Clause legislation narrowly, in order to avoid saddling the States with obligations that they did not anticipate.

The majority's approach in this case turns this Spending Clause presumption on its head. We have held that, in enacting IDEA, Congress wished to require "States to educate handicapped children with nonhandicapped children whenever possible." Congress, however, also took steps to limit the fiscal burdens that States must bear in attempting to achieve this laudable goal. These steps include requiring States to provide an education that is only "appropriate" rather than requiring them to maximize the potential of disabled students, see 20 U.S.C. § 1400(c); recognizing that integration into the public school environment is not always possible, see § 1412(5), and clarifying that, with a few exceptions, public schools need not provide "medical services" for disabled students, §§ 1401(a)(17) and (18).

For this reason, we have previously recognized that Congress did not intend to "impose upon the States a burden of unspecified proportions and weight" in enacting IDEA. These federalism concerns require us to interpret IDEA's related services provision, consistent with *Tatro*, as follows: Department of Education regulations require districts to provide disabled children with health-related services that school nurses can perform as part of their normal duties. This reading of *Tatro,* although less broad than the majority's, is equally plausible and certainly more consistent with our obligation to interpret Spending Clause legislation narrowly. Before concluding that the district was required to provide clean intermittent catheterization for Amber Tatro, we observed that school nurses in the district were authorized to perform services that were "difficult to distinguish from the provision of [clean intermittent catheterization] to the handicapped." We concluded that "it would be strange indeed if Congress, in attempting to extend special services to handicapped children, were unwilling to guarantee them services of a kind that are routinely provided to the nonhandicapped."

Unlike clean intermittent catheterization, however, a school nurse cannot provide the services that respondent requires, and continue to perform her normal duties. To the contrary, because respondent requires continuous, one-on-one care throughout the entire school day, all agree that the district must hire an additional employee to attend solely to respondent. This will cost a minimum of $18,000 per year. Although the majority recognizes this fact, it nonetheless concludes that the "more extensive" nature of the services that respondent needs is irrelevant to the question whether those services fall under the medical services exclusion. This approach disregards the constitutionally mandated principles of construction applicable to Spending Clause legislation and blindsides unwary States with fiscal obligations that they could not have anticipated.

For the foregoing reasons, I respectfully dissent.

POSTSCRIPT

Should Children with Disabilities Be Provided with Extraordinary Care in Order to Attend Regular Classes in Public Schools?

Like many cases decided by the Rehnquist court, this case ultimately comes down to an issue of federalism. Justice Thomas, joined in dissent by Justice Kennedy, is concerned about the financial burdens that local school districts will face under the weight of federal mandates. Indeed, Thomas suggests that Justice Stevens willfully ignores such concerns. Nonetheless, Stevens was able to carry six other votes in this decision.

For some background information on this issue, consult Stephen B. Thomas's *Health Related Legal Issues in Education* (Education Law Association, 1987), which provides a general treatment of the subject. In addition, see Rex R. Schultze, "Reading, Writing and Ritalin: The Responsibility of Public School Districts to Administer Medications to Students," 32 *Creighton Law Review* 793 (1999) for coverage of a different but related question. To fully comprehend the discussion in *Garret F.,* read the Court's earlier decision in this area, *Irving Independent School District v. Tatro,* 468 U.S. 883 (1984). Finally, there are several Web sites that contain pertinent information. See, for example, the Council for Disability Rights site at http://www.disabilityrights.org and the Disability Rights Education and Defense Fund site at http://www.dredf.org.

ISSUE 19

Do Race-Conscious Programs in Public University Admissions Policies Violate the Fourteenth Amendment's Guarantee of Equal Protection Under the Law?

YES: Clarence Thomas, from Dissenting Opinion, *Barbara Grutter v. Lee Bollinger et al.*, U.S. Supreme Court (June 23, 2003)

NO: Sandra Day O'Connor, from Majority Opinion, *Barbara Grutter v. Lee Bollinger et al.*, U.S. Supreme Court (June 23, 2003)

ISSUE SUMMARY

YES: Supreme Court Justice Clarence Thomas argues that the University of Michigan Law School's admissions policy discriminates on the basis of race and is therefore in violation of the Fourteenth Amendment's equal protection clause.

NO: Supreme Court Justice Sandra Day O'Connor holds that the admissions policy of the University of Michigan Law School, which makes race one factor among many in the process of creating a diverse student body, does not violate the Constitution's guarantee of equal protection under the law.

Affirmative action continues to be one of the most hotly debated issues in the United States. Proponents justify the use of affirmative action policies by arguing that government should utilize race-conscious programs both to redress the continuing effects of past racial discrimination and to achieve more racially diverse educational and work environments. Opponents of affirmative action view it as unnecessary and unfair, arguing that it is, in essence, nothing more than "reverse discrimination" and, as such, a violation of the Fourteenth Amendment's guarantee of equal protection under the law. Opponents also assert that affirmative action policies stigmatize the beneficiaries of such programs, marking them as unable to succeed on their own merits.

For the past 25 years, since the U.S. Supreme Court's decision in *Regents of the University of California v. Bakke*, 438 U.S. 265 (1978) held that race could be taken into account in a public university's admissions decisions, opponents of affirmative action have pressed their challenge to its legality. In other words, rather than settling the matter, the *Bakke* decision only seems to have provided both sides in this debate with the resources for its continuation. Why? The *Bakke* Court was deeply divided, producing six separate opinions, none of which were able to garner a majority of the Court. Justice Lewis F. Powell was joined by four other members of the Court in invalidating the admissions policy of the University of California at Davis Medical School—a race-based "set aside"—on the grounds that it constituted an impermissible racial classification. However, Powell was joined by four different members of the Court in holding that public universities may nonetheless use race as one factor in the admissions decision. Because of the splintered nature of the Court's statement on affirmative action, and because of the inherently contested nature of the problem of race in American law and politics, further litigation was almost inevitable. And while the Court did not revisit the specific question presented in *Bakke* for another 25 years, it did speak to several closely related legal questions. In two important cases in the intervening decades, *City of Richmond v. J. A. Croson Co.*, 488 U.S. 469 (1989) and *Adarand Constructors, Inc. v. Pena*, 515 U.S. 200 (1995), the Court held that the only constitutionally legitimate use of racial preferences was to remedy historically specific instances of racial discrimination.

In 1996 Barbara Grutter, a state resident, applied for admission to the University of Michigan Law School. When filling out her application form, Grutter identified herself as "white" in response to a question that asked each applicant to disclose his or her race. Although she was initially placed on a waiting list, Grutter was ultimately denied admission to the school. Six months later, Grutter (represented by the CIR) filed a class action suit in federal district court on behalf of herself and all others from "disfavored racial groups" who had been denied admission to the law school because of its policy and practice of applying different admissions standards depending upon the race of the applicant. Grutter contended that the law school's admissions policy discriminated against her on the basis of race, thereby denying her equal protection under the law in violation of the Fourteenth Amendment.

After a 13-day trial, the District Court for the Eastern District of Michigan concluded that the law school's use of race as a factor in its admissions decisions was unconstitutional. During the spring of 2002, the U.S. Court of Appeals for the Sixth Circuit reversed the lower court's decision, holding that the law school could consider race as one factor in the admissions process in order to advance the compelling state interest of achieving a diverse student population. With a conflicting interpretation of a similar admissions policy coming from the Fifth Circuit, the stage was set for the U.S. Supreme Court to speak once again to this issue. The following readings are from Justices Clarence Thomas's and Sandra Day O'Connor's opinions from the case.

Dissenting Opinion of Clarence Thomas

Grutter *v.* Bollinger

Frederick Douglass, speaking to a group of abolitionists almost 140 years ago, delivered a message lost on today's majority:

> "[I]n regard to the colored people, there is always more that is benevolent, I perceive, than just, manifested towards us. What I ask for the negro is not benevolence, not pity, not sympathy, but simply *justice.* The American people have always been anxious to know what they shall do with us. . . . I have had but one answer from the beginning. Do nothing with us! Your doing with us has already played the mischief with us. Do nothing with us! If the apples will not remain on the tree of their own strength, if they are worm-eaten at the core, if they are early ripe and disposed to fall, let them fall! . . . And if the negro cannot stand on his own legs, let him fall also. All I ask is, give him a chance to stand on his own legs! Let him alone! . . . [Y]our interference is doing him positive injury." What the Black Man Wants: An Address Delivered in Boston, Massachusetts, on 26 January 1865, reprinted in 4 The Frederick Douglass Papers 59, 68 (J. Blassingame & J. McKivigan eds. 1991) (emphasis in original).

Like Douglass, I believe blacks can achieve in every avenue of American life without the meddling of university administrators. Because I wish to see all students succeed whatever their color, I share, in some respect, the sympathies of those who sponsor the type of discrimination advanced by the University of Michigan Law School (Law School). The Constitution does not, however, tolerate institutional devotion to the status quo in admissions policies when such devotion ripens into racial discrimination. Nor does the Constitution countenance the unprecedented deference the Court gives to the Law School, an approach inconsistent with the very concept of "strict scrutiny."

No one would argue that a university could set up a lower general admission standard and then impose heightened requirements only on black applicants. Similarly, a university may not maintain a high admission standard and grant exemptions to favored races. The Law School, of its own choosing, and for its own purposes, maintains an exclusionary admissions

From *Barbara Grutter v. Lee Bollinger et al.,* 539 U.S. ___ (2003). Some case citations omitted.

system that it knows produces racially disproportionate results. Racial discrimination is not a permissible solution to the self-inflicted wounds of this elitist admissions policy.

The majority upholds the Law School's racial discrimination not by interpreting the people's Constitution, but by responding to a faddish slogan of the cognoscenti. Nevertheless, I concur in part in the Court's opinion. First, I agree with the Court insofar as its decision, which approves of only one racial classification, confirms that further use of race in admissions remains unlawful. Second, I agree with the Court's holding that racial discrimination in higher education admissions will be illegal in 25 years. See *ante,* at 31 (stating that racial discrimination will no longer be narrowly tailored, or "necessary to further" a compelling state interest, in 25 years). I respectfully dissent from the remainder of the Court's opinion and the judgment, however, because I believe that the Law School's current use of race violates the Equal Protection Clause and that the Constitution means the same thing today as it will in 300 months.

I

. . . The Constitution abhors classifications based on race, not only because those classifications can harm favored races or are based on illegitimate motives, but also because every time the government places citizens on racial registers and makes race relevant to the provision of burdens or benefits, it demeans us all. "Purchased at the price of immeasurable human suffering, the equal protection principle reflects our Nation's understanding that such classifications ultimately have a destructive impact on the individual and our society." *Adarand Construction, Inc.* v. *Peña,* 515 U.S. 200, 240 (1995) (Thomas, J., concurring in part and concurring in judgment).

II

Unlike the majority, I seek to define with precision the interest being asserted by the Law School before determining whether that interest is so compelling as to justify racial discrimination. The Law School maintains that it wishes to obtain "educational benefits that flow from student body diversity," Brief for Respondents Bollinger et al. 14. This statement must be evaluated carefully, because it implies that both "diversity" and "educational benefits" are components of the Law School's compelling state interest. Additionally, the Law School's refusal to entertain certain changes in its admissions process and status indicates that the compelling state interest it seeks to validate is actually broader than might appear at first glance.

Undoubtedly there are other ways to "better" the education of law students aside from ensuring that the student body contains a "critical mass" of underrepresented minority students. Attaining "diversity," whatever it means, is the mechanism by which the Law School obtains educational benefits, not an end of itself. The Law School, however, apparently believes that only a racially mixed student body can lead to the educational benefits it seeks. How, then, is the Law School's interest in these allegedly unique educational "benefits" *not* simply the forbidden interest in "racial balancing," *ante,* at 17, that the majority expressly rejects?

A distinction between these two ideas (unique educational benefits based on racial aesthetics and race for its own sake) is purely sophistic—so much so that the majority uses them interchangeably. The Law School's argument, as facile as it is, can only be understood in one way: Classroom aesthetics yields educational benefits, racially discriminatory admissions policies are required to achieve the right racial mix, and therefore the policies are required to achieve the educational benefits. It is the *educational benefits* that are the end, or allegedly compelling state interest, not "diversity."

One must also consider the Law School's refusal to entertain changes to its current admissions system that might produce the same educational benefits. The Law School adamantly disclaims any race-neutral alternative that would reduce "academic selectivity," which would in turn "require the Law School to become a very different institution, and to sacrifice a core part of its educational mission." Brief for Respondents Bollinger et al. 33–36. In other words, the Law School seeks to improve marginally the education it offers without sacrificing too much of its exclusivity and elite status.

The proffered interest that the majority vindicates today, then, is not simply "diversity." Instead the Court upholds the use of racial discrimination as a tool to advance the Law School's interest in offering a marginally superior education while maintaining an elite institution. Unless each constituent part of this state interest is of pressing public necessity, the Law School's use of race is unconstitutional. I find each of them to fall far short of this standard.

III

A

A close reading of the Court's opinion reveals that all of its legal work is done through one conclusory statement: The Law School has a "compelling interest in securing the educational benefits of a diverse student body." *Ante,* at 21. No serious effort is made to explain how these benefits fit with the state interests the Court has recognized (or rejected) as compelling, see Part I, *supra,* or to place any theoretical constraints on an enterprising court's desire to discover still more justifications for racial discrimination. In the absence of any explanation, one might expect the Court to fall back on the judicial policy of *stare decisis.* But the Court eschews even this weak defense of its holding, shunning an analysis of the extent to which Justice Powell's opinion in *Regents of Univ. of Cal.* v. *Bakke,* 438 U.S. 265 (1978), is binding, *ante,* at 13, in favor of an unfounded wholesale adoption of it.

Justice Powell's opinion in *Bakke* and the Court's decision today rest on the fundamentally flawed proposition that racial discrimination can be contextualized so that a goal, such as classroom aesthetics, can be compelling in one context but not in another. This "we know it when we see it" approach to evaluating state interests is not capable of judicial application. Today, the

Court insists on radically expanding the range of permissible uses of race to something as trivial (by comparison) as the assembling of a law school class. I can only presume that the majority's failure to justify its decision by reference to any principle arises from the absence of any such principle. . . .

IV

The interest in remaining elite and exclusive that the majority thinks so obviously critical requires the use of admissions "standards" that, in turn, create the Law School's "need" to discriminate on the basis of race. The Court validates these admissions standards by concluding that alternatives that would require "a dramatic sacrifice of . . . the academic quality of all admitted students" need not be considered before racial discrimination can be employed.[1] In the majority's view, such methods are not required by the "narrow tailoring" prong of strict scrutiny because that inquiry demands, in this context, that any race-neutral alternative work "'about as well.'" The majority errs, however, because race-neutral alternatives must only be "workable" and do "about as well" *in vindicating the compelling state interest.* The Court never explicitly holds that the Law School's desire to retain the status quo in "academic selectivity" is itself a compelling state interest, and, as I have demonstrated, it is not. Therefore, the Law School should be forced to choose between its classroom aesthetic and its exclusionary admissions system—it cannot have it both ways.

With the adoption of different admissions methods, such as accepting all students who meet minimum qualifications, the Law School could achieve its vision of the racially aesthetic student body without the use of racial discrimination. The Law School concedes this, but the Court holds, implicitly and under the guise of narrow tailoring, that the Law School has a compelling state interest in doing what it wants to do. I cannot agree. First, under strict scrutiny, the Law School's assessment of the benefits of racial discrimination and devotion to the admissions status quo are not entitled to any sort of deference, grounded in the First Amendment or anywhere else. Second, even if its "academic selectivity" must be maintained at all costs along with racial discrimination, the Court ignores the fact that other top law schools have succeeded in meeting their aesthetic demands without racial discrimination. . . .

V

Putting aside the absence of any legal support for the majority's reflexive deference, there is much to be said for the view that the use of tests and other measures to "predict" academic performance is a poor substitute for a system that gives every applicant a chance to prove he can succeed in the study of law. The rallying cry that in the absence of racial discrimination in admissions there would be a true meritocracy ignores the fact that the entire process is poisoned by numerous exceptions to "merit." For example, in the national debate on racial discrimination in higher education admissions, much has been made of the fact that elite institutions utilize a so-called "legacy" preference to give the children of alumni an advantage in admissions. This, and other, exceptions to a "true" meritocracy give the lie to protestations that merit admissions are in fact the order of the day at the Nation's universities. The Equal Protection Clause does not, however, prohibit the use of unseemly legacy preferences or many other kinds of arbitrary admissions procedures. What the Equal Protection Clause does prohibit are classifications made on the basis of race. So while legacy preferences can stand under the Constitution, racial discrimination cannot.[2] I will not twist the Constitution to invalidate legacy preferences or otherwise impose my vision of higher education admissions on the Nation. The majority should similarly stay its impulse to validate faddish racial discrimination the Constitution clearly forbids.

In any event, there is nothing ancient, honorable, or constitutionally protected about "selective" admissions. The University of Michigan should be well aware that alternative methods have historically been used for the admission of students, for it brought to this country the German certificate system in the late-19th century. See H. Wechsler, The Qualified Student 16–39 (1977) (hereinafter Qualified Student). Under this system, a secondary school was certified by a university so that any graduate who completed the course offered by the school was offered admission to the university. The certification regime supplemented, and later virtually replaced (at least in the Midwest), the prior regime of rigorous subject-matter entrance examinations. The facially race-neutral "percent plans" now used in Texas, California, and Florida are in many ways the descendents of the certificate system.

Certification was replaced by selective admissions in the beginning of the 20th century, as universities sought to exercise more control over the composition of their student bodies. Since its inception, selective admissions has been the vehicle for racial, ethnic, and religious tinkering and experimentation by university administrators. The initial driving force for the relocation of the selective function from the high school to the universities was the same desire to select racial winners and losers that the Law School exhibits today. Columbia, Harvard, and others infamously determined that they had "too many" Jews, just as today the Law School argues it would have "too many" whites if it could not discriminate in its admissions process. See Qualified Student 155–168 (Columbia); H. Broun & G. Britt, Christians Only: A Study in Prejudice 53–54 (1931) (Harvard).

. . . [N]o modern law school can claim ignorance of the poor performance of blacks, relatively speaking, on the Law School Admissions Test (LSAT). Nevertheless, law schools continue to use the test and then attempt to "correct" for black underperformance by using racial discrimination in admissions so as to obtain their aesthetic student body. The Law School's continued adherence to measures it knows produce racially skewed results is not entitled to deference by this Court. The Law School itself admits that the test is imperfect, as it must, given that it regularly admits students who score at or below 150 (the national median) on the test. See App. 156–203 (showing that, between 1995 and 2000, the Law School admitted 37 students—27 of whom were black; 31 of whom were "underrepresented minorities"—with LSAT scores of 150 or lower). And the Law School's *amici* cannot seem to agree on the fundamental question whether the test itself is useful. Compare Brief for Law School Admission Council as *Amicus Curiae* 12 ("LSAT scores . . . are an effective predictor of students' performance in law school") with Brief for Harvard Black Law Students Association et al. as *Amici Curiae* 27 ("Whether [the LSAT] measure[s] objective merit . . . is certainly questionable").

Having decided to use the LSAT, the Law School must accept the constitutional burdens that come with this decision. The Law School may freely continue to employ the LSAT and other allegedly merit-based standards in whatever fashion it likes. What the Equal Protection Clause forbids, but the Court today allows, is the use of these standards hand-in-hand with racial discrimination. An infinite variety of admissions methods are available to the Law School. Considering all of the radical thinking that has historically occurred at this country's universities, the Law School's intractable approach toward admissions is striking.

The Court will not even deign to make the Law School try other methods, however, preferring instead to grant a 25-year license to violate the Constitution. And the same Court that had the courage to order the desegregation of all public schools in the South now fears, on the basis of platitudes rather than principle, to force the Law School to abandon a decidedly imperfect admissions regime that provides the basis for racial discrimination.

VI

The absence of any articulated legal principle supporting the majority's principal holding suggests another rationale. I believe what lies beneath the Court's decision today are the benighted notions that one can tell when racial discrimination benefits (rather than hurts) minority groups, see *Adarand*, 515 U.S., at 239 (Scalia, J., concurring in part and concurring in judgment), and that racial discrimination is necessary to remedy general societal ills. This Court's precedents supposedly settled both issues, but clearly the majority still cannot commit to the principle that racial classifications are *per se* harmful and that almost no amount of benefit in the eye of the beholder can justify such classifications. . . .

The silence in this case is deafening to those of us who view higher education's purpose as imparting knowledge and skills to students, rather than a communal, rubber-stamp, credentialing process. The Law School is not looking for those students who, despite a lower LSAT score or undergraduate grade point average, will succeed in the study of law. The Law School seeks only a facade—it is sufficient that the class looks right, even if it does not perform right.

The Law School tantalizes unprepared students with the promise of a University of Michigan degree and all of the opportunities that it offers. These overmatched students take the bait, only to find that they cannot succeed in the cauldron of competition. And this mismatch crisis is not restricted to elite institutions. See T. Sowell, Race and Culture 176–177 (1994) ("Even if most minority students are able to meet the normal standards at the 'average' range of colleges and universities, the systematic mismatching of minority students begun at the top can mean that such students are generally overmatched throughout all levels of higher education"). Indeed, to cover the tracks of the aestheticists, this cruel farce of racial discrimination must continue—in selection for the Michigan Law Review, see University of Michigan Law School Student Handbook 2002–2003, pp. 39–40 (noting the presence of a "diversity plan" for admission to the review), and in hiring at law firms and for judicial clerkships—until the "beneficiaries" are no longer tolerated. While these students may graduate with law degrees, there is no evidence that they have received a qualitatively better legal education (or become better lawyers) than if they had gone to a less "elite" law school for which they were better prepared. And the aestheticists will never address the real problems facing "underrepresented minorities," instead continuing their social experiments on other people's children. . . .

ᴄᴀⱺᴠ

. . . [T]he majority has placed its *imprimatur* on a practice that can only weaken the principle of equality embodied in the Declaration of Independence and the Equal Protection Clause. "Our Constitution is color-blind, and neither knows nor tolerates classes among citizens." *Plessy* v. *Ferguson,* 163 U.S. 537, 559 (1896) (Harlan, J., dissenting). It has been nearly 140 years since Frederick Douglass asked the intellectual ancestors of the Law School to "[d]o nothing with us!" and the Nation adopted the Fourteenth Amendment. Now we must wait another 25 years to see this principle of equality vindicated. I therefore respectfully dissent from the remainder of the Court's opinion and the judgment.

Notes

1. The Court refers to this component of the Law School's compelling state interest variously as "academic quality," avoiding "sacrifice [of] a vital component of its educational mission," and "academic selectivity." *Ante,* at 27–28.

2. Were this Court to have the courage to forbid the use of racial discrimination in admissions, legacy preferences (and similar practices) might quickly become less popular—a possibility not lost, I am certain, on the elites (both individual and institutional) supporting the Law School in this case.

Majority Opinion

Grutter *v.* Bollinger

Justice O'Connor delivered the opinion of the Court.

This case requires us to decide whether the use of race as a factor in student admissions by the University of Michigan Law School (Law School) is unlawful.

I

A

The Law School ranks among the Nation's top law schools. It receives more than 3,500 applications each year for a class of around 350 students. Seeking to "admit a group of students who individually and collectively are among the most capable," the Law School looks for individuals with "substantial promise for success in law school" and "a strong likelihood of succeeding in the practice of law and contributing in diverse ways to the well-being of others." App. 110. More broadly, the Law School seeks "a mix of students with varying backgrounds and experiences who will respect and learn from each other." *Ibid.* In 1992, the dean of the Law School charged a faculty committee with crafting a written admissions policy to implement these goals. In particular, the Law School sought to ensure that its efforts to achieve student body diversity complied with this Court's most recent ruling on the use of race in university admissions. See *Regents of Univ. of Cal.* v. *Bakke*, 438 U.S. 265 (1978). Upon the unanimous adoption of the committee's report by the Law School faculty, it became the Law School's official admissions policy.

The hallmark of that policy is its focus on academic ability coupled with a flexible assessment of applicants' talents, experiences, and potential "to contribute to the learning of those around them." The policy requires admissions officials to evaluate each applicant based on all the information available in the file, including a personal statement, letters of recommendation, and an essay describing the ways in which the applicant will contribute to the life and diversity of the Law School. In reviewing an applicant's file, admissions officials must consider the applicant's undergraduate grade point average (GPA) and Law School Admissions Test (LSAT) score because they are important (if imperfect) predictors of academic success in law school. The policy stresses that "no applicant should be

From *Barbara Grutter v. Lee Bollinger et al.*, 539 U.S. ___ (2003). Some notes and case citations omitted.

admitted unless we expect that applicant to do well enough to graduate with no serious academic problems."

The policy makes clear, however, that even the highest possible score does not guarantee admission to the Law School. Nor does a low score automatically disqualify an applicant. Rather, the policy requires admissions officials to look beyond grades and test scores to other criteria that are important to the Law School's educational objectives. So-called "'soft' variables" such as "the enthusiasm of recommenders, the quality of the undergraduate institution, the quality of the applicant's essay, and the areas and difficulty of undergraduate course selection" are all brought to bear in assessing an "applicant's likely contributions to the intellectual and social life of the institution."

The policy aspires to "achieve that diversity which has the potential to enrich everyone's education and thus make a law school class stronger than the sum of its parts." The policy does not restrict the types of diversity contributions eligible for "substantial weight" in the admissions process, but instead recognizes "many possible bases for diversity admissions." The policy does, however, reaffirm the Law School's longstanding commitment to "one particular type of diversity," that is, "racial and ethnic diversity with special reference to the inclusion of students from groups which have been historically discriminated against, like African-Americans, Hispanics and Native Americans, who without this commitment might not be represented in our student body in meaningful numbers." By enrolling a "'critical mass' of [underrepresented] minority students," the Law School seeks to "ensur[e] their ability to make unique contributions to the character of the Law School."

The policy does not define diversity "solely in terms of racial and ethnic status." Nor is the policy "insensitive to the competition among all students for admission to the [L]aw [S]chool." Rather, the policy seeks to guide admissions officers in "producing classes both diverse and academically outstanding, classes made up of students who promise to continue the tradition of outstanding contribution by Michigan Graduates to the legal profession."

B

. . . We granted certiorari, 537 U.S. 1043 (2002), to resolve the disagreement among the Courts of Appeals on a question of national importance: Whether diversity is a compelling interest that can justify the narrowly tailored use of race in selecting applicants for admission to public universities. Compare *Hopwood* v. *Texas,* 78 F.3d 932 (CA5 1996) (*Hopwood I*) (holding that diversity is not a compelling state interest), with *Smith* v. *University of Wash. Law School,* 233 F.3d 1188 (CA9 2000) (holding that it is).

II . . .

B

The Equal Protection Clause provides that no State shall "deny to any person within its jurisdiction the equal protection of the laws." U.S. Const., Amdt. 14,

§2. Because the Fourteenth Amendment "protect[s] *persons,* not *groups,*" all "governmental action based on race—a *group* classification long recognized as in most circumstances irrelevant and therefore prohibited—should be subjected to detailed judicial inquiry to ensure that the *personal* right to equal protection of the laws has not been infringed." *Adarand Constructors, Inc.* v. *Peña,* 515 U.S. 200, 227 (1995) (emphasis in original; internal quotation marks and citation omitted). We are a "free people whose institutions are founded upon the doctrine of equality." *Loving* v. *Virginia,* 388 U.S. 1, 11 (1967) (internal quotation marks and citation omitted). It follows from that principle that "government may treat people differently because of their race only for the most compelling reasons." *Adarand Constructors, Inc.* v. *Peña,* 515 U.S., at 227.

We have held that all racial classifications imposed by government "must be analyzed by a reviewing court under strict scrutiny." This means that such classifications are constitutional only if they are narrowly tailored to further compelling governmental interests. "Absent searching judicial inquiry into the justification for such race-based measures," we have no way to determine what "classifications are 'benign' or 'remedial' and what classifications are in fact motivated by illegitimate notions of racial inferiority or simple racial politics." *Richmond* v. *J. A. Croson Co.,* 488 U.S. 469, 493 (1989) (plurality opinion). We apply strict scrutiny to all racial classifications to "'smoke out' illegitimate uses of race by assuring that [government] is pursuing a goal important enough to warrant use of a highly suspect tool." *Ibid.*

Strict scrutiny is not "strict in theory, but fatal in fact." *Adarand Constructors, Inc.* v. *Peña, supra,* at 237 (internal quotation marks and citation omitted). Although all governmental uses of race are subject to strict scrutiny, not all are invalidated by it. As we have explained, "whenever the government treats any person unequally because of his or her race, that person has suffered an injury that falls squarely within the language and spirit of the Constitution's guarantee of equal protection." 515 U.S., at 229–230. But that observation "says nothing about the ultimate validity of any particular law; that determination is the job of the court applying strict scrutiny." *Id.,* at 230. When race-based action is necessary to further a compelling governmental interest, such action does not violate the constitutional guarantee of equal protection so long as the narrow-tailoring requirement is also satisfied.

Context matters when reviewing race-based governmental action under the Equal Protection Clause. See *Gomillion* v. *Lightfoot,* 364 U.S. 339, 343–344 (1960) (admonishing that, "in dealing with claims under broad provisions of the Constitution, which derive content by an interpretive process of inclusion and exclusion, it is imperative that generalizations, based on and qualified by the concrete situations that gave rise to them, must not be applied out of context in disregard of variant controlling facts"). In *Adarand Constructors, Inc.* v. *Peña,* we made clear that strict scrutiny must take "'relevant differences' into account." 515 U.S., at 228. Indeed, as we explained, that is its "fundamental purpose." *Ibid.* Not every decision influenced by race is equally objectionable and strict scrutiny is designed to provide a framework for carefully examining the importance and the sincerity of the reasons advanced by the governmental decisionmaker for the use of race in that particular context.

III

A

With these principles in mind, we turn to the question whether the Law School's use of race is justified by a compelling state interest. Before this Court, as they have throughout this litigation, respondents assert only one justification for their use of race in the admissions process: obtaining "the educational benefits that flow from a diverse student body." Brief for Respondents Bollinger et al. i. In other words, the Law School asks us to recognize, in the context of higher education, a compelling state interest in student body diversity.

We first wish to dispel the notion that the Law School's argument has been foreclosed, either expressly or implicitly, by our affirmative-action cases decided since *Bakke*. It is true that some language in those opinions might be read to suggest that remedying past discrimination is the only permissible justification for race-based governmental action. See, *e.g., Richmond* v. *J. A. Croson Co., supra,* at 493 (plurality opinion) (stating that unless classifications based on race are "strictly reserved for remedial settings, they may in fact promote notions of racial inferiority and lead to a politics of racial hostility"). But we have never held that the only governmental use of race that can survive strict scrutiny is remedying past discrimination. Nor, since *Bakke,* have we directly addressed the use of race in the context of public higher education. Today, we hold that the Law School has a compelling interest in attaining a diverse student body.

The Law School's educational judgment that such diversity is essential to its educational mission is one to which we defer. The Law School's assessment that diversity will, in fact, yield educational benefits is substantiated by respondents and their *amici*. Our scrutiny of the interest asserted by the Law School is no less strict for taking into account complex educational judgments in an area that lies primarily within the expertise of the university. Our holding today is in keeping with our tradition of giving a degree of deference to a university's academic decisions, within constitutionally prescribed limits.

We have long recognized that, given the important purpose of public education and the expansive freedoms of speech and thought associated with the university environment, universities occupy a special niche in our constitutional tradition. In announcing the principle of student body diversity as a compelling state interest, Justice Powell invoked our cases recognizing a constitutional dimension, grounded in the First Amendment, of educational autonomy: "The freedom of a university to make its own judgments as to education includes the selection of its student body." *Bakke, supra,* at 312. From this premise, Justice Powell reasoned that by claiming "the right to select those students who will contribute the most to the 'robust exchange of ideas,'" a university "seek[s] to achieve a goal that is of paramount importance in the fulfillment of its mission." 438 U.S., at 313 (quoting *Keyishian* v. *Board of Regents of Univ. of State of N.Y., supra,* at 603). Our conclusion that the Law School has a compelling interest in a diverse student body is informed by our view that attaining a diverse student body is at the heart of the Law School's proper institutional mission, and that "good faith" on the part of a university is "presumed" absent "a showing to the contrary." 438 U.S., at 318–319.

As part of its goal of "assembling a class that is both exceptionally academically qualified and broadly diverse," the Law School seeks to "enroll a 'critical mass' of minority students." Brief for Respondents Bollinger et al. 13. The Law School's interest is not simply "to assure within its student body some specified percentage of a particular group merely because of its race or ethnic origin." *Bakke,* 438 U.S., at 307 (opinion of Powell, J.). That would amount to outright racial balancing, which is patently unconstitutional. *Ibid.; Freeman* v. *Pitts,* 503 U.S. 467, 494 (1992) ("Racial balance is not to be achieved for its own sake"); *Richmond* v. *J. A. Croson Co.,* 488 U.S., at 507. Rather, the Law School's concept of critical mass is defined by reference to the educational benefits that diversity is designed to produce.

These benefits are substantial. As the District Court emphasized, the Law School's admissions policy promotes "cross-racial understanding," helps to break down racial stereotypes, and "enables [students] to better understand persons of different races." App. to Pet. for Cert. 246a. These benefits are "important and laudable," because "classroom discussion is livelier, more spirited, and simply more enlightening and interesting" when the students have "the greatest possible variety of backgrounds."

The Law School's claim of a compelling interest is further bolstered by its *amici,* who point to the educational benefits that flow from student body diversity. In addition to the expert studies and reports entered into evidence at trial, numerous studies show that student body diversity promotes learning outcomes, and "better prepares students for an increasingly diverse workforce and society, and better prepares them as professionals." Brief for American Educational Research Association et al. as *Amici Curiae* 3; see, *e.g.,* W. Bowen & D. Bok, The Shape of the River (1998); Diversity Challenged: Evidence on the Impact of Affirmative Action (G. Orfield & M. Kurlaender eds. 2001); Compelling Interest: Examining the Evidence on Racial Dynamics in Colleges and Universities (M. Chang, D. Witt, J. Jones, & K. Hakuta eds. 2003).

These benefits are not theoretical but real, as major American businesses have made clear that the skills needed in today's increasingly global marketplace can only be developed through exposure to widely diverse people, cultures, ideas, and viewpoints. Brief for 3M et al. as *Amici Curiae* 5; Brief for General Motors Corp. as *Amicus Curiae* 3–4. What is more, high-ranking retired officers and civilian leaders of the United States military assert that, "[b]ased on [their] decades of experience," a "highly qualified, racially diverse officer corps . . . is essential to the military's ability to fulfill its principle mission to provide national security." Brief for Julius W. Becton, Jr. et al. as *Amici Curiae* 27. The primary sources for the Nation's officer corps are the service academies and the Reserve Officers Training Corps (ROTC), the latter comprising students already admitted to participating colleges and universities. *Id.,* at 5. At present, "the military cannot achieve an officer corps that is *both* highly qualified *and* racially diverse unless the service academies and the ROTC used limited race-conscious recruiting and admissions policies." *Ibid.* (emphasis in original). To fulfill its mission, the military "must be selective in admissions for training and education for the officer corps, *and* it must train and educate a highly qualified, racially diverse officer corps in a racially diverse setting." *Id.,* at 29 (emphasis in original). We agree that "[i]t requires only a small step from this analysis to conclude that our country's other most selective institutions must remain both diverse and selective." *Ibid.*

We have repeatedly acknowledged the overriding importance of preparing students for work and citizenship, describing education as pivotal to "sustaining our political and cultural heritage" with a fundamental role in maintaining the fabric of society. *Plyler* v. *Doe,* 457 U.S. 202, 221 (1982). This Court has long recognized that "education . . . is the very foundation of good citizenship." *Brown* v. *Board of Education,* 347 U.S. 483, 493 (1954). For this reason, the diffusion of knowledge and opportunity through public institutions of higher education must be accessible to all individuals regardless of race or ethnicity. The United States, as *amicus curiae,* affirms that "[e]nsuring that public institutions are open and available to all segments of American society, including people of all races and ethnicities, represents a paramount government objective." Brief for United States as *Amicus Curiae* 13. And, "[n]owhere is the importance of such openness more acute than in the context of higher education." *Ibid.* Effective participation by members of all racial and ethnic groups in the civic life of our Nation is essential if the dream of one Nation, indivisible, is to be realized.

Moreover, universities, and in particular, law schools, represent the training ground for a large number of our Nation's leaders. *Sweatt* v. *Painter,* 339 U.S. 629, 634 (1950) (describing law school as a "proving ground for legal learning and practice"). Individuals with law degrees occupy roughly half the state governorships, more than half the seats in the United States Senate, and more than a third of the seats in the United States House of Representatives. See Brief for Association of American Law Schools as *Amicus Curiae* 5–6. The pattern is even more striking when it comes to highly selective law schools. A handful of these schools accounts for 25 of the 100 United States Senators, 74 United States Courts of Appeals judges, and nearly 200 of the more than 600 United States District Court judges. *Id.,* at 6.

In order to cultivate a set of leaders with legitimacy in the eyes of the citizenry, it is necessary that the path to leadership be visibly open to talented and qualified individuals of every race and ethnicity. All members of our heterogeneous society must have confidence in the openness and integrity of the educational institutions that provide this training. As we have recognized, law schools "cannot be effective in isolation from the individuals and institutions with which the law interacts." See *Sweatt* v. *Painter, supra,* at 634. Access to legal education (and thus the legal profession) must be inclusive of talented and qualified individuals of every race and ethnicity, so that all members of our heterogeneous society may participate in the educational institutions that provide the training and education necessary to succeed in America.

The Law School does not premise its need for critical mass on "any belief that minority students always (or even consistently) express some characteristic minority viewpoint on any issue." Brief for Respondent Bollinger et al. 30. To the contrary, diminishing the force of such stereotypes is both a crucial part of the Law School's mission, and one that it cannot accomplish with only token numbers of minority students. Just as growing up in a particular region or having particular professional experiences is likely to affect an individual's views, so too is one's own, unique experience of being a racial minority in a society, like our own, in which race unfortunately still matters. The Law School has determined, based on its experience and expertise, that a "critical mass" of underrepresented minorities is necessary to further its compelling interest in securing the educational benefits of a diverse student body.

B

Even in the limited circumstance when drawing racial distinctions is permissible to further a compelling state interest, government is still "constrained in how it may pursue that end: [T]he means chosen to accomplish the [government's] asserted purpose must be specifically and narrowly framed to accomplish that purpose." *Shaw* v. *Hunt,* 517 U.S. 899, 908 (1996) (internal quotation marks and citation omitted). The purpose of the narrow tailoring requirement is to ensure that "the means chosen 'fit' . . . th[e] compelling goal so closely that there is little or no possibility that the motive for the classification was illegitimate racial prejudice or stereotype."

Since *Bakke,* we have had no occasion to define the contours of the narrow-tailoring inquiry with respect to race-conscious university admissions programs. That inquiry must be calibrated to fit the distinct issues raised by the use of race to achieve student body diversity in public higher education. Contrary to Justice Kennedy's assertions, we do not "abandon[ ] strict scrutiny," see *post,* at 8 (dissenting opinion). Rather, as we have already explained, *ante,* at 15, we adhere to *Adarand's* teaching that the very purpose of strict scrutiny is to take such "relevant differences into account."

To be narrowly tailored, a race-conscious admissions program cannot use a quota system—it cannot "insulat[e] each category of applicants with certain desired qualifications from competition with all other applicants." *Bakke, supra,* at 315 (opinion of Powell, J.). Instead, a university may consider race or ethnicity only as a "'plus' in a particular applicant's file," without "insulat[ing] the individual from comparison with all other candidates for the available seats." In other words, an admissions program must be "flexible enough to consider all pertinent elements of diversity in light of the particular qualifications of each applicant, and to place them on the same footing for consideration, although not necessarily according them the same weight."

We find that the Law School's admissions program bears the hallmarks of a narrowly tailored plan. As Justice Powell made clear in *Bakke,* truly individualized consideration demands that race be used in a flexible, nonmechanical way. It follows from this mandate that universities cannot establish quotas for members of certain racial groups or put members of those groups on separate admissions tracks. Nor can universities insulate applicants who belong to certain racial or ethnic groups from the competition for admission. *Ibid.* Universities can, however, consider race or ethnicity more flexibly as a "plus" factor in the context of individualized consideration of each and every applicant.

. . . The importance of this individualized consideration in the context of a race-conscious admissions program is paramount.

. . . Unlike the program at issue in *Gratz* v. *Bollinger,* the Law School awards no mechanical, predetermined diversity "bonuses" based on race or ethnicity. . . .

We also find that, like the Harvard plan Justice Powell referenced in *Bakke,* the Law School's race-conscious admissions program adequately ensures that all factors that may contribute to student body diversity are meaningfully considered alongside race in admissions decisions. With respect to the use of race itself, all underrepresented minority students admitted by the Law School have been deemed qualified. By virtue of our Nation's struggle with racial inequality, such students are both likely to have experiences of particular importance to the Law School's mission, and less likely to be admitted in meaningful numbers on criteria that ignore those experiences.

The Law School does not, however, limit in any way the broad range of qualities and experiences that may be considered valuable contributions to student body diversity. To the contrary, the 1992 policy makes clear "[t]here are many possible bases for diversity admissions," and provides examples of admittees who have lived or traveled widely abroad, are fluent in several languages, have overcome personal adversity and family hardship, have exceptional records of extensive community service, and have had successful careers in other fields. The Law School seriously considers each "applicant's promise of making a notable contribution to the class by way of a particular strength, attainment, or characteristic—*e.g.,* an unusual intellectual achievement, employment experience, nonacademic performance, or personal background." *Id.,* at 83–84. All applicants have the opportunity to highlight their own potential diversity contributions through the submission of a personal statement, letters of recommendation, and an essay describing the ways in which the applicant will contribute to the life and diversity of the Law School.

What is more, the Law School actually gives substantial weight to diversity factors besides race. The Law School frequently accepts nonminority applicants with grades and test scores lower than underrepresented minority applicants (and other nonminority applicants) who are rejected. This shows that the Law School seriously weighs many other diversity factors besides race that can make a real and dispositive difference for nonminority applicants as well. By this flexible approach, the Law School sufficiently takes into account, in practice as well as in theory, a wide variety of characteristics besides race and ethnicity that contribute to a diverse student body. . . .

We are mindful, however, that "[a] core purpose of the Fourteenth Amendment was to do away with all governmentally imposed discrimination based on race." *Palmore* v. *Sidoti,* 466 U.S. 429, 432 (1984). Accordingly, race-conscious admissions policies must be limited in time. This requirement reflects that racial classifications, however compelling their goals, are potentially so dangerous that they may be employed no more broadly than the interest demands. Enshrining a permanent justification for racial preferences would offend this fundamental equal protection principle. We see no reason to exempt race-conscious admissions programs from the requirement that all governmental use of race must have a logical end point. The Law School, too, concedes that all "race-conscious programs must have reasonable durational limits."

In the context of higher education, the durational requirement can be met by sunset provisions in race-conscious admissions policies and periodic reviews to determine whether racial preferences are still necessary to achieve student body diversity. . . .

We take the Law School at its word that it would "like nothing better than to find a race-neutral admissions formula" and will terminate its race-conscious admissions program as soon as practicable. It has been 25 years since Justice Powell first approved the use of race to further an interest in student body diversity in the context of public higher education. Since that time, the number of minority applicants with high grades and test scores has indeed increased. We expect that 25 years from now, the use of racial preferences will no longer be necessary to further the interest approved today.

IV

In summary, the Equal Protection Clause does not prohibit the Law School's narrowly tailored use of race in admissions decisions to further a compelling interest in obtaining the educational benefits that flow from a diverse student body. Consequently, petitioner's statutory claims based on Title VI and 42 U.S.C. §1981 also fail. The judgment of the Court of Appeals for the Sixth Circuit, accordingly, is affirmed.

It is so ordered.

POSTSCRIPT

Do Race-Conscious Programs in Public University Admissions Policies Violate the Fourteenth Amendment's Guarantee of Equal Protection Under the Law?

In 1954 the landmark civil rights case *Brown v. Board of Education*, 347 U.S. 483 (1954) was decided. *Brown* was the culmination of the desegregation strategy of the National Association for the Advancement of Colored People (NAACP) Legal Defense Fund; it promised the beginning of a new era of equal justice under law for America's racial minorities. For many, the promise of *Brown* was a nation that had overcome the vestiges of past practices of racial discrimination and that stood at the threshold of a truly color-blind society. But that promise has been elusive. Not too long after *Brown* was decided, it became apparent to some that in order to bring about racial justice, it would still be necessary to continue to take race into account in many important public policy decisions. The late justice Harry A. Blackmun lent an eloquent voice to this position in his opinion in *Regents of the University of California v. Bakke*, 438 U.S. 265 (1978). There he announced that he yielded

> to no one in [his] earnest hope that the time will come when an "affirmative action" program is unnecessary, and is, in truth, only a relic of the past. . . . At some time, beyond any period of what some would claim is only transitional inequality, the United States must and will reach a stage of maturity where action along this line is no longer necessary. Then persons will be regarded as persons, and discrimination of the type we address today will be an ugly feature of history that is instructive but that is behind us.

For some, race-conscious remedies designed to cure the ills of past discrimination have done nothing to ease racial tensions and have resulted only in creating new problems, such as punishing "innocent" people—Barbara Grutter, for example—for the sins of others. For others, race-conscious programs have threatened the very integrity of the Constitution, risking one of its most sacred principles: that all stand equal before the law, regardless of race, class, or other personal characteristics. Yet the fact remains that, nearly half a century after *Brown*, far too many of America's colleges and universities would remain predominantly white but for race-conscious admissions programs of the sort at issue in *Grutter v. Bollinger*. None of the Supreme Court justices seem to disagree on that single point; the question is what to do about it.

Prior to the decision in *Grutter*, it was unclear whether the Court would continue to allow race to be taken into account for any purpose other than providing a remedy for past discrimination. Indeed, many have argued that race can be taken into account only for such purposes. The *Grutter* majority breaks rank with this, however, and says that forward-looking, utilitarian justifications are also sufficient to justify race-conscious college admissions policies; that is, the achievement of *diversity* in the university classroom is a compelling state interest. Even after *Grutter*, however, it is still not entirely clear what the Court means by "diversity." Furthermore, one might reasonably question whether such diversity policies are synonymous with *affirmative action*. Wasn't the original goal of affirmative action to "level the playing field," to offer opportunities to those who have not had them? More specifically, wasn't the original goal of affirmative action to remedy the present effects of past discrimination? According to the *Grutter* majority, diversity is justified because it will be good for all students—the white majority as well as underrepresented groups—and for the educational institution as a whole. One might reasonably ask whether the Court is authorizing the university to use underrepresented students of color for purely instrumental reasons.

Those who wish to read further on this issue might begin with a study by Derek Bok and William Bowen, former presidents of Harvard and Princeton Universities: *The Shape of the River: Long-Term Consequences of Considering Race in College and University Admissions* (Princeton University Press, 1998). In addition, Michel Rosenfeld's *Affirmative Action and Justice: A Philosophical and Constitutional Inquiry* (Yale University Press, 1991) provides a thoughtful and challenging study of many of the important issues involved here. Further, readers might be interested in visiting the Web site of the Center for Individual Rights (CIR) at http://www.cir-usa.org. The CIR is a nonprofit, tax-exempt public interest law firm, which provided legal representation for Grutter in her suit against the University of Michigan Law School. Finally, visit the University of Michigan Web site http://www.umich.edu/~urel/admissions/legal/grutter/ for useful information about *Grutter* and for many of the legal documents filed in this case.

Contributors to This Volume

EDITOR

ETHAN KATSH is professor of legal studies and director of the Center for Information Technology and Dispute Resolution at the University of Massachusetts at Amherst (http://www.odr.info). A graduate of the Yale Law School, he has authored three books on law and technology: *Law in a Digital World* (Oxford University Press, 1995), *The Electronic Media and the Transformation of Law* (Oxford University Press, 1989), and, with Professor Janet Rifkin, *Online Dispute Resolution: Resolving Conflicts in Cyberspace* (2001). Professor Katsh conducted the pilot online dispute-resolution project for eBay and is involved in many activities designed to resolve disputes using the Internet. He may be reached at Katsh@legal.umass.edu.

AUTHORS

AMERICAN CIVIL LIBERTIES UNION (ACLU) has the mission to preserve all of these protections and guarantees: Your First Amendment rights—freedom of speech, association, and assembly; freedom of the press; and freedom of religion supported by the strict separation of church and state. Your right to equal protection under the law—equal treatment regardless of race, sex, religion or national origin, your right to due process—fair treatment by the government whenever the loss of your liberty or property is at stake. Your right to privacy—freedom from unwarranted government intrusion into your personal and private affairs.

RICHARD C. BARTH was appointed assistant secretary for the Office of Policy Development in the Department of Homeland Security Department on August 28, 2006. In that position, he is the principal action officer for coordinating policy among DHS entities, as well as with state and federal agencies, and foreign governments. Prior to assuming this position, Assistant Secretary Barth was corporate vice president and director, Homeland Security Strategy, for Motorola's Government Relations Office in Washington, D.C.

STEPHEN BREYER is an associate justice of the U.S. Supreme Court. He received an A.B. from Stanford University, a B.A. from Magdalen College, Oxford, and an LL.B. from Harvard Law School. He served as a law clerk to Justice Arthur Goldberg of the Supreme Court of the United States during the 1964 term. Prior to being appointed as a judge of the United States Court of Appeals for the First Circuit, he was a professor at Harvard Law School. From 1990 to 1994, he served as chief judge for the First Circuit Court of Appeals. President Clinton nominated him as an associate justice of the Supreme Court in 1994.

ROBERT CORDY is associate justice of the Massachusetts Supreme Judicial Court. He received a J.D. from Harvard Law School in 1974. Prior to being appointed to the bench, he was a partner at the law firm of McDermott, Will & Emery.

ROBERT DELAHUNTY is associate professor of law at the University of St. Thomas School of Law. Prior to taking this position, he served in various positions at the U.S. Department of Justice, most recently in the Office of Legal Counsel. During 2002–2003, he was deputy general counsel at the White House Office of Homeland Security.

RUTH BADER GINSBURG is an associate justice of the U.S. Supreme Court. She graduated at the top of her law school class at Columbia University and taught at Rutgers and Columbia Law Schools. She served as director of the ACLU Women's Rights Project, and between 1972 and 1978 she argued six cases involving sex-role stereotyping before the Court and won five. She was appointed to the Supreme Court by President Bill Clinton in 1993.

ANTHONY KENNEDY is an associate justice of the U.S. Supreme Court. He received his LL.B. from Harvard Law School in 1961 and worked for law firms in San Francisco and Sacremento, California, until he was nominated by President Gerald Ford to the U.S. Court of Appeals for the Ninth Circuit in 1975. He was nominated by President Ronald Reagan to the Supreme Court in 1988.

ROBERT B. KING is a judge for the Fourth Circuit United States Court of Appeals. He was appointed to this position by President Bill Clinton in 1998. Judge King was appointed United States Attorney for southern West Virginia by President Jimmy Carter in 1977 and served in that position until 1981. He was in private practice from 1981 until his appointment by President Clinton in 1998.

JAMES P. LOGAN received a B.S. degree from the University of Nevada at Reno and a law degree from McGeorge School of Law, University of the Pacific. He is an attorney with the State of Nevada Public Defenders Office where he has been an Appellate Deputy since 1990.

MARGARET MARSHALL is chief justice of the Massachusetts Supreme Judicial Court. A native of South Africa, she graduated from Witwatersrand University in Johannesburg in 1966 and later received a J.D. from Yale Law School. Before her appointment to the Supreme Judicial Court, she was vice president and general counsel of Harvard University. She was appointed as an associate justice of the Supreme Judicial Court in November 1996 and named chief justice in September 1999.

SANDRA DAY O'CONNOR was an associate justice of the U.S. Supreme Court. She worked in various legal capacities both in the United States and in Germany until she was appointed to the Arizona State Senate in 1969. She served as a state senator for four years and served in the Arizona judiciary for six years before she was nominated to the Supreme Court by President Ronald Reagan in 1981.

WILLIAM H. REHNQUIST (1924–2005) became the 16th chief justice of the U.S. Supreme Court in 1986. He engaged in a general practice of law with primary emphasis on civil litigation for 16 years before being appointed assistant attorney general, Office of Legal Counsel, by President Richard Nixon in 1969. He was nominated by Nixon to the Supreme Court in 1972.

STEPHEN REINHARDT is a judge on the U.S. Court of Appeals for the Ninth Circuit in Seattle, Washington.

ANTONIN SCALIA is an associate justice of the U.S. Supreme Court. He taught law at the University of Virginia, the American Enterprise Institute, Georgetown University, and the University of Chicago before being nominated to the U.S. Court of Appeals by President Ronald Reagan in 1982. He served in that capacity until he was nominated by Reagan to the Supreme Court in 1986.

DAVID SOUTER is an associate justice of the U.S. Supreme Court and a former judge for the U.S. Court of Appeals for the First Circuit in Boston, Massachusetts. He was nominated by President George Bush to the Supreme Court in 1990.

TIMOTHY D. SPARAPANI is legislative counsel on Privacy for the American Civil Liberties Union. He is a graduate of the University of Michigan Law School and previously was associated with the law firm of Dickstein, Shapiro, Morin & Oshinsky.

JOHN PAUL STEVENS is an associate justice of the U.S. Supreme Court. He worked in law firms in Chicago, Illinois, for 20 years before being nominated by President Richard Nixon to the U.S. Court of Appeals in 1970. He served in that capacity until he was nominated to the Supreme Court by President Gerald Ford in 1975.

CLARENCE THOMAS is an associate justice of the U.S. Supreme Court. A former judge on the U.S. Court of Appeals for the District of Columbia, he was nominated by President George Bush to the Supreme Court in 1991. He received his J.D. from the Yale University School of Law in 1974.

271 UNITED KINGDOM AND EUROPEAN PARLIAMENTARIANS make up the amicus group. The amicus group numbers 271, comprising 186 members of the Houses of parliament of the United Kingdom of Great Britain and Northern Ireland (the "UK Parliament") and 85 current or former Members of the European parliament and a vice president of the European Commission. The amicus group spans the political spectrum. It includes senior figures from all the major political parties in the United Kingdom, 5 retired law Lords, 9 judges in the highest court in the UK, including a former Lord Chancellor, or senior lawyers, some of whom have held high judicial office, 11 bishops of the Church of England, and former Cabinet ministers.

THE UNITED STATES DEPARTMENT OF JUSTICE has a mission to enforce the law and defend the interests of the United States according to the law; to ensure public safety against threats foreign and domestic; to provide federal leadership in preventing and controlling crime; to seek just punishment for those guilty of unlawful behavior; and to ensure fair and impartial administration of justice for all Americans.

THE UNITED STATES SUPREME COURT consists of the Chief Justice of the United States and such number of Associate Justices as may be fixed by Congress. Power to nominate the Justices is vested in the President of the United States, and appointments are made with the advice and consent of the Senate.

JOHN YOO is a professor of law at the University of California at Berkeley School of Law (Boalt Hall), where he has taught since 1993. From 2001 to 2003, he served as a deputy assistant attorney general in the Office of Legal Counsel of the U.S. Department of Justice, where he worked on issues involving foreign affairs, national security, and the separation of powers. He served as general counsel of the U.S. Senate Judiciary Committee from 1995 to 1996, where he advised on constitutional issues and judicial nominations.